SANDER'S FISHING GUIDE 1

Western New York Edition

John M. Sander

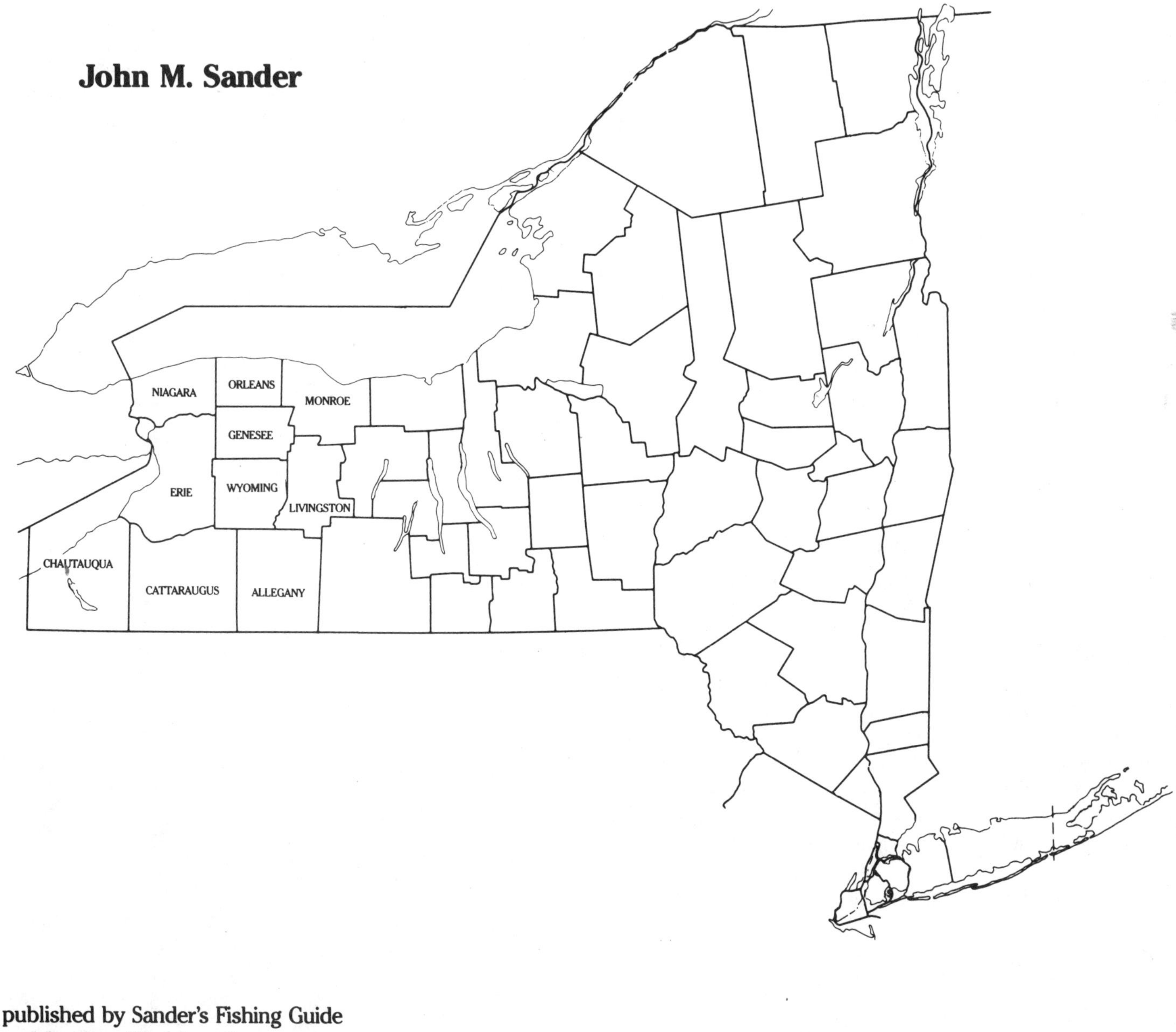

published by Sander's Fishing Guide
and Services Directory, Inc.
P.O. Box 0624, Amherst, NY 14226

Revised Edition

Also available from Sander's Fishing Guides:

Sander's Fishing Guide No. 2 - Finger Lakes Region Edition. A comprehensive guide to 255 lakes and streams in the Central New York area.

Cover Design: Rose Hoth

Cover Photo: The author shows off a typical fall rainbow from the lower Niagara River. Caught on a flyrod, it fell for a white rabbit fur streamer, and weighed in at 5 pounds.

Printed in the United States of America.

ACKNOWLEDGMENTS

I would like to thank the following organizations for their cooperation in the preparation of this book:

Empire State/Lake Ontario Trout and Salmon Derby, Inc; Heather Printing; JTEK CADD Services; Muskie Inc; the New York State Department of Environmental Conservation, Regions 8 and 9; the New York State Sea Grant Institute; the State University of New York at Buffalo, Department of Geography; Trout Unlimited, Western New York Chapter; the United States Fish and Wildlife Service.

I would also like to thank the following individuals for their contributions to this project:

Warren Berry, Mike Bleech, Jim Bokar, Don Cook, Paul Cybart, Gordy Dekdabrun, George Dovolos, Jim Hanley, Bill Hilts, Jr., Pat Inzer, Spike Kelderhouse, Rick Kinecki, Stan Koprevich, Dan Kosowski, John Kowalczyk, John Long, Sr., Ted Newman, Mike Ostrowski, Derwood Say, Rick Schleyer, George Skinner, Joe Urso, and the late Bob Wunder.

Finally, I would like to give special thanks to the following individuals for their contributions to the production of this book:

Michelle Green for her work in laying out this book, Michelle Pfister and Denise Kobbler for graphics work, Andrea Harnack for her renderings of trout flies, Cheryl McCaffery and Rob Jordan for their work in designing and drawing many of the maps, Ken Gravelle for taking many of the photographs, Rick Kustich for numerous articles and photographs, Rose Hoth for cover design, the staff at Yearke Graphics for typesetting, and the staff at Partner's Press.

FOREWORD

Seven long years have passed since I wrote and published the original Sander's Fishing Guide to Western New York, and it has been four years since that tome went out of print. Much has happened to the region's fisheries in the intervening years (thankfully most of it good), but the basic reason for writing a guide such as this has not changed. Therefore, I have reprinted, with minor revisons, the foreward to the original edition.

It could be argued that the love of fishing is one of the single greatest common denominators among men and women. Few of us haven't at one time or another taken rod in hand and revelled in the anticipation of a strike, the fight of an unseen opponent, and, hopefully, the landing of the quarry, be it a humble blue gill or mighty muskellunge. Unfortunately, we fishermen are all too often creatures of habit. We become familiar with a few select streams or lakes and concentrate our efforts on these, ignoring opportunities that are often only over the next rise. We allow this sense of familiarity or ignorance of viable alternatives to harden into a narrow perspective that keeps us on a lake long after its productivity has diminished or crowds have turned a favorite stream into a seasonal zoo.

The sad part about this situation is that in western New York it is entirely unnecessary. The ten-county area covered in this guide is blessed, in terms of variety, quality, and quantity, with some of the best freshwater fishing in the entire United States!

This hasn't always been the case, however. Only 25 years ago the combined effects of overharvesting, pollution, and the introduction of non-native species such as sea lamprey and alewives had decimated the formerly sensational fishing that was found in Lake Erie, Lake Ontario, and their tributaries. Environmental degradation also affected many inland lakes and streams, resulting in the proliferation of rough fish, stunted fish, and the depression or outright elimination of game species populations. Consequently, this region developed a well-deserved reputation for having limited angling opportunities. Unfortunately, this reputation still persists in the minds of many people, not only those from outside the area, but with local people as well.

The quality of our lakes and streams began to improve in the late 1960s and early 1970s. At that time, growing concern over the plight of our environment forced the enactment of legislation designed to halt, or at least slow down, the discharge of pollutants into lakes and streams. In addition, programs were started to repair, where possible, some of the damage that had accumulated over decades of neglect. The success of these programs, though still qualified in many respects, are nevertheless impressive.

The most spectacular successes, at least as far as fishermen are concerned, have been achieved with the Great Lakes stocking programs being carried on by the state, provincial, and federal governments of the United States and Canada. Beginning experimentally with a few thousand fish, these stocking efforts now involve the distribution of millions of fish in the Great Lakes and their tributaries each year. Chinook salmon, coho salmon, lake trout, brown trout, rainbow trout, and steelhead are now drawing anglers from all over the world to Lake Erie and Lake Ontario. And if recent stocking experiments are successful, one of the most renowned game fish of North America, the Atlantic Salmon, will also be making a comeback.

In addition to the rejuvenated cold-water fishing, our Great Lakes are once again gaining recognition for their outstanding angling for warm-water species. The New York portions of Lake Erie and Lake Ontario have arguably the best smallmouth bass fishing in the world. Walleye have made a strong comeback in eastern Lake Erie, and both lakes have tremendous populations of panfish, including yellow perch, white perch, silver bass, and rock bass. All of this adds up to a rather impressive turnaround for two lakes that only a few years ago were being written off by many people as lost causes!

The Great Lakes and their tributaries are not only benefactors of the environmental cleanup and fish management programs. The New York State Department of Environmental Conservation has a long-standing and ambitious program of augmenting the fish stocks in over 100 lakes and streams in western New York. While the major portion of this program involves the stocking of trout streams and trout ponds, a considerable amount of effort is directed to the maintenance of wild trout streams, such as the Wiscoy, Pardee Hollow Creek, and Mill Creek. In addition, a number of conservation minded fishing organizations, such as Trout Unlimited, are often directly involved in stream renovation projects, affording anglers the chance to experience a uniquely satisfying aspect of their avocation.

Warm-water species are also being stocked in several areas. Silver Lake is currently at the top of the Conservation Department's walleye stocking program, and the results there have been impressive. A walleye stocking program carried on by the Niagara River Anglers' Association has greatly improved the quality of the walleye fishing in the lower Niagara River.

As far as major inland lakes are concerned, this region is uniquely endowed. Chautauqua Lake has some of the finest muskie fishing in the entire northeastern United States thanks in part to having the world's largest muskie hatchery right on its shore, at Prendergast Point. The huge Allegheny Reservoir, already a highly productive impoundment, is being managed by the U.S. Fish and Wildlife Service in hopes of soon developing a truly spectacular fishery, especially for walleye. Numerous other lakes, including Conesus, Hemlock, Rushford, and Cuba are known across the state for the quality and diversity of their angling opportunities. And these represent only a small portion of the lakes and ponds found in western New York.

Until the publication of the original Sander's Fishing Guide to Western New York in 1985, the greatest obstacle to experiencing much of this piscatorial bounty had been the lack of a comprehensive source of information on what is available. Pamphlets distributed by the Department of Environmental Conservation cover the entire state and, thus, give only a cursory description of the lakes and streams in any particular area. Even local tackle shops are often ill-equipped to give detailed information on any more than a handful of sites. So the perennial question asked by worm dunkers and fly fishermen alike, "Where can you fish around here?" often goes unanswered or is only partially satisfied by a number of stock answers. Hopefully, this new and greatly improved edition will help remedy the situation and let people know once and for all that western New York has fishing worth bragging about.

Those of you familiar with the original guide to western New York will immediately recognize the improvements that have been made to this new edition. Changes in typesetting and layout make the text much easier to read. Interspersed throughout the book are beautifully drawn trout flies, which greatly enhance the overall aesthetics of the book and actually make the text easier to read by providing visual islands. (Reproductions of these flies can be obtained by using the order form in the back of this book.) All maps have been redrawn and updated by professional cartographers and graphic artists. With regard to the information contained in this new edition, the most important change is an increased reliance on guest articles. These articles present a wealth of first-hand information that no single individual could provide. These and numerous other improvements make this edition an easier to use and more complete reference guide.

Tight lines!

John Sander

TABLE OF CONTENTS

PART I - INLAND WATERS

Italicized numbers indicate maps.

Italicized numbers indicate maps.

Italicized numbers indicate maps.

HOW TO USE YOUR WESTERN NEW YORK FISHING GUIDE

This book was designed to be a comprehensive introduction to the wide range of angling opportunities available in Western New York. While some of this area's streams and lakes are heavily fished, many go virtually unnoticed because few people realize that they exist. To remedy this situation, we have endeavored to provide you with three basic categories of information: 1) how to locate a particular stream or lake on a map, especially topographical maps; 2) how to access the site in the field; and 3) what general set of conditions and facilities to expect when you get there. While most of the information contained in this guide is self-explanatory a number of points should be clarified in order for you to fully utilize the information provided.

A. **Map Coordinates** - These coordinates are provided for each lake and stream. (In the case of a stream or river, the coordinates correspond to the location of the mouth.) These coordinates make it possible to locate the position of the stream or lake on any map that is delineated in terms of latitude and longitude, such as a topographical map (see below), regardless of whether or not the name of the stream or lake appears on the map.

B. **USGS Maps** - U.S. Geological Survey topographical maps are by far the best field maps available, and when purchased will provide you with a wealth of information on alternative access sites, terrain, the locations of tributaries, and much more. In the case of streams and rivers, the first map refers to the mouth and the most downstream portions of the stream. The maps that follow cover progressively upstream sections until the final map, which covers the headwaters of the stream.

C. **Access** - For each lake, all launch sites that we were able to locate and verify were open to the general public are listed, as are all principal roads surrounding the lake. For streams and rivers, naturally we could not list every road or bridge crossing. Instead, usually only one access is given. Keep in mind that these are only recommendations. The ability to access a stream via a particular road crossing can change abruptly due to posting by landowners. Therefore, it would be a good idea to always have an alternate access road in mind before you head for a particular stream. For streams that are stocked, the given access road will always put you onto a section of the stream that is stocked.

D. **Notes** - A very important aspect of this guide is the note space left at the end of each entry. This space was provided in order for you to: (1) keep a record of any important additional information (alternate access sites, data on a particular hole, etc.) not found in this guide; (2) to keep an updated record of any major changes that take place on a stream or lake; and (3) to note any errors of omission or commission that may have occurred in the writing of this guide (heaven forbid!). This will enable you to maintain your guide as a reliable source of information for many years.

E. **Log Sheets** - The log sheets found at the end of the book will help you to record the one thing that no book can provide you with: experience. If used faithfully, logs can turn even an unsuccessful fishing trip into a learning experience and increase your chances becoming a successful angler.

CASSADAGA CREEK

Map Coordinates	42° 05′ 30″ 79° 08′ 13″
USGS Maps	Jamestown, Gerry, Ellery Center, Cassadaga
Township(s)	Ellicott, Gerry, Stockton
Access	Love Road (upper section); paralleled by Route 380 between Stockton and Ross Mills (lower section)
Principal Species	Brown Trout (stocked), Muskellunge, Northern Pike, Smallmouth Bass, Bullhead, panfish

Cassadaga Creek is a large, slow-moving stream that provides very good fishing for both warm-water and cold-water species.

The upper portion of the stream, from its source at Lower Cassadaga Lake down to its junction with Bear Lake Outlet, is primarily trout water. This section averages 15 to 20 feet in width, and has a gravel and sand bottom. It is surrounded by open fields and woodlands, and has intermittent bank cover. Although subject to severe fluctuations in water flow, it is, nevertheless, fishable all trout season.

The spring fishing in the upper section of Cassadaga Creek is quite good due to the generous number of fish that are stocked here. In March and April, 3,600 brown trout yearlings are released in the 5.2-mile section between Bear Lake Outlet and Love Road. There are extensive public fishing rights on the trout section of this stream.

Below the mouth of Bear Lake Outlet, warm-water species begin to predominate in Cassadaga Creek. There are plenty of smallmouth bass, muskellunge (especially between Ross Mills and South Stockton), northern pike, bullhead, and panfish. The northern pike can be taken in any number, any size, all year. Ice fishing is permitted.

About 500 muskie are stocked in Cassadaga Creek each year, between Ross Mills and South Stockton. If you plan to fish for muskies, be sure to have the special license that is required in Chautauqua County.

From South Stockton to the confluence with Conewango Creek, Cassadaga Creek is a part of the Cassadaga/Conewango Waterway. This is a county-operated system designed to increase public access to and utilization of these two important streams. There is a county-maintained Adirondack lean-to shelter with privy, located on several acres of county-owned land off Route 380, about 1 mile north of Ross Mills. To facilitate canoeing on Cassadaga Creek, five launch sites (canoes and cartop boats only) with parking areas have been constructed. They are located in the following areas: On County Road 71, just north of the village of South Stockton; on County Route 314, near the village of Red Bird; on Miller Road, off Route 380, one mile above Kimball Stand; on Knight Road, off Route 380, near Ross Mills; and at the confluence with the Chadakoin River, just below the Southern Tier Expressway.

NOTES: ____________________

____

____

PART I
INLAND WATERS

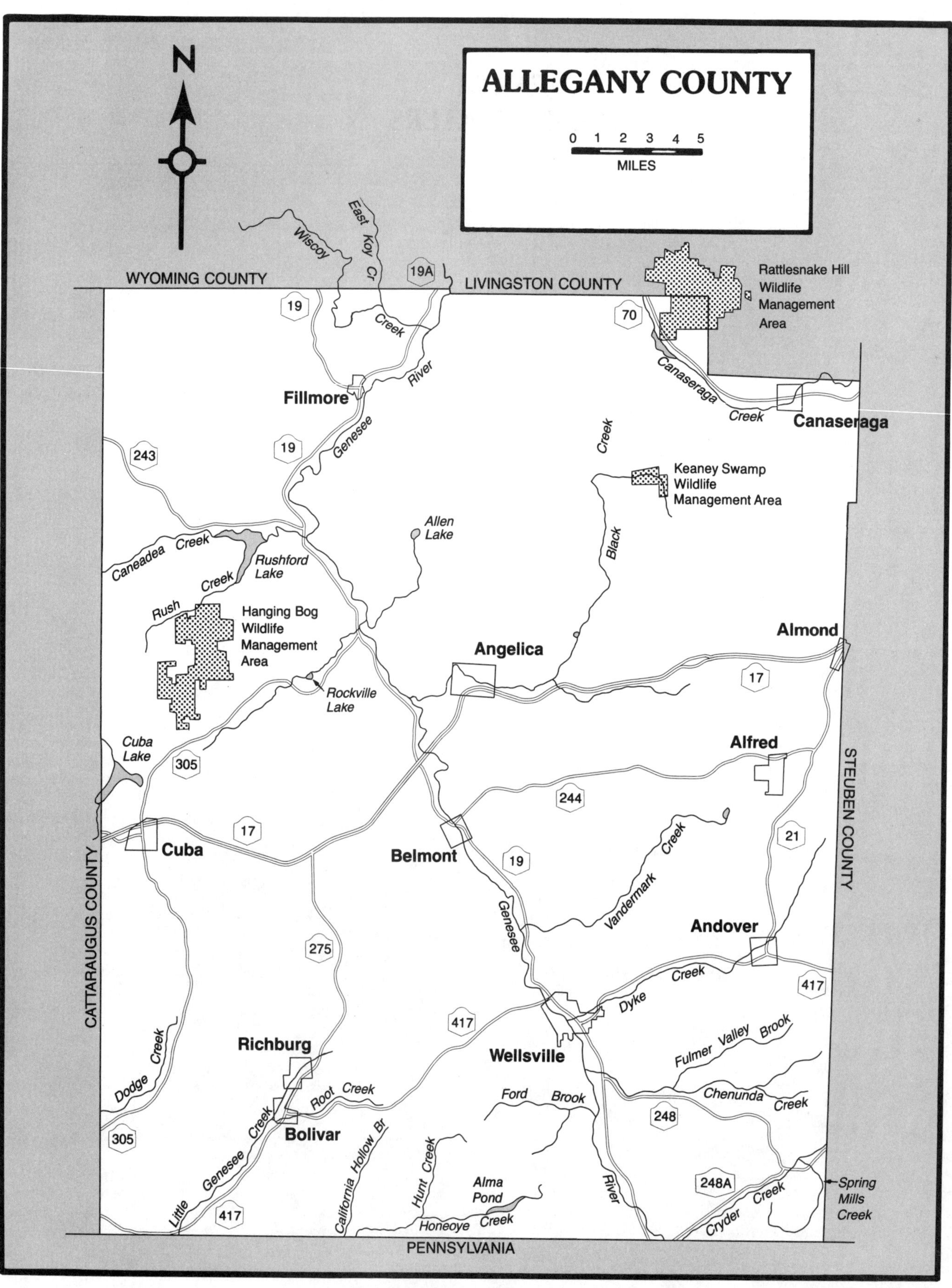
ALLEGANY COUNTY
0 1 2 3 4 5
MILES
N
WYOMING COUNTY
LIVINGSTON COUNTY
STEUBEN COUNTY
CATTARAUGUS COUNTY
PENNSYLVANIA
Rattlesnake Hill Wildlife Management Area
Keaney Swamp Wildlife Management Area
Hanging Bog Wildlife Management Area
Fillmore
Canaseraga
Angelica
Almond
Alfred
Cuba
Belmont
Andover
Wellsville
Richburg
Bolivar
Wiscoy
East Koy Cr
Creek
Genesee River
Canaseraga Creek
Black Creek
Allen Lake
Caneadea Creek
Rushford Lake
Rush Creek
Rockville Lake
Cuba Lake
Vandermark Creek
Dyke Creek
Fulmer Valley Brook
Chenunda Creek
Ford Brook
Root Creek
Dodge Creek
Little Genesee Creek
California Hollow Br
Hunt Creek
Alma Pond
Honeoye Creek
Cryder Creek
Spring Mills Creek
19A
19
70
243
17
305
244
21
275
417
248
248A

ALLEGANY COUNTY STREAMS AND RIVERS

BLACK CREEK

Map Coordinates .... 42° 18′ 18″ 75° 57′ 33″
USGS Map(s) .... West Almond, Birdsall
Township(s) .... Angelica, West Almond
Access .... The bridge crossing on County Road 16
Principal Species .... Brown Trout (stocked)

Averaging about 15 feet in width, Black Creek has good water quality and a bottom of gravel with some rubble. It is surrounded by pastureland and woodland, and most sections have a good amount of alder bank cover. There are several large, old beaver impoundments along the middle and upper reaches that are reported to hold modest-size largemouth bass and panfish. The headwaters, which flow through the Keaney Swamp Wildlife Management Area, may harbor some trout. The middle and upper sections of this stream are probably fishable all trout season.

In March and April, Black Creek is stocked with a total of 1,700 brown trout yearlings in the 3-mile section between the bridge crossings on County Road 16, which is labelled Route 408 on some older maps.

NOTES: ________________________________

____

____

CALIFORNIA HOLLOW BROOK

Map Coordinates .... 42° 00′ 00″ 78° 06′ 56″
USGS Map(s) .... Allentown
Township(s) .... Bolivar
Access .... South Bolivar Road (County Road 33)
Principal Species .... Brown Trout (wild), Brook Trout (stocked)

California Hollow Brook is a small stream averaging about 10 feet in width. Surrounded by woodland and pastureland, this stream has extensive bank cover. With the exception of the warm, marshy headwaters, California Hollow Brook has cold, high-quality water and a bottom of rock and rubble. It holds a significant number of wild brown trout and is fishable all trout season.

In the spring, California Hollow Brook is stocked with 1,100 brook trout yearlings in the 3-mile section immediately upstream of South Bolivar.

NOTES: ________________________________

____

____

CANASERGA CREEK - **See Livingston County Streams and Rivers.**

CANEADEA CREEK

Map Coordinates .... 42° 22′ 58″ 78° 09′ 14″
USGS Map(s) .... Houghton, Freedom, Rawson
Township(s) .... Rushford
Access .... Hardy Corners Road
Principal Species .... Rainbow Trout (stocked), Smallmouth Bass

Caneadea Creek is one of two streams dammed to form Rushford Lake (the other is Rush Creek). It averages 15 feet in width and has a gravel bottom. Though the stream is surrounded primarily by woodland, most sections have rather sparse bank cover.

Caneadea Creek is stocked annually with 1,400 rainbow trout yearlings, from its confluence with Rushford Lake upstream to Hardy Corners. However, due to fishing pressure and the effects of excessively warm water, rainbows not caught by early June will have moved down into Rushford Lake. There is no spawning run of rainbow trout into this stream.

Aside from stocked trout, Caneadea Creek also holds limited numbers of smallmouth bass throughout much of its length.

NOTES: ________________________________

____

____

CHENUNDA CREEK

Map Coordinates .... 42° 05′ 26″ 77° 56′ 09″
USGS Map(s) .... Wellsville South, Whitesville
Township(s) .... Willing, Independence
Access .... State Route 248
Principal Species .... Brown Trout (stocked)

Chenunda Creek is a small tributary of the Genesee River averaging 10 to 12 feet in width. It has a gravel bottom and intermittent bank cover. It is surrounded by woodland and pastureland, and is fishable only during the early months of trout season.

In the fall, Chenunda Creek is stocked with 200 brown trout fingerlings, from 0.4 mile below Fulmer Valley Road upstream to Hallsport.

NOTES: ________________________________

____

____

CRYDER CREEK

Map Coordinates .... 41° 59′ 53″ 77° 52′ 12″
USGS Map(s) .... Ulysses, Whitesville, Rexville
Township(s) .... Independence, Willing (Allegany County); West Union (Steuben County)
Access .... State Route 248A - see below
Principal Species .... Brown Trout (stocked), Brook Trout (stocked)

Cryder Creek is a major tributary of the upper Genesee River. The Allegany County section averages 25 to 30 feet in width and has a bottom composed primarily of gravel, with some silt in the lower end. Bordered by pastureland and woodland, this stream has good bank cover and is fishable all trout season. There are public fishing rights along the entire Allegany County portion of this stream, with a few intermittent exceptions (be sure to check for signs indicating public access).

In March and April, the 7-mile section of Cryder Creek downstream of the mouth of Wileyville Creek, in Whitesville, is stocked with a total of 2,400 brown trout yearlings.

The Steuben County portion of the creek, which is known locally as Marsh Creek, is a typical brook trout stream. Flowing along a valley bottom, it is a silt- and gravel-bottomed, alder-lined stream averaging 15 to 20 feet in width. This reach of the stream is much flatter and slower moving than the Allegany County section, and there are some very substantial beaver ponds here. Fishing on this part of Cryder Creek is sustained by stocking, but some wild trout might be found near the mouths of some of the larger tributaries, such as Wileyville Creek.

A log book can be an invaluable addition to an angler's tackle box. Fishing is a learning experience. If used properly, logs will not only help you figure out what you are doing right, but just as important, what you are doing wrong. This can turn a bad day on the water into a valuable learning experience. Sample log sheets are located at the end of this book.

In the spring, 600 brook trout yearlings are stocked in the 3-mile section of Cryder Creek above Wileyville Creek.

NOTE: On current topographical maps (Rexville) the stream paralleled by Route 248 is shown as Marsh Creek. The DEC considers this to be the main stream of Cryder Creek, not the stream that is paralleled by County Road 124, which is south of Marsh Creek. The information pertaining to the Steuben County section of Cryder Creek refers to the stream shown as Marsh Creek.

NOTES: ______________________________

____

____

DODGE CREEK

Map Coordinates .... 42° 02′ 07″ 78° 20′ 38″
USGS Map(s) .... Portville, Bolivar, Friendship
Township(s) .... Genesee
Access .... Hooker Road
Principal Species .... Brown Trout (stocked)

Dodge Creek averages about 15 feet in width, has a bottom composed of gravel with some silt, and is surrounded by woodland and pastureland. Bank cover on this stream is sporadic. Although normally fishable only during the first few months of trout season, a cool, rainy summer could make trout fishing possible all season. It should be noted that much of Dodge Creek is posted and permission should be obtained before fishing here. However, many of the posted signs are for hunting and now say that fishing is permitted.

In March and April, Dodge Creek is stocked with a total of 1,800 brown trout yearlings, from Yubadam Road upstream 6.3 miles to West Clarksville. In the fall, Tributary 17 of Dodge Creek, located just north of West Clarksville, is stocked with 500 brown trout fingerlings. This tributary is a good trout fishing stream in its own right.

NOTES: ______________________________

____

____

DYKE CREEK

Map Coordinates .... 42° 07′ 06″ 77° 56′ 48″
USGS Map(s) .... Wellsville South, Wellsville North, Andover
Township(s) .... Wellsville, Andover
Access .... State Route 417
Principal Species .... Brown Trout (stocked)

Dyke Creek averages 15 feet in width and has a gravel and silt bottom. The surrounding woodland and pastureland provide good bank cover. Although fishable all trout season, the fishing is of marginal quality during the summer due to high water temperatures.

In March and April, Dyke Creek is stocked with a total of 2,100 brown trout yearlings, from the Preheator Company in Wellsville to just below Andover.

NOTES: ______________________________

____

____

FORD BOOK (Main Branch)

Map Coordinates .... 42° 03′ 54″ 77° 55′ 31″
USGS Map(s) .... Wellsville South, Allentown
Township(s) .... Willing, Alma
Access .... South branch of Ford Brook Road
Principal Species .... Brown Trout (stocked and wild)

This small stream averages 10 feet in width and has a gravel bottom. The surrounding pastureland and woodland provide only intermittent bank cover. Ford Brook is fishable primarily in the spring and fall, but its headwaters hold some nice wild brown trout year-round. There is evidence of some oil seepage from nearby wells, but this does not appear to be a serious problem.

In the fall, Ford Brook is stocked with 200 brown trout fingerlings, from one-half mile below the south branch of Ford Brook Road to one-half mile above the road.

NOTES: ______________________________

____

____

FULMER VALLEY BROOK

Map Coordinates .... 42° 04′ 54″ 77° 02′ 55″
USGS Map(s) .... Whitesville
Township(s) .... Willing, Wellsville
Access .... Fulmer Valley Road
Principal Species .... Brook Trout (stocked and wild)

This small stream averages 10 to 15 feet in width and has a gravel bottom. Surrounded mainly by woodland, Fulmer Valley Brook has only intermittent bank cover. This is a high-quality trout stream that is fishable all season. It has wild brook trout throughout its length, and many of its tributaries also hold good numbers of wild trout.

In the fall, the lower 2-mile stretch of Fulmer Valley Brook is stocked with 500 brook trout fingerlings.

NOTES: ______________________________

____

____

GENESEE RIVER (State Line to Mount Morris Dam)

Map Coordinates .... 42° 44′ 00″ 77° 56′ 00″
USGS Map(s) .... Mount Morris, Nunda, Portageville, Fillmore, Houghton, Black Creek, Angelica, Belmont, Wellsville North, Wellsville South
Location .... Counties of Allegany and Wyoming
Access .... Routes 19 and 19A (see article)
Principal Species .... Brown Trout (stocked), Rainbow Trout (stocked), Brook Trout (wild), Largemouth Bass, Smallmouth Bass, Walleye, Panfish

Originating in the hills of Pennsylvania and flowing north to Lake Ontario, the New York portion of the Genesee River can be divided into fairly well-delineated cold- and warm-water sections.

The cold water section of the Genesee River flows from the state line to the dam in the town of Belmont. This portion of the Genesee can be characterized as a wide, fast moving, gravel-bottomed river. It has good insect hatches, notably between Wellsville and Belmont, numerous stretches of well-shaded banks, and the water is usually clear.

While there is little or no natural reproduction of trout in this part of the Genesee, trout populations are maintained by a substantial stocking program carried out by the DEC. In March, April, and May a total of 15,000 brown trout yearlings are stocked in the 19-mile stretch of river between the dam in Belmont and the state line. In addition, 6,200 rainbow trout yearlings are stocked in the 9-mile section between Wellsville and the state line. The Genesee River also regularly receives excess breeding stock, which can noticeably improve the spring fishing.

Trout can be taken from this river, from the dam in Belmont upstream to the Pennsylvania state line, all year, any size, 10 fish per day. Ice fishing is permitted.

Beginning in 1990, the 2.5-mile section of the river immediately downstream of the Route 19 bridge crossing in Shongo became a no-kill area. Trout may be taken all year, but must be released. Only artificial lures may be used on this section of the river.

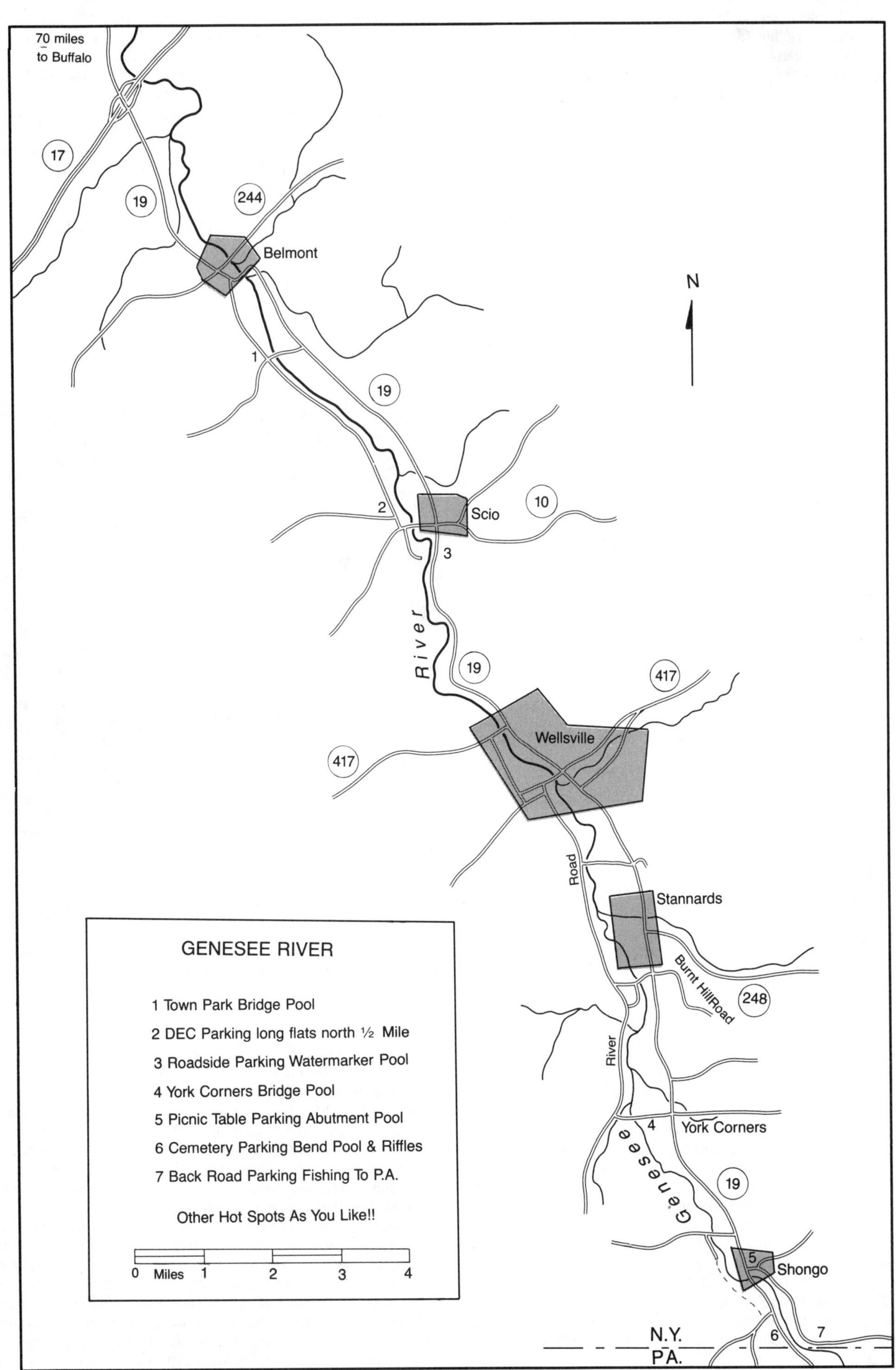
70 miles
to Buffalo
17
19
244
Belmont
N
1
19
2
Scio
10
3
River
19
417
Wellsville
417
Road
Stannards
Burnt HillRoad
248
River
4
York Corners
Genesee
19
5
Shongo
N.Y.
P.A.
6
7
GENESEE RIVER
1 Town Park Bridge Pool
2 DEC Parking long flats north ½ Mile
3 Roadside Parking Watermarker Pool
4 York Corners Bridge Pool
5 Picnic Table Parking Abutment Pool
6 Cemetery Parking Bend Pool & Riffles
7 Back Road Parking Fishing To P.A.
Other Hot Spots As You Like!!
0 Miles 1 2 3 4

Though the Genesee River above Belmont is primarily a cold-water fishery, there is also the possibility of catching black bass, primarily smallmouth. These fish are neither large nor numerous, but above Belmont the fishing for largemouth and smallmouth bass is unrestricted; they can be taken in any number, at any size, all year. Ice fishing for bass is permitted. Check for current regulations.

From the dam at Belmont to the dam at Mount Morris the Genesee River is primarily a warm-water fishery. It is characterized by few insect hatches, some turbidity, very few weeds, and generally unshaded banks. The fishing for smallmouth bass is good spring, summer, and fall, and there are large numbers of carp, suckers, yellow perch, and bullhead. There is also a limited number of walleye between the dams at Mount Morris and Belmont. In Letchworth State Park there are a number of deep, shaded pools that hold brown and rainbow trout, but access to the Genesee River from the park is prohibited in most areas due to the dangerous nature of the gorge that the river flows through. A real hotspot in this section of the river is the pool at the base of the dam in Belmont, where practically every species that inhabits the Genesee can be caught.

The Genesee River, from the state line to the town of Fillmore, is paralleled at varying proximities by State Route 19. Access to this section of the river is facilitated by nearly 15 miles of public fishing rights between the state line and Belmont. Also, there are four state-maintained public parking areas on the Genesee River between the state line and the town of Scio. They are located at: the Route 19 bridge crossing in the town of Shongo; the bridge crossing on Graves Road, just off Route 19, about 1 mile north of Shongo; on Jack Bridge Road, off River Road, just south of Stannards; and the Knight Creek Road bridge crossing in the town of Scio.

Below Fillmore the river is roughly paralleled by State Route 19A to the town of Portageville at the southern end of Letchworth State Park.

The following article deals with the many varied aspects of fishing the Genesee River. It was written by two members of Trout Unlimited.

THE UPPER GENESEE RIVER

By Paul Maciejewski and Al Himmel

Since the Genesee is a relatively large body of water, its water shed is extensive, and the many small feeder streams have a profound effect upon the main river's conditions. Before one makes the trip to Wellsville, it would be wise to have a contact in the area to determine what the situation is relative to fishing. Too often the fisherman arrives on the scene to find the river running over its banks and totally unfishable.

Belfast to Wellsville

The Genesee River offers a perfect mix of water types, regardless of a trout fisherman's preference. The flow varies from riffles to flats, deep pools to white waters, with numerous slow runs thrown in. The brown trout is the principal quarry in the river, although there are many rainbows to be had, along with the rare-to-be-seen brook trout.

There are many access points for fishing. Starting at the dam, you may fish the slow runs by parking along Route 19 for about a half-mile or so. The road then moves away from the river until past the town of Scio, when it is again visible on and off until the city of Wellsville. The closer to Wellsville you get, the poorer the fishing becomes, because of the flood control projects having channelized the stream-bed. An alternate approach to the stream is to turn right at the first road from Belmont, which then takes you to a bridge crossing the river, and an intersection with Back River Road. Various types of water exist in this section between here and Scio. Access is easy and can be found just by looking. Another popular spot is at the end of Back River Road, where another bridge crosses Knight Road. From here an angler may work in both directions.

Wading the stream is by far the best way to fish the Genesee River, since it is generally large water in these stretches, but the person without waders can still find gravel banks to stand on without much difficulty.

Like most other trout waters, the insect life is varied. There are seldom any extremely heavy hatches, but instead there seems to be a more constant pattern of emergence. Some of the most productive flies are as follows: Caddis in the 14 to 18 size range (the fish seem to prefer grey, cream, or a rusty-orange color); Light Cahills in sizes 12 to 18 for when the waters warm up slightly; and the Adams, an all-around good choice for the dry fly fisherman since it imitates so much. For the heavier waters, make sure you take along some good floaters like the Wulff series or Humpy. Since the river is often flowing through brush and fields, later in the season don't forget to bring some crickets, hoppers, and ants for some good action. For the wet fly enthusiast, caddis pupa, Cahills (both light and dark), Picket Pins, and Hare's Ears in sizes 8 to 16 all work well. Small streamers like the Black Ghost and Grey Ghost will also the job. The fly fisherman would be wise to use a rod for 4- to 6-pound line in any length he or she prefers. Not forgetting the spin fisherman, any ultra-light rod and reel combination spooled with 2- to 4-pound-test line will work the best. A heavier line is much more visible to the fish, and using it gives fewer strikes. Lures that are productive are the smaller size Mepps and Rooster Tail spinners in the lighter colors, and small spoons in chrome or brass finish.

This fish is typical of the brown trout caught in the upper Genesee River. Photo courtesy Rick Kustich.

Whatever your choice of lure or fly, the Genesee River offers some fine fishing. The only thing to remember is that any stream can only hold so many fish; so keep only what you are going to use, and gently release the rest. They will be there for you to pursue the next time!

Wellsville to Shongo

Below Wellsville access is almost unrestricted, since both Route 19 or the back road parallel the river. There are some posted sections, but these are relatively short and can be avoided by parking well away from those areas. Along the back road there is an old railroad bed that also parallels the river and can be used to hike along to gain entry wherever one desires. Bridge access and parking is found at Stannards, Yorks Corners, and Shongo, with several other crossroads also available from Route 19.

Fish along this 15-mile stretch range from the usual stockers to monster rainbows, lunker browns, an occasional brookie, and leaping bass. It is always a thrill to wonder which of the species is on the line. To locate the best fishing takes a lifetime of experience, so it is best to have a friend act as guide if one is available. Dwayne Wilson of Trout Unlimited is the resident expert, having been brought up in Wellsville by a trout fishing, fly-tying father, and competing with two older fishing brothers. Barring such expert advice, the easiest section

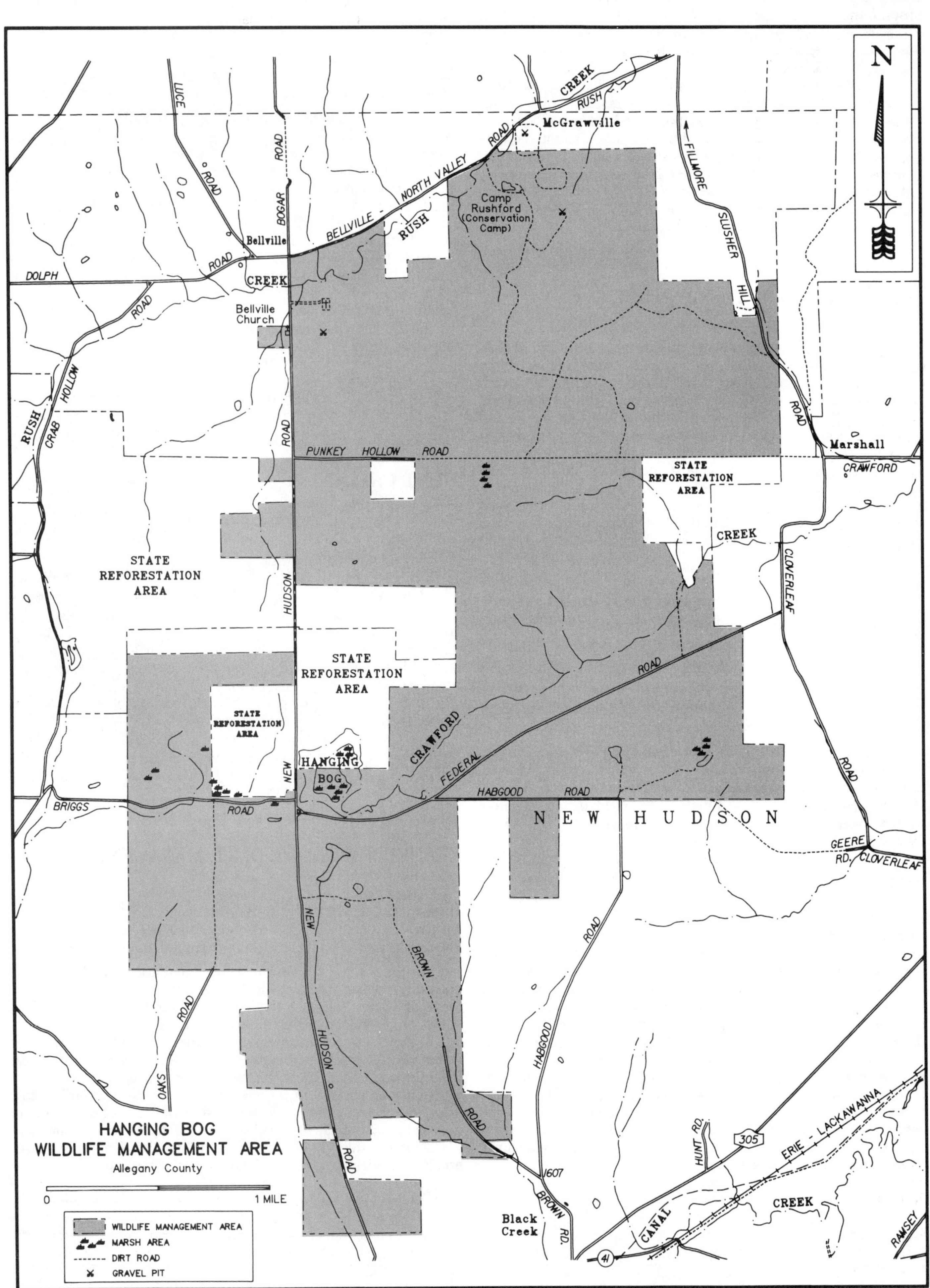
N
HANGING BOG
WILDLIFE MANAGEMENT AREA
Allegany County
0
1 MILE
WILDLIFE MANAGEMENT AREA
MARSH AREA
DIRT ROAD
GRAVEL PIT
McGrawville
Camp Rushford (Conservation Camp)
Bellville
Bellville Church
Marshall
STATE REFORESTATION AREA
HANGING BOG
NEW HUDSON
Black Creek
PUNKEY HOLLOW ROAD
HABGOOD ROAD
CRAWFORD ROAD
FEDERAL ROAD
BRIGGS ROAD
NEW HUDSON ROAD
BROWN ROAD
OAKS ROAD
CLOVERLEAF ROAD
GEERE RD.
SLUSHER HILL ROAD
FILLMORE
ERIE - LACKAWANNA
CANAL
CREEK
HUNT RD.
305
41
1607
RAMSEY

to fish "cold" is from Shongo to the state line. Parking is possible on either Route 19 or on the other side of the river, where a dirt road also parallels the stream, as does the old railroad bed. A half-mile walk upstream from the old bridge abutment should bring you to some excellent fishing.

Since the water conditions are so variable, the Genesee offers something for everyone. Deep, still pools for quiet sit-down fishing, rushing meanders through eroded pastures, and rocky-bottomed riffles can be found in almost any of the sections illustrated on the map. Be sure to wear polaroid glasses so you can see the trout that lie motionless at the bottom of some treefall, and then wonder why and what it is that would make them rise to a fly or chase a moving spinner. If western-like conditions can be found in this part of the state, for sure the Genesee River has that potential.

FLIES FOR THE GENESEE RIVER

By Warren Hammond and Leo Baldwin

From April 1 to June 1, good dry flies to use are: the size 12 Quill Gordon, size 14 Dark Hendrickson, and size 12 March Brown. From June through July, there is a 5 p.m. to 6 p.m. hatch of mayflies, which can be matched with size 12 and 14 Yellow May Flies and size 14 and 16 Light Cahill dry flies. Also from May through July, the size 12 and 14 Renegade and Royal Coachman are good attractor flies for both the brown trout and rainbows. A size 14 to 18 Adams dry fly works well through the season. In late August into October, small (size 20) black ants and tiny tricos (size 20 to 26) work well. An Isonychia hatch sometimes occurs in late September, and a size 12 Grey Drake or Grey Comparadun will work during this period. For the browns a good wet fly is an orange-bodied, grizzly-hackled wooly worm tied on a size 10 or 12 3 XL hook.

For information on the Genesee River from the Mount Morris Dam to Lake Ontario see Monroe County Streams and Rivers.

NOTES: ______________________________

____

____

HANGING BOG WILDLIFE MANAGEMENT AREA

Map Coordinates .... 42° 19′ 03″ 78° 14′ 02″
USGS Map(s) .... Black Creek, Rawson
Township(s) .... New Hudson
Access .... New Hudson Road - see map
Principal Species .... Rainbow Trout (wild), Panfish

The Hanging Bog Wildlife Management Area is a 4,571-acre tract of state-owned land. It consists of rolling hills, extensive forestlands, ponds, and marshes.

There are limited fishing opportunities in Hanging Bog, but the remoteness and beauty of the area make the fishing that is available attractive. Wild rainbow trout are found in the upper sections of Rush Creek, which flows through the northern portion of the area. These fish are a nonmigratory strain and remain in this portion of the stream all year. Some of the larger pools hold trout in excess of 12 inches, but most of these rainbows will be a bit on the small side. In addition, the small ponds and marshes in the management area provide angling for bullheads, pumpkinseeds, rock bass, and crappies. Because of the high acidity and low nutrient content of the water in these ponds, these fish never get very large, but their vast numbers can provide fast action. This is an ideal area to introduce children to the pleasures of fishing.

NOTES: ______________________________

____

____

HONEOYE CREEK

Map Coordinates .... 41° 58′ 06″ 78° 11′ 47″
USGS Map(s) .... Allentown, Wellsville South
Township(s) .... Bolivar, Alma
Access .... Pump Station Road
Principal Species .... Brown Trout (stocked and wild)

Honeoye is a small stream averaging 12 to 15 feet in width. It has a gravel and silt bottom and very brushy banks. There is a slight problem with oil seepage from nearby wells, but it does not seem to affect the quality of the fishing. Fishable all season, there are wild brown trout in this stream in the vicinity of Alma.

The section of the stream between the village of Alma and Alma Pond meanders through extensive wetlands and beaver impoundments. Although very difficult to fish, a persistent angler will be well-rewarded for his efforts. Some of the region's largest brown trout are found in this stretch of Honeoye Creek. There are no public fishing rights sections here, so anglers are advised to obtain permission to fish this portion of the stream.

In the fall, Honeoye Creek is stocked with 2,100 brown trout fingerlings, from the state line to the mouth of Hunt Creek near Alma.

NOTES: ______________________________

____

____

HUNT CREEK

Map Coordinates .... 42° 00′ 35″ 78° 03′ 31″
USGS Map(s) .... Allentown
Township(s) .... Alma
Access .... County Road 18
Principal Species .... Brown Trout (stocked and wild)

Hunt Creek averages about 12 feet in width and has a gravel bottom. The surrounding woodlands and alders provide good bank cover, and the water is of very good quality. There are wild brown trout in the headwaters of this stream, which is fishable all trout season. If an angler is willing to fight the thick bank cover, some nice holdover browns can be taken from this stream.

In the fall, the lowermost 2.3-mile section of Hunt Creek is stocked with 1,200 brown trout fingerlings.

NOTES: ______________________________

____

____

KEANEY SWAMP WILDLIFE MANAGEMENT AREA

Map Coordinates .... 42° 25′ 27″ 77° 54′ 21″
USGS Map(s) .... Birdsall
Township(s) .... Birdsall
Access .... County Road 15A - see map
Principal Species .... Brown Trout, Largemouth Bass

The Keaney Swamp Wildlife Management Area is a 707-acre tract consisting primarily of wetlands and upland stands of hardwoods. Much of Keaney Swamp is boarded by state reforestation land. The entire area is drained by the headwaters of Black Creek.

Keaney Swamp is maintained primarily as a wetland habitat for waterfowl. Other wildlife that use the area include beaver, woodcock, ruffed grouse, cottontail rabbits, mink, and raccoon.

Activities allowed in the swamp by the DEC include hunting, trapping, and camping (by permission of the regional wildlife manager). Of interest to fishermen are the fishing opportunities in Black Creek, which holds brown trout, and the numerous beaver ponds in the vicinity, some of which hold largemouth bass.

NOTES: ______________________________

____

____

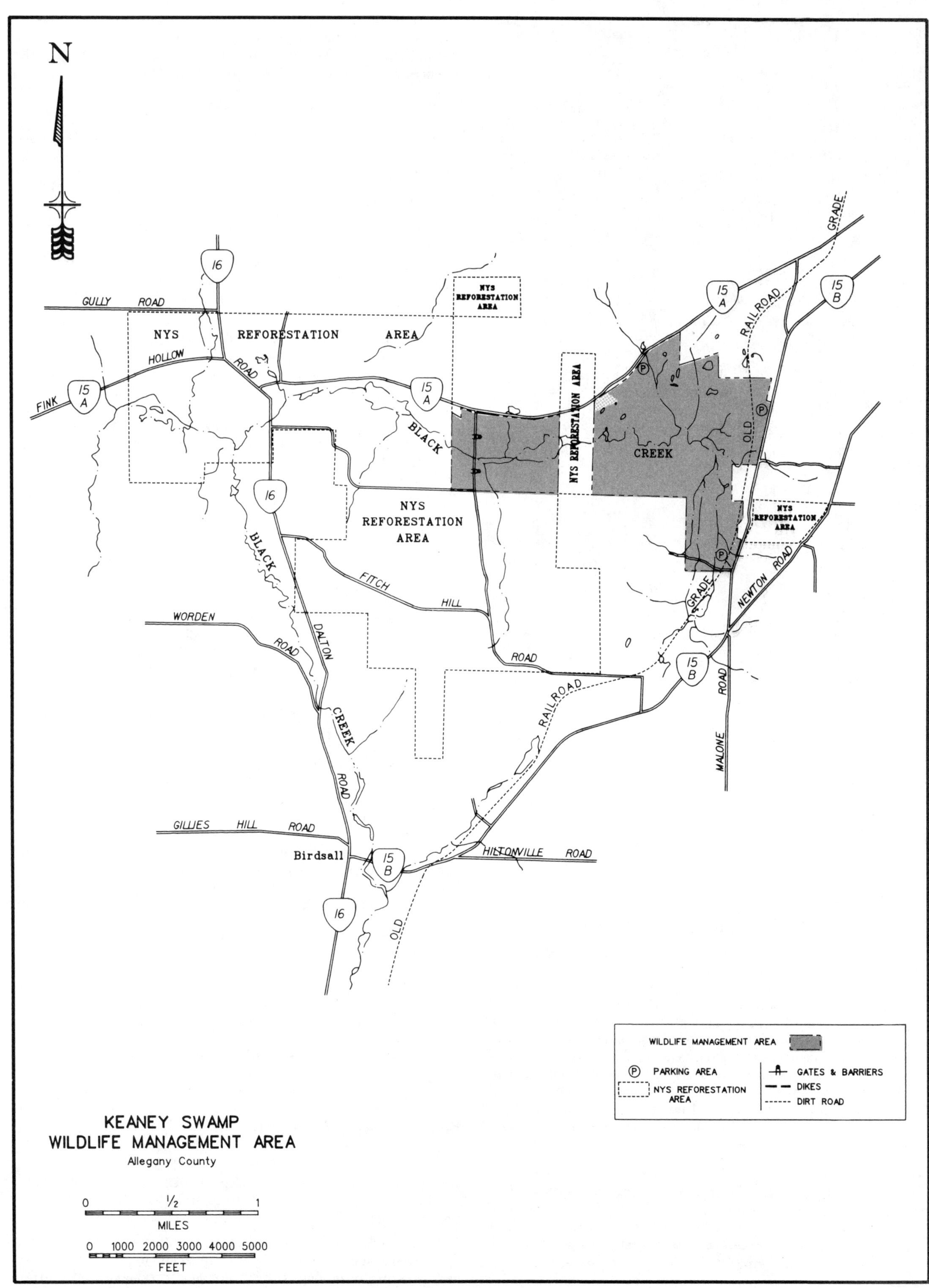
N
GULLY ROAD
NYS REFORESTATION AREA
NYS REFORESTATION AREA
HOLLOW ROAD
FINK
15 A
15 A
15 A
16
16
16
BLACK
BLACK CREEK
NYS REFORESTATION AREA
CREEK
NYS REFORESTATION AREA
NYS REFORESTATION AREA
RAILROAD
GRADE
OLD
15 B
15 B
15 B
FITCH HILL ROAD
WORDEN ROAD
DALTON
CREEK
ROAD
NEWTON ROAD
MALONE ROAD
GRADE
RAILROAD
GILLIES HILL ROAD
Birdsall
HILTONVILLE ROAD
OLD
WILDLIFE MANAGEMENT AREA
PARKING AREA
NYS REFORESTATION AREA
GATES & BARRIERS
DIKES
DIRT ROAD
KEANEY SWAMP
WILDLIFE MANAGEMENT AREA
Allegany County
0 1/2 1
MILES
0 1000 2000 3000 4000 5000
FEET

Portions of Rush Creek flow through the Hanging Bog Wildlife Management Area and a state reforestation tract. These well-shaded stretches provide fair to good fishing for wild rainbow trout in the spring and fall.

LITTLE GENESEE CREEK

Map Coordinates .... 41° 59′ 43″ 78° 15′ 12″
USGS Map(s) .... Bullis Mills, Shinglehouse, Bolivar
Township(s) .... Genesee, Bolivar
Access .... State Route 417
Principal Species .... Brown Trout (stocked)

Unlike most streams in Allegany County, Little Genesee Creek is not a tributary of the Genesee river. It flows into the Allegany River via Oswayo Creek. Averaging about 30 feet in width in the lower reaches, it has a bottom of gravel and silt. The bank cover is intermittent. Fishable during the first few months of trout season, Little Genesee Creek flows through woodland and pastureland. There is some slight seepage from nearby oil wells, and while this has not yet affected the quality of the fishing, recent reports from the DEC indicate that it has now affected the flavor of the fish. Public fishing rights exist on 2.8 miles of the stream between Bolivar and the state line. These sections are not continuous, so anglers should look for appropriate signs and parking areas.

The DEC has purchased miles of fishing easements along many of the streams in western New York. These easements provide public access to some of the best trout streams in the area. However, these are still private property. Respect the land and the landowner's rights.

In the spring, Little Genesee Creek is stocked with 2,400 brown trout yearlings in the 6.3-mile section between Bolivar and the state line. In the fall, it is stocked with 2,000 brown trout fingerlings in the 5-mile section immediately above the village of Bolivar.

NOTES: ____________________

ROOT CREEK

Map Coordinates .... 42° 03′ 30″ 78° 10′ 50″
USGS Map(s) .... Bolivar, Allentown
Township(s) .... Bolivar
Access .... State Route 417
Principal Species .... Brown Trout (stocked and wild)

Flowing mostly through farmland, Root Creek is a small stream averaging about 10 feet in width. It has a bottom of gravel and silt, good water quality, and a lot of bank cover. A good population of wild brown trout can be found throughout its entire length. Although fishable all season, spring and fall are the most productive times here.

In the fall, Root Creek is stocked with 1,100 brown trout fingerlings in the 3.5-mile section just upstream of the road crossing at Route 417.

NOTES: ____________________

RUSH CREEK

Map Coordinates .... 42° 21′ 34″ 78° 12′ 13″
USGS Map(s) .... Rawson, Black Creek
Township(s) .... Rushford, New Hudson
Access .... Rush Creek Road
Principal Species .... Rainbow Trout (wild)

Rush Creek is one of two streams dammed to form Rushford Lake (the other is Caneadea Creek). It averages 12 to 15 feet in width, has a gravel bottom, and a good amount of bank cover. The headwaters of Rush Creek, near the village of Bellville, flow through state forest land and the Hanging Bog Wildlife Management Area.

Although fishable all season, Rush Creek has a problem with high water temperatures in the summer. This is caused in part by the presence of beaver ponds and bogs along its course.

The entire stream holds a fair number of nonmigratory wild rainbow trout, and there is a fair run of rainbows from Rushford Lake here in the spring. Due to the rising water temperature, however, most lake-run fish will have moved down into Rushford Lake by late spring.

In 1983, Rush Creek was deleted from the state stocking program.

NOTES: ____________________

SPRING MILLS CREEK

Map Coordinates .... 42° 02′ 26″ 77° 46′ 03″
USGS Map(s) .... Whitesville, Rexville
Township(s) .... Independence
Access .... Mills Road (County Road 19)
Principal Species .... Brown Trout (stocked and wild)

Spring Mills Creek is a very small tributary of Cryder Creek. It averages about 8 feet in width, has a gravel and bedrock bottom, and very good water quality. The surrounding woodlands and pasturelands provide intermittent bank cover. This stream is fishable all season and there are wild brown trout throughout its length.

In the fall, the lowermost 3.5-mile section of Spring Mills Creek is stocked with 900 brown trout fingerlings.

NOTES: ______________________________

____

____

VANDERMARK CREEK

Map Coordinates .... 42° 10′ 09″ 77° 58′ 48″
USGS Map(s) .... Wellsville North, Andover
Township(s) .... Scio, Ward
Access .... Vandermark Road (County Road 10)
Principal Species .... Brown Trout (stocked), Brook Trout (wild)

Vandermark Creek is a small tributary of the Genesee River. Averaging 15 feet in width, it has a gravel bottom, good water quality, and has generally good bank cover, at least in the stocked sections. Vandermark Creek is surrounded primarily by woodland, and is fishable all trout season. There is a fair number of native brook trout in its headwaters.

In the fall, this stream is stocked with 500 brown trout fingerlings in the 2.5-mile section just upstream of the crossing of County Road 10, near Duke Road.

NOTES: ______________________________

____

____

WISCOY CREEK - **See Wyoming County Streams and Rivers.**

ALLEGANY COUNTY LAKES AND PONDS

ALLEN LAKE

Location

Map Coordinates .... 42° 23′ 45″ 78° 04′ 00″
USGS Map(s) .... Fillmore
Township .... Allen
Access .... Vincent Road

Physical Characteristics

Area .... 50 acres
Shoreline .... 1.5 miles
Elevation .... 1,899 feet
Maximum Depth .... 25 feet
Mean Depth .... 12 feet
Bottom Type .... Clay

Chemical Characteristics

Water .... Clear
pH .... Slightly alkaline
Oxygen .... Good throughout lake

Plant Life

Rooted vegetation is very limited.

Species Information

Rainbow Trout .... Abundant; growth rate good to excellent
Brook Trout .... Abundant; growth rate good to excellent
Brown Bullhead .... Common; growth rate good

Boat Launch Sites

Cartop boats and canoes can be launched from a ramp at the southwest corner of the lake, off Vincent Road. Outboard motors are prohibited. Electric motors are allowed.

General Information

Allen Lake is an artificial impoundment of a branch of Wigwam Creek. Located on the 2,200-acre Allen Lake State Forest, it was intended to be exclusively a trout lake and is heavily stocked. Each year, approximately 2,800 brook trout and 2,800 rainbow trout yearlings are stocked here, in addition to a fair number of excess breeder stock. The fish winter over in this lake quite well, and it is not uncommon for the rainbows to reach lengths in excess of 20 inches and the brookies to top 12 inches.

A productive method for fishing Allen Lake is to wade out and fish in the early morning or evening. Trout can usually be taken in this manner as late as early June. The bottom is firm, and you can cover a lot of water by wading. Fly fishing is especially productive while the fish are in shallow, but small spinners and jigging spoons also work well.

For shore-bound fisherman the riprap along the south side of the lake provides good access. Using small hooks baited with night-crawlers, white worms, canned kernel corn, or marshmallows, cast out into 10 to 20 feet of water. If necessary, use two small splitshot attached about 18 inches above the hook to get some distance. Let the bait slowly drift to the bottom. A majority of the fish taken from this lake are probably taken in this way.

The deepest part of the lake, near the dike, is productive even in the warmest summer months due to the presence of springs. The trout congregate in these cool, deep areas all summer long. They can be taken from these depths by trolling with spoons or plugs. Some anglers do well at night fishing under bright lights suspended over the water.

Bottom fishing for bullhead in the spring is also very productive, despite the fact that the DEC occasionally tries to eliminate these and other non-trout species from the lake.

Trout can be taken from Allen Lake from 1 April to 30 November any size, any species, 5 per day. The use of fish or fish eggs, dead or alive, for bait is prohibited. Ice fishing is prohibited. Camping and picnicing are permitted on the state-owned land adjacent to the lake, but not directly on the lake perimeter.

NOTES: ______________________________

____

____

Small lakes can provide some of the best early season trout fishing. Many, such as Allen Lake, are heavily stocked with yearling trout. In addition, large excess breeder trout are occasionally stocked in these lakes.

ALMA POND

Location

Map Coordinates .... 42° 00′ 49″ 78° 00′ 25″
USGS Map(s) .... Allentown, Wellsville South
Township .... Alma
Access .... Four Mile Road

Physical Characteristics

Area .... 35 acres
Shoreline .... 1.2 miles
Elevation .... 1,571 feet
Maximum Depth .... 8 feet
Mean Depth .... 4 feet
Bottom Type .... Muck

Chemical Characteristics

Water .... Always turbid due to the activity of bullheads and carp, and from summer algae blooms
pH .... Slightly alkaline
Oxygen .... Occasionally low, particularly in winter. Significant winterkills of fish occur here every few years.

Plant Life

Rooted aquatic vegetation is limited in this lake.

Boat Launch Sites

Cartop boats and canoes can be launched from an area by the dam on the western end of the lake.

Species Information

Largemouth Bass .... Common; growth rate good
Smallmouth Bass .... Uncommon; growth rate unknown
Tiger Muskellunge .... Common; growth rate good
Northern Pike .... Common; growth rate good
Carp .... Common; growth rate good
Brown Bullhead .... Common; growth rate good
Brown Trout .... Uncommon; growth rate not available

Also found in Alma Pond are crappies, rock bass, bluegills, and suckers.

General Information

Located just north of the Pennsylvania border, Alma Pond is an artificial impoundment of Honeoye Creek. On current topographical maps and DOT maps it is listed as Beaver Lake. Although stocked annually with 200 tiger muskie fingerlings, an angler is much more likely to catch either largemouth bass or northern pike from this pond. Both species exhibit good growth rates and it is not uncommon for a real lunker to be pulled from here. Woody debris in the form of brush piles, snags and tree stumps is located throughout the pond making fishing difficult, but it provides excellent habitat and cover for the fish. The trout found here are strays from the creek.

In the winter, Alma Pond is a popular ice fishing spot with the locals, providing good catches of northern pike and an occasional muskie.

NOTES: ______________________________

____

____

CUBA LAKE

Location

Map Coordinates .... 42° 14′ 11″ 78° 18′ 27″
USGS Map(s) .... Cuba, Rawson
Township(s) .... Cuba
Access .... West Shore Road

Physical Characteristics

Area .... 492.8 acres
Shoreline .... 6 miles
Elevation .... 1,560 feet
Maximum Depth .... 46 feet
Mean Depth .... Approximately 20 feet
Bottom Type .... Muck, some gravel and rubble

Chemical Characteristics

Water .... Clear
pH .... Alkaline
Oxygen .... Generally good; poor in summer at depths greater than 20 feet.

Plant Life

Extensive weed beds are found along the northern shore. In the summer the weeds can cover as much as 40 percent of the lake.

Boat Launch Sites

1. Public launch site (gravel) off West Shore Road at Oil Creek inlet.
2. Public launch site (gravel) on South Shore Road near the outlet.

Species Information

Walleye .... **Commmon; growth rate fair**

Though there is some natural reproduction of walleye in this lake, the population is sustained by stocking. Walleye have been stocked here since the 1920s, and the DEC now stocks 2,500,000 walleye fry here each year. The population has rebounded in recent years, but they are still plagued by rather poor growth rates. The average 5- to 6-year-old walleye in this lake is only 15 inches in length. Occasionally, an angler will take a lunker-size fish, but these are rare, consisting of very old females or the odd-ball fish that just naturally grows faster than his siblings. The reason(s) that the walleye grow slowly in Cuba Lake is unknown.

The best walleye fishing on Cuba Lake occurs early in the season, before the weeds have had a chance to take over a large portion of the lake. Low-light periods (early morning, evenings, and cloudy days) provide the best fishing. Jigs are the lure of choice at this time of year. Plain 1/4- to 1/2-ounce plain jigs in black, white, or yellow are popular on this lake. Bucktail jigs in black and white, brown and white or black and orange will also work well. Plain or bucktail, they can be fished clean or tipped with a minnow.

Early in the season the walleye will be found close to shore in water as shallow as 3 to 5 feet when light intensity is low, prowling the emerging weedlines. While it is true that you can pick up fish trolling or wind-drifting these shallows, you are more likely to spook them than catch them. A better approach is to use these methods to locate schools of fish and then to anchor. Use fore and aft anchors to prevent the boat from swinging. Then fan cast toward the shallows, varying your lure colors, depths, and retrieval speeds until you find a combination that works.

When the sun is high in the sky, try fishing off deep points for spring walleyes. Larger size jigs are more appropriate when fishing deeper waters.

As spring gives way to summer, the walleye move out into deeper water. However, on this lake they can not move into water deeper than 20 feet, due to poor oxygen levels below that depth. That forces them to concentrate along deep weedlines or in the weeds themselves. Trolling along the weedlines with deep diving crankbaits such as Hot-N Tots and Killer Bs can be very productive during periods of low light.

While the majority of the walleye found in the weedbeds won't be actively feeding, the fish found in the weeds but near the outer edge can be enticed to strike. Anchor well outside of the weedline and cast into the weeds with a floating jig tipped with worms or leeches weighted with a little splitshot. The trick is to let the jig settle completely and then retrieve it very slowly. This will decrease your chances of getting snagged, and the slow crawl of the lure through the weeds will often cause a less-than-active walleye to strike. Because the weeds provide ample shade, these fish can be pursued even during the brightest days. Unfortunately, this is also the time when you find the greatest amount of boat traffic on the lake, which can shut the fishing down.

In the fall changing weather conditions cause the lake to become more homogeneous in terms of temperature and oxygen distribution. This enables the fish to begin moving into deeper waters. Until the lake freezes over, you will still find some good walleye fishing close to shore along weedlines early in the morning and in the evening, but the overall pattern is for the fish is to begin moving into progressively deeper water during the day. The same tackle and techniques that worked during the summer months should also work well here during the fall.

For reasons unknown to this writer relatively few walleye are reported taken from Cuba Lake during the winter months. It might be due to the fact that many people concentrate on the great yellow perch fishing. Also, the abundance of perch here could have a negative impact on the quality of the winter walleye fishing, much as it does on Oneida Lake.

If you do plan on fishing for walleye through the ice try using half ounce Swedish Pimples, Russian jigs or bucktail jigs dressed with a perch eye or small minnow. Tip-ups baited with buckeye minnows or shiners are also effective.

Smallmouth Bass .... **Very common; growth rate fair to good**

Most of the smallmouth bass taken from Cuba Lake are a bit on the small side, but what they lack in size they make up for in numbers. Frequenting rock and rubble bottomed areas, they are found mainly in the extreme eastern end of the lake and on the few rocky points scattered around the lake.

Early in the season, try fishing along developing weedlines with eighth-ounce bucktail jigs. Later in the summer, when the weedlines have developed, fish rocky areas and points using soft-shelled crabs, bucktail or plain jigs (to oz.) tipped with twister tails or leeches, and small crankbaits.

In the fall, smallmouth often go on a feeding binge, resulting in some of the best fishing of the year. Try switching to jigs baited with shiners. Still-fishing with 3- to 4-inch shiners in the deeper parts of the lake can be extremely effective in October and November. Look for rocky bottomed areas and fish the shiner right on the bottom.

Largemouth Bass .... **Very common; growth rate fair to good**

Largemouth bass are arguably the most sought after species in Cuba Lake. This is due to their abundance here and the growing popularity of bass fishing in this region. Fortunately, the growing pressure has not yet hurt their numbers.

Early in the season, small spinners will be the most effective lures. One-eighth to one-sixteenth oz. Panther Martins fished in shallow coves with emerging weeds will produce good numbers of fish. As the water temperatures rise, gradually switch to slightly larger spinners, spinnerbaits, top surface baits, and small, shallow-running crankbaits.

Later in the season, when the weeds have fully emerged, work the weedlines using black or purple plastic worms for fast action. The most productive areas are located on the western side of the lake, from the inlet around to the launch site on South Shore Road. Spinnerbaits and buzzbaits worked over the tops of weedbeds also work well.

In the fall, largemouth tend to orient more off deep weedlines and drop-offs, though some fish can still be taken in shallow water during extended warm spells. Large, slowly worked spinnerbaits, followed by deep-diving crankbaits are the most productive lures during this period. Small jigs dressed with a pork rind or a small minnow will also take fish if worked very slowly. Remember that as the water temperatures fall the bass become slow moving, necessitating a slower retrieve.

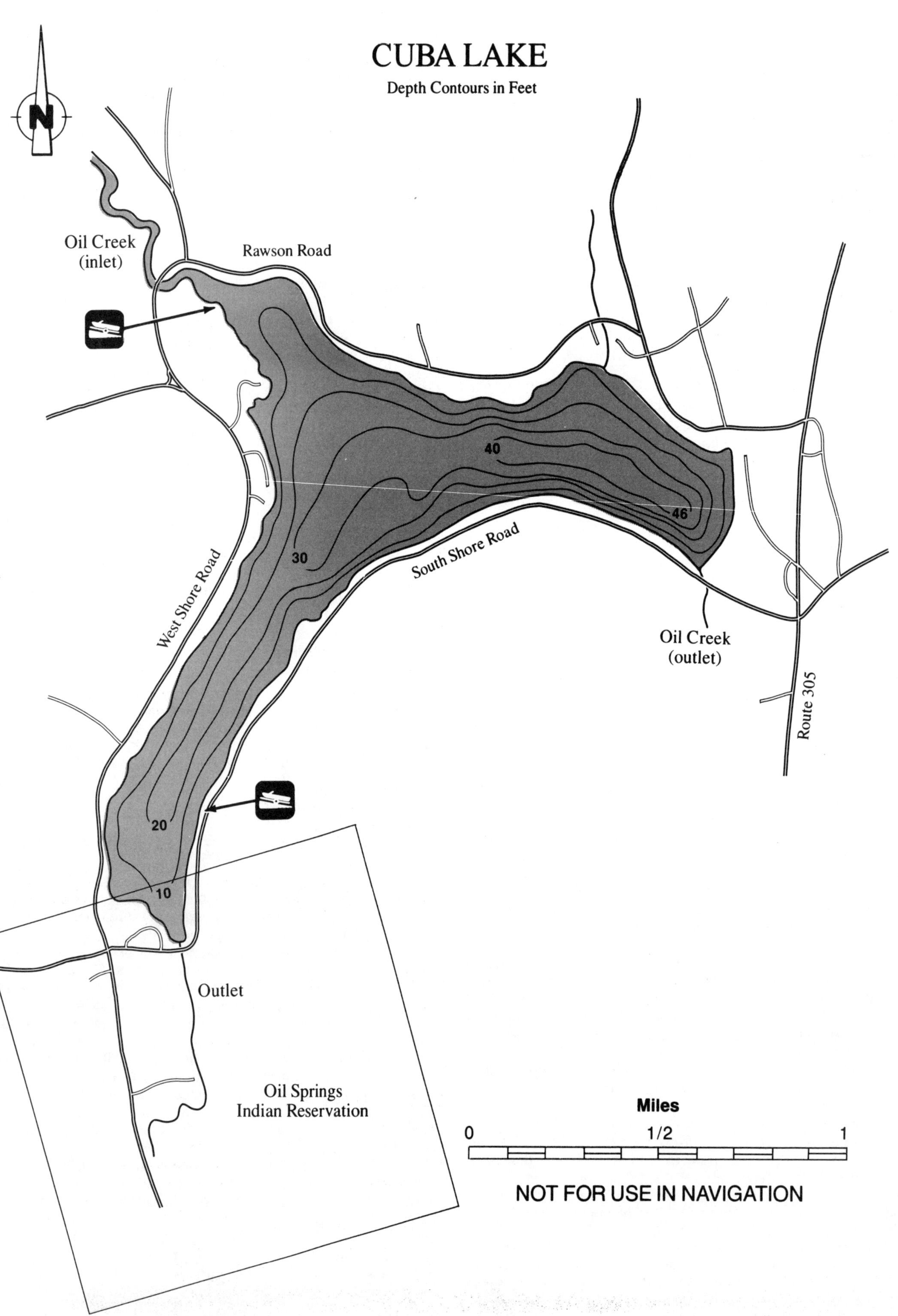
CUBA LAKE
Depth Contours in Feet
N
Oil Creek
(inlet)
Rawson Road
40
46
30
South Shore Road
West Shore Road
Oil Creek
(outlet)
Route 305
20
10
Outlet
Oil Springs
Indian Reservation
Miles
0
1/2
1
NOT FOR USE IN NAVIGATION

Yellow Perch .... **Abundant; growth rate good**

Unlike most of the panfish found in Cuba Lake, yellow perch exhibit good growth rates. Many an angler here has filled a 5-gallon pail with 10- to 12-inch perch.

Immediately after ice-out, large numbers of perch will be found in shallow bays. A productive method for taking springtime perch is to anchor along the edges of dormant weedlines and still fish with grubs, worms or minnows. The use of a perch rig or spreader will significantly increase your catch. Fish the bait near, but not on, the bottom.

As the lake warms, the schools of perch become less concentrated and more migratory, and, therefore, harder to catch. For most of the summer, when the weeds are at their fullest, you can take perch by fishing with worms or small crabs along deep weedlines. Another area to try is in the deep open pockets often found in weedbeds. Approach these pockets as quietly as possible to avoid spooking the fish. Your probably not going to take great numbers of fish, but your efforts will be rewarded

Yellow perch will also be found on deep rocky points in the summer. Still fish these areas with minnows, crayfish, or small jigs tipped with minnows. The bait should be close to the bottom. Don't waste all day on one point. Keep moving until you find some action and move on when the fish have stopped biting.

In the fall, perch fishing usually picks up considerably. The fish become more schooled up and can be found along deep weedlines and on deep rocky points in large numbers. Minnows fished close to the bottom work well. Again, the use of a spreader will increase your catch. Small jigs will also catch perch in the fall, but you have to work the jig with a slow, deliberate stroke rather than the sharp, pumping action used in the summer.

In the winter, the perch fishing on Cuba Lake can be excellent. Many of the deep, dormant weedlines will be productive. A popular spot with the locals is the deepest area of the lake near the dam. Standard techniques, such as tip-ups baited with small minnows, and small jigs tipped with perch eyes or mousey grubs will take impressive numbers of perch.

Tiger Muskellunge .... **Uncommon; growth rate unknown**

Tiger muskellunge (a northern pike/muskellunge hybrid) were first stocked in Cuba Lake in 1972. They were stocked annually from 1976 to 1981 when the program was terminated. What remains is a nonbreeding remnant population whose continued existence in this lake is open to question. With an average life-span of about 10 years, most of the tiger muskies stocked here have already been removed from the fishery.

The muskies that do remain can provide you with a memorable experience. Reaching a length in excess of 50 inches, these toothsome predators can give you the fight of a lifetime. The most productive areas are the weedbeds at the western end of the lake near the inlet, and in the weedy bay on the northeast side of the lake. Casting with large jerkbaits, such as the Suick, or musky spinners, like the Mepps Musky Killer, accounts for most of the fish taken. Tiger muskies can also be taken by trolling deep-diving Pikie Minnows, Flatfish, and Brooks Reefers along deep weedlines. Trollers might want to consider using lead core line to keep their lures 15 to 25 feet down. Unlike many fish, tiger muskies often feed best late in the morning and early afternoon.

Additional Species

In addition to the species listed above, Cuba Lake also has significant populations of black crappie, rock bass, carp, and suckers.

General Information

Located just north of the town of Cuba, this lake is an artificial impoundment of Oil (Rawson) Creek. At the time of its creation in 1858 it was the largest man-made body of water in the world. Extensive weed beds (at times overly extensive) provide habitat for walleye, largemouth and smallmouth bass, perch, and tiger muskies. A present overabundance of predator species has made growth rates for some of these species less than optimum. Perch are an exception to this. Large numbers of good size perch are harvested through the ice here each winter.

Cuba lake is presently supervised by the Allegany State Park Commission, but is in the process of being turned over to a quasi-public recreation district. The extreme western end of the lake is on the Oil Springs Indian Reservation.

The DEC stocks 2,500,000 walleye fry here annually.

NOTES: ____________________

____

____

ROCKVILLE LAKE

Location

Map Coordinates .... 42° 18′ 22″ 78° 05′ 53″
USGS Map(s) .... Black Creek
Township(s) .... Belfast
Access .... Lake Road, off Route 305

Physical Characteristics

Area .... 25 acres
Shoreline .... 1.10 miles
Elevation .... 1,412 feet
Maximum Depth .... 10 feet
Mean Depth .... 5 feet
Bottom Type .... Clay, muck

Chemical Characteristics

Water .... Turbid
pH .... Slightly alkaline
Oxygen .... Fair to good at all depths

Plant Life

Rooted vegetation is very limited.

Species Information

Largemouth Bass .... Common; growth rate fair to good
Northern Pike .... Common; growth rate fair
Tiger Muskellunge .... Uncommon; growth rate unknown
Carp .... Common; growth rate fair to good
Suckers .... Common; growth rate fair to good.

Boat Launch Sites

There is one launch site for cartop boats.

General Information

Rockville Lake is a small impoundment of Black Creek (not the Black Creek mentioned in the stream section). The quality of fishing on this lake is only fair, though at times it can provide some big fish. The population of largemouth bass is self-sustaining. Northern pike and tiger muskies are remnant populations. The DEC no longer stocks this lake.

NOTES: ____________________

____

____

RUSHFORD LAKE

Location

Map Coordinates .... 42° 22′ 49″ 78° 11′ 01″
USGS Map(s) .... Houghton, Black Creek
Township(s) .... Rushford, Caneadea
Access .... Route 243 and Balcom Beach Road

Physical Characteristics

Area .... 550 acres
Shoreline .... 5.30 miles
Elevation .... 1,440 feet
Maximum Depth .... 120 feet
Mean Depth .... Not available
Bottom Type .... Clay, muck, limited gravel

RUSHFORD LAKE
Depth Contours in Feet
N
Balcomb
Beach
Road
Route 243
Lake Road
SHANGRI-LA POINT
Outlet
100
120
Dam
HODGESON'S
Hillcrest Road
50
PIRATES COVE
Hillcrest Road
25
10
Rush Creek
(inlet)
Miles
0
1/2
1
NOT FOR USE IN NAVIGATION

Chemical Characteristics

Water	Clear to slightly turbid
pH	Slightly alkaline
Oxygen	Generally good; can be deficient in the deepest parts of the lake in the summer.

Plant Life

Vegetation is quite limited and is found primarily in the shallows of the southern and western arms and in a few bays along the northern shore. Extreme fluctuations in water level and steep slopes combine to keep weed growth down.

Boat Launch Sites

1. Public launch site (gravel ramp) at foot of Balcom Beach Road, off Route 243. From Memorial Day to Labor Day (Monday to Thursday) launching is free. From Friday to Sunday boats with motors up to 25 hp are charged $4. Boats with motors over 25 hp are charged $15. Before Memorial Day and after Labor Day launching is free.

Species Information

Smallmouth Bass .... Common; growth rate fair

Smallmouth bass are one of the primary predators in Rushford Lake. Though the majority tend to run a bit on the small side, a few 4- to 5-pound fish are taken here each year.

Rushford Lake is at full pool by early May, and for a number of reasons the lake is slow to warm up in the spring. Because of this, smallmouth are usually on or just coming off their spawning beds when bass season opens. Initially, anglers should start looking for fish in shallow water, 3 to 12 feet deep. Because the fish are going to be concentrated near the shore, the early part of the season is one of the most productive periods on Rushford Lake for bass fishing. The spawning beds, docks and areas where you find shallow shelves adjacent to steep drop-offs are going to be especially good.

The local fishermen I spoke with all preferred using live minnows early in the season. If casting is your preference, they recommended using small spinners and jigs.

When the temperature of the water approaches 60 degrees, smallmouth bass will begin to drop down into deeper water (10 to 25 feet) in the daytime, and orient along deep weedlines, rocky ledges and submerged points. They return to the shallows in the early morning and evening. Live minnows (golden shiners if possible) are very effective for taking these fish, as are small crabs. Stan Koprevich, who lives on the lake and fishes it as often as possible, recommends catching a good wind drift or using a trolling motor to work these areas. Stan likes to fish with a minnow on a size 4 hook (size 6 for smaller minnows). He doesn't usually use any weight. He feels that this allows the minnow to swim more freely, and a more active bait will attract more bass. If the drift isn't to fast, Stan also leaves the bail open, giving the minnow even more freedom of movement. As an alternative to drifting live minnows Stan recommends trolling with small sinking Rapalas or silver X-4 Flatfish.

Small plain or bucktail jigs tipped with a minnow or Mister Twister tail will also work well when cast shoreward and slowly worked out toward deeper water. These are particularly effective in areas where the bottom drops off fast such as along the cliffs on the

An artificial impoundment, Rushford Lake is drawn down as much as 65 feet in the fall. Though this has a detrimental effect on the biology of the lake, the fishing here is still quite good. Note the exposed shoreline.

southwest side of the outlet near the dam or practically anywhere in the southern arm of the lake.

From dusk to dawn smallmouth bass come into very shallow water to feed. These are often big fish that come into these waters to feed on large minnows. Hula-poppers and jitterbugs can be very effective on these fish.

While the majority of the waters in this lake under 40 feet deep probably hold at least some smallmouth, naturally some areas are going to be better than others. Many of the locations that follow were recommended by Jim Bokor, an avid fisherman who has fished this lake for years:

1. Pirates Cove. There is a small gravel bar near the mouth of the cove that is excellent for bass all summer long;
2. The ledges on the main point southwest of the dam. This area holds a lot of bass, but they tend to run on the small side. There is a ledge on this point that protrudes out about 30 feet and is particularly good for bass in August. Jim does very well here using spinners and worms fished close to the bottom;
3. The ledges on the south corner near the dam. This is one area of the lake favored by big smallmouth. Large bucktail jigs, worked properly, should be very effective here;
4. The buoys on the north side of the lake, about three-fifths of a mile west of the dam. The bass fishing is good on the outside of the buoys where the shallows drop off into deep water;
5. The buoys one-quarter mile east of Shangra La Point. The buoys mark a bar. Fish on the outside of the bar where it drops off into deep water;
6. Shangra La Point. This is a small point of stone and gravel about 30 feet wide that drops off into deep water. Fish the deeper outside edges;
7. The ledges one-quarter mile west of the launch at Balcom Beach;
8. The submerged islands in the northwest arm of the lake. At times the grass will grow right to the surface here. This area is good for smallmouth all summer long. Jim says that spinners or jigs dressed with small white Mister Twister tails work well in this area;
9. The buoys on the southwest side of the west arm of the lake. These are located near the inlet. Fish along the outside edge of the buoys; and
10. The point at Hodges. This is the point on the south side of the bay that lies on the west side of the lake. There is a small bar off this point that is strewn with boulders and old stumps. Fish the outside edge of the bar.

They begin drawing this lake down in late September, at a rate of around 3 feet per day. Fortunately, this doesn't seem to hurt the bass fishing at all. The fish are already moving into deeper water by this time, and simply continue to follow this pattern. As is the case on many other lakes, the smallmouth bass in Rushford Lake go on a feeding binge in the fall.

Rainbow Trout .... Common; growth good

Rushford Lake has a good population of rainbow trout. In the spring, when the water levels are low, rainbows will be found near shore in fairly shallow water seeking preferred water temperatures and forage fish (alewives are abundant in this lake). Stan Koprevich and Jim Bokor both feel that the shallows near the mouths of Caneadea Creek and Rush Creek, the flats just off the launch at Balcom Beach and the waters near the dam offer the best fishing early in the season. Jim also says that the flats directly across from Hodges are good early on.

Stan does a lot of trout fishing here and says that the early season can be divided into two distinct periods. The first period runs from April 1 and lasts about three weeks, or until the lake is stocked with trout. During this time Stan fishes with minnows right on the bottom. Use slip sinkers when fishing on the bottom to allow the bait to swim freely. Mornings and evenings are the most productive times, but during the spring trout can also be taken with fair regularity during the day. Toward the end of April, just before any trout are stocked here, Stan will switch to fishing a minnow under a bobber. He doesn't usually use any splitshot when using a bobber, preferring instead to let the minnow swim freely.

Flatlining is another method that is highly productive for trout in the spring. Jointed Rapalas, silver or blue Flatfish, Sutton spoons or any other lure that imitates an alewife will be productive when slowly trolled along the shore. Johnson Sprites also work well here. This shallow water trolling is productive until early June.

The second phase of the spring fishery begins after the lake is stocked, which occurs in late April and early May. Rushford Lake get an annual stocking of 3,800 rainbow trout yearlings. Once these fish are present, Stan switches to spincasting. He has found that these newly arrived hatchery fish are easily taken by casting small (1/16 oz.) Panther Martins and Rooster Tails. Stan uses 6-pound-test line and a large splitshot to get long casts.

As water temperatures rise, the trout will begin to move out into deeper water. Some fish will continue to be caught in the shallows as late as early July, but most rainbows will have migrated toward the deep water near the dam by early summer. There is some oxygen deficiency in the deepest parts of the lake. This, plus the fact that the surface water temperatures are generally too warm, eventually forces the trout into a fairly restricted band of suitable water, making the fishing all the more easy.

Once the trout have become established in the deep water near the dam, they tend to spread out over the thermocline in search of baitfish, and become a bit difficult to find, at least during the day. But the night time is a different story. Stan does very well at night using live bait. He uses a large sinker to get the bait down to where the fish have found preferred temperatures. This can be anywhere from 20 to 90 feet down in the summer, but Stan has found that most often the trout will be found 30 to 40 feet down in the water column. He strongly recommends that when you do get a strike, note what depth your bait is at and work that part of the water column thoroughly. I'm not sure what type of rig Stan uses, but I would recommend using an English bait hook and a barrel sinker as the terminal tackle. The hook is sewed under the back skin of the bait with a baiting needle along the dorsal fin. The hook should be inserted in such a way that the hooks lie on the head of the bait, with the points facing toward the tail. If done properly, the bait, such as an alwife, will live for quite a long time, and its ability to swim will not be greatly impeded. The snell of the hook should be attached with a small snap swivel to the main line. This not only allows you to change hooks rapidly, but also keeps the barrel sinker away from the bait. More than one bait can be fished from a line if leaders are attached to the main line at 10-foot intervals. This allows you to cover a greater part of the water column, increasing your chances of success. Night fishing for rainbows using this method is good from sundown to sunrise.

In the fall, two changes take place that affect the trout fishing on Rushford Lake. First, by the middle of September the fish are entering their spawning phase. This will cause them to become more structure oriented and they can again be taken in the areas that were productive in the spring, at least for a few weeks. Second, the lake is drawn down beginning in late September at a rate of about 3 feet per day. This causes the fish (all species) to increasingly concentrate in the area by the dam. When this happens, the trout fishing can be excellent. I have been down on the exposed ledges off the point just to the northwest of the dam in the fall, when the lake was about one-half drawn down. The whole area was alive with trout constantly rising to the surface. The same methods that worked in the spring will also work well in the fall.

Trout can be taken here from April 1 to November 30, any size, 5 per day. Ice fishing is not permitted.

Additional Species

Rushford Lake has a number of species that individually are only of secondary importance, but when taken together constitute a major part of this fishery.

Brown trout are stocked here at the rate of 1,800 yearlings per year. They will often be found in the same areas as the rainbows, and can be taken with the same methods.

A springtime favorite on Rushford Lake are the abundant crappies. Reaching up to 1 pound in size, they are caught in good numbers from mid-April to mid-May. The most productive areas are the drop-offs adjacent to the dam. Small spinners and jigs, or minnows fished under a bobber are very effective. For some real excitement, Stan Koprevich recommends using a light fly rod to cast small, white pork rinds on a size 6 hook. The best crappie fishing will be early in the morning and in the evening.

Carp can be found in practically any shallow area of the lake in the spring, especially if there are any weeds present. An especially good spot is the small cove on the south side of the west arm of the lake near the inlet. If you've ever had a desire to try bowfishing for carp, Jim Bokor says this is the place to start. They are always in this cove in good number in the morning.

Bullhead can also be found in most of the shallow parts of the lake. They are abundant, and range from one-half to 1 pound in size. The best bullhead fishing takes place in the spring.

A relatively new introduction to Rushford Lake are walleye. It is not known how they got into the lake. They were first seen in the summer of 1988 by anglers fishing near the dam. All the fish taken so far have been small, and they certainly don't constitute any sort of a fishery yet. Whether or not they will become one is unknown, but it is a situation worth keeping an eye on.

Rounding out the species found in this lake are rock bass, yellow perch, sunfish, and suckers. Lake trout, until recently found in this lake, are no longer present.

General Information

Rushford Lake was formed by the damming of Rush Creek and Caneadea Creek in 1925. This was done by the Rochester Gas and Electric Company to help regulate the flow of water in the Genesee River. Several years ago, the lake was sold by RG and E to the Rushford Lake Recreational District, a quasi-public agency.

The lake is usually at full water capacity in late spring and summer, but is drawn down by as much as 65 feet in the fall and winter. This has a detrimental effect on the growth rate of some fish species, and definitely inhibits the growth of weeds. It also precludes ice fishing in the winter (ice fishing is strictly prohibited). The lake is usually iced up until late March.

There is rather little public shore access on this lake. Shore bound anglers can access the lake at the public launch on Balcom Beach Road and at the public beach on the extreme south end of the lake, by the mouth of Rush Creek. Additional shore access can be found adjacent to the dam in October and November when the water levels are low. This area can be reached by driving to the foot of Lake Road and walking down a foot path.

NOTES: ______________________________

____

____

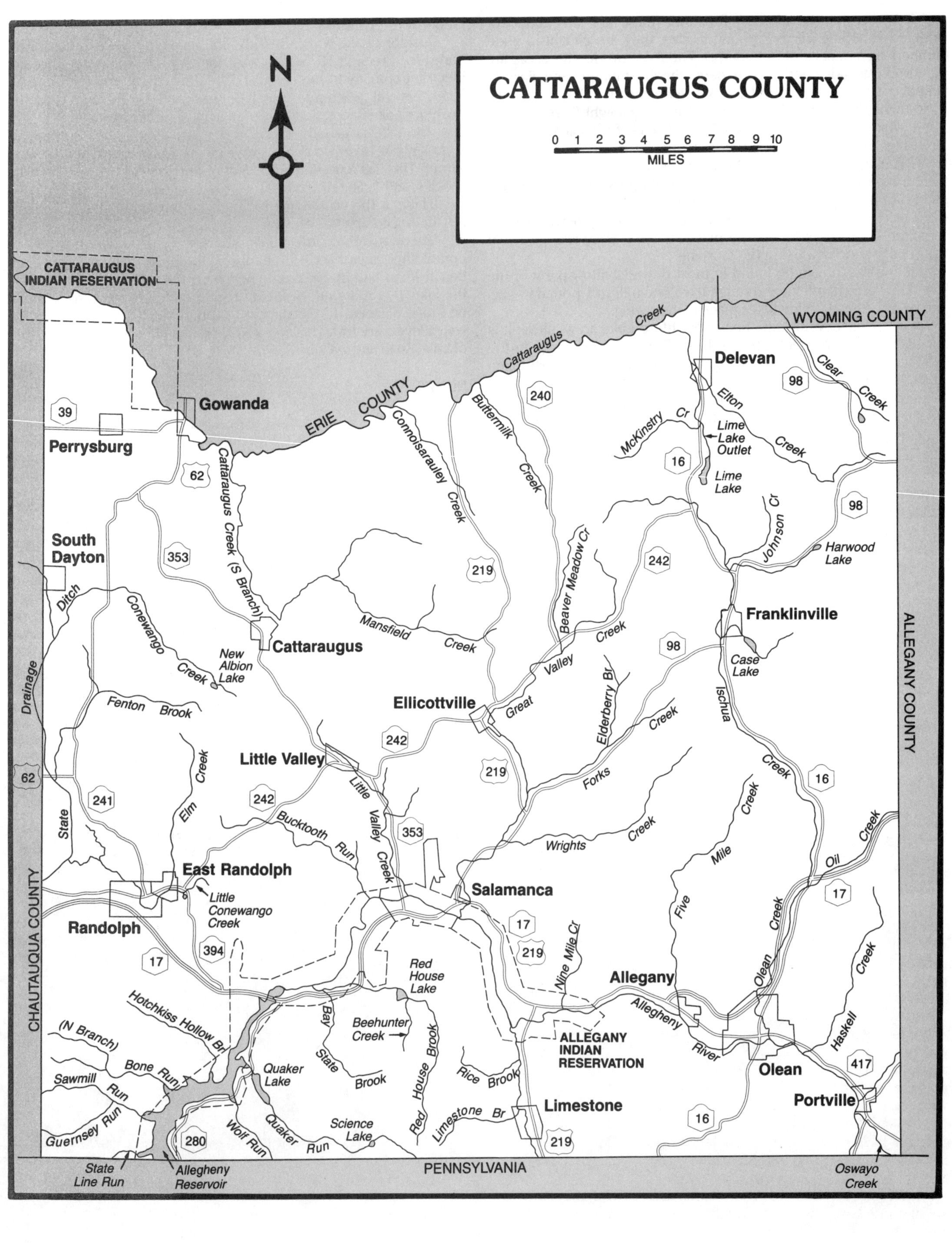
CATTARAUGUS COUNTY
0 1 2 3 4 5 6 7 8 9 10
MILES
N
CATTARAUGUS INDIAN RESERVATION
WYOMING COUNTY
ERIE COUNTY
ALLEGANY COUNTY
CHAUTAUQUA COUNTY
PENNSYLVANIA
Gowanda
Perrysburg
South Dayton
Delevan
Franklinville
Cattaraugus
Ellicottville
Little Valley
East Randolph
Randolph
Salamanca
Allegany
Olean
Portville
Limestone
Cattaraugus Creek
Cattaraugus Creek (S Branch)
Connoisarauley Creek
Buttermilk Creek
Clear Creek
Elton Creek
McKinstry Cr
Lime Lake Outlet
Lime Lake
Johnson Cr
Harwood Lake
Beaver Meadow Cr
Mansfield Creek
Great Valley Creek
Case Lake
Ischua Creek
Elderberry Br
Forks Creek
Conewango Creek
New Albion Lake
Fenton Brook
Elm Creek
Ditch
Drainage
State Ditch
Bucktooth Run
Little Valley Creek
Wrights Creek
Five Mile Creek
Oil Creek
Olean Creek
Haskell Creek
Little Conewango Creek
Red House Lake
Nine Mile Cr
Allegheny River
ALLEGANY INDIAN RESERVATION
Hotchkiss Hollow Br
(N Branch)
Bone Run
Sawmill Run
Guernsey Run
Bay State Brook
Beehunter Creek
Red House Brook
Quaker Lake
Rice Brook
Limestone Br
Wolf Run
Quaker Run
Science Lake
State Line Run
Allegheny Reservoir
Oswayo Creek
39
62
353
240
219
98
16
242
241
17
394
280
417

CATTARAUGUS COUNTY STREAMS AND RIVERS

ALLEGHENY RIVER

Map Coordinates	40° 26′ 36″ 80° 00′ 55″
USGS Map(s)	Steamburg, Red House, Little Valley
Location	Southern Cattaraugus County
Access	Readily accessible from many bridge crossings between Salamanca and Portville - see below
Principal Species	Muskellunge, Northern Pike, Walleye, Smallmouth Bass, Channel Catfish, Panfish

The New York portion of the Allegheny River is a wide, slow-moving, silt-bottomed river with numerous deep holes providing good fishing opportunities for many warm-water species.

Wood pilings, which date from turn-of-the-century logging operations, line the river on both sides in many areas. Many of these pilings barely reach the surface. They pose a hazard to power boats, but they also provide shelter to many types of fish, especially muskellunge and northern pike. Unfortunately, they are having a detrimental affect on the overall productivity of the river. The DEC reports that the pilings cause the river to be artificially channeled. This results in excessive flooding and a loss of backwater habitat, the latter of which could have a serious affect on the muskies and northern pike.

Muskellunge, which are stocked throughout the river, can be taken in both the summer and the fall. They are frequently found in the large pools that form below most bridges. While muskies can be taken throughout the river, the most productive waters are the pools between Olean and Portville. The best pool is reputed to be below the bridge at Steam Valley. This bridge pool is well known for producing large numbers of fish, not only muskies, but also walleye and smallmouth bass. Other muskie hotspots are the mouths of major tributaries, such as Olean Creek, Oswayo Creek, and Tunungwant Creek. Jerk-baits are generally considered to be the most productive means of taking these hard-fighting fish. Be sure to check for current Cattaraugus County muskie regulations.

Northern pike are a fairly recent introduction to this river. They were stocked in the Allegheny Reservoir by the U.S. Fish and Wildlife Service and then rapidly invaded other parts of the river system. Northerns are now very common in the New York section of the Allegheny River. They can be found practically everywhere to some degree, but the best areas are along the old pilings that line some parts of the river, at the confluence with Olean Creek, the oxbows near Salamanca, and the section near Red House Brook. The spring is an especially productive time to fish for these toothsome predators.

The Allegheny River is one of the few bodies of water in Western New York where muskellunge and northerns co-exist. Unfortunately, the muskie population here could be in a state of irreversible decline due to competition from its more voracious cousin. Though smaller in size (at least in North America), northern pike will usually out-compete muskies for food and habitat. The river is managed as a muskie fishery by the DEC; to help protect muskies, northern pike are subject to unrestricted fishing in the Allegheny River, i.e., any number, any size, all year long.

Another important game fish found in this river are walleye. Walleye fishing in the Allegheny is quite good in the spring and fall. They can be taken under any major bridge where the current has scooped out a deep pool. An especially productive section of the river is the reach between Salamanca and the reservoir. Every spring tremendous numbers of walleye run up the river from the reservoir to spawn, and the fishing at this time can be incredible. This is a good section for fishing from shore or in waders. Most of the walleye taken here weigh 2 to 3 pounds, but occasionally a lunker tipping the scales at 7 or 8 pounds is reported.

In addition to the above species, there are healthy populations of smallmouth bass, rock bass, carp, suckers, and catfish throughout the Allegheny River. The state record catfish came out of the Allegheny River and weighed well over 20 pounds. There might also be a few American eels swimming about in this river. They were stocked in the system years ago by Fish and Wildlife and a remnant population might still be holding on. Don't be surprised if after landing an especially hard fighting fish it gets up and runs away. There are a lot of very large salamanders known as Hellbenders in this river.

To get to many of these fish you're probably best off using a canoe, particularly during periods of low water when the fish are forced to concentrate in the larger pools. You might have to pull the canoe over some of the shallows, but its often the only way to get to the really good fishing.

Access to the Allegheny River presents no problems. Boat launch sites are found on the reservoir at Onoville, Highbanks, and at Allegany State Park (see Allegheny Reservoir), at a state-operated site on Olean Creek off Giles Hollow Road, 6 miles north of Olean, (hand launch only), at Veterans Bridge where the Southern Tier Expressway crosses the river in the town of Allegany (on the south side of the river on River Road) and at the South Olean bridge launch site, at Route 16 and West River Road. Bank access can readily be had from many of the bridge crossings in Salamanca, Allegany, Olean, and Portville. It should be remembered that the Allegheny River, from the Town of Vandalia to the Allegheny Reservoir, is on the Allegany Indian Reservation, and a Seneca Nation fishing license is required.

NOTES: ____

ALLEGANY STATE PARK

Map Coordinates	42° 03′ 12″ 78° 48′ 35″
USGS Map(s)	Steamburg, Red House, Little Valley, Salamanca, Limestone
Location	Southern Cattaraugus County
Access	Entrances off Route 17 (Southern Tier Expressway)
Principal Species	Brown Trout (stocked and wild), Brook Trout (stocked and wild), Rainbow Trout (stocked and wild), Largemouth Bass, Panfish

Nestled in the scenic, wooded hills of southern Cattaraugus County, Allegany State Park is the largest park in the state park system, measuring over 62,000 acres in size. The park is set up to accommodate practically every type of outdoor activity. There are an incredible 747 cabin, tent, and trailer sites available for use throughout the year. Additional facilities include: 80 miles of hiking trails, nature interpretive trails and programs, an outdoor amphitheater for cultural events, 25 miles of groomed cross-country ski trails, over 50 miles of prepared snowmobile trails with a link up to the Alleghany National Forest and the Pennsylvania State Forest Trail System, which contain over 500 miles of trails, 3 miles of paved bicycle trails, numerous scenic overlooks, more than 50,000 acres of diversified terrain open to hunting, and of course a multitude of fishable lakes and streams. Additional information on Allegany State Park can be obtained by calling: (716) 354-2182 or (716) 354-2545.

The following article was written by Neal Wilson, an avid angler of these waters and a member of Trout Unlimited.

THE STREAMS OF ALLEGANY STATE PARK

By Neal Wilson

Allegany State Park, the largest division in the state park system, offers the fisherman a wide variety of fishing choices. Three lakes (Quaker, Red House, and Science) are all stocked with either browns, rainbows, or brook trout, in addition to having populations of panfish, and, in the case of Red House Lake, bass. This makes them excellent for family fishing. Two medium-size streams, Quaker Run and Red House Brook, are stocked with brook and brown trout. Numerous small streams, often no more than 5 feet across, are found in the park. Limestone Brook, Rice Brook, Wolf Run, Bay State

Brook, and Beehunter Creek all receive some stocked trout each year, as well as holding populations of wild brook and brown trout. Stoddard Creek, McIntosh Creek, Stoney Brook, Bova Creek, Coon Run, Murray Brook, Yaeger Brook, and Cain Hollow Creek are not stocked, but do contain wild brook and brown trout (see map).

All of the streams in Allegany State Park are of a freestone type (rock, gravel, and boulder bottom), spring fed, and fishable to some degree the whole season. Even during dry seasons, there is still enough water flow in the smallest streams to make fishing worthwhile and challenging. If you like to fish beaver ponds, try Red House Brook, Bay State Brook, and Wolf Run. They have beaver dams scattered along their lengths. During the first month of the season Red House Brook and Quaker Run receive extremely heavy fishing pressure, but after that all the streams are nearly devoid of fishermen.

If you are a fisherman who likes the peace and solitude of fishing for wild trout in beautiful surroundings, then I highly recommend you try Allegany's smaller streams. The brook trout don't get big; if you catch one over 6 inches it's a big one for that stream (my personal best was a brookie just over 12 inches). And they are beautifully colored fish. The wild browns run larger than the brook trout, but they are not quite as plentiful, and they're harder to catch and land. A 17-inch wild brown is the largest fish I have ever caught on one of Allegany's smaller streams.

The park's small streams flow through heavily wooded valleys that shade them from the sun, keeping water temperatures cold enough for the trout to remain active all season. However, in low water conditions extreme care should be taken, as the trout are very spooky in the gin-clear water.

In terms of tackle to use on these waters, I recommend a matched 5 1/2- to 6-foot ultra-light outfit spooled with 4-pound-test line for the bait and spinner fisherman. For bait I suggest night-crawlers cut in half. Threaded them onto a size 6, 8, or 10 bait-hold hook so that the bend of the hook comes out of the worm about a half inch from the end of the worm. My second choice for bait are large mealworms. For these I use a size 12 or 14 single-egg hook. Hook the mealworm through a couple of body segments in the back. Use just enough weight to get your offering to the bottom, so that it drifts and bounces naturally along the bottom with the current. For the spinner fisherman, use your favorite lure type. My personal choice is a small Panther Martin. Size 0 or 1 spinners work best on this type of water.

For the fly fisherman, a 7 1/2-foot 4 or 5 weight matched outfit is perfect for these streams. An 8- or 9-foot 6 weight outfit is called for on the lakes. As to choice of flies, I recommend using the Hairwing Coachman, Adams, Light Cahills, and caddis flies in sizes 14 to 18. In the nymph category, I recommend the gold-ribbed Hare's Ear, yellow and green Caddis Pupa, and March Browns in sizes 12 to 16.

A park fishing permit is required for fishing in Allegany State Park. It is free and can be obtained at the park police office in the Red House Administration Building. The permit has a map of the park streams and roads.

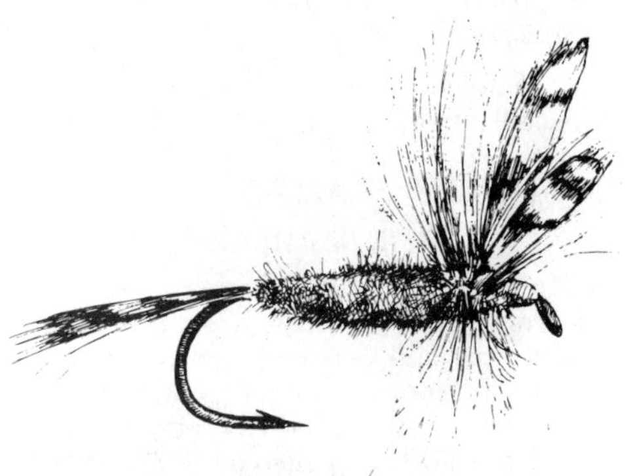

A popular generic pattern, the Adams can be used to imitate numerous insects by varying the size of the fly.

Brook trout can be found in the headwaters of many, if not most, of the trout streams found in Cattaraugus County. They will seldom reach more than 9 inches, but occasionally a fish over 12 inches will be encountered. A good way to begin your search for these wily and elusive fish is to obtain a topographical map of an area and look for headwaters in wooded areas. Brook trout need cold water, and the shade of trees keeps the stream water cool even in summer. Carrying a thermometer will also help; brook trout are seldom found in water over 65 degrees.

For more information on fishing in Allegany State Park see: Bay State Brook, Beehunter Creek, Limestone Brook, Quaker Run, Quaker Lake, Red house Brook, Red House Lake, Rice Brook, Science Lake, and Wolf Run.

NOTES: ______________________________

____

____

BAY STATE BROOK

Map Coordinates .... 42° 05′ 40″ 78° 48′ 15″
USGS Map(s) .... Red House
Location .... Allegany State Park
Access .... Paralleled by Bay State Road
Principal Species .... Brown Trout (stocked and wild), Brook Trout (wild)

Bay State Brook is a small stream averaging about 10 feet in width. It has a gravel and rubble bottom and a good amount of bank cover. It is surrounded by woodlands that shade its waters and keep temperatures down. Fishable to some extent all season, easy fishing is found here only during the early months of trout season. Like most of the small streams in Allegany State Park, it may hold wild brook and/or brown trout in its upper reaches. A state park fishing permit is required.

In the fall, the 2.5-mile section of Bay State Brook upstream of the park boundary is stocked with 700 brown trout fingerlings.

NOTES: ______________________________

____

____

BEAVER MEADOW CREEK

Map Coordinates .... 42° 19′ 13″ 78° 36′ 24″
USGS Map(s) .... Ashford, Ellicottville
Township(s) .... Ellicottville
Access .... County Road 32
Principal Species .... Brown Trout (stocked and wild)

Beaver Meadow Creek averages about 15 feet in width. It has a bottom of rubble, gravel, and silt. The water is generally clear and of good quality, but little insect life is to be found here. Bordered by woodlands and open fields, most of this stream has intermittent bank cover, except in the headwaters, which are rather overgrown with brush.

Fishable all season, Beaver Meadow Creek forms a large pond below Fancy Tract Road. There are some posted areas above the road, but the state has public fishing rights south of Route 75 and east of Route 32.

In the fall, a 3.5-mile section of this stream is stocked with 800 brown trout fingerlings, from Fancy Tract Road upstream to the mouth of Carter Brook. The headwaters hold some wild brown trout.

NOTES: ______________________________

____

____

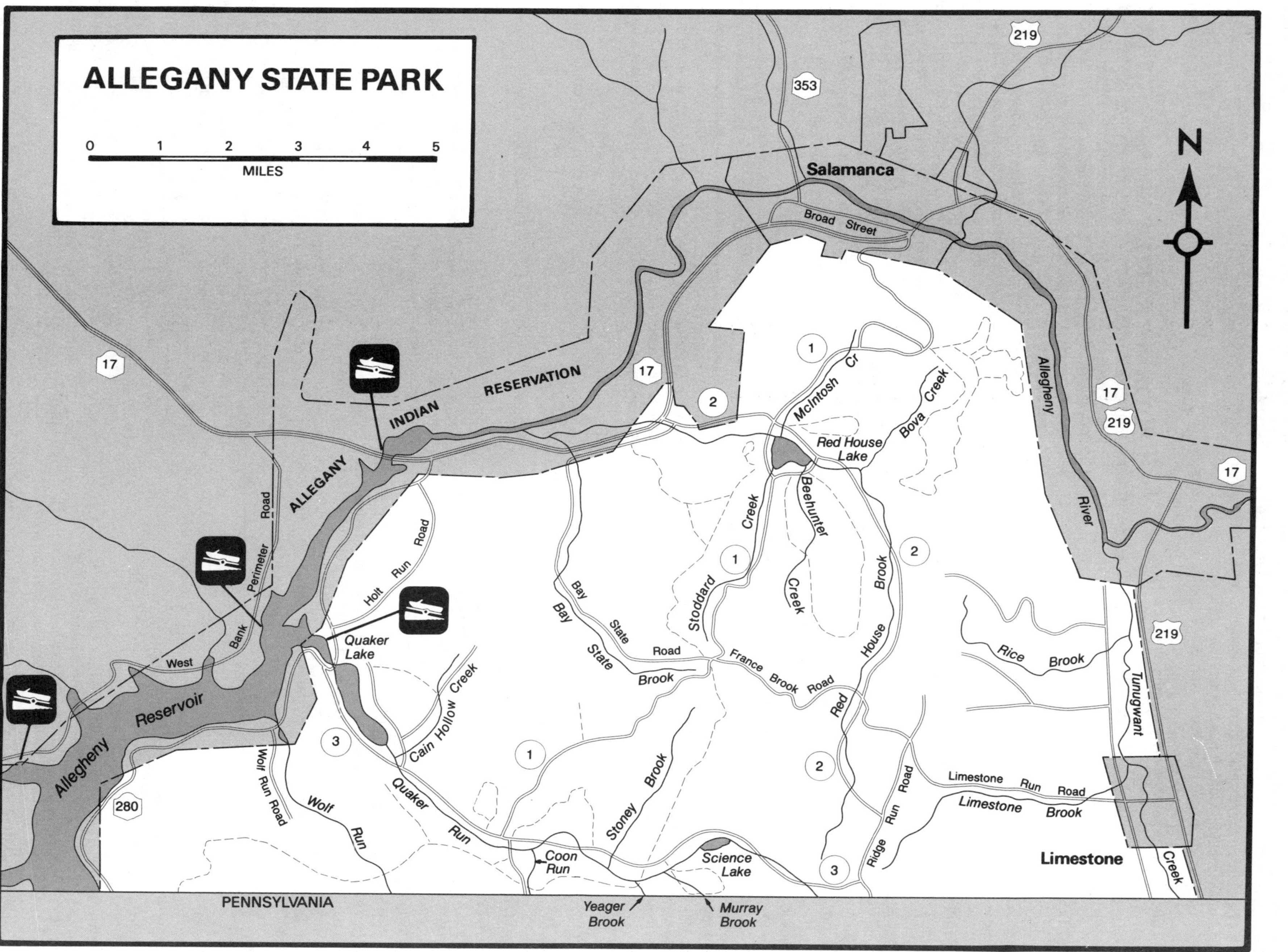

ALLEGANY STATE PARK
0
1
2
3
4
5
MILES
N
Salamanca
Broad Street
Allegheny River
219
17
353
Tunugwant Creek
Limestone
Limestone Run Road
Limestone Brook
Rice Brook
Bova Creek
McIntosh Cr
Red House Lake
Beehunter Creek
Red House Brook
Ridge Run Road
France Brook Road
Stoddard Creek
Bay State Road
Bay State Brook
Stoney Brook
Science Lake
Murray Brook
Yeager Brook
Coon Run
Cain Hollow Creek
Quaker Run
Holt Run Road
Quaker Lake
Wolf Run
Wolf Run Road
ALLEGANY INDIAN RESERVATION
West Bank Perimeter Road
Allegheny Reservoir
280
PENNSYLVANIA

BEEHUNTER CREEK

Map Coordinates .... 42° 05′ 57″ 78° 44′ 19″
USGS Map(s) .... Knapp Creek
Location .... Allegany State Park
Access .... Paralleled by Beehunter Trail
Principal Species .... Brook Trout (stocked and wild)

Beehunter Creek, also known as Beeline Creek, averages a diminutive 5 feet in width. It has a gravel bottom and very good bank cover. Although it may hold some wild brook and/or brown trout, thereby providing some fishing all season long, in all practicality it is only fishable during the early months of trout season. A state park fishing permit is required.

In the fall, the lower end of Beehunter Creek is stocked with 300 brook trout fingerlings.

NOTES: ______________________________

BONE RUN (Main Branch)

Map Coordinates .... 42° 01′ 50″ 78° 56′ 38″
USGS Map(s) .... Steamburg, Ivory
Township(s) .... South Valley
Access .... County Road 33
Principal Species .... Rainbow Trout (stocked)

Bone Run is a fair-quality trout stream that averages about 15 feet in width. A very secluded stream, it runs through a mix of meadows and woodland. It has a good amount of bank cover, but no overhanging canopy. The bottom consists mainly of rubble, with some gravel and muck. Although there is a good flow of water here all year and fish can be taken all season, the best fishing is to be had during the first months of trout season and in the fall.

In the spring, the lower 3 miles of Bone Run is stocked with 900 rainbow trout yearlings. It is possible that there are some wild trout in the headwaters of this stream.

NOTES: ______________________________

BONE RUN (North Branch)

Map Coordinates .... 41° 10′ 50″ 78° 56′ 38″
USGS Map(s) .... Jamestown, Ivory
Township(s) .... South Valley
Access .... Bone Run Road
Principal Species .... Brook Trout (stocked)

The north branch of Bone Run averages 15 feet in width. It has a gravel and rubble bottom and a lot of bank cover. Surrounded primarily by woodlands, this stream is fishable only during the first few months of trout season.

In the fall, the lower end of this stream is stocked with 300 brook trout fingerlings.

NOTES: ______________________________

BUCKTOOTH RUN (West Branch)

Map Coordinates .... 42° 09′ 42″ 78° 46′ 21″
USGS Map(s) .... Little Valley
Township(s) .... Little Valley, Salamanca
Access .... Bucktooth Run Road
Principal Species .... Brown Trout (stocked and wild), Brook Trout (stocked and wild)

This small trout stream averages 10 feet in width, has a rock and gravel bottom, and generally clear water. Bucktooth Run is bordered by woodlands, which provide a lot of bank cover. Though it is essentially fishable only during the early part of trout season, parts of this stream might hold some wild brook or brown trout.

In the fall, the lower 2.5-mile section of Bucktooth Run is stocked with 500 brown trout fingerlings.

NOTES: ______________________________

BUTTERMILK CREEK

Map Coordinates .... 42° 29′ 02″ 78° 40′ 36″
USGS Map(s) .... Ashford Hollow, West Valley
Township(s) .... Ashford
Access .... Bord Road
Principal Species .... Brook Trout (stocked)

This stream averages about 10 feet in width and has a gravel and clay bottom. Woodland and pastureland provide the stream with intermittent bank cover. It is usually fishable only during the first few months of trout season. There are many productive pools on this stream and a number of very productive tributaries. Buttermilk Creek is posted in the vicinity of the Nuclear Fuel Service Center.

In the fall, Buttermilk Creek is stocked with 300 brook trout fingerlings in the 1-mile section just above Ashford Hollow Road. In addition, Tributary 47 (near the junction of Ashford Hollow Road and West Valley Road) is stocked in its lower portions with 300 brook trout fingerlings in the fall.

NOTES: ______________________________

CATTARAUGUS CREEK (South Branch)

Map Coordinates .... 42° 25′ 30″ 78° 53′ 30″
USGS Map(s) .... Gowanda, Cattaraugus, Collins Center
Township(s) .... Otto and East Otto
Access .... East Otto Road (upper section), Point Peter Road or Forty Road (lower section)
Principal Species .... Brown Trout (stocked), Rainbow Trout (stocked), Salmon

The south branch of Cattaraugus Creek can be divided into two distinct sections: the stocked section, which is located between East Otto and the headwaters; and the lower section, which lies between the junction with the main branch of Cattaraugus Creek and a 20-foot falls located about 2 miles upstream of the mouth.

The stocked portion of the stream averages about 15 feet in width. It has a rocky bottom and is usually milky in color. Surrounded by pasture land and open fields, there is intermittent bank cover along the stream. Public fishing rights are owned by the state above and below the junction with Mansfield Creek.

There is a fair amount of insect life here, and the water is suitable for fly fishing. Bait fishing would be difficult due to the large numbers of dace and chubs in this section.

In the fall, a 6.4-mile section of this stream is stocked with 1,800 brown trout fingerlings, from East Otto to its source.

The lower portion of the south branch is a part of the legendary Zoar Valley. This area is a mixture of private lands, Nature Conservancy lands, and state-owned property. It is readily accessed by Point peter Road or Forty Road, both of which dead-end near the stream. At the end of Point Peter Road there is a parking area and a path leading directly to the stream; at the end of Forty Road you have to park at a barrier and walk down a gravel path to the old bridge that used to connect the two roads.

This portion of the stream is difficult to characterize. In some areas the stream is 100 feet wide and only 1 foot deep. A few hundred yards downstream it can be 15 feet wide and 8 feet deep. The bottom consists primarily of shale and rubble, but there are significant areas of sand and bedrock. There almost no bank cover over this water. The stream flows through a gorge that is 200 to 300 feet deep and over 100 feet wide.

The best fishing in the lower section of the stream is from the late fall to early spring. Significant numbers of stray Lake Erie rainbow trout run up the south branch as far as the falls to spawn during this period. Some stray salmon are also found here in the fall. There are some resident rainbows in the stream in the deeper pools near the falls all year long.

The property above and below the falls is heavily posted. Remember to get permission before fishing on this part of the stream.

NOTES: ____

____

____

The south branch of Cattaraugus Creek flows through one of the most beautiful areas in western New York, the Zoar Valley Multiple Use Area. Nestled in a rugged, steep-sided gorge, the area offers numerous ways to enjoy the outdoors, including fishing.

CLEAR CREEK

Map Coordinates .... 42° 32′ 05″ 78° 25′ 22″
USGS Map(s) .... Arcade, Delavan, Freedom
Township(s) .... Freedom
Access .... Route 98 and Bray Road
Principal Species .... Brown Trout (stocked and wild), Rainbow Trout (wild)

Clear Creek averages 15 to 20 feet wide in sections. It has a rock and gravel bottom and usually clear water. Although the surrounding woodlands and pasturelands provide a lot of bank cover, the stream is still suitable for fly fishing.

Clear Creek is fishable all season. There are wild brown trout throughout its length, and a small run of wild rainbows occurs here each spring. The most productive area is near a small tributary near Sandusky.

In the spring, a 5-mile section of this stream is stocked with 1,800 brown trout yearlings, from Bray Road upstream to Phillippi Road.

In the following article, John O'Neil of Trout Unlimited discusses his experiences on this productive and underfished stream.

CLEAR CREEK

By John O'Neil

Forty miles from Buffalo and just south of Arcade, Clear Creek flows through Cattaraugus and Wyoming counties. A small stream, Clear Creek holds an excellent population of wild trout, although it does receive an annual stocking of hatchery fish. The creek runs through pastures, farm fields, and brush, not to mention several back yards.

The stream bed is composed primarily of gravel, rock, and sand. It also has one of the steepest gradients of any trout stream in western New York. Combine these two factors with a heavy spring runoff, and favorite pools of years past may not only no longer exist, but could be high and dry the following season.

Regardless of these conditions the trout fend rather well for themselves, taking up residence in new lies when and where the stream settles. Unfortunately, the same cannot be said for the insect life. This upheaval depletes populations and may be one reason for the generally small size of mature trout.

The trout do have a few things in their favor, namely, very good water quality, augmented by numerous spring seeps, which keep the water temperature under 70 degrees even in the hot summer months, and only a moderate amount of fishing pressure.

The trout population of Clear Creek seems to be about 70 percent rainbows and 30 percent brown trout; at least that's a rough estimate based on their susceptibility to my own angling efforts. Add a very occasional brook trout, and it keeps things interesting. Rainbow trout are everywhere in the stream but seem to prefer the faster riffles and the heads of small pools. They don't grow big, but they are awfully fiesty. Average size is about 7 inches, and anything over 10 inches is bragging size. The brown trout are partial to the pools, and on Clear Creek that means any water over 18 inches deep. They don't put on the acrobatics of the rainbow, but grow a bit bigger and fight with determination.

Early season means bait or spin fishing. And although some fishermen are content to flail away with weighted nymphs, to be effective you must be bumping bottom in the deeper pools. To do this you are left to your own devices. But a light line adorned with the proper number of split shots to keep the bait bouncing along the bottom seems to be the way to go. Spin fishermen may prefer casting upstream and allowing their lures to sink before retreiving them with the current. Small spinners seem to work best in this manner.

As May rolls around, the fly fisherman comes into his own. Despite a lack of any large hatches, the fish here are quite receptive to the artificials. Any of the old standards seems to work well. Use Adams, Hendricksons, and dark caddis imitations early; as the season progresses, lighter-colored patterns, such as Cahills and Ausable Wulfs, work well. Sizes 14 and 16 are ideal. Nymphs and wet flies are also effective, and again selectivity isn't a problem. Hare's Ears, caddis pupae, or just about any suggestive type pattern all produce fish.

To get to Clear Creek from Buffalo take Route 16 south to Yorkshire, then East on Route 39 to Route 98 in the Village of Arcade. Route 98 parallels the stream from near its confluence with Cattaraugus Creek in town to near its headwaters crossing it in the town of Sandusky.

The state has fishing rights from Arcade upstream to Galen Hill

Road and has also provided fishermen with several parking areas starting at Bray Road.

On this stream one spot seems to be as good or as bad as the next, and access is no problem. Under the bridge is as good as hiking a mile away. If fishing can be relaxing, Clear Creek is a relaxing place to fish, but being small it cannot endure much pressure or abuse. I'm sure the trout of Clear Creek will be good to you, so please be good to them.

NOTES: ______________________________

____

____

CONEWANGO CREEK - See Chautauqua County Streams and Rivers.

CONNOISARAULEY CREEK

Map Coordinates .... 42° 28′ 23″ 78° 44′ 59″
USGS Map(s) .... Ashford Hollow, Ellicottville
Township(s) .... East Otto
Access .... Connoisarauley Road
Principal Species .... Brown Trout (stocked), Chinook Salmon

This is a small, lightly fished stream, averaging 8 to 10 feet in width. The bottom consists of rock and clay, and the water is normally clear. The surrounding pastureland and woodland provide only intermittent bank cover. Connoisarauley Creek is a very picturesque stream. This is especially true where it flows through a small gorge.

In the fall, limited numbers of stray salmon and trout can be found in the section of the stream below a falls located about 1 mile upstream of Cattaraugus Creek. Much of the lower section of the stream is posted.

In the spring, Connoisarauley Creek is stocked with 300 brown trout yearlings in the 1.5-mile section above Ashford Hollow. The stocked section is fishable only during the first few months of trout season, with bait fishing being the most productive method.

NOTES: ______________________________

____

____

The lower end of Connoisarauley Creek is very picturesque, especially where it flows through a small gorge. Limited numbers of trout and salmon can be found here in the fall.

ELDERBERRY BROOK

Map Coordinates .... 42° 13′ 50″ 78° 37′ 55″
USGS Map(s) .... Salamanca
Township(s) .... Great Valley
Access .... Martin Road, west of Route 98
Principal Species .... Brown Trout (wild)

Elderberry Brook, known also as Plum Brook, is a small tributary of Forks Creek averaging no more than 5 feet in width. It has a gravel and silt bottom, and the water is generally clear. Surrounded by swampy pastureland, this is a very brushy stream and is fishable only during the early months of trout season.

Elderberry Brook is not stocked.

NOTES: ______________________________

____

____

ELM CREEK

Map Coordinates .... 42° 09′ 19″ 78° 57′ 59″
USGS Map(s) .... Randolph
Township(s) .... Conewango
Access .... Elm Creek Road (County Road 7)
Principal Species .... Brown Trout (stocked)

This is a small stream averaging 10 feet in width. It has a gravel bottom and generally clear water. Surrounded by woodland and pastureland, Elm Creek has intermittent bank cover and is fishable all season.

Elm Creek is a high-quality stream that occasionally gives up a large fish. It is heavily fished, but for its size it is also quite heavily stocked.

In the spring, a 3-mile section of Elm Creek, from its mouth upstream to the dam at Walker Road, is stocked with 1,400 brown trout yearlings.

Above the dam at Walker Road, this stream forms what is called the Elm Creek Watershed Pond. This is a permanent 6-acre impoundment that provides very good spring fishing for brown trout. The pond is difficult to see from the road, being secluded by a stand of trees. Though there is no launch site here, you could carry a small boat or canoe to the pond.

In the spring, the pond is stocked with 600 brown trout yearlings.

NOTES: ______________________________

____

____

ELTON CREEK

Map Coordinates .... 42° 31′ 10″ 78° 31′ 10″
USGS Map(s) .... Sardinia, Arcade, Delavan, Freedom
Township(s) .... Yorkshire, Freedom, Farmersville
Access .... Route 98
Principal Species .... Brown Trout (stocked), Brook Trout (stocked and wild), Rainbow Trout (wild)

Elton Creek is a large stream averaging 30 feet in width. It has a bottom of gravel and rock, is surrounded by open pastureland and woodland, and has a lot of overhanging bank cover. This stream muddies quickly after a rain. The stream bed is unstable and likely to change yearly due to spring floods.

There is a negligible amount of insect life on Elton Creek, but it is a good fly fishing stream, nevertheless. It is also a good spin fishing stream. There are several large holes, one at the Swanson Hill Road Bridge and another just west of Farmersville Station.

The state has public fishing rights from the Delevan Village line to just east of County Road 73 (look for the DEC signs indicating PFR sections). However, from County Road 73 upstream to Route 98 there are a lot of posted sections.

In March and April, Elton Creek is stocked with 3,200 brown trout yearlings in the 9.5-mile section from the stream's mouth to just above Blue Street. In the fall, it is stocked with 1,000 brown trout fingerlings, from Farmersville Station to .5 mile above the Route 98 Bridge. The small tributary that is crossed by Route 243 is occasionally stocked with brook trout.

In addition to the stocked fish, Elton Creek has a healthy population of wild brook trout in its headwaters and some wild rainbow trout in its lower portions. This stream is fishable all season.

NOTES: ______________________________

____

____

FENTON BROOK

Map Coordinates .... 42° 13′ 45″ 78° 03′ 00″
USGS Map(s) .... Kennedy, Cherry Creek, New Albion
Township(s) .... Leon
Access .... Flat Iron Road
Principal Species .... Brown Trout (stocked)

This stream averages 20 feet in width, has a gravel bottom, and very good water quality. Though bordered primarily by woodlands, a section of Fenton Brook runs through the village of Leon; however, this has not affected the water quality since the closing of the milk plant a number of years ago.

Under normal circumstances Fenton Brook would be fishable all trout season. However, due to the easy access of the stream and the resulting high fishing pressure that depletes the stocked fish, it qualifies as an early season put-and-take stream. Posting is prevalent, but some posting signs stipulate that fishing is permitted.

In March and April, Fenton Brook is stocked with 1,600 brown trout yearlings, from Flat Iron Road upstream to the village of Leon.

NOTES: ______________________________

____

____

FIVE MILE CREEK

Map Coordinates .... 42° 05′ 35″ 78° 30′ 23″
USGS Map(s) .... Olean, Hinsdale, Humphrey
Township(s) .... Allegany
Access .... Paralleled by County Road 19
Principal Species .... Brown Trout (stocked)

Five Mile Creek averages 10 feet in width, has a gravel and silt bottom, and very good water quality. The stream is surrounded by woodland and farmland, which provides the stream with intermittent bank cover.

New York is one of the most diverse and beautiful states in the country, and has a lot more to offer the outdoor enthusiast than just great fishing. An excellent source of what the state has in terms of outdoor recreation is the Department of Environmental Conservation (DEC). Contact your local DEC office for pamphlets on fishing, hunting, boating, camping, cross-country skiing, and many other activities.

A very good early-season trout stream, the best section of Five Mile Creek is from Wing Hollow Road (near the ski resort) to Church Road. The headwaters possibly hold some wild brown trout.

In the spring, a 6.2-mile section of Five Mile Creek is stocked with 1,000 brown trout yearlings, from just below Etons Cross Road to one-quarter mile above Cooper Hill Road.

NOTES: ______________________________

____

____

FORKS CREEK

Map Coordinates .... 42° 13′ 32″ 78° 37′ 59″
USGS Map(s) .... Salamanca, Humphrey
Township(s) .... Great Valley, Humphrey
Access .... Paralleled by Route 98 north of Martin Road
Principal Species .... Brown Trout (stocked), Smallmouth Bass

Forks Creek averages about 20 feet in width, has a bottom of rock, gravel, and silt, and has generally clear, good-quality water. The bordering farmland and woodland provide a lot of bank cover, and there are some swamps along the stream as well.

There are many large, deep holes on this stream. They hold quite a few chubs and suckers, and some smallmouth bass. Bait fishing for trout would be difficult here, but there is a substantial amount of insect life on Forks Creek, making fly fishing productive through the summer months. This is also a good spin fishing stream.

In the spring, a 5-mile section of Forks Creek, from its mouth up to Morgan Hollow Road, is stocked with 1,500 brown trout yearlings.

NOTES: ______________________________

____

____

GREAT VALLEY CREEK

Map Coordinates .... 42° 09′ 05″ 78° 41′ 30″
USGS Map(s) .... Salamanca, Ellicottville, Ashford
Township(s) .... Ellicottville
Access .... Route 219, Route 242
Principal Species .... Brown Trout (stocked), Rainbow Trout (stocked)

This is a gravel- and silt-bottomed stream averaging 15 to 20 feet in width. The surrounding woodlands and open fields provide intermittent bank cover.

Great Valley Creek is not a high-quality stream, and is only fishable during the early months of trout season.

In the spring, this stream is stocked with 400 brown trout yearlings in the 2-mile section above Bryant Hill Road. In addition, 1,500 rainbow trout yearlings are stocked here in the spring in the 3-mile section between the confluence with Wrights Creek, above the Village of Peth, upstream to the confluence with Forks Creek, near Martin Road.

NOTES: ______________________________

____

____

GUERNSEY RUN

Map Coordinates .... 42° 00′ 50″ 79° 02′ 45″
USGS Map(s) .... Ivory
Township(s) .... South Valley
Access .... Guernsey Road, south of County Road 89
Principal Species .... Brown Trout (stocked and wild), Brook Trout (stocked and wild)

Guernsey Run averages 10 feet in width. Plentiful bank cover is provided by the surrounding woodlands. This gravel-bottomed stream is generally fishable only during the early months of trout season, although the headwaters could possibly hold some wild brook and/or brown trout all year long.

In the fall, the lower 1-mile section of Guernsey Run is stocked with 200 brown trout fingerlings.

NOTES: ______________________________

HASKELL CREEK

Map Coordinates .... 42° 03′ 55″ 78° 23′ 32″
USGS Map(s) .... Olean, Portville, Cuba
Township(s) .... Portville
Access .... Jollytown Road Bridge
Principal Species .... Brown Trout (stocked)

Haskell Creek is a slow-moving stream with a bottom of gravel, rock, and sand. It averages about 15 feet in width. The surrounding woodlands and pasturelands provide intermittent bank cover.

This stream is fishable all season. The moderate amount of insect life found on Haskell Creek makes fly fishing a possibility, and spin fishing is also productive. Bait fishing, however, could be difficult because of the numerous chubs and minnows present in the stream. Some sections of the creek are posted.

In the spring, the 2-mile section of Haskell Creek just above the Haskell Road Bridge is stocked with 600 brown trout yearlings.

NOTES: ______________________________

MUDDLER MINNOW

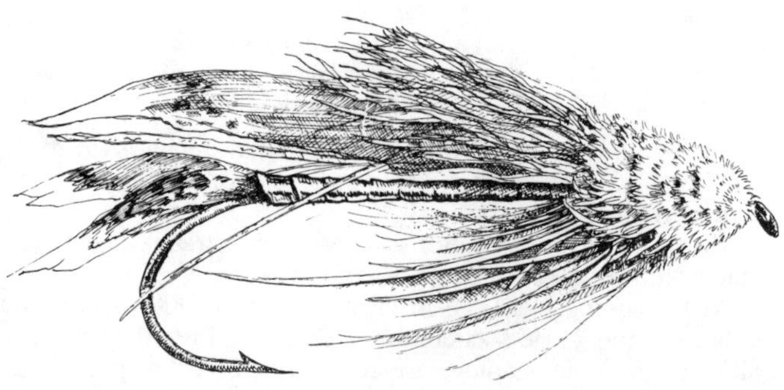

The Muddler Minnow is an excellent imitator of small bait fish and is as effective on bass as it is on trout and salmon.

HOTCHKISS HOLLOW BROOK

Map Coordinates .... 42° 02′ 36″ 78° 55′ 26″
USGS Map(s) .... Steamburg
Township(s) .... Cold Spring
Access .... Paralleled by Hotchkiss Hollow Road
Principal Species .... Brook Trout (stocked)

This gravel-bottomed stream averages about 8 feet in width. Surrounded by woodlands, the stream has a lot of overhanging bank cover. Hotchkiss Hollow Brook is normally fishable only in the spring.

In the fall, the 1.5-mile section of the stream immediately above the boundary of the Allegany Indian Reservation is stocked with 300 brook trout fingerlings.

NOTES: ______________________________

ISCHUA CREEK

Map Coordinates .... 42° 10′ 11″ 78° 23′ 22″
USGS Map(s) .... Hinsdale, Franklinville, Delevan, West Valley
Township(s) .... Machias, Franklinville, Ischua, Hinsdale
Access .... Paralleled by Route 16 below Franklinville
Principal Species .... Brown Trout (stocked and wild), Brook Trout (stocked), Smallmouth Bass, Largemouth Bass, Northern Pike, Carp, Panfish

Passing through several townships in Cattaraugus County, Ischua Creek is listed among the top 50 trout streams in New York State. It flows southward, closely paralleled by Route 16 below Franklinville, until reaching Hinsdale, where it joins with Oil creek to become Olean Creek.

Ischua Creek averages 25 to 30 feet in width, and has a good flow of water all year. Above Franklinville, the bottom consists of gravel and sand. There is a fair amount of bank cover on this section, but not too much for fly fishing. Below Franklinville, the bottom consists more of silt and rock, and the bank cover is more intermittent. There is some pollution in the Franklinville area, but it does not seem to affect the quality of the fishing.

Ischua Creek is an excellent fly fishing stream, with good hatches of mayflies in late May and June. Nymph and spin fishing also produce well all during trout season, especially when the stream is rising. Bait fishing can be pretty difficult in the summer because of the enormous numbers of chubs in the stream.

In addition to the excellent trout fishing, Ischua Creek also provides limited opportunities to take such warm-water species as largemouth and smallmouth bass, northern pike, and carp. This is especially true in the downstream portions of the stream. The fishing for largemouth and smallmouth bass is unrestricted above Hinsdale, i. e., any number, any size, all year. Ice fishing is permitted.

Ischua Creek flows primarily through pasturelands, sections of which are posted. The state owns public fishing rights on the following sections: between Route 242 and Route 16; above and below the intersection of Route 16 and Route 98; and below Farewell Road for approximately 1 mile. Don't limit yourself to these areas, though, for a polite request will often result in permission to fish some very productive sections of the stream.

The spring stocking of Ischua Creek, by far the largest stream stocking program in Cattaraugus County, goes as follows: from the stream mouth to Pierce Hill Road - 8,100 brown trout yearlings (March, April, and May); from Pierce Hill Road to Franklinville - 7,200 brown trout yearlings (March, April, and May); and from Franklinville to Gulf Creek - 5,400 Brown trout yearlings (March, April, and May).

In the fall, 2,200 brown trout fingerlings are stocked between the mouth of Gulf Creek and Sisson Road in the township of Machias. Several small tributaries of Ischua Creek are also stocked the fall.

Tributary 11, which is accessible from Williams Hollow Road, receives 300 brook trout fingerlings, and the lower portion of Tributary 35, which is accessible from Very Road just south of Felton Hill Road, is stocked with 100 brown trout fingerlings.

In addition to the stocked trout, there is a substantial amount of natural reproduction of brown trout in Ischua Creek, especially above Franklinville. Wild brown trout can be found in large numbers in many of the small tributaries as well.

The following article provides first-hand impressions of Ischua Creek as seen through the eyes of two members of Trout Unlimited.

ISCHUA CREEK

By Gordon Deitrick and Bob Janiga

This stream follows State Route 16 through the townships of Ischua, Franklin, and Machias, starting west of the Village of Machias and flowing south to the Village of Hinsdale, where it meets Oil Creek and becomes Olean Creek. Listed among the state's top 50 trout streams, it is a large stream that carries a good amount of water year round. It is stocked from its mouth at Hinsdale to practically its source above Machias. In addition to the stocking, there is a fair amount of natural reproduction. This stream averages 25 feet in width, and in the upper stretches runs over gravel and sand, but from Franklinville south the bottom is mostly silt and rock. There is some pollution in the Franklinville area, but it doesn't seem to affect the fishing. The Ischua flows through open pasture, some of which is posted. There are some public fishing rights where the stream runs between Route 242 and Route 16, also above and below the intersections of Routes 98 and 16, and below Farewell Road for approximately 1 mile.

This is a fly fishing stream, with good hatches of mayflies in late May and June. Nymph and spin fishing are good all season, especially when the stream is rising. Bait fishing is hectic in June, July, and August, as the stream is loaded with chubs. For something different try fly fishing at night (muddler minnows and dark streamers). Check current regulations.

The Upper Ischua

To reach this section of the Ischua, take Route 16 south, go through Machias and about 2 to 3 miles further south you'll pass under a railroad viaduct (almost at the junction with Route 98). That's the spot, though access is also possible from Brown Road and Fox Road south of Machias.

The immediate area near the Route 16 bridge is abundant with stocked trout (in fact, the Ischua receives the largest stocking in Cattaraugus County). Upstream areas are spotty, some good, some poor, but though the trout are fewer in number they tend to be larger than average. The stream is of medium width, has a gentle flow over gravel, and is lined with lush foliage, but it is not overgrown. Fly fishing is certainly possible, for there are abundant fly hatches in the early season; the fly fishing should be good prior to the 4th of July.

I like to fish the stream with ultra-light spinning gear, using 1/16- to 1/8-ounce spinners (Panther Martins are especially successful). Fish upstream all the way to Brown Road, but the fishing gets poor upstream of Brown Road. There are some nice deep holes in this section, and a beaver dam with its pond between the two Route 16 bridges, holding bass. The pond is too deep to wade through and skirting it is difficult, but possible.

The Ischua in this section is especially good after a rain storm when its waters are rising, for spinners, and should be equally good with nymphs. The bait fisherman, however, will find that the Ischua is also one of the best chub streams in western New York.

Ischua Creek below Franklinville

This stretch of stream varies from 20 to 40 feet wide, with a very heavy runoff in early spring. It is used by canoeists. The stream bottom is silty gravel and clay. Bait and spin fishing are favored in April and May, for this stream is usually silty until about mid-June, especially below the Town of Cadiz to Olean. Fly fishing from June to September is effective. You may fish for bass from Hinsdale upstream, so beware: your supposed lunker brown may turn out to be a smallmouth bass.

Ischua Creek is the most heavily stocked stream in Cattaraugus County, with a total annual allotment of 16,500 trout. The stream has good carry-over, resulting in some of the largest brown trout of any stream in the region.

There is good access in Cadiz at Route 98 at Cooney Road. The water between Cooney Road to Pierce Hill is very slow, deep, and silty. There is some excellent fishing around the town of Ischua, with access at Baxter Mill Road or Dutch Hill Road. Here you will find several fallen trees in the water, which usually shelter some big browns or bass. Unfortunately, the carp population is also large.

From the Town of Ischua downstream to Hinsdale, in early July, I have seen several good stonefly hatches, mostly giant golden. The stream's best hatches are usually the Grey Fox, Green Drake, Grey Caddis, Tan Caddis, Trico, and Golden Stone. The Green Drake hatches late here, sometimes even after the sun goes down (hint). Near Hinsdale there is access at Phillips Road near the Olean airport. This section, since it flows through pastureland, has some open area. You will notice a long (huge!) pool from the bridge upstream. This deep pool definitely has trout in it (I guarantee it), so watch for rises. Please return Floyd, the large trout who lives under a tree lying in the water on the left side near the head of the pool. If he's too smart for you, there is plenty of pretty water downstream for a couple of miles.

NOTES: ______________________________

____

____

JOHNSON CREEK

Map Coordinates .... 42° 22′ 05″ 78° 27′ 30″
USGS Map(s) .... Franklinville
Township(s) .... Franklinville
Access .... Paralleled by Laidlaw Road (County Road 80)
Principal Species .... Brown Trout (stocked and wild)

Johnson Creek averages about 5 feet in width, has a bottom of gravel and silt, and is surrounded by pastureland and woodland. It is quite brushy for most of its length. Fishable all trout season, there is a fair amount of wild brown trout in the upper portions of the creek. Bait or nymph fishing works best here.

In the fall, the 2-mile section of this stream from just below the Laidlaw Road bridge crossing (near Pigeon Road) upstream to Tributary 3 is stocked with 600 brown trout yearlings.

NOTES: ______________________________

____

____

LIME LAKE OUTLET

Map Coordinates .... 42° 29′ 40″ 78° 29′ 16″
USGS Map(s) .... Delevan
Township(s) .... Machias, Yorkshire
Access .... access and parking off Route 16, just north of Lime Lake
Principal Species .... Brown Trout (stocked and wild), Brook Trout (wild)

This northern outlet of Lime Lake is a very heavily fished stream that flows through woodlands, swamps, and open fields. It has a gravel bottom, very good water quality, and lots of bank cover.

There are native brook trout in the headwaters of Lime Lake Outlet and a good population of wild brown trout throughout the stream. These fish grow to a quite respectable size. The sections east of Route 16 are too small and brushy for fly fishing, but are good for bait and spin fishing. The state has purchased public fishing rights from the Route 16 bridge crossing to the village of Delevan.

In March and April, Lime Lake Outlet is stocked with 3,200 brown trout yearlings along its entire length.

NOTES: ______________________________

____

____

LIMESTONE BROOK

Map Coordinates .... 42° 01′ 46″ 78° 38′ 24″
USGS Map(s) .... Limestone
Location .... Allegany State Park
Access .... Paralleled by Limestone Run Road
Principal Species .... Brown Trout (stocked)

This stream averages 6 feet in width, has a gravel and rubble bottom, and is surrounded by woodlands and pastureland.

Limestone Brook is fishable in most sections only during the first few months of trout season. There might be some limited fishing for wild brown and brook trout in small spring-fed pools during the summer. Limestone Brook is too brushy and small for fly fishing.

In the fall, the 3-mile section just upstream of the Allegany State Park boundary is stocked with 500 brown trout fingerlings. A state park fishing permit is required.

NOTES: ______________________________

____

____

LITTLE CONEWANGO CREEK

Map Coordinates .... 42° 11′ 07″ 79° 00′ 32″
USGS Map(s) .... Kennedy, Randolph, Steamburg
Township(s) .... Mansfield, New Albion
Access .... Paralleled by Route 53
Principal Species .... Brown Trout (stocked), Brook Trout (stocked), Smallmouth Bass, Muskellunge

Little Conewango Creek averages 10 to 15 feet in width, and has a bottom of gravel and sand, becoming silt below the town of Randolph. The stream becomes very muddy and roily in the spring. The surrounding farmlands, woodlands and, swamps provide intermittent bank cover.

Trout are the main species in this stream and they can be caught here all season long. Occasionally, the section of the stream below the town of Randolph yields a nice muskellunge or smallmouth bass.

The state owns public fishing rights on practically the entire length of Little Conewango Creek.

In the spring, 3,000 brown trout yearlings are stocked in Little Conewango Creek in the 5.5-mile section just above the town of Randolph. In the fall, tributary 1, just below Swamp Road, is stocked in its lower portions with 200 brook trout fingerlings.

NOTES: ______________________________

____

____

LITTLE VALLEY CREEK

Map Coordinates .... 42° 09′ 50″ 78° 44′ 34″
USGS Map(s) .... Salamanca, Cattaraugus
Township(s) .... Mansfield, New Albion
Access .... Paralleled by Route 53
Principal Species .... Brook Trout (stocked)

This stream averages 15 feet in width, has a rock and gravel bottom, and very good water quality. Surrounded by pastureland and woodland, most of this stream has intermittent bank cover. Some areas are posted. It is fishable all season and is suitable for fly fishing.

In the spring, Little Valley Creek is stocked with 200 brook trout yearlings from approximately 1 mile below Kahler Hill Road upstream 3 miles to Lynlyco Lake Outlet.

NOTES: ______________________________

____

____

MANSFIELD CREEK

Map Coordinates .... 42° 27′ 38″ 78° 28′ 57″
USGS Map(s) .... Cattaraugus, Ellicottville
Township(s) .... Mansfield
Access .... Maple Road (see below)
Principal Species .... Brown Trout (stocked)

Averaging 20 feet in width, Mansfield Creek has a bottom of gravel and clay, which causes it to become muddy quickly after a rain. The surrounding woodlands and pasturelands provide only intermittent bank cover. This stream is fishable all trout season.

Mansfield Creek is a good quality fly fishing stream, particularly in July and August, with good hatches of mayflies and some stoneflies. It is also a better than average spinning stream, but large numbers of chubs and dace hinder bait fishing during the summer months.

There is a public parking area for fishermen near the intersection of Maple Road and Toad Hollow Road. Public Fishing rights extend from Toad Hollow Road downstream to approximately 1 mile west of Thompson Road, with a few intermittent exceptions south of the intersection of Hart Road and Maple Road.

In March and April, Mansfield Creek is stocked with 3,400 brown trout yearlings in the 5.5-mile section between the stream mouth and the town of Maples.

NOTES: ______________________________

____

____

McKINSTRY CREEK

Map Coordinates .... 42° 27′ 38″ 78° 28′ 57″
USGS Map(s) .... Delevan, West Valley
Township(s) .... Yorkshire
Access .... Route 16 south of Delevan
Principal Species .... Brown Trout (stocked and wild)

McKinstry Creek averages 10 feet in width, has a gravel bottom, and clear, good quality water. Surrounded by farmland, woodland, and recreational land, there is a lot of bank cover on this stream.

There are large numbers of large wild brown trout throughout the stream, and it is fishable all trout season. The extensive bank cover on this stream makes it somewhat unsuitable for fly fishing. But bait and spin fishing are both very productive methods here. Public fishing rights extend from the town of Delevan to Camp Arrowhead.

In the spring, the lowermost 4-mile section of McKinstry Creek is stocked with 800 brown trout yearlings.

NOTES: ______________________________

____

____

NINE MILE CREEK

Map Coordinates .... 42° 05′ 25″ 78° 34′ 44″
USGS Map(s) .... Knapp Creek, Humphery
Township(s) .... Allegany
Access .... Paralleled by North Nine Mile Road
Principal Species .... Brown Trout (wild)

This small stream averages 10 feet in width, and has a bottom of gravel and mud. It is surrounded by farmland and woodland, and has a lot of bank cover. Nine Mile Creek is an adequate bait or spin fishing stream, but not worth a special trip. It is not stocked, and below Vandalia it is on the Allegany Indian Reservation. Much of this stream is posted, but many of the farmers will allow fishing upon request.

NOTES: ______________________________

____

____

OLEAN CREEK

Map Coordinates .... 42° 04′ 32″ 78° 25′ 23″
USGS Map(s) .... Olean, Hinsdale
Township(s) .... Hinsdale, Olean
Access .... Launch site on Giles Hollow Road off Route 16.
Principal Species .... Brown Trout (stocked), Muskellunge, Smallmouth Bass, Northern Pike, Walleye, Panfish

Olean Creek is formed by the joining of Ischua Creek and Oil Creek. It is a large stream, averaging 35 to 40 feet in width, and has a silt and rock bottom.

Though there is a small section of Olean Creek near Hinsdale that is marginally capable of holding trout, for the most part warm-water species predominate in this stream. Muskellunge, smallmouth bass, walleyes, and panfish can be caught here. The fishing for northern pike is unrestricted, i.e., any number, any size, all year long. Ice fishing is also permitted.

There is a state-maintained access site on Giles Hollow Road, off Route 16, 6 miles north of Olean. It provides parking for 30 cars and a boat launch site (hand launch).

Olean Creek is annually stocked with 600 muskellunge fingerlings between Olean and Hinsdale. A large pool known as Olean Creek Pond, which is really nothing more than a wide spot in the stream, is stocked with 200 brown trout yearlings. This pond is rather warm for trout in the summer, but it does provide some good trout fishing in the spring.

NOTES: ______________________________

____

____

Many of the trout caught in western New York originate in the state trout hatchery in Randolph.

OSWAYO CREEK

Map Coordinates .... 42° 01′ 38″ 78° 20′ 51″
USGS Map(s) .... Portville, Bullis Mills
Township(s) .... Portville
Access .... Route 305
Principle Species .... Muskellunge, Smallmouth Bass, Walleye, Northern Pike

The fishing in Oswayo Creek is very similar to that in the Allegany River. There are good numbers of smallmouth bass, walleyes, and northern pike, and good-size muskellunge can be caught here. As in the case of the Allegany River, however, the number of muskies may be dwindling due to fierce competition from an expanding northern pike population. Unlike the Allegany River, northern pike fishing is subject to current state regulations.

Oswayo Creek is not presently stocked.

NOTES: ______________________________

____

____

QUAKER RUN

Map Coordinates .... 42° 03′ 23″ 78° 53′ 45″
USGS Map(s) .... Steamburg, Red House, Limestone
Location .... Allegany State Park
Access .... Paralleled by State Park Route 3
Principal Species .... Brown Trout (stocked and wild), Rainbow Trout (wild), Brook Trout (wild)

This stream averages about 12 feet in width, has a bottom of gravel and rock, and is surrounded by picturesque, hilly woodlands. There is a lot of bank cover on this stream, but it is still suitable for fly fishing, especially in the half-mile section above Quaker Lake. There are good populations of wild brown trout and rainbow trout throughout the stream, and fish of respectable size are caught here each year. Quaker Run is fishable all trout season. A state park fishing permit is required.

In the spring, 2,500 brown trout yearlings and 1,700 brook trout yearlings are stocked the length of Quaker Run below the dam.

NOTES: ______________________________

____

____

RED HOUSE BROOK

Map Coordinates .... 42° 02′ 16″ 78° 49′ 17″
USGS Maps .... Red House, Limestone
Location .... Allegany State Park
Access .... Paralleled by State Park Route 2 and County Road 43
Principal Species .... Brook Trout (stocked)

Red House Brook averages 15 feet in width below the dam at Red House Lake, and narrows to 10 feet above the first bridge upstream from Red House Lake. It has a gravel and rock bottom, and clear, fast-moving water. Red House Brook is surrounded by woodlands and has intermittent bank cover.

This stream is suitable for fly fishing below the dam and upstream from the lake to the first bridge. It is fishable all trout season, except in very dry years. Even then, however, a few fish might be taken from some larger pools.

A state park fishing permit is required, and where the stream runs on the Allegany Indian Reservation, about 2 miles downstream of the dam, an Indian license is required.

In the spring, nearly the entire state park section of this stream is stocked with 2,500 brook trout yearlings.

NOTES: ______________________________

____

____

If there is a lack of rain during the summer months, many of the smaller streams in Allegany State Park will stop flowing and dry to pools. Brook trout and brown trout residing in these streams will then be concentrated in the larger pools. Angling for these fish is difficult at best; they are extremely wary because of their situation. However, by approaching a pool stealthily and being extra careful in your presentation, very rewarding summer trout fishing can be experienced.

RICE BROOK

Map Coordinates .... 42° 03′ 40″ 78° 38′ 29″
USGS Map(s) .... Limestone
Location .... Allegany State Park
Access .... Irish Brook Road
Principal Species .... Brown Trout (stocked)

Rice Brook averages about 8 feet in width and has a gravel bottom. It is surrounded by woodlands and has a lot of bank cover.

This stream is fishable only during the early months of trout season, with the exception of some pools that stay well-watered all year long.

In the fall, the lower 1.6-mile section of Rice Brook is stocked with 600 brown trout fingerlings.

A state park fishing permit is required.

NOTES: ______________________________

____

____

SAWMILL RUN (Main Branch)

Map Coordinates .... 42° 01′ 28″ 78° 57′ 30″
USGS Map(s) .... Steamburg
Township(s) .... South Valley
Access .... Sawmill Run Road (County Road 89)
Principal Species .... Brook Trout (stocked and wild)

The main branch of Sawmill Run averages about 12 feet in width, has a gravel and rubble bottom, and is surrounded by woodlands, some of which are state-owned.

This stream is fishable during the first few months of trout season. The banks are too brushy for fly fishing, but bait and spinners work well here. There are beaver ponds on this stream, and they provide some habitat for small native brook trout.

In the fall, the lower 3-mile section of Sawmill Run is stocked with 500 brook trout fingerlings.

NOTES: ______________________________

____

____

SAW MILL RUN (North Branch)

Map Coordinates .... 42° 01′ 28″ 78° 57′ 30″
USGS Map(s) .... Steamburg
Township(s) .... South Valley
Access .... Sawmill Run Road (County Road 89)
Principal Species .... Brook Trout (wild), Brown Trout (stocked)

The north branch of Sawmill Run averages about 10 feet in width, has a gravel and rubble bottom, and is surrounded by woodlands, some of which are state-owned.

This stream is fishable during the first few months of trout season. The banks are too brushy for fly fishing, but bait and spinners work well. There are beaver ponds on this stream, and they provide some habitat for small native brook trout.

In the fall, the lower 2-mile section of the north branch of Sawmill Run is stocked with 300 brown trout fingerlings.

NOTES: ______________________________

____

____

SAWMILL RUN (South Branch)

Map Coordinates .... 42° 02′ 01″ 78° 59′ 47″
USGS Map(s) .... Steamburg, Ivory
Township(s) .... South Valley
Access .... Paralleled by South Sawmill Run Road and Gurnsey Hollow Road
Principal Species .... Brook Trout (wild)

This stream averages 10 feet in width and flows through a picturesque woodland, some of which is state-owned. The stream is too brushy for fly fishing, but spinners and bait work well here. There are numerous small brook trout throughout much of this stream.

The south branch of Sawmill Run is not stocked.

NOTES: ______________________________

____

____

STATE LINE RUN

Map Coordinates .... 42° 00′ 04″ 78° 57′ 42″
USGS Map(s) .... Steamburg, Cornplanter Run, Ivory
Township(s) .... South Valley
Access .... Brown Road, south of Onoville
Principal Species .... Brown Trout (stocked)

State Line Run averages 8 feet in width, has a gravel bottom, and is surrounded by woodlands, which provide a lot of bank cover. It is fishable only during the first few months of trout season.

In the fall, this stream is stocked with 300 brown trout fingerlings along its entire length.

NOTES: ______________________________

____

____

WOLF RUN

Map Coordinates .... 42° 07′ 17″ 78° 53′ 38″
USGS Map(s) .... Steamburg, Red House
Location .... Allegany State Park
Access .... Wolf Run Road
Principal Species .... Brook Trout (stocked)

This stream averages 8 feet in width, has a gravel and rock bottom, and is surrounded by woodlands, which provide a good amount of bank cover. There are a few fish-holding pools that can be fished all season long, but most fishing must be done on fast, straight-flowing water. Most of Wolf Run is fishable only during the first few months of trout season.

In the spring, Wolf Run is stocked with 200 brook trout yearlings from Browns Hollow to the state line.

NOTES: ______________________________

____

____

WRIGHTS CREEK

Map Coordinates .... 42° 11′ 49″ 78° 39′ 30″
USGS Map(s) .... Salamanca, Humphery, Hinsdale
Township(s) .... Great Valley, Humphrey
Access .... Paralleled by Bozard Hill Road
Principal Species .... Brown Trout (stocked)

Wrights Creek is a small, high-quality trout stream averaging 6 to 8 feet in width. It has a gravel bottom and very good water quality. This lightly fished stream is surrounded primarily by pastureland and has only intermittent bank cover. The best fishing occurs during the first few months of trout season. Wrights Creek is a bait and spin fishing stream.

In the spring, a 3-mile section of this stream is stocked with 800 brown trout yearlings, from Humphrey Center upstream almost to its source.

NOTES: ______________________________

____

____

CATTARAUGUS COUNTY LAKES AND PONDS

ALLEGHENY (KINZUA) RESERVOIR

Location

Map Coordinates	41° 50′ 17″ 79° 00′ 10″
USGS Map(s)	Steamburg, Red House
Township(s)	South Valley, Cold Spring
Access	Paralleled by West Bank Perimeter Road and Route 280

Physical Characteristics

Area	5,000 acres (New York section)
Shoreline	40 miles (New York section)
Elevation	1,328 feet (normal pool)
Maximum Depth	45 feet (normal pool)
Mean Depth	Not available
Bottom Type	Muck, gravel, rock

Chemical Characteristics

Water	Clear to slightly turbid
pH	Alkaline
Oxygen	Good throughout the lake all year

Plant Life

Extensive weedbeds are found in the shallow northern end. Limited beds exist in bays and shallow near-shore areas in the remainder of the reservoir. Algal blooms are inconspicuous.

Boat Launch Sites

1. An informal gravel ramp capable of handling trailer launchings is located near the western end of the Southern Tier Expressway crossing and is accessible from old Route 17 out of Steamburg - no charge.
2. High Banks Campground, off West Bank Perimeter Road. Take the Southern Tier Expressway to Exit 17, go south 3 miles to campground; launch ramp, docks - fee.
3. Onoville Marina, off West Bank Perimeter Road. Take the Southern Tier Expressway to Exit 17, go south 8 miles to marina; full service marina - fee.
4. Allegheny State Park (Quaker Area). Friends Boat Launch Site on Route 280, 2.5 miles south of Route 17 from Exit 18. Concrete ramp, parking for 35 cars and trailers, - no charge.

Additional launch sites are located just over the Pennsylvania state line at Willow Bay, off Route 346 (east side of reservoir) and at Webb's Ferry, just south of the state line (west side of reservoir). Due to fluctuating water levels and the presence of submerged obstructions, caution is advised when boating here.

Species Information

Walleye .... Common; growth rate good

Walleye are unquestionably the fish most sought after by anglers here. Millions of fry are stocked in the reservoir by the U.S. Fish and Wildlife Service at irregular intervals. These stocked walleye are augmented by a fair amount of natural reproduction in the lower reaches of the Allegheny River above the reservoir. What all this adds up to is one heck of a lot of walleye in the reservoir.

The walleye from the Allegheny Reservoir don't usually attain what you would call bragging size, although a few lunkers are occasionally taken here. In fact, two Pennsylvania state record walleye were caught in the reservoir in 1980. Generally, though, they run in the 1 to 2 pound category, but this is changing for the better with the successful introduction of rainbow smelt as a forage base. Fish in the 2 to 3 pound category are now becoming more common. The smelt could also become an important fishery in their own right.

The most productive season for taking walleyes in the Allegheny Reservoir is the spring. At this time they move in great numbers into the shallow sections of the reservoir to spawn and are fairly easy to locate. They are especially concentrated in the upper end where the river flows into the reservoir. Great numbers of fish migrate into this area, and some walleye actually move as far upstream as to re-enter Pennsylvania on the east side of Allegany State Park.

While the head of the reservoir gets the greatest number of fish, other areas can also be very productive in the spring if you know where to look. Dan Kosowski, a friend of mine and avid Kinzua walleye fisherman, generously confided to me his favorite spring hotspots one afternoon. The following list probably doesn't exhaust the total number of sites that hold fish, but it should provide you with more than enough water to check out in May and June.

Site A: This is a stretch of near-shore mud flats about 400 yards long. When the reservoir is at a high pool level and there is a north wind blowing against the shore, this is one of the most consistent areas Dan knows of for good near-shore fishing. The wind roils the water, making it off-color. Dan has found that without a north wind the fishing here is not very good. He normally fishes in 8 to 10 feet of water using a size 4 silver Indiana blade spinner dressed with fire beads.

Site B: This is a point on the south side of the mouth of Pierce Run. This is one of the few spots Dan has found to be especially productive at night, at least in the New York portion of the reservoir. The wind doesn't play a critical role here. Anchor up close to shore and cast a jig tipped with a worm. Work the jig down the face of the steep drop-offs. Dan recommends using chartreuse jigs in this reservoir unless the water is particularly muddy, in which case he uses black.

Site C: The shoreline between the mouths of Bone Run and Sawmill Run provides excellent jig fishing early in the morning, just as the sun is coming up, and one hour before and after dusk. This is another site that is productive when the pool levels are high and the water is roiled. When you think that the rest of the reservoir is too high and muddy, this area will usually be productive. Some fish will be caught here as late as the first week of July, but the fishing is best in May and early June. Dan has observed that an indication that the area holds actively feeding walleye are the presence of carp rolling along the shore. Look for south or southeast winds. When the wind is right, drift northward along the shore, bouncing a jig tipped with a worm on the bottom. Trolling parallel to shore with crankbaits in the late morning and early afternoon can also be productive here, but it can be a trying experience due to the large amount of brushpiles along this shore.

Site D: This is the shoreline that lies on the southeast side of New York's share of the reservoir, about one-half mile north of the state line. There is a lot of rubble in this area, and the bottom drops off quickly. Dan has had great success here long-line trolling in 10 to 15 feet of water parallel to shore using crankbaits. He recommends using Rapala Countdowns (7s and 9s) in silver and black and weighting them in such a way that the crankbait lightly tunks the bottom. This is a productive area in the middle of the day, and Dan claims to have limited out often in an afternoon. Fish will also be found along this shoreline during low-light periods. It is one of the few areas in the New York portion of the reservoir that Dan has found to be productive from May through August. Northwest, west, and southwest winds provide the best conditions for fishing here.

Site E: This area is about one mile downstream of the Route 17 bridge, where Route 280 runs right along the shore. This is where Dan has consistently caught the biggest walleyes. It appears that a lot of spent females in the 4 to 5 pound class congregate in this area before returning to the deeper parts of the reservoir. The site is most productive in mid-May and early June, and the middle of the day seems to produce the best fishing. Dan suggests using long lines and trolling parallel to shore with crankbaits. Start trolling in about 15 feet of water and slowly work your way in toward shallower water until you start picking up fish. This site is good in anything except a strong east wind.

Site F: This site is located just out from High Banks Campground on the east side of a submerged island. Good fishing here is limited to May and June, and only early in the day. It is convenient having the campground's launch ramp nearby, but the amount of boat traffic in this area readily puts the fish down by late morning. Dan's recommendation is to use chartreuse jigs tipped with a worm. Slowly bounce the jig along the bottom, being sure to fish just to the east of the old river channel, not in it. A westerly wind favors the fishing here.

ALLEGHENY (KINZUA) RESERVOIR

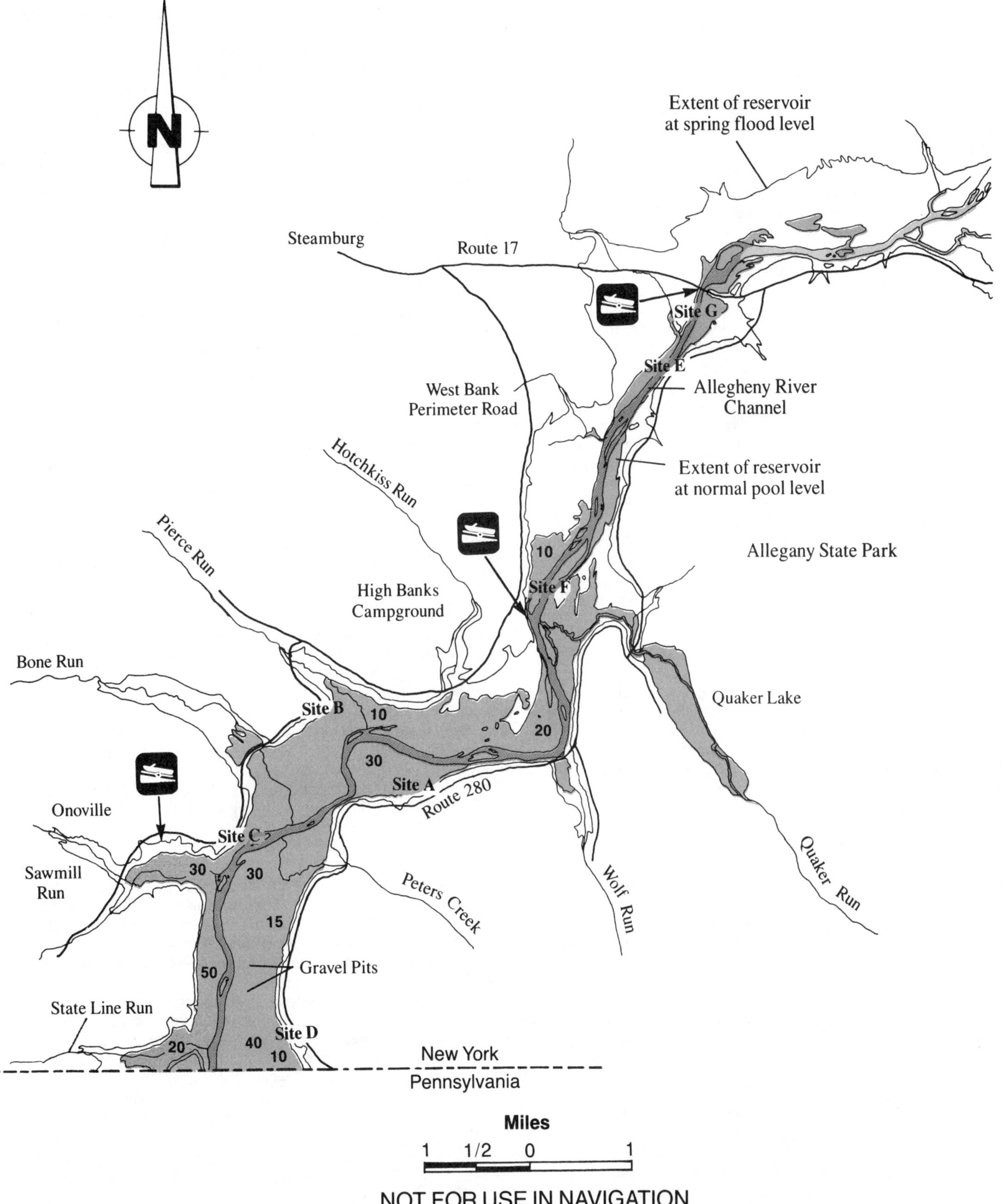

Site G: Immediately downstream of the Route 17 Bridge there is a shallow, flat-bottomed area along the east side of the old river channel. This area is excellent for walleye in early May. It is close to the lower reaches of the river where many of the fish spawn, and as the fish begin moving back down to the deeper parts of the reservoir the concentrations of walleye on these flats can be incredible. Dan prefers to anchor in this area rather than troll. He casts chartreuse jigs tipped with a minnow and slowly works it over the bottom. If there is no action here or it is too congested with boats, simply move over to Site H.

Site H: This area is located just to the south and east of Site G. If you locate it on the topographical map titled "Red House" you will see that it is an old railroad grade. In early May this grade is usually submerged under 5 to 10 feet of water. Troll with long lines parallel to it with crankbaits.

Regardless of whether he's trolling crankbaits, casting jigs, or drifting worms, Dan always prefers to keep his presentation very close to the bottom. Experience has taught him that in the spring that is where the walleye in this reservoir are feeding.

Through July and August the walleye will still be found as far upstream as the bridge crossing at Route 17. However, they will be caught in these relatively shallow waters with decreasing frequency. By the end of August, the deep channel off of High Banks Campground will pretty much mark the upstream limit of really good walleye fishing in the reservoir. After that time start looking for walleyes in at least 25 feet of water in the daytime and 15 to 20 feet at dusk and dawn.

Because walleye are a very mobile species of fish, it is difficult to say that any particular area is always going to be productive. Weather conditions, the time of year, and the movement of bait fish are all going to play a part in where these fish are going to locate. But there are some areas of the reservoir that do produce more walleyes through the summer than others. Two well-known areas are the waters off of Wolf Run and Quaker Run.

Another friend of mine, Mike Ostrowski, has provided me with information on several areas that he feels are better than average walleye producers in the summer. The first area is at the large point on the south side of the bay at State Line Run, right at the New York border. Mike does very well here either still fishing or drifting worms and minnows.

A second area that Mike has had a lot of success in is found almost directly between the bays at State Line Run and Sawmill Run. If you look on a topographical map, you will see what appear to be several depressions adjacent to the old river channel in this area. These are what used to be ponds before the reservoir was flooded. Still fishing over these holes with worms or minnows has proven to be very effective for Mike. He also claims that with a favorable wind (a southwest wind is best) drifting over these holes with jigs can also be very productive.

A third area that Mike has done well at is along the mouth of the culvert at Bone Run. Bait fish congregate at the mouth of the culvert, and the walleye move in at dusk to feed on them. You don't need a boat to fish here. Cast from shore with large Rapala-type lures or still fish with worms and minnows. The riprap along the shore here is also a hotspot for smallmouth bass in the summer.

If trolling is your style of fishing, Mike recommends two of Dan Kosowski's favorite spring haunts, the areas marked A and C on your map. Troll upstream along these shorelines in 15 to 25 feet of water.

Some species of fish, such as the walleye, have cone-shaped teeth that are only sharp at the point. The teeth of these fish are not likely to cut your line. However, some species, such as northern pike and muskellunge, have teeth that are razor sharp at the point and knife-edged along the side. The teeth of these fish can easily cut through a light line. It is advisable to use a steel or heavy monofilament leader when angling for fish that are equipped with such teeth. Contrary to what many fishermen believe, if used properly a steel leader will not seriously reduce the number of strikes, especially in the case of muskellunge.

There are a lot of branches and brush piles along the sides of this reservoir. This means that you are likely to hang up often while trolling, and that can be very expensive. If you want to avoid this expense, be prepared to do some backing up, and use heavier than normal line, 10- to 14-pound-test at most. This should allow you to free most of your lures. Line heavier than this will dampen the action of your lure.

If you are really serious about catching walleye in this reservoir in the summer, it's a good idea to come down here in the dead of winter. The Alleghany Reservoir is drawn down tremendously in the winter, exposing a great deal of structure that is submerged in the summer. Casual readings from a depth finder or even the most recent topographical maps can't give you the detailed information that an on-site inspection can.

As the weather warms and the water levels drop, the walleye begin to move back into increasingly deeper, cooler water. By late summer they will often be found in 40 to 50 feet of water. They continue to move into deeper water (up to 60 feet) through the fall and early winter. Their requirement for deep water in the winter restricts the areas where they are likely to be found in the New York section of the reservoir due to the drawn down pool level at this time of year. Two highly productive spots for taking walleye through the ice include the deep channel just off of High Banks Camp Ground and the waters off of Onoville Marina. Later in the winter and early spring, the fish will again begin to move into shallower water in anticipation of their spawning run.

Northern Pike .... Common; growth very good

Northern pike were first introduced into the reservoir in 1968 in an attempt to control the rapidly growing populations of carp and other rough fish. Stocking continued until 1970, and natural reproduction has maintained a healthy population of pike ever since. Most of these toothsome predators fall in the 18- to 26-inch category, but many fish in excess of 30 pounds have been taken here, including three Pennsylvania state records.

Northerns are found throughout the shallower portions of the reservoir, and most fish are taken in less than 20 feet of water. There are, however, a number of areas in the New York section that regularly produce better than average catches of fish. In the main channel of the reservoir the western shore, from the state line north to Onoville, and the eastern shore, from the mouth of Wolf Run north to Quaker Bay, consistently produce good numbers of fish. All of the shallow, weedy bays will hold some northerns. Particularly good fishing can be found in State Line Bay, off the marina at Onoville (especially through the ice), along the culvert at the mouth of Bone Run, in the overflow area of the bay at the mouth of Pierce Run, and in the east side of the overflow area bisected by the Route 17 bridge crossing.

Above the Route 17 bridge crossing, northern pike can be found almost anywhere, at least in the spring when pool levels are still high. Great numbers of pike move up into this shallow area to spawn in the spring. Especially productive are the three large man-made excavations known as borrow pits. These pits, which are found alongside the main body of the reservoir on the Allegany Indian Reservation, were created when gravel was taken for construction of the Southern Tier Expressway (Route 17). One pit is visible from the Red House exit of the Expressway, and can be reached via old Route 17. The other two can be reached from the Steamburg exit and old Route 417.

If water levels in the reservoir are high enough, these borrow pits fill with water. When this happens, tremendous numbers of northerns seek out these pits to spawn in, at times resulting in remarkable concentrations of fish. Very often a large portion of these fish will be stranded in the pits when water levels in the reservoir fall. Most northerns will prefer to remain in the pits if the water level in the connecting channels fall below 18 inches. Information from the DEC indicates that these trapped fish will survive quite well, providing an additional fishing resource. These pits also hold large numbers of carp, crappies, rock bass, and yellow perch. Be sure to have a Seneca Nation fishing license when fishing in the pits.

Shortly after spawning, most northern pike will seek out adjacent flats in 10 to 20 feet of water, relating to rock piles, small patches of weeds, or small drop-offs. For the best early season pike action, try still fishing with live bait, preferably large shiners (8 to 12 inches). Large chubs and suckers will also work. These baits can also be used while backtrolling or drifting very slowly over the flats. During the first few weeks of the season, northerns will tend to be close to the bottom. To keep your bait near the bottom, be sure to use a sinker. However, by the end of May the northerns will have sufficiently recuperated from their spawning rituals to become more active and aggressive. Then you'll want to fish without a sinker, using a bobber to keep your bait off the bottom and out from the cover of emerging weeds. The late spring is also a good time to begin using spinners, such as the Mepps Aglia, Panther Martin, or Vibrax. Spinnerbaits tipped with a minnow will also produce fish in the late spring and early summer. Although they will catch fish later in the summer, they're definitely more effective in the late spring/early summer period.

In the summer, most northerns move to deeper weedlines, though smaller fish will always be found in the shallow bays. These fish can be taken using a number of methods. Troll the inside, then the outside weedlines, using large spinnerbaits tipped with a minnow (4- to 6-inch shiners, chubs, or suckers), large silver flatfish, crankbaits, or large spoons, such as the classic red and white Dardevle. Play with the trolling depth as you work the weedlines, but keep in mind most northern are taken from less than 20 feet of water.

If trolling isn't to your liking, fan casting can also be productive, and it allows you to learn the structure of a particular area very quickly. All of the above hardware will work, but for a little variety, try using salt-water flies. Several anglers I know use large (5- to 15-inch) flies on other lakes with considerable success, and there is no reason that they wouldn't work well here. Whether trolling or casting, be sure to use a short wire leader or 20- to 30-pound shock tippet. Northern pike have teeth as sharp as razor blades and your going to lose a lot of fish and a lot of tackle if you don't.

Most of the really big northern pike come from weedlines in close juxtaposition to relatively deep, cool water. If you're looking to fish exclusively for large pike, look for these areas and concentrate your efforts there. The trick to fishing for these trophy-size northerns is to use large baits. Try using a 12-inch sucker hooked through the upper lip with a size 2 short-shank hook fished from a slip-bobber. A bait this size will usually only attract the attention of the large northern pike.

In the fall, another method is added to your angling arsenal, namely, jigs. The variety of jigs that will work in the fall is very wide, but they all have something in common - they are big. Half-ounce and 1-ounce jigs dressed with a bucktail, a plastic waterdog (5- to 7-inch size), or a 4- to 6-inch Mister Twister tail will all take pike from this reservoir. The fall is also a good time to use large (5- to 15-inch) minnow imitations, such as a jointed Rapala.

One of the most productive periods for harvesting pike on this or any other lake is the winter, immediately after the lake freezes. A majority of the northern pike will be found in shallow water, 5 to 10 feet deep, primarily in the weedy bays. There could also be some good ice fishing in the borrow pits mentioned above. As the season progresses, however, pike have a tendency to follow the bait fish and small panfish, such as yellow perch, into increasingly deeper water (20 to 30 feet), and the success rate for taking northerns falls. Toward the end of the winter most pike will move to the north end of the reservoir to be near their spawning grounds.

Standard ice fishing techniques can be used here. A tip-up baited with a large sucker or shiner hooked through the back is about a fancy as you have to get. Size 2 or 4 hooks are the most commonly used, and most veteran pike fishermen prefer braided nylon line terminating in either a short wire leader or a heavy duty (40- to 60-pound) monofilament shock tippet. A short-handled gaff is good to have around too. A lot of pike, especially the big ones, are lost at the hole, while they're being landed. A gaff will eliminate this problem.

When ice fishing on the Alleghany Reservoir, there are a couple of things to keep in mind. First is the fact that water levels are often drawn down here, leaving the ice cover unsupported and potentially unstable. You can avoid this problem by fishing in the borrow pits. Second, there are numerous gas seeps and springs in the reservoir, and these can seriously undermine the thickness of the ice in localized areas.

If you do plan to fish here in the winter, try to get current reports on conditions. A hotline exists for the Pennsylvania section of the reservoir, and it gives information on pool levels. The number for this hotline is given at the end of this article.

Smallmouth Bass .... **Very common; growth rate good**

Smallmouth bass are known to be plentiful in the Allegheny Reservoir, but for some reason relatively few are taken from the New York section. There has been some speculation over the years as to the cause of this, but no one has yet come up with a totally acceptable theory. One possibility is that many, if not most, of the smallmouth here are pelagic. This means that they are not structure-oriented, as is usually the case, but tend to move out into open water, high up in the water column. Contrary to what most people believe, it is not that uncommon for smallmouth bass to do this. It has been documented in Lake Erie and all of the larger Finger Lakes. If this is true, the bass are probably feeding on schools of young yellow perch, and possibly on smelt, both of which are also pelagic.

This isn't to say that traditional structure fishing wouldn't be productive. There are some areas where regular bass fishing techniques do work well. Look for deep structure, such as the old river channel or deep rocky points, for the best results. The channel just off High Banks Campground is often productive, as are the flats on the east side of the reservoir between the mouth of Peters Creek and the state line, and the riprap along the mouth of the culvert at Bone Run.

Brown Trout .... **Common; growth very good**

The U.S. Fish and Wildlife Service has had some success in stocking brown trout in the Allegheny Reservoir, and stockings do continue sporadically. These stocked fish are greatly augmented by the large numbers of browns that migrate into the reservoir from the many streams that feed into it. A major portion of the brown trout in the tributaries that survive to the age of 2 years move down into the reservoir, taking up permanent residence. These fish commonly reach a size of 5 to 10 pounds, due to the greater abundance of forage. Brown trout over 15 pounds are not uncommon.

Most of the brown trout in the reservoir are found in the Pennsylvania section, where deeper, cooler water is more available. But a sizable population is also found in New York waters. The old tributary mouths are by far the most productive areas for taking browns here. Often these sites are associated with springs that keep the water cool enough for trout. A notable example of this is the mouth of Cold Spring Brook. Try fishing the old stream mouths in the spring. Trolling with Rapala type plugs in 5 to 10 feet of water, or casting large spoons can be very effective on these fish.

Muskellunge .... **Common; growth good**

There is a sizable population of muskellunge in this reservoir, and to ensure their continued survival the U.S. Fish and Wildlife Service stocks muskies here. They grow big on the abundant forage in the reservoir, and trophy-size fish in excess of 45 pounds have been taken. Unfortunately, most muskies are found in the Pennsylvania section of the lake.

In New York's waters the muskie fishing is usually only fair. But in the early spring and fall large fish do move into the bays in New York. These large predators are also found in the old river channel all year long, but they are very difficult to locate and catch. For the most part, muskellunge are a bonus fish in this part of the reservoir.

Channel Catfish .... **Very common; growth rate very good**

Channel catfish were first introduced into the reservoir by stocking in 1968. The stocking program was discontinued in 1971. Natural reproduction has now made them abundant in most of the lake. Feeding heavily on the reservoir's abundant crayfish population, catfish here regularly reach 6 to 8 pounds, and 15-pound channel cats are not uncommon.

Catfish are not a popular quarry, and this has helped to maintain their large population. This is unfortunate, for they are amongst the finest tasting fish to be caught in fresh water.

The southern tier of western New York is a sportsman's paradise. As shown in these photos of Cattaraugus County, the vast majority of the region is rural, and consists of a mix of forested, rolling hills, deep gorges, and numerous streams, rivers, ponds, and lakes.

The best time to angle for these piscatorial delicacies is at night. They frequent rocky shorelines and bars, feeding heavily on crayfish. Catfish will also be found in bays and backwaters that have a silt and mud bottom.

Popular methods for taking catfish include still fishing with crayfish, stinkbaits, chicken guts, minnows, or big gobs night-crawlers. They will also hit small spinners.

Yellow Perch .... **Common; growth rate good**

Yellow perch were abundant in the reservoir in the early 1970s, but their population has declined steadily since then. This could be due to a number of factors. Yellow perch have a tendency to exhibit fluctuating reproductive success, resulting in periods of boom and bust. There is also the strong possibility that the perch are suffering from overpredation. They serve as a major forage base for nearly every predatory species in the lake. If this is the case, the situation could improve soon, given the successful introduction of rainbow smelt into the reservoir in the past few years.

The best perch fishing takes place in April and May when the fish school up to spawn. Concentrate on shallow areas with submerged brush, or bottoms of sand and gravel. Still fishing with small worms or minnows usually works best. Keep the bait a few inches off the bottom. Yellow perch can also be taken in good numbers in the late fall and early winter. Concentrate on the deep water at the south end of the New York portion of the reservoir. Still fishing with minnows is the most common method used during this period. Perch can be taken through the ice on Kinzua, primarily from the lower end. Two noted hotspots for big perch in the winter are the deep waters just out from the launch at Onoville and from the deep channel off Highbanks Campground. The borrow pits at the north end of the reservoir are reported to offer good winter perch fishing, and the ice there is much more stable than on the main body of the reservoir.

Additional Species

In addition to the above species, Kinzua Reservoir also has good fishing for a number of fish of secondary importance. Often you can find some good fishing for white crappies here in the spring, but their numbers are a far cry from what they were in the early 1970s. Fish in the 10 to 12 inch range are common, and they can be found schooled up in shallow water in the late spring and early summer as they spawn. Check the mouths of tributaries, shallow bays, and rocky points. Minnows and small bucktail jigs work best. If you don't get a hit after a few casts, move on to another site.

Rock bass are found through the reservoir. They favor shallow, rocky areas and can be taken with small spinners, minnows, or worms. On ultra-light tackle rock bass can provide some fast action and fine table fare.

Brown Bullhead are found in most of the shallower areas of the reservoir. Averaging 8 to 14 inches, they feed mainly at night and favor bottoms of mud and sand. The best time to fish for bullhead is in the spring, when they move in great numbers into the shallows to spawn. Stinkbaits, worms, and chicken guts will take most of the fish. Unlike channel cats, bullheads will only rarely take a lure.

Rainbow trout were stocked in the reservoir, but they are not commonly taken in the New York section. Two areas where they are occasionally found are the bays associated with Quaker Run and Sawmill Run.

Rounding out the fish population in the reservoir are carp, bluegills, white bass, and an occasional largemouth bass.

General Information

The Allegheny Reservoir, popularly known as the Kinzua Reservoir, is an impoundment of the Allegheny River. It was created by the construction of the Kinzua Dam in Pennsylvania in 1966. Designed for the purposes of flood control and recreation, the fertile waters of the reservoir provide habitat for an amazing variety fish. It is establishing itself as one of the better fisheries in the western part of the state, although it has had to contend with the problem of fluctuating fish populations. These are caused by several factors: The reservoir is relatively new, a number of stocking programs have been tried here with varying degrees of success, the bait fish population has been altered, and water levels fluctuate drastically over the course of the year. All of these factors combine to make the system basically unstable.

The major drawback to fishing the Allegheny Reservoir is the confusing license situation. The reservoir straddles two states, New York and Pennsylvania, and roughly 95 per cent of the New York portion is within the boundaries of the Allegany Indian Reservation. In order to avoid fishing in areas for which you do not hold an appropriate license, it would be necessary to have a license for all three jurisdictions, a rather expensive proposition.

But fishing here can be well worth the money and effort. The reservoir is greatly underfished, at least in the New York section, and some trophy fish are just waiting to be landed.

For fishing, camping and license information contact the following agencies:

Seneca Nation of Indians
Clerk's Office, Haley Building
P.O. Box 231
Salamanca, New York 14760

Allegheny State Park Commission
Salamanca, New York 14779

Onoville Marina County Park
303 Court Street
Little Valley, New York 14755

New York State Department of Environmental Conservation
Region 9
128 South Street
Olean, New York 14760

Allegheny Reservoir Hotline: (814)-726-0164

A very informative brochure titled "The Allegheny Reservoir Fisheries Guide" can be obtained by contacting:

U.S. Army Corp of Engineers
Kinzua Dam
P.O. Box 983
Warren, PA 16365
(814)-726-0678

NOTES: ______________________________

____

____

CASE LAKE

Location

Map Coordinates .... 42° 18′ 55″ 78° 26′ 00″
USGS Map(s) .... Franklinville (not on current editions)
Township(s) .... Franklin
Access .... Abbotts Road

Physical Characteristics

Area .... 80 acres
Shoreline .... 2.5 miles
Elevation .... 1,675 feet
Maximum Depth .... 40 feet
Mean Depth .... 15 feet
Bottom Type .... Muck, gravel

Chemical Characteristics

Water .... Clear
pH .... Slightly alkaline
Oxygen .... Very good throughout the lake all year

LIME LAKE
Depth Contours in Feet
Route 16
Potter Road
Railroad Grade
Lake Road
Hazelmere Road
5
10
20
30
35
Feet
0
500
1,00
NOT FOR USE IN NAVIGATION

Plant Life

This lake has sparse bottom vegetation except in shallow areas, primarily along the east shore and in the south end.

Species Information

Rainbow Trout .... Abundant; growth rate good to excellent
Brook Trout .... Abundant; growth rate good to excellent
Largemouth Bass .... Common; growth rate good

Boat Launch Sites

The state maintains a public access area and hand launch site for cartop boats and canoes (electric motors only), with parking for 52 cars. There is also an impromptu launch site on the east side of the lake on Abbotts Road, just before the turn-off for the main parking area.

General Information

Case Lake is an 80-acre impoundment formed by the damming of Gates Creek. It is surrounded by woodlands and is suitable for fly fishing. This is a two-story lake, meaning it supports populations of both warm- and cold-water species.

Trout can be caught here all year, any size, five per day. Ice fishing is allowed. Check for current regulations.

Case Lake is stocked annually with 1,800 rainbow trout and 1,800 brown trout yearlings. Large numbers of excess breeders are also released here.

In addition to its fine trout fishing, Case Lake also has a good population of largemouth bass, which provide the best action during the summer months. Various panfish species are also plentiful.

NOTES: ____________________

HARWOOD LAKE

Location

Map Coordinates .... 42° 23′ 00″ 78° 22′ 45″
USGS Map(s) .... Delevan
Township(s) .... Farmersville
Access .... Route 98, 5 miles east of Route 16

Physical Characteristics

Area .... 38 acres
Shoreline .... Data not available
Elevation .... 1,820 feet
Maximum Depth .... 12 feet
Mean Depth .... 8 feet
Bottom Type .... Muck, clay

Chemical Characteristics

Water .... Clear to slightly turbid
pH .... Slightly alkaline
Oxygen .... Good throughout lake all year

Plant Life

Sparse bottom vegetation exists here, with the exception of the small bays on the north side of the lake.

Species Information

Brook Trout .... Abundant; growth rate good to excellent
Rainbow Trout .... Abundant; growth rate good to excellent

Boat Launch Sites

Cartop boats and canoes can be launched from shore. The state maintains a parking area for 25 cars.

General Information

Harwood Lake is a picturesque little trout lake that receives a great deal of fishing pressure. It is adjacent to a tract of government-owned land that was reforested 30 years ago and is state-maintained.

Still fishing from the bank is prevalent on this lake, but small boats are both allowed and practical. Gas engines are prohibited. Excellent hatches of insects just before sundown provide better than average fly fishing opportunities. Trout can be taken from the lake from April 1 to November 30, any size, 5 per day. Ice fishing is prohibited. It is illegal to use or possess live or dead bait here.

In the spring, 2,500 brook trout yearlings and 2,100 rainbow trout yearlings are stocked in Harwood Lake. Occasionally, large breeders are stocked here, as well.

The state has completed a fishing ramp for wheelchairs and restroom facilities for the handicapped.

NOTES: ____________________

LIME LAKE

Location

Map Coordinates .... 42° 26′ 06″ 78° 28′ 33″
USGS Map(s) .... Delevan
Township(s) .... Machias
Access .... Off Route 16

Physical Characteristics

Area .... 256 acres
Shoreline .... 3.79 miles
Elevation .... 1,636 feet
Maximum Depth .... 38 feet
Mean Depth .... Approximately 14 feet
Bottom Type .... Gravel, muck

Lime Lake is one of the most productive bass lakes in western New York. The lunker proudly displayed by this young angler weighed in at 5 pounds.

Chemical Characteristics

Water .... Generally clear except during algal blooms
pH .... Slightly alkaline
Oxygen .... Usually good throughout the lake; levels could be slightly deficient during periods of algal blooms.

Plant Life

Weed beds are extensive in Lime Lake. Upwards of 90 percent of the lake is treated every year for weed control and algal blooms are recurrent.

Species Information

Largemouth Bass .... Abundant; growth rate good
Chain Pickerel .... Common; growth rate good
Tiger Muskellunge .... Common; growth rate data not available
Yellow Perch .... Abundant; growth rate fair
Rock Bass .... Abundant; growth rate fair
Bullhead .... Abundant; growth rate fair
Pumpkinseeds .... Abundant; growth rate fair

Boat Launch Sites

The DEC has recently purchased an access site for cartop boats and canoes on Lime Lake. It is located on the east side of the lake. Look for the yellow DEC access signs.

General Information

Created in 1839, Lime Lake is an impoundment formed by damming the outlets of what where originally three separate ponds. Almost entirely fed by cold spring water, this lake has the unique distinction of emptying into two separate drainage systems. Its water eventually finds its way into the north Atlantic Ocean and the Gulf of Mexico.

Studies by the DEC indicate that Lime Lake has an excellent population of largemouth bass and panfish. Their distribution is such that nearly any section of the lake should produce well. There is also a growing population of tiger muskellunge.

Lime Lake is stocked with 1,500 tiger muskellunge fingerlings annually.

NOTES: ______________________________

____

____

NEW ALBION LAKE

Location

Map Coordinates .... 42° 18′ 00″ 78° 54′ 45″
USGS Map(s) .... New Albion (not on current editions)
Township(s) .... New Albion
Access .... Mosher Hollow Road, northwest of the Village of New Albion

Physical Characteristics

Area .... 50 acres
Shoreline .... Data not available
Elevation .... 1,381 feet
Maximum Depth .... 16 feet
Mean Depth .... 7 feet
Bottom Type .... Muck

Chemical Characteristics

Water .... Clear
pH .... Slightly alkaline
Oxygen .... Good throughout lake

Plant Life

Scattered weed beds are found in the shallower parts of the lake.

Species Information

Rainbow Trout .... Abundant; growth rate good
Brown Trout .... Abundant; growth rate good

Boat Launch Sites

The state maintains a launch site for canoes and cartop boats (electric motors only) and a parking area off Mosher Hollow Road.

General Information

New Albion Lake is an impoundment of the upper section of Conewango Creek. First opened to the public in the spring of 1983, this lake provides excellent trout fishing all season long. There is a state-maintained launch site and parking area. In addition, the state has constructed a special fishing access ramp and restroom facilities for the handicapped.

This lake is intended to be a trout-only type of lake, but warmwater species indigenous to Conewango Creek, such as chubs and smallmouth bass, will be present, at least for a while.

Trout can be taken from April 1 to November 30, any size, 5 per day. Ice fishing is prohibited. Check for current regulations.

In the spring, New Albion Lake is stocked with 2,800 rainbow trout yearlings and 2,800 brown trout yearlings.

NOTES: ______________________________

____

____

QUAKER LAKE

Location

Map Coordinates .... 42° 02′ 30″ 78° 52′ 00″
USGS Map(s) .... Red House
Location .... Allegany State Park
Access .... State Park Route 3

Physical Characteristics

Area .... 270 acres
Shoreline .... 3.5 miles
Elevation .... 1,365 feet
Maximum Depth .... 42 feet
Mean Depth .... 15 feet
Bottom Type .... Clay, gravel, rock

Chemical Characteristics

Water .... Clear
pH .... Slightly alkaline
Oxygen .... Good throughout lake all year

Plant Life

Vegetation is sparse except in some shallow areas.

Species Information

Rainbow Trout .... Abundant; growth rate good to excellent
Brown Trout .... Abundant; growth rate good to excellent
Also present are numerous panfish

Boat Launch Sites

Cartop boats and canoes can be launched from shore (no motors allowed).

General Information

Quaker Lake is an artificial impoundment fed primarily by Quaker Run. This is an excellent location for a family fishing trip. A State Park permit is required to fish here.

Approximately 4,200 rainbow trout and 4,200 brown trout are released into Quaker Lake annually. Excess breding stock from state hatcheries, some in the 4 to 5 pound category are regularly released here, as well. Occasionally, wild rainbow trout and brown drop down into Quaker Lake from Quaker Run.

NOTES: ______________________________

____

____

RED HOUSE LAKE

Location

Map Coordinates .... 46° 06′ 13″   78° 44′ 41″
USGS Map(s) .... Limestone
Location .... Allegany State Park
Access .... State Park Route 1

Physical Characteristics

Area .... 90 acres
Shoreline .... 1.90 miles
Elevation .... 1,410 feet
Maximum Depth .... 20 feet
Mean Depth .... 7 feet
Bottom Type .... Muck, gravel

Chemical Characteristics

Water .... Clear
pH .... Alkaline
Oxygen .... Good throughout the lake all year

Plant Life

Rooted vegetation is very limited except in shallow areas.

Species Information

Rainbow Trout .... Abundant; growth rate good to excellent
Brown Trout .... Abundant; growth rate good to excellent
Largemouth Bass .... Common; growth rate fair to good

Boat Launch Sites

The state maintains a launch site (hand launch only) and parking area. Boats and canoes can be rented at the lake.

General Information

Red House Lake is an artificial impoundment of Red House Brook. It is a two-story lake, having both cold- and warm-water environments. It has very good populations of largemouth bass and panfish, as well as brown trout and rainbow trout. Like Quaker lake, this is an excellent location for family fishing. Keep in mind that this lake is usually not free of ice until late April. Don't plan any early fishing trips without first checking with park officials. A state park permit is required.

In the spring, Redhouse Lake is stocked with 1,000 brown trout yearlings.

SCIENCE LAKE

Location

Map Coordinates .... 42° 00′ 37″   78° 46′ 03″
USGS Map(s) .... Red House
Location .... Allegany State Park
Access .... State Park Route 3

Physical Characteristics

Area .... 2 acres
Shoreline .... 33 miles
Elevation .... 1,840 feet
Maximum Depth .... 15 feet
Mean Depth .... 7 feet
Bottom Type .... Muck

Chemical Characteristics

Water .... Clear to slightly turbid
pH .... Slightly alkaline
Oxygen .... Good throughout the lake all year

Plant Life

Bottom Vegetation is very limited.

Species Information

Brook Trout .... Abundant; growth good to excellent

Boat Launch Sites

No launch facilities are available.

General Information

Although very small, Science Lake is a very heavily stocked lake and a good location for family fishing trips.

In the spring, 800 brook trout fingerlings are stocked in Science Lake. Periodically, large excess breeders from state hatcheries are also released here.

A State Park permit is required to fish here.

NOTES: ______________________________

The many streams and lakes in Allegany State Park offer a wide variety of fishing opportunities. Red House Lake, pictured at right, provides good fishing for bass and trout.

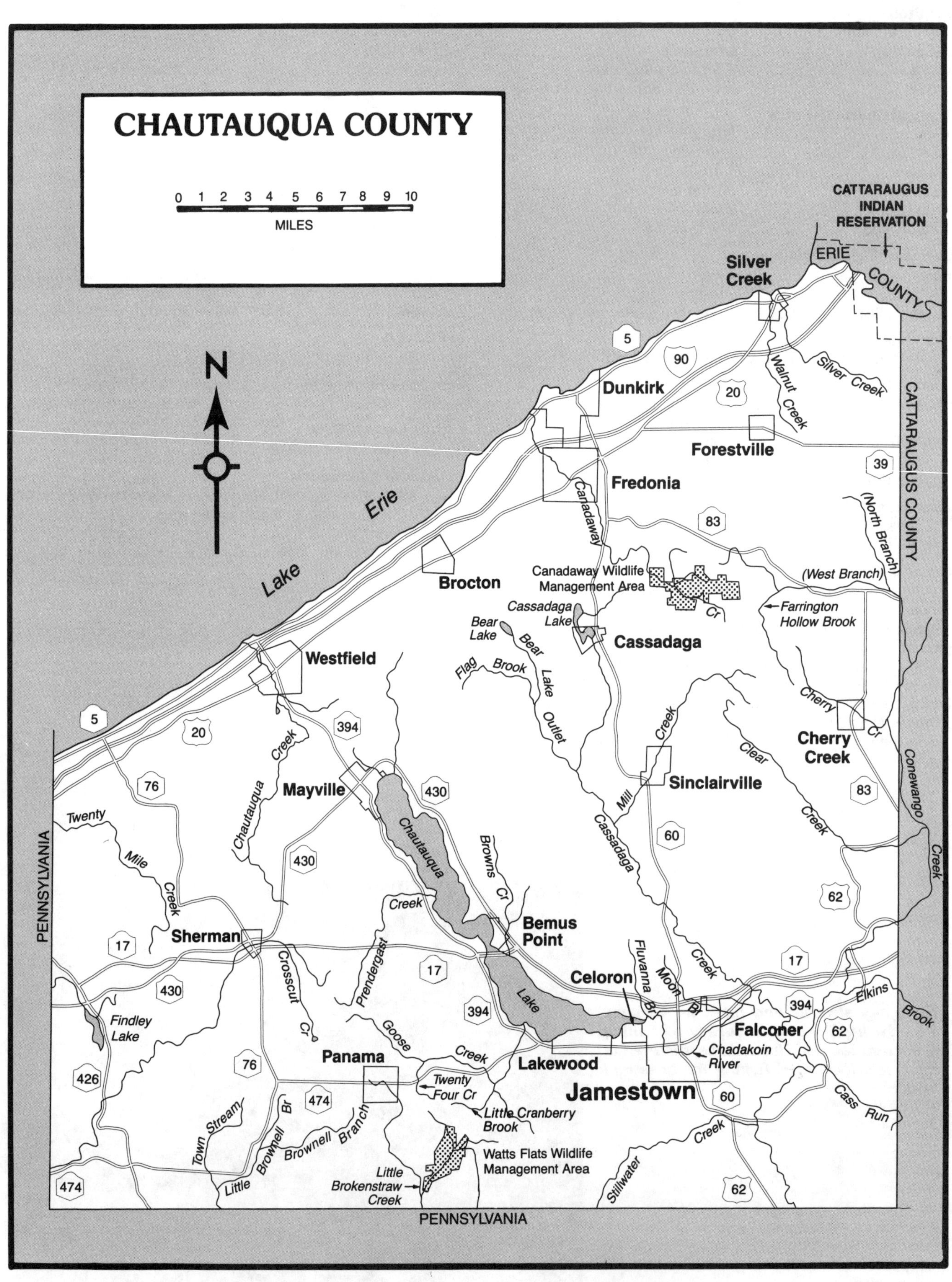

CHAUTAUQUA COUNTY
0 1 2 3 4 5 6 7 8 9 10
MILES
N
CATTARAUGUS INDIAN RESERVATION
ERIE COUNTY
CATTARAUGUS COUNTY
PENNSYLVANIA
PENNSYLVANIA
Lake Erie
Silver Creek
Dunkirk
Forestville
Fredonia
Brocton
Westfield
Cassadaga
Mayville
Sinclairville
Cherry Creek
Sherman
Bemus Point
Celoron
Falconer
Lakewood
Panama
Jamestown
Canadaway Wildlife Management Area
Cassadaga Lake
Bear Lake
Bear Lake Outlet
Flag Brook
Farrington Hollow Brook
(North Branch)
(West Branch)
Walnut Creek
Silver Creek
Canadaway Cr
Cherry Cr
Clear Creek
Mill Creek
Cassadaga Creek
Conewango Creek
Chautauqua Creek
Twenty Mile Creek
Chautauqua Lake
Browns Cr
Prendergast Creek
Crosscut Cr
Findley Lake
Goose Creek
Fluvanna Br
Moon Br
Chadakoin River
Elkins Brook
Cass Run
Twenty Four Cr
Little Cranberry Brook
Watts Flats Wildlife Management Area
Little Brokenstraw Creek
Town Stream
Little Brownell Br
Brownell Branch
Stillwater Creek
5
90
20
39
83
394
430
76
17
60
62
426
474

CHAUTAUQUA COUNTY STREAMS AND RIVERS

BEAR LAKE OUTLET

Map coordinates .... 42° 15′ 42″ 79° 19′ 34″
USGS Map(s) .... Cassadaga, Hartfield
Township(s) .... Stockton
Access .... Bridge crossing at Route 380
Principal Species .... Rainbow Trout (stocked), Smallmouth Bass, Muskellunge, Northern Pike, Bullhead

Bear Lake Outlet is a clear, slow-moving stream averaging 15 to 20 feet in width. It has a gravel bottom and is surrounded by farmland and some woodland, making it brushy in some sections.

This stream has a good indigenous population of smallmouth bass, and bullhead and muskellunge are also caught here. There is unrestricted fishing for northern pike in this stream. They can be taken any size, any number, all year. Ice fishing is permitted.

In addition to holding warm-water species, Bear Lake Outlet is stocked with trout. In the spring, 1,200 rainbow trout yearlings are released in the 2.9-mile section between Cemetery Road and the bridge at Route 380.

NOTES: ______________________________

BROWNELL BRANCH

Map Coordinates .... 42° 01′ 03″ 79° 35′ 51″
USGS Map(s) .... North Clymer
Township(s) .... Clymer, Harmony
Access .... Einnick Road, north of Brownell Road
Principal Species .... Brown Trout (wild), Brook Trout (stocked and wild)

This stream averages about 8 feet in width, has a gravel bottom, and is fishable all trout season. It is surrounded by woodlands and wooded marshlands, and has rather brushy bank cover. East of County Road 628, it flows through a state reforestation area.

In the spring, Brownell Branch is stocked with 500 brook trout yearlings in the 1.2-mile section just above the stream mouth. There are wild brown trout throughout the stream as well, and they grow to a respectable size.

NOTES: ______________________________

BROWNS CREEK

Map Coordinates .... 42° 10′ 07″ 79° 22′ 56″
USGS Map(s) .... Chautauqua
Township(s) .... Ellery
Access .... Hayner Road
Principal Species .... Brown Trout (stocked)

Browns Creek joins Bemus Creek just before emptying into Chautauqua Lake. It has a bottom of silt and sand, little bank cover, and is fishable only during the first few months of trout season.

Like Cattaraugus County, brook trout can be found in the headwaters of many of the Chautauqua County trout streams that lie east of the ridge that parallels Lake Erie. And they will be found in same type of areas - higher elevation headwaters situated in woodlands. Fishing headwaters can be difficult; they are almost always small and brushy, and the fish are seldom more than 9 inches. Use the lightest tackle available when pursuing these fish, and be very careful in your approach and presentation.

In the fall, 200 brown trout fingerlings are released in the 1-mile section of Browns Creek between Hayner Road and Walker Road.

NOTES: ______________________________

CANADAWAY CREEK

Map Coordinates .... 42° 28′ 37″ 79° 22′ 07″
USGS Map(s) .... Dunkirk, Cassadaga, Hamlet
Township(s) .... Dunkirk, Pomfret, Arkwright
Access .... Route 5 bridge crossing in Dunkirk
Principal Species .... Rainbow Trout (stocked and wild), Brown Trout, Coho Salmon, Chinook Salmon

Emptying into Lake Erie west of the town of Dunkirk, Canadaway Creek is a gravel- and shale-bottomed stream that gets a good run of steelhead in the spring. It also has good fall runs of coho, chinook, steelhead, and brown trout. These fish can run up as far as the falls at Laona. Snagging is allowed from August 15 to November 15, between Route 20 and the aforementioned falls.

There is limited natural reproduction of rainbow trout in Canadaway Creek in the section above Laona, which can be accessed in the Canadaway Creek Wildlife Management Area.

The lower end of Canadaway Creek is stocked with 20,000 coho salmon fingerlings in the fall.

NOTES: ______________________________

CANADAWAY CREEK WILDLIFE MANAGEMENT AREA

Map Coordinates .... 42° 22′ 30″ 79° 14′ 00″
USGS Map(s) .... Hamlet
Township(s) .... Arkwright
Access .... Cassadaga Road (Route 312), Center Road (Route 369)
Principal Species .... Rainbow Trout (wild), Largemouth Bass

This is a 2,180-acre preserve consisting of deeply wooded hills through which flow the headwaters of Canadaway Creek. The area is home to a wide variety of flora and fauna, and provides opportunities for numerous outdoor activities. Cross-country skiing (trail and free-form), hiking, and horseback riding are popular here. The diverse habitat supports numerous game species, including deer, grouse, mink, fox, and rabbit, making the area popular with hunters and trappers. For the fisherman there are several small ponds that hold modest-size bass and trout, and there are limited numbers of wild rainbow trout in Canadaway Creek.

NOTES: ______________________________

CASS RUN

Map Coordinates .... 42° 05′ 11″ 79° 07′ 52″
USGS Map(s) .... Jamestown, Ivory
Township(s) .... Carroll
Access .... Paralleled by Harrington Road
Principal Species .... Brown Trout (stocked)

Cass Run is a good-quality trout stream averaging 15 feet in width. It has a bottom of gravel and rubble. Surrounded primarily by

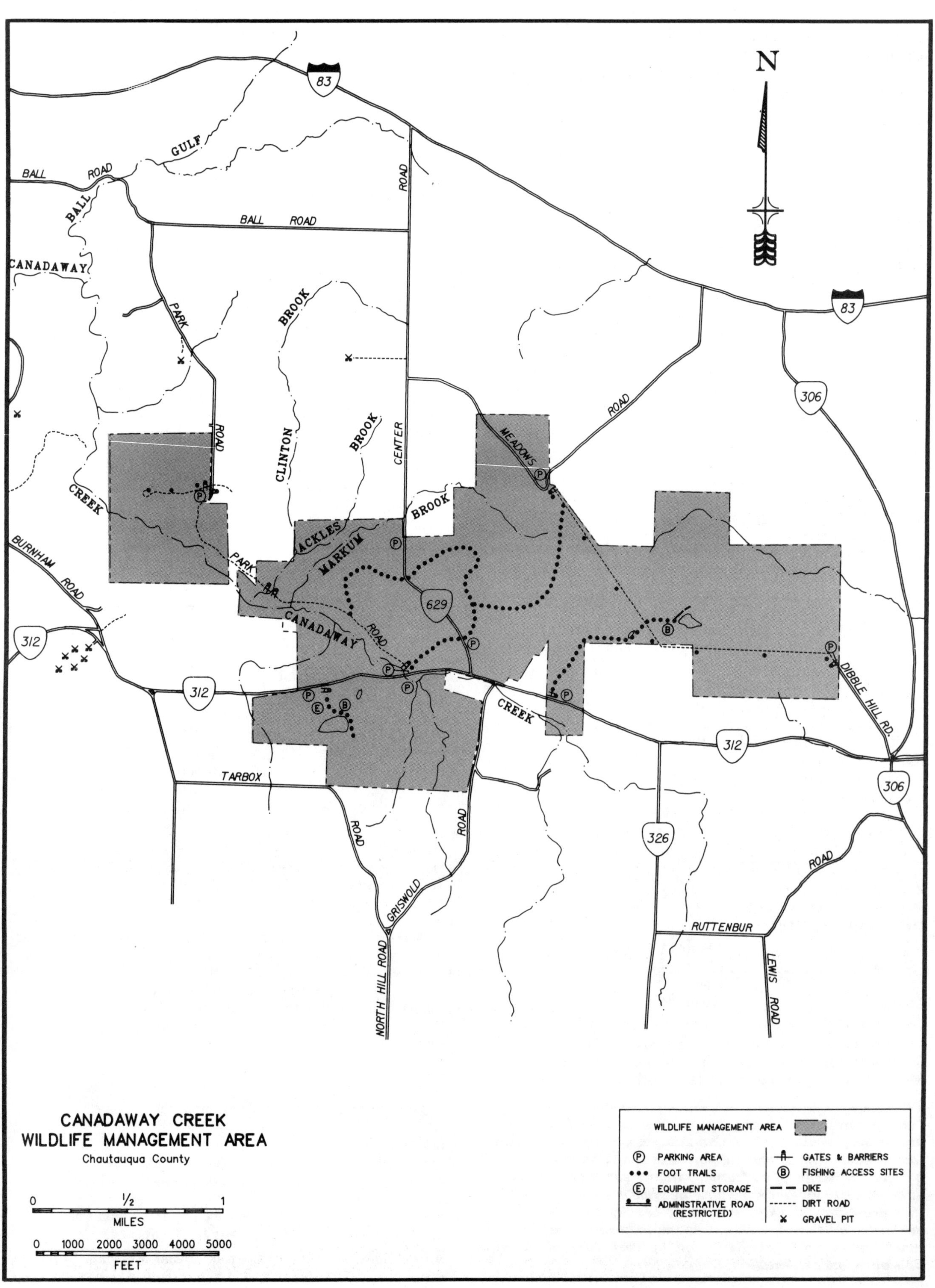

CANADAWAY CREEK
WILDLIFE MANAGEMENT AREA
Chautauqua County
0 1/2 1
MILES
0 1000 2000 3000 4000 5000
FEET
WILDLIFE MANAGEMENT AREA
PARKING AREA
FOOT TRAILS
EQUIPMENT STORAGE
ADMINISTRATIVE ROAD (RESTRICTED)
GATES & BARRIERS
FISHING ACCESS SITES
DIKE
DIRT ROAD
GRAVEL PIT
N
83
306
312
326
629
BALL ROAD
GULF
CANADAWAY
PARK ROAD
BROOK
CLINTON
CENTER ROAD
MEADOWS ROAD
CREEK
BURNHAM ROAD
MARKUM
CANADAWAY ROAD
TARBOX ROAD
GRISWOLD ROAD
NORTH HILL ROAD
RUTTENBUR ROAD
LEWIS ROAD
DIBBLE HILL RD.

woodlands, this stream has intermittent bank cover and is fishable all trout season.

In the spring, the lowermost 3-mile section of Cass Run is stocked with 1,100 brown trout yearlings.

NOTES: ____

____

____

CASSADAGA CREEK

Map Coordinates	42° 05′ 30″ 79° 08′ 13″
USGS Map(s)	Jamestown, Gerry, Ellery Center, Cassadaga
Township(s)	Ellicott, Gerry, Stockton
Access	Love Road (upper section); paralleled by Route 380 between Stockton and Ross Mills (lower section)
Principal Species	Brown Trout (stocked), Muskellunge, Northern Pike, Smallmouth Bass, Bullhead, Panfish

Cassadaga Creek is a large, slow-moving stream that provides very good fishing for both warm-water and cold-water species. The upper portion of the stream, from its source at Lower Cassadaga Lake down to its junction with Bear Lake Outlet, is primarily trout water. This section averages 15 to 20 feet in width and has a gravel and sand bottom. It is surrounded by open fields and woodlands, and has intermittent bank cover. Although subject to severe fluctuations in water flow, it is, nevertheless, fishable all trout season.

The spring fishing in the upper section of Cassadaga Creek is quite good due to the generous number of fish that are stocked here. In March and April, 3,600 brown trout yearlings are released in the 5.2-mile section between Bear Lake Outlet and Love Road. There are extensive public fishing rights on the trout section of this stream.

Below the mouth of Bear Lake Outlet, warm-water species begin to predominate in Cassadaga Creek. There are plenty of smallmouth bass, muskellunge (especially between Ross Mills and South Stockton), northern pike, bullhead, and panfish. The northern pike can be taken in any number, any size, all year. Ice fishing is permitted.

About 500 muskies are stocked in Cassadaga Creek each year, between Ross Mills and South Stockton. If you plan to fish for muskies, be sure to have the special license that is required in Chautauqua County.

From South Stockton to its confluence with Conewango Creek, Cassadaga Creek is a part of the Cassadaga/Conewango Waterway. This is a county-operated system designed to increase public access to and utilization of these two important streams. There is a county-maintained Adirondack lean-to shelter with privy, located on several acres of county-owned land off Route 380, about 1 mile north of Ross Mills. To facilitate canoeing on Cassadaga Creek, five launch sites (canoes and cartop boats only) with parking areas have been constructed. They are located in the following areas: On County Road 71, just north of the village of South Stockton; on County Route 314, near the village of Red Bird; on Miller Road, off Route 380, one mile above Kimball Stand; on Knight Road, off Route 380, near Ross Mills; and at the confluence with the Chadakoin River, just below the Southern Tier Expressway.

NOTES: ____

____

____

Northern pike and muskellunge are very similar in appearance, but they are easy to differentiate if you know what to look for. Northern pike have five or fewer sensory pores on the underside of their lower jaw; muskellunge have six to nine such pores. Also, on northerns the entire cheek is scaled, but muskies have no scales on the lower half of their cheeks.

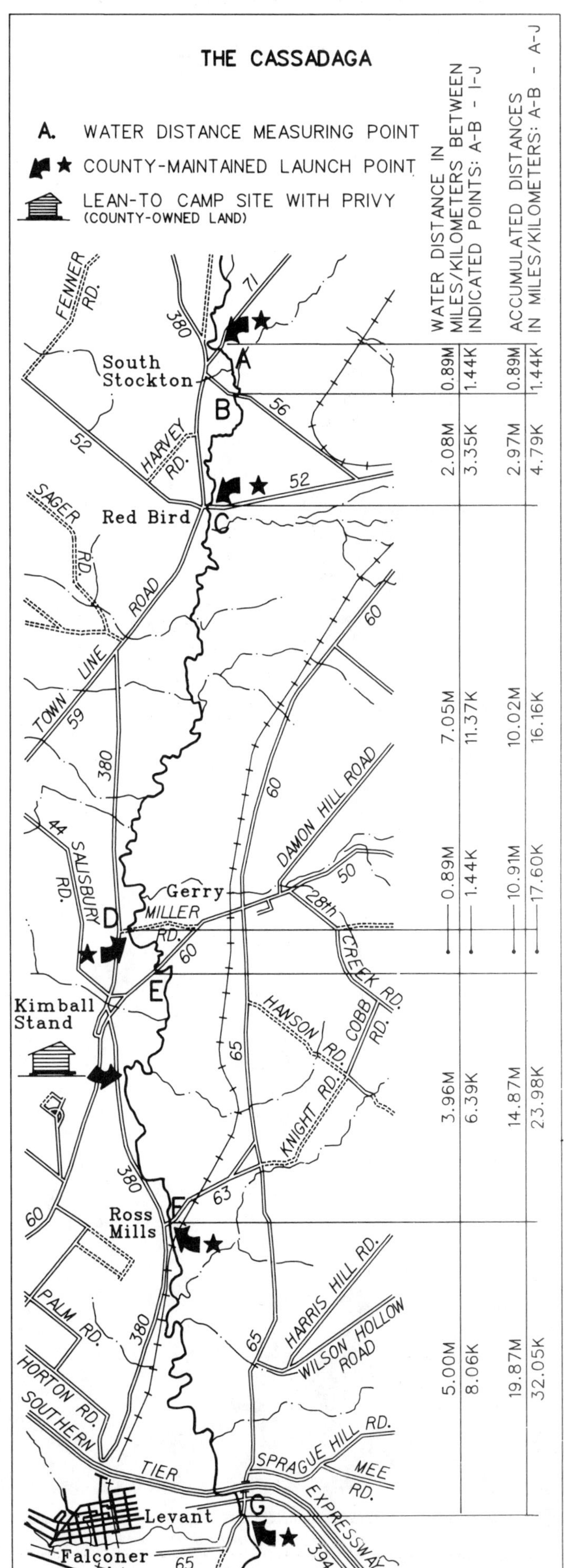

CHADAKOIN RIVER

Map Coordinates	42° 07′ 54″ 79° 10′ 52″
USGS Map(s)	Gerry, Jamestown, Lakewood
Township(s)	Jamestown, Ellicott
Access	McCrae launch ramp at Jones and Gifford Avenue
Principal Species	Largemouth Bass, Smallmouth Bass, Northern Pike, Panfish

The Chadakoin River is the outlet of Chautauqua Lake. A dam just below the municipal boat launch ramp in Jamestown divides the river in to two sections. At present, the best fishing is in the upper end of the river where largemouth bass, smallmouth bass, and panfish such as crappies are taken in good numbers. Further downstream, the fishing degrades due to the large infusion of excessively warm water from a power plant in Jamestown. The warm-water discharge is scheduled to be terminated at the end of 1991 and the quality of the fishing here should improve thereafter.

Access to the lower portion of the Chadakoin River is found next to Hill's Department Store on Market Street. Largemouth bass, smallmouth bass, and northern pike can be found in this section, but the fishing is mediocre at best.

NOTES: ______________________________

____

____

The Chadakoin is a shallow, sluggish river that provides some of the best fishing for largemouth bass in Chautauqua County. Because the banks are so heavily wooded, it is easy to forget that the river flows through the middle of a highly developed area. Photo courtesy Mike Bleech.

CHAUTAUQUA CREEK

Map Coordinates .... 42° 20′ 16″ 79° 36′ 25″
USGS Map(s) .... Westfield, Sherman
Township(s) .... Westfield, Chautauqua
Access .... Nettle Hill Road (upper section); Route 5 bridge crossing (lower section)
Principal Species .... Rainbow Trout (stocked and wild), Brown Trout (stocked and wild), Coho Salmon

Chautauqua Creek empties into Lake Erie just west of Barcelona Harbor. The lower portion of this stream, below the Westfield Water Works Dam, is accessible from the bridge crossing at Route 5. There are very good runs of steelhead here in the spring, and a few brown trout are usually caught as well. In the fall, beginning in late September, steelhead, brown trout, and cohos are all taken in significant numbers. With the exception of the coho, these fish will linger in Chautauqua Creek until early spring, providing some excellent cold weather fishing. Special Great Lakes regulations apply to the lower portions of the stream. Snagging is allowed from U.S. Route 20 upstream to the Waterworks Dam from August 15 to November 15.

In the spring, the lower end of Chautauqua Creek is stocked with 18,000 steelhead yearlings, 18,000 skamania rainbow yearlings, and 45,000 coho fingerlings.

Above the Waterworks Dam, Chautauqua Creek averages 12 to 15 feet in width and has a bedrock bottom with some pockets of gravel. It is fishable all trout season and regular state rules apply. This part of the stream runs through a deep, wooded gorge and has limited bank cover. For those who enjoy solitude while fishing, upper Chautauqua Creek is highly recommended. There are wild brown trout and rainbow trout throughout this stream, and some of them reach a very respectable size.

The state has purchased public fishing rights on several tracts of land about one mile south of the town of Westfield, off Route 17. Also, there are almost continuous public fishing rights from Nettle Hill Road downstream to one-half mile below Taylor Road.

In the spring, the upper reach of Chautauqua Creek is stocked with 700 brown trout yearlings in the 1.5-mile section from Lyons Road upstream to Nettle Hill Road.

NOTES: ______________________________

____

____

CHERRY CREEK

Map Coordinates .... 42° 17′ 39″ 79° 04′ 09″
USGS Map(s) .... Cherry Creek, Hamlet
Township(s) .... Cherry Creek
Access .... Farrington Hollow Road,
Principal Species .... Brown Trout (wild)

Cherry Creek is one of the better quality trout streams in Chautauqua County. It averages about 15 feet in width, has a gravel bottom, and is fishable all trout season. Surrounded by woodland and pastureland, there is good bank cover on most of stream.

Cherry Creek is not stocked. There is, however, sufficient natural reproduction to provide excellent quality trout fishing, and large wild brown trout can be caught throughout the stream.

NOTES: ______________________________

____

____

CLEAR CREEK

Map Coordinates .... 42° 13′ 39″ 79° 02′ 17″
USGS Maps .... Kennedy, Gerry, Hamlet
Township(s) .... Cherry, Ellington
Access .... Paralleled by Route 62 east of Ellington
Principal Species .... Brown Trout (stocked and wild)

Clear Creek fluctuates between 10 and 20 feet in width, has a gravel and sand bottom, and excellent water quality. It is surrounded by woodlands and is fishable all season. Problems with erosion prevent Clear Creek from reaching its full potential as a trout stream. There is little bank cover due to the poor stability of its banks, though fish can be caught even in the fully denuded sections. There are good numbers of wild brown trout in this stream and they grow to a respectable size. There are extensive public fishing rights along almost the entire length of the stream.

In March and April, Clear Creek is stocked with 1,800 brown trout yearlings in the 2.5-mile section immediately above the stream mouth. In the fall, 3,800 brown trout fingerlings are stocked here, from 5.5 miles above the Route 62 bridge crossing to one-half mile below the bridge.

NOTES: ______________________________

____

____

Streams offer more than just the opportunity to fish. They are highways to the outdoors, providing access to areas that are often otherwise inaccessible. The author and his dog, Gretchen, walk the length of many streams in the summer and fall to learn more about them and their surroundings.

CONEWANGO CREEK

Map Coordinates	41° 50′ 28″ 79° 08′ 44″
USGS Map(s)	Russell, Jamestown, Ivory, Kennedy, Cherry Creek, New Albion
Location	Counties of Chautauqua and Cattaraugus
Access	Mosher Hollow Road (upper section), launch site at Route 62 (lower section); see text
Principal Species	Brown Trout (stocked and wild), Muskellunge, Northern Pike, Smallmouth Bass, Largemouth Bass, Bullhead, Walleye, panfish

Beginning near the village of New Albion in Cattaraugus County, Conewango Creek is a long, diversified stream that offers anglers a wide variety of fishing opportunities. The upper portion, from New Albion Lake (see Cattaraugus County Lakes) to the state drainage ditch, is a fair-quality trout stream averaging 15 to 20 feet in width. It has a silt and gravel bottom, and is surrounded by woodlands, swamps, and pastures. There is intermittent bank cover along this section of the Conewango. This reach of the stream is fishable all trout season.

There is a good population of wild brown trout here, as well as a few hatchery fish that migrate down out of the stocked sections of the north and west branches of the Conewango. These fish often attain a good size. Although not numerous, there are some smallmouth bass and northern pike in the upper Conewango as well. This section of the stream is not stocked.

Near Cherry Creek Road, just below where it crosses into Chautauqua County, Conewango Creek enters the state drainage ditch, a wide, silt-bottomed channel. The state drainage ditch is, as the name suggests, an artificial cut made to facilitate drainage along Conewango Creek. But don't get the impression that this is a straight cut, denuded of vegetation and lacking in character. To the contrary, it is reminiscent of the backwaters of a southern swamp. The ditch is approximately 9 miles in length and runs from Leon Road down to Goodwins Landing. Its width varies from 15 feet in the upper reaches to as much as 60 feet near the end. A good way to fish this water is by canoe. There is an impromptu launch site for canoes and cartop boats just outside of Randolph, near to where the railroad crosses old Route 17. Though the upper section gets shallow at times, further downstream it is anywhere from 5 to 20 feet deep. Some portions are completely choked with overhanging branches, especially in the upper reaches. The water is slow moving and murky, looking almost totally stagnant. If you plan on fishing here in warm weather, be sure to bring along plenty of insect repellant. The bugs are plentiful here, and voracious.

The most important species found in the ditch are muskellunge. The state annually stocks 900 muskie fingerlings in this water, and they do quite well here, feeding on populations of crappies, suckers, small bass, and trout. The trout are stocked fish that made the unfortunate mistake of migrating down from the more hospitable waters of Little Conewango Creek. If they aren't taken by a fisherman they're almost certain to become a meal for a muskie or big northern. Also found here are good populations of largemouth bass, bullheads, and some northern pike. The pike are a relatively new introduction to this drainage, having migrated up from the Allegany River via Conewango Creek.

From the state drainage ditch to the state line, Conewango Creek averages 40 to 60 feet in width. It has a silt bottom and is primarily a deep, sluggish, warm-water stream. Crisscrossed by Route 62, this portion of the Conewango has good to excellent fishing for muskellunge, northern pike, smallmouth bass, and bullhead, with limited fishing for largemouth bass, crappies, and walleyes.

Below the confluence with Little Conewango Creek, brown trout can be found in this stream and, although not present in great numbers, they generally run large in size. When water levels are high in the spring and fall, these trout will often be found in or near the lower sections of such cold-water tributaries as Cass Run, Elkins Brook, and Clear Creek.

Conewango Creek is regularly stocked with muskellunge. Each

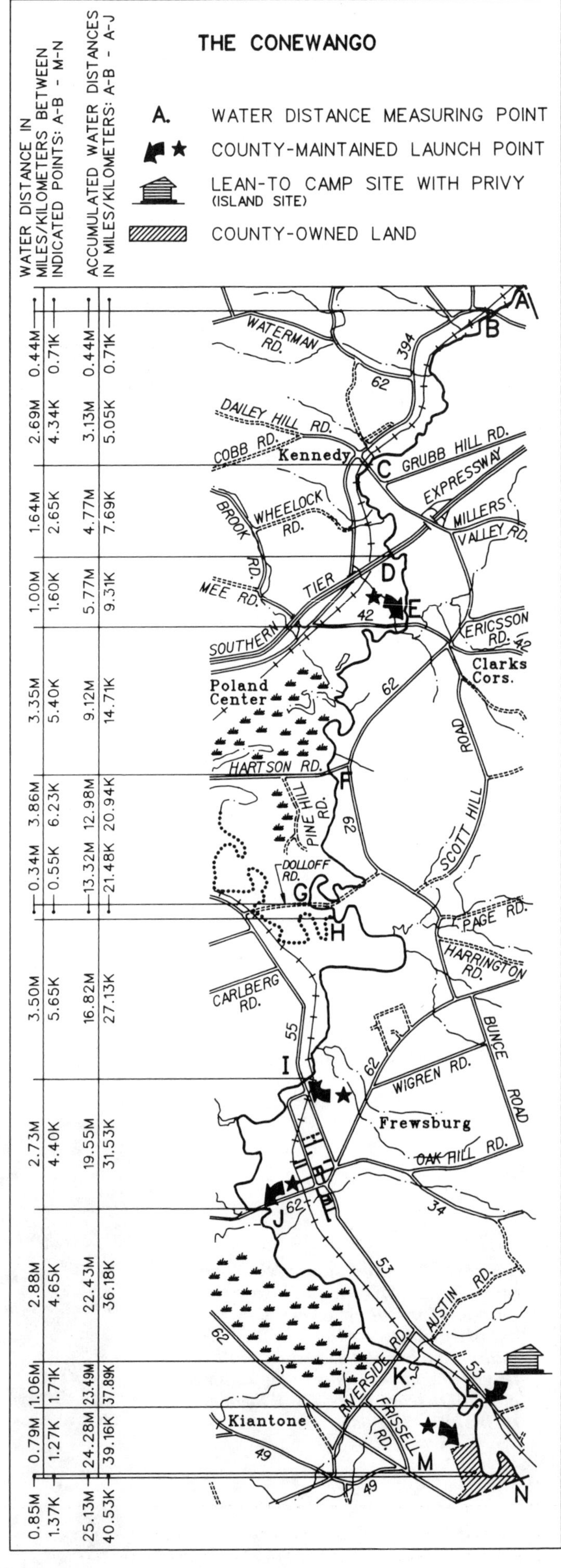

year approximately 950 muskie fingerlings are released between the state line and the confluence with Cassadaga Creek. Be sure to check for current Chautauqua County muskie regulations. In order to protect the muskie population in Conewango Creek, the DEC allows the more competitive northern pike to be taken all year, any size, any number. Ice fishing is permitted.

From its final crossing into Chautauqua County (one-half mile above the bridge crossing at Route 394) to the state line, Conewango Creek is administered as part of the Cassadaga/Conewango Waterway. This is a county-operated system designed to increase access to and utilization of this important stream. The county maintains an Adirondack-type lean-to shelter and privy on a county-owned island one mile below Riverside Road. Four boat launch sites with parking areas (small boats and canoes only) have been constructed at the following sites: one-half mile west of Frissell Road, just above the state line; the bridge crossing at Route 62, one-half mile west of Frewsburg; the bridge crossing at County Route 317, north of Frewsburg; and the bridge crossing on County Route 42, one mile below the Southern Tier Expressway.

NOTES: ____________________

ZUG BUG

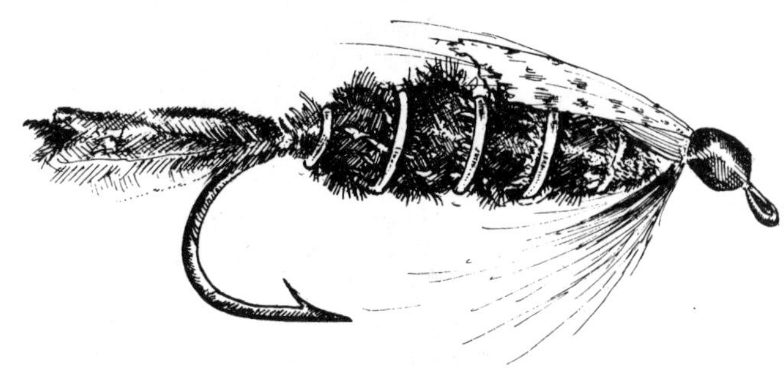

The Zug Bug is a very effective fly on lakes and ponds as well as on streams. It imitates a wide range of nymphs.

CONEWANGO CREEK (North Branch)

Map Coordinates .... 42° 22′ 06″ 79° 03′ 58″
USGS Map(s) .... Cherry Creek, Perrysburg
Township(s) .... Villanova
Access .... Roughly paralleled by Hanover Road
Principal Species .... Brown Trout (stocked)

The north branch of Conewango Creek averages 10 to 15 feet in width, has a gravel bottom, and is fishable all trout season. It is surrounded by woodlands and farmlands, and has a substantial amount of bank cover.

In the fall, this branch of Conewango Creek is stocked with 300 brown trout fingerlings, from the bridge crossing at Hanover Road upstream 1.7 miles to Bartlett Road.

NOTES: ____________________

CONEWANGO CREEK (West Branch)

Map Coordinates .... 42° 19′ 31″ 79° 03′ 05″
USGS Map(s) .... Cherry Creek, Perrysburg, Hamlet, Forestville
Township(s) .... Villanova
Access .... Route 83
Principal Species .... Brown Trout (stocked)

The west branch of Conewango Creek averages 15 feet in width. It has a gravel bottom and is fishable all trout season. Surrounded by woodlands and farmlands, there is a lot of bank cover along this stream.

In the spring, this stream is stocked with 800 brown trout yearlings, from South Hill Road upstream 1.6 miles to Wentworth Road.

NOTES: ____________________

For information on fishing in central New York, obtain a copy of Sander's Fishing Guide No. 2 - The Finger Lakes Region. An order form is located in the back of this book.

CROSSCUT CREEK

Map Coordinates .... 42° 09′ 25″ 79° 35′ 05″
USGS Map(s) .... Sherman
Township(s) .... Sherman
Access .... Waits Corners Road
Principal Species .... Brown Trout (stocked)

Crosscut Creek, known also as Waits Corners Creek, averages 8 feet in width. It has a silt and sand bottom and is fishable only during the early months of trout season. Surrounded by woodlands and farmlands, there is a lot of bank cover along this stream.

In the fall, Crosscut Creek is stocked with 400 brown trout fingerlings, from its mouth near Waits Corners Road upstream 1.5 miles to Freeman Road.

NOTES: ____________________

ELKINS BROOK

Map Coordinates .... 42° 07′ 51″ 79° 05′ 47″
USGS Map(s) .... Kennedy, Ivory
Township(s) .... Randolph (Cattaraugus County), Poland (Chautauqua County)
Access .... Miller Valley Road
Principal Species .... Brown Trout (wild)

Elkins Brook averages 5 feet in width, has a gravel bottom, and very clear, high-quality water. Surrounded by pasturelands, this stream has intermittent bank cover.

Elkins Brook is most productive during the first few months of trout season. The best fishing is found downstream of County Road #8. When the water levels are high, some good-size fish usually make their way up this stream from the Conewango, and the deep pools that are formed at times of high water are often quite productive. Elkins Brook is not stocked, but there are good numbers of wild brown trout throughout the stream, especially in the spring. Keep in mind that this stream is heavily posted, and permission to fish here should be obtained from the landowner.

NOTES: ____________________

FARRINGTON HOLLOW BROOK

Map Coordinates .... 42° 22′ 10″   78° 09′ 30″
USGS Map(s) .... Hamlet
Township(s) .... Villanova and Cherry Creek
Access .... Hamlet Road
Principal Species .... Brown Trout (stocked)

This stream is a small tributary of the west branch of Conewango Creek. It averages 10 feet in width and has a sand and gravel bottom. It is surrounded by open fields, woodlands, and swamps, and there is a lot of bank cover along the stream.

Farrington Hollow Brook is fishable only during the first few months of trout season. Most of the bridge pools are fairly productive.

In the spring, 400 brown trout yearlings are stocked in the lowermost 1.2-mile portion of the stream.

NOTES: ______________________________

This is one of the ponds found on the Canadaway Creek Wildlife Management Area. These ponds hold modest numbers of trout and bass and provide fishing ina truly remote setting.

FLAG BROOK

Map Coordinates .... 42° 18′ 15″   79° 21′ 41″
USGS Map(s) .... Cassadaga, Hartfield
Township(s) .... Stockton
Access .... Dean Road
Principal Species .... Brown Trout (stocked)

Flag Brook is a small tributary of Bear Lake Outlet. It averages 15 feet in width and has a gravel bottom. Surrounded by open fields and woodlands, there is intermittent bank cover on this stream. Flag Brook is fishable only during the early months of trout season.

In the fall, a 1.8-mile section of Flag Brook is stocked with 900 brown trout fingerlings, from one-half mile above the confluence with Bear Lake Outlet to the mouth of the stream's second major tributary.

NOTES: ______________________________

FLUVANNA BROOK

Map Coordinates .... 42° 06′ 55″   79° 16′ 55″
USGS Map(s) .... Lakewood
Township(s) .... Ellicott
Access .... Paralleled by Strunk Road
Principal Species .... Brook Trout (stocked)

This stream averages about 8 feet in width, has a silt and sand bottom, and is surrounded by residential areas and patches of woodlands. It is fishable only during the early months of trout season.

In the fall, the 1-mile section of Fluvanna Brook immediately above the stream's mouth is stocked with 300 brook trout fingerlings.

NOTES: ______________________________

GOOSE CREEK

Map Coordinates .... 42° 06′ 39″   79° 22′ 14″
USGS Map(s) .... Lakewood, Panama
Township(s) .... Busti and North Harmony
Access .... Wall Road
Principal Species .... Brown Trout (stocked and wild)

Goose Creek is a large, high-quality trout stream averaging 15 to 20 feet in width. It has a bottom of gravel and sand, going to silt in its lower portions. Emptying into Chautauqua Lake at Ashville Bay, it is surrounded primarily by woodlands and wooded marshlands. There is a lot of bank cover on this stream.

When judged strictly on its fish-holding potential, Goose Creek would be considered fishable all season. Due to heavy fishing pressure, however, its more accessible sections are pretty much fished out by early summer. The more remote, off-road sections of the stream do hold fish all season, though, and there are numerous wild brown trout in this stream's headwaters.

In the April and May, a 7.7-mile section of this stream is stocked with 3,600 brown trout yearlings, from the village of Ashville upstream to Wall Road. In the fall, Tributary 6 of Goose Creek, which is accessible from Demmings Road, is stocked with 600 Brook trout fingerlings in the 1-mile section immediately above the stream mouth. This small stream might sustain some fishing pressure, but most of the fish stocked here will eventually drop down into Goose Creek.

There are extensive public fishing rights on Goose Creek above the village of Blockville.

NOTES: ______________________________

LITTLE BROKENSTRAW CREEK

Map Coordinates .... 41° 49′ 59″   79° 23′ 03″
USGS Map(s) .... Lottville, Panama, North Clymer
Township(s) .... Harmony
Access .... Wilcox Road
Principal Species .... Brown Trout (stocked)

Little Brokenstraw Creek is a marginal-quality trout stream. It averages 15 to 20 feet in width, has a gravel bottom, and is fishable only during the early months of trout season. Surrounded by woodlands and wooded marshlands, it has intermittent bank cover.

In the spring, Little Brokenstraw Creek is stocked with 1,600 brown trout yearlings, from the village of Niobe upstream 4 miles to the first road crossing above Wilcox Road.

NOTES: ______________________________

LITTLE BROWNELL BROOK

Map Coordinates .... 42° 02′ 15″ 79° 35′ 15″
USGS Map(s) .... North Clymer
Township(s) .... Clymer
Access .... Paralleled by Route 474
Principal Species .... Brown Trout (wild), Brook Trout (stocked)

Little Brownell Brook averages about 10 feet in width, has a gravel bottom, and is surrounded by woodlands and wooded marshlands, which provide a lot of bank cover along this stream. Little Brownell Brook is fishable all trout season.

In the fall, the lowermost 1.4-mile section of this stream is stocked with 500 brook trout fingerlings. There are also limited numbers of wild brown trout throughout Little Brownell Brook.

NOTES: ______________________________

LITTLE CRANBERRY BROOK

Map Coordinates .... 42° 04′ 00″ 79° 23′ 22″
USGS Map(s) .... Panama
Township(s) .... Harmony
Access .... Waltonian Drive
Principal Species .... Brown Trout (wild), Brook Trout (stocked)

This small tributary of Goose Creek averages 10 feet in width and has a gravel and rubble bottom. Little Cranberry Brook flows through woodlands and has a good amount of bank cover.

This stream is usually only fishable during the first half of trout season. However, some wild brown trout might be found in the areas below Waltonian Road all season long.

In the fall, the lowermost 1.6-mile section of this stream is stocked with 500 brook trout fingerlings. Tributary 4, which joins Little Cranberry Brook one-quarter mile above Waltonian Drive, is stocked with 200 brook trout fingerlings along its entirety. This stream could handle some fishing pressure, but most of the fish stocked here will eventually drop down into Little Cranberry Brook.

NOTES: ______________________________

MILL CREEK

Map Coordinates .... 42° 13′ 45″ 79° 17′ 45″
USGS Map(s) .... Ellery Center, Cassadaga, Hamlet
Township(s) .... Gerry and Charlotte
Access .... Route 60
Principal Species .... Brown Trout (stocked)

Mill Creek is a large, marginal-quality trout stream averaging 20 feet in width. It has a bottom of gravel and sand, intermittent bank cover, and is fishable only during the first few months of trout season. Surrounded by woodlands and pasturelands, Mill Creek is a wild stream with very unstable banks.

In the spring, this stream is stocked with 1,600 brown trout yearlings, from its mouth upstream 3.9 miles to the town of Sinclarville.

NOTES: ______________________________

MOON BROOK

Map Coordinates .... 42° 06′ 57″ 79° 11′ 57″
USGS Map(s) .... Jamestown, Gerry, Ellery Center
Township(s) .... Ellicott
Access .... Curtis Road
Principal Species .... Brook Trout (stocked)

Moon Brook is a small stream that empties into the Chadakoin River in Falconer. Rock- and gravel-bottomed, it flows through a mix of meadows and woodlands in its upper sections, grading down to primarily residential surroundings in its lower end. Moon Brook does have a fair amount of carry-over, and is best fished in the fall.

In the fall, the DEC stocks Moon Brook with 300 brook trout fingerlings in the 1-mile section that begins 1 mile above the stream mouth.

NOTES: ______________________________

PRENDERGAST CREEK

Map Coordinates .... 42° 11′ 07″ 79° 26′ 36″
USGS Map(s) .... Chautauqua, Sherman
Township(s) .... Chautauqua, North Harmony
Access .... Route 394
Principal Species .... Brown Trout (stocked and wild)

Prendergast Creek is a high-quality trout stream averaging 15 to 20 feet in width. It has a bottom of sand and gravel and flows through woodlands and open fields. This stream has a lot of bank cover and is fishable all season.

There is a good population of wild brown trout throughout Prendergast Creek, and in the spring a 1.7-mile section of the stream just above the bridge at Route 394 is stocked with 1,200 brown trout yearlings

NOTES: ______________________________

SILVER CREEK

Map Coordinates .... 42° 32′ 46″ 79° 10′ 10″
USGS Map(s) .... Silver Creek
Township(s) .... Hanover
Access .... Bridge crossing at Route 5
Principal Species .... Rainbow Trout (stocked), Brown Trout (stocked), Coho Salmon, Chinook Salmon

Silver Creek and its sister stream, Walnut Creek, come together in the town of Silver Creek, and shortly thereafter they empty into Lake Erie. These are spawning streams for salmonids in the spring

Monofilament lines and leaders eventually develop small nicks and cracks that can result in line breakage. Before needlessly loosing a fish, check for line damage by rubbing it with a cotton ball. Cotton fibers will catch in damaged areas, indicating whether or not the line should be replaced. Lines that are tightly coiled after casting should also be replaced.

and fall. In the spring, steelhead and brown trout can be caught here, primarily between the Route 5 bridge and the lake. Shore fishing in and around the stream mouth in springtime produces some nice catches of coho and chinook. In the fall, this stream has tremendous fishing for brown trout, and steelhead, coho, and chinook are often caught here as well. Shore fishing around the mouth of Silver Creek in the fall is especially productive for brown trout.

NOTES: ______________________________

____

____

STILLWATER CREEK

Map Coordinates .... 42° 03′ 02″ 79° 10′ 42″
USGS Map(s) .... Jamestown, Lakewood, Sugar Grove
Township(s) .... Busti
Access .... Simmons Road
Principal Species .... Brown Trout (stocked)

Stillwater Creek is a large, marginal-quality trout stream. Averaging about 20 feet in width, it has a gravel and silt bottom. It is surrounded by marshlands, farmlands, and woodlands. It is fishable only during the early months of trout season.

In the spring, the 2.2-mile section of Stillwater Creek between Donelson Road and the state road is stocked with 700 brown trout yearlings.

NOTES: ______________________________

____

____

TOWN STREAM

Map Coordinates .... 42° 01′ 00″ 79° 37′ 40″
USGS Map(s) .... Clymer
Township(s) .... Clymer
Access .... Route 74
Principal Species .... Brook Trout (stocked and wild)

Town Stream averages 8 to 10 feet in width, has a gravel and sand bottom, and is surrounded mostly by open fields. There is good bank cover along this stream and it is usually fishable all trout season. There could be some wild brook trout in the section just above Clymer Pond.

In the fall, the lower 1-mile section of Town Stream is stocked with 400 brook trout fingerlings.

NOTES: ______________________________

____

____

TELLICO

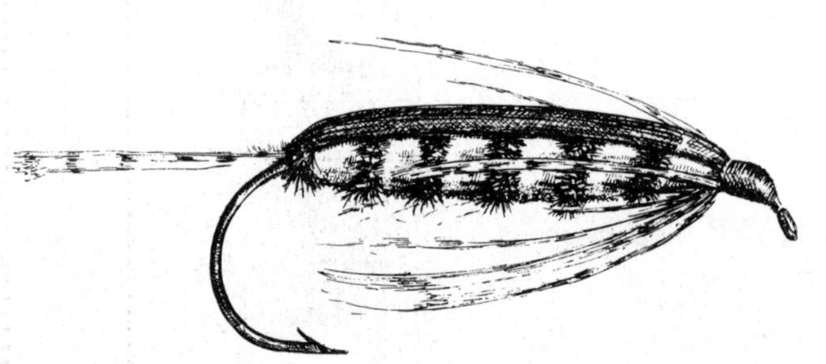

Tellico's colors, which are due to the use of peacock herl and yellow floss, make it an extremely attractive pattern. It imitates the stonefly nymphs present in many ponds and streams.

TWENTY FOUR CREEK

Map Coordinates .... 42° 05′ 12″ 79° 27′ 00″
USGS Map(s) .... Panama
Township(s) .... Harmony, North Harmony
Access .... Route 74
Principal Species .... Brown Trout (stocked)

This tributary of Goose Creek averages 8 to 10 feet in width, has a gravel bottom, and is surrounded by woodlands. This stream has a lot of bank cover. It is fishable only during the early months of trout season.

In the fall, Twenty Four Creek is stocked with 200 brown trout fingerlings at the Route 74 bridge crossing.

NOTES: ______________________________

____

____

TWENTY MILE CREEK

Map Coordinates .... 42° 15′ 47″ 79° 47′ 05″
USGS Map(s) .... Northeast, South Ripley
Township(s) .... Mina, Ripley
Access .... Post Road
Principal Species .... Rainbow Trout (stocked and wild), Brown Trout (stocked), Coho Salmon

Twenty Mile Creek is a shallow stream averaging 15 to 20 feet in width. It has a bottom of bedrock and shale. A tributary of Lake Erie, this stream gets a good run of steelhead in the spring, as well as a few brown trout. In the fall, starting in late September, Twenty Mile Creek gets substantial runs of steelhead and coho salmon. The steelhead usually can be caught here until the beginning of the following spring.

Normally, Great Lakes fishing regulations would apply to the angling for these fish. However, there is no really impassible barrier on this stream (coho have been caught almost throughout Twenty Mile Creek), so the interpretation of the rules is uncertain.

Aside from the lake-run fish, this stream has a good population of wild rainbow trout, primarily in the 4-mile section immediately above the state line. The state stocks a 9-mile section of Twenty Mile Creek, from the state line upstream to Raters Corners, with 1,100 rainbow trout yearlings every spring.

NOTES: ______________________________

____

____

WATTS FLATS WILDLIFE MANAGEMENT AREA

Map Coordinates .... 42° 02′ 00″ 79° 29′ 30″
USGS Map(s) .... Panama
Township(s) .... Harmony
Access .... Green Flat Road, Dale Swamp Road
Principal Species .... Northern Pike, Bullhead, Panfish

This is an 1,100-acre preserve consisting of swamps, open-water wetlands, and woodlands. Its purpose is to provide a wetland environment for a large number of species, including beaver, mink, raccoon, deer, and various water fowl such as mallards, wood ducks and herons.

Drained principally by the east branch of Little Brokenstraw Creek, the many streams and ponds in this area have populations of northern pike, bullhead, and panfish. Bullfrogs are also quite common and can be taken by any individual who holds a fishing license or small game license. There are public parking areas on Dale Swamp Road and Green Flat road.

NOTES: ____________________

____

____

Wetlands, such as the Watts Flats Wildlife Management Area pictured at right, are among the most productive and diverse environments in nature. They provide habitats for hundreds of species of aquatic, amphibious, and terrestrial species.

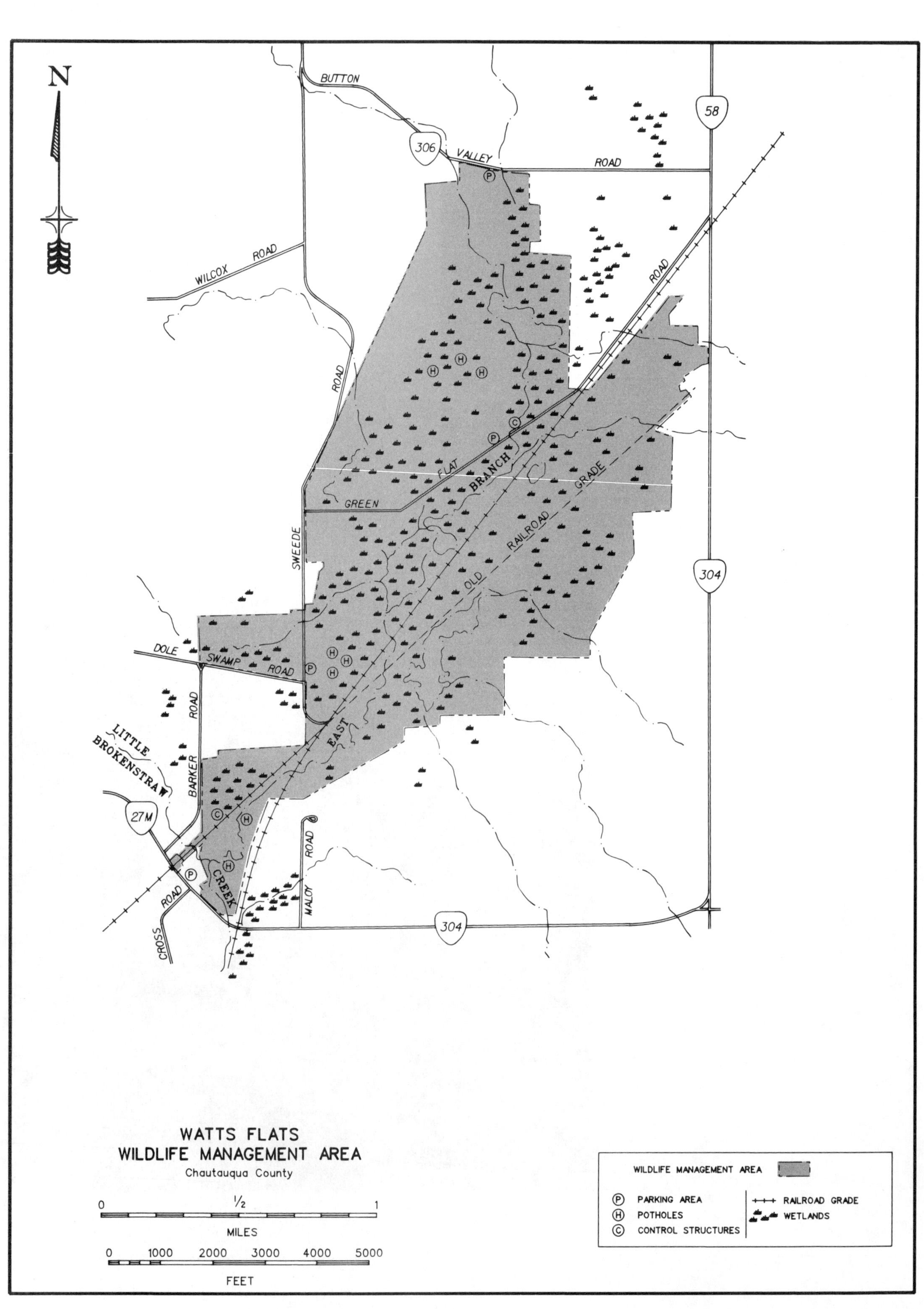
N
BUTTON
306
VALLEY
ROAD
58
WILCOX ROAD
ROAD
ROAD
FLAT
BRANCH
GREEN
SWEEDE
GRADE
RAILROAD
OLD
304
DOLE
SWAMP
ROAD
ROAD
BARKER
LITTLE
BROKENSTRAW
EAST
27M
CREEK
ROAD
CROSS
MALOY
ROAD
304
WATTS FLATS
WILDLIFE MANAGEMENT AREA
Chautauqua County
0
½
1
MILES
0
1000
2000
3000
4000
5000
FEET
WILDLIFE MANAGEMENT AREA
PARKING AREA
POTHOLES
CONTROL STRUCTURES
RAILROAD GRADE
WETLANDS

CHAUTAUQUA COUNTY LAKES AND PONDS

BEAR LAKE

Location

Map Coordinates	42° 20′ 17″ 79° 22′ 36″
USGS Map(s)	Hartfield
Township(s)	Pomfret, Stockton
Access	Bear Lake Road

Physical Characteristics

Area	141 acres
Shoreline	2.50 miles
Elevation	1,315 feet
Maximum Depth	35 feet
Mean Depth	15 feet
Bottom Type	Gravel, muck

Chemical Characteristics

Water	Clear to slightly turbid
pH	Alkaline
Oxygen	Good throughout the lake all year

Plant Life

Extensive weed beds are found along the entire shore of the lake.

Species Information

Muskellunge	Common; growth rate good
Northern Pike	Common; growth rate good
Largemouth Bass	Common; growth rate good
Smallmouth Bass	Common; growth rate good
Bullhead	Common; growth rate good

Also present are numerous panfish, including yellow perch, crappie, and pumpkinseeds.

Boat Launch Sites

1. The Clever Store on Bear lake Road. Gravel launch ramps - fee.
2. New York State (DEC) access site on Bear Lake Road. Cartop and canoe launching and parking - no charge.

General Information

Nestled in the hills of northern Chautauqua County, this clear, spring-fed lake is highly productive for many warm-water species of fish. Extensive weed beds and lily pads provide excellent habitat for largemouth and smallmouth bass, northern pike, and muskie. The fishing on Bear Lake peaks in the spring and again in early fall. Because it is protected by wooded hills, Bear Lake is calm even on windy days. Conveniently located 8 miles from Dunkirk and Mayville, it provides an excellent alternative to Lakes Erie and Chautauqua when they're too rough to fish.

Everything that you would need to fish here is available at the Clever Store, including bait, tackle, boats, gas, launch ramps, and camp sites. Be sure to check in at the store for good, up-to-date information on fishing activity on Bear Lake, or to register for one of the fishing contests that are constantly being held here.

Bear Lake is stocked annually with 800 muskie fingerlings.

NOTES: ______________________________

____

____

CASSADAGA LAKE

Location

Map Coordinates	42° 20′ 33″ 79° 19′ 18″
USGS Map(s)	Cassadaga
Township(s)	Pomfret, Stockton
Access	Route 60

Physical Characteristics

Area	211 acres
Shoreline	5.10 miles
Elevation	1304 feet
Maximum Depth	60 feet
Mean Depth	Not available
Bottom Type	Muck

Chemical Characteristics

Water	Slightly turbid
pH	Alkaline
Oxygen	Generally good; deficient below 20 feet in summer

Plant Life

Weed beds are extensive throughout this lake. Severe algal blooms occur in the summer.

Species Information

Muskellunge	Common; growth rate very good
Northern Pike	Uncommon; growth rate good
Largemouth Bass	Very common; growth rate good
Smallmouth Bass	Common; growth rate good
Yellow Perch	Abundant; growth rate fair
Crappie	Common; growth rate fair
Bullhead	Common; growth rate good
Pumpkinseeds	Abundant; growth rate fair

Boat Launch Sites

1. New York State - DEC - maintained launch site off Route 60 on middle lake in the hamlet of Lily Dale - no charge.

General Information

Cassadaga Lake is actually an interconnected set of three separate lakes. A popular summer resort area, the lake is heavily utilized by fishermen, boaters, and skiers, but this appears to have little effect on fish populations. What might affect the angling here is the overabundance of vegetation, which chokes sections of this lake in the summer.

It's never too early to teach your children the pleasures of fishing. Katie Gravelle, age 2, caught this pumpkinseed by herself while vacationing on Chautauqua Lake.

To the best of my knowledge, no depth map exists for Cassadaga Lake. This is probably due to the difficulty in charting the highly undulating bottom of the lake. The many hills and valleys provide good habitat for populations of muskie, largemouth and smallmouth bass, and panfish. A relatively new inhabitant of this lake is the northern pike, which appears to be establishing itself in the lower lake. These species can all be taken in the spring, summer, and fall, although heavy weed growth and competition from boaters and water skiers for use of the lake can hinder fishing in the summer. There is at present little ice fishing activity here in the winter.

NOTES: ____

____

____

CHAUTAUQUA LAKE

Location

Map Coordinates	42° 11′ 01″ 79° 25′ 32″
USGS Map(s)	Chautauqua, Lakewood, Panama, Ellery Center
Township(s)	Chautauqua, Ellery, North Harmony, Ellicott, Busti
Access	Paralleled by Route 17 and Route 394; - see launch sites below

Physical Characteristics

	Upper Basin	Lower Basin
Area	7,000 acres	6,100 acres
Shoreline	22.20 miles	20.25 miles
Elevation	1,308 feet	1,308 feet
Maximum Depth	77 feet	19 feet
Mean Depth	30 feet	15 feet
Bottom Type	Gravel, rubble	Mud, sand

Chemical Characteristics

	Upper Basin	Lower Basin
Water	Clear	Usually turbid
pH	Slightly alkaline	Slightly alkaline
Oxygen	Generally very good, but can be slightly depleted below 20 feet in the summer	Good all year

Plant Life

In the upper basin, weed beds are found in almost all shallow bays to a depth of 12 feet and throughout the extreme northern portion of the Lake. They are extensive throughout the lower basin.

Boat Launch Sites

1. Prendergast Point on Route 394 in the village of Chautauqua. Hard-surface ramp, parking for 40 cars and trailers - no charge.
2. Chautauqua Lake Boat Yard on Route 394 in Mayville. Single hard-surface ramp - free
3. Ashville Bay Marina on Route 394 in Ashville Bay. Full service marina, single hard-surface ramp - fee.
4. Maple Bay Marina on Route 494 in Ashville Bay. Full service marina, single hard-surface ramp - fee.
5. Bemus Point on Route 430 in the hamlet of Bemus Point. Single hard-surface ramp, parking for 30 cars and trailers - no charge.
6. Long Point State Park off Route 430, between Bemus Point and Maple Springs. Full service marina, hard-surface ramp - no charge (possible park user fee).

Additional launch facilities are located on the Chadakoin River in Celeron and other boating facilities are available at other marinas around the lake.

Species Information

Muskellunge .... **Very common; growth rate good to excellent**

Chautauqua Lake is renowned for the quality of its muskellunge (or muskie as they are commonly called) fishing. It is one of the few lakes in New York State (or anywhere for that matter) where you can honestly say that they are almost abundant. That they are so plentiful is do in part to the presence of the world's largest muskie hatchery at Prendergast Point. This hatchery supplies the lake with an incredible 40,000 muskie fry each year.

The muskies do well in this lake largely because of the excellent forage base available to them. Every year fish in excess of 50 inches are caught here. A fish of this size will commonly weigh over 35 pounds! The largest recorded muskie taken from Chautauqua Lake weighed 44 pounds. It was caught on live bait off Lighthouse Point.

Although muskie season doesn't officially open here until the third Saturday in June, many of these fish are caught and released in the spring. The fishing continues to be good after opening day and remains so until around the end of July, at which time it slacks off considerably. It picks up again in the fall. One of the best kept secrets about this lake is the high-quality muskie fishing to be found here after most people have called it quits on boat fishing for the year. You can have the lake and some of the finest muskie fishing to be found anywhere all to yourself in the month of October if your willing to brave a little chilly weather.

To protect the quality of the muskie fishing in this lake, the DEC has imposed the following special regulations: Unlike most of New York State, Chautauqua's muskie season closes on October 31, and it is no longer augmented by a partial open season in the winter; a special license, which can be obtained from license agents in Chautauqua County or the DEC offices in Olean and Buffalo, is required; seals are furnished with the special license and must be affixed to the fish immediately on taking; creel limits are one fish per day and no more than five per season; the minimum length is 40 inches; landing nets are permitted, but gaff hooks and clubs are prohibited; and the special license must be filled in and returned to the DEC within five days after the close of the season. Be sure to check your regulations guide for current regulations.

The source for most of my information on Chautauqua Lake muskie fishing was Spike Kelderhouse, a veteran Chautauqua Lake guide and angler. Much of what follows is based on Spike's 50 years of fishing and guiding on the lake.

A popular method for catching muskies on this lake is trolling. Spike trolls what he refers to as "courses." These are trolling lanes that are defined by fixed objects along the shore, such as points, bays, or major landmarks. These courses seldom cross the lake from side to side. Instead, they run nearly parallel to shore at specific depths.

There are slight differences in the way Spike trolls courses, depending on the basin he is in. Trolling depth is one such difference. Nettings by the DEC have shown that in the upper basin, few muskies are found in the 5- to 10-foot depth range. Therefore, trolling depths in the upper basin must be at least deeper than 10 feet. In the lower basin, were the average depth is only 15 feet, the fish will be found in shallower water, usually between 5 and 10 feet.

Another difference concerns weeds. Spike claims that for many years it wasn't important to closely follow the weedlines in the upper basin. Trolling out in open water was far more productive than being tight up against the weeds. However, in recent years he has found it necessary to get in closer (but not tight) to the weedlines. I have heard similar stories from other anglers on the lake. The reason(s) for this is unknown. The lower basin is so shallow that weeds can be found almost anywhere. Consequently, weedlines are not a major consideration in the lower half of the lake.

In both basins the muskies will tend to orient off rocky ledges, weedlines, creek mouths, and on shoals.

With regard to tackle, Spike recommends a medium-action boat rod, 5 to 10 feet in length for trolling. Run long rods off the side of the boat, and the shorter rods right off the back. You can often catch muskies in or near the prop wash.

At one time he tried using light-action spinning rods for muskies, but had to give the idea up. While trolling in this lake you are almost always going to pick up weeds on your lures. Because spinning reels use monofilament line, the line and lures can not be hauled in hand over hand very easily. Usually, you have to stop the boat and reel the line in. This is time consuming and disruptive. With the heavier braided lines used on level-wind reels you can bring the lines in hand over hand without getting tangled, clean off the lures, and quickly resume fishing.

Spike now recommends using a Penn 309 reel, or something comparable. This is a large-capacity, level-wind reel. A Penn 209 is a lighter reel, but could also be used.

Popular trolling lures for muskies include big (6-inch or larger), deep-diving Pikie Minnows, Brooks Reefers, original Creek Chubs, Swim Wiz, Cisco Kids, and Flatfish. Good colors include combinations of yellow, orange, black, and chartreuse.

Because of the speeds at which you need to troll in order to trigger a strike, most experienced muskie fishermen use weighted dacron line or lead core lines to keep the bait down. Thirty-pound dacron line should be sufficient for muskie fishing. When using lead core line, 40-pound line is good enough. Another advantage to dacron and lead core lines is that you can easily stack lines using dacron and lead core combinations. The dacron can be fished long and shallow, while the lead core is fished close and deep, even right in the prop wash.

Spike doesn't like monofilament lines for several reasons. It is hard to manage and keep clean when trolling for muskies. It is also difficult to know just how much line is out, unless you are using one of the new line counter reels. And it can't be marked with a pen or magic marker. The chemicals in the ink can cause the line to deteriorate. Dacron line, however, can be marked with a pen or magic marker at measured intervals. Lead core line comes marked; the line changes color at 10-yard intervals.

An important thing to remember when trolling is that outriggers and downriggers don't work well for muskies. Often, when you hook a muskie he isn't actually hooked - he's just mouthing the bait or lure. Therefore, you must be able to keep the line taut, or the fish can easily spit out the bait or lure without being hooked. If the line is taut his chances of being hooked when he tries to spit out the bait are good. The problem with downriggers and outriggers is the fact that they allow too much play in the line between the time when the fish hits the lure and the angler sets the hook.

In the summer, the courses that Spike trolls in the upper basin run from the south side of Tom's Point to the tower at Chautauqua Institute, from the south end of Bemus Bay up to the north side of Long Point, and from Midway Park up to Chedwell. Later in the season, the course that runs from Sunset Bay to the tip of Long Point, just skirting the underwater point in Warner Bay, is very productive.

In the lower basin, he recommends that you start trolling at the bridge and chart a course that just skirts Cheney Point. Continue on down to the point at Ashville Bay, go a little past Ashville and then cross the lake to the Grey Barns, which are located just north of Bellview. Go up along the shore and head toward Arnold's Bay. You can troll through the bay, or bypass it. (Arnold's Bay is best when fished in the fall). Head toward the bridges and go back through the course. This course could be extended down as far as Sherman's bay and is productive through August. Another good course runs right down the middle of the lower basin. This course is also productive until late August.

Casting is another method of taking muskies and it accounts for the largest percentage of muskies taken from Chautauqua Lake. If you're going to use jerkbaits, Spike recommends using Suicks or Bagleys. You get a good workout if you're using these baits properly, but fishing jerkbaits is arguably the most productive method for taking Chautauqua Lake muskies. If fishing with spinners is more to your liking, big bucktail spinners, such as the Mepps Muskie Killer and Giant Killer are very effective. Spike recommends using a stiff rod for casting, such as an Ugly Stick or other baitcasting rods. You need a rod with a strong base and a stiff tip. Your usual spincasting rod just doesn't have enough backbone in the top section (tip) to work the lure effectively. You could also use a medium- to light-weight trolling rod. However, you can use a spincasting rod or baitcasting rod when you are using crankbaits.

During periods of low light, crankbaits, jerkbaits, and spinnerbaits are typically worked over weed beds or along weedlines. During periods of bright sun, move to the outer edges of the weeds or out into open water off weed beds. Productive weed beds in the summer

Captain Warren Berry, one of the top muskie guides in the state, shows off a 30-pound Chautauqua Lake muskie. The fish was caught aboard Warren's boat, "The Frenchman."

are found at Prendergast Point, in Whitney Bay, off Woodlawn, just to the north of Tom's Point, in Bemus Bay, just downlake of the state launch on Long Point, on both sides of Long Point, off Chedwell, and in Dewittville Bay. Fishing off the end of long docks and around large, moored boats is also productive. The advantage that you have with fishing crankbaits and jerkbaits is that you can concentrate your efforts on a given area and cover it thoroughly. The disadvantage is that you are limited in the amount of area that you can cover.

Live-baiting is another method that can be used to take muskies. Spike uses two long rods (minimum 8 feet, but preferably 10 to 12 feet) when fishing with live bait. The rods have to be this long if you're using Spike's method, because when you're live-baiting you typically fish 6 to 10 feet down and you're using a fixed position bobber. If the rod is shorter than the distance between the bobber and the bait, you won't be able to reel the fish in all of the way, and your chances of losing the fish are that much greater. The bobber serves two purposes - it keeps the bait out of the weeds and it acts as a strike indicator. A good bait for this type of fishing is a 6- to 8-inch horndace. Suckers are also a good choice because they tend to stay as far down as they possibly can. With other baits you usually have to put some wrap-around weight on the line 12 to 14 inches above the bait to keep it down. Spike likes to use live-baiting while slowly rowing or drifting; don't row too fast or you'll drown the bait. As soon as you see the bobber go down, stop the boat and give the fish a lot of free line so that it can do what it wants with the bait. Often, live-baiting is done at night. This is done in part because of the extensive recreational use of the lake during the day. When live-baiting at night, the slow clicking of the reel is the indication that you might have a strike. After stopping the boat and giving the fish some slack line, look for the bobber with a flashlight, but try not to shine the light directly on the bobber - that could spook the fish. You can put florescent orange tape on the top of the bobber to make it stand out better. Check the bobber periodically to see if it moves when you stop rowing. If it doesn't, the bait might either be dead or covered with weeds. Muskies won't usually hit on a bait that appears to be dead. The style of bobber normally used in this type of fishing is a long stem balsa wood bobber, 6 to 10 inches long. The hook used is a large, barbed, short-shanked hook with a long wire leader. The bait is hooked through both lips, from the bottom up. English style hooks, which are sewn through the back of the bait, can also be used.

Unquestionably, the most productive time for taking muskies is in the fall. The fall is a good time for muskies for several reasons: The weeds are dying off, making casting, trolling, and bait fishing all more easy; the female muskies are feeding more heavily and opportunistically, and the winds are more favorable here in the fall, i.e., more from the west, bearing out the old fishing adage "when the wind is from the west the fish bite the best."

In the fall the muskie fishing picks up considerably from its mid-summer doldrums. Depending on who you talk to, either live bait fishing or trolling is the most productive method in the fall. In fact, both can be very effective.

As soon as the lake temperatures begin to fall, female muskies start to feed more heavily, and for this reason live-baiting becomes highly productive. Fish the bait on the edge of the weedline or over the weeds. When the temperatures start to fall the weeds begin to die back, and weed beds that were right to the surface in the summer will now have 2 to 4 feet of water over them, opening these areas to live bait fishing and trolling.

The northern end of the lake is very good in the fall. There are a lot of weed beds here. Fish with live bait along the weedlines in the late summer and fall. Dewittville Bay, Bemus Bay, and Long Point all produce well in the fall.

Trolling is still very productive at this time of year. The major course to follow in the northern basin is from the bell tower at Chautauqua Institute around the northern end of the lake to Point Chautauqua. In the lower basin, the course that runs from the ferry down along Arnold's Bay to Cheny Barn is recommended.

An old-fashioned, but highly effective, method for catching muskies in the fall is called skittering. It is done with two, and only two, people in a boat. One man stands in the back of the boat and fishes, while the other man rows the boat backwards. By doing this, the man fishing comes up on the fish first and there is less chance of the fish being spooked. Row slowly along the weedline. They used to skitter in this lake using 14- to 17-foot bamboo rods known as Calcutta rods. These rods are still popular in the South, where they are used for bass and panfish. If you are going to use a Calcutta rod, be sure that it has a pretty substantial tip, like a trolling rod, not like the limber rods used for panfish. A reel is used with enough line to allow the fish to make a good run, but you don't need a lot of line because in skittering you don't have to cast. You use the same type and size of chubs as in live-baiting. The difference is that you must let the bait die before you use it. Spike says that it is better to let the bait die naturally, rather than to kill it yourself. When it is dead hook the bait through the corner of the mouth and eye on the same side of the head. To present the bait, let out about the same amount of line as the length of the rod. Then swing the bait out forward from the stern of the boat (i.e., in the direction that you are rowing). Don't reel the bait back in. Instead, work it back and forth across the stern in a sweeping motion. If you get a strike, don't set the hook. Give the fish slack and let it run with the bait. Only set the hook when you think that the fish has had enough time to turn the bait and set the hook.

Fishing for muskies is no longer allowed on Chautauqua Lake in the winter. However, many fish are caught by anglers ice fishing for walleye and perch. All of these muskies must be released. When releasing the fish, try to do so without pulling the fish's head out of the hole. In the winter, the gills and eyes of the fish can be severely damaged by exposure to the frigid, dry air. This can occur in less than a minute.

Walleye .... Abundant; growth rate good

Chautauqua Lake is currently one of the top walleye-producing lakes in New York State. Historically, however, walleye were an insignificant species in this lake. The first recorded attempts to stock walleye here took place between 1903 and 1908, when over 5 million fry were introduced into the lake. These efforts were unsuccessful. There are several confirmed reports of walleye being caught in this lake between 1937 and the late 1950s. The origin of these fish is uncertain; they could be the result of sporadic reproduction of the earlier fry stockings or the unauthorized released of walleye into the lake.

Walleye did not become a factor in this lake until 1962. In that year the first successful year-class was recorded. The growth of the walleye population from that period onward was rapid. By the late 1970s, walleyes rivaled muskies in abundance, a position they still hold today.

Chautauqua Lake walleye are well fed and occasionally attain a weight of 10 pounds or more, but 1 to 2 pounds is more the norm. Really large fish are rather uncommon.

The walleye in this lake, as in many lakes, tend to school up according to size. Large fish are often solitary. Size is in part a function of age and nearly all of the fish from a given year- class will have been removed from the population by disease, predation, or angling before they all reach a large size. In addition, it has been shown that there are several behavioral categories of walleye in this lake. The majority of fish belong to one of several groups whose home territory consists of a particular area of the lake and who tend to orient along or just inside weedlines. However, there is a smaller group of walleye who are essentially nomadic. Unlike the majority of Chautauqua Lake walleye, these nomadic fish are less structure-oriented, solitary, and, when found in water over 30 feet deep, are usually suspended. The fish in this group also tend to be significantly larger than the more structure-oriented fish.

When the season first opens, walleye are most often found close to shore in water 3 to 10 feet deep. A number of techniques can be used to take these fish. Trolling is probably the most popular method. Troll very slowly in shallow water, starting just before sundown. The fishing should be good until just before sunup. A good way to troll for walleyes is with a small engine (6 hp) or electric trolling motor and a 14- to 16-foot boat. With only two or three people on board you can fish comfortably and quietly. Using this type of setup you can run lines as short as 30 to 40 feet. With larger boats and motors, you have to run longer lines, often up to 100 feet, to avoid spooking the fish. Popular lures include Rebels, Rapalas, and other similar stickbaits. Use a large split-shot about 3 feet above the lure and troll in 3 to 10 feet of water just off dock edges, buoy lines, and along old weedlines. Trolling seems to produce the best results, both in terms of numbers of fish caught and in the size of the fish caught. This method turns up a few huge lunkers every year. One important thing to keep in mind is that, usually, people don't use planer boards when trolling here at night. There is too much of a likelihood of catching a buoy or other angler.

Casting from shore with jigs and Rapala-type baits can also be very productive early in the season. Fish can be taken all night long, but just before sunup is often the best time to cast for walleye from shore.

Whether you are fishing from a boat or from shore, a good method for finding walleye in the shallows is to fish with a lantern. Sweep the lantern over the water. Because of the highly reflective eyes of the walleye, you will often be able to see their eyes glow in the water. Quickly note where you've spotted their eyes and remove the lantern so as not to spook the fish. Carefully cast a little beyond the fish and work the lure to where it was spotted.

Because of the number of walleye currently in the lake, practically the entire shoreline can be good at night early on. This goes for both basins of the lake. But there are a few areas that traditionally produce more early season walleye than others.

In the upper basin, early season hotspots are found off Maple Springs, from Midway Park up to Dewittville, and on Prendergast Point. Dewittville Creek and Prendergast Creek both get good runs of spawning walleye in the spring, so there should be some good fishing off the mouths of those streams when the season opens. In the lower Basin, productive areas include much of the shoreline from Cheny Point down to Sherman's Bay, from Lakecrest down to Greenhurst, the Lakewood Bar, the Grass Islands, and the area known as "The Crib". The Bar, Crib, and Islands are all marked with buoys.

Good early season night fishing generally lasts three to four weeks. After this many anglers switch from night fishing to daytime fishing. But some walleyes continue to be taken in near- shore areas at night.

In the summer, the majority of walleyes in this lake orient to weedlines. As soon as good weedlines have been established, troll along emerging lines or still fish close to the weeds.

For still fishing, Spike Kelderhouse recommends using a light spinning outfit, a size 4 hook baited with a night crawler, and a splitshot 24 to 36 inches above the hook. Anchor just off a weedline and cast over the weeds. Slowly retrieve the bait until it drops down the edge of the weeds. Then, very slowly retrieve it toward the boat. If you can't find any fish on what are usually productive weedlines, try exploring just inside the edges of the weeds. Often the fish will be forced to move into the weeds for cover or to forage.

Another proven method is to backtroll while fishing with a Lindy Rig and worm combination or a floating jig head and worm. Fish these tight along the weedlines. If the wind is just right, you can also pick up fish by drifting along weedlines with these rigs. Leeches are also a good walleye bait, but they are more expensive and difficult to put on a worm harness because they are not that long. They can be trolled or cast. They have the added advantage of also being excellent bait for smallmouth bass. Trolling and drifting with worms or leeches is productive until the temperature of the lake starts to drop.

Generally speaking, you don't have to fish very deep for the walleye in Chautauqua Lake in the summer. Most fish are going to be taken in less than 15 feet of water in the summer. Contrary to popular belief, the walleye in Chautauqua Lake do not migrate into deeper water during the day to avoid bright sunlight. Studies have shown that, because of the poor light penetration in this lake, the fish are not forced to move deeper during sunny periods.

Nearly the entire perimeter of Chautauqua Lake will hold some walleyes at this time of year, at least as long as their population remains up and there is no major die-off as there was in the lower basin in the late 1970s. But there are some areas that are more consistent producers than others.

In the upper basin, try the areas around the Bell Tower, Prendergast Point, Dewittville Bay, and Maple Springs. They used to catch a fair number of walleye in the deep holes of the lake in the summer. They used heavy drop sinkers, a 3-foot leader, and a worm harness. Spike feels that this is no longer productive, and that the walleye have moved into shallower waters in the summer. This could be in response to a change in the baitfish population, such as a decline in the number of young of the year yellow perch. These are a favorite walleye food and are benthic in the early part of their life cycle. A decline in the abundance of food in the deeper parts of the lake would force the walleye into shallower water or at least to suspend higher up in the water column.

In the lower basin, good walleye fishing can be found around Cheney Point, under the bridge, at Bemus Point, off Bemus Creek, around the point that lies just below the Stow Ferry on the west side of the lake, and around the Crib, the Grass Islands, and Lakewood Bar.

Throughout the summer, some walleye will move into the shallows at night to feed. Don't hesitate to cast into any well-lit section of the lake shore. Bright lights attract insects and insects attract bait fish, which in turn attract walleye. Many a bass fisherman has been surprised by a walleye at the end of his line by casting into well-lit waters that aren't generally known for walleye.

There is a transition period between the summer and fall walleye fishing and it is marked by a considerable decline in the quality of the fishing. This is due to the turning over of the waters in the upper basin. In the late summer or early fall, Chautauqua Lake begins to cool off. As near-surface water temperatures fall, the colder water begins to sink and the thermocline begins to break up. The lake turns over and this radically alters the distribution of oxygen in the water, and brings very clear water to the surface. The light-shy walleye are forced into deeper water to find amenable conditions of light and oxygen. It is during this reorientation period that the quality of the fishing slacks off.

Once the walleye have settled into their early fall patterns, they will usually be found in 20 to 25 feet of water. This means that, in the fall, the overwhelming majority of the fish are going to be taken from the upper basin of the lake. As water temperatures continue to drop, the fish will move into increasingly deeper water. By mid-October they are usually found in 25 to 35 feet of water, and by December they will be in 35 to 45 feet of water. This is about as deep as they will go. Most walleyes in this lake are taken in water no deeper than 45 feet. They are seldom taken from the deepest holes, but they will often be taken on the edges of these holes.

Anglers here usually go back to fishing with artificials in the fall. Many stop trolling in favor of vertical jigging. Popular jigs include Sonars, Jigging Rapalas, and Swedish Pimples. These are very effective when fished outside deep weedlines and off points.

One reason that anglers jig rather than troll in the fall is that the depths at which walleyes are usually caught in the fall (35+ feet) are difficult to reach with conventional trolling techniques.

Productive areas in the upper basin in the fall center on deep, undulating flats. Look for 25 to 40 feet of water off Woodlawn, Whitney Bay, and Prendergast Point. Other productive fall areas include the middle section of the lake, from Long Point to Bemus Point.

In the winter, most anglers concentrate their efforts on fishing the upper basin, though an occasional walleye will still be caught in the lower basin. Using tip-ups baited with 3-inch minnows is probably the most popular technique for taking walleyes here in the winter. Jigging with Swedish Pimples, Jigging Rapalas, and Little Johns also accounts for a lot of walleye. Don't forget that to be worked properly a Jigging Rapala needs to be jigged with long, hard strokes, whereas the Swedish Pimple and Little Johns are worked with a shorter stroke. These jigs can be tipped with minnows for added attraction.

The area between Long Point and Dewittville Bay is the hotspot in the winter. Especially productive are the drop-offs between the Vikings (just a little north of Midway Park) and Dewittville Bay. The bar out from Warner Bay is also good in the winter. Good fishing can be found anywhere from 20 to 40 feet down in these areas.

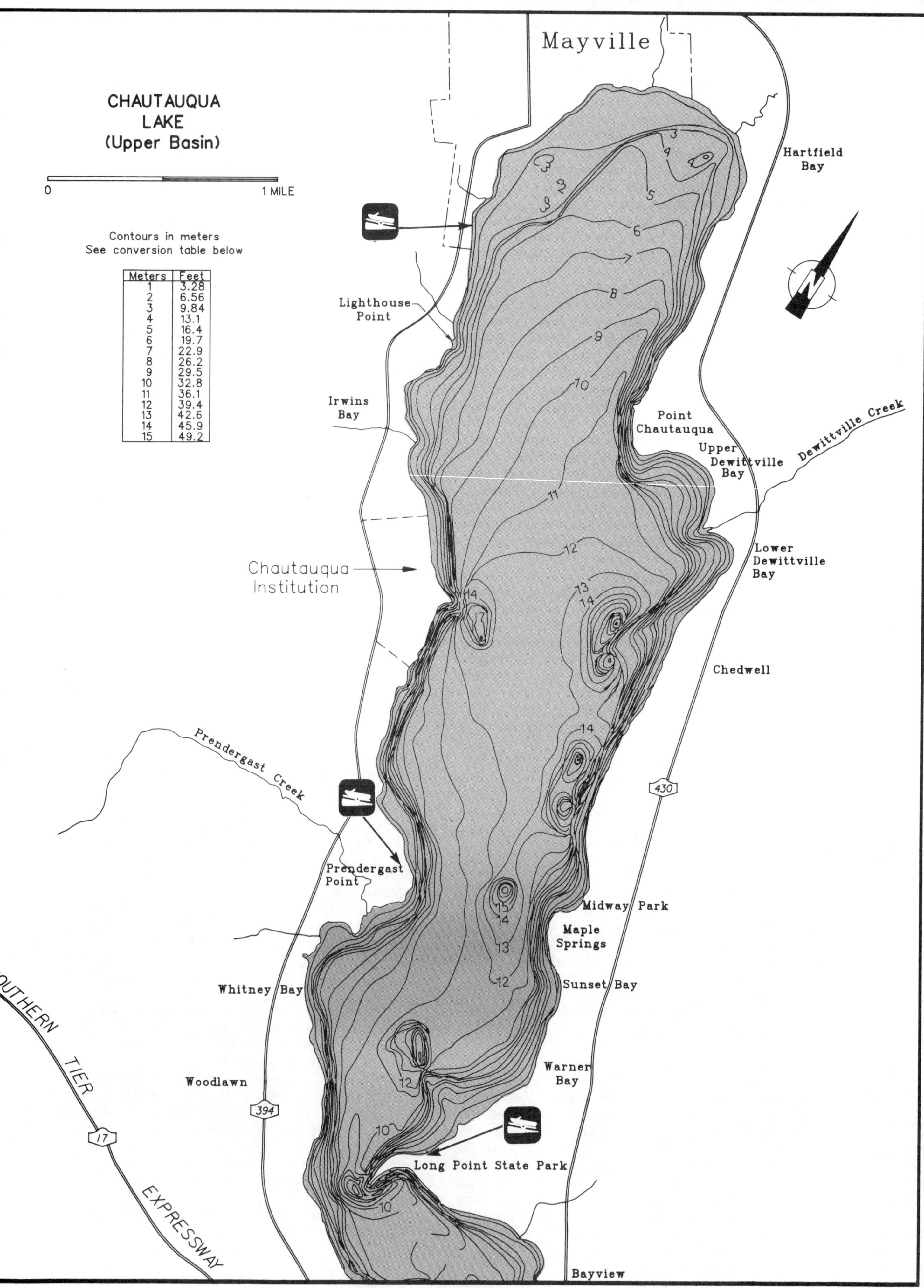

Meters	Feet
1	3.28
2	6.56
3	9.84
4	13.1
5	16.4
6	19.7
7	22.9
8	26.2
9	29.5
10	32.8
11	36.1
12	39.4
13	42.6
14	45.9
15	49.2

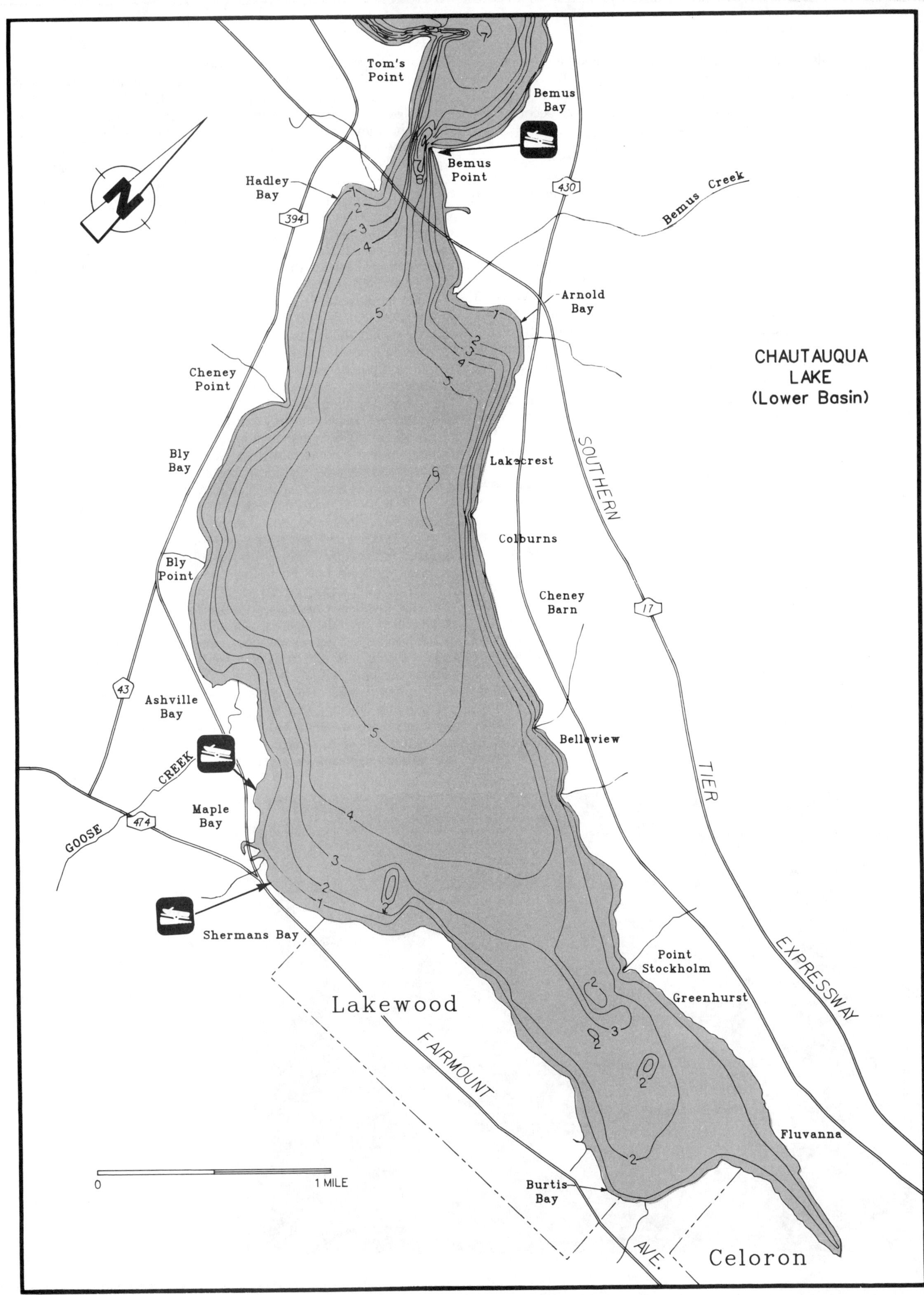
CHAUTAUQUA
LAKE
(Lower Basin)
Tom's Point
Bemus Bay
Bemus Point
Bemus Creek
Hadley Bay
394
430
Arnold Bay
Cheney Point
Bly Bay
Lakecrest
SOUTHERN
Colburns
Bly Point
Cheney Barn
17
43
Ashville Bay
Belleview
TIER
CREEK
Maple Bay
GOOSE
474
Shermans Bay
Point Stockholm
EXPRESSWAY
Greenhurst
Lakewood
FAIRMOUNT
Fluvanna
0
1 MILE
Burtis Bay
AVE.
Celoron

In late winter, anglers begin finding fish moving into shallower waters in response to increasing spawning urges. The waters off several of the major streams where the fish will spawn, such as Dewittville Creek, Prendergast Creek, and Goose Creek become very productive just before the close of the season.

Largemouth Bass .... Common; growth rate good

Largemouth bass have long been a popular quarry on Chautauqua Lake, but in the past decade their popularity has sky-rocketed. Numerous bass tournaments are now held on the lake each year, which is an indication of the quality of this fishery.

Both basins of the lake offer good fishing for largemouth bass. Extensive weedbeds and docks provide plenty of cover for the fish.

In the southern basin, the area around the bridges and essentially every bay provide good fishing for largemouth. Also good in the southern basin, at least until the weeds get too thick, are the Grass Island, the Lakewood Bar, and the Crib. The mouth of the Chadakoin River and the river itself are also prime fishing areas for largemouth. Fishermen often pick up a few in the spring while fishing for crappies in the southern basin.

In the northern basin, almost the entire lake from Chautauqua Institute around to Dewittville Bay is good. Look for areas where there is shallow water close to deep weedlines. If there are a lot of docks along the shoreline, so much the better. Another productive area in the northern basin is Whitney Bay. The situation here is almost ideal for bass fishing. The shallow waters of the bay have numerous patches of lily pads relatively close to deep water, a situation much favored by largemouth bass.

In the very northern end of the lake is an area known as "The Flats." Relatively shallow and flat, this is an area of patchy weed beds that provides better than average bass fishing. Terry Jones, a friend of mine and an avid bass fisherman, likes to fish the docks along the Flats. These docks are prime bass holding areas because they aren't chocked with weeds and because the water in this area is generally clearer than in other parts of the lake. Terry feels that these docks get less pressure than the docks on other parts of Chautauqua. Start fishing under and around docks from the start of the season. Hot, sunny days early in the season are especially good for dock fishing. The pilings of the docks are warmed by the sun, and they in turn warm the water around them. This slight increase in water temperature is enough to attract numerous bass. Later in the year, when the water temperatures in the shallows begin to cool down, fishing under docks becomes less productive.

When dock fishing, Terry recommends using a straight plastic worm, rather than a one that has a curled tail. The flat tail of the curled worms, like the Mister Twister, adhere more easily to the dock, and they tend to wrap around your line if not cast correctly. Terry also suggests pegging the sinker so that it stays directly in front of the worm. This will keep the lure and sinker from cartwheeling when you cast.

Two techniques employed by anglers who fish docks often are known as skipping and pitching. Skipping basically is casting the bait or lure side-armed with a spinning rod. Pitching is an under-hand method of casting that allows you to make a very quiet and accurate presentation. Both of these methods are good for getting under docks and overhanging brush and trees.

During the summer and early fall, try fishing in the open pockets of weedbeds rather than along weedlines. Many fishermen feel that the largemouth in this lake are forced to hold closer to the weedlines than normal in some areas, or actually hold in the weeds, due to direct or indirect competition from the muskies and walleyes. Flipping is a very productive technique for taking fish that hold in the weeds. There are several variations on flipping, but they are all fairly similar. Keeping as quiet as possible, a shallow-draft boat is maneuvered close to openings in a thick weed bed by means of a trolling motor equipped with a weed guard. The boat is then stopped, and the angler either makes a short cast to the opening or, if the opening is very close, he carefully drops the lure down in the water. Bass hold close to the edges of these pockets, waiting to ambush small fish, frogs, or other prey. A well-presented worm or jig 'n pig is often irresistible. This method must be done with a very stiff rod and the drag should be set tight. As soon as the fish hits the bait, the hook must be set hard and fast. The idea is to get the fish turned and moving toward you as quickly as possible. By horsing it in this manner, you don't give the fish the opportunity to get tangled in the weeds, which it will naturally attempt to do as soon as the hook is set. Terry's standard flipping rig consists of a stiff rod (some stores now sell rods designed especially for this type of fishing) equipped with a left-handed level-wind reel wound with 14- to 17-pound-test line. He prefers to use a left-handed reel when he's pitching and flipping because you don't have to switch hands after each presentation, as you would if you were using a regular reel. Jig 'n pigs top Terry's list of bass baits. Six-inch purple worms and white spinnerbaits also work very well.

The author and fishing companion Joe Gravelle boated this impressive catch of panfish in just over an hour while fishing in Ashville Bay.

Of course, not all largemouth bass are going to be caught in the weeds. In many parts of the lake, bass are caught by anglers using the time-honored method of working weedlines with crankbaits, spinnerbaits, plastic worms, live bait, or jig 'n pigs. If the water is clear, Terry likes to use a black, blue, and purple jig 'n pig, i.e. a black and blue pork rind and a purple jig head. If the water is murky, he will go to a black and green pork rind and a black, chartreuse, or green jig head. The depth of the water determines the size of the jig to use. The deeper the water the larger the jig.

After the lake turns over in the fall, the bass move out to the deeper weedlines. Largemouth bass go on a feeding binge in the fall in order to fatten up for the winter. You can expect increased feeding activity until the water temperatures go below the mid-50s. Then the fishing slows, but largemouth can still be taken on live bait until the end of the season.

Smallmouth Bass .... Common; growth good

Both basins of Chautauqua Lake offer good, sometimes excellent, fishing for smallmouth bass. Traditional smallmouth structure (i.e., shoals, drop-offs, points, etc.) is found primarily in the upper basin. Some of the most productive areas are off Mayville, off Point Chautauqua, along the drop-offs between Midway Park and Dewittville Bay, the Big Bar, which is located just north of Long Point in Warner Bay, in Bemus Bay, and along Tom's Point. However, most of the points and ledges in the upper basin hold some smallmouth.

In the lower basin, the shoreline between Colburn's and Greenhurst holds a pretty good population of bass. The problem here is that the bass are often going to hold close to very small pockets of rock and rubble, which are often no larger than the average living room. The hardest part to catching the fish will be finding these disparate pockets.

Contrary to what many people believe, smallmouth bass can be found in weedy areas. This is especially true on this lake, where traditional structure is often lacking. Smallmouth are often encountered by walleye fishermen trolling along weedlines. Popular baits in the summer include medium to large soft-shelled crabs, minnows, worms, and leeches. Fish these close to the bottom, using as little splitshot as possible. In the fall, still fishing with large minnows over rocky areas and shoals or jigging along ledges are highly productive techniques.

Crappies .... Abundant; growth very good

Just as the ice is leaving the lake, huge schools of crappies move into shallow bays, shorelines, boat slips, and boat channels to spawn. They will be found in these areas until late May.

The spring crappie fishing on Chautauqua Lake has to be seen to be believed. Often before the ice is completely off the lake, fantastic numbers of these tasty fish begin to congregate in bays and near-shore areas to spawn. This takes place primarily in the lower basin. Information from fishermen and nettings by the DEC indicate that Arnold's Bay, Bly Bay, Maple Bay, and Ashville Bay are usually the most productive areas in the lower basin. However, good action can be found in almost any bay, around docks, and boat slips. Also, don't forget to check out the mouths of streams, submerged brush piles, or brushy shorelines.

In the northern basin, Whitney Bay is always an exceptionally good area for crappie fishing.

Fishing for crappies is a simple matter. Use ultra-light rods rigged with light line and very small (1/32- to 1/16-ounce) white, soft-bodied jigs. For added effect the jig can be tipped with a minnow. Minnows fished on a small hook also work well. The jig or minnow should be fished about 3 feet below a small bobber. When fishing with just a minnow, use a small split-shot to keep the bait down. Be sure not to set the hook too hard when crappie fishing. They have soft mouths, and you can easily tear the hook right out if you're not careful.

By the time summer rolls around the schools of crappie will have dispersed and the fish will have moved out in to deeper water. But they can often be found near submerged structure.

In the fall, the near-shore crappie fishing picks up again. Although its very good at this time, it doesn't quite match up to the spring fishing. The techniques used to take crappies in the fall are the same as in the spring. This continues on into the winter, and many fisherman harvest good numbers of these fish through the ice.

General Information

Chautauqua Lake is one of New York State's greatest vacation attractions. The region is popular not only for its tremendous fishing, but for such varied things as the world famous Chautauqua Institute, regional wineries, and exquisite scenery. Because it is a well-established resort area, Chautauqua Lake is serviced by numerous marinas, camp grounds, hotels, and resorts. For a very informative treatment of these facilities and other useful information on the Chautauqua region obtain a copy of the Chautauqua County Travel Guide. Its pages are full of useful information about the area. To get a copy contact:

The Chautauqua County Vacationland Association Inc.
2 North Erie Street
Mayville, New York 14757
Phone (716) 753-4304

The following article was written by Mike Bleech, one of the area's top outdoor writers and a Chautauqua Lake fisherman of considerable experience. Here he gives his impression of the lake's diversity and quality.

FISHING AT CHAUTAUQUA LAKE

By Mike Bleech

Chautauqua Lake rates among the great fishing lakes of North America. It provides outstanding fishing for muskellunge, walleyes, largemouth bass, smallmouth bass, crappies, yellow perch, blue gills, and bullheads. This is one of those rare lakes that has both lots of fish, and big fish, even though fishing pressure is heavy. If you know what to do, and when to do it, you can have year around good fishing at Chautauqua.

Chautauqua is one of my 'home' lakes. I can have my boat on the water within an hour of the instant I get the notion to go fishing, so I spend a lot of time on its water. I would like to share some of this time with you. The object will be to help you have good fishing results at this lake, no matter when you visit. We will look at a year of fishing at Chautauqua Lake, beginning with New Year's Day . . .

WINTER

It's New Year's Day. Not many ice fishermen will be on the lake early today. The rolling hills that surround the lake are covered with a couple inches of snow. The temperature was in the low 20s at the crack of dawn, but by the time we get to the lake it has warmed (?) to the high 20s. We tell ourselves that the walleyes usually do not hit very good until late afternoon, usually, so in mid-afternoon we are actually early. We drill our holes over about 30 feet of water, just a short walk south of the public access at Prendergast Point. There is 4 1/2 inches of ice. It might not be safe closer to the center of the lake. This is clear ice, with no snow on it.

We are fortunate to be here now, because the fishing typically drops off somewhat when there is snow on the ice. As expected, the walleyes start hitting about 4:30, and during the 45 minutes before darkness, we catch a few dozen walleyes, including enough to fill our limits. That is a typical good day of early ice fishing at Chautauqua. Limit catches are common, particularly among the regulars. Sometimes you might catch walleyes almost as fast as you can get your bait or lure down to them! But of course, there are some slow times, too.

There is good ice fishing through the winter for yellow perch and sunfish. Some of the best of this action is in the Mayville area. Tiny jigs tipped with grubs are the top sunfish lures. They are also effective for perch. Many perch anglers prefer to use small minnows.

Walleyes hold most ice anglers' attention until the season closes on March 15. You are liable to find walleyes anywhere in the basin of the upper half of the lake, from Bemus Bay north past Point Chautauqua. Some of the more popular areas are Long Point, Prendergast Point, Maple Springs, the Chautauqua Institute, and Point Chautauqua. The most productive water is generally at least 30 feet deep.

For many anglers the fishing season on Chautauqua Lake starts with the spring crappie fishing, when tremendous numbers of crappies move into the shallows to spawn around docks and brush piles. Hundreds of anglers are drawn to the lake at this time, resulting in scenes such as that pictured here. Photo courtesy Mike Bleech.

Late ice fishing for crappies is one of the highlights of the fishing year at Chautauqua Lake! Action gets fast during the last couple weeks of safe ice, which usually occurs in late March. It is not unusual for anglers to fill a five-gallon bucket with slab crappies. The measure of the crappie fishing is how many crappies it takes to fill the bucket. The fewer it takes, the better the fishing is. A 35 crappie bucket means you have caught some mighty nice crappies!

The late ice crappie hotspots are Ashville Bay, Maple Bay, Burtis Bay, and Bemus Bay. You will easily recognize the current hotspots by the clusters of anglers and ice shanties. Most ice anglers use either small minnows or small jigs. Jigs, such as the Swedish Pimple, Rapala Jig, Airplane Jig, or various leadhead jigs, are usually tipped with grubs. Move minnows or jigs frequently, but do not make long or fast jig movements, and pause a few seconds between movements. Crappie hits are often difficult to detect, so be alert!

SPRING

The great spring crappie fishing continues after the ice leaves the lake, and may last through June, depending on the current crappie population. Some of the best fishing will be during the first week after the ice leaves, weather permitting. During the first warm weekend of open water there will be a flotilla of crappie anglers divided into groups at the various hotspots. The early open-water crappie action is in the shallow bays where the water is quickest to warm. Bemus Bay, Ashville Bay, Maple Bay, Arnolds Bay, and Whitney Bay are all likely places to find hungry crappies during April. During peak crappie population years, there will be good crappie fishing all around the lake.

My favorite fishing method here for springtime crappies is jigging under a float. I use 1/32-ounce or 1/16-ounce leadheads, and a wide assortment of plastic bodies. Color is a serious consideration. The most productive colors at Chautauqua Lake have been smoke with silver glitter, blue with silver glitter, chartreuse, white, purple, and yellow.

The jig is always at the depth I want it to be when it is suspended beneath a float. This is handy for keeping the jig above weeds, and it allows very slow retrieves. One of the best tactics is to let the waves do the jigging. But the most helpful advantage of the float is that strikes are easy to see. Crappies are notoriously light strikers!

If Lake Erie was not just a few miles to the northwest folks would say that Chautauqua Lake has the best walleye fishing in the country. The season opener on the first Saturday of May is the start of another of my most enjoyable fishing patterns - bar hopping for walleyes. The walleyes here are abundant and fast growing, and there is no more pleasant way to catch them than in shallow water, during the still of night.

Dave Peterson taught me this pattern soon after I returned home from Vietnam in the early 1970s. It was the best welcome home I got. We often caught (and still do) walleyes by the dozens, including a few around the 10-pound mark. Dave, 'Doc' Myers, and I shared an amazing night of walleye action with this pattern.

Doc and I met Dave at the Bait Pond, a bait and tackle business operated by Dave and his family, along Route 394 near Cheney Point. From there we drove to Dewittville, near the northeast corner of the lake, where we waded out onto a long shallow bar to cast for walleyes.

Walleyes move over the shallow bars under the cover of darkness to feed on minnows. Oftentimes when the walleyes move in, you can see or hear them attacking minnows near the surface. We cast for them with a variety of lures, including crankbaits and jigs. Most often we use minnow-shaped lures. My favorite in this situation - that is, when the walleyes are near the surface - is a jointed Rebel Minnow. I retrieve the lure very slowly, so that it is just a couple inches below the surface.

When a walleye takes this lure it is usually felt only as a light tick, or like the lure picked up a small piece of floating weed. Set the hook quickly if you get even the hint of a strike!

Dave, Doc, and I started catching walleyes as soon as we started casting that evening. We had hits on nearly every cast! Several times I lost a fish, then hooked another before getting the lure retrieved.

After an hour or so of this, I felt a funny bumping on my feet. I shined my light into the water by my feet, and saw a school of keeper-sized walleyes using my feet for cover!

I pulled enough line off my reel so that my lure hung about 3 feet below my rod tip, then I pulled the lure through the water right there in front of me. Several walleyes scrambled for the lure. I hooked a 16 incher and pulled it from the water.

Since I had not yet kept any walleyes, I put that one on my rope stringer and lowered it into the water. That did not bother the other walleyes a bit. I filled out my limit with 16- to 18-inch walleyes right there at my rod tip.

SUMMER

Chautauqua Lake buzzes with activity during the summer. Though just a decade ago there were few bass anglers, now there are more bass boats than water skiers, and that is a bunch! This lake now gets so much attention for its largemouth bass, smallmouth bass, walleyes, and crappies that it almost escapes notice that it has long been billed as the best muskie lake in the world.

The season for bass and muskellunge opens on the third Saturday of June. This weekend is generally one of the best of the year for anglers, as both muskies and bass are active.

Muskies are the top fresh-water game-fish trophy. They provide a real challenge. Your best opportunity to tie into a muskie might be with one of the area guides. Captain Warren Berry (Box 231, Ashville, NY 14710), who operates 'the Frenchman Boat' is one of the top muskie guides in the country.

Should you decide to try for the muskies on your own, you are apt to find muskies anywhere in the lake. The deep edges of the weedlines are likely places to connect with a hungry muskie. While trolling and jerkbaiting are the most popular methods, your chances for success might be better if you use big, black jigs.

Like most lakes in New York, the largemouth bass were mostly ignored until the bass boom crept into the state during the early 1980s. Smallmouth bass have long been popular here, but it was not until a large-scale bass study from 1977 to 1980 that it was learned that Chautauqua Lake has twice as many largemouths as smallmouths.

Largemouth bass are abundant in the weedlines. Flipping is the hot method for getting those bass out of the weeds. The top lure is a jig 'n pig in various combinations of black, black, and black. Work slowly, covering every pocket that you can slide your jig 'n pig into. There are some big bass in these weed beds - and don't be surprised if a walleye or muskie grabs the lure.

One of the best, but least-known, methods for catching big walleyes during mid-summer is flipping in the weedlines with a slight variation in the jig 'n pig. Instead of a black Arkie jig, use chartreuse. And instead of a black pork frog, use a chartreuse, yellow, or white Uncle Josh Ripple Rind.

Walleyes often pick up the jig while it is on the bottom, as opposed to largemouth bass that usually grab the lure while it is sinking. So, leave the jig 'n pig on bottom longer than you might while flipping for bass.

You can escape fishing and boating pressure by fishing during the nighttime. I believe, based on experience, that the best summertime fishing hours at Chautauqua Lake are from 3:00 a.m. until boating and fishing activity begins to pick up in the mid-morning. If you wait until 7:00 a.m. to get on the water you will have missed the best of this fishing.

My pal Bill Anderson and I had the kind of night anglers dream about one early July morning. Bill is an early morning person, and I am a late night person. So we compromised and left home at 2 o'clock in the morning.

We began fishing between Long Point and Maple Springs, casting surface lures over a rocky, mostly weed-free area. By the time we fished through the area we had planned to fish, roughly the north side of Big Bar, we had caught and released a dozen smallmouths. The biggest were in the 3-pound class, which is not especially big for this lake, and most of the bass were much smaller. Up to this point it was a nice bit of fishing, but nothing out of the ordinary here.

Next we fished Whitney Bay, working south from Prendergast Point. We still used the same surface lures, an Ugly Albert and a buzzbait, but instead of the rocky structure we now retrieved the lures over weeds and soft bottom. The wind was at our backs, so

Some of the best fishing on Chautauqua Lake takes place in the fall. With a majority of the pleasure boaters and fair-weather fishermen off the water, the serious fisherman can pursue trophy-sized bass, muskie, and walleye almost anywhere on the lake and any time of day. The muskie fishing is especially good at this time of year. Photo courtesy Mike Bleech.

we moved through this area rather quickly. Bill had a big muskie on for a few seconds, and we each caught a couple respectable largemouths.

We debated about working through that area again. That would have been a logical decision, in view of our success during the first pass. But we do not always make our decisions because they seem most logical. After all, we do this fishing thing for fun. Instead of going back through that productive water in Whitney Bay, we fished from Victoria, which is right across the lake from Long Point, to Tom's Point. This produced several modest-sized smallmouths on the rocky area of Victoria Point, a half-dozen good largemouths, all over 3 1/2 pounds, from the weed cover, and a dandy smallmouth from a rocky slot through the weeds.

The first light of dawn appeared while we were anchored along the outer edge of a weedline, near the Route 17 bridge. Up to this point we had released everything we caught. But here we put our limits of walleyes in the livewell. None of them were huge, but the smallest was 2 1/2 pounds.

The wind had made an abrupt shift. It was a bit stronger, and coming from the northeast while we were catching the walleyes. They struck minnow-shaped lures retrieved slowly, just under the surface. Bill missed another big muskie here, too. He had cast to it after seeing it roll.

The walleyes continued to hit until the sun was slightly above the horizon. It was at this point, when we pulled the anchor to move on, that we took notice of what an outstanding fishing outing this was!

Our next stop, the last stop of the morning, was in a rocky area along the central-eastern side of the lower lake. The game plan here was soft-shelled crayfish for smallmouths. We had stopped to visit with Dave Peterson the day before, and had bought a dozen soft-shells from him.

A 5-pound smallmouth rewarded my efforts here. We caught several, including some others to 4 1/2 pounds. Bill took a couple of these on a white Mister Twister jig. This jig, which Bill was casting with an ultra-light outfit, also yielded a 3-foot muskie. Bill released it in good condition.

It was close to 9:00 a.m. when we quit fishing and headed for the boat access area at Prendergast, where we had launched about 6 hours earlier. It had been a great night and morning of fishing, even for Chautauqua Lake!

FALL

If I could fish Chautauqua Lake during only one week of the year, I would want it to be during fall. I would choose a week in late October, mainly because muskie season closes on the last day of this month. I would hope for balmy, Indian summer weather, and water temperature in the 40s. Nighttime air temperatures might drop around the freezing point, but during the day it would climb into the 50s or 60s.

You would like this fishing. Most of the anglers and nearly all of the pleasure boaters are gone for the season. The rich, summertime food supply for the game fish has been whittled away, so that the game fish have to hunt longer for their meals, and they are more receptive to anglers' offerings. The walleyes, smallmouths, and largemouths will be congregated in definable areas, so once we find them we can usually catch a few. And best of all, fall is trophy time!

We could start the day at one of the points that extend underwater. I would like to anchor near some irregular structure in depths from 6 to 12 feet. We would use large minnows, 6 to 8 inches in length. We would also have a couple dozen smaller minnows, because it is likely that we will find some big yellow perch. Our primary target would be trophy-sized smallmouth bass! But we might catch more walleyes than bass, which would not be a disappointment.

In the evening, and on into the night, we could troll live bait for muskies. This is done along the deep edges of the weedlines, using live baits that might be a foot long. The baits are hung beneath floats, so that they are within a couple feet of bottom. This is a slow trolling presentation. Either row or use an electric motor on its slow speed.

Muskies like dark, nasty nights. Dave Peterson taught me about live baiting for muskies, and he taught me about catching muskies in bad weather. He proved it to my brother by guiding him to his biggest Chautauqua Lake muskie, so far, a 24 1/2 pounder, on a night that was so windy, dark, and rainy that I was afraid the muskie might get them into the water before they could get the muskie into the boat. The storm had driven me off the water even before they hooked the muskie. I rowed out to look for them, fearing they might have trouble, and found them fighting Greg's trophy.

Muskie fishing is generally good right up to the close of season. Smallmouth bass action will continue until the water temperature drops below the low 40s, and largemouth bass will get sluggish at about the same time. Walleye and yellow perch might provide good fishing until ice-up.

If we tried to take advantage of all the fishing peaks at Chautauqua Lake we would have to move to the lake shore. Long dry spells are not the norm here. You could vacation here most any week and expect to have some good fishing, as long as you are flexible.

Ice fishing is very popular on Chautauqua Lake. The winter provides excellent fishing for crappies, walleye, and occasionally yellow perch. Photo courtesy Mike Bleech

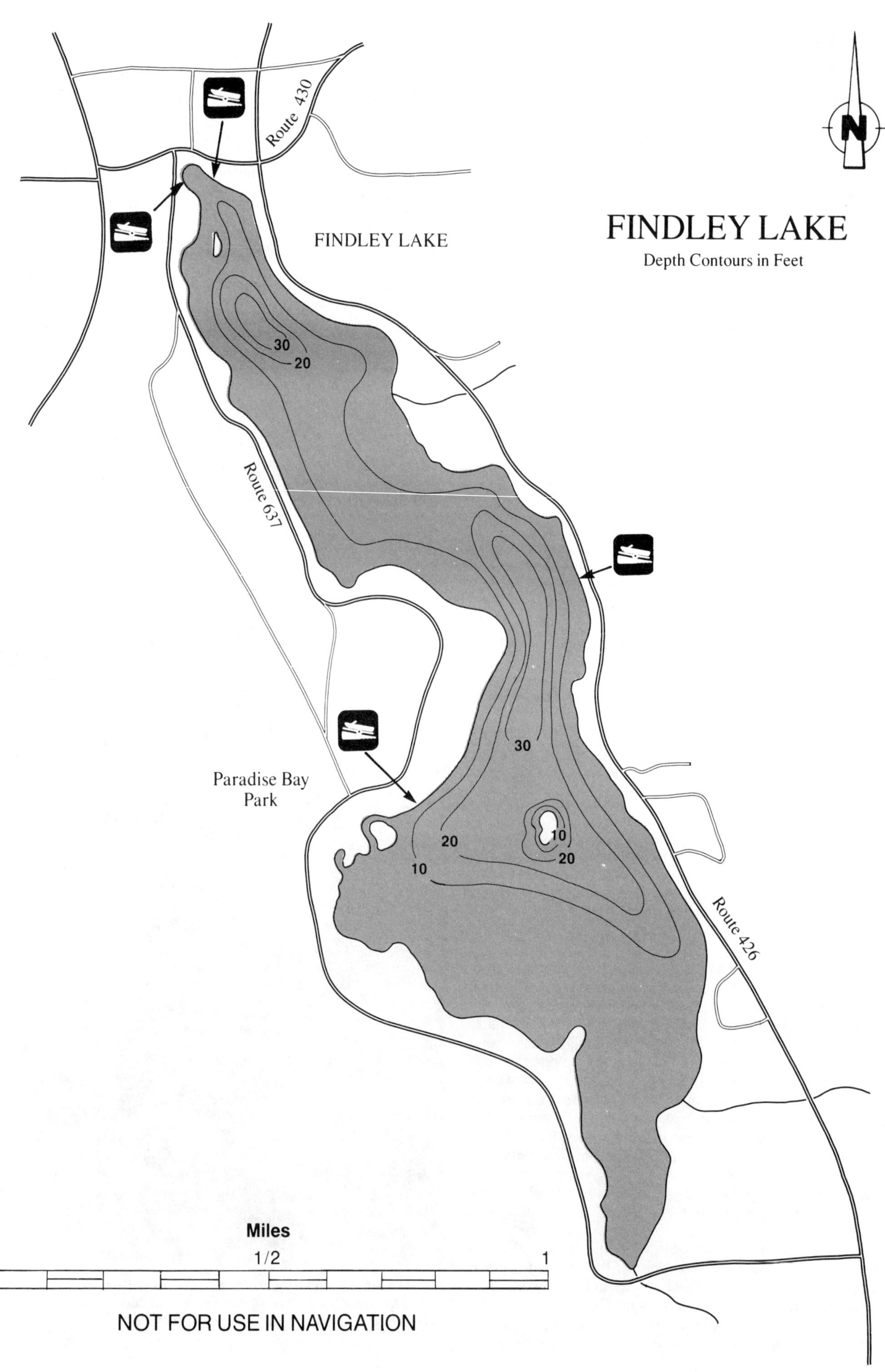

FINDLEY LAKE
Depth Contours in Feet
FINDLEY LAKE
Route 430
Route 637
Route 426
Paradise Bay Park
30
20
30
20
10
10
20
Miles
0
1/2
1
NOT FOR USE IN NAVIGATION

FINDLEY LAKE

Location

Map Coordinates	42° 07′ 09″ 79° 44′ 04″
USGS Map(s)	Clymer
Township(s)	Mina
Access	Route 426, Route 637

Physical Characteristics

Area	275 acres
Shoreline	5.50 miles
Elevation	1,420 feet
Maximum Depth	35 feet
Mean Depth	40 feet
Bottom Type	Muck, sand, gravel

Chemical Characteristics

Water	Generally clear
pH	Slightly alkaline
Oxygen	Usually good throughout the lake; could be deficient in deepest water during the summer.

Plant Life

Vegetation is abundant throughout the lake; most of the lake is treated every year for weed control.

Species Information

Tiger Muskellunge	Common; growth rate good
Walleye	Uncommon; growth rate good
Largemouth Bass	Common; growth rate good
Yellow Perch	Common; growth rate good
Northern Pike	Uncommon; growth rate good
Bullhead	Common; growth rate good
Crappie	Common; growth rate fair

Boat Launch Sites

1. New York State access site off Route 430 at the north end of the lake. Cartop and canoe launching - no charge.
2. Public Launch ramp on Route 430. Concrete ramp - no charge.
3. New York State access site off Route 426, 1 1/2 miles south of the village of Findley. Cartop boats and canoes only - no charge.
4. Paradise Bay Campground off Route 637. Trailer launch site - fee.

General Information

There are unsubstantiated claims that Findley is one of the most productive muskie (tiger) lakes, for its size, in the country. That may or may not be true, but this certainly is a good quality lake for species such as muskie, largemouth bass, and panfish. Hidden away in the extreme southwestern corner of New York State, Findley Lake is relatively unknown and, consequently, gets little fishing pressure. It is readily accessible to boat fishermen, but shore-bound anglers will find this a difficult lake to fish due to the fact that much of the shoreline is very swampy. When Lake Erie is kicking up because of the wind, Findley will be much calmer and should prove to be a good alternative location. Its many panfish also make it an ideal lake for introducing children to the pleasures of angling. In the winter, ice fishing is a popular pasttime and good catches of perch are supplimented by an occassional walleye and muskie.

Findley lake is stocked annually with 1,700 tiger muskie fingerlings and 4,500 walleye fingerlings.

NOTES: ____________________

ERIE COUNTY
0 1 2 3 4 5
MILES
N
NIAGARA COUNTY
TONAWANDA INDIAN RESERVATION
GENESEE COUNTY
WYOMING COUNTY
CATTARAUGUS COUNTY
CHAUTAUQUA COUNTY
CATTARAUGUS INDIAN RESERVATION
Lake Erie
Buffalo
Tonawanda
Kenmore
Williamsville
Akron
Depew
Lancaster
Alden
Sloan
Lackawanna
Blasdell
East Aurora
Orchard Park
Hamburg
Angola
Farnham
North Collins
Springville
Gowanda
Burnt Ship Creek
Big Six Mile Creek
Woods Cr
Spicer Cr
West River Pkwy
Niagara River
LaSalle Lake
Tillman Road Wildlife Management Area
Tifft Nature Preserve
Tonawanda Creek
Murder Cr
Ellicott Creek
Cayuga Creek
Little Buffalo Creek
Buffalo Creek
Cazenovia
Smoke Cr
Cazenovia Creek
Hunters Creek
Cazenovia Creek (East Branch)
Cazenovia Creek (West Branch)
Eighteen Mile Creek (Main Branch)
Eighteen Mile Creek (South Br)
Little Sister Cr
Big Sister Cr
Delaware Creek
Muddy Cr
Clear Creek
(North Branch)
(Main Branch)
Derby
Spooner Cr
Spring Br
Coon Br
Hosmer Br
Cattaraugus Creek
190
990
78
93
263
290
5
90
384
33
20
62
354
400
358
240
219
20A
277
75
249
438
39
16

ERIE COUNTY STREAMS AND RIVERS

BIG SISTER CREEK

Map Coordinates .... 42° 39′ 55″ 79° 03′ 48″
USGS Map(s) .... Angola, Eden, North Collins
Township(s) .... Evans
Access .... Bennett Park (the old Buffalo Municipal Beach)
Principal Species .... Brown Trout, Rainbow Trout, Coho Salmon, Chinook Salmon, Panfish

Big Sister Creek averages about 15 feet in width. The action here is pretty much limited to the spring and fall runs of trout and salmon, and the quality of the fishing during these spawning runs is heavily dependant upon rainfall. If the rainfall has been sufficient, the fishing in this stream can be quite good, and the fish can run right up into the headwaters.

The mouth of Big Sister Creek is posted on both sides for about 200 yards, but there is easy access where the stream flows through Bennett Park. Wade fishing or boat fishing just off the mouth of the stream in Lake Erie is often very productive.

This stream is not stocked.

NOTES: ____________________

____

____

BIG SIX MILE CREEK

Map Coordinates .... 43° 01′ 36″ 79° 00′ 43″
USGS Map(s) .... Niagara Falls, Tonawanda West
Township(s) .... Grand Island
Access .... Big Six Mile Creek Marina, off Whitehaven Road
Principal Species .... Bullhead, Northern Pike, Panfish

For the most part, Big Six Mile Creek is simply a state-operated marina (Big Six Mile Marina). There is no fishing in the marina during boating season, but the creek mouth, on which a small breakwall is located, is fishable most of the year.

In the early spring, bullhead, yellow perch, rock bass, and northern pike can be caught in this creek. In the winter, perch, smelt, and an occasional northern pike can be taken through the ice in the vicinity of the marina.

NOTES: ____________________

____

____

BUFFALO CREEK

Map Coordinates .... 42° 52′ 15″ 78° 47′ 15″
USGS Map(s) .... Buffalo SE, Orchard Park, East Aurora, Strykersville
Location .... Counties of Erie and Wyoming
Access .... Factory Road (upper section), Harlem Road (lower section)
Principal Species .... Brown Trout (stocked and wild), Rainbow Trout (stocked), Largemouth Bass, Smallmouth Bass, Panfish

The headwaters of Buffalo Creek average about 10 feet in width. The bottom is predominantly gravel in this section and the water quality is very good. Surrounded for the most part by woodlands, the stream has a good amount of bank cover and is fishable all trout season. Although the portion of the stream that runs through county forest land is off limits and other sections have posted areas, the upper reaches of Buffalo Creek are still worth investigating, for they hold a fair number of wild brown trout.

Below Day Road, Buffalo Creek meanders through farmland into Wyoming County. This section of the stream averages 15 to 20 feet in width, has a gravel bottom, and intermittent bank cover. It is fishable all season here, but due to rather high water temperatures, the fishing can be a bit spotty in the summer. There are no wild trout in this part of Buffalo Creek, but a 4-mile section, from Factory Road in Strykersville upstream to the Erie County line, is stocked in the spring with 1,500 brown trout yearlings.

Below Factory Road, Buffalo Creek re-enters Erie County. For most of the remainder of its course it averages about 30 feet in width, has a gravel and bedrock bottom, and intermittent bank cover. Warm-water species begin to predominate around Wales, and good catches of largemouth and smallmouth bass are not uncommon. In the spring there is an excellent run of suckers in this stream. If the rainfall is sufficient there is a moderately good run of trout in the spring, and trout and salmon in the fall, as far upstream as the dam in Elma.

Two especially productive areas of Buffalo Creek are the confluence of Buffalo and Cayuga Creeks (brown trout) and the wing dams near Harlem Road and Union Road (bass and trout). Closer to the mouth of Buffalo Creek, nearly every species of fish that inhabits the Niagara River can be caught, with the possible exceptions of northern pike and walleye.

NOTES: ____________________

____

____

PEACOCK SOFT HACKLE

This fly pulsates as it moves through the water. Fished deep, it imitates caddis fly nymphs; fished in shallow water, it imitates the emergent fly.

BURNT SHIP CREEK

Map Coordinates .... 43° 03′ 40″ 78° 59′ 55″
USGS Map(s) .... Tonawanda West
Township(s) .... Grand Island
Access .... East River Road, West River Parkway
Principal Species .... Northern Pike, Bullhead, Smallmouth Bass, Carp, Panfish

Burnt Ship Creek forms a narrow channel separating Buckhorn Island from Grand Island. Access to either end of this channel is by way of two narrow dirt roads off of East River Road and the West River Parkway. The western end is a major spawning ground for northern pike and bullhead, and large numbers of both species can be caught here in the spring. The bullhead fishing lasts all year and night fishing is always very productive.

If the water levels are high enough, this would be an excellent body of water to take a canoe or cartop boat through for some interesting springtime fishing, as it is surrounded primarily by a large, mostly undisturbed, marsh.

NOTES: ____

____

____

CATTARAUGUS CREEK (Main Branch)

Map Coordinates .... 42° 34′ 14″ 79° 08′ 15″
USGS Map(s) .... Silver Creek, Farnham, North Collins, Gowanda, Collins Center, Ashford Hollow, Sardinia, Arcade, Bliss, Johnsonburg
Location .... Southern boundary of Erie County, Wyoming County
Access .... Paralleled by Route 39 (upper section); piers and launch site at mouth (off Route 5)
Principal Species .... Brown Trout (stocked and wild), Rainbow Trout (stocked and wild), Brook Trout (wild), Coho Salmon, Chinook Salmon, Smallmouth Bass, Largemouth Bass, Bullhead, Panfish

Beginning in southwestern Wyoming County and flowing generally westward to empty into Lake Erie near the town of Irving, Cattaraugus Creek has established itself as one of the finest trout and salmon streams in New York State. Very long and circuitous, this stream defines the entire southern boundary of Erie County.

In terms of its characteristics, Cattaraugus Creek can be divided into two major sections. The lower Cattaraugus, from Lake Erie upstream to the dam at Springville, averages between 50 feet and 100 feet in width, depending upon the flow. The lower reaches of Cattaraugus Creek are very prone to floods, and the banks and the stream bottom tend to get scoured often. It has a gravel bottom below Gowanda, with gravel and shale between Gowanda and Springville. The water quality is generally good, though it tends to be muddy after a rain. There is little bank cover, as much of this section of the stream flows through a steep-sided gorge. The surroundings vary from open fields, farmland, and some woodland below Gowanda to primarily woodlands above Gowanda.

GOOFUS BUG

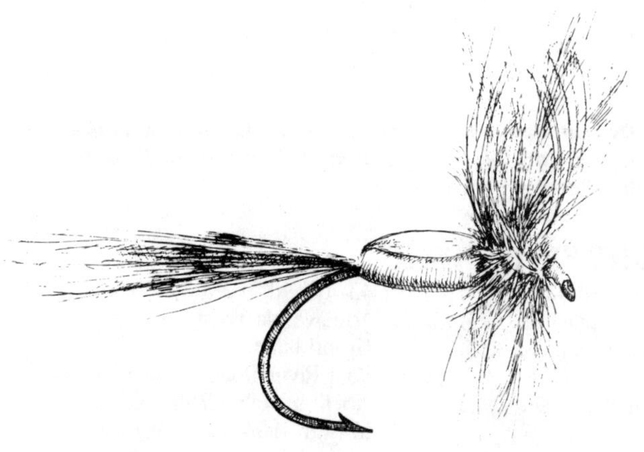

The Goofus Bug is a "do everything" type of dry fly. Tied with deer body hair for good buoyancy, it is especially effective on fast moving water.

It is in the fall that Cattaraugus Creek earns its reputation as a top quality stream. Beginning in September, enormous numbers of coho salmon and a fair number of chinook salmon move into the stream from Lake Erie. These fish can be caught in great numbers up as far upstream as the Springville Dam until late November. The dam is located on Scoby Hill Road off Route 219. Don't neglect to try some of the tributaries, such as Clear Creek, Spring Brook, and Spooner Brook, all of which partake in this annual flood of fish. The most productive method for taking these fish is drift fishing with egg sacs or yarn flies. Spin fishing also works well.

Immediately above the Indian reservation is the snagging section of the stream. This can be reached from Taylor Hollow Road or Route 62 in Gowanda. Snagging for salmon is permitted on Cattaraugus Creek between the Aldrich Street Extension bridge and the mouth of Point Peter Brook from September 1 to November 15.

Just as the salmon runs are dying out, the Cattaraugus gets a fresh influx of trout. The vast majority of these trout are going to be rainbows and steelhead. Only occasionally do significant numbers of brown trout spawn here in the fall. As with the salmon, these fish will run as far upstream as the dam in Springville. A large percentage will even work their way up into the headwaters of such tributaries as Clear Creek, Spooner Creek, Connoisarauley Creek, and Derby Brook. Most of the browns that run here will be out of the stream by late December, but the fishing for steelhead will last through the winter and actually peak in early spring.

The lower section of Cattaraugus Creek is stocked annually with 90,000 coho salmon and 57,000 steelhead.

Access to the lower Cattaraugus is more than adequate. The mouth of the stream can be fished from two large piers built by the Army Corps of Engineers. The southern pier is at the foot of Allegany Road in the village of Sunset Bay. There is a state-operated boat launch with double hard-surface ramps and parking for 60 cars and trailers near the mouth of the creek. The northern pier is on the Cattaraugus Indian Reservation. It can be reached by taking the unnamed right fork off Route 5 across from the Indian Bingo Building, just south of the village of Farnham. If you don't have an Indian fishing license, practically the entire stream below Gowanda is off limits. The only exception, other than the piers, is the south side of Cattaraugus Creek from the south pier upstream to about one-quarter mile above Routes 5 and 20. If you do possess an Indian license, there are innumerable dirt roads off Four Mile Level Road that lead right to the stream, and the fishing pressure on the reservation section is very light. Above Gowanda is a large tract of state-owned land. This entire section of Cattaraugus Creek is accessible only by canoe due to the deep gorge that it runs through. The remainder of the lower Cattaraugus is loosely paralleled by Gowanda Zoar Valley Road. There are no public fishing rights in this area, and there is a lot of posting, especially near the Springville Dam and just above the previously mentioned state-owned land. There are, however, sufficient unposted areas to make a trip to this section worthwhile.

There are also warm-water fish in Cattaraugus Creek. Smallmouth bass congregate in this stream to spawn in large numbers, but by the opening of bass season most have already moved out into Lake Erie. Bullhead, yellow perch, sheepshead, pumpkinseeds, and rock bass are always available in Cattaraugus Creek. Limited numbers of walleye are also taken here in the spring and early summer, primarily between the railroad bridges in the town of Irving and the creek mouth. The number of walleye taken here, though, don't really reflect the quantity that are present, for the extreme lower portion of Cattaraugus Creek is one of the primary walleye spawning areas in the eastern part of Lake Erie. In the summer, fishing generally tapers off in the lower Cattaraugus Creek. It is limited primarily to indigenous smallmouth bass, which tend to run smaller than the bass that spawn here in the spring, small numbers of wild rainbow trout, and rough fish such as bullhead, rock bass, and sheepshead.

Above the dam in Springville is the upper Cattaraugus. The stream is paralleled by Route 39 between Springville and the bridge at Route 16. This portion of the stream averages 20 to 40 feet in width, depending on flow. It has a bottom of gravel and silt and tends to be cloudy, especially after a rain, due to the clay banks of many of its tributaries. It flows through farms and woodlands, but there is relatively little bank cover on this section. This portion of the upper Cattaraugus is suitable for fly, spinning, and bait fishing. There are some wild brown trout and rainbow trout in this reach, but the vast majority of the fish are stocked trout. The portion of the stream between Springville and the bridge at Route 16 is heavily stocked. This is also one of the most heavily fished stretches of water in western New York early in the season. Fish can be found here all year, but the best fishing will be over by early summer.

From the Route 16 bridge to Arcade Center, the fishing is a bit spotty, particularly in the summer. However, even in the summer a fair number of fish, both browns and rainbows, can be taken from several spring-fed pools near the town of Arcade. Access to this part of the stream is from Bixby Hill Road or West Avenue in Arcade. Fishing pressure in this area is light, especially if you are willing to walk a little upstream or downstream of the bridges. The cover here is open enough for fly fishing.

From Arcade Center to just below East Arcade the stream is a bit brushy and narrow, but very productive. There are a number of large pools that yield fish, many of them wild, even during the warmest summer months. Access to this section is from Genesee Road and Cattaraugus Road, where the state has obtained public fishing rights. Fly fishing is possible here, and the May fly hatches in this area are very good.

The section of the stream from just below East Arcade to Java Lake is somewhat swampy and very brushy. The fish, mostly wild brown trout, are numerous but tend to run on the small side. It is possible that wild brook trout are also in the headwaters.

The upper Cattaraugus is very heavily stocked. In the spring, 10,600 brown trout yearlings are released in this stream, from West Townline Road to 1 mile above the village of East Arcade, a distance of 18.2 miles. There are public fishing rights on this section extending from approximately 1 mile below the Yorkshire Corners bridge on Route 16 to 2 miles above the bridge. In Wyoming County public fishing rights extend from Arcade to 1 mile above East Arcade. Look for the yellow DEC signs indicating public access.

NOTES: ______________________________

____

____

Cattaraugus Creek is one of the largest and most diverse streams in western New York. Below the town of Springville, the creek flows through a deep, scenic gorge.

CAYUGA CREEK

Map Coordinates	42° 52′ 12″ 78° 47′ 11″
USGS Map(s)	Buffalo SE, Buffalo NE, Lancaster, Clarence
Township(s)	Cheektowaga, Lancaster
Access	Harlem Road, Union Road
Principal Species	Brown Trout, Smallmouth Bass

Cayuga Creek is a bedrock- and silt-bottomed stream that is surrounded by residential areas in its most productive sections. Due to high water temperatures in the summer, there are no resident trout in this stream. However, if there is sufficient rainfall in the spring and fall, brown trout and an occasional salmon can be caught here, especially if you concentrate on the area near the confluence with Buffalo Creek. The lower portions also hold large numbers of suckers, some very large carp, and numerous smallmouth bass.

This stream is not stocked.

NOTES: ______________________________

____

____

Contrary to what many people think, you don't have to be able to cast a great distance to be a good fly fisherman. Accurate casting of a fly 30 to 40 feet is usually adequate on most streams in western New York.

CAZENOVIA CREEK (East Branch)

Map Coordinates	42° 45′ 38″ 78° 38′ 43″
USGS Map(s)	Orchard Park, East Aurora, Holland, Sardinia
Township(s)	Aurora, Wales, Holland, Sardinia
Access	Route 16
Principal Species	Brown Trout (stocked), Smallmouth Bass, Bullhead

Beginning near the town of Chaffee in southern Erie County and flowing north to join the west branch of Cazenovia Creek just south of Route 20A, the east branch of Cazenovia Creek can be divided into cold-water and warm-water sections. The cold-water portion of this stream, which is closely paralleled by Route 16, runs from just north of Chaffee to just north of Holland. This section averages 10 to 15 feet in width and has a gravel and bedrock bottom. The surrounding farmlands and pastures provide the stream with intermittent bank cover. Due to heavy fishing pressure in the spring and high water temperatures in the summer, the stream is fishable only during the first few months of trout season.

In the spring, the east branch of Cazenovia Creek is stocked with 3,100 brown trout yearlings, from Blakely Corners Road upstream 13 miles to Savage Road.

The remainder of the east branch is a warm-water fishery that can get excessively warm in the summer. However, good catches of smallmouth bass, carp, suckers, and bullhead are not uncommon.

NOTES: ______________________________

____

____

CAZENOVIA CREEK (Main Branch)

Map Coordinates .... 42° 51′ 40″ 78° 49″ 37″
USGS Map(s) .... Buffalo SE, Orchard Park
Township(s) .... Buffalo, West Seneca, Elma, Aurora
Access .... Seneca Street
Principal Species .... Smallmouth Bass

The main branch of Cazenovia Creek provides good fishing for smallmouth bass. Fly fishing for bass on warm summer evenings is popular on this stream. Minnow and crayfish imitations and streamer flies are very effective, especially in the faster sections. In the lower reaches much of the stream is slate bottomed. There are numerous undercuts in the slate and the bass will often use these as cover as they wait to ambush baitfish. Subsurface lures and poppers work best in this section.

NOTES: ________________________________

____

____

CAZENOVIA CREEK (West Branch)

Map Coordinates .... 42° 45′ 38″ 78° 38′ 43″
USGS Map(s) .... Orchard Park, Colden, Springville
Township(s) .... Aurora, Colden, Concord
Access .... Paralleled by Route 240
Principal Species .... Brook Trout (wild), Brown Trout (wild)

The west branch of Cazenovia Creek averages 10 to 15 feet in width, has a gravel bottom, and a good year-round flow of water. The water is usually clear, but the stream will muddy up after a heavy rain. Bank cover is intermittent along the stream and most sections can be fly fished.

The fishable section of this stream runs from the hamlet of Footes, which is about 1.5 miles south of Kissing Bridge, to the village of West Falls. The best fishing is found between Footes and Colden. Locals refer to the section downstream of West Falls as "The Sewer." It is polluted and much too warm in the summer to support any fish. There is little posting on the stream, and some sections can be accessed from an old railroad grade as well as from Route 240.

Most of the fish in the west branch are wild brook trout and brown trout, and there are reports of some very big browns coming from the stretch near Kissing Bridge. The west branch is only lightly fished and is well worth investigating.

NOTES: ________________________________

____

____

CLEAR CREEK (Main Branch)

Map Coordinates .... 42° 32′ 26″ 79° 01′ 38″
USGS Map(s) .... Farnham, North Collins, Gowanda, Collins Center
Township(s) .... Collins, the Cattaraugus Indian Reservation
Access .... Taylor Hollow Road
Principal Species .... Brook Trout (wild), Rainbow Trout, Chinook Salmon, Coho Salmon

This tributary of Cattaraugus Creek averages 15 to 20 feet in width. It flows primarily through farmlands, which provide intermittent bank cover in most sections, but bank cover is lacking along some stretches due to serious bank erosion. Though Clear Creek itself is gravel bottomed, it tends to muddy quickly after a heavy rainfall due to the clay and silt banks of many of its tributaries.

This stream is fishable all season, as there are limited numbers of wild brook trout in the upper section, some of which reach a respectable size. But the summer months are not highly productive due to high water temperatures.

In the spring and fall, there are substantial runs of trout and salmon up Clear Creek by way of Cattaraugus Creek. The most productive section is on the Indian Reservation, which begins just below Taylor Hollow Road.

Clear Creek is not stocked.

NOTES: ________________________________

____

____

CLEAR CREEK (North Branch)

Map Coordinates .... 42° 31′ 11″ 78° 57′ 00″
USGS Map(s) .... North Collins, Langford
Township(s) .... Collins, North Collins
Access .... Taylor Hollow Road
Principal Species .... Rainbow Trout, Chinook Salmon, Coho Salmon

This tributary of Clear Creek averages 15 feet in width, has a gravel and bedrock bottom, and very good water quality. Surrounded by farms and woodlands, there is intermittent bank cover on this stream. It tends to get a bit warm in the summer, but fish can be taken here all season.

There are wild rainbow trout throughout this stream, though they tend to be small. There is a moderate run of salmon here, via Cattaraugus Creek, in the fall, and lake-run rainbow trout can be found here from late fall through spring. The most productive area is from the stream mouth, which is just below Taylor Hollow Road and is on the Cattaraugus Indian Reservation, upstream to Jennings Road.

The north branch of Clear Creek is not stocked.

NOTES: ________________________________

____

____

COON BROOK

Map Coordinates 42 27 29 78 47 11
USGS Map(s) .... Collins Center, Langford
Township(s) .... Collins
Access .... Zoar Valley Road
Principal Species .... Brown Trout, Rainbow Trout

Coon Brook is a small tributary of Cattaraugus Creek averaging about 6 feet in width. This gravel-bottomed stream has a good year-round flow of water. Because it has such a high gradient, there are not many pools of any size on Coon Brook. There is intermittent cover along its banks, but a good fly fisherman will find much of the stream fishable. It takes a heavy rain to muddy Coon Brook, so you might want to keep it in mind when other streams in the area are running too off-color.

Coon Brook almost always has something to offer. Because it is so well watered, large brown trout from Cattaraugus Creek can make their way into this stream all year, and there are reports that even the very upper reaches of Coon Brook hold big browns, some of which are wild. These fish are augmented in the fall by fair runs of rainbows, most of which will be found no further up than Zoar Valley Road. There is also the possibility of a few salmon making their way into Coon Brook in the early fall.

NOTES: ________________________________

____

____

DELAWARE CREEK

Map Coordinates .... 42° 38′ 40″ 79° 03′ 50″
USGS Map(s) .... Angola, Farnham, North Collins
Township(s) .... Evans
Access .... Most easily approach from Lake Erie
Principal Species .... Rainbow Trout, Chinook Salmon, Coho Salmon

Delaware Creek is now so heavily posted that it is essentially closed to public fishing. If rainfall has been sufficient, there are fair to good runs of salmon up this stream in the fall, and trout, primarily rainbows, can be found here from late fall through spring. These fish can run as far up as the headwaters of the stream. Although much of the stream is no longer accessible, good fishing can still be had by fishing just off the mouth of Delaware Creek from a boat, or by casting from shore on either side of the mouth.

Delaware Creek is not stocked.

NOTES: ______________________________

____

____

DERBY BROOK

Map Coordinates .... 42° 28′ 26″ 78° 44′ 59″
USGS Map(s) .... Ashford Hollow, Collins Center, Langford
Township(s) .... Concord
Access .... Road crossing at Route 39
Principal Species .... Rainbow Trout, Coho Salmon

Derby Brook is a small tributary of Cattaraugus Creek. This gravel- and cobble-bottomed stream averages no more than 10 feet in width, though it does have some sizeable pools. It has a good flow of water all year, and only a heavy rain will cause it to muddy. It is surrounded by woodlands and farms, and there is a considerable amount of bank cover along its course, especially above Route 39. Beginning about 50 yards below Route 39 the stream enters a woods and is more open. Much of Derby Brook is posted, but you can generally obtain permission to fish here.

Most of the fishing in Derby Brook is dependant on runs of fish from Lake Erie. In the fall, a few salmon will make their way into the stream via Cattaraugus Creek, but this hardly constitutes a fishery. More substantial are the runs of rainbows that occur in the late fall and spring. A lot of these fish will stack up in front of a small spillway below Grote Road (shown on some maps as Hoffman Road), but many of them will make their way over it and run up as far as Route 39.

NOTES: ______________________________

____

____

EIGHTEEN MILE CREEK (Main Branch)

Map Coordinates .... 42° 43′ 05″ 78° 58′ 10″
USGS Map(s) .... Eden, Hamburg, Colden, Springville
Township(s) .... Hamburg, Boston, Concord
Access .... Parking for pay on Lake Shore Road (lower section); paralleled by old Route 219 (upper section)
Principal Species .... Rainbow Trout, Brook Trout (wild), Brown Trout (wild), Chinook Salmon, Coho Salmon, Smallmouth Bass, Bullhead

The main branch of Eighteen Mile Creek averages about 15 feet in width and has a bottom of bedrock, with some gravel above the mouth of the south branch. It tends to get cloudy after a heavy rain, although it clears up in a day or two. Flowing through a gorge for much of its length, there is little bank cover to be found here due to the surrounding terrain.

In the fall, there are good runs of chinook salmon and coho salmon in this stream. Like Cattaraugus Creek, relatively few brown trout run up this stream in the fall. Good numbers of rainbow trout are in the stream from late fall through spring. Normally, these fish will not be able to run up further than an impassable barrier near the mouth of the south branch; however, when water levels are high, it is possible for the fish to move as far up as the town of North Boston. Current regulations restrict snagging of salmon to the section of Eighteen Mile Creek from U.S. Route 20 upstream to Mayer Road in North Boston. Eighteen Mile Creek is stocked annually with 12,500 steelhead and 22,500 coho salmon.

Eighteen mile Creek is usually a very low, clear-running stream. After a heavy rainfall, it gets muddy, but it clears quickly. The best time to fish the stream is after a rain when the water is still up and green. Don't wait until the water has subsided and is gin clear. The best time to fish for trout in the lower portion of the stream is in the early morning and evening.

In the summer, smallmouth bass can be taken in good numbers in Eighteen Mile Creek at least as far up as the hamlet of Creekside. Rough fish such as bullheads, suckers, and carp are also available. Otherwise, fishing opportunities in the lower portion of this stream are minimal in the summer.

Access to Eighteen Mile Creek is good. There is a new pay-for-parking area near the bridge on Lake Shore Road. Further upstream the creek can be accessed by way of the Conrail tracks and the old Versailles Road bridge in North Evans. At Route 20 there is parking at the cemetery and an access road leading down to the stream. Further upstream along North Creek Road, there is an access point about 1.5 miles east of Route 20, where a road leads down to the confluence of the main and south branches of the stream.

Above Fowlerville, the headwaters of Eighteen Mile Creek are good trout water. The stream in this section averages about 5 feet in width, has a gravel and rubble bottom, and good water quality. It flows through farms and woodlands, and is fishable all season. It is open enough for fly fishing. There is a lot of posting in this area, but if you can obtain access you will find some decent fishing for wild rainbow trout and brown trout. In the headwaters there are fair numbers of brook trout, some of which are reported to be over 12 inches in length.

NOTES: ______________________________

____

____

EIGHTEEN MILE CREEK (South Branch)

Map Coordinates .... 42° 41′ 30″ 78° 54′ 00″
USGS Map(s) .... Hamburg, Langford
Township(s) .... Eden, North Collins, Concord
Access .... Jennings Road (lower section); paralleled by New Oregon Road (upper section)
Principal Species .... Brown Trout (wild), Brook Trout (wild), Rainbow Trout, Chinook Salmon, Coho Salmon

The south branch of Eighteen Mile Creek can be divided into two main sections. The first, from the mouth upstream to Route 75, is accessible from Jennings Road. It averages about 20 feet in width, has a bottom of bedrock with some pockets of gravel, and intermittent bank cover. The water in the south branch generally runs clearer than in the main branch of the stream.

There are good runs of coho salmon and chinook salmon here in the fall. Although the regulations stipulate that snagging is allowed up as far upstream as Route 75, it is doubtful that any of these fish will be able to get above the dam at Crommers Mill on Church Road. Rainbow Trout also run this stream, and will be found in good numbers from late fall through spring. The south branch of Eighteen Mile Creek is stocked annually with 12,500 steelhead and 22,500 coho salmon.

The second section of this stream, above Route 75, is partly paralleled by New Oregon Road. It averages 10 to 15 feet in width, has a bottom of gravel and rock, and very good water quality. Surrounded by farms and woodlands, there is intermittent bank cover along this section of the stream. Between New Oregon and Wyandale the stream has a lot of deep holes that hold some very big trout. There are a lot of wild rainbow trout and brown trout in the upper portion of the stream, especially above the village of New Oregon.

The headwaters of this stream are located south of Genesee Road near the hamlet of Wyandale. The stream is small here, only about 5 feet wide, but there are some decent holes. There are wild brown trout in this section, with a smattering of wild brook trout. This uppermost section is fishable all season. Posting is prevalent in this area, so access could be a problem.

NOTES: ______________________________

____

____

ELLICOTT CREEK

Map Coordinates .... 43° 01′ 16″ 78° 52′ 38″
USGS Map(s) .... Tonawanda West, Tonawanda East, Buffalo NE, Lancaster, Clarence, Corfu
Township(s) .... Tonawanda, Amherst, Cheektowaga, Lancaster, Alden
Access .... Ellicott Creek Park, Glen Park, Harris Hill Road
Principal Species .... Brown Trout, Rainbow Trout, Northern Pike, Smallmouth Bass, Panfish

Ellicott Creek is an underrated fishery. The waters below the falls in Williamsville, which can be accessed from Glen Park, provide fair to good trout fishing in the spring and fall.

Ellicott Creek is a stream with a sullied reputation. To many people, its name is synonymous with sewage, conjuring up images of an inky, foul-smelling, and nearly stagnant creek. While some sections of this stream have been heavily abused, for the most part it is a jewel in the rough.

The lower half of Ellicott Creek flows through a heavily populated area. It is wide, slow moving, and carries a heavy silt load. But its turbid waters do provide some remarkably good fishing. Northern pike are common in most of the lower creek and can be caught throughout the year. Smallmouth bass can be caught near the mouth of the creek. In the spring and fall, a surprising number of big trout from the Niagara River migrate up the creek as far upstream as the falls in Williamsville.

Above the falls in Williamsville, Ellicott Creek offers fair fishing for northern pike and panfish. Panfish and trout are occasionally stocked in the vicinity of the Island Park in Williamsville. The state is considering stocking the section of the creek between Transit Road and Stoney Road in Lancaster with trout.

NOTES: ______________________________

____

____

HOSMER BROOK

Map Coordinates .... 42° 31′ 40″ 78° 30′ 31″
USGS Map(s) .... Arcade, Sardinia
Township(s) .... Sardinia
Access .... Road crossings at Route 39 and Genesee Road
Principal Species .... Brown Trout (stocked and wild), Rainbow Trout (wild), Brook Trout (wild)

Hosmer Brook, known also as Sardinia Brook, is one of the very few high-quality trout streams in Erie County. This stream holds many wild brook trout and rainbow trout. In addition, approximately 500 brown trout yearlings are stocked in the 2-mile section between the mouth of the stream and Genesee Road every spring.

When I first started to fish this stream nearly 10 years ago, the vast majority of the fish that I caught were stocked brown trout. Only occasionally did I come across a wild brook or rainbow trout, and when I did, the fish were very small, averaging perhaps 6 inches in length.

Over the years, however, there was a gradual change in the ratio of wild to stocked fish in this stream. I was seeing more wild fish, particularly rainbows, and their size was increasing dramatically. By the summer of 1990, I was catching more wild rainbows than stocked browns, and wild fish over 12 inches were not uncommon. I mention this only because Hosmer Brook is such a fragile resource, and because there are so few streams in this area with a good population of wild rainbow trout. If you find this stream as pleasurable to fish as I do, please return the wild fish to the stream.

The following article, written by Gordy Deitrick of Trout Unlimited, explains just what is necessary to fish this fine little stream.

HOSMER BROOK

By Gordy Deitrick

Hosmer Brook is the place to go when all the other streams are bad. It is stable water, almost always clear, even when all the surrounding streams are cloudy. It holds native brook trout, and a chance for large browns in the section south of Sardinia. The stream is located about 1 mile west of Route 16 on Route 39 (or Genesee Road). It runs under the road in the village of Sardinia, where there is good fishing upstream and down. You can also start at the confluence with Cattaraugus Creek, which is located by taking a left turn in Sardinia on Savage Road and proceeding south. Hosmer Brook is just to the left (east) of the highway bridge.

The lower section of the brook up to Route 39 is primarily worm and spinning water, except of the first quarter mile, which is open.

Fish the runs and crevices, especially along the concrete retaining wall. After this first quarter mile the woods begin, with a full canopy of trees overhead and many downed trees laying across the stream. The holes are small and filled with brush. If you must fish flies, dappling is the technique to use, for backcasting is difficult at best; and even with the spinning rod, dappling a small Mepps spinner into the pockets is a good method. It's hands and knees fishing, and even then you'll spook more fish than you catch. The town is about a mile upstream, and the closer to the town you get the more open the stream and the deeper the holes. Also, the bigger the trout, with some lunkers who probably migrated upstream from the Cattaraugus. The remains of an old dam are just downstream from Route 39. It's brushy, filled with trash, and difficult to get around, but by all means fish all the pockets in the debris. The Route 39 bridge forms a sort of dam, with a falls and a pool just below, which is always heavily stocked and may also contain a large migrating brown.

Upstream from the Route 39 bridge, the stream is open, old meadowland mostly, and suitable for fly fishing as well as spinning. The first 100 yards upstream is the only part of the stream that is not public fishing, but it has never been posted. (Note: When fishing on this unposted property stay as close to the stream as possible and do not bother any animals that you may encounter; otherwise, you might find posted signs the next time you come around) The area is generally open, though the stream is protected by overhanging grasses and brush. Good flies are polly-wing spinners and the Poul Jorgensen style caddis nymphs. About a quarter mile upstream, the pastureland ends and the stream becomes brushier, but it can still be fly fished. Even though there's a residence on your left, you'll find plenty of trout in this area. After another quarter mile of open water, you'll hit heavy brush and another patch of woods upstream to Genesee Road. The fishing's good in the woods, with some nice deep holes, but for the spinner fisherman. Fly casting becomes almost impossible until you cross Genesee Road, about 1 mile north of Route 39.

The property immediately downstream of Genesee Road is posted on both sides (but not to the fisherman working upstream in the woods, however). The property upstream of Genesee Road is the site of an old Trout Unlimited stream improvement project. Note the willows planted by Trout Unlimited in 1975 and trimmed in 1985. Above these willows the upstream side is open pastureland and very suitable for fly fishing. Light Cahills on a summer evening at dusk may well bring you a nice rainbow, which are in this section of the stream. About a half mile upstream begins an alder swamp, and this marks, unfortunately, the upper limit of fishing on a very nice little stream.

NOTES: ____________________

____

____

HUNTER CREEK

Map Coordinates .... 42° 45′ 43″ 78° 31′ 28″
USGS Map(s) .... East Aurora, Holland, Strykersville
Township(s) .... Wales, Holland
Access .... Road crossings at Hunter Creek Road and Warner Hill Road
Principal Species .... Brook Trout (wild)

Hunter Creek is a small tributary of Buffalo Creek. It averages about 10 feet in width, has a rock and gravel bottom, and flows through woodlands and pastures. There is quite a bit of overhanging vegetation, providing lots of cover for the small brook trout that are found here.

NOTES: ____________________

____

____

LITTLE BUFFALO CREEK

Map Coordinates .... 42° 53′ 21″ 78° 38′ 37″
USGS Map(s) .... Lancaster, Clarence, East Aurora, Cowelsville
Township(s) .... Lancaster, Elma, Marilla
Access .... Route 354
Principal Species .... Brown Trout (stocked)

Little Buffalo Creek averages 10 to 15 feet in width and has a gravel and silt bottom. It flows through farmland and residential areas. With the exception of the stocked section, there is a lack of bank cover on this stream, and as a result it tends to get too warm to fish in the summer months. But there are some big holes on this stream that produce well in the early part of trout season. Until recent years there was a lot of posting on this stream, but much of the posting has been lifted.

In the fall, 2,000 brown trout yearlings are stocked in Little Buffalo Creek in the 7-mile section from one-half mile below Williams Street in Lancaster upstream to one-half mile above the village of Marilla.

NOTES: ____________________

____

____

Hosmer Brook is one of the finest trout streams in Erie Country. Its deep, clear pools and cold, spring-fed waters provide habitat for large numbers of stocked brown trout and wild rainbow trout.

LITTLE SISTER CREEK

Map Coordinates .... 42° 40′ 06″ 79° 03′ 46″
USGS Map(s) .... Angola, Eden
Township(s) .... Evans
Access .... Most easily approached by boat from Lake Erie
Principal Species .... Brown Trout, Rainbow Trout, Chinook Salmon Coho Salmon

Little Sister Creek, like Delaware and Muddy creeks, is now so heavily posted that it is virtually inaccessible to shore-bound fishermen. Fishing now is restricted to boat fishing off the stream mouth in lake Erie, and it can be quite productive. If rainfall has been sufficient, there are fair to good runs of salmon up this stream in the fall, and good runs of trout in the fall and spring.

NOTES: ________________________________

____

____

MUDDY CREEK

Map Coordinates .... 42° 37′ 31″ 79° 05′ 44″
USGS Map(s) .... Angola, Eden
Township(s) .... Evans
Access .... Most easily approached by boat from Lake Erie
Principal Species .... Brown Trout, Rainbow Trout, Chinook Salmon Coho Salmon

For all practical purposes, Muddy Creek is inaccessible to fishermen due to heavy posting. This is unfortunate, because if there has been sufficient rainfall, this stream gets a fair run of salmon in the fall, and good runs of trout in the fall and spring. All of these fish can run as far up as the headwaters of the stream. Although not as productive as Delaware, Little Sister, or Big Sister Creeks, boat fishing near the mouth of Muddy Creek in Lake Erie can result in some good catches of trout and salmon.

NOTES: ________________________________

____

____

BLACK NOSE DACE

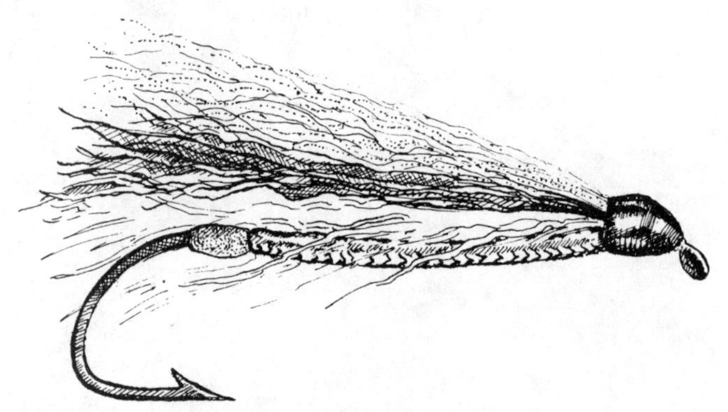

This popular pattern imitates the dace and shiners common to many of the waters in western New York.

MURDER CREEK

Map Coordinates .... 43° 04′ 53″ 78° 31′ 06″
USGS Map(s) .... Wolcottsville, Akron, Corfu, Alexander
Township(s) .... Newstead
Access .... Paralleled by Route 93
Principal Species .... Walleye, Northern Pike, Panfish

Murder Creek is a small tributary of Tonawanda Creek. It is best known as the stream that flows through Akron Park. Between the village of Akron and the confluence with Tonawanda Creek, this stream harbors a fair number of walleye, some of which reach a very respectable size. The stream also holds a limited number of northern pike.

NOTES: ________________________________

____

____

SMOKE CREEK

Map Coordinates .... 42° 48′ 40″ 78° 51′ 50″
USGS Map(s) .... Buffalo SE, Orchard Park, Colden
Township(s) .... Lackawanna, Orchard Park
Access .... Probably best approached by boat from Lake Erie
Principal Species .... Walleye, Smallmouth Bass

The rocky shoal at the mouth of Smoke Creek is one of the principal spawning grounds for walleye in the eastern basin of Lake Erie. A significant number of these fish find their way into the stream, and many are still there after the season opens. Smallmouth bass also move into Smoke Creek in the late spring and early summer, providing a fair fishery after bass season opens. Few of the walleye and bass will move further upstream than the crossing at Route 62.

NOTES: ________________________________

____

____

SPICER CREEK

Map Coordinates .... 43° 01′ 31″ 78° 53′ 39″
USGS Map(s) .... Tonawanda West, Buffalo NW
Township(s) .... Grand Island
Access .... East River Road
Principal Species .... Northern Pike, Bullhead, Panfish

Spicer Creek is primarily a spring spawning ground for northern pike, bullhead, and a limited number of crappies. Fishing in the spring can be quite good, and bullhead can be taken all summer from the creek mouth at night. Because much of the stream is surrounded by swamps, access to the stream mouth is best achieved by boat.

NOTES: ________________________________

____

____

SPOONER CREEK

Map Coordinates .... 42° 29′ 09″ 78° 43′ 03″
USGS Map(s) .... Ashford Hollow, Springville
Township(s) .... Concord
Access .... There is an impromptu pull-off and parking area on Route 39 approximately 1 mile west of Springville.
Principal Species .... Rainbow Trout

Spooner Creek, which is known locally as Spooner Gulf, is a small tributary of Cattaraugus Creek. Averaging about 10 feet in width, most of the stream is gravel bottomed, except in the lower sections were there is a considerable amount of silt. This is a very well-watered stream, and the pools upstream of Concord Road are every bit as big and deep as those below Route 39. The water here generally runs clear, especially above Concord Road. But steady rains or snow melt will bring in silt and clay from tributaries, and it will take several days for the lower sections of the stream to clear up. Spooner Creek runs through a wooded area, but the bank cover along the stream is intermittent at best, and most of the stream can be fly fished. Much of the stream is posted; however, with the exception of the stretch that run through a private sportsmen's club (the quarter-mile section immediately above Zoar Valley Road) you can usually obtain permission to fish the stream. Downstream of Zoar Valley Road, most of the posted signs are for hunting.

The fishing in Spooner Creek is dependant on runs of fish from Lake Erie. In the fall, a few salmon will make their way into the stream via Cattaraugus Creek, but this hardly constitutes a fishery. More substantial are the runs of rainbows that occur from fall through spring. If rainfall has been sufficient, these fish can be found as far upstream as a small spillway below Trevitt Road, about 2 miles upstream of Route 39. The pool below this spillway is very popular and productive. There is no part of the stream that is unproductive, but the most popular section with local anglers is the section that flows between Trevitt Road and Concord Road. There are a lot of nice pools in this section. Although there is some posting along this stretch, most landowners will grant you permission to fish here.

One of my sources of information on the small tributaries of Cattaraugus Creek, including Spooner Creek, was a gentleman by the name of Ted Newman. I first met Ted while fishing on Spooner Creek and was immediately impressed with the breadth and depth of his knowledge regarding local streams, and in his mastery of the art of fly fishing (I have seen Ted cast as many as four fly rods at once, two forward, two backward). Ted fly fishes Spooner Creek often. For the fly fisherman, he recommends brown and yellow wooly worms tied on a size 2 or 4 hook. Worms, egg sacs, and small spinners worked along an undercut bank will also take a lot of fish.

If you are prone to cabin fever in the winter, this is a good stream to keep in mind. Unless the weather has been very cold for an extended period, Spooner Creek can be fished through the winter.

NOTES: ______________________________

____

____

Many of the small tributaries of Cattaraugus Creek below the dam in Springville offer excellent fishing steelhead in the spring, often right up into their headwaters. Streams such as Coon Brook, Derby Brook, and Spooner Creek should not be overlooked. The stream pictured here is Spooner Creek.

SPRING BROOK

Map Coordinates	42° 28′ 48″ 78° 41′ 06″
USGS Map(s)	Ashford Hollow, Springville
Township(s)	Concord
Access	Road crossing at North Street in Springville
Principal Species	Brook Trout (wild), Brown Trout (stocked)

Spring Brook is a small, high-quality tributary of Cattaraugus Creek. It averages 6 to 10 feet in width and has a gravel and silt bottom. The stream is watered primarily by springs, which supply it with a good flow of water all year, even in dry summer months. The stream usually runs clear; nothing short of a flash flood after a heavy rain will muddy it. The surroundings are a mix of farms, woodlands, and residential areas, and part of the stream flows right through the village of Springville. Bank cover is intermittent, but many sections are open enough to fly fish.

Spring Brook is fishable from its junction with Cattaraugus Creek upstream to Middle Road. Above Middle Road the stream flows through swamps and is too difficult to access. Most of the stream is not posted, and residents don't seem to mind fishermen. However, it is heavily posted just downstream of Middle Road. You must get permission from the farmer to fish on that section, but it could be worth your while. There are rumors of some very large brook trout in that section.

The most popular stretch of the stream with local fishermen is between Cattaraugus Creek and North Street. Above the spillway in Springville, there are good numbers of wild brook trout, while below the spillway are numerous big browns that migrate up from Cattaraugus Creek. The stream is above the Springville Dam, so there aren't any runs of trout or salmon from Lake Erie.

Spring Brook is a unique and fragile resource. To preserve the quality of fishing on this stream, you should consider releasing the wild brook trout that you catch here.

NOTES: ______________________________

____

____

WOODS CREEK

Map Coordinates	43° 03′ 45″ 78° 58′ 37″
USGS Map(s)	Tonawanda West
Township(s)	Grand Island
Access	East River Parkway
Principal Species	Northern Pike, Largemouth Bass, Bullhead, Carp, Panfish

The lower end of Woods Creek is one of the few remaining spawning sites for northern pike in the Niagara River. The stream also has a large resident population of northern pike. Large numbers of bullhead and carp spawn here in early spring, providing excellent fishing in March and April. In addition, rock bass, yellow perch, and smallmouth bass can be caught near the mouth of the stream in the summer.

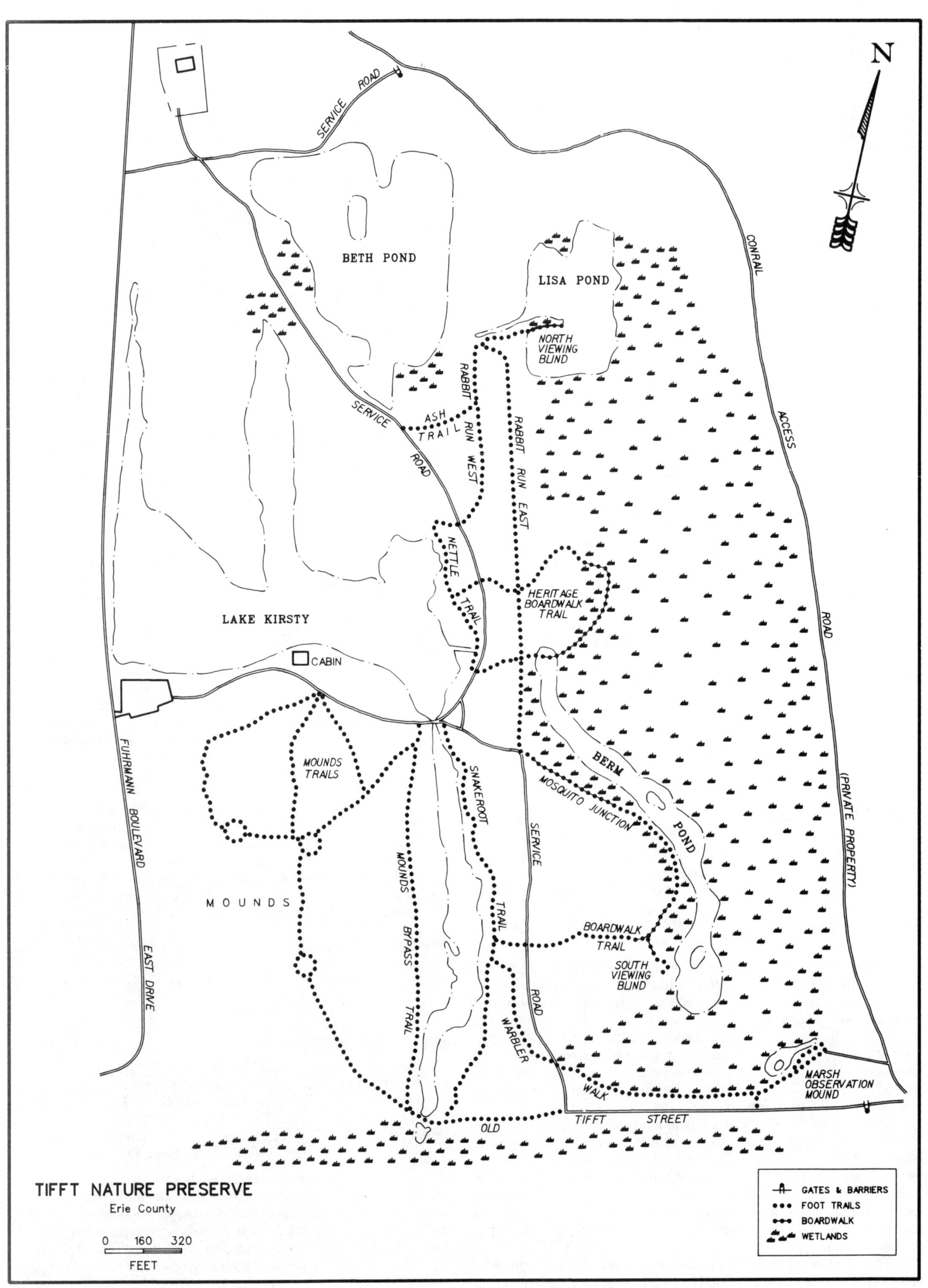
N
SERVICE ROAD
BETH POND
LISA POND
NORTH VIEWING BLIND
CONRAIL
ACCESS
ROAD
(PRIVATE PROPERTY)
RABBIT RUN WEST
RABBIT RUN EAST
ASH TRAIL
SERVICE ROAD
NETTLE TRAIL
HERITAGE BOARDWALK TRAIL
LAKE KIRSTY
CABIN
BERM POND
MOSQUITO JUNCTION
MOUNDS TRAILS
SNAKEROOT TRAIL
SERVICE ROAD
FUHRMANN BOULEVARD
EAST DRIVE
MOUNDS
MOUNDS BYPASS TRAIL
BOARDWALK TRAIL
SOUTH VIEWING BLIND
WARBLER WALK
MARSH OBSERVATION MOUND
OLD TIFFT STREET
TIFFT NATURE PRESERVE
Erie County
0 160 320
FEET
GATES & BARRIERS
FOOT TRAILS
BOARDWALK
WETLANDS

ERIE COUNTY LAKES AND PONDS

LASALLE LAKE

Location

Map Coordinates	43° 00′ 07″ 78° 46′ 37″
USGS Map(s)	Buffalo NE
Township(s)	Amherst
Access	Frontier Road

Physical Characteristics

Area	Approximately 30 acres
Shoreline	2 miles
Elevation	572 feet
Maximum Depth	18 feet
Mean Depth	6 feet
Bottom Type	Bedrock, silt

Chemical Characteristics

Water	Clear
pH	Alkaline
Oxygen	Good

Plant Life

Extensive weed beds are found throughout the larger lake. The smaller lake is ringed with a weedline.

Species Information

Largemouth Bass	Common; growth rate good
Smallmouth Bass	Uncommon; growth rate fair
Northern Pike	Uncommon; growth rate fair
Black Crappie	Common; growth rate good
Bluegills	Abundant; growth rate poor

Boat Launch Sites

Boating on both lakes is strictly prohibited.

General Information

Lasalle Lake and its small companion lake were developed as a means to drain the low-lying land where the north campus of the State University of New York at Buffalo is located. Despite their small size, both lakes offer good fishing for largemouth bass and panfish. Situated in a park-like setting, this is an ideal place to take children for a afternoon of fishing.

Access to the lakes is limited to the shore. Boating, wading, and ice fishing are forbidden.

NOTES: ______________________________

TIFFT NATURE PRESERVE

Location

Map Coordinates	42° 50′ 36″ 78° 51′ 06″
USGS Map(s)	Buffalo SE
Township(s)	Buffalo
Access	Fuhrmann Boulevard

Physical Characteristics

Area	11.8 acres (Lake Kirsty)
Shoreline	1.5 miles
Elevation	571 feet
Maximum Depth	8 feet
Mean Depth	Not available
Bottom Type	Muck

Chemical Characteristics

Water	Slightly turbid
pH	Alkaline
Oxygen	Good throughout Lake Kirsty

Plant Life

Weeds are found throughout Lake Kirsty.

Species Information

Northern Pike	Common; growth rate unknown
Largemouth Bass	Common; growth rate unknown
Yellow Perch	Common; growth rate unknown

Also available are suckers, freshwater drum, bullhead, and panfish.

Boat Launch Sites

Boating on Lake Kirsty is prohibited.

General Information

The Tifft Nature Preserve is a unique wetland tract located in the City of Buffalo and administered by the Buffalo Museum of Science. It offers such outdoor activities as bird-watching, hiking, snowshoeing, and picnicing.

Fishing in the preserve is restricted to the west, south, and east shoreline of Lake Kirsty. This lake is connected to Lake Erie and nearly every species of fish found in Lake Erie, with the probable exception of trout and salmon, can be caught in Lake Kirsty.

NOTES: ______________________________

Lasalle Lake, which is located entirely on the north campus of the State University of New York at Buffalo, offers good fishing for bass and panfish. Situated in a large park-like setting, this is an ideal location for teaching children the pleasures of fishing.

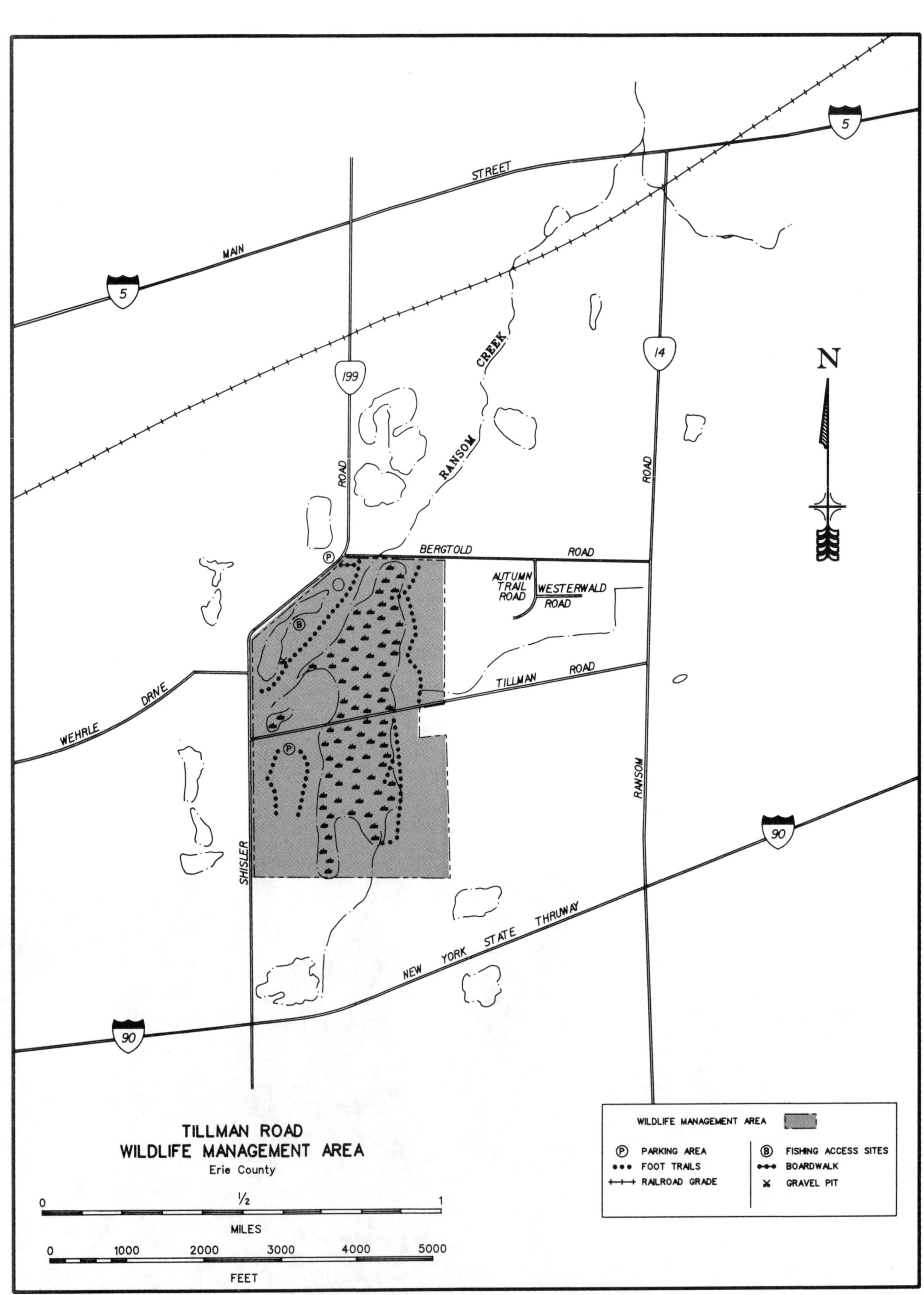
MAIN
STREET
5
5
199
ROAD
14
ROAD
RANSOM CREEK
N
BERGTOLD
ROAD
AUTUMN TRAIL ROAD
WESTERWALD ROAD
TILLMAN
ROAD
WEHRLE
DRIVE
SHISLER
RANSOM
90
90
NEW
YORK
STATE
THRUWAY
TILLMAN ROAD
WILDLIFE MANAGEMENT AREA
Erie County
0
½
1
MILES
0
1000
2000
3000
4000
5000
FEET
WILDLIFE MANAGEMENT AREA
PARKING AREA
FOOT TRAILS
RAILROAD GRADE
FISHING ACCESS SITES
BOARDWALK
GRAVEL PIT

TILLMAN ROAD WILDLIFE MANAGEMENT AREA

Location

Map Coordinates .... 42° 29′ 18″ 78° 27′ 30″
USGS Map(s) .... Clarence
Township(s) .... Clarence
Access .... Wehrle Drive

Physical Characteristics

Area .... 235 acres
Shoreline .... 1 mile
Elevation 635
Maximum Depth .... Not available
Mean Depth .... Approximately 4 feet
Bottom Type .... Sand, muck

Chemical Characteristics

Water .... Clear
pH .... Alkaline
Oxygen .... Good in all the ponds

Plant Life

Weed beds are extensive, choking much of the ponds.

Species Information

Largemouth Bass .... Common; growth rate fair
Pumpkinseeds .... Abundant; growth rate good

Boat Launch Sites

Boating is prohibited without written permission of the DEC.

General Information

This 235-acre parcel of land was acquired by the state in 1977. Its diverse habitat is comprised of emergent marsh, open water, deciduous swamp, and hardwood forest. The most distinguishing feature of the area is an 80-acre cattail marsh that attracts large numbers of migrating birds in the spring and fall.

Tillman Road offers a wide variety of recreational uses including bird watching, hiking, cross-country skiing, and fishing. The fishing is limited to several small ponds along Wehrle Drive. Don't be fooled by the size of the smaller ponds. They all hold fish. If you do fish here, consider returning the fish to the water. Otherwise, these ponds could be fished out in a few years. Use of a boat on these ponds without permission of the DEC is prohibited.

NOTES: ____________________

In addition to the larger lakes in the county, the following small ponds, which are located in municipal parks, are stocked each year with varying types of panfish. These ponds provide recreational fishing opportunities for children.

COMO PARK LAKE

Map Coordinates .... 42° 53′ 21″ 78° 39′ 31″
USGS Map(s) .... Lancaster
Township(s) .... Lancaster
Access .... Pardee Road
Principal Species .... Panfish

This 8-acre lake is stocked each year with 2,000 panfish.

NOTES: ____________________

DELAWARE PARK LAKE

Map Coordinates .... 42° 56′ 06″ 78° 51′ 48″
USGS Map(s) .... Buffalo NE
Township(s) .... Buffalo
Access .... Elmwood Avenue
Principal Species .... Panfish

This 25-acre lake is stocked each year with 4,000 panfish.

NOTES: ____________________

SOUTH PARK LAKE

Map Coordinates .... 42° 49′ 45″ 78° 49′ 47″
USGS Map(s) .... Buffalo SE
Township(s) .... Lackawanna
Access .... Off Ridge Road
Principal Species .... Panfish

This 23-acre lake is stocked each year with 2,000 panfish.

NOTES: ____________________

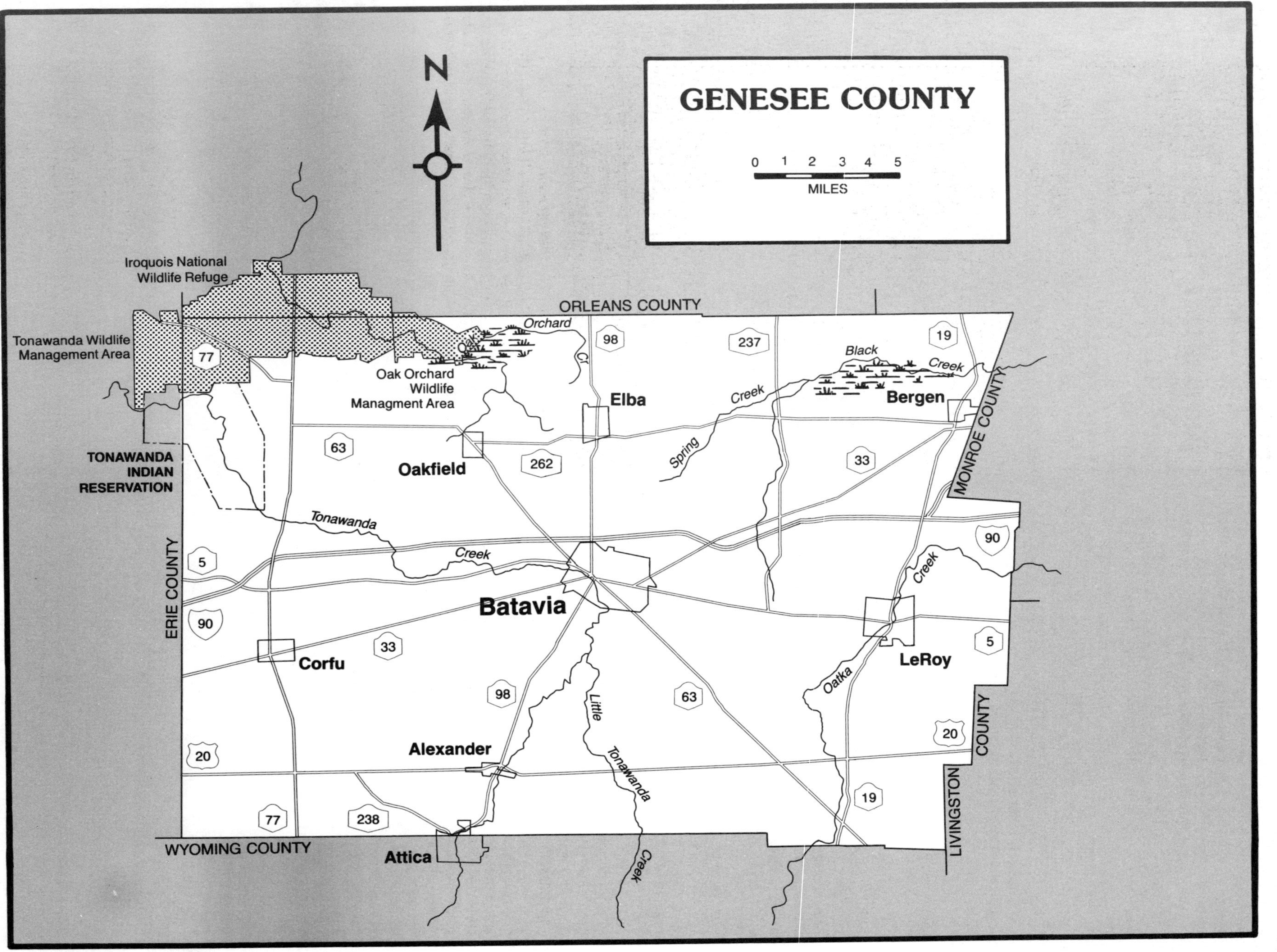

GENESEE COUNTY
0 1 2 3 4 5
MILES
N
ORLEANS COUNTY
MONROE COUNTY
LIVINGSTON COUNTY
WYOMING COUNTY
ERIE COUNTY
Iroquois National Wildlife Refuge
Tonawanda Wildlife Management Area
TONAWANDA INDIAN RESERVATION
Oak Orchard Wildlife Managment Area
Batavia
Bergen
Elba
Oakfield
LeRoy
Alexander
Attica
Corfu
Black Creek
Spring Creek
Orchard Cr
Tonawanda Creek
Little Tonawanda Creek
Oatka Creek
19
237
98
262
63
33
90
5
20
77
238

GENESEE COUNTY STREAMS AND RIVERS

LITTLE TONAWANDA CREEK

Map Coordinates .... 42° 57′ 34″ 78° 11′ 48″
USGS Map(s) .... Batavia South, Dale
Township(s) .... Alexandria, Bethany (Genesee County); Middlebury (Wyoming County)
Access .... Roughly paralleled by Dale Road
Principal Species .... Brown Trout (stocked and wild)

Little Tonawanda Creek begins in the hills north of Warsaw and flows north to join Tonawanda Creek just south of Batavia. This stream averages 12 to 15 feet in width, has a silt and gravel bottom, and good water quality. Surrounded by woodlands, open fields, and swamps, there is generally a lot of bank cover along this stream, which keeps it cool and makes it fishable all trout season. Little Tonawanda Creek and several of its tributaries flow through sections of the Carlton Hill Multiple Use Area in the township of Middlebury. The public has fishing rights on waters in the multiple use area, although obtaining access to other sections of this stream is usually not a problem. There are wild brown trout throughout Little Tonawanda Creek, especially in the Wyoming County portion. In Genesee County, where the stream can be accessed from Conway Road, the browns are fewer in number, but fish up to 16 inches were handled during an electroshocking survey conducted by the DEC.

In the spring, this stream is stocked with 800 brown trout yearlings from West Middlebury Road upstream 3.2 miles to the village of Dale.

NOTES: ____________________

OAK ORCHARD WILDLIFE MANAGEMENT AREA

Map Coordinates .... 43° 07′ 16″ 78° 17′ 30″
USGS Map(s) .... Oakfield, Knowlesville
Township(s) .... Alabama, Oakfield
Access .... Knowlesville Road
Principal Species .... Northern Pike, Panfish, Carp

The Oak Orchard Wildlife Management Area is a 2,500-acre tract of man-made and natural wetlands. Its primary function is to provide habitat to the thousands of waterfowl that stop in this region during their yearly migrations.

The area provides opportunities for outdoor activities, including hiking, hunting, cross-country skiing, and photography. The tract is drained by Oak Orchard Creek, which has a good population of northern pike, panfish, and possibly some bass. Small boats are allowed on the stream, but some restrictions apply. Check with the DEC or the refuge headquarters before boating in this area.

NOTES: ____________________

The Oak Orchard Wildlife Management Area is part of a vast wetlands complex encompassing over 19,000 acres. Though its primary purpose is to provide sanctuary for waterfowl, the area does provide fishing opportunities; northern pike, carp, and panfish are found in Oak Orchard Creek, which flows through the refuge, and in many of the area's impoundments.

SPRING CREEK

Map Coordinates .... 43° 05′ 56″ 78° 02′ 51″
USGS Map(s) .... Byron, Batavia North
Township(s) .... Byron, Elba
Access .... Transit Road (Route 78)
Principal Species .... Brown Trout (stocked and wild)

Spring Creek is a small tributary of Black Creek (see Monroe County Streams). It averages 10 to 15 feet in width, has a gravel bottom, and good water quality. Surrounded primarily by farmland, with some woodlands and swamps near Transit Road, there is intermittent bank cover on this stream. There are a few wild brown trout throughout Spring Creek, and it is probably fishable all trout season, although it is of marginal quality in the summer.

In the spring, Spring Creek is stocked with 200 brown trout yearlings from the mouth of tributary No. 3, just above Tower Hill Road, upstream to the mouth of tributary No. 7, one-half mile above Transit Road.

NOTES: ____________________

TONAWANDA WILDLIFE MANAGEMENT AREA

Map Coordinates .... 43° 06′ 41″ 78° 26′ 51″
USGS Map(s) .... Medina, Akron
Township(s) .... Royalton, Alabama, Shelby
Access .... Meadville Road
Principal Species .... Smallmouth Bass, Largemouth Bass, Walleye, Northern Pike

The Tonawanda Wildlife Management Area is located halfway between Lockport and Batavia along Route 77 in Genesee and Niagara Counties. It is bounded on the south by the Tonawanda Indian Reservation. This 5,600-acre wetland tract is the westernmost of the two state waterfowl areas.

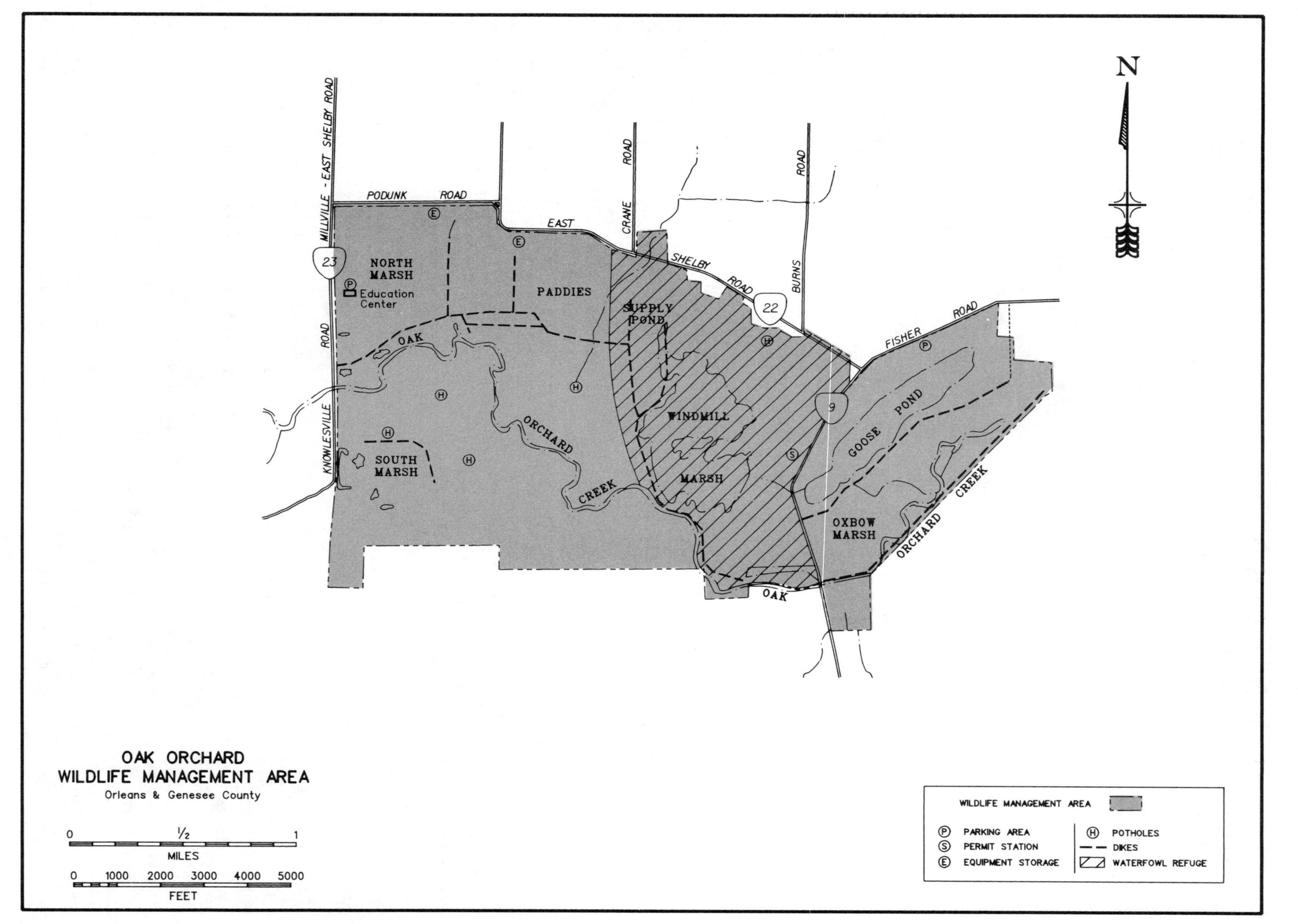
N
MILLVILLE - EAST SHELBY ROAD
PODUNK ROAD
EAST SHELBY ROAD
CRANE ROAD
BURNS ROAD
FISHER ROAD
KNOWLESVILLE ROAD
23
22
9
NORTH MARSH
Education Center
PADDIES
SUPPLY POND
WINDMILL MARSH
GOOSE POND
OXBOW MARSH
SOUTH MARSH
OAK ORCHARD CREEK
ORCHARD CREEK
OAK
OAK ORCHARD
WILDLIFE MANAGEMENT AREA
Orleans & Genesee County
0
1/2
1
MILES
0
1000
2000
3000
4000
5000
FEET
WILDLIFE MANAGEMENT AREA
P PARKING AREA
S PERMIT STATION
E EQUIPMENT STORAGE
H POTHOLES
DIKES
WATERFOWL REFUGE

Each spring, great numbers of Canada geese and ducks, including blacks, mallards, American widgeon, pintails, teal, shovelers, ringnecks, and others stop here to rest and feed before continuing north, while some remain to nest on the area. The best time to view the outstanding waterfowl concentrations is from early March through the middle of May.

Tonawanda Creek flows through a small part of the wildlife area and provides good fishing for a number of species. Walleye in the 6- to 8-pound class have been taken in this section in recent years, and 4-pound fish are not uncommon. Other species commonly found in this reach of Tonawanda Creek include largemouth bass, smallmouth bass, and northern pike. A little known secret is that rainbow trout from Lake Erie will migrate up into this area in the spring.

NOTES: ______________________________

____

____

The Oak Orchard Creek Wildlife Management Area has numerous small impoundments and channels that provide fishing for northern pike, carp, and panfish. Oak Orchard Creek also flows through the area, providing additional fishing opportunities.

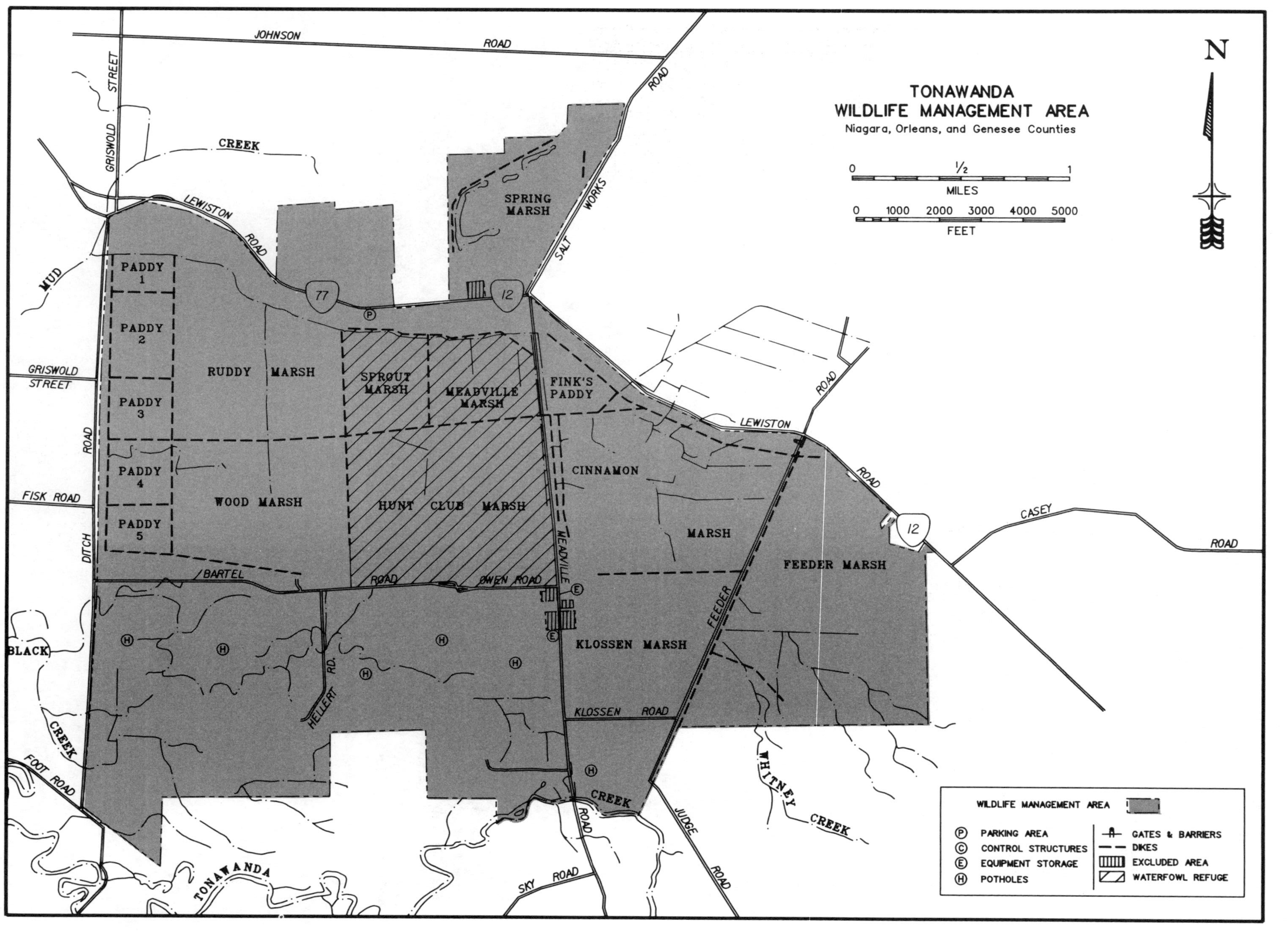
TONAWANDA
WILDLIFE MANAGEMENT AREA
Niagara, Orleans, and Genesee Counties
0
½
1
MILES
0 1000 2000 3000 4000 5000
FEET
N
JOHNSON ROAD
GRISWOLD STREET
CREEK
MUD
LEWISTON ROAD
SPRING MARSH
SALT WORKS ROAD
77
12
PADDY 1
PADDY 2
PADDY 3
PADDY 4
PADDY 5
RUDDY MARSH
SPROUT MARSH
MEADVILLE MARSH
FINK'S PADDY
WOOD MARSH
HUNT CLUB MARSH
CINNAMON MARSH
FEEDER MARSH
KLOSSEN MARSH
GRISWOLD STREET
ROAD
FISK ROAD
DITCH
BARTEL ROAD
OWEN ROAD
MEADVILLE
HELLERT RD.
KLOSSEN ROAD
FEEDER
LEWISTON ROAD
CASEY ROAD
BLACK
CREEK
FOOT ROAD
TONAWANDA
CREEK
SKY ROAD
ROAD
JUDGE ROAD
WHITNEY CREEK
WILDLIFE MANAGEMENT AREA
PARKING AREA
CONTROL STRUCTURES
EQUIPMENT STORAGE
POTHOLES
GATES & BARRIERS
DIKES
EXCLUDED AREA
WATERFOWL REFUGE

Genesee County is blessed with an abundance of natural and man-made wetlands, including wet meadows, marshlands, and wooded swamps. Most of these wetlands are located in a 20,000-acre complex consisting of the Iroquois National Wildlife Refuge, and the Tonawanda and Oak Orchard State Wildlife Management Areas. These beautiful and fragile environments are managed by the state and federal governments primarily as habitats for numerous species of migratory waterfowl. Fishing in the streams and ponds found in these wetlands is often outstanding.

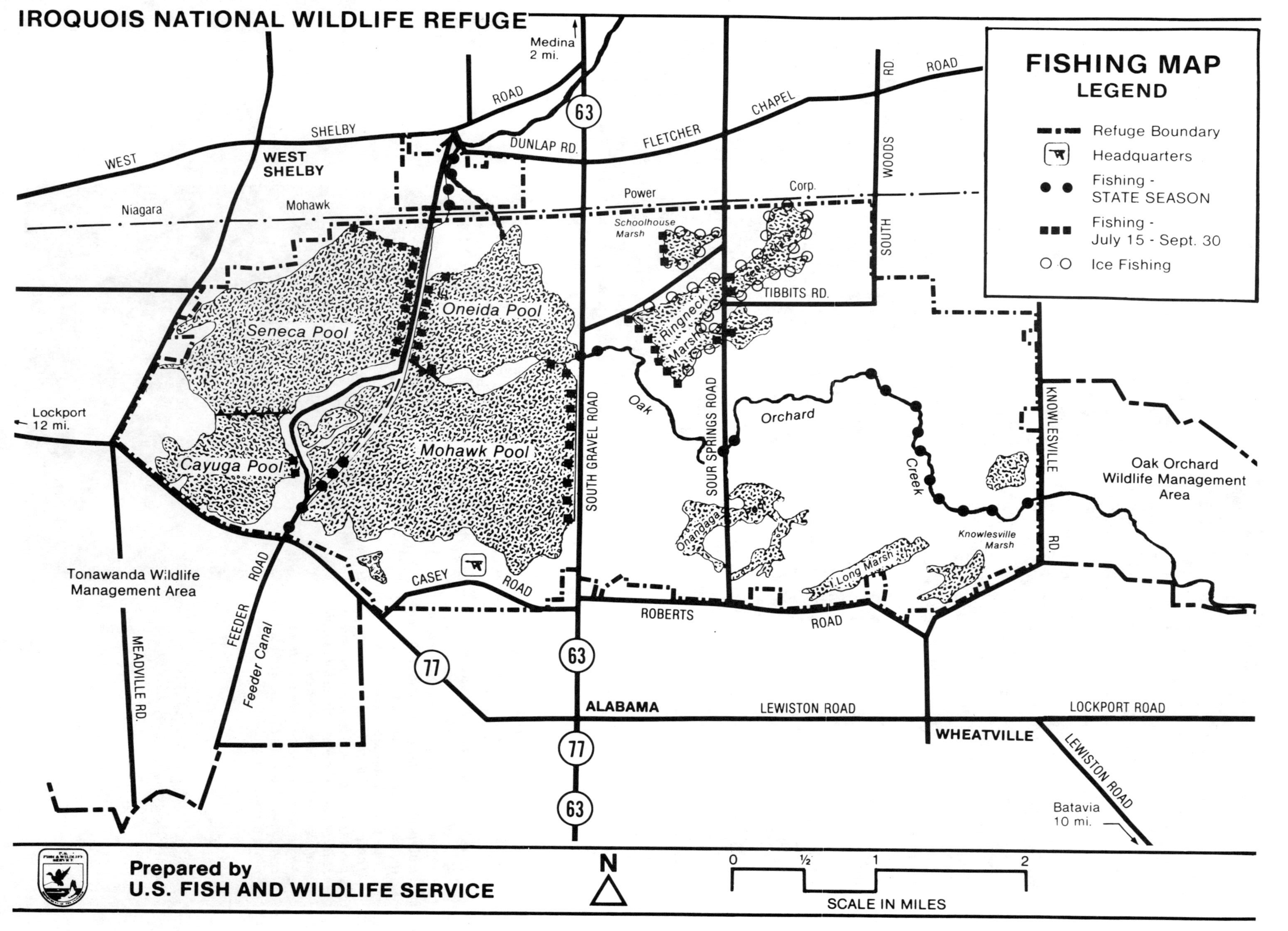

IROQUOIS NATIONAL WILDLIFE REFUGE
FISHING MAP
LEGEND
Refuge Boundary
Headquarters
Fishing - STATE SEASON
Fishing - July 15 - Sept. 30
Ice Fishing
Medina 2 mi.
Lockport 12 mi.
Batavia 10 mi.
WEST SHELBY ROAD
WEST SHELBY
DUNLAP RD.
FLETCHER CHAPEL ROAD
SOUTH WOODS RD
Niagara Mohawk Power Corp.
Schoolhouse Marsh
Ringneck Marsh
TIBBITS RD.
Seneca Pool
Oneida Pool
Cayuga Pool
Mohawk Pool
SOUTH GRAVEL ROAD
SOUR SPRINGS ROAD
Oak Orchard Creek
Onandaga Pool
Long Marsh
Knowlesville Marsh
KNOWLESVILLE RD.
Oak Orchard Wildlife Management Area
Tonawanda Wildlife Management Area
FEEDER ROAD
Feeder Canal
MEADVILLE RD.
CASEY ROAD
ROBERTS ROAD
63
77
ALABAMA
WHEATVILLE
LEWISTON ROAD
LOCKPORT ROAD
N
0 ½ 1 2
SCALE IN MILES
Prepared by
U.S. FISH AND WILDLIFE SERVICE

GENESEE COUNTY LAKES AND PONDS

IROQUOIS NATIONAL WILDLIFE REFUGE

Oak Orchard Creek (Upper Section)

Map Coordinates .... 43° 07′ 00″ 78° 23′ 00″
USGS Map(s) .... Medina, Knowlesville, Akron, Oakfield
Township(s) .... Alabama, Shelby
Access .... Bisected by Route 63 (see map)
Principal Species .... Northern Pike, Bullhead, Largemouth Bass, panfish

The Iroquois National Wildlife Refuge is a 10,818-acre area that has been set aside primarily to provide wetland habitat for migratory waterfowl. Combined with the state wildlife management units that are contiguous with the refuge (Tonawanda and Oak Orchard Wildlife Management Areas), this area, which consists of approximately 20,000 acres of marshland, wooded swampland, wet meadows, pasture, and farmland, is the remnant of what was once a large postglacial lake.

The swamps and marshes of this refuge would normally be dry between the months of April and November. However, through the use of dikes about 4,000 acres can be flooded, and water flow through Oak Orchard Creek can be maintained all year.

Fishing is allowed in the refuge, and the primary species sought here is northern pike. There are a lot of them, and some attain a respectable size. There are also bullhead and panfish here. Largemouth bass were available in good numbers in Ringneck Marsh, but a severe cold spell in the winter of 1976/1977 wiped out most of their population. Reportedly, they have made something of a comeback.

Sport fishing in the Iroquois National Wildlife Refuge is permitted on all waters designated by signs as open in accordance with specified dates. Sport fishing shall be in accordance with all applicable state regulations subject to the following special conditions:

1. All waters will be closed to fishing from 1 March through 14 July, and from 1 October through 30 November, except those portions of the feeder canal and Oak Orchard Creek designated by signs as open.
2. Ice fishing will be permitted only on Ringneck, Schoolhouse, and Center Marshes. Ice fishing will only be permitted during the period from December 15 through the last day of February.
3. With the exception of ice fishing, fishing on all refuge impoundments will be limited to posted areas on dikes and roads. No wading or swimming is permitted.
4. No boats or other flotation devices will be permitted, except that boats without motors may be used on Oak Orchard Creek from Knowlesville Road to a cable 2 miles westward. Firearms are not permitted in boats.
5. Leaving boats, structures or other equipment on the refuge overnight is not permitted.

Further general regulations designed to protect the fragile nature of the refuge include:

6. Motor vehicles, including snowmobiles, are restricted to state roadways.
7. Firearms are permitted only on open areas during hunting seasons.
8. Picking flowers, shrubs, or other vegetation is not allowed.
9. Camping, picnicing, and fires are prohibited.
10. All areas of the refuge except roads, overlooks, and designated trails are closed to the public between 1 March and 15 July - the waterfowl nesting season.
11. Refuge areas are open only from dawn to dusk.

Although the above regulations might seem somewhat restrictive, they are necessary, and they should not keep you from enjoying the experience of fishing, hunting, or hiking in this unique environment. For further information, contact:

Refuge Manager
Iroquois National Wildlife Refuge
P.O. Box 517, Casey Road
Alabama, NY 14003
Telephone: (716) 948-5445

NOTES: ______________________________

____

____

The canal that feeds the four major pools in the western half of the Iroquois national Wildlife Refuge can be accessed from a parking area off Dunlop Road near West Shelby Road. A path parallels the canal for several miles providing plenty of fishing for northern pike.

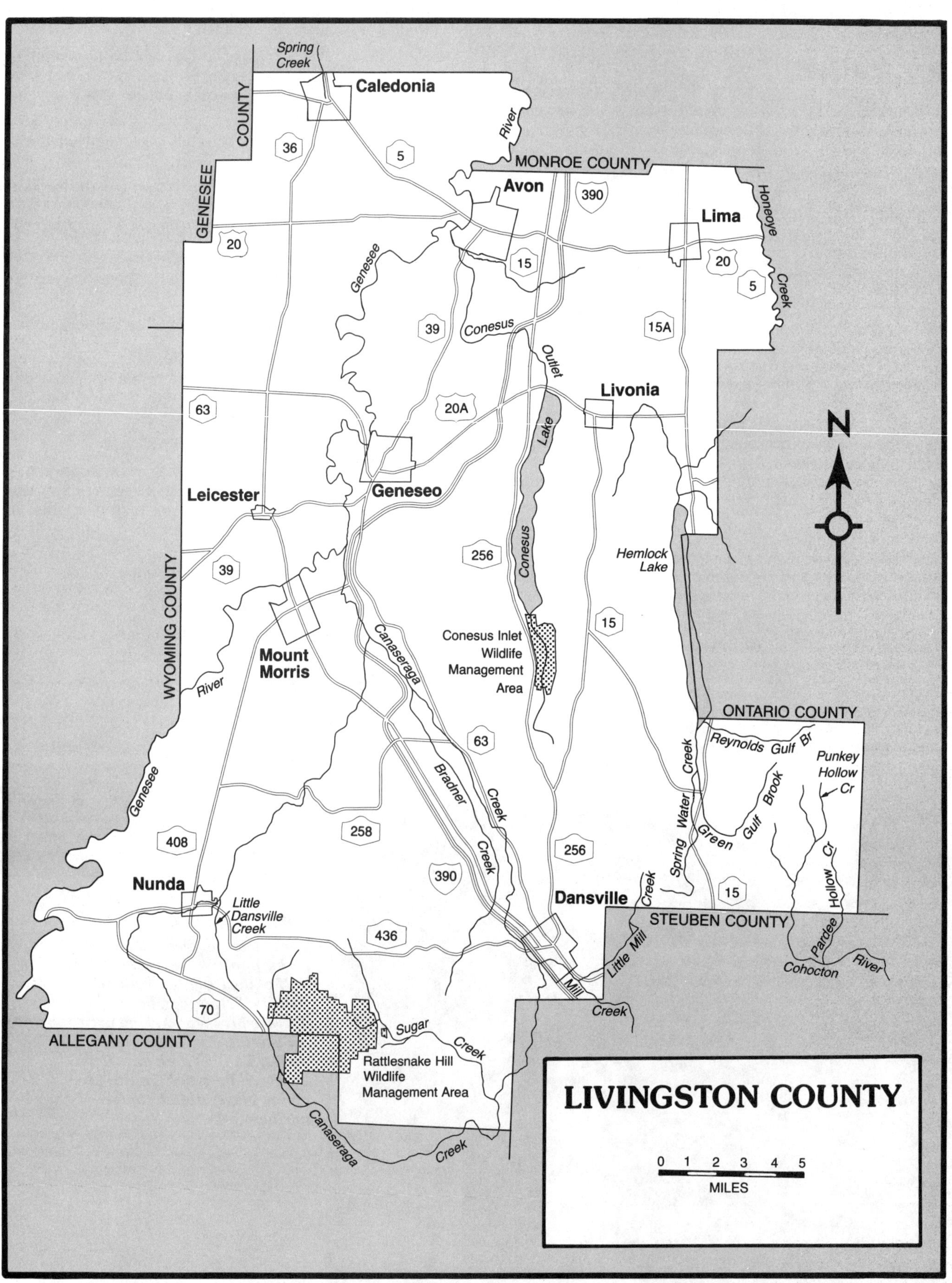
LIVINGSTON COUNTY
Caledonia
Avon
Lima
Livonia
Geneseo
Leicester
Mount Morris
Nunda
Dansville
Spring Creek
MONROE COUNTY
GENESEE COUNTY
WYOMING COUNTY
ONTARIO COUNTY
STEUBEN COUNTY
ALLEGANY COUNTY
Honeoye Creek
Conesus Outlet
Conesus Lake
Hemlock Lake
Genesee River
Canaseraga Creek
Bradner Creek
Spring Water Creek
Reynolds Gulf Br
Punkey Hollow Cr
Green Gulf Brook
Hollow Cr
Pardee Hollow
Cohocton River
Little Mill Creek
Mill Creek
Little Dansville Creek
Sugar Creek
Conesus Inlet Wildlife Management Area
Rattlesnake Hill Wildlife Management Area
N
0 1 2 3 4 5
MILES

LIVINGSTON COUNTY STREAMS AND RIVERS

BRADNER CREEK

Map Coordinates .... 42° 41′ 02″ 77° 47′ 55″
USGS Map(s) .... Sonyea, Dansville, Ossian
Township(s) .... Groveland, West Sparta
Access .... Everman Road, off Route 36
Principal Species .... Brown Trout (wild)

Bradner Creek averages 10 feet in width and has a gravel bottom and very good water quality. The bordering woodlands provide a fair amount of bank cover. This stream is fishable all trout season and holds wild brown trout throughout its length. It might also hold some wild brook trout.

Bradner Creek is not stocked.

NOTES: ______________________________

CANASERAGA CREEK

Map Coordinates .... 42° 15′ 19″ 77° 50′ 27″
USGS Map(s) .... Geneseo, Sonyea, Conesus, Dansville
Location .... Counties of Allegany, Livingston, and Steuben
Access .... Newville Road (upper section), Route 70 (stocked section)
Principal Species .... Brown Trout (stocked and wild), Largemouth Bass, Smallmouth Bass, Bullhead, Panfish

The upper reaches of this stream vary in width from 10 to 15 feet. It has a gravel, silt, and bedrock bottom, a good amount of bank cover, and is surrounded by dense woodlands. There are a lot of small wild brown trout in this section of Canaseraga Creek. The most productive seasons to fish here are the spring and fall,

Below the Rattlesnake Hill Wildlife Management Area in Allegany County and Steuben County, the stream flows through less heavily wooded areas. It tends to be muddy after a heavy rain and the stream banks are subject to considerable erosion. Near the village of Canaseraga the stream flows through a large swamp that tends to warm the stream and make it marginal habitat for trout in the summer. These swamps, however, hold a lot of largemouth bass and bullhead.

As Canaseraga Creek re-enters Livingston County, bank cover becomes more prevalent and the stream again becomes hospitable to trout. The trout are less numerous than in the upper reaches, but their size increases, and 20-inch browns are not uncommon.

From Dansville to the confluence with the Genesee River, Canaseraga Creek is primarily a warm-water stream of mediocre productivity, with northern pike and smallmouth bass making up the bulk of the fish caught. Walleye enter the lower reaches of Canaseraga Creek in the spring, and there can be some good fishing for these fish early in the season.

In the spring, the Steuben County portion of Canaseraga Creek is stocked with 2,300 brown trout yearlings. In the fall, the Allegany County portion of this stream is stocked with 2,800 brown trout fingerlings, from the Steuben County line upstream to the village of Swain.

NOTES: ______________________________

Fish are very sensitive to sound. They can detect the sound of your footstep from a considerable distance as it is transmitted from the ground to the water. However, sound is not transmitted very efficiently from air to water. Therefore, fish can not hear you talk, and whispering is unnecessary.

COHOCTON RIVER (Headwaters to Tributary 22)

Map Coordinates .... 42° 19′ 25″ 77° 18′ 00″
USGS Map(s) .... Bath, Rheims, Avoca, Naples, Wayland, Springwater
Location .... Counties of Livingston and Steuben
Access .... Paralleled by Route 36 (headwaters) and by Route 415 (stocked section)
Principal Species .... Brown Trout (stocked and wild), Brook Trout (wild), Smallmouth Bass

Originating in the hills near Tabor Corners in Livingston County, the upper Cohocton River is surrounded mainly by farmlands and swamps. It averages 10 to 15 feet in width, has a gravel and rubble bottom, and excellent water quality. There is a lot of bank cover along the Cohocton in this region, enough to make fly fishing impractical until you get below the Steuben County line.

The river is not stocked in Livingston County, but is managed as a wild trout stream. The uppermost section contains large numbers of wild brook trout. Below Scribner Road wild brown trout begin to predominate. There are several deep, productive holes on this section of the river. A partially effective brown trout barrier dam near the county line acts as a pool digger and is a genuine hot spot. Fishing pressure on the upper Cohocton is quite light after Memorial Day, as is the case with most streams in Livingston County. Trout can be taken from this portion of the river all year, any size, five per day.

Access to the upper Cohocton is facilitated by public fishing rights that extend for about one-half mile above and below Scribner Road and along Tabor Corners Road near the county line. Usually, permission to fish on private lands is granted to those who request it.

The Steuben County section of the river is stocked in the spring with a total of 10,200 brown trout yearlings, from Goff Creek, just below Avoca, upstream to the mouth of Spring Brook, near the town of Cohocton. In Steuben County trout can be taken all year, with a 9-inch minimum size limit, five per day except in the following areas:

1. From the north boundary of the U.S. Veteran's Facility upstream to the Route 415 bridge; and
2. From the north boundary of the village of Avoca upstream to the mouth of Neil Creek.

In these sections trout can be taken all year, with a 12-inch minimum size limit, three per day, using artificial lures only. Be sure to check for current regulations.

The trout section of the Cohocton River is described in the following article.

THE COHOCTON RIVER

By John Monnin

The Cohocton River, a good trout stream about 50 miles east of the Wiscoy, starts in the town of Springwater, in Livingston County, and flows southeast to Painted Post where it joins the Chemung River. Route 15 parallels the stream southward from Cohocton.

There are a number of good sections from the V.A. Hospital in Bath upstream to its source. An artificials-only section, beginning at the hospital and running upstream to Knights Brook, holds some real nice brown trout. From Avoca upstream 1.75 miles is another artificial-lures-only section, and this, along with a section in the town of Wallace, are the most popular sections of the river, both heavily stocked and heavily fished. From Wallace upstream to the town of Cohocton the fishing is spotty, with the road and rail bridges the best bets for the man who fishes salted minnows and night crawlers.

The section between Cohocton and Atlanta runs through mostly swampy ground, and one should use a boat or a canoe. Start at the railroad bridge about halfway between the two towns and work upstream to Atlanta with spinners, which are probably too deadly and should be outlawed (guess what I'm going to use when I fish the Cohocton?). Once in Atlanta, the section behind the old church is good with nymphs, especially the March Brown; and the section between River Street bridge and Beecher Road bridge is very good with night crawlers along the undercut banks. Both sections hold native brookies and stocked browns, which will rise late in the day to a Royal Coachman or a size 14 Light or Dark Cahill. There are also many native brook trout in the section upstream from Parks Road who like nothing more than a salted minnow, but will settle for a small Coachman streamer or size 14 Picket Pin fished slow and deep.

The next section is further upstream at the town of Springwater. To get there from Atlanta, go west on Route 21 from Parks Road. At the bridge where Route 21 crosses the Cohocton, turn right on County Road 37 and go upstream about one mile to a sign saying "Welcome to Springwater". There is a white house on the left, then a chicken yard where you can park. Although the stream is public fishing, access is limited by posting, so you can only get to the stream by means of the ditch by the chicken yard. It's worth the trouble, for this section produces 20-inch trout early in the season. There is a fish trap built here to keep trash fish out of the upstream brook trout spawning grounds. Fish just below the trap and the first bend above it, for though the stream is small here, these are two very good pools.

Further upstream at Scribner Road, there is more public fishing access. The stream is small, but the holes are productive - a DEC electroshocking has produced a 24-inch brown here. And if you like the tasty brook trout, here's where to get them, especially at the cemetery upstream and the old beaver dam.

Though best as a bait stream, the Cohocton does produce with flies in the evening when the sun is off the water. Try a Blue Dun wet in the swamp section, or a dry Royal Coachman at Beecher Road bridge and at the burned-down lumber yard in the south end of Atlanta. A Cahill also works well in the dusk between sunset and dark.

NOTE: The map coordinates given for the Cohocton River actually correspond to the mouth of Tributary 22, the most downstream point of the river that is classified as trout water. The map reference numbers, as well as the article prepared by John Monnin, also deal exclusively with this cold-water section of the Cohocton.

NOTES: ______________________________

____

____

CONESUS INLET FISH AND WILDLIFE MANAGEMENT AREA

Map Coordinates	42° 43′ 30″ 77° 43′ 00″
USGS Map(s)	Conesus
Township(s)	Conesus
Access	Route 256 (West Swamp Road)
Principal Species	Northern Pike, Largemouth Bass, Bullhead, Walleye, Carp, Suckers, Panfish

Located at the southern end of Conesus Lake, this area contains over 1,100 acres of swamps and open fields. It is drained by the principal inlet of Conesus Lake. The area is managed primarily as a spawning ground for northern pike and as a refuge for waterfowl.

Excellent fishing for northern pike, largemouth bass, and brown bullhead can be found in the inlet and in the southern portion of the lake. Other species that can be found here include walleye, carp, and suckers. In addition to the inlet, there are several small ponds that may provide some fishing opportunities. Fishing is allowed in this area in accordance with state fishing regulations. There are seven public parking areas on East and West Swamp Roads, as well as a public launch site for cartop boats and canoes on the north side of the management area on the west side of the inlet.

NOTES: ______________________________

____

____

GREEN GULF BROOK

Map Coordinates	42° 38′ 53″ 77° 35′ 57″
USGS Map(s)	Wayland, Springwater
Township(s)	Springwater
Access	Kellogg Road west of Route 15
Principal Species	Brook Trout (wild), Rainbow Trout (wild), Brown Trout (wild)

Green Gulf Brook, also known as Limekiln Brook, averages about 8 feet in width, has a gravel bottom, and excellent water quality.

Located at the southern end of Conesus Lake, the Conesus Inlet Wildlife Management Area provides access to the southern end of the lake and the inlet, both of which offer good fishing for northern pike, largemouth bass, and bullhead.

Surrounded by swamps, woodlands and suburban areas, it has a fair amount of bank cover.

This stream is fishable all trout season. About 1 mile above the mouth of this stream is an impassible water falls. There is a good population of wild brook trout above the falls, while below, rainbow and brown trout predominate. From early winter to spring there is a good run of rainbow trout from Hemlock Lake via Springwater Creek.

This stream is not stocked.

NOTES: ______________________________

____

____

LITTLE DANSVILLE CREEK

Map Coordinates .... 42° 34′ 55″ 77′ 55′ 25″
USGS Map(s) .... Nunda
Township(s) .... Nunda
Access .... Chidesy Road
Principal Species .... Brown Trout (stocked and wild)

Little Dansville Creek, known also as Newville Creek, averages 10 feet in width and has a gravel and rubble bottom. Bank cover on this stream is intermittent. It is surrounded primarily by woodlands.

The stream is fishable all season, although the summer months are not highly productive. There are wild brown trout throughout Little Dansville Creek, and they generally see few anglers.

In the fall, the lower 3-mile portion of this stream is stocked with 1,000 brown trout fingerlings.

NOTES: ______________________________

____

____

LITTLE MILL CREEK

Map Coordinates .... 42° 32′ 48″ 77° 40′ 57″
USGS Map(s) .... Dansville, Conesus
Township(s) .... North Dansville
Access .... Route 63
Principal Species .... Brown Trout (wild), Brook Trout (wild)

Little Mill Creek is a small tributary of Mill Creek. This stream averages about 8 feet in width. It has a gravel bottom and good water quality. Surrounded by woodlands, there is a lot of bank cover along the stream.

Fishable all season, Little Mill Creek is loaded with wild brook and brown trout. It is heavily posted but certainly worth getting permission to fish on.

Little Mill Creek is not stocked.

NOTES: ______________________________

____

____

MILL CREEK

Map Coordinates .... 42° 33′ 10″ 77° 42′ 23″
USGS Map(s) .... Dansville, Wayland
Township(s) .... North Dansville (Livingston County), Wayland (Steuben County)
Access .... Crossed by Schwarzenback Highway in Patchinville and paralleled by Michigan Road near Perkinsville - see below
Principal Species .... Brook Trout (wild), Brown Trout (wild)

Mill Creek is a little-known, very underutilized trout stream in the northwest corner of Steuben County and southern Livingston County. This relative anonymity is ironic, for Mill Creek is unquestionably one of the finest wild trout streams in the region, if not the state. Given its size, there are few streams more productive than Mill. During a recent survey, an electroshocking of a 500-foot section of the stream produced an incredible 300 trout. Not bad for a stream that only averages 10 to 15 feet in width.

The uppermost reach of Mill Creek, above the hamlet of Patchinville, is a small, wild brook trout stream flowing through remote, picturesque woodlands. This section averages only 4 to 6 feet in width, but there is a very good year-round flow of cold water, enough to sustain quite a good population of trout. The bottom consists primarily of gravel. The stream is thickly hedged by alders, making any type of fishing difficult but a little persistence will almost certainly pay off. There are very few dace or chubs in Mill Creek, so the old-fashioned method of drifting a worm, salted minnow, or very small spinner into the numerous pools or submerged root tangles will prove to be very productive for trout.

In the middle section of the stream, below Patchinville, you start picking up wild brown trout, and they quickly come to dominate the fishery. The reach of Mill Creek between Patchinville and Perkinsville is similar in characteristics to the upper reaches of the stream. However, there are some important differences. Close to Perkinsville Mill Creek is influenced by the Marlbed Ponds, warm-water impoundments that drain into the stream, resulting in the presence of some carp and suckers. This in no way affects the trout fishing. Also, there is some siltation in the stream where it runs along an old railroad grade and the water in this section is usually a little milky in color. The middle reach of the stream is a bit more open than the headwaters, averaging perhaps 10 feet in width. Most of this section is still too restricted for fly fishing, but there are a few spots where it could be done. However, much of the fishing will still involve drifting a small worm or working small spinners, and this will put you into some of the best trout fishing around. As in the headwaters, there are plenty of deep pools, submerged roots and trout, lots of trout. So many, in fact, that they generally run a little on the small size, only 8 to 10 inches (this is the reason there are no size restrictions on trout in Mill Creek). Some fish, though, do get up to a respectable 16 to 18 inches.

By the time the stream enters Perkinsville, it is exclusively brown trout water. In Perkinsville Mill Creek goes under County Road 91 and over a small falls. The pool below this falls holds some nice browns. Fish up to 5 pounds have been reportedly taken there.

Below Perkinsville the fishing is a bit easier, at least in terms of the mechanics. Mill Creek begins to widen out at this point, and although still heavily rimmed by alders and willows, there is some encroachment of the stream by farmland. Most of it is probably not open enough for fly fishing, but you could toss a spinner a short distance. This lower section of Mill Creek, from Perkinsville to its confluence with Canaseraga Creek in Dansville, is the least productive part of the stream. There is a lot of siltation in this reach and gravel areas, pools and other fish-holding areas are less frequent. This is not to say that there are not trout here, but the massive density of fish found above Perkinsville does not exist in this reach. The browns do run much larger here, so there is some compensation, and they can be found right down to the mouth of the stream.

To facilitate access to this remarkable fishery, the state has obtained 1.42 miles of public fishing easement along the stream, on the section just above Perkinsville, where it runs along Michigan Road. Also, the old railroad grade provides good access to this section of the stream. The grade parallels Mill Creek for at least one-

Polarized sunglasses enable you to see through the glare of the water's surface, a big advantage when scouting for fish or their lairs. They also protect your eyes from the harmful effects of ultraviolet radiation that reflects off the water and can cause cancer. Amber-colored lenses provide the best vision on small streams. On shallow lakes tan lenses are recommended, while grey lenses are best for deeper lakes.

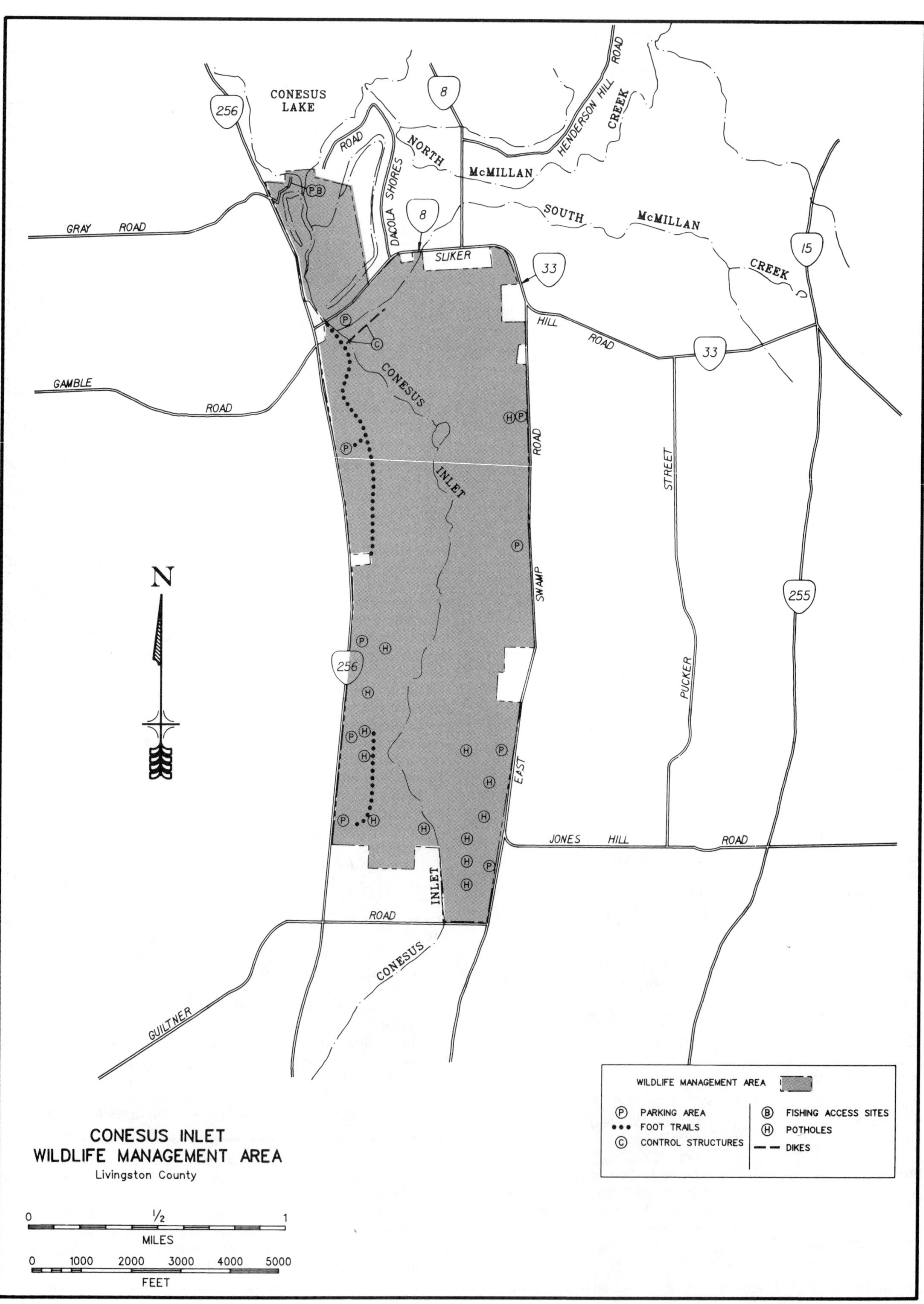
CONESUS LAKE
256
8
ROAD
NORTH
McMILLAN
HENDERSON HILL ROAD
CREEK
DACOLA SHORES
SOUTH
McMILLAN
CREEK
15
GRAY ROAD
SLIKER
33
HILL
ROAD
33
GAMBLE
ROAD
CONESUS
INLET
ROAD
STREET
SWAMP
255
N
256
PUCKER
EAST
JONES HILL ROAD
INLET
ROAD
CONESUS
GUILTNER
WILDLIFE MANAGEMENT AREA
PARKING AREA
FOOT TRAILS
CONTROL STRUCTURES
FISHING ACCESS SITES
POTHOLES
DIKES
CONESUS INLET
WILDLIFE MANAGEMENT AREA
Livingston County
0
1/2
1
MILES
0
1000
2000
3000
4000
5000
FEET

half mile starting at County Road 91, in Perkinsville. You will often have to climb down a steep hillside to get to the stream, but its the easiest way to get to some of more remote sections. You can get to the grade by walking about 200 yards downstream of County Road 91.

Mill Creek is not stocked. It is managed as a wild trout stream. Trout can be taken from this stream all year, any size, 10 fish per day. Be sure to check for current regulations.

NOTES: ______________________________

PARDEE HOLLOW CREEK

Map Coordinates .... 42° 33′ 54″ 77° 30′ 34″
USGS Map(s) .... Wayland
Township(s) .... Springwater
Access .... Miller Road
Principal Species .... Brook Trout (wild)

Pardee Hollow Creek is a high-quality trout stream that averages about 8 feet in width, has a gravel bottom and excellent water quality. Flowing through woodlands, it has a lot of bank cover and is fishable all season.

This stream is not stocked. It is managed as a wild brook trout stream.

NOTES: ______________________________

PUNKEY HOLLOW CREEK

Map Coordinates .... 42° 36′ 45″ 77° 31′ 15″
USGS Map(s) .... Wayland, Springwater
Township(s) .... Springwater
Access .... Pardee Hollow Road
Principal Species .... Brook Trout (wild)

This is a small gravel- and rubble-bottomed stream averaging about 8 feet in width. Surrounded by woodlands and fields, it has good bank cover and an unusually good volume of water.

Punkey Hollow Creek is full of wild Brook trout and is fishable all season. Unfortunately, this stream is heavily posted. Punkey Hollow Creek is not stocked.

NOTES: ______________________________

RATTLESNAKE HILL WILDLIFE MANAGEMENT AREA

Map Coordinates .... 42° 35′ 00″ 77° 51′ 00″
USGS Map(s) .... Nunda, Ossian
Township(s) .... Nunda, Ossian, Grove
Access .... Ebert Road
Principle Species .... Brown Trout (wild), Brook Trout (stocked and wild), Largemouth Bass

The Rattlesnake Hill Wildlife Management Area is a 5,100-acre tract of wilderness used by the DEC as a game management unit. A variety of woodland species, such as deer, ruffed grouse, and squirrel can be hunted here. There is limited hunting for waterfowl as well.

Of interest to fishermen are the numerous small ponds found in the Rattlesnake Hill area. Two of the deeper ponds are stocked each fall with 200 brook trout fingerlings apiece. Several other ponds contain medium-size largemouth bass. For the stream fisherman, the headwaters of Canaseraga Creek and a section of Sugar Creek are nearby and both have populations of wild brook and brown trout.

There are numerous hiking and cross-country skiing trails in the Rattlesnake Hill Management Area, and camping is allowed here (by permit).

NOTES: ______________________________

Mill Creek is one of the most productive trout streams in Western New York, but it gets little attention from area fishermen. This is due in part to its location; Mill Creek meanders through some of the more remote regions of Livingston and Steuben counties.

REYNOLDS GULF BROOK

Map Coordinates .... 42° 40′ 15″ 77° 36′ 00″
USGS Map(s) .... Springwater
Township(s) .... Springwater
Access .... Paralleled by Reynolds Gulf Road
Principal Species .... Brook Trout (wild), Rainbow Trout (wild)

Reynolds Gulf Brook averages 10 feet in width and has a gravel bottom and excellent water quality. The surrounding woodlands provide a lot of bank cover.

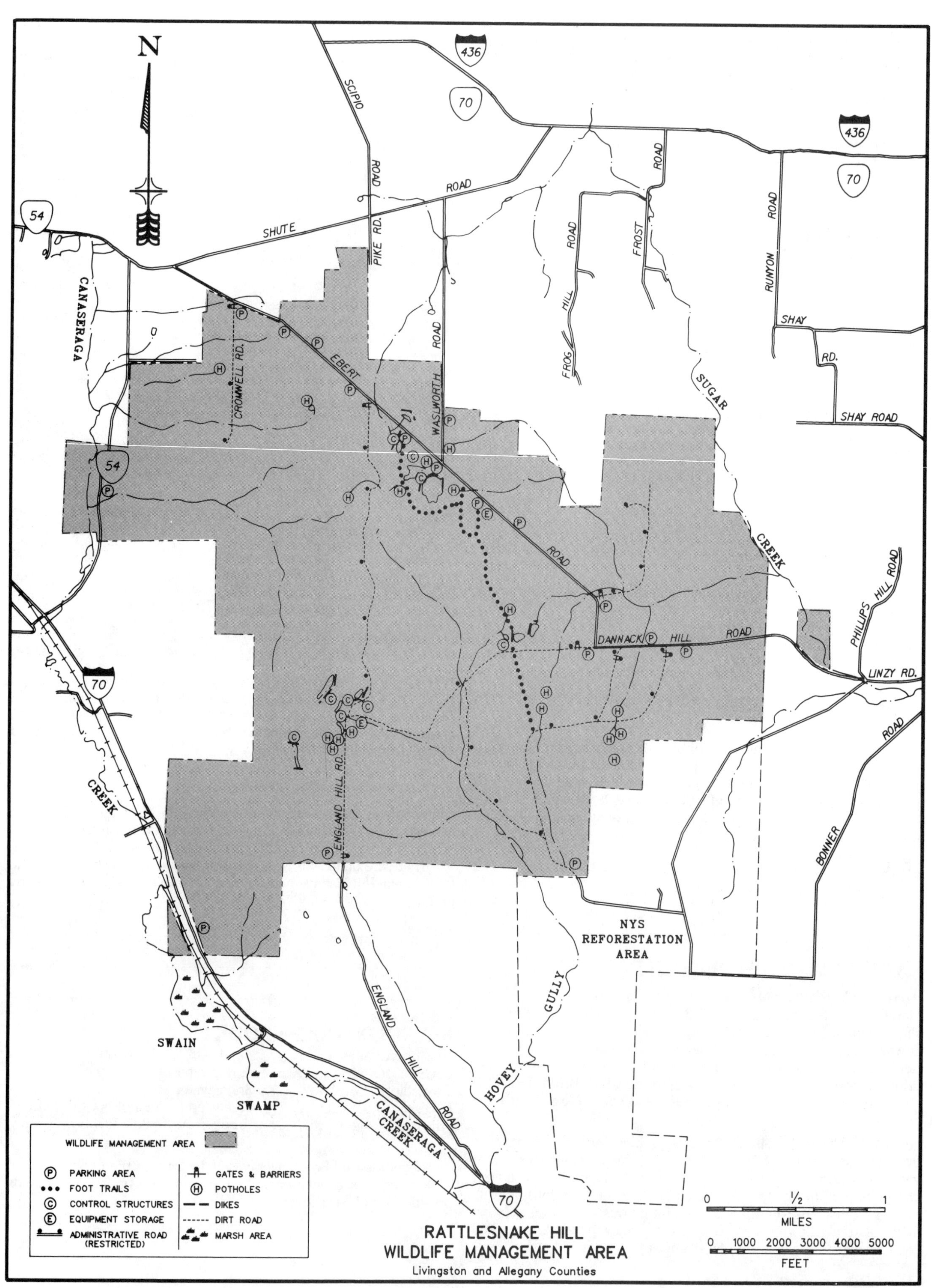

RATTLESNAKE HILL
WILDLIFE MANAGEMENT AREA
Livingston and Allegany Counties

This stream has wild brook trout throughout its length, and there is also a small run of adult rainbow trout here in the spring and fall. Reynolds Gulf Brook is usually fishable only during the early spring and fall.

This stream is not stocked.

NOTES: ______________________________

____

____

SPRING CREEK

Map Coordinates .... 43° 11′ 18″ 77° 51′ 55″
USGS Map(s) .... Caledonia
Township(s) .... Caledonia, Mumford
Access .... State Hatchery property off Route 36
Principal Species .... Brown Trout (wild), Brook Trout (wild), Rainbow Trout (wild)

Spring Creek, often referred to as Spring Brook, is the source of water for the Caledonia State Fish Hatchery. Accessible from within the town of Caledonia, this stream averages 20 to 25 feet in width. It has a limestone bottom (there is some gravel and rubble) and is fed by extremely cold springs. There is only intermittent bank cover on this stream, and as the accompanying article indicates, fly fishing is the method most often used.

Spring Creek is managed as a wild trout stream, although some hatchery fish do occasionally escape into its waters. There are tremendous numbers of wild brown trout, rainbow trout, and brook trout in this stream, and they can be taken all year, five per day, minimum size 9 inches.

There is a special regulation section on the property of the state fish hatchery where trout can be taken all year between the hours of 8:30 a.m. and 4:30 p.m., three per day, minimum size 10 inches, artificial lures only. Be sure to check for current regulations.

The following article is reprinted courtesy of Trout Unlimited.

SPRING CREEK

By Wayne Hadley

Spring Creek runs like a slightly haggard jewel through the villages of Caledonia and Mumford. Its ecology and the experience of fishing it are unlike those of any other stream in western New York. It is a limestone stream, slow-flowing, clear, and home to the most cynical trout available locally. If you wish to fish bait, fling spinning lures, or kill trout, kindly cease reading at this point. Simply put, there are already a host of fisherman dedicated to this stream, very little public access, and its trout are frequently recycled as evidenced by hook scars and imbedded flies fished on too light tippets.

If you've not fished this type of water before, go read Marinaro, Fox, or Koch. They know a whole lot more about it than I do. I'd recommend lines of 3 to 5 DTF, rods from 7 feet to 8 feet, and a single-action reel capable of yielding line smoothly to very light pressure. Leader tippets should be long, limp, and seldom larger than 5X. Flies are a matter of personal choice, but I'll give you my suggestions knowing most of you will ignore them. Think small. A size 12 is a big fly at Spring Creek.

There are four major food types I find worthwhile to imitate. Good tiers would no doubt suggest that my tying looked as though it had been plucked from my navel, but never mind. The trout occasionally oblige anyway.

The scuds, or freshwater shrimp, are a staple, most effective for me early and late in the season. Tied on short-shank salmon egg hooks (perish the thought) from size 12 to 16, weighted or unweighted, and with all fur bodies of tan, olive, or grey they catch fish. Like every other pattern here, dead drift works best. With scuds, scratch bottom and where possible fish to individual trout.

You'll learn a lot of trout behavior this way, and at least in my case, considerable humility. A local pattern called Nickel Nymph (for the hook plating, not the price) is popular in the early season and looks like a scud to me.

Two mayfly types are abundant and important. The smaller is blue- or gray-winged and about a size 18. It may hatch at any time throughout the season. I hate it. Simply because I can't catch a damn thing when it hatches. Maybe no-hackles or thorax dries would work. My nymphs are a failure for this one as well. I think the little devils swim like hell and I can't imitate them adequately, Schweibert to the contrary.

The most anticipated forage (seems like a crass way to categorize such delicately beautiful little beasts) is the Bright Fox. It hatches in May and June in numbers that overwhelm me. They're bluish- to yellow-winged, with yellowish to orangish bodies. Hooks should be size 16 to 18. Dead-drifted grayish nymphal imitations work well for me before the hatch gets too heavy. When this hatch is at its peak, I give up. Carpet, masses, hordes, zillions describe its abundance. My imitations, at least, don't stand much chance. I've sometimes honestly felt that the fish took only those flies that flapped their wings. Mine don't. The fish get exceedingly blase about feeding, but if you're desperate, frustrated, compulsive, or just damn stubborn, try dappling a damp fly. Just dangle the leader from the rod tip and float it over a riser again and again. A low way to catch a trout, but it sometimes works for me. Otherwise, quit fishing and, like me, just watch the emergence and appreciate all the beautiful things we don't know about flies and fish and fishermen. Light Cahill-hued dries pushed a little toward the yellow end of the spectrum and tied in any style but navel fuzz will take fish. I cling feverishly to a badly chewed quill-bodied emerging nymph tied on a light wire hook, the last of several given me by a Spring Creek regular. They were deadly fished just under the film, but I've never been able to match the quill colors in the body. Help gratefully accepted. My own creations work, but not nearly so well.

The fourth and last of the major food items is the midge. Big midges. Dry imitations will take fish on occasion, but mostly I like the pupae. The standard here is the Bonbright, a quill-bodied, fur-thoraxed tie on hooks from size 12 to 18. Quill colors vary, but red (yeah red) peacock quills work best for me. Tie on light or heavy wire hooks for various water depths and circumstances. A few lightly weighted with fuse wire will sometimes help reach a deep lying fish.

LIGHT CAHILL

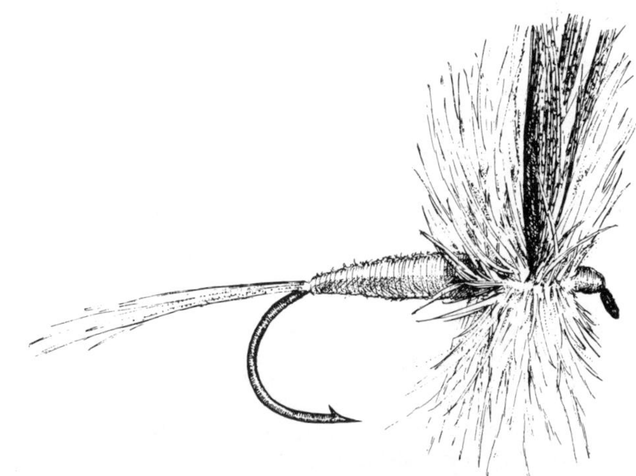

The Light Cahill is a popular dry fly that imitates many of the sulphur flies in the western New York area. By varying its size, this fly can be productive all season. Its coloration makes it especially effective just before dark.

Day in and day out, this is the fly of choice. My greatest success comes with a very dead drift and it must pass close to a feeding fish. Be patient; they'll do their part if you'll do yours. Auxiliary flies of value include all of the terrestrials. Jassids, which I suspect look a lot like adult midges, are good at times. Green inchworms can produce when they're making their suicide descents, and a beetle or ant may get you some action all through summer. Sneakily presented damsel fly nymphs snugged close to the moss beds in summer can sometimes make the day. I am not going to discuss night fishing or the use of small, somber, lightly dressed maribou streamers because they are too good for all but very honest men. Cut back that leader to 2X or more. There are some major surprises finning quietly under those moss beds.

The fish: There are browns, rainbows, and brooks here in descending order of abundance and average size, and ascending order of catchability. I'm always amazed to see how different trout species vary in susceptibility to angling. As a gross approximation, I'd say there are twenty browns here for every rainbow or brookie and about equal numbers of the latter two species (I once witnessed an electroshocking effort here). On some days I've caught nothing but brook trout. The same phenomenon can, by the way, be observed among the browns, rainbows, and cutthroats of Armstrong Spring Creek. Don't be misled: none of them are easy. Someone once said that all limestone fish were browns - intellectually. All species are in good condition and the browns will out jump any I've ever encountered. Depending on the area, sizes run from 6 inches to 15 inches, with an average around 10 inches. There are a lot of larger fish, but light tippets and abundant snags make landing one more luck than skill. Colors of all species are truly spectacular, the result I suspect of rich diet and clear water. The browns and brookies are the most vividly hued I've ever seen. Admire and release!

If by now you've noticed a lot of what and how in comparison to where, you're catching on. The very limited easy access will be self-evident. Please, this is an incredibly heavily utilized resource of high quality in a densely populated area. Do not contribute to a decrease in access currently open by rude or thoughtless behavior. Much of the small access could be closed by the stupidity of a few fishermen.

Etiquette: Place a lot of fishermen in a little space, mix well, and watch the fist fights. It isn't usually a problem here. Angler densities can be high, particularly on holidays, weekends, and any time the bright fox hatch is on. Crowding is inescapable, but can be endurable with a little common sense and consideration. On this stream location isn't important. There are fish everywhere and the ones around the bend will be no bigger or easier than the ones sipping midges under your rod tip. Wading in the weed-filled, silty water will annoy everyone downstream. Find a place that looks good, plant your feet and stay there. Within casting range are a lot more fish than you can catch.

Spring Creek is a thing of beauty, if a little frayed at the edges. And, like a lovely woman victimized by age, deserves the very gentlest handling. Treat it gently; it cannot be replaced.

NOTES: ______________________________

____

____

GOLD-RIBBED HARE'S EAR (nymph)

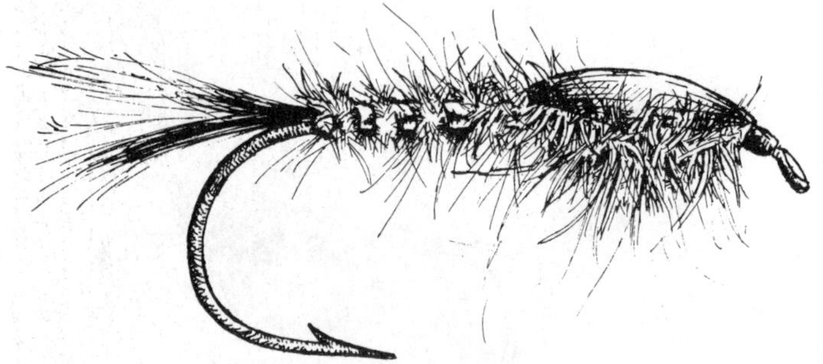

Imitating numerous types of insects, the Gold-Ribbed Hare's Ear nymph pattern can be fished effectively almost anywhere. It will attract bass and panfish as well as trout.

GRAY GHOST

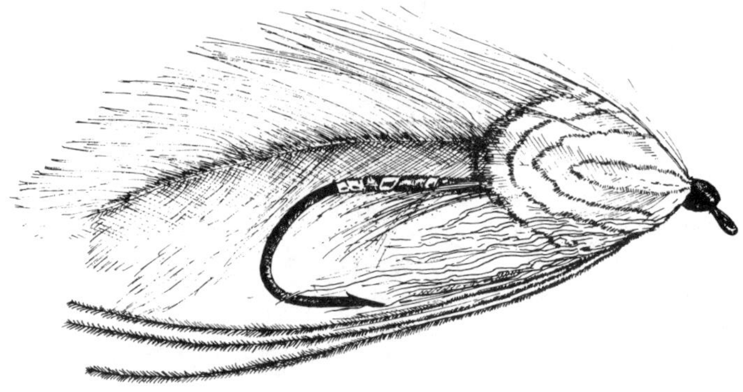

The Gray Ghost is a pale imitation of the emerald shiner, which is found in many of the waters of western New York. Commonly used to catch trout, it is also a good pattern for bass when tied on a larger hook. This pattern will produce well through most of the daylight hours.

SPRINGWATER CREEK

Map Coordinates	42° 40′ 05″ 77° 36′ 03″
USGS Map(s)	Springwater, Wayland
Township(s)	Springwater
Access	Kellogg Road
Principal Species	Brook Trout (wild), Rainbow Trout (wild)

Springwater Creek averages 12 to 15 feet in width and has a gravel bottom and excellent water quality. Surrounded primarily by woodlands, there is extensive bank cover on this stream.

The upper portion of Springwater Creek is also known as Pokamoonshine Hollow Creek and is accessible from Pokamoonshine Road. It is similar to the lower sections of the stream. It is full of wild brook trout and is fishable all season.

Springwater Creek itself has a healthy population of rainbow trout and there is a good spawning run of these fish in the early spring and in the fall. The most productive method for taking these rainbows is fishing with egg sacs. The state owns extensive public fishing rights on this stream, from Kellogg Road to just above Depot

Road, with a few intermittent exceptions. Fishing is allowed on Springwater Creek from Kellogg Road to Hemlock Lake by permit only, which is free and can be obtained by sending a self-addressed, stamped envelope to:

City of Rochester
Department of Environmental Services
Bureau of Water
10 Felix Street
Rochester, NY 14608

NOTES: ______________________________

____

____

SUGAR CREEK

Map Coordinates .... 42° 29′ 06″ 77° 44′ 00″
USGS Map(s) .... Arkport, Dansville, Ossian
Township(s) .... Ossian
Access .... Linzy Road
Principal Species .... Brown Trout (stocked), Brook Trout (wild)

Sugar Creek averages 10 to 12 feet in width and has a predominantly gravel bottom and excellent water quality. This tributary of Canaseraga Creek is surrounded by woodlands and there is extensive bank cover for most of its length.

There are wild brook trout throughout this stream, and it is fishable all season. In the fall, the lowermost 2-mile section of Sugar Creek is stocked with 1,100 brown trout fingerlings.

NOTES: ______________________________

____

____

The Rattlesnake Hill Wildlife Management Area has numerous small ponds connected by a series of rails. Several of these ponds are stocked by the state with brook trout, and most of the larger ponds contain brown trout and bass.

LIVINGSTON COUNTY LAKES AND PONDS

CONESUS LAKE

Location

Map coordinates .... 42° 47′ 12″ 77° 43′ 00″
USGS Map(s) .... Livonia, Conesus
Township(s) .... Conesus, Geneseo, Groveland, Livonia
Access .... Paralleled by East Lake Road (County Road 8) and West Lake Road (Route 256)

Physical Characteristics

Area .... 3,420 acres
Shoreline .... 18.47 miles
Elevation .... 818 feet
Maximum Depth .... 69 feet
Mean Depth .... 38 feet
Bottom Type .... Muck, gravel, and sand
Mean Thermocline .... 36 feet

Chemical Characteristics

Water Clarity .... Clear
pH .... Alkaline
Oxygen .... Good throughout the lake except during the summer in water below the thermocline

Plant Life

There are significant weed beds in the northern end of the lake to a depth of about 15 feet. Weed beds are also present in the southern end of the lake to 15 feet. There are sporadic patches of weed in all of the major bays and coves. There is a slight problem with algae blooms here in the late summer.

Boat Launch Sites

1. Bob's Bait and Tackle at Lakeville Road and Route 15. Private launch for small boats rented at Bob's Bait and Tackle.

2. New York State launch site off East Lake Road, just south of McPherson Point. Hard-surface launch ramps, two floating docks, and parking for 70 cars and trailers. This is the principal launch site on the lake - no charge.

3. Leisure Time Marina, 2365 East Lake Road, Conesus. Private trailer launch ramp, marine supplies, boat rentals, gas - fee.

4. New York State fishermen access site off Route 256 at the southern end of the lake. Hand launching for cartop boats and canoes, parking for 40 cars - no charge.

5. A state-maintained parking area and launch site for cartop boats and canoes has been constructed on the outlet on the north end of the lake south of Route 20A. This site is also meant to serve as a public access point for ice fishing.

Species Information

Note: In the early 1980s, alewives were introduced into Conesus Lake. Shortly thereafter, their population exploded and they are now the dominant fish species in the lake. Their dominance of the lake has resulted in a number of significant changes in the biology of the lake. First and foremost is the affect this has had on the yellow perch population. Until recently, Conesus was one of the top yellow perch lakes in the state. The winter harvest alone was estimated to be in excess of 175,000 fish per year. The alewives wiped out an important forage base for the perch, a crustacean known as Daphnia pulex. The immediate effect of this has been to greatly slow down the growth rate of the yellow perch. Most of the perch taken here now are emaciated. In addition, although it is not known for sure, there is a very good possibility that the alewives are feeding on the perch fry, thereby reducing the actual numbers of yellow perch that survive to enter the fishery (it was just such a situation that so greatly depressed the perch fishing in Lake Ontario).

Another result of the presence of alewives in Conesus Lake concerns the abundance of plankton. Before the alewives took over, the population of plankton was kept in check by the large population of Daphnia pulex. Now that these crustaceans have been eliminated, Conesus Lake is generally less clear than in previous years (to see how this factor can affect your choice of tackle see the sections on smallmouth bass and largemouth bass), and it is experiencing slightly more significant algae blooms in the late summer. This hasn't greatly affected the fishing here yet, but it could if the situation gets much worse.

The abundance of alewives in Conesus Lake is so great that it has actually impacted on the composition of terrestrial wildlife around the lake. The DEC has received reports of large numbers of gulls on the lake, feeding on dead alewives. This is indicative of the far-reaching effects that a non-native species can have on a lake. It is hoped that a point of equilibrium will be reached whereby the alewives will be kept in check by predation from such species as northern pike, largemouth bass, smallmouth bass, and walleye. Until this occurs, the only definite thing that can be said about Conesus Lake is that its species structure is in a state of severe flux.

Yellow Perch .... **Abundant; growth rate fair**

Until the invasion of alewives in the early 1980s, yellow perch were arguably the most popular fish found in Conesus Lake. Despite its relatively small size, this lake was consistently one of the top perch-producing lakes in the state.

Early in the year, right after ice-out, many anglers concentrate their perch fishing efforts on the deep narrows between Long Point and McPherson Point. This natural bottleneck has good perch habitat and serves to concentrate the schools of perch as they migrate around the lake. Another spring hotspot is the cove between McPherson Point and Old Orchard Point. This cove, in fact, is one of the most productive areas for perch on Conesus Lake, from ice-up until late June. The waters off Maple Bay also provide some early spring perch action. Later in the spring, yellow perch are known to concentrate on the outside edges of the weed beds off Walkley's Landing, along the weed beds off Eagle Point, and along the weed beds between McPherson Point and Old Orchard Point.

A popular and productive method for taking springtime perch is to anchor along the edges of dormant weed beds and still fish with worms, grubs, or minnows. The use of perch rigs (spreaders) will increase your catch considerably.

Later in the year, as the summer sun warms the waters of Conesus Lake, the perch school-up less and become much more migratory, making them decidedly harder to find. They will most often be found over hard, rocky bottoms and near structure associated with deep water. For the most part, yellow perch are taken incidentally in the summer, usually by anglers fishing for smallmouth bass with small spinners or jigs. If you're really serious about fishing for perch in the summer, check out the points, especially on the southwest side of the lake.

Between Long Point and Maple Beach there are several points running into deep water. Still fish the points with small crayfish or minnows, or use small jigs tipped with minnows. Keep moving until you find some action.

In the fall, the perch fishing picks up considerably. Yellow perch begin to move into very deep water by mid-October, and there is relatively little really deep water in Conesus Lake. Very productive areas will include the hole directly across from Cottonwood Point, the narrows between McPherson Point and Long Point, and the deep water off Eagle Point. Minnows fished close to the bottom are probably be your best bet. Again, use spreaders to take full advantage of the multitudinous perch just waiting for something to hit on.

It is in the winter that Conesus Lake earns its reputation as one of the top yellow perch lakes in the state. Standard tip-ups will work well on this lake, but the most popular method here for taking buckets full of perch is jigging. The most popular jig is the classic "Conesus Jig" either in silver or copper. These are available from local tackle shops. Other standard ice fishing jigs, such as the red or white Russian jig or the Swedish pimple, are also effective. Tipping the jig with a mousey grub, an oak leaf grub, or a perch eye will increase your chances of success. Keep moving and changing jigs until you locate a school and then get ready for some real action.

There is a general tendency for yellow perch to move into increasingly deeper waters in the fall and winter. However, there is a short period in the early winter when the perch are going to be found in the shallow portions of the lake in 10 to 20 feet of water.

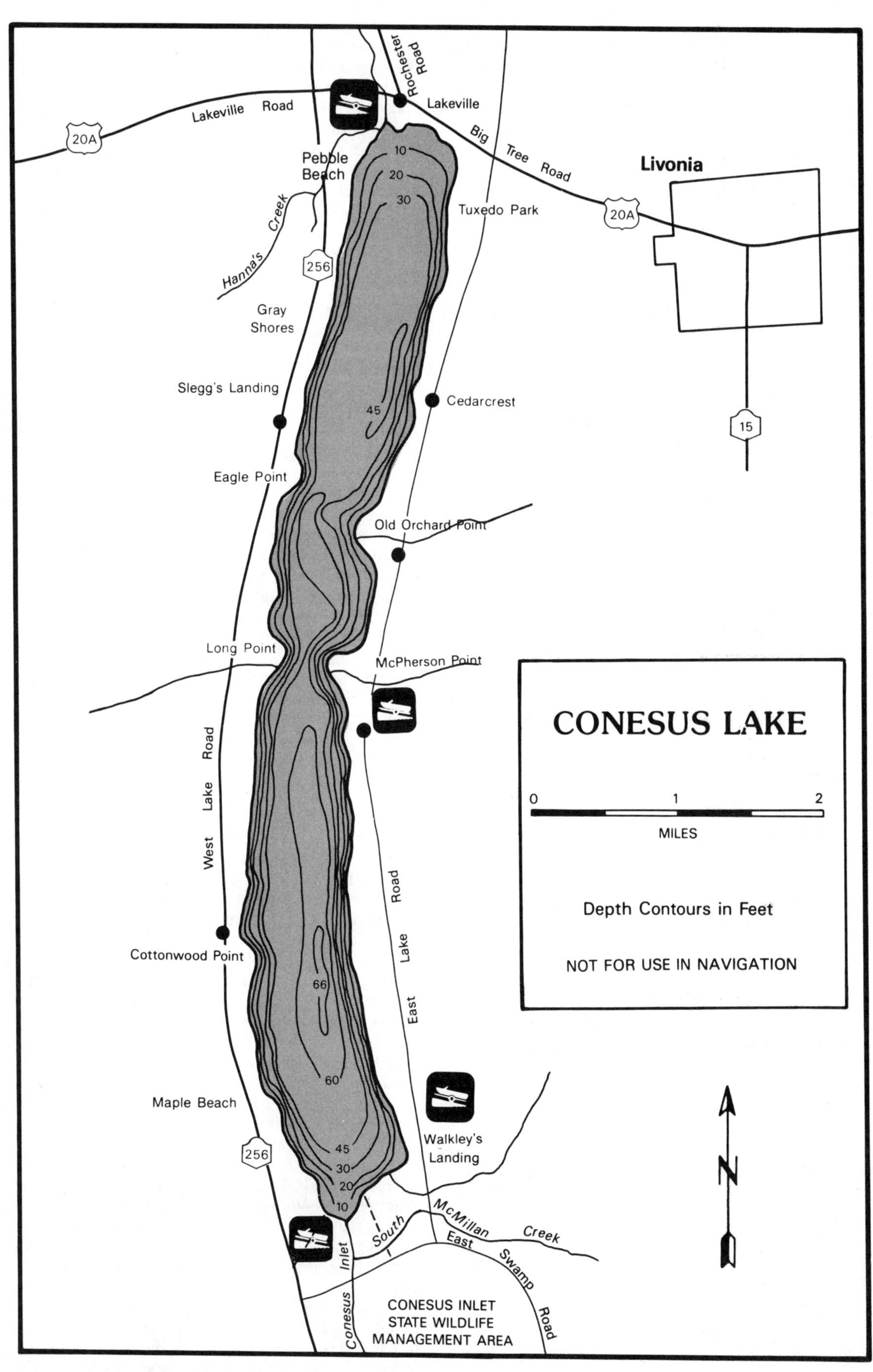
CONESUS LAKE
0
1
2
MILES
Depth Contours in Feet
NOT FOR USE IN NAVIGATION
Rochester Road
Lakeville
Lakeville Road
20A
Big Tree Road
Livonia
20A
Pebble Beach
Hanna's Creek
256
Tuxedo Park
Gray Shores
Slegg's Landing
Cedarcrest
15
Eagle Point
Old Orchard Point
Long Point
McPherson Point
West Lake Road
East Lake Road
Cottonwood Point
Maple Beach
256
Walkley's Landing
McMillan Creek
East Swamp Road
South
Conesus Inlet
CONESUS INLET STATE WILDLIFE MANAGEMENT AREA
10
20
30
45
66
60
45
30
20
10
N

This occurs just after safe ice has formed over the shallows, but before ice has formed over the rest of the lake. The perch are drawn in by bait fish seeking shelter in the dimly lit waters under the ice. On Conesus Lake this means that most of the early ice fishing will take place near the northern end of the lake The south end of the lake does have shallow water, but the relatively warm water from the inlet keeps that end ice-free longer than the north end. Even when it does freeze, the south end can be treacherous to venture out on. As the ice and snowpack thicken, the plants in the northern end are cut off from sunlight and the oxygen levels diminish. This will force the yellow perch to move into progressively deeper water, i.e., southward. Once the perch begin this migration, the only way to find out where they're hitting is to check with local tackle shops or to follow the crowds on the ice.

There are three major access points on Conesus Lake for winter anglers. There is popular, but informal, access via the water authority property on the northwest side of the lake, between Slegg's Landing and Gray Shores. There is a DEC parking and access site at the south end of the lake, off Route 256. And there is a public boat launch and access site south of McPherson Point. This site is the most popular because it has plenty of parking and provides good access to the bottleneck that concentrates the perch as they migrate southward.

Smallmouth Bass .... Common; growth rate good

There are a lot of smallmouth bass in Conesus Lake, but their habitat is surprisingly limited. Therefore, if you know how to read the lake and familiarize yourself with some of the bass hangouts, you're likely to find some good and consistent fishing for smallmouth bass here.

When bass season opens, most of the female smallmouth in this lake will be spawned out. A majority of the females will disperse throughout various habitats in the lake, exhibiting no tendency to concentrate in particular areas. However, adult males will linger in the shallows, protecting nest and fry from predators. Because they aggressively protect their nests, they can be taken very easily early in the season. It really makes sense to avoid taking smallmouth bass until the water temperature in the shallows warms up into the low 60s. For every adult bass harvested from the nesting area, hundreds of unprotected bass fry will perish due to predation.

Once the 60 degree mark is reached, adult smallmouth will switch from paternal chores to active feeding habits. Adult fish will begin to be found in 10 to 25 feet of water near deep weedlines, rocky ledges, and off submerged points. They can be taken on small jigs (1/8 to 1/4 ounce) dressed with bucktails or Mister Twisters.

SHAD IMITATION

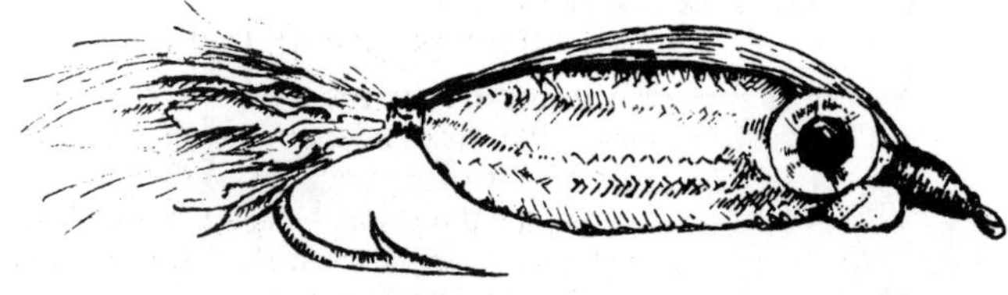

Shad imitations are commonly used to catch trout and salmon in lakes, but they are also very effective in the lower ends of feeder streams.

Grape, chartreuse, and yellow are productive colors on this lake. Crankbaits, such as Hot 'n Tots or Bagley's Killer Bs, will also be effective. For the fly fisherman, leech patterns in claret or white or crayfish patterns can be deadly effective. In the early morning (6 a.m. to 9 a.m.) small spinners and bluegill poppers will take bass as they feed near shore in shallow water. The same is true in the evening (7 p.m. to dark). You will want to keep your hardware as small as possible when fishing in this lake because the water is so clear (unless algae blooms are becoming a problem; see note above) the bass get a good chance to give it a visual inspection, and they're less likely to be put off by a small jig or popper. Natural baits will also work well. Crayfish or minnows fished close to the bottom over rocky points or other structure near deep water will usually produce fish

A majority of the best smallmouth habitat is found in the lower end of Conesus Lake and most of it is on the western side of the lake. All of the points between Long Point and Maple Beach hold smallmouth bass and some are better than others, so you'll have to do some investigating. The south side of Long Point is exceptionally productive. Good fishing can also be found just south of Eagle Point, off Old Orchard Point, and on the north side of McPherson Point. There is some fishing for smallmouth between Gray Shores and Pebble Beach, and off the point at Cedar Crest, but its rather sporadic.

Conesus Lake is fairly regular in shape. It doesn't have a lot of exaggerated points or coves, and this makes for fairly simple trolling. You can hit a lot of smallmouth water while trolling, and you certainly will catch fish, but fan casting from an anchored boat does have some advantages. It doesn't waste time (a lot of the water you'll cover while trolling this lake won't have smallmouth habitat) and it allows you to familiarize yourself completely with specific points, drop-offs, and weedlines.

Although some smallmouth bass will continue to be taken in the shallows during periods of low light, there is a general tendency for them to move into increasingly by deeper water, beginning around the end of August. Begin to concentrate your efforts on the rocky points, fishing with crabs or minnows in 20 to 40 feet of water, or trolling deep-diving crankbaits. In October and early November smallmouth bass usually go on a pre-winter feeding binge. At that time, live bait or small jigs fished over deep bottom structure can be incredibly effective.

Northern Pike .... Common; growth rate good

Northern pike are well-distributed throughout Conesus Lake and exhibit good growth rates. Conesus northerns average 25 to 30 inches, but fish considerably larger have been taken, particularly from the weed beds just above and below Cottonwood Point.

While they can be found nearly everywhere in the lake where weeds exist, there are four areas of particular importance: the extreme northern end of the lake, the extreme southern end of the lake, the cove between McPherson Point and Old Orchard Point, and the stretch of shoreline between Long Point and the south side of Cottonwood Point.

At the southern end of Conesus Lake is the Conesus Inlet Fish and Wildlife Management Area. This marshy tract is drained by Conesus Inlet and was obtained by the DEC to serve primarily as a spawning ground for northern pike. Because a majority of the northern in this lake spawn here, the lower end of Conesus is the place to concentrate your early season efforts.

Shortly after spawning, most northern pike will seek out adjacent flats in 10 to 20 feet of water, relating to rock piles, small patches of weeds, or small drop-offs. For the best early season pike action, try still fishing with live bait, preferably large shiners (8 to 12 inches). Large chubs and suckers will also work well. These baits can also be used while backtrolling or drifting very slowly over the flats.

During the first few weeks of the season, northerns will tend to be close to the bottom. To keep your bait near the bottom, be sure to use a sinker. However, by the end of May the northerns will have sufficiently recuperated from their spawning rituals to become more active and aggressive. Then you'll want to fish without a sinker, using a bobber to keep your bait off the bottom and out from the cover of emerging weeds. The late spring is also a good time to begin using spinners, such as the Mepps Aglia, Panther Martin, or Vibrax. Spinnerbaits tipped with a minnow will also produce fish. Although they will catch fish later in the season, they are definitely more effective during the late spring/early summer period.

In the summer, northerns can be taken using a number of methods. Conesus Lake has well-defined structure, making it an easy lake to troll. Troll the inside then the outside weedlines using large spinnerbaits tipped with a minnow (4- to 6-inch shiners, chubs, or suckers), large silver flatfish, crankbaits, or large spoons, such as the classic red and white Dardevle. Play with the trolling depth as you work the weedlines, but keep in mind that most northerns are taken from this lake in less the 30 feet of water.

If trolling isn't to your liking, fan casting can also be productive, and it allows you to learn the structure of a particular area very quickly. All of the above hardware will work, but for a little variety try using salt water flies. Several local anglers use large (5- to 15-inch) flies here with considerable success. Whether trolling or casting, be sure to use a short wire leader or a 20- to 30-pound shock tippet. Northern pike have teeth as sharp as razor blades and your going to lose a lot of fish and a lot of tackle if you don't.

Most of the really big northern pike seem to come from the weed beds just north and south of Cottonwood Point. This may be due to the close juxtaposition of shallow weedlines and relatively deep, cool water, a situation generally favored by large northern pike. If you're looking to fish exclusively for large pike, this would be the area in which to concentrate your efforts. The trick to fishing for these trophy-size northerns is to use large baits. Try using a 12-inch sucker hooked through the upper lip with a size 2 short-shank hook. Fish the bait below a slip-bobber. A bait this size will usually only attract the attention of the large northern pike, and at the same time you won't be bothered by any pesky largemouth bass that hold in the same areas.

In the fall, another method is added to your angling arsenal, namely, jigs. The variety of jigs that will work in the fall is very wide, but they all have something in common - they are big. Half ounce and 1-ounce jigs dressed with a bucktail, a 5- to 7-inch plastic waterdog, or a 4- to 6-inch Mister Twister tail will all take pike from this lake. The fall is also a good time to use large (5- to 15-inch) minnow imitations, such as a jointed Rapala.

One of the most productive pike harvesting times on Conesus Lake, or any other lake for that matter, is the winter, immediately after the lake freezes. A majority of the northern pike will be found in water 5 to 15 feet deep, primarily in the weedy bays or at the north and south ends of the lake. As the season progresses, however, they have a tendency to follow the bait fish, such as the yellow perch, into increasingly deeper water. Later still, their spawning urge awakens and a majority of the pike will head for the south end of the lake to be near their spawning grounds.

Standard ice fishing techniques are used on Conesus Lake. A tip-up baited with a large sucker or shiner hooked through the back is about a fancy as you have to get. Size 2 or 4 hooks are the most commonly used, and most veteran pike fishermen prefer braided nylon line terminating in either a short wire leader or a heavy-duty (40- to 60-pound test) monofilament shock tippet. A short-handed gaff is good to have around too. A lot of pike, especially the big ones, are lost at the hole while they're being landed. A gaff will eliminate this problem.

Keep in mind that the water from the inlet is warmer than the lake and can make the ice on the south end of the lake less safe than ice on other parts of the lake.

While fishing for northern pike, don't be surprised if after close inspection, some of the smaller northerns you catch turn out to be chain pickerel. Pickerel are present in Conesus Lake, though in far fewer numbers than northerns. Closely related to northerns, they are similar in appearance, often inhabit the same areas, and can be caught with the same techniques.

Largemouth Bass .... Common; growth rate good

There is a wide variety of habitat for largemouth bass in this lake, from the slowly tapering flats at the north end of the lake to the deeper weedlines at the outer edges of the larger bays.

Early in the season, before the lake reaches its maximum average temperature, spinners will usually be the most effective lure here. This is especially true in the first few weeks after the opening of the season. Start out with smaller spinners, (such as an 1/8- to 1/16-ounce Panther Martin), and fish the shallow, weedy coves.

The shallow water at the extreme southern end of the lake and the tapering flats at the northern end should also be productive at this time of the year. As the waters warm, gradually switch to slightly larger spinners, spinnerbaits, top surface baits, and small shallow-running crankbaits. Plastic worms worked very slowly through weed beds will also produce well.

In July, August, and September, largemouth bass can be taken in 5 to 15 feet of water, depending on conditions. The bay between McPherson Point and Old Orchard Point, the shallow water just south of McPherson Point, and the small cove on the southwest side of the lake are all consistent producers. Random populations of largemouth bass are also found between Tuxedo Park and Old Orchard Point, and from the state boat launch site near McPherson Point half way down to Walkley's Landing.

Because many of the areas where largemouth bass are likely to be found are well-defined but intermittent weed beds, fan casting is probably the best method to use on Conesus Lake. Trolling would, however, be a more appropriate way to fish in the areas where bass are randomly and thinly distributed.

Conesus Lake is usually a very clear lake. Because of this, many local anglers prefer to use smaller than usual tackle. In the summer, 1/2- to 1/4-ounce jigs dressed with a 1 1/2-inch Mister Twister tail are highly effective. Small spinnerbaits, while not nearly as effective later on as they were early in the season, will still take fish. For really fast action, try fishing with small jigs or spinnerbaits along the inside edge of weed beds or around docks just at daybreak. Later, work the outer edge with jigs or deep diving crankbaits. For areas with extensive shallow weed growth, buzzbaits worked over the weeds just after daybreak and just at sunset will produce a lot of action. Dusk, dawn, and overcast periods are also a good time to try plastic worms, frogs (real or imitation), and top water spoons.

In the fall, largemouth bass tend to orient more off drop-offs and deep weedlines, though some fish can still be taken in the shallows during extended warm spells. Spinnerbaits again become top bass producers, followed by deep-diving crankbaits and buzzbaits. When the water cools below 55 degrees, small jigs dressed with a minnow or pork rind will take fish if worked very slowly. Remember, as the water cools down, the metabolism and reactions of fish slow down, necessitating a slower retrieve.

When the lake is almost cold enough to freeze over, largemouth bass will still be feeding, but not very aggressively. Stationary fishing with small live baits or jigs is about the most effective method for taking these lethargic bass.

Walleye .... Uncommon; growth rate good

In the late 1960s the DEC estimated the adult walleye population of Conesus Lake at 12,000. By 1986, this estimate had dropped to 2,000 adult walleye. The reason(s) for this precipitous drop is not known. About all that can be said for the walleye fishing in this lake is that there are some real lunkers in Conesus, but they are few and far between, and most walleye are only taken incidentally, usually by bass fishermen.

Even given these circumstances, fewer than expected walleye are currently being caught. They are feeding on alewives, which invaded the lake in the early 1980s, and show little interest in traditional walleye lures presented in traditional ways. If you're really intent upon taking one of the huge walleye still left in the lake, it might be a good idea to adopt the downrigger strategies used successfully by Lake Erie fishermen for suspended walleyes.

The walleye fishing in Conesus Lake might be down, but it could rebound explosively. Conesus Lake has generally good walleye habitat. If some of the important limiting factors, which are currently unknown, are suddenly removed, the walleye fishing could return to its former glory very quickly.

To promote the return of the walleye fishery, the state has put the lake on the top of its walleye stocking list. At the present time,

Conesus Lake is stocked with 25,000 advanced (i.e., jumbo) walleye fingerlings (until recently, walleye fry were stocked here to the tune of 15,900,000 per year, but to no avail). This has resulted in the recruitment of juvenile walleye in this lake for the first time in many years. The policy of stocking fingerling walleye will continue for at least two more years, after which it will be evaluated by the DEC. Based on preliminary evidence, however, the DEC is encouraged by the results.

Additional Species

In addition to the species listed above, Conesus Lake also has populations of chain pickerel (see northern pike), carp, white suckers, brown bullhead, rock bass, bluegill, and pumpkinseeds.

General Information

Conesus Lake is the most westerly of the Finger Lakes. Relatively small and shallow, it is, nevertheless, one of the most productive and popular lakes in New York State. Recent studies by the DEC indicate that most of the game species in the lake are in good shape in terms of population and growth rate. The notable exceptions are walleye, which have been in decline for over a decade, and yellow perch, which are being severely impacted by alewives. What effect the dominance of alewives in this lake will have on other species is not yet known.

The habitat exists in Conesus Lake for a cold-water fishery, and attempts were made in the 1960s and 1970s to establish a trout population in the lake. Unfortunately, low survival of the trout yearlings, probably due to predation by northern pike, doomed the experiment to failure.

A major problem on Conesus Lake is lack of public access. Almost the entire perimeter of the lake is privately owned. The best access is limited to three parcels of land owned by the state, which are located on the outlet just south of Route 20A, just south of McPherson Point, and at the southern end of the lake.

NOTES: ______________________________

____

____

HEMLOCK LAKE

Location

Map Coordinates	42° 42′ 39″ 77° 36′ 28″
USGS Map(s)	Springwater, Honeoye
Township(s)	Conesus, Livonia, Springwater (Livingston County); Canadice (Ontario County)
Access	Paralleled by Route 15A

Physical Characteristics

Area	1,800 acres
Shoreline	17.10 miles
Elevation	905 feet
Maximum Depth	91 feet
Mean Depth	45 feet
Bottom Type	Muck, rock, clay
Mean Thermocline	28 feet

Chemical Characteristics

Water Clarity	Clear
pH	Alkaline
Oxygen	Always good throughout the shallow areas of the lake. Oxygen depletion occurs in water below 60 feet during the summer. This does not jeopardize the survival of any species. It does affect how salmonids should be fished. It confines them to a narrow stratum in the water column.

Plant Life

Extensive weed beds (primarily water milfoil) occur at the southern end of the lake. Intermittent weed beds are found along the eastern and western sides of the lake. Weeds are also present at the northern end of Hemlock Lake, but to a much lesser extent than in the south end. Algae blooms are not a severe problem on this lake, but do occur.

Boat Launch Sites

1. The City of Rochester has an unimproved access point and gravel ramp off Rix Hill Road in the small park along the northeast corner of the lake.

2. An unimproved access site and gravel ramp is also found at the southeast corner of the lake off Route 15A.

Species Information

Trout and Salmon .... Common; growth rate very good

Hemlock Lake has very good populations of lake trout, rainbow trout, and brown trout. A lesser population of Atlantic salmon is found here, as are a small, and soon to be eliminated, number of brook trout.

Studies by the DEC indicate that lake trout are the dominant predator in this lake and that these lakers are possibly the fastest growing of their kind in the entire northeastern United States. A 5- to 6-year old lake trout from Hemlock Lake averages close to 10 pounds, and the DEC has handled several fish from 14 to over 20 pounds. Unfortunately, creel census figures indicate that the harvest of lake trout is extremely low here, although the population is very healthy. State fisheries biologists aren't sure why this is so, but hypothesize that they might be feeding so heavily on forage fish, which are abundant here, that lures go unnoticed.

Rainbow trout were established in Hemlock Lake in the late 1940s, and have been an important tributary fishery since that time. With the development of modern techniques for deep-water salmonid fishing in the late 1970s and 1980s, a very significant lake fishery has developed here for rainbows. At present, the population of rainbow trout in Hemlock Lake is considered to be at an optimum level by fisheries management personnel. Unlike lake trout, of which 85 per cent are stocked fish, all of the rainbow trout in this lake are wild, having been bred in the high-quality waters of the Springwater Creek system. The average rainbow taken from Hemlock Lake is a 3- to 4-year old fish weighing less than 2 pounds. However, older fish weighing over 10 pounds are taken occasionally in the lake and from Springwater Creek during spawning runs.

Over the past few years, the DEC has managed to establish a fair fishery for landlocked Atlantic salmon in this lake. One of the most highly prized gamefish in North America, these hard fighting salmon are currently sustained solely by stocking and it is not expected that a naturally self-sustaining population will develop.

Brown trout have also been established in this lake recently, and they provide some very good angling. Their numbers are maintained solely by stocking. Though they grow well here, indicating that they are feeding heavily on the abundant forage fish, browns are taken fairly easily from Hemlock Lake. This is in sharp contrast to the poor harvest of lake trout, which is thought to be due to a dense forage base.

Soon after ice-out, trout will be found in shallow areas of Hemlock Lake. Trolling with long lines or planer boards, using Little Cleos, Rapalas, or Rebels is a very productive method for taking springtime trout. Slow drifting along the shore, working a very small jig tipped with a minnow slowly along the bottom, is also highly effective for brown trout and rainbow trout. Be sure to use a light line (4-pound test).

In the spring, try fishing with cut smelt for lake trout. Cast out, using a slip sinker to take the bait to the bottom. Many veteran trout fishermen feel that it is necessary to use a slip sinker and to leave the reel bail open to avoid spooking the fish as they mouth the bait. Close the bail and set the hook after the second run has started to ensure that the trout has the whole bait in its mouth.

While you're at Hemlock Lake in the spring, don't neglect the excellent run of rainbows that takes place in Springwater Creek.

In the summer, deep-water fishing techniques are necessary to take trout and salmon from Hemlock Lake. These techniques include still fishing, thermoclining, copper-line fishing, and downrigger fishing.

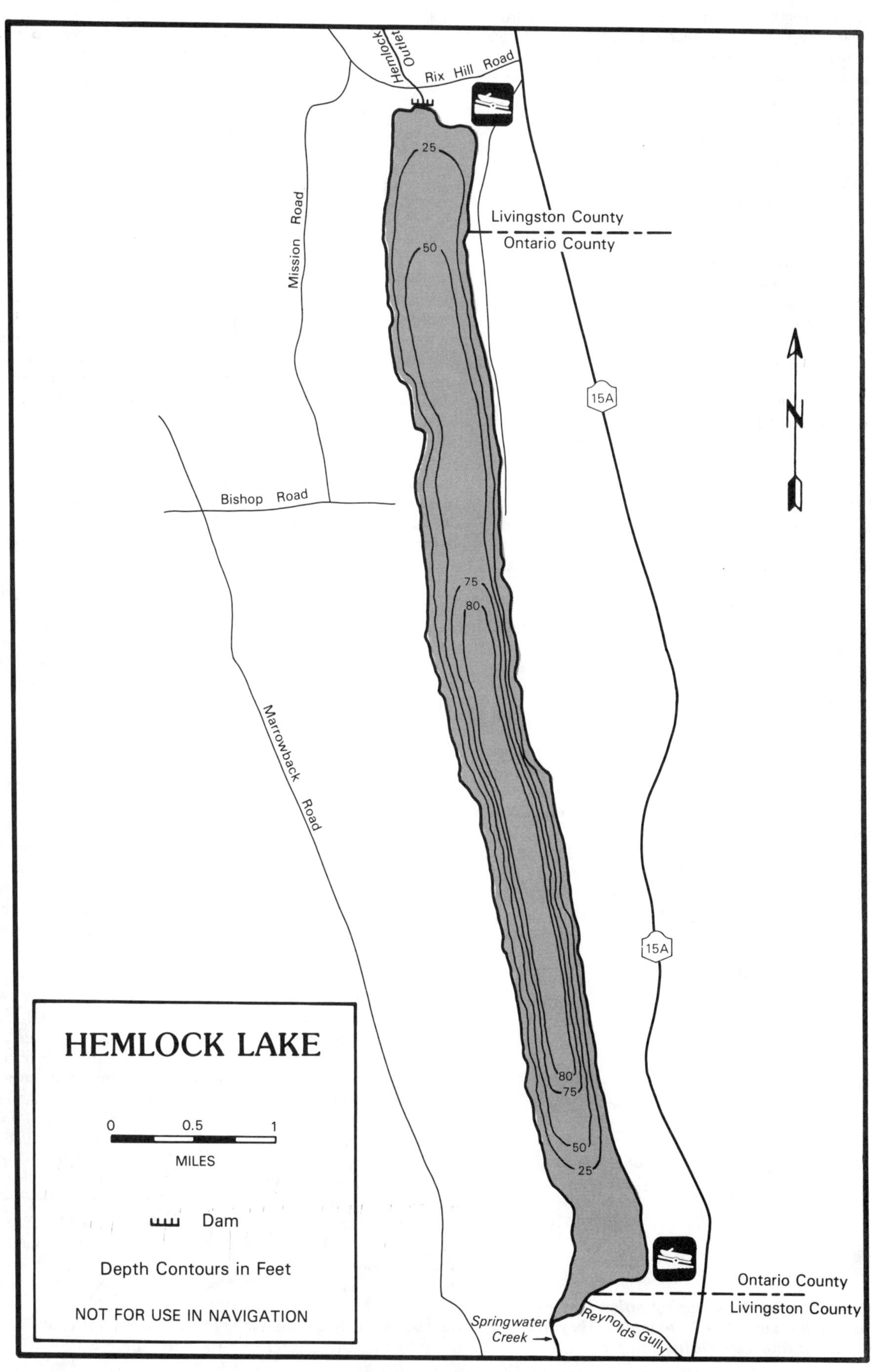

Hemlock Outlet
Rix Hill Road
Mission Road
Livingston County
Ontario County
15A
N
Bishop Road
Marrowback Road
25
50
75
80
HEMLOCK LAKE
0
0.5
1
MILES
Dam
Depth Contours in Feet
NOT FOR USE IN NAVIGATION
Ontario County
Livingston County
Springwater Creek
Reynolds Gully

Beginning in the late summer or early fall, the trout and salmon start to move back into shallower waters, some to feed, others to spawn. All of the techniques and tackle that worked in the spring will also work well in the fall.

Finger Lakes fishing regulations allow trout to be taken from Hemlock Lake all year long, which means ice fishing for trout is legal here. The lake usually freezes over entirely, but the north and south ends are accessible first. A majority of the ice fishing takes place at the south end of the lake, but there is nothing to indicate that the north end is any less productive then the south, at least in terms of trout. (Note: The city of Rochester prohibits ice fishing at the extreme north end of Hemlock Lake where the water intake is located.) Tip-ups baited with minnows are productive, as are various jigging lures, such as the Swedish pimple, Russian jig, or the Rapala jigging minnow. Certain cold-weather fly patterns can also be used, such as the lead wing Coachman or any shrimp imitation.

Hemlock Lake is currently stocked annually with 3,600 lake trout yearlings, 7,300 lake trout fingerlings, 5,000 brown trout yearlings, and 4,100 Atlantic salmon yearlings. Brook trout, which have been stocked here in recent years, have removed from the stocking list for Hemlock Lake.

Chain Pickerel .... Common; growth rate very good

Chain pickerel are commonly found anywhere in Hemlock Lake where weed beds exist. They aren't nearly as popular with fishermen as smallmouth bass and lake trout, but they do provide some very good angling. The pickerel in Hemlock Lake are larger than those found in Honeoye Lake. Pickerel taken from Hemlock Lake commonly reach 18 to 24 inches in length.

Chain pickerel are found throughout more of this lake than you would initially think. The weed-choked southern end is undoubtedly the most productive area for these toothy predators, but the thick weed beds of the northern end also hold pickerel, as do the intermittent weeds along the periphery of the lake.

Early in the season, spinners, such as the Mepps Aglia or Panther Martin, are effective pickerel lures. Spoons, such as Little Cleos or Daredevles, also work well early on, particularly if fished slowly to impart a fluttering motion rather than a fast spin. Spinnerbaits also work very well at this time of year.

In June, July, and August pickerel can be taken with a variety of lures. The larger pickerel are often taken by trolling the outside weedlines with deep-diving crankbaits, silver and blue flatfish, and spoons. For fishing in the weed beds at the southern end of Hemlock Lake, use weedless lures, such as Johnson's Silver Minnow, Texas-rigged worms, or the Mean Mister Twister.

In the fall, live baits, including small suckers, shiners, and minnows, are top pickerel producers. The same hardware that worked throughout the summer months can also be used in the fall, but spinnerbaits are often better, returning to the level of effectiveness that they displayed in the spring.

BASS POPPER

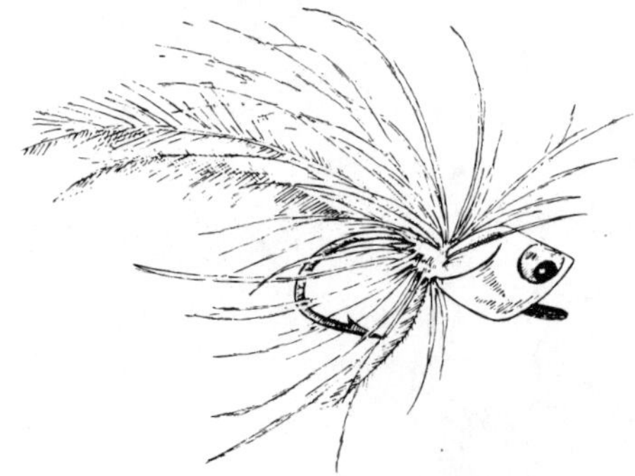

Bass poppers attract fish by the gurgling noise they produce when "popped" along the surface of the water. They are very effective on bass and panfish, especially at night.

Chain pickerel are a popular quarry through the ice on Hemlock Lake. An overwhelming majority of the ice fishing takes place on the southern end of the lake, and the weed beds located there provide some good winter pickerel fishing. Tip-ups baited with live minnows, chubs, or small suckers are always good when used over shallow weedlines (10 feet or less). Cut smelt, which is very popular with many northern pike fishermen, should also work well for pickerel.

Largemouth Bass .... Common; growth rate very good

Despite the fact that their overall habitat is rather restricted in this lake, largemouth bass are present in significant numbers and have a better then average growth rate. Local anglers estimate that the average Hemlock Lake largemouth weighs a solid 2 pounds. Bass weighing 4 to 5 pounds are taken here each year.

Largemouth bass are limited to areas of the lake that exhibit significant weed growth. The lower end of the lake has extensive weed beds and accounts for a majority of the largemouth taken in the lake. While nearly the entire lower end of Hemlock Lake has a good habitat, an especially productive feature is the old, submerged creek bed. When the lake was first dammed up at the north end the south end was permanently flooded, but the creek bed is still discernable. Deep-diving crankbaits, plastic worms, bucktail jigs, and jigs dressed with Mister Twister tails are all effective for working the creek bed, weedlines, or the naturally occurring openings in the weed beds. For working the tops of submerged weed beds use a top water plug or surface spoons.

Largemouth bass are also found at the north-end of the lake, along the west side of the lake between the gauging station and Mission Point (the point, in fact, is pretty good), and along the east side as far south as the launch site. Scattered populations of largemouth can also be found elsewhere in Hemlock Lake wherever weed beds exist.

Smallmouth bass .... Common; growth rate good

According to DEC surveys, smallmouth bass are currently the single most sought often warm-water quarry in Hemlock Lake. They are randomly distributed along the east and west sides of the lake, favoring rocky points and drop-offs. The points on the northwest side of the lake are considered by the anglers we interviewed to be about the most productive on the lake for smallmouth. But nearly any rocky point or steep, rocky ledge on this lake should hold a few smallmouth. One suggestion for locating probable smallmouth habitat is to check out the mouths of the numerous streams that feed Hemlock Lake. Where a stream empties into the lake there is usually an out-wash of rubble. Smallmouth will often be found on or near these small gravel beds. Once a likely area has been located, drift over the site, casting 1/8- to 1/4-ounce bucktail jigs or jigs dressed with black, yellow, or white Mister Twister tails. Deep-diving crankbaits, such as the Hot 'n Tot, Wiggle Wart, or Mann's Deep Hog and Deep Pig can also be used.

Additional Species

Hemlock Lake hosts a number of species of secondary importance. Rock bass are abundant in the lake, but get very little attention from area anglers. They are well-distributed along the periphery of the lake, inhabiting much the same water as smallmouth bass. Smelt, so important to the maintenance of the lake's trout and salmon population, are abundant, but contribute little to the fishery in terms of overall harvest. Some smelt are taken through the ice, but the vast majority are taken during their spawning run in two small tributaries on the northwest corner of the lake (smelt apparently never run in the lakes main tributary, Springwater Creek). There is a popular, but short-lived, fishery for brown bullhead in the spring of the year. Yellow perch can be found in many parts of the lake. Their numbers are only fair at best, but this lake's perch are usually big. The trick to taking them seems to be fishing in deep water (but above the level of oxygen depletion) as close to the steep sides of the lake as possible. Rounding out the available species in Hemlock Lake are bluegills, pumpkinseeds, white suckers, and carp, the last of which are often taken by lake trout fishermen in the lake's hypolimion, the cold layer of water below the thermocline.

Historically, whitefish and walleye were important species in Hemlock Lake, but their populations have suffered an all but total collapse.

General Information

Hemlock Lake lies 25 miles south of the city of Rochester and serves as a principle source of water for that city. To ensure the purity of the lake's water, the lake and the surrounding countryside have been maintained in a nearly pristine state. There is almost no development on the lake's periphery, providing fishermen a unique wilderness setting close to a major metropolitan area.

The major problem on Hemlock Lake is the lack of adequate access. The two unimproved launch sites are capable of handling the small boats allowed on the lake, but they are located at either end of this 7-mile long body of water. This means that a long boat ride faces anyone who wishes to fish the central portion of Hemlock Lake. Shore access is even worse. Almost the entire shoreline of the lake is open to public access, but, with the exception of the north and south ends of the lake, there are no nearby roads, greatly restricting the areas of the lake available to shore fishing. This problem is compounded in the winter by the fact that the access road at the south end of the lake, where a majority of the ice fishing takes place, is not plowed. If you don't use a snowmobile its a long, cold walk from Route 15A to the ice fishing areas.

If you plan on fishing Hemlock Lake, be aware that special regulations apply here. Boats are permitted on the lake, but are restricted to a maximum of 16 feet. Motors are restricted to 10 horsepower. Fishing is by permit only, which can be obtained (free) by sending a stamped, self-addressed envelope to:

City of Rochester
Watershed Permit
7412 Rix Hill Road
Hemlock, NY 14466
(716) 367-3250

NOTES: ______________________________

____

____

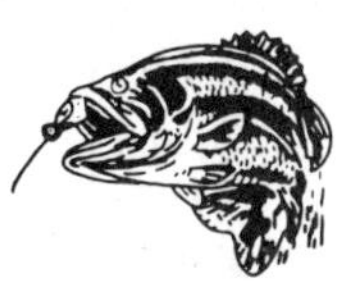

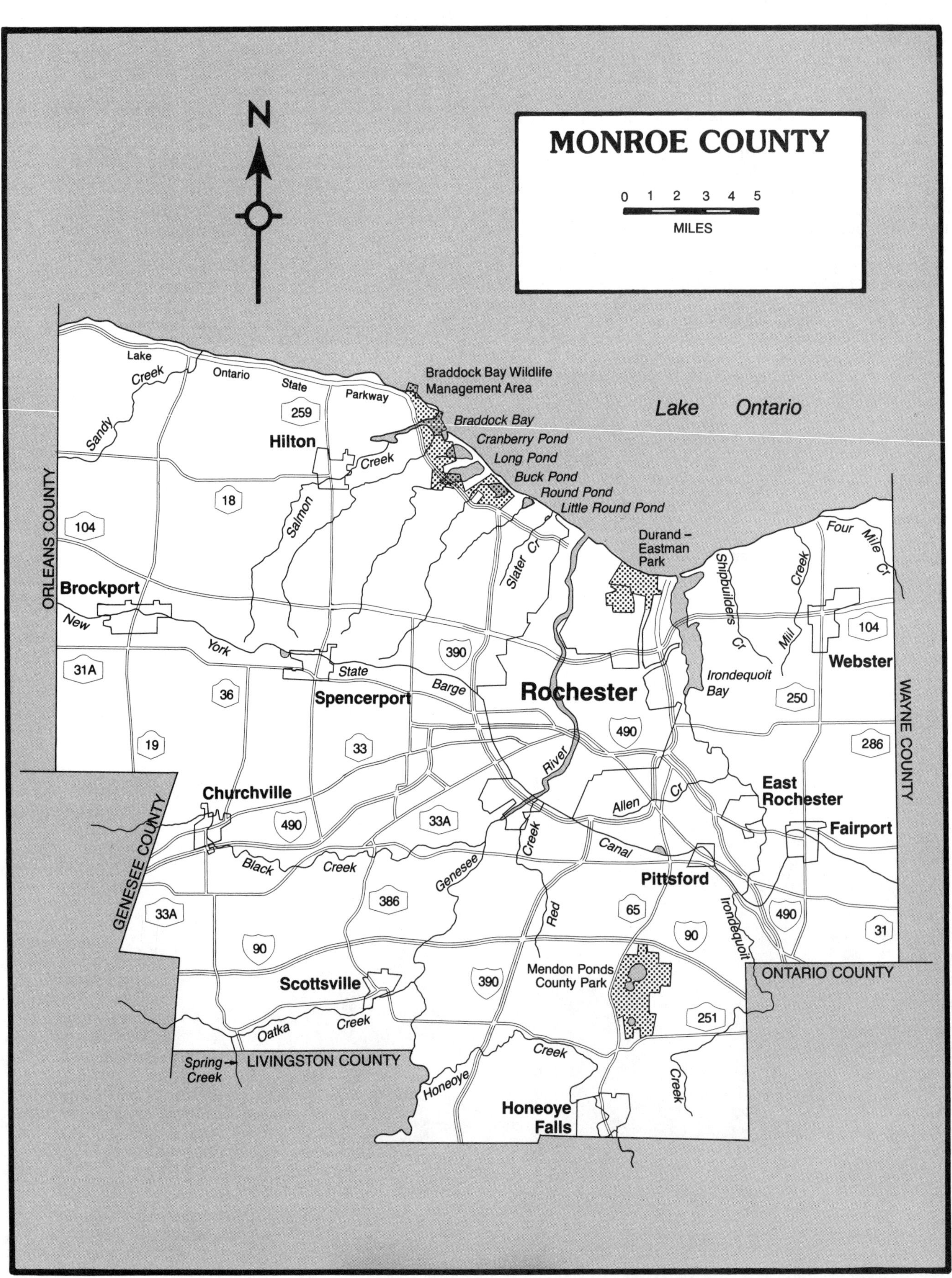
MONROE COUNTY
0 1 2 3 4 5
MILES
N
Lake Ontario
Lake Ontario State Parkway
Braddock Bay Wildlife Management Area
Braddock Bay
Cranberry Pond
Long Pond
Buck Pond
Round Pond
Little Round Pond
Durand - Eastman Park
Sandy Creek
Salmon Creek
Slater Cr
Four Mile Cr
Shipbuilders Cr
Mill Creek
Irondequoit Bay
Hilton
Brockport
Spencerport
Rochester
Webster
Churchville
East Rochester
Fairport
Pittsford
Scottsville
Honeoye Falls
New York State Barge Canal
Genesee River
Allen Cr
Black Creek
Red Creek
Irondequoit Creek
Oatka Creek
Honeoye Creek
Spring Creek
Mendon Ponds County Park
ORLEANS COUNTY
GENESEE COUNTY
WAYNE COUNTY
ONTARIO COUNTY
LIVINGSTON COUNTY
259
18
104
31A
36
19
33
390
490
33A
386
90
65
250
286
31
251

MONROE COUNTY STREAMS AND RIVERS

ALLEN CREEK

Map Coordinates .... 43° 07′ 56″ 77° 30′ 02″
USGS Map(s) .... Rochester East, Pittsford
Township(s) .... Henrietta, Pittsford, Penfield, Brighton
Access .... Allen Creek Road, Winton Road
Principal Species .... Rainbow Trout (stocked), Panfish

Allen Creek is a tributary of Irondequoit Creek. Its lower portions can hold fair numbers of steelhead if water levels are sufficient in the spring and fall. More consistent, however, are the panfish and rough fish, such as rock bass, carp, and suckers. They can be caught here throughout the spring, summer, and fall.

This creek runs through heavily populated areas and is primarily bordered by private property. Be sure to get landowners permission before fishing from such property.

Allen Creek is not stocked.

NOTES: ______________________________

____

____

BLACK CREEK

Map Coordinates .... 43° 05′ 04″ 77° 40′ 49″
USGS Map(s) .... West Henrietta, Clifton, Churchville, Byron
Township(s) .... Chili, Riga (Monroe County); Bergen, Byron (Genesee County)
Access .... Route 383 (Scottsville Road)
Principal Species .... Largemouth Bass, Smallmouth Bass, Northern Pike, Walleye, Bullhead, Panfish

Black Creek is a warm-water stream of mediocre quality. The best fishing is found in the wide, lower section near its confluence with the Genesee River. In this area there is good walleye fishing in the summer, roughly from the middle of June to late July. Small jigs in combination with worms work well on these fish, particularly in the evening. Bullhead, panfish, and northern pike are also common in this section of the stream. A fair number of largemouth bass, smallmouth bass, and northern pike are distributed throughout the middle and upper portions of the creek.

There is additional parking and access available at Black Creek Park off Route 33A (Chili-Riga Center Road) and Churchville Park on Route 33 (Buffalo Road).

Black Creek is not stocked. However, Spring Creek, a tributary of Black Creek in Genesee County, has both stocked and wild brown trout.

NOTES: ______________________________

____

____

FOUR MILE CREEK

Map Coordinates .... 43° 16′ 01″ 77° 26′ 03″
USGS Map(s) .... Ninemile Point, Webster, Ontario
Township(s) .... Webster
Access .... Lake Road
Principal Species .... Rainbow Trout (stocked), Brown Trout (stocked)

This small stream gets a good run of rainbow trout in the early spring. The water level in Four Mile Creek is usually quite low in the fall, but fair numbers of rainbow trout and brown trout still make their way into its lower reaches. They can only go up as far as the old dam near Lake Road.

The state is tentatively planning to purchase public fishing rights on part of this stream, but has not done so as of Spring 1991. Presently, it is not heavily posted below Lake Road.

Four Mile Creek is not stocked.

NOTES: ______________________________

____

____

GENESEE RIVER (Mount Morris Dam to Lake Ontario)

Map Coordinates .... 43° 15′ 30″ 77° 36′ 09″
USGS Map(s) .... Rochester East, Rochester West, West Henrietta, Rush, Caledonia, Geneseo, Sonyea
Location .... Counties of Livingston and Monroe
Access .... See access list below
Principal Species .... Brown Trout, Rainbow Trout, Chinook Salmon, Coho Salmon, Smallmouth Bass, Channel Catfish, Largemouth Bass, Bullhead, Northern Pike, Walleye, Panfish

The lower portion of the Genesee River is one of the most diverse and exciting streams in western New York. It combines beautiful, varying scenery with bountiful angling for over a dozen species of fish, in areas ranging from metropolitan sprawl to backwoods solitude.

As it flows northward from Mount Morris toward Rochester, the Genesee River is a gently winding, warm-water stream. This section is quite scenic, and solitude is readily available. It offers fishermen such species as largemouth and smallmouth bass, bullhead, channel catfish, walleye, crappies, carp, and suckers. All of these fish are fairly common throughout the river. The walleye population, which until recently was rather low, seems to be on the rebound, judging from the increasing numbers being caught. Very good catches of walleye are not uncommon in the stretch of river immediately below the Mount Morris Dam.

The Livingston County section of the Genesee River can be accessed from almost any road crossing, but they tend to be rather spread out. One should, instead, consider canoeing this water. To traverse its length would take several days of very pleasant canoeing. It would also enable the angler to investigate some of the

MICKEY FINN

The brightly colored Mickey Finn is one of the most popular trout flies. It imitates a wide range of forage fish.

more remote, and possibly more productive, stretches of the river seldom seen by fishermen.

As the Genesee flows into Monroe County and the City of Rochester, it undergoes some major changes. Cascading over a series of falls, the river enters a steep-sided gorge. Once over the final (lower) falls, which is located near Driving Park Avenue, the fish population changes, reflecting the presence of Lake Ontario species. The lake-run species found here include brown trout, rainbow trout, coho salmon, chinook salmon, white bass, yellow perch, white perch, smelt, northern pike, bowfin, sheepshead, rock bass and American eel. With the possible except of largemouth bass, all the species found in the upper river are also available here.

Information from the DEC indicates that resident fish populations are fairly evenly distributed through out the Genesee River, both above and below the falls. Below the lower falls, these fish are supplemented by the seasonal influx of tremendous numbers of lake fish.

The most notable of the seasonal species, not surprisingly, are the trout and salmon. In the spring, rainbow trout (steelhead) and brown trout are caught here by the thousands. Lake trout are also available at this time, from the piers at the mouth of the river. Late summer and fall brings in coho and chinook salmon in great numbers, followed later by brown trout and rainbow trout. Trout, in fact, can be found in this section of the Genesee River throughout the fall, winter, and spring; it's even possible that a few remain in the river through the summer. All of the salmonids will run up as far as the base of the lower falls during their spawning runs. They tend to stack up in the stretch of water between Seth Green Island and the falls. This area is naturally very popular with fishermen and gets quite a bit of fishing pressure, so you may want to try some of the other public access areas. They all produce well when the fish are in and are often less crowded.

Snagging for salmon is permitted on the Genesee River from the Stutson Street bridge upstream to the lower falls. Be sure to check for current regulations.

The lower Genesee River is stocked annually with 270,000 chinook salmon, 25,000 coho salmon, and 20,000 rainbow trout (steelhead).

Because of the enormous quality and popularity of trout and salmon fishing in the Genesee below the lower falls, many people tend to forget that this stretch of water is also a high-quality fishery for other species. In some years, there is an excellent run of smelt up the river early in the spring, and dipping for these tasty little fish between Seth Green Island and the falls is very popular and productive. Other lake-run fish that tend to congregate in the river include smallmouth bass, bullhead, channel catfish, white perch, rock bass (near the piers), walleye, and sheepshead.

Because the Genesee River flows through a heavily populated area, it gets a great deal of attention from those who live nearby. To facilitate the utilization of this waterway, a number of access areas have been developed by the city of Rochester, the county of Monroe, and by the state. They include:

East Shore Access

1. There is a state fishing area and free parking lot off the circle at the north end of Saint Paul Boulevard. You can fish a few steps from the parking lot or walk through the Coast Guard grounds to reach Summerville Pier.
2. Access to the lower falls and Seth Green Island is via a Rochester Gas & Electric Corporation roadway off Seth Green Drive, at the intersection of Saint Paul Street and Norton Street. Public parking is limited, however.
3. Seneca Park parallels the river for a considerable distance, and there is free parking within the park. It is located off Saint Paul Boulevard about 1 mile north of Route 104. Several rough footpaths lead down to the river's edge. They can be dangerous, so use them at your own discretion.
4. Genesee Valley Park East at Elmwood Avenue and Wilson Boulevard has a launch site for cartop boats and canoes, and provides bank access.

West Shore Access

1. Most convenient access is in Charlotte. Take Lake Avenue to the north end. At the traffic light turn right into the parking lot for Ontario Beach Park. From there you can walk onto Charlotte Pier.
2. Just south of the above lot and practically joined to it is a county boat launch site with multiple hard-surface ramps and parking facilities. There is a modest fee during the height of the fishing season. When the launch closes "officially" you can launch without charge.
3. An unimproved footpath in Maplewood Park near Driving Park Bridge will take you to the water. The path begins with a ramp, but quickly turns into a narrow path. Again, it's rough walking and you need to use caution.
4. Genesee Valley Park West at Elmwood Avenue and Plymouth Avenue has a launch site for cartop boats and canoes, and provides some bank access.
5. Turning Point Park off Boxart Street at Lake Avenue has a

The lower falls of the Genesee River, which is located just upstream of the bridge on Driving Park Avenue. In the fall, trout and salmon stack up in this portion of the river, which can be accessed from a path in Maplewood Park.

launch site for cartop boats and canoes, and bank access.

6. During the fall chinook runs, a fish-cleaning service runs a free ferry from the east shore, near the power company roadway, to the west shore.
7. There is a DEC fishing access site at Brown's Bridge on Route 253. It has a launch site for cartop boats and canoes, parking for 12 cars, and bank access.

In addition to the above sites, a number of marinas also service the Genesee River in the Rochester area. These include:

1. River View Yacht Basin, 18 Pettin Street extension, off River Street, west side of river. Full-service marina, single ramp - fee.
2. Shumway Marine, 70 Pattonwood Drive, east side of river. Full-service marina, single ramp - fee.
3. Voyager Boat Sales, under the Stuttson Street bridge, east side of the river. Full-service marina, single ramp - fee.

The following article was written by Bob Wunder, who for several years has done an excellent job putting together the weekly Monroe County Fishing Hotline (716) 987-8800.

FISHING THE GENESEE RIVER

By Bob Wunder

Charlie Fredericks held his breath as I slid the net under the big fish. Then I lifted and Charlie let out a whoop of victory. It was a fat, silvery rainbow just in from Lake Ontario. It would go 14 pounds, maybe more. He removed the green glow bug from the corner of the trout's jaw and squatted to ease the fish back into the water. We could see the trout's gills and fins working as my partner held it by the tail. Then there was a surge and the fish disappeared. "This beats Alaska," my guest grinned.

Charlie should know. Now retired from the presidency of a major Manhattan advertising agency, Charlie spends his time chasing fish, especially trout. He has a weekend camp on the Delaware River and also manages several trips each year to trout waters in other states. His travels have taken him to some of Alaska's premier rainbow trout rivers. He says the fishing here is better. In both numbers and size.

We were fishing the Genesee River a scant three miles from downtown Rochester, New York. The river begins as a trickle in northern Pennsylvania and winds more than 100 miles north, passing through the heart of Rochester and entering Lake Ontario about five miles downstream. There is an upper falls smack in the middle of the city and a lower falls perhaps a mile below that. The latter is an impassable barrier to migrating rainbows that move up from the lake in the spring and fall.

"I don't get them this big in Alaska," Charlie said. There was more than a little awe in his voice. The fact that we were taking big rainbows within the city limits may have had something to do with it. One does not expect urban fishing to match that of wilderness waters.

We were fishing the current on the west side of Seth Green Island, virtually beneath the city's Driving Park Bridge. The fall run was in full swing, and the water in front of us was alive with rainbows. None looked smaller than 5 pounds and there were some that appeared even bigger than the fish Charlie has just released.

Most area fishermen know about the good spring and fall action. But not everyone realizes that the excellent fishing extends through the winter months. Some who fish the river all winter maintain that the rainbows spend the cold months in Lake Ontario, off the river mouth. When the temperature rises above freezing and there is a mini-thaw, the rainbows offshore feel the change and respond. They start upstream in a false spawning run. The trout linger in the Genesee for a day or two until the temperature drops. Then they drift back to the lake to await the next false signal.

Others take a different view. Carl Widmer, regional fisheries manager of the state's Department of Environmental Conservation (DEC), says, "Lots of rainbows enter the river in the fall and remain all winter." Whatever the pattern — it may be a combination of both resident and migrating fish — the fall run can begin anywhere from the middle to the end of October. Good fishing can extend into early April. That's six months of excitement, give or take a few weeks.

According to Widmer, the trout consist of both domestic rainbows raised at the nearby Caledonia hatchery and steelhead that have been developed from a strain of fish from the state of Washington. DEC studies show that the steelhead strain is predominant. Best news of all, the trout in the Genesee run big, with 10- to 15-pound fish common and some running to 20 pounds.

How good is the fishing? Rochester guide Cas Pizzo fishes the Genesee regularly after he ends his Lake Ontario charter service in late autumn. He feels that the fishing is superior to that of the more famous Niagara River 80 miles to the west. "They both give up about the same number of fish," he says, "but the rainbows in the Genesee run consistently larger."

The big trout congregate in the fast water below the lower falls. Most anglers wade and use spinning or fly-fishing gear. With a fly-fishing outfit you have your choice of using a weight-forward floating line or 10-pound monofilament line. A glow bug is the preferred lure, especially in chartreuse, but take along orange, yellow, and orange/yellow bugs as well. Egg sacs are also popular. You'll need split-shot 18 inches or so above the bait to get it to tick along the bottom.

Jim Cronin, one of the best trout men on the river, likes a 9-foot, 9-weight fly rod. He tapes on a spinning reel filled with 8-pound mono and a 6-pound leader. A big rainbow can rampage downstream where it's too deep to follow. The lighter leader permits him to break off an uncontrollable fish without losing a lot of line. Instead of split-shot added to the leader in the conventional fashion, Jim uses a Slinky Drifter filled with buckshot. His system works. His best fish last year was 22 pounds.

Taxidermist Paul Adams recommends large egg sacs. "The bigger, the better," he advises. "For some reason, the rainbows here like bigger baits. Start with a bag the size of a quarter. And don't be afraid to go to a bag as big as a golf ball. You might feel foolish, but it works. If you have only dime-size bags, use two or three together to present a large bait."

Rainbows aren't the only attraction in the river. In the spring and fall, chinook (king) salmon run up the river. September through November are the best months. That's when the piers at the river mouth see a lot of action. You can fish from both Charlotte (west) and Summerville (east) piers. Both offer free public access. The Summerville Pier seems to produce more fish. Opinion is divided on whether the river channel itself or the open lake side is best. It can change one day to the next, so try both. As a bonus, you might tie into one of the huge brown trout that move into the river during the tail end of the fall salmon run. And don't be surprised to hook a coho (silver) salmon. Pier fishermen like 3/4- and 1-ounce spoons for chinooks. The spoons are heavy enough to cast a good distance, an important consideration when trout and salmon hold tantalizingly offshore. Smaller sizes are generally preferred for browns, rainbows, and cohos. Try a silver spoon with a splash of red, green, or blue as a secondary color. Little Cleos, Kastmasters, and Pirates are good bets.

Mike Kennan, one of Lake Ontario's most successful charter captains, says fish run bigger in fall. His findings:

	Spring (pounds)	Fall (pounds)
Chinook	3 - 20	18 - 40
Coho	1/2 - 5	10 - 20
Rainbow	2 - 20	5 - 20
Brown	2 - 12	8 - 20

The Genesee also offers excellent walleye fishing. Again, not everyone is aware of it. The most successful walleye anglers keep quiet about their catches. The best fishing is from mid-July into August, with fish ranging from 2 to 7 pounds. One angler does well fishing jigs tipped with 3-inch Mr. Twisters in white, yellow, or chartreuse.

Walleyes here hang in pockets below boulders, especially along the west side of Seth Green Island. Fish the natural curves of the river bank the same way you would fish a trout stream. The best approach, according to Paul Adams, is to position yourself above the fish and feed your lure down to them, letting it drift into the pockets and work in the current. Small Rebels, Rapalas, and similar plugs are favorites. He likes silver and black combinations in discolored water, silver and blue when the river is running clear. Don't look for deep water here. The pockets run 2 to 3 feet in depth, with an occasional hole 6 feet deep.

Some walleye experts on the river swear by bait. They suggest crabs, minnows, and worms in that order. When you're working the water for walleyes, you might also hang a smallmouth now and then.

Panfish are present, but they naturally take a back seat to the trout and salmon. You can take bluegills, pumpkinseeds, bullheads, and white bass in the river's slower stretches. White perch and sheepshead tend to stay near the mouth and provide good action for pier fishermen. In the spring, sufficient numbers of smelt sometimes run the river to provide good catches by dipping, but in recent years they have not been present in numbers large enough to constitute a significant fishery.

Yellow perch fishing from the piers has been popular for decades. The DEC has noted a decline in the size and numbers of perch in recent years. It is attributed to a booming population of sawbellies (alewives). When one species abounds, the other suffers. A high mortality rate among sawbellies, such as that of 1971, usually brings six or seven years of outstanding perch fishing in the lake and river.

The Genesee at first glance is deceiving. Except for the area immediately near the lower falls, it does not look like trout water. The bottom here is rock and rubble, but downstream it is mud. Once you leave the riffles, the river is flat and slow with no appreciable current. But conditions can change. The city's storm sewers feed into the river and a rainstorm can quickly raise the level and muddy the water to make the river unfishable for days.

The river is also shallower than one would suspect. The main channel, which is dredged regularly to accommodate commercial lake vessels, is approximately 20 feet deep. Below Seth Green Island depth is about 12 feet. A few holes near the island can reach 6 feet, but depth here is generally less.

Wherever you fish the Genesee, lower falls to the mouth, you can expect to tangle with big fish, so be prepared. Don't go too light with your tackle. Use a rod with backbone and a line that matches the size of the fish. Note for pier fishermen: be sure you bring a long-handled net. You may even want to tape an extension onto the handle for added reach when the water is low.

Access to the Genesee River is fairly good, especially considering that you are in a populated area. Your best bet is to fish from a boat so you can cover the whole stretch from the mouth up to the lower falls, trolling plugs and spoons during the runs. At the falls, you can beach your boat and wade or fish from shore.

For a free Monroe County fishing information packet contact:

Convention & Visitors Bureau
126 Andrews Street
Rochester, New York 14604
(716)-546-3070

For up-to-the-minute river conditions call any of the tackle shops listed in the Rochester telephone directory.

NOTES: ______________________________

____

____

Atlantic salmon were once native to Lake Ontario, and provided a fishery of immense proportions. Their demise was primarily due to overharvesting, deforestation of the lake's watershed, and the effects of industrialization along the shore of the lake. The DEC is currently attempting to re-establish Atlantic salmon as a sport fishery in the lake, and the results look promising.

HONEOYE CREEK

Map Coordinates	42° 58′ 16″ 77° 43′ 08″
USGS Map(s)	Rush, Honeoye Falls, Honeoye
Township(s)	Rush
Access	Fishell Road
Principal Species	Walleye, Smallmouth Bass, Panfish

The best fishing on Honeoye Creek is in the stretch between its confluence with the Genesee River and West Henrietta Road. There are abundant smallmouth bass and panfish throughout this section. Walleye are commonly caught nearer the stream mouth. Coarse fish such as carp and suckers are also found here.

Access to Honeoye Creek is facilitated by a state-maintained launch site for cartop boats and canoes. It is located off Fishell Road, one-quarter mile west of Route 15 (West Henrietta Road).

This creek is not stocked.

NOTES: ______________________________

____

____

IRONDEQUOIT CREEK

Map Coordinates	43° 10′ 39″ 77° 31′ 33″
USGS Map(s)	Rochester East, Webster, Fairport, Honeoye Falls
Township(s)	Penfield, Perinton, Mendon (Monroe County); Victor (Ontario County)
Access	Cartop boat and canoe access site off Route 404; Ellison Park, on Route 286 (Blossom Road); Penfield Linear Park, south of Route 441, handicapped access available; Panorama Plaza; Powder Mills Park, off Route 96 (Pittsford-Victor Road), handicapped access available; town access site, on Main Street in Fishers, north of Route 251.
Principal Species	Rainbow Trout (stocked), Brown Trout (stocked and wild), Atlantic Salmon, Northern Pike, Bullhead, Panfish

Not too long ago, Irondequoit Creek was a heavily polluted stream of little value to fishermen. In recent years, however, it has been returned to a relatively clean state. This turn around has been accomplished by putting an end to the dumping of municipal sewage into the stream, with the result that today it ranks as one of the top rainbow trout (steelhead) streams in New York State.

In the spring 24,000 rainbow trout yearlings (steelhead) are stocked in Irondequoit Creek. Tremendous numbers of these big, hard-fighting fish can be found in Irondequoit Creek from mid-fall until late spring. They will run at least as far up as the town of Fishers in Ontario County. If water levels are sufficiently high, steelhead will also be found in several tributary streams, most notably Allen Creek, north of Route 441.

Irondequoit Creek is not an important salmon stream. A few coho and chinook do stray into the lower creek in the fall; a majority of these fish taken in the vicinity of Ellison Park. In recent years, the DEC tried stocking this and several other streams with Atlantic salmon with the hope of re-establishing a self-sustaining population of these fish. Unfortunately, this policy did not succeed due to predation by other salmonids that crowd into Irondequoit Bay in the spring. However, Atlantic salmon are now being stocked off the mouth of Irondequoit Creek. The numbers of fish being harvested aren't impressive yet, but it is hoped that this will improve with time. Most of the Atlantic salmon are caught in the lake, not in the creek.

Due to the changes in the Atlantic salmon stocking policy, the special regulations that were in effect on Irondequoit Creek for the past several years have been lifted. Consult your regulations guide for current regulations.

Above Fairport Road, south of East Rochester, Irondequoit Creek is a good-quality inland trout stream. Averaging 10 to 20 feet in width, it is surrounded mainly by residential areas and park land, but does run through a wooded area near Bushnell Basin. This section of the stream is fishable all trout season. Wild browns can be found in fairly good numbers as far upstream as the mouth of Trout Brook, near Bloomfield Road in Mendon Township.

The County of Monroe maintains a hatchery at Powder Mills Park. This facility has always provided large numbers of brown trout for Irondequoit Creek. Recently, however, the hatchery has switched to stocking rainbow trout. At various times during the year, local sportsmen's groups, in cooperation with the hatchery, hold fishing derbies for children and senior citizens in Powder Mills Park. The creek will usually be posted with "no fishing" signs a few days prior to the event and hatchery fish will be stocked specifically for the derby. A few breeder fish are added to the stocking to give the participants the opportunity to take a 6- to 10-pound brown trout.

In the spring, 1,300 brown trout yearlings are stocked in the 2-mile section of Irondequoit Creek between the New York State Barge Canal and the boundary of Powder Mills Park. An additional 300 brown trout yearlings are stocked between the Monroe/Ontario County line and the mouth of Trout Brook. In Ontario County, Irondequoit Creek is stocked with 500 brown trout from the county line upstream 0.8 mile to the hamlet of Fishers.

A number of warm-water species are found in Irondequoit Creek, including northern pike, bullhead, rock bass, and an occasional walleye. Northerns can be found in the very lowest reaches of the creek all year long. In the spring, they run up Irondequoit Creek at least as far as Allen Creek to spawn. A limited run of suckers also takes place here in the spring.

A major problem on Irondequoit Creek is access. It is very heavily posted, especially below the New York State Barge Canal. There are tentative plans for the state to acquire public fishing rights on the creek, but none have been obtained as of Spring 1991.

NOTES: ____________________

Once of little value to fishermen, Irondequoit Creek is now one of the top steelhead streams in New York State. It also provides fishing for brown trout and northern pike.

MILL CREEK

Map Coordinates	43° 15′ 38″ 77° 27′ 06″
USGS Map(s)	Ninemile Point, Webster
Township(s)	Webster
Access	Webster Beach Park, off Route 18 (Lake Road)
Principal Species	Rainbow Trout, Brown Trout, Chinook Salmon, Coho Salmon, Smallmouth Bass, Largemouth Bass, Panfish

Mill Creek is a small stream that gets a very good run of rainbow trout in the spring, as well as a significant number of coho jacks. In the fall rainbow trout, brown trout, and stray salmon are often caught here in large numbers.

In addition to the cold-water species, smallmouth bass, yellow perch, and other panfish are found in the lower section of the creek in the spring, summer, and fall.

Access to Mill Creek is essentially limited to the portion that flows through Webster Beach Park; the rest of the creek is heavily posted. There is a 200-foot public fishing pier adjacent to the creek mouth.

Mill Creek is not stocked.

NOTES: ____________________

NEW YORK STATE BARGE CANAL - See Orleans County Streams and Rivers.

OATKA CREEK (Lower Section)

Map Coordinates	43° 01′ 27″ 77° 43′ 48″
USGS Map(s)	West Henrietta, Clifton, Caledonia, LeRoy
Township(s)	Wheatland (Monroe County), LeRoy (Genesee County)
Access	Oatka Trail, Oatka Creek Park
Principal Species	Brown Trout (stocked and wild), Rainbow Trout, Brook Trout, Northern Pike, Largemouth Bass, Smallmouth Bass, Panfish

As it leaves the town of LeRoy in Genesee County, this stream is a low-quality, warm-water fishery that all but dries up in the summer. However, at an area known as the Blue Hole, near Circular Hill Road, the Oatka receives a strong influx of cold spring water and again becomes habitable by trout. Further downstream, at Mumford, the quality of the stream is again reinforced by the cold, clear waters of the famed Spring Creek (see Livingston County). The result is a trout stream that ranks as one of the finest in New York State.

Surrounded by farmland and park land, the lower Oatka is a slowly meandering stream that averages about 75 feet in width. It has a gravel and slate bottom with pockets of silt. The water is usually quite clear, and there is a substantial amount of aquatic vegetation throughout much of its length.

Fishable all year, the Oatka has a good population of wild brown trout, primarily between Circular Hill Road and Scottsville. Rainbows are only occasionally taken here, and these fish are probably

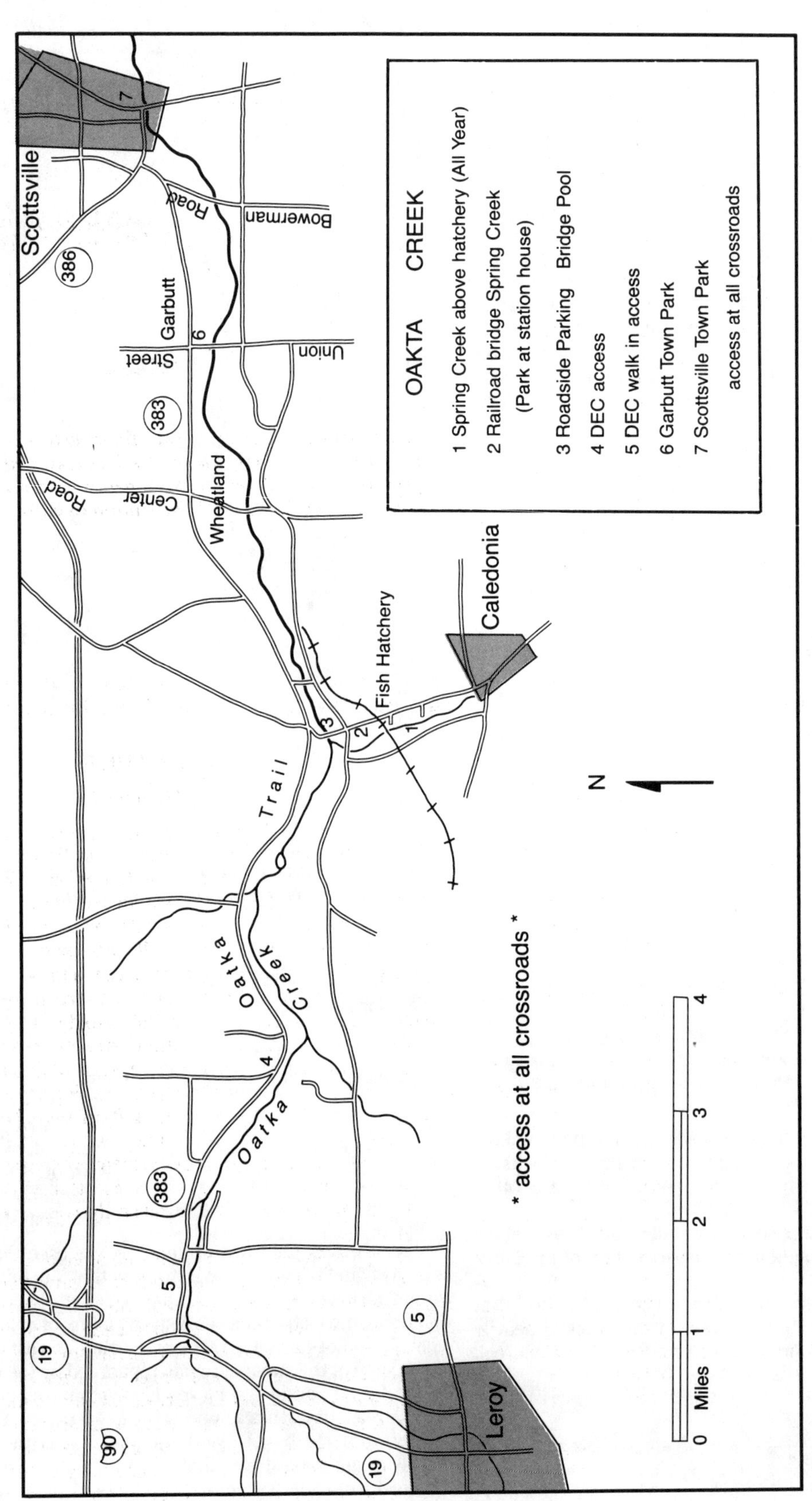
OAKTA CREEK
1 Spring Creek above hatchery (All Year)
2 Railroad bridge Spring Creek
(Park at station house)
3 Roadside Parking Bridge Pool
4 DEC access
5 DEC walk in access
6 Garbutt Town Park
7 Scottsville Town Park
access at all crossroads
* access at all crossroads *
Scottsville
Caledonia
Leroy
Fish Hatchery
Oatka Creek
Oatka Trail
Wheatland Center Road
Bowerman Road
Union Street
Garbutt
386
383
5
19
90
N
0 Miles 1 2 3 4

escapees from the Caledonia Fish Hatchery. In addition to trout, the section of Oatka Creek near the Genesee River is a good northern pike stream. Largemouth and smallmouth bass are also taken with regularity in the lower portions of the stream.

In the spring, the 1.9-mile section of Oatka Creek between Scottsville and the old dam above Bowerman Road is stocked with a total of 6,300 brown trout yearlings. Trout can be taken all year on Oatka Creek, any size, 10 per day with the following exception: From the dam above Bowerman Road upstream to the Twin Bridges (near Route 36), trout can be taken all year, minimum size 12 inches, 3 per day, and only artificial lures can be used. However, since the fish in this section are almost entirely native trout, this would be a good area to practice catch-and-release fishing. The state has purchased intermittent areas of public fishing rights between Perry Road in Genesee County and the Twin Bridges, and some landowners will permit access through their property on request.

The nutrient-rich waters of the lower Oatka produce a wide variety of aquatic insects. For this reason it is a very good fly-fishing stream. In addition, most of the lower section is large enough to make casting easy. However, this does not necessarily mean that the fishing is easy. The native trout of the Oatka can provide quite a challenge to the fly fisherman.

Good fly fishing can be experienced in the middle of winter here. Dead-drifted olive and tan scud patterns and a variety of nymphs such as the hare's ear and the red fox squirrel tail worked near the bottom can produce fast action. On warm sunny winter days, when the water temperature increases slightly, the angler may even be able to find a few trout feeding at the surface on midges.

The scud and nymph patterns work well into early spring. This is when the fishing really picks up. The middle of April marks the beginning of a progression of good hatches that last into early summer. The first is the famous Hendrickson hatch. Thick hatches of duns can be experienced on the Oatka's fertile waters. The hatch usually occurs in the early afternoon. There can also be good spinner falls at dusk. The hatch normally lasts through the end of April.

The Hendricksons are followed by the tan caddis hatch in early May. Good action can be encountered throughout the day. Sometimes this hatch is best approached with an emerging caddis fished just below the surface or in the surface film. Caddis action can last well into May and overlap the emergence of the March Brown hatch in the middle of the month and the Gray Fox hatch toward the end of the month. Both of these mayflies normally hatch in the afternoon, although they may begin to emerge in the late morning. However, their emergence on the Oatka can be somewhat sporadic. For this reason, the most consistent action can sometimes be found by dead-drifting nymphs, which represent these mayflies, in the morning, prior to the hatch.

The sulphur hatch, which occurs from the end of May until about the middle of June, can be considered the highlight of the season. The daily emergence of this majestic mayfly usually triggers good surface activity. The hatch normally begins in the late afternoon and lasts until dusk. Usually a spinner fall follows the hatch near dark. The balmy evening temperatures of late spring coupled with good action make this hatch a joy to fish.

As the season moves into summer, the fishing gets a little tougher. The water is normally low and clear. Good tiny Blue Wing Olive hatches can be experienced in the early summer, however. A good time to try a variety of terrestrials is when the water is low and clear and there is no visible surface activity. Some midge hatches can also be found in the summer. The most productive time to fish the Oatka in the summer is in the early morning while the water is still cool. Small nymphs work especially well if there is no surface activity.

As the season moves into fall, there is only sporadic hatch activity. Terrestrials continue to be a good choice. Streamer patterns and wooly buggers can produce in the fall, especially when the water has risen and is a little off-color. Actually, these patterns work well anytime during the year when these water conditions exist. The Oatka tends to muddy after a downpour. For this reason it is a good idea to try to get the latest water conditions after there has been a heavy rain.

AMERICAN MARCH BROWN (nymph)

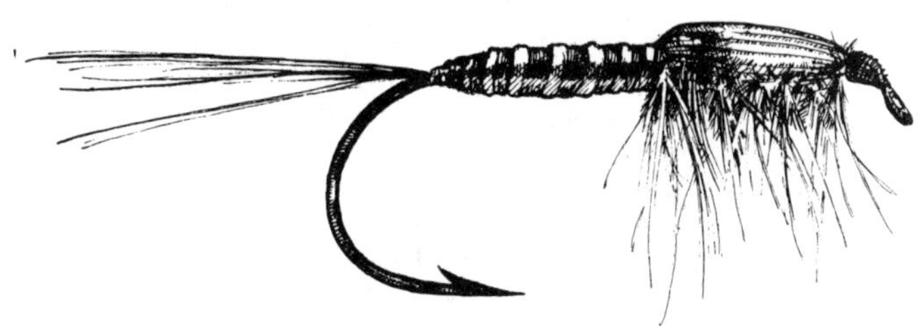

March brown hatches occur intermittently from early afternoon to just before dusk. This classic pattern imitates the nymphs that are active just prior to these hatches. Consequently, it produces well from noon to dusk.

The following article was written by Al Himmel, an avid fly fisherman and an active member of Trout Unlimited.

OATKA CREEK

By Al Himmel

Oatka Creek can be divided into two stretches: One, from LeRoy to Mumford, is accessible from two public fisherman parking areas, the bridge at Mumford, and the bridge at LeRoy. Most of the remaining land is posted along Oatka Trail, but can be accessed at one point for a parking fee deposited in a can on a fence. The second stretch, from Mumford to Scottsville, can be accessed at bridges in Mumford, Garbutt, and Scottsville, but almost all of the posted sections belong to fishing clubs and are posted as patrolled. Upstream from the bridge, at the Rubberoid Plant, the stream can be fished up to the club posting, and upstream from Scottsville bridge on Route 251 it can be fished by permission of the owner. In the town of Scottsville itself there is streamside parking behind the warehouse and there is no posting; however, a short hike through the bushes is required, and the stream divides into two branches. Upstream there is some local stream improvement where posting begins. The final access point is at the town of Scottsville park, on the creek. Locals fish this area with bait extensively, so one may have to wade some to avoid the youngsters.

Generally, Oatka Creek is a difficult stream to fish during the late season, since nutrient levels produce a profusion of green slimy algae under which the trout hide, oblivious to all that transpires above. Additionally, there are many deep holes filled with siltation into which waders can sink hip deep. Stream improvement on Oatka has been almost non-existent in recent years, so that recognizable holding sites are few and far between. Long hours of searching and wading are required to obtain a book on this stream. Additionally, stocking is done exclusively at the bridge access points so that early season success is not indicative of all season activity. That these fish find hiding places and carry over is evidenced by a recent catch recorded on worms in May: 13 trout, from 8 to 16 inches, all deeply colored, including brookies, rainbow, and browns. The large rainbows were probably escapees from the Caledonia hatchery. One or more 20- to 24-inch trout are taken every year in the spring, usually by youngsters fishing worms or minnows in their favorite deep hole. Oatka is definitely a bait fisherman's paradise if he finds a deep holding pool at a more remote section. Not long ago, a Caledonia lad recorded a 28-inch fish.

For the fly fisherman, it is necessary to decide to fish Oatka early and often until the Hendricksons begin, and then to follow the hatching sequence by fishing regularly. The best place to start is at Garbutt or the fishing access point nearest LeRoy. The Garbutt stretch is characterized by several old bridge abutments that hold trout, but as all flyers know, the time of day and year will determine whether there are rising trout or absolute solitude. The March Brown hatch is usually good in this section.

Upstream from the Mumford bridge, the junction of Spring Creek forms one of the most superb fly fishing pools - if the cows do not interfere. Further upstream some truly beautiful fallen tree pools hold the big ones, but ducks often resent the intrusion and create a furor, which must be allowed to subside. Still further upstream posting begins, but there is a riffle at the end of the posted section that can be most productive.

The blue silo section on Oatka Trail is heavily stocked and fished. The secret here is to avoid the weekends and early mornings. Most of the bait fisherman leave about 4 p.m. All in all, Oatka is a puzzle, a pleasure, and a headache. The fisherman who is willing to use various methods and learn the secrets can find large trout, northerns, and sometimes highly productive trout fishing.

For information on the upper section of Oatka Creek see the section on Wyoming County streams and rivers.

NOTES: ______________________________

____

____

RED CREEK

Map Coordinates .... 43° 07′ 11″ 77° 38′ 23
USGS Map(s) .... West Henrietta
Township(s) .... Brighton
Access .... Genesee Valley Park East
Principal Species .... Northern Pike, Bullhead, Panfish

This small stream empties into the New York State Barge Canal just east of the Genesee River. Surrounded by park land, this is a good location for introducing children to the pleasures of fishing. A site for launching cartop boats and canoes exists at the stream mouth.

Red Creek is not stocked.

NOTES: ______________________________

____

____

HORNBERG

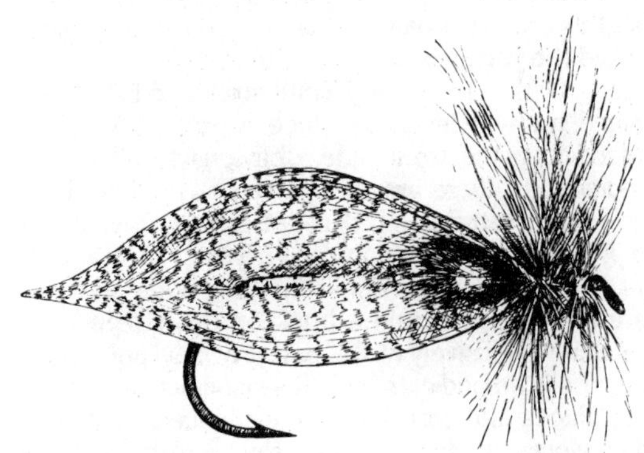

Resembling numerous types of bait fish, the Hornberg is an old standby from the early days of fly fishing. It can be fished wet or dry depending on how it is dressed.

SALMON CREEK

Map Coordinates .... 43° 18′ 55″ 77° 43′ 48″
USGS Map(s) .... Braddock Heights, Hilton, Spencerport
Township(s) .... Greece, Parma
Access .... Braddock Bay Park Marina
Principal Species .... Rainbow Trout, Brown Trout, Chinook Salmon, Coho Salmon, Northern Pike, Bullhead, Smallmouth Bass, Largemouth Bass, Yellow Perch, Panfish

This stream is the primary tributary of Braddock Bay. In the spring, Salmon Creek gets an excellent run of rainbows and a few brown trout. In the early fall chinook salmon, coho salmon, and brown trout are very abundant, followed in the late fall and winter by rainbow trout. All of these fish can be found in good numbers as far upstream as the dam just above Parma Center Road. Snagging for Salmon is allowed on Salmon Creek, from the Lake Ontario Parkway upstream to the Parma Dam.

Salmon Creek is also an important warm-water fishery. Northern pike, largemouth bass, and smallmouth bass are common throughout the creek and are especially abundant just above and below the Ontario Parkway. Bullhead and other panfish are also quite common in the lower section of the creek, especially in the spring.

Access other than by canoe or small boat is a problem here due to heavy posting above Manitou Road. However, the state is in the process of obtaining public fishing rights on Salmon Creek.

Salmon Creek is stocked annually with a total of 10,000 rainbow trout (steelhead).

NOTES: ______________________________

____

____

SANDY CREEK

Map Coordinates .... 43° 21′ 07″ 77° 53′ 30″
USGS Map(s) .... Hamlin, Kendall
Township(s) .... Hamlin (Monroe County), Kendall, Murray (Orleans County)
Access .... State-operated launch ramp on east side of creek off Ontario State Parkway.
Principal Species .... Rainbow Trout, Brown Trout, Chinook Salmon, Coho Salmon, Northern Pike, Smallmouth Bass, Bullhead, Panfish

Sandy Creek offers good to excellent fishing for coho salmon and chinook salmon in the fall. These are followed by good runs of brown trout and, in the late fall and spring, by rainbow trout. Although much of the fishing activity takes place in the lower portions of the creek, the trout and salmon will run at least as far upstream as the town of Murray in Orleans County. Sandy Creek forks above the town and both forks probably hold fish. Snagging for salmon is allowed between the Ontario Parkway and the bridge crossing at Route 104.

Northern pike and smallmouth bass are found throughout the creek, with the best catches coming from the Monroe County section. Bullhead and panfish are caught in good numbers in the lower section of the creek in the spring, summer, and fall.

Sandy Creek is heavily posted. Cartop boats and canoes provide access to much of the stream that would otherwise be unapproachable. They can be launched from the marina on the west side of the creek. The state has purchased public fishing rights on large sections of Sandy Creek near the crossing of Church Road and near the intersection of Route 18 and Redman Road.

Sandy Creek is stocked annually with a total of 180,000 chinook salmon, 30,000 coho salmon, and 13,300 rainbow trout (steelhead).

NOTES: ______________________________

____

____

SHIPBUILDERS CREEK

Map Coordinates .... 43° 15′ 00″ 77° 29′ 55″
USGS Map(s) .... Rochester East, Webster
Township(s) .... Webster
Access .... Closed by posting; approach at mouth via lake
Principal Species .... Rainbow Trout, Brown Trout

Rainbow trout and brown trout are abundant in the lower portion of this creek in the spring and fall, but access is difficult due to posting. Smelt fishing (netting) is very productive near the creek mouth.

Ship Builders Creek is not stocked.

NOTES: ______________________________

____

____

SLATER CREEK

Map Coordinates .... 43° 16′ 10″ 77° 37′ 36″
USGS Map(s) .... Braddock Heights, Rochester West
Township(s) .... Greece
Access .... Off Beach Avenue, near the Russell Station
Principal Species .... Rainbow Trout, Brown Trout, Chinook Salmon, Coho Salmon, Smallmouth Bass, Northern Pike, Bullhead, Panfish

The Russell Station has a warm-water discharge that enters Lake Ontario via Slater Creek. As with other such discharges, huge numbers of cold-water and warm-water species are attracted to the area year round.

In the spring, tremendous numbers of rainbow trout are found here, as well as a good number of brown trout. In the fall, there is excellent fishing for coho salmon and chinook salmon, followed by brown trout and later by rainbow trout. The creek forms a large pool (Little Round Pond) just above Beach Avenue. This pool is ice free all winter and the fishing for salmonids is quite good here, even in mid-winter.

Warm-water fish are also attracted to the discharge area. Most of the species that inhabit Lake Ontario can be found here in abundance year round, including northern pike, smallmouth bass, crappie, rock bass, silver bass, yellow perch, white perch, bullhead, burbot, carp, and suckers.

The state owns the property on both sides of the stream mouth, as well as most of the property that borders on Little Round Pond.

The rough water to the right of the two anglers pictures here is the outflow from the Russell Station power plant. The warm water from the station serves as a strong attractant to many of the species found in Lake Ontario, including bass, trout, and salmon.

A state-maintained site on the east side of the pond provides a launch site for cartop boats and parking for about 40 cars.

Slater Creek is not stocked.

NOTES: ______________________________

____

____

SPRING CREEK - See Livingston County Streams and Rivers.

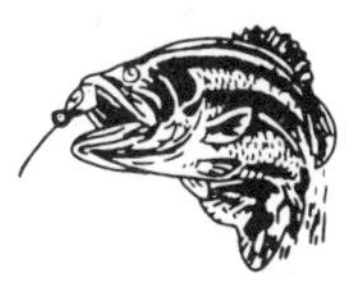

MONROE COUNTY LAKES AND PONDS

BRADDOCK BAY

Location

Map Coordinates .... 43° 18′ 45″ 77° 42′ 50″
USGS Map(s) .... Braddock Heights
Township(s) .... Greece
Access .... Braddock Bay State Park

Physical Characteristics

Area .... 256 acres
Shoreline .... Approximately 5 miles
Elevation .... 249 feet
Maximum Depth .... Varies due to shifting sand bars
Mean Depth .... Approximately 4 feet
Bottom Type .... Sand, muck

Chemical Characteristics

Water .... Clarity varies with conditions
pH .... Alkaline
Oxygen .... Good at all depths all year

Plant Life

Extensive weed beds exist along the periphery of the bay.

Species Information

Largemouth Bass .... Common; growth rate good
Rock Bass .... Common; growth rate good
Yellow Perch .... Common; growth rate good
Black Crappie .... Common; growth rate good
Brown Bullhead .... Abundant; growth rate good
Northern Pike .... Common; growth rate fair to good
Walleye .... Uncommon; growth rate good
White Perch .... Seasonal (spring)
Silver Bass .... Common; growth rate good
Channel Catfish .... Common; growth rate good
Carp .... Common; growth rate good
Bowfin .... Uncommon; growth rate good
Pumpkinseed .... Common; growth rate fair to good
Chinook Salmon .... Seasonal (fall)
Coho Salmon .... Seasonal (spring and fall)
Rainbow Trout .... Seasonal (spring and fall)
Brown Trout .... Seasonal (spring and fall)
American Eel .... Possession prohibited

Boat Launch Sites

1. Braddock Bait and Tackle - 327 Manitou Beach Road, Hilton. Tackle, hard-surface ramp - fee.
2. Parkway Marina - 320 Manitou Road, Hilton. Full service marina, single hard-surface ramp - fee.
3. Braddock Bay State Park - 194 Braddock Road, off East Manitou Road, Greece. City-owned, full-service marina, double hard-surface ramps - fee.

NOTE: Braddock Bay is very shallow and the mouth is subject to shoaling. Caution is advised when attempting to access or exit this bay, especially during low-water periods.

General Information

Braddock Bay is one of the most productive areas on the southern shore of Lake Ontario. Soon after ice-out, great numbers of bullhead and white perch move into the bay to spawn and are easily taken by shore fishermen. Shortly afterwards, smelt can be found near the mouth of the bay and along the near-shore areas of Lake Ontario, though few are taken in the bay itself. Coho salmon, brown trout, and rainbow trout are also found in the near-shore areas, as well as in the bay, in the spring. Northern pike, largemouth bass, and smallmouth bass are found in the streams that feed into Braddock Bay, most notably Salmon Creek.

During the summer and fall, there is very good angling for largemouth bass, northern pike, panfish, and rough fish in Braddock Bay, while smallmouth bass and yellow perch can be taken just outside the mouth of the bay in Lake Ontario. Walleye can also be found in the bay in the summer, but unsuccessful spawning in recent years has greatly reduced their numbers.

As fall approaches, large numbers of salmon begin to move into the shallow waters of Lake Ontario in anticipation of the fall spawning runs. When conditions are right, they will move into Braddock Bay on their way into Salmon Creek. They are followed later in the fall by brown trout and rainbow trout. The large concentrations of these fish in the bay and its feeder streams makes for some of the most exciting fishing to be found in western New York.

Ice fishing is a popular sport on Braddock Bay. Northern pike, yellow perch, and other panfish are abundant. In addition to these species, significant numbers of brown trout and rainbow trout will linger in the bay during the winter and are a real challenge when taken through the ice.

NOTES: ______________________________

____

____

When drift fishing with minnows or other swimming baits, hook the bait through the lips to for a more natural presentation. When still fishing, this effect is usually achieved by hooking the bait through the dorsal area.

BUCK POND

Location

Map Coordinates .... 43° 16′ 50″ 77° 40′ 03″
USGS Map(s) .... Braddock Heights
Township(s) .... Greece
Access .... Edgemere Drive

Physical Characteristics

Area .... 187 acres
Shoreline .... 3.58 miles
Elevation .... 249 feet
Maximum Depth .... 5 feet
Mean Depth .... 4 feet
Bottom Type .... Muck, sand

Chemical Characteristics

Water .... Clarity varies with conditions
pH .... Alkaline
Oxygen .... Good throughout the pond all year

Plant Life

Extensive weed beds exist throughout the pond.

Species Information

Largemouth Bass .... Common; growth rate good
Rock Bass .... Common; growth rate good
Yellow Perch .... Common; growth rate good
Black Crappie .... Common; growth rate good
Brown Bullhead .... Abundant; growth rate good
Northern Pike .... Common; growth rate fair to good
Walleye .... Uncommon; growth rate good
White Perch .... Seasonal (spring)
Silver Bass .... Common; growth rate good
Channel Catfish .... Common; growth rate good
Carp .... Common; growth rate good
Sunfish .... Common; growth rate fair to good
Chinook Salmon .... Seasonal (fall)
Coho Salmon .... Seasonal (spring and fall)
Rainbow Trout .... Seasonal (spring and fall)
Brown trout .... Seasonal (spring and fall)

Boat Launch Sites

None; shore access only.

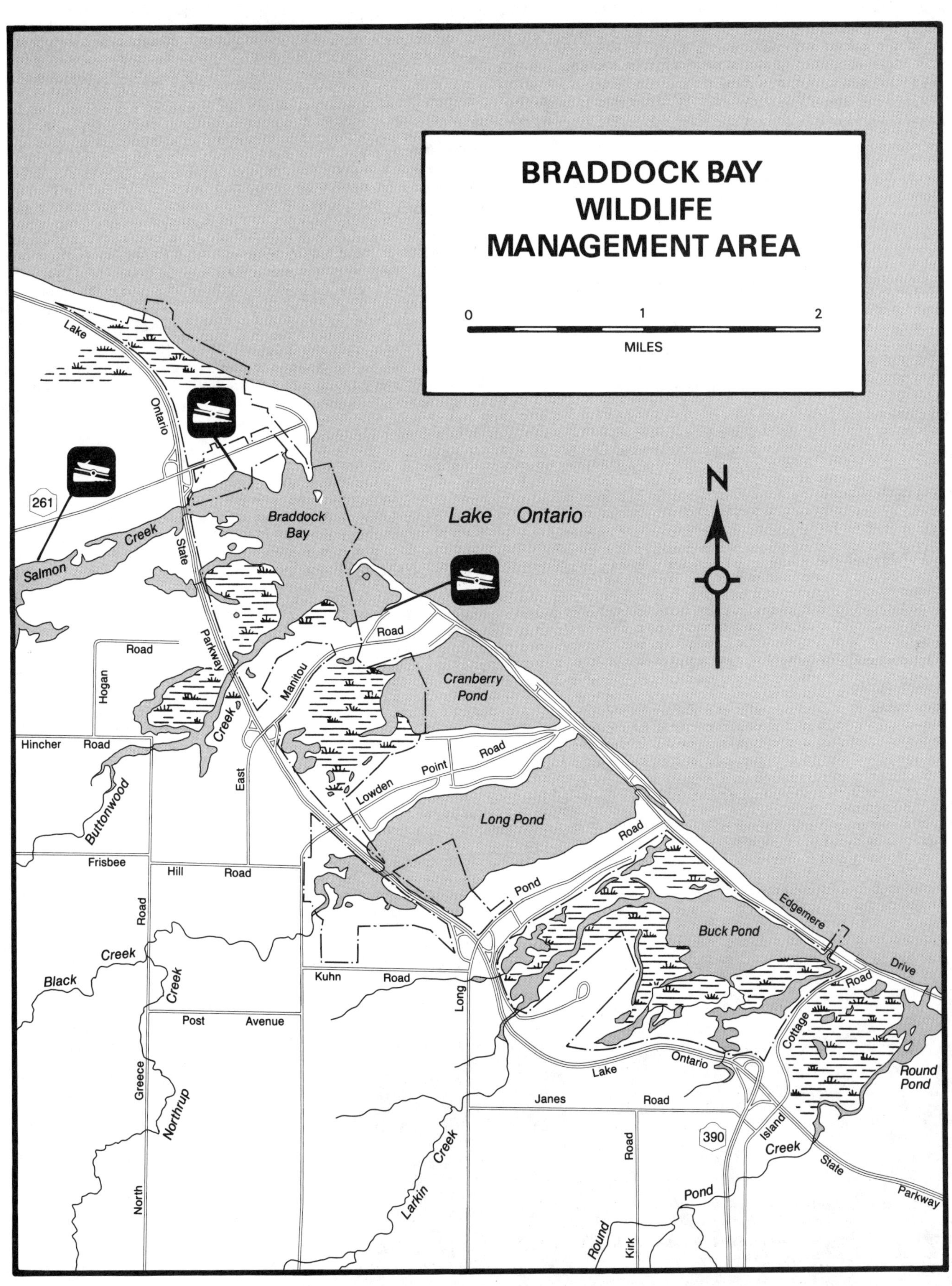
BRADDOCK BAY
WILDLIFE
MANAGEMENT AREA
0
1
2
MILES
N
Lake Ontario
Braddock Bay
Cranberry Pond
Long Pond
Buck Pond
Round Pond
261
390
Lake Ontario State Parkway
Salmon Creek
Manitou Road
Hogan Road
Hincher Road
Creek
East
Buttonwood
Lowden Point Road
Frisbee Road
Hill Road
Pond Road
Edgemere Drive
Black Creek
Creek
Kuhn Road
Long Pond Road
Post Avenue
Cottage Road
Lake Ontario
Greece
North
Northrup
Janes Road
Larkin Creek
Road
Island Creek
State Parkway
Pond
Round
Kirk

General Information

Probably the best fishing on Buck Pond is found in the spring, when bullhead and white perch move in from Lake Ontario to spawn. The other species listed above are all available in varying numbers, primarily in the spring and fall, including some stray trout and salmon. Because access is limited to the shallow shoreline along Edgemere Drive, fishing opportunities in the summer are somewhat limited. During the winter the entire pond is accessible through the ice. The ice fishing here is exceptionally good, especially for northern pike.

NOTES: ______________________________

____

____

CRANBERRY POND

Location

Map Coordinates	43° 18′ 02″ 77° 41′ 49″
USGS Map(s)	Braddock Heights
Township(s)	Greece
Access	Edgemere Drive

Physical Characteristics

Area	226 acres
Shoreline	2.81 miles
Elevation	249 feet
Maximum Depth	9 feet
Mean Depth	6 feet
Bottom Type	Muck, sand

Chemical Characteristics

Water	Clarity varies with conditions
pH	Alkaline
Oxygen	Good throughout the pond all year

Plant Life

Extensive weed beds exist throughout the pond.

Species Information

Largemouth Bass	Common; growth rate good
Rock Bass	Common; growth rate good
Yellow Perch	Common; growth rate good
Black Crappie	Common; growth rate good
Brown Bullhead	Abundant; growth rate good
Northern Pike	Common; growth rate fair to good
Walleye	Uncommon; growth rate good
White Perch	Seasonal (spring)
Silver Bass	Common; growth rate good
Channel Catfish	Common; growth rate good
Carp	Common; growth rate good
Bowfin	Uncommon; growth rate good
Pumpkinseed	Common; growth rate fair to good
Chinook Salmon	Seasonal (fall)
Coho Salmon	Seasonal (spring and fall)
Rainbow Trout	Seasonal (spring and fall)
Brown Trout	Seasonal (spring and fall)

Boat Launch Sites

There is an unimproved gravel ramp at the northwest corner of the pond for small boats only - no charge.

General Information

The principal species found in Cranberry Pond are brown bullhead and white perch, which come into the pond from Lake Ontario in the spring to spawn. Fair to good numbers of the other listed species are also caught here, primarily in the spring and fall, including a significant number of stray trout and salmon. With the exception of one unimproved gravel ramp for small boats, fishing is restricted to the shallow shoreline along Edgemere Drive, and this somewhat limits the fishing opportunities in the summer. In the winter, ice fishing is popular on Cranberry Pond, and good numbers of northern pike and panfish, as well as an occasional trout, are taken.

NOTES: ______________________________

____

____

IRONDEQUOIT BAY

Location

Map Coordinates	43° 16′ 28″ 77° 38′ 44″
USGS Map(s)	Braddock Heights
Township(s)	Irondequoit, Webster, and Penfield
Access	Lake Road (northern shore); Irondequoit Bay Park East, off Route 404 on east side of bay; Irondequoit Bay Park West, on Bay Front South Road on the west side of the bay.

Irondequoit Bay, seen here from the bridge at Route 104, is essentially a separate lake; its connection to Lake Ontario is very tenuous. Once heavily polluted, the bay has re-established its reputation as an excellent fishery.

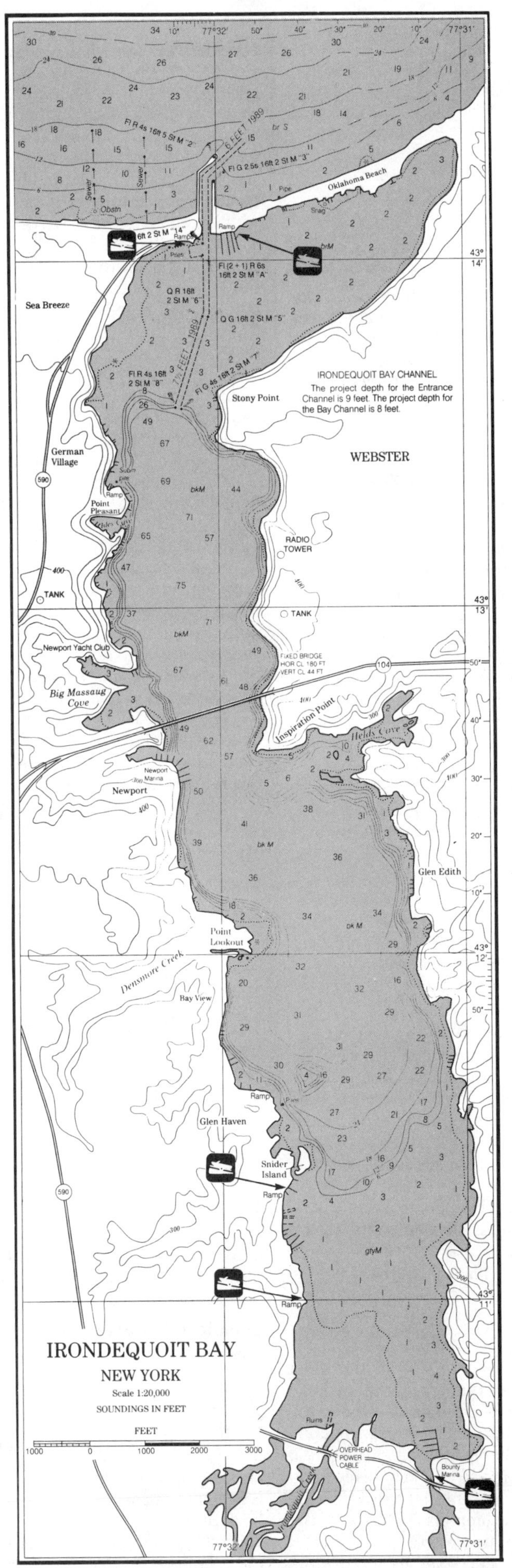
IRONDEQUOIT BAY
NEW YORK
Scale 1:20,000
SOUNDINGS IN FEET
FEET
IRONDEQUOIT BAY CHANNEL
The project depth for the Entrance Channel is 9 feet. The project depth for the Bay Channel is 8 feet.
Sea Breeze
Oklahoma Beach
Stony Point
WEBSTER
German Village
Point Pleasant
RADIO TOWER
TANK
Newport Yacht Club
Big Massaug Cove
FIXED BRIDGE HOR CL 180 FT VERT CL 44 FT
Inspiration Point
Newport
Newport Marina
Glen Edith
Point Lookout
Densmore Creek
Bay View
Glen Haven
Snider Island
Ramp
OVERHEAD POWER CABLE
Bounty Marina
77°32′
77°31′

Physical Characteristics

Area	1,654 acres
Shoreline	Not available
Elevation	249 feet
Maximum Depth	76 feet
Mean Depth	22 feet
Bottom Type	Muck, sand

Chemical Characteristics

Water	Slightly turbid
pH	Unknown
Oxygen	The waters of Irondequoit Bay stratify in the summer, with dissolved oxygen becoming deficient below 15 feet. Eutrophication and stagnation also contribute to poor oxygen levels in the bay, particularly in the summer.

Plant Life

Weed beds exist in the shallow northern and southern ends of the bay and intermittently along the eastern and western shores. Extensive algal blooms occur during the summer months, seriously hindering the growth of rooted aquatic plants.

Species Information

Largemouth Bass	Common; growth rate good
Smallmouth Bass	Common; growth rate good
Northern Pike	Common; growth rate good
White Perch	Seasonal (spring)
Brown Bullhead	Very common; growth rate good
Carp	Common; growth rate good
Black Crappie	Common; growth rate fair to good
Rock Bass	Common; growth rate fair to good
Silver Bass	Common; growth rate good
Suckers	Common; growth rate good
Channel Catfish	Uncommon; growth rate good
Bowfin	Uncommon; growth rate good
Longnose Gar	Uncommon; growth rate unknown
Sheepshead	Common; growth rate fair to good
Yellow Perch	Common; growth rate good
Pumpkinseed	Common; growth rate fair
Smelt	Seasonal (spring)
Brown Trout	Seasonal (spring and fall)
Rainbow Trout	Seasonal (spring and fall)
Coho Salmon	Seasonal (spring and fall)
Chinook Salmon	Seasonal (fall)

Boat Launch Sites

1. Mayer's Marine, Lake Road (Route 18) at Irondequoit Bay outlet. Marine supplies, boat rentals; single ramp - fee.
2. New York State-maintained launch site off Lake Road (Route 18) at northwest corner of the bay. Small unimproved site suitable for small trailerable boats, cartop boats, and canoes - no charge.
3. Sutter's Marine, 512 Bay Front South. Marine supplies, single ramp - fee.
4. Monroe County launch site off Bay Front South Road. Small, hard-surface ramp suitable for small trailerable boats, cartop boats, and canoes - no charge.
5. New York State launch site on Route 404 (Empire Blvd.) at the southern end of the bay. Launch site for cartop boats and canoes - no charge.

General Information

A century ago, Irondequoit Bay ranked as one of the most productive and diverse fisheries on the southern shore of Lake Ontario. Muskellunge, blue pike, and walleye plied its waters and the quality of fishing for largemouth and smallmouth bass, yellow perch, northern pike, trout, and panfish would boggle the mind of anyone familiar with the bay today. The sport fishing in the bay declined in the twentieth century, due to increased salinity from road de-icing salt, the dumping of sewage, and the proliferation of carp, to the point where its reputation was as sullied as its waters.

In recent years, however, steps have been taken to improve the water quality in the bay, and this has already resulted in a considerable improvement in the fishing here.

The muskie and blue pike are gone now, and walleye are only rarely taken in Irondequoit Bay. But the many coves, drop-offs and shallows of this lake (although classified as a bay, it has only a tenuous connection with Lake Ontario) provide angling for a wide variety of warm- and cold-water species. The most abundant fish are white perch and brown bullhead, both of which are taken in great quantity, primarily in the spring. Other panfish that can be taken here with varying degrees of success include yellow perch, black crappie, rock bass, silver bass, smelt, and sunfish. Northern pike, though not as plentiful as in the old days, are still common in the shallows of the southern end of Irondequoit Bay. Carp are also quite common in this area. Largemouth bass are found throughout the bay, and the fishing for these tenacious fighters is very good all season long. Especially productive areas for bass are Held's Cove, Big Massaug Cove, and along the drop-offs in the central portion of the bay. Smallmouth bass, while not as plentiful as their largemouth cousins, can be found in most bays and along the shallow, near-shore waters of the central area. The western shore seems to be more productive than the eastern for smallmouth.

Cold-water species have returned to Irondequoit Bay, thanks to the DEC stocking program. In the spring, huge numbers of rainbow trout stack up in the southern area of the bay, very close to the mouth of Irondequoit Creek, in anticipation of their spawning run. Numerous brown trout, holdovers from the spawning run of the previous fall, can be taken in the spring by trolling along the western shore, between Point Pleasant and Point Lookout. The shallow northern end also holds numerous trout and salmon (coho) in the spring and is a popular bank fishing area. In the fall, Irondequoit Bay has excellent fishing for brown trout and rainbow trout, and a few coho and chinook salmon will stray into the bay, as well.

Ice fishing is becoming increasingly popular on this bay, though you still don't have to worry about crowds. Good catches of northern pike, yellow perch, smelt, brown trout, and rainbow trout can be taken through the ice, but you might have to hunt around a little for good locations. Not enough information has been generated yet to establish a consensus as to where the best hard-water angling areas are.

NOTES: ______________________________

____

____

LONG POND

Location

Map Coordinates	43° 17′ 22″ 77° 41′ 29″
USGS Map(s)	Braddock Heights
Township(s)	Greece
Access	Edgemere Drive

Physical Characteristics

Area	450 acres
Shoreline	5.5 miles
Elevation	249 feet
Maximum Depth	8 feet
Mean Depth	5 feet
Bottom Type	Muck, sand

Chemical Characteristics

Water	Clarity varies with conditions
pH	Alkaline
Oxygen	Good throughout the pond all year

Plant Life

Extensive weed beds are found throughout the pond.

Species Information

Largemouth Bass	Common; growth rate good
Rock Bass	Common; growth rate good
Yellow Perch	Common; growth rate good
Black Crappie	Common; growth rate good
Brown Bullhead	Abundant; growth rate good

In Monroe County, the shore of Lake Ontario forms numerous small bays that are almost completely cut off from the lake. These protected bays can be fished when the lake is too rough. They offer good fishing for panfish, bass, northern pike, and seasonal fishing for trout and salmon.

Northern Pike	Common; growth rate fair to good
Walleye	Uncommon; growth rate good
White Perch	Seasonal (spring)
Silver Bass	Common; growth rate good
Channel Catfish	Common; growth rate good
Carp	Common; growth rate good
Bowfin	Uncommon; growth rate good
Pumpkinseed	Common; growth rate fair to good
Chinook Salmon	Seasonal (fall)
Coho Salmon	Seasonal (spring and fall)
Rainbow Trout	Seasonal (spring and fall)
Brown Trout	Seasonal (spring and fall)

Boat Launch Sites

None; shore access only.

General Information

White perch and brown bullhead are the principal species found in Long Pond. In the spring, they can be taken in great numbers from the pond and the outlet when they migrate in from Lake Ontario to spawn. The other species listed are available in fair to good numbers, primarily in the spring and fall, including good numbers of trout and salmon. Access to Long Pond is limited to the shoreline and outlet along Edgemere Drive, and this somewhat restricts the fishing opportunities in the warm summer months. During the winter, ice fishing is popular on Long Pond, and good numbers of northern pike and panfish, as well as an occasional trout, are caught through the ice.

NOTES: ____________________

ROUND POND

Location

Map Coordinates	43° 16′ 28″ 77° 38′ 44″
USGS Map(s)	Braddock Heights
Township(s)	Greece
Access	Edgemere Drive

Physical Characteristics

Area	53 acres
Shoreline	3.46 miles
Elevation	249 feet
Maximum Depth	5 feet
Mean Depth	3 feet
Bottom Type	Muck, sand

Chemical Characteristics

Water	Clarity varies with conditions
pH	Alkaline
Oxygen	Good in the pond all year

Plant Life

Extensive weed beds are found through the pond.

Species Information

Largemouth Bass	Common; growth rate good
Rock Bass	Common; growth rate good
Yellow Perch	Common; growth rate good
Black Crappie	Common; growth rate good
Brown Bullhead	Abundant; growth rate good
Northern Pike	Common; growth rate good
Walleye	Uncommon; growth rate good
Pumpkinseed	Common; growth rate fair to good
White Perch	Seasonal (spring)
Silver Bass	Common; growth rate good

Channel Catfish	Common; growth rate good
Carp	Common; growth rate good
Chinook Salmon	Seasonal (fall)
Coho Salmon	Seasonal (spring and fall)
Rainbow Trout	Seasonal (spring and fall)
Brown Trout	Seasonal (spring and fail)

Boat Launch Sites

None; shore access only.

General Information

White perch and brown bullhead are the principal species found in Round Pond. They are taken in good numbers in the spring when they migrate in from Lake Ontario to spawn. The other species listed are found here in varying concentrations, primarily in the spring and fall. The fishing for trout and salmon is very limited, as is the ice fishing, due to the shallow water depths. Fishing is limited to the shallow shoreline and outlet along Edgemere Drive.

NOTES: ______________________________

In addition to the large lakes and ponds in Monroe County, there are a number of very small ponds that are a part of the Rochester Urban fishing Program. This program is designed to increase the fishing opportunities available to the urban residents of Monroe County. Although generally small, the following ponds should not be overlooked, for they provide good fishing for many species of warm water fish, as well as other recreational opportunities.

COBBS HILL PARK RESERVOIR (Lake Riley)

Map Coordinates	43° 08′ 16″ 77° 34′ 19″
USGS Map(s)	Rochester East
Township(s)	City of Rochester
Access	off Route 31 (Monroe Avenue) or Culver Road
Area	5 acres
Principal Species	Largemouth Bass, Smallmouth Bass, Brown Bullhead, Bluegill, Bowfin, Carp, Channel Catfish, Black Crappie, White Perch, Suckers

This small lake is stocked yearly with varying species of fish. It offers good bank fishing, and is an excellent location for introducing children to the world of angling. Parking is available nearby.

Boats are not allowed.

NOTES: ______________________________

BRIGHTON PARK POND

Map Coordinates	43° 06′ 00″ 77° 35′ 30″
USGS Map(s)	(Not on current topographical maps)
Township(s)	Brighton
Access	Westfall Road and Clinton Avenue
Area	16 acres
Principal Species	Largemouth bass, Bluegill

Brighton Pond is operated by the Town of Brighton Parks and Recreation Department. A permit is required to fish the pond.

NOTES: ______________________________

DURAND-EASTMAN PARK PONDS

Map Coordinates	43° 13′ 48″ 77° 33′ 40″
USGS Map(s)	Rochester East
Township(s)	City of Rochester
Access	Lake Shore Boulevard
Area	Durand Lake - 19 acres; Eastman Lake - 19.2 acres
Principal Species	Largemouth Bass, Bluegill, Brown Bullhead, White perch, Yellow Perch

Nestled in a large, wooded area adjacent to Lake Ontario, Durand-Eastman Park provides good to excellent fishing for largemouth bass in the spring and late summer. Yellow perch are also quite abundant and can be taken through the ice in winter.

Shore fishing is permitted anywhere on the ponds. Boats are not allowed.

NOTES: ______________________________

MAPLEWOOD PARK POND

Map Coordinates	43° 10′ 59″ 77° 37′ 51″
USGS Map(s)	Rochester East, Rochester West
Township(s)	City of Rochester
Access	Maplewood Drive
Area	1 acre
Principal Species	Rock Bass, White Bass, Bluegill, Brown Bullhead, Carp, Black Crappie, White Perch

This park provides family picnicing and fishing opportunities. Fishing is from the shore only. This pond is stocked yearly with panfish.

NOTES: ______________________________

M.C.C. POND

Map Coordinates	43° 06′ 04″ 77° 36′ 37″
USGS Map(s)	Pittsford
Location	Monroe Community College Campus
Access	Campus roads off Route 15A
Area	5 acres
Principal Species	Bluegill, Brown Bullhead, Carp, Black Crappie

The fish population is this pond is maintained by an inlet that connects it to the New York State Barge Canal. Fishing is allowed from 8:45 a.m to 8:45 p.m., and only on days in which classes are in session. Parking is available nearly.

NOTES: ______________________________

Numerous ponds are located in the Rochester area, and many of them are located in parks that are readily accessible to the public. Most of these ponds are stocked with panfish, and several of them also provide good fishing for such game species as largemouth bass and northern pike. They are ideal locatins for teaching children the fundamentals of fishing.

MENDON PONDS PARK

Map Coordinates .... 43° 01′ 18″ 77° 34′ 19″
USGS Map(s) .... Pittsford, Honeoye Falls
Township(s) .... Mendon
Access .... Douglas Road
Area .... Hundred Acre Pond - 105 acres; Quaker Pond - 26 acres; Deep Pond - 13 acres; Round Pond - 5 acres; Lost pond - 1 acre
Species .... Largemouth Bass, Bluegill, Brown Bullhead, Black Crappie, Northern Pike, Suckers, Carp

The five ponds in this park all provide good to excellent fishing for largemouth bass and northern pike. Boats are allowed on all of them and are necessary on Quaker and Deep Ponds, due to marshy shorelines. Launching is facilitated on Hundred Acre Pond by a launch site at the southeast corner of the pond, off Douglas road. Ice fishing is allowed on all the ponds and can be very productive.

NOTES: ______________________________

____

____

SENECA PARK POND

Map Coordinates .... 43° 01′ 35″ 77° 37′ 10″
USGS Map(s) .... Rochester East, Rochester West
Township(s) .... City of Rochester
Access .... Off St. Paul Boulevard
Area .... 4 acres
Principal Species .... Smallmouth Bass, Largemouth Bass, Brown Bullhead, Rock Bass, Bluegill, Bowfin, Channel Catfish, Carp, Suckers

This is an ideal location for a family picnic and fishing trip. The pond is stocked annually and is very productive. Parking is available in designated areas around the pond. Boats and ice fishing are not allowed.

NOTES: ______________________________

____

____

Unlike most other areas of western New York, bow fishing for carp is very popular in the Rochester area.

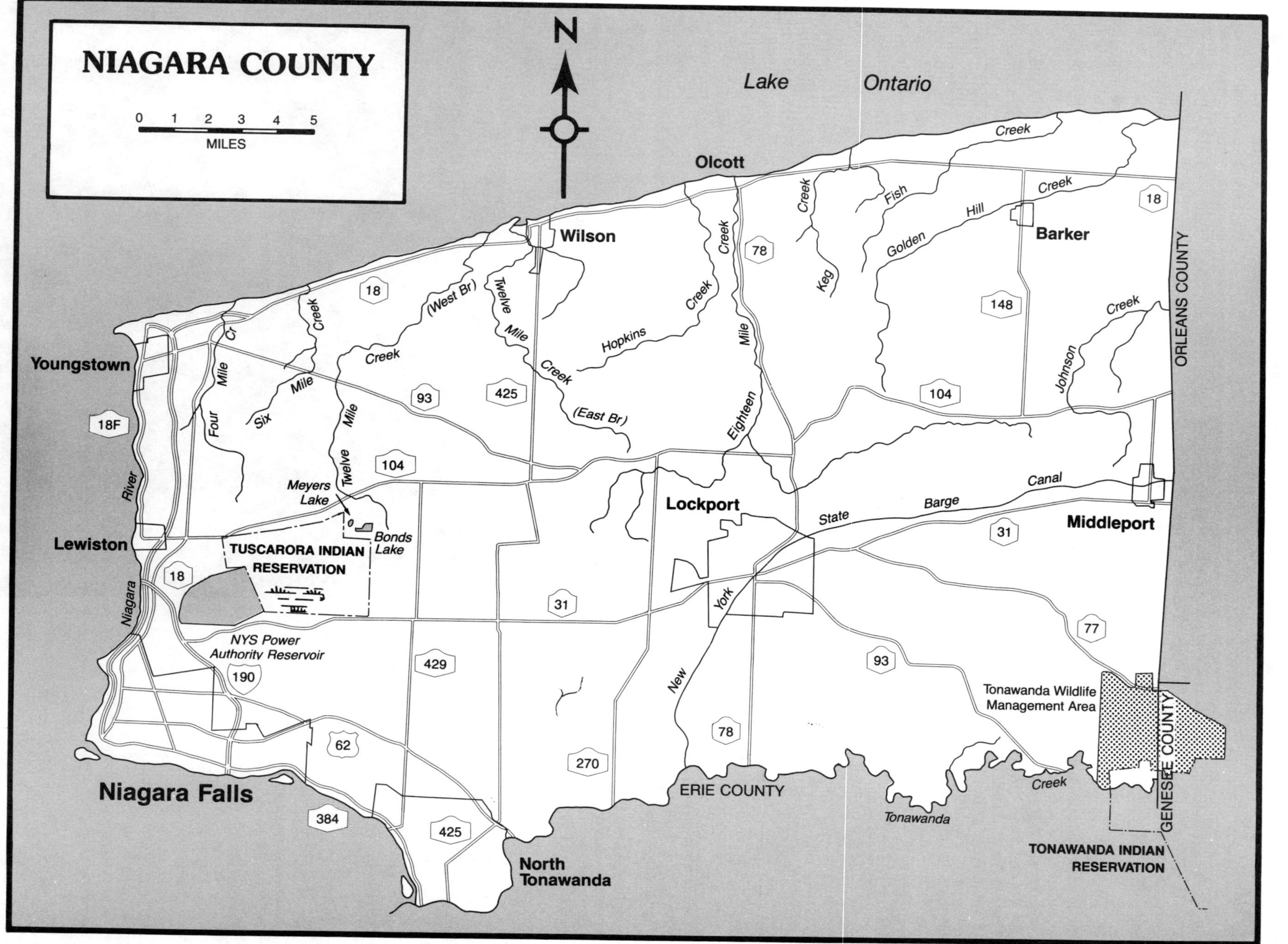
NIAGARA COUNTY
0 1 2 3 4 5
MILES
N
Lake Ontario
Olcott
Wilson
Barker
Youngstown
Lewiston
Lockport
Middleport
Niagara Falls
North Tonawanda
ORLEANS COUNTY
GENESEE COUNTY
ERIE COUNTY
TONAWANDA INDIAN RESERVATION
Tonawanda Wildlife Management Area
TUSCARORA INDIAN RESERVATION
Meyers Lake
Bonds Lake
NYS Power Authority Reservoir
Niagara River
New York State Barge Canal
Tonawanda Creek
Johnson Creek
Golden Hill Creek
Fish Creek
Keg Creek
Eighteen Mile Creek
Hopkins Creek
Twelve Mile Creek (East Br)
Twelve Mile Creek (West Br)
Twelve Mile Creek
Six Mile Creek
Four Mile Cr
18
18F
104
148
78
93
31
77
425
429
270
62
384
190

NIAGARA COUNTY STREAMS AND RIVERS

EIGHTEEN MILE CREEK

Map Coordinates .... 43° 20′ 21″ 78° 45′ 08″
USGS Map(s) .... Newfane, Lockport
Township(s) .... Newfane
Access .... Fisherman's Park, off Route 78 in Burt; Newfane Town Marina in Olcott
Principal Species .... Rainbow Trout, Brown Trout, Coho Salmon, Chinook Salmon, Channel Catfish, Largemouth Bass, Smallmouth Bass, Black Crappie, Northern Pike, Bullhead, Panfish

Eighteen Mile Creek is the largest stream in Niagara County, aside from the Niagara River. It provides excellent angling opportunities for both warm- and cold-water species. The variety of species available and the ease of access make this a place to fish almost anytime of the year.

The entire section of the creek above the dam in Burt is very lightly fished. The steepness of the high banks makes shore fishing almost impossible, and the dam keeps trout and salmon out. Some bass and panfish can be had from a canoe, though, which can be put in the water near the Ide Road Bridge, just off Lockport-Olcott Road (Route 78) in Newfane. The deep water directly behind the dam is said to hold some good-size northern pike. It is accessible from a canoe, but caution is advised.

The overwhelming majority of fishing on this stream takes place between the dam at Burt and the piers at Olcott. This stretch of the stream is accessible in two areas as far as shore fishing is concerned. The first area is from the dam to Fisherman's Park in Burt; the second is the section from the bridge at Route 18 to the piers . There are two large piers in Olcott where the creek empties into Lake Ontario. The west pier can be reached by turning down Jackson Street off Route 18, by the Olcott Bait and Tackle Shop, and following it down to the lake, where it becomes Beach Street. There is a grass parking area on the corner of Beach Street and Van Buren Street, but parking in the nearby Yacht Club lot is not permitted. Additional parking can be found at the town marina. The east pier can be accessed by way of a marked pathway that runs along Hedley's.

The intervening area between Fisherman's Park and the bridge at Route 18 is inaccessible by foot due to very high, steep banks. If you have a small boat or canoe, however, this middle section can provide excellent fishing for bass and northern pike, as well as seasonal fishing for trout and salmon.

The majority of the fishing on this stream is for trout and salmon, and anglers come from all over New York, Pennsylvania, and Ohio to experience it. The fishing bonanza starts in the late summer when great numbers of chinook salmon begin congregating off the piers in Olcott, just prior to their spawning runs. The piers are usually crowded, but the fishing can be fast and furious.

As soon as conditions are right in the stream, the salmon will quickly move upstream and they get corralled at the base of the dam in Burt. The pool at the base of the dam is one of the most popular spots for trout and salmon in all of Niagara County. It can be reached by walking upstream from Fisherman's Park. This is a very popular spot with snaggers. Salmon can be snagged between the railroad bridge upstream to the dam from August 15 to November 15.

The salmon are followed in the late fall by excellent runs of rainbow trout and brown trout. The fishing for brown trout peaks in the late fall, but some browns will hold in the creek all winter. Good fishing for rainbows will be found throughout this creek from late fall through early spring. The stretch between the railroad bridge and the dam is especially productive for rainbows in the late fall and winter. The pool at the base of the dam usually has some open water all winter.

The excellent fishing continues in the spring. Chinook and coho salmon and rainbow trout can be caught from the piers or just off them, often in great numbers.

Although the pool at the base of the dam usually gets most of the attention, other sections of the stream are also productive. As the water leaves the pool and flows towards Fisherman's Park a quarter mile away, it is quick and rather shallow. This stretch is excellent for drifting eggs. It's more challenging than the pool at the base of the dam, and offers a little more elbowroom.

Further downstream, just past the old railroad trestle that crosses the stream immediately upstream of Fisherman's Park, Eighteen Mile Creek becomes rather slow flowing and murky. This is a good spot for fly fishing or wading out to cast into the otherwise unreachable areas.

Some pleasant fishing is also found on Eighteen Mile Creek in the Newfane town marina and under the Route 18 bridge, which is just upstream of the marina. Panfish and bass are normally found here in spring through fall. This area is popular with live-bait fisherman, and it is also a good place to cast for trout and salmon when the piers get too crowded. Parking is available very close to the water, and fishing from a wheelchair is possible at the marina dock.

In the spring, Eighteen Mile Creek is stocked with 180,000 chinook salmon.

While most people concentrate on the trout and salmon fishing on Eighteen Mile Creek, the fine warm-water fishing should not be overlooked. Northern pike, smallmouth bass, rock bass, black crappie, bullhead, perch, and silver bass all come into this creek each spring in great numbers to spawn. In the late summer and fall, anyone with a small boat or canoe and the patience to investigate the many weedlines and brush piles can easily find enough smallmouth bass, northern pike, bullhead, and panfish to fill a stringer. Don't be too surprised if you come across an occasional largemouth bass or walleye. They are in this creek too, though not in large numbers.

NOTES: ____________________

FISH CREEK

Map Coordinates .... 43° 22′ 14″ 78° 32′ 11″
USGS Map(s) .... Barker, Newfane
Township(s) .... Somerset
Access .... Lower Lake Road
Principal Species .... Rainbow Trout, Brown Trout, Bullhead, Panfish

This is a small, mediocre-quality stream that is best known for hosting an excellent run of suckers in the spring. Bullhead fishing is also quite good here just after ice out.

As with many other small streams that empty into Lake Ontario, there is a recurring sand bar at the mouth of Fish Creek that can prevent trout and salmon from entering. However, when rainfall has been sufficient, good numbers of steelhead and brown trout are taken here in the spring and fall, at least as far up as Route 18. A few salmon will also stray up this stream in the fall.

Fish Creek is not stocked.

NOTES: ____________________

Many of the larger streams in western New York, including Niagara County's Eighteen Mile Creek, have populations of northern pike. Often overlooked by anglers seeking more glamorous species such as salmon or bass, northern pike are voracious fighers, and can test your angling skills to the limit. They are usually caught with live bait or large spinners and spoons. For a real thrill, try fly fishing for northerns. Use a medium-weight fly rod, weight-forward fly line, and big streamers or bucktail flies. If the northerns are feeding on the surface, big popping bass bugs and flies that imitate minnows will also work well.

The Burt Dam area has been popular with snaggers and fishermen for years. In the early fall, salmon running up Eighteen Mile Creek to spawn stack up here like cord wood. Later in the season, brown trout and rainbow trout can be found near the dam.

FOUR MILE CREEK

Map Coordinates .... 43° 16′ 38″ 78° 59′ 56″
USGS Map(s) .... Six Mile Creek, Fort Niagara, Lewiston
Township(s) .... Porter
Access .... Woodcliff Road off Route 18F; Four Mile Creek State Park off Route 18F
Principal Species .... Rainbow Trout, Brown Trout, Bullhead, Largemouth Bass, Panfish

Often overlooked by anglers, this is a small stream that gets a fair to good run of steelhead in the spring, and steelhead, brown trout, and a few salmon in the fall. Most of the fishing is done on the section below Route 18F. Although closed off by a large sand bar in the summer months, a few brown trout are occasionally taken from deep, shaded pools all summer long.

There is some warm-water fishing in Four Mile Creek, primarily for bullhead and rock bass in the spring. The large pool at the mouth of the stream holds numerous panfish, largemouth bass, and a few northern pike.

NOTES: ______________________________

____

____

GOLDEN HILL CREEK

Map Coordinates .... 43° 22′ 16″ 78° 28′ 31″
USGS Map(s) .... Lyndonville, Newfane
Township(s) .... Somerset
Access .... Golden Hill State Park, off Route 18
Principal Species .... Rainbow Trout, Brown Trout, Walleye, Panfish

Although not stocked, this small stream gets a fair run of steelhead in the spring and fall, and brown trout can be caught at the creek mouth, primarily in the spring. Most of the angling here is for warm-water species. There is excellent spring fishing for bullheads and perch in the small cove at the mouth of the stream. Occasionally walleye are also caught in the lower section of the stream.

There is a single, hard-surface launch ramp and parking for 50 cars and trailers at Golden Hill State Park.

NOTES: ______________________________

____

____

HOPKINS CREEK

Map Coordinates .... 43° 20′ 04″ 78° 44′ 49″
USGS Map(s) .... Newfane, Wilson
Township(s) .... Newfane
Access .... Coomer Road, just south of Route 18
Principal Species .... Rainbow Trout, Brown Trout, Bullhead, Northern Pike, Panfish

Located about one and one-half miles west of Olcott Harbor, this stream is very heavily posted and is accessible only on a small section south of Route 18. Generally, there is sufficient water in Hopkins Creek to allow fairly large numbers of steelhead to run beyond the posted area in the spring and late fall. The creek mouth, which is only accessible by boat, provides very good angling for spring and fall lake trout and brown trout. Salmon are taken here on occasion.

Hopkins Creek is also known for its warm-water fishing. There is an excellent run of bullhead here, often as early as late February. This is followed later in the spring by runs of suckers and rock bass. The pool that is formed by the creek mouth is a consistent producer of northern pike, primarily in the spring and late summer, and panfish.

Hopkins Creek is not stocked.

NOTES: ______________________________

____

____

KEG CREEK

Map Coordinates .... 43° 21′ 09″ 78° 39′ 10″
USGS Map(s) .... Newfane
Township(s) .... Newfane
Access .... Route 18, 4 miles east of Olcott Harbor
Principal Species .... Rainbow Trout, Brown Trout, Chinook Salmon, Coho Salmon

This is a small, gravel- and silt-bottomed stream averaging no more than 15 feet in width. It is surrounded by farmland and wooded marshland, and has intermittent bank cover. As with many of the small streams that feed Lake Ontario, Keg Creek has low summertime water levels. In some years it just about dries up. It also has a recurring sand bar at its mouth, which can prevent fish from migrating into it.

These problems notwithstanding, when brought back to life by spring or autumn rains this stream ranks as one of the top steelhead streams in western New York. Every spring thousands of these fish come here to spawn. They return again in the fall, accompanied by numerous brown trout and a fair number of coho and chinook salmon. Other species, such as bass and panfish, are seldom taken. Although the marshy, reedy sections of the creek should hold them, access to these areas tends to be difficult.

The best fishing on Keg Creek is found between Route 18 and the lake. A well-worn path follows the stream for about half of this distance to where high banks rise above the marshy part of the creek. This marshy stretch, which continues almost to the lake, generally isn't fishable from shore, but could be waded. To get to the lake, follow the high bank along side of an apple orchard to where a woods begins. Follow the woods around to the right and take the first path to the left, which ends on the beach.

As this stream gently twists and turns on its journey to the lake, occasional deep pools and undercut banks are formed. These areas often hold some very big trout in the spring and fall. Fish found in these areas can be quite a challenge because they're very wary. Many a spinner can buzz past their noses without so much as a second glance. Try these spots out if you want to put your egg drifting or fly fishing abilities to the test.

The mouth of Keg Creek is found just down the beach to the left of the path. It forms a very wide, shallow pool which narrows down to just a few feet across as it reaches the lake. This area gets stagnant unless there is sufficient rainfall to keep it flowing. When the water is moving, the mouth is a good spot for both trout and salmon, which sometimes look like torpedoes ripping through the shallow water. Fishing the lake itself in this area can be equally productive, with the added incentive of lake trout and other species being available. The rocky ledges to the right of the path are good, as are the bluffs on the other side of the creek.

While most of the fishing is done downstream of Route 18, the upper portion of Keg Creek also provides some good fishing, especially in spring. If rainfall has been adequate, some steelhead might be found as far up as Swigert Road, although the first half mile or so is the place to concentrate. This is usually an overlooked stretch of stream, not nearly so crowded as the lower section.

It should be noted that the state does not own fishing rights on Keg Creek. Access to this to this high-quality stream is granted through the generosity of private land owners and could easily be lost if their property is abused. Please conduct yourself like the guest you are and be sure to carry out whatever you carry in.

In the spring, Keg Creek is stocked with 11,100 rainbow trout (steelhead).

NOTES: ______________________________

____

____

THE NEW YORK STATE BARGE CANAL - See Orleans County Streams and Rivers.

SIX MILE CREEK

Map Coordinates .... 43° 17′ 05″ 78° 57′ 26″
USGS Map(s) .... Six Mile Creek, Ransomville
Township(s) .... Porter
Access .... Route 18
Principal Species .... Rainbow Trout, Brown Trout

This is a very small stream of marginal quality. If rainfall has been sufficient, there is a fair run of steelhead here in the spring and fall. A few brown trout are also taken here in the fall, as well as an occasional salmon.

Six Mile Creek is not stocked.

NOTES: ______________________________

____

____

TONAWANDA CREEK

Map Coordinates .... 43° 01′ 25″ 78° 52′ 55″
USGS Map(s) .... Tonawanda West, Tonawanda East Clarence Center, Wolcottsville, Akron, Oakfield, Batavia North, Batavia South, Attica
Location .... Counties of Erie, Niagara, Genesee, and Wyoming
Access .... Route 98 (stocked section), Tonawanda Creek Road (lower section)
Principal Species .... Brown Trout (stocked and wild), Brook Trout (wild), Largemouth Bass, Smallmouth Bass, Northern Pike, Bullhead, Walleye, Panfish

Rising out of the glacial moraines of west-central Wyoming County, the upper portion of Tonawanda Creek, above Varysburg, is a spring-fed trout stream of fair to good quality. This section averages 15 to 20 feet in width and has a bottom of gravel and silt. Although adversely affected by erosion and generally poor bank cover, this section is, nevertheless, fishable all trout season.

The stream forks near the junction of Maxon Road and Route 98, and both branches have good populations of wild brown trout and occasionally give up a nice brook trout. The east branch has a number of small tributaries that also hold numerous wild brook and brown trout.

In March and May, the upper section of Tonawanda Creek is stocked with a total of 2,400 brown trout yearlings, from Varysburg upstream 6 miles to North Java Station, near County Road 9.

Between Varysburg and the Tonawanda Wildlife Management Area high water temperatures make Tonawanda Creek a trout stream of marginal quality. In fact, warm-water species begin to predominate. Largemouth bass, smallmouth bass, bullhead, and northern pike can all be caught in this section. Especially productive is the fishing for smallmouth bass upstream of Indian Falls.

In the vicinity of the wildlife area, the quality of the stream has improved in recent years. This is especially true of the walleye fishing. Previously, the walleye were only caught in this section in the spring. Now they are being taken through the season. Their size has also improved. Several fish in the 6 to 8 pound class have been taken in this section in recent years, and 4-pound fish are not uncommon. Walleye can be caught in Tonawanda Creek as far upstream as Indian Falls near Route 77.

Other species commonly found in this reach of Tonawanda Creek include largemouth bass, smallmouth bass, and northern pike. A little known secret is that rainbow trout from Lake Erie will migrate as far upstream as Indian Falls in the spring. Unfortunately, access to most of the stream between the falls and the wildlife area is restricted due to posting or because it is on the Tonawanda Indian Reservation.

Between the Tonawanda Wildlife Management Area and the confluence with the New York State Barge Canal, Tonawanda Creek is a warm-water fishery of considerable potential. There is excellent spring fishing for northern pike near the mouths of Mud Creek, Ransom Creek, Sawyer Creek, and the confluence with the Barge Canal. Smallmouth bass, rock bass, crappies, bullhead, and suckers are all plentiful, and good numbers of walleye are taken in deeper pools above and below Route 78 (Transit Road). In the summer of 1990, several walleye in the 6 to 8 pound category were taken in this area.

NOTES: ______________________________

____

____

Unless there is an impassible barrier preventing further migration, many of the fish that live in the Great Lakes but spawn in streams will swim upstream incredible distances. In Tonawanda Creek, rainbows from Lake Erie and the Niagara River will migrate upstream as much as 30 miles to spawn.

Olcott Harbor at the mouth of Eighteen Mile Creek is one of the busiest ports on Lake Ontario. It is well equipped to service boaters and anglers.

TWELVE MILE CREEK (East Branch)

Map Coordinates .... 43° 18′ 41″ 78° 51′ 15″
USGS Map(s) .... Wilson, Cambria
Township(s) .... Wilson
Access .... Wilson-Tuscarora State Park, the piers at Wilson Harbor
Principal Species .... Rainbow Trout, Brown Trout, Chinook Salmon, Coho Salmon, Largemouth Bass, Smallmouth Bass, Northern Pike, Bullhead, Yellow Perch, Panfish

The east branch of Twelve Mile Creek enters Lake Ontario via Wilson Harbor. There are two piers at Wilson Harbor, but only the east pier is readily accessible. The west pier is only connected to land by a corrugated steel wall, though you could tie your boat up to it and fish. These piers provide some truly excellent fishing. Almost any time of year something is bound to be hitting here, from yellow perch and northern pike in the summer to trout and salmon in the spring and fall.

The fishing starts here soon after ice-out. Bullhead fishing is excellent in the harbor in the late winter and early spring, and a few are even taken through the summer. Rock bass, northern pike, yellow perch, silver bass, and crappies are all caught in large numbers during the spring. With the exception of northern pike, which are found throughout Twelve Mile Creek, most of these fish will be caught in the harbor or from the piers. The perch fishing can be especially good. If the perch population in Lake Ontario is at one of its peaks, it is easy to fill a 5-gallon pail with 10- to 14-inch fish in an afternoon. Fish with minnows or worms on spreaders for the best results. The lakeward side of the east pier usually offers the best fishing.

During the summer and early fall, water levels are quite low in this creek, but largemouth bass, smallmouth bass, northern pike, and panfish can all be found in the harbor and along the piers. A noted hotspot for largemouth bass and northern pike is along the back corner of the west pier, which unfortunately is accessible only by boat. In the winter ice fishing is a possibility in the back bay of Wilson Harbor. Yellow perch, smelt, largemouth bass, and northern pike all hang in this protected area, awaiting the arrival of spring.

Cold-water species also abound in Twelve Mile Creek. In the spring and fall, there is good to excellent fishing here for steelhead and brown trout. Chinook and coho salmon are also taken here in the fall, both in the creek and just off the creek mouth. These fish will run up at least as far as the section of stream that parallels Youngstown Road. Unlike Eighteen Mile Creek, snagging for salmon is prohibited on this stream.

In the spring, Twelve Mile Creek is stocked with 13,300 rainbow trout (steelhead) and 60,000 chinook salmon.

To facilitate access to this stream, the state has purchased public fishing rights along Twelve Mile Creek between Wilson-Tuscarora State Park and Braley Road.

NOTES: ____________________

TWELVE MILE CREEK (West Branch)

Map Coordinates .... 43° 18′ 41″ 78° 51′ 20″
USGS Map(s) .... Wilson, Six Mile Creek
Township(s) .... Wilson
Access .... Wilson-Tuscarora State Park, bridge crossing at Route 18
Principal Species .... Rainbow Trout, Brown Trout, Largemouth Bass, Smallmouth Bass, Northern Pike, Bullhead, Panfish

This is a wide, sluggish stream that empties into Lake Ontario just west of Wilson Harbor. Most of the angling done here is for warm-water species. It is one of the area's top producers of bullhead in the spring, and these tasty fish can be taken from the pool at the mouth of the stream all summer. There is also good spring fishing for rock bass, crappies, silver bass, and perch in the lower portion of the creek. Largemouth bass, smallmouth bass, and northern pike can be caught throughout the west branch in the spring, summer, and fall. In the spring the creek mouth is one of the areas hotspots for dipping smelt. Brown trout, coho salmon, and chinook salmon can be taken here in the fall, and rainbow trout (steelhead) can be caught here in the spring and fall.

To facilitate access to this stream, the state has purchased public fishing rights along the west branch of Twelve Mile Creek above and below Youngstown Road.

In the spring, the west branch of Twelve Mile Creek is stocked with 13,300 rainbow trout (steelhead).

NOTES: ____________________

Rainbow trout migrating up Tonawanda Creek from the Niagara River can run as far upstream as this falls, which is located just off Route 77 in the hamlet of Indian Falls. Though much of the stream in this area is either posted or located on the Tonawanda Indian Reservation, the sections that can be accessed offer good seasonal fishing for northern pike, bass, trout, and walleye.

NIAGARA COUNTY LAKES AND PONDS

BONDS LAKE COUNTY PARK

Location

Map Coordinates	43° 10′ 48″ 78° 55′ 04″
USGS Map(s)	Ransomville
Township(s)	Lewiston
Access	Lower Mountain Road (Bonds Lake), Black Nose Spring Road (Meyers Lake)

Physical Characteristics

Area	32 acres (Bonds Lake), 12 acres (Meyers Lake)
Shoreline	1.1 miles (Bonds Lake) 0.65 miles (Meyers Lake)
Elevation	548 feet
Maximum Depth	Not available
Mean Depth	Not available
Bottom Type	Bedrock, muck, gravel

Chemical Characteristics

Water	Clear
pH	Alkaline
Oxygen	Good all year in both lakes.

Plant Life

There is considerable rooted vegetation in both lakes.

Species Information

Largemouth Bass	Common; growth rate fair to good

Also available are numerous panfish.

Boat Launch Sites

A launch site exists on the western end of Bonds Lake; motors are prohibited.

Bonds Lake and Meyers Lake, both located in Bonds Lake County Park, are ideal locations for teaching children the fundamentals of fishing.

General Information

Bonds Lake and Meyers Lake are shallow ponds that offer surprisingly good fishing for largemouth bass and panfish. This 600-acre park is ideal for family picnicing and fishing in the summer, and provides opportunities for numerous activities in the winter, including tobogganing, cross-country skiing, and downhill skiing.

These lakes are not stocked.

NOTES: ______________________________

____

____

NEW YORK STATE POWER AUTHORITY RESERVOIR

Location

Map Coordinates	43° 08′ 30″ 79 00′ 00″
USGS Map(s)	Lewiston, Ransomville
Township(s)	Lewiston
Access	Route 253 (Military Road)

Physical Characteristics

Area	1,900 acres
Shoreline	6.7 miles
Elevation	655 feet
Maximum Depth	56 feet
Mean Depth	Fluctuates
Bottom Type	Large rocks, rubble, gravel

Chemical Characteristics

Water	Clear
pH	Alkaline
Oxygen	Good throughout the lake all year

Plant Life

Limited vegetation exists, primarily in the shallow eastern end of the reservoir.

Species Information

Yellow Perch	Abundant; growth rate good
Silver Bass	Common; growth rate good
Rock Bass	Common; growth rate good
Smallmouth Bass	Common; growth rate good
Brown Trout	Uncommon; growth rate good
Northern Pike	Uncommon; growth rate good
Muskellunge	Rare; growth rate not available

Boat Launch Sites

At present boats are not allowed on this impoundment. However, opening the reservoir to cartop boats and canoes is being considered by the Power Authority.

General Information

Located adjacent to Reservoir State Park, this 1900-acre impoundment is a great place for family fishing. Constructed as part of the pump generating station of the Robert Moses Power Project, the reservoir is deepest in the western end and slopes upward toward the shallow eastern end. It is filled to capacity during the weekend and drawn down about 5 feet per day until it is at its shallowest on Friday, often exposing a considerable amount of bottom structure in the eastern end.

Nearly every species of fish found in the Niagara River can be taken here, and the angling for certain species is exceptionally good. Yellow perch are the most abundant fish in the reservoir, and great numbers are taken in the spring, and to a lesser extent, in the fall.

Night fishing for bass can be very productive during the summer on gin-clear lakes that provide little action during the day. Bright sunlight and warm surface temperatures force the fish to seek out shaded areas or deep water. At night, they come up from the depths and out of heavy cover to feed.

Smallmouth bass and northern pike are also quite common. When fishing for these and other species, it is recommended that you use a bobber; the reservoir is lined with large rocks and snagging can be a problem when attempting to fish on the bottom.

The public is allowed to fish here from April 1 to October 31. Because of the routine draw-downs, ice fishing is precluded and access during the winter months is prohibited. The eastern end of the reservoir is adjacent to the Tuscarora Indian Reservation and is not open to public access.

The reservoir is not stocked.

NOTES: ______________________________

____

____

The backbay of Wilson Harbor offers excellent fishing for largemouth bass, northern pike, and panfish.

The 1,900-acre Power Authority Reservoir is open to public fishing and every species of fish found in the Niagara River can be caught here. Because of the rocky shoreline and bottom, the use of a bobber is recommended when fishing the reservoir to avoid snagging.

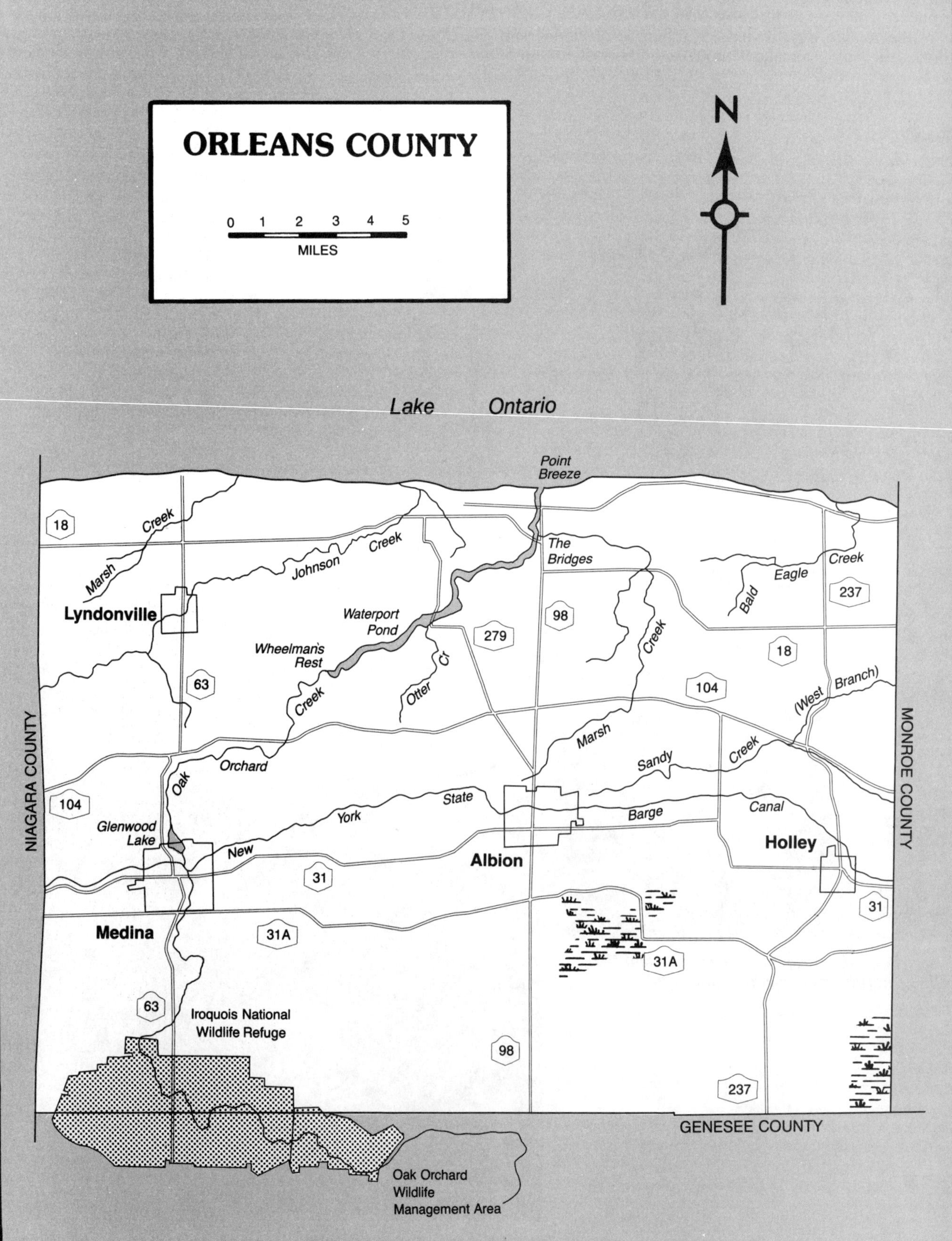
ORLEANS COUNTY
0 1 2 3 4 5
MILES
N
Lake Ontario
Point Breeze
The Bridges
Marsh Creek
Johnson Creek
Lyndonville
Waterport Pond
Wheelman's Rest
Oak Orchard Creek
Otter Cr
Eagle Creek
Bald
Creek
Marsh
Sandy Creek
(West Branch)
Glenwood Lake
New York State Barge Canal
Albion
Holley
Medina
Iroquois National Wildlife Refuge
Oak Orchard Wildlife Management Area
NIAGARA COUNTY
MONROE COUNTY
GENESEE COUNTY
18
63
279
98
237
104
31
31A

ORLEANS COUNTY STREAMS AND RIVERS

BALD EAGLE CREEK

Map Coordinates .... 42° 22′ 02″ 78° 01′ 50″
USGS Map(s) .... Kendall
Township(s) .... Kendall
Access .... Bald Eagle Marina, off Route 237
Principal Species .... Brown Trout, Rainbow Trout, Bullhead, Panfish

Although small, Bald Eagle Creek offers a variety of angling opportunities. It gets a good run of steelhead in the spring, and in the fall, steelhead, brown trout, and an occasional salmon are taken in its lower portion.

Warm-water species, including bullhead, yellow perch, and rock bass are also found in Bald Eagle Harbor in the spring. In the winter, ice fishing in the harbor often results in some fine catches of perch and smelt, with an occasional walleye or trout (steelhead and browns), rounding out the fare this stream has to offer.

Bald Eagle Creek is not stocked.

NOTES: ____

____

____

JOHNSON CREEK

Map Coordinates .... 43° 22′ 21″ 78° 16′ 07″
USGS Map(s) .... Ashwood, Lyndonville
Township(s) .... Carlton, Yates
Access .... Yates-Carlton Townline Road; Lakeside Beach State Park
Principal Species .... Brown Trout, Rainbow Trout, Northern Pike, Largemouth Bass, Smallmouth Bass, Bullhead

Johnson Creek offers better than average fishing opportunities for both cold- and warm-water species. The steelhead run in the spring is excellent, and the same can be said for the fall runs of steelhead and brown trout. Considering the fact that they are not stocked in this stream, a surprising number of salmon are also caught here in the fall. There is more than adequate water in Johnson Creek for the salmonids to run as far up as the dam in Lyndonville.

Warm-water fishing on this stream begins just after ice-out. Large, lake-run bullheads spawn here in March, April, and May. While they can be found throughout the creek, a majority of them will be taken between the bridge crossing at Route 18 and the lake. Northern pike can also be found throughout Johnson Creek in the spring. Resident populations of largemouth and smallmouth bass are found below the Lyndonville Dam, and they are taken in quantity during the summer and early fall. The best catches are had downstream of Route 18, partially due to the periodic influx of smallmouth from Lake Ontario. These lake-run fish are often substantially larger than their stream-bound kin. In the fall, northern pike are again taken, and Johnson Creek is one of the few streams in this area with a significant fall run of bullhead.

Johnson Creek is surrounded by orchards and farmland, and it is very heavily posted. The best way to fish this stream is to drift-fish with a canoe, which can be put in at one of the many bridge crossings between Lyndonville and Kuckville.

This stream is not stocked.

NOTES: ____

____

____

MARSH CREEK

Map Coordinates .... 43° 21′ 08″ 78° 11′ 33″
USGS Map(s) .... Kent
Township(s) .... Carlton
Access .... The bridges at Oak Orchard Creek; bridge crossings at Route 18 or Route 104
Principal Species .... Chinook Salmon, Brown Trout, Rainbow Trout, Smallmouth Bass, Largemouth Bass, Northern Pike

Marsh Creek is a major tributary of the lower Oak Orchard Creek. It is fishable at least as far upstream as Route 104, but above the first three-quarters mile the creek gets very narrow and shallow. Steelhead are caught here in the spring, and steelhead, brown trout, and a few salmon are taken in the fall.

More important than the trout or salmon is the fishing for warm-water species. There is very good angling for both largemouth and smallmouth bass all season long in the lower section of the creek. For those intrepid enough to investigate the narrow upper section, there are numerous productive holes where you can turn up largemouth all season, as well as an occasional northern pike. Northerns can also be caught in the wide mouth of Marsh Creek, with the most productive times being late spring and early fall.

Marsh Creek is not stocked.

NOTES: ____

____

____

Many streams that are not stocked by the state nevertheless get good runs of trout and salmon in the fall. Dale Froman caught this 30-pound chinook salmon in Johnson Creek. Photo courtesy Don Cook.

NEW YORK STATE BARGE CANAL (Western Section)

Map Coordinates .... 42° 31′ 40″ 78° 30′ 31″
USGS Map(s) .... Tonawanda West, Tonawanda East, Clarence Center, Lockport, Gasport, Medina, Knowlesville, Albion, Holley, Brockport, Spencerport, Rochester West, West Henrietta, Pittsford, Fairport
Location .... Counties of Niagara, Orleans, and Monroe
Access .... Paralleled by Route 31 between Lockport and Rochester. See also below.
Principal Species .... Smallmouth Bass, Largemouth Bass, Northern Pike, Walleye, Channel Catfish, Bullhead, Panfish

First opened in 1825, the New York State Barge Canal was initially designed to promote the growth of commerce in the state. Today, the canal also serves as a major recreational waterway, providing many opportunities to the outdoor enthusiast.

For the fisherman, the canal offers angling for a wide variety of warm-water species. In recent years, anglers have discovered that the canal has good populations of largemouth and smallmouth bass, and it is rapidly earning a reputation as one of the top bass waters in this part of the state. Northern pike, channel catfish, bullhead, yellow perch, white perch, rock bass, silver bass, pumpkinseeds, and crappies are also found throughout the western section of the canal. Occasionally, big walleye are found in the canal, primarily west of Lockport. (The extreme western portion of the canal, from the town of Pendleton to the Niagara River, is actually the lower reaches of Tonawanda Creek, which itself has a fair walleye population.) Once in a great while a trout or salmon will stray into the canal from the Niagara River, and more than one bass fisherman has been surprised to have a large trout or salmon run away with his hook, line, and sinker (including this writer).

The most productive areas on the canal are the widewater turnarounds, which are located intermittently along the waterway. These weedy backwaters provide habitat for nearly every species of fish that inhabit the canal. Often found in conjunction with parks and marine facilities, these widewater areas are ideal locations for family fishing. Other highly productive areas to check out include the spillways at the locks along the canal. These often provide good walleye fishing from mid-May to early August.

The western end of the canal would probably be much more productive were it not for the fact that much of it is drained each winter. This has a detrimental effect on both the fish and plant life in the canal, and greatly limits the opportunities for ice fishing.

Access to the canal is facilitated by a number of newly completed trails. The longest section closely parallels the canal between Lockport and Rochester for a distance of 60 miles. Smaller trails are found in Erie County, in the town of Amherst (3 miles), and in Monroe County, between the towns of Pittsford and Fairport (5 miles). These trails not only provide bank access to the canal, but also serve as recreational highways to hikers, cross-country skiers, and bicyclers. They are interspersed with picnic areas equipped with picnic tables and grills.

Boating on the barge canal, which is allowed from May to November, is very popular, with 90,000 lock passages by recreational boats being recorded each year. Use of this waterway and its lock system is toll-free and requires no special permits. There are no restrictions on the size of boats or motors, but the maximum speed on the canal is 10 mph. Be sure to check with the New York State Department of Transportation for a complete list of regulations.

Boat Launch Sites (going from west to east)

Niagara County

1. North Tonawanda City Park - on Sweeney Street one-half mile from Niagara Rive; multiple hard-surface ramps, parking - no charge.
2. Botanical Park - Sweeney Street at East Robinson Road; state-maintained, multiple hard-surface ramps, parking - no charge.
3. West Canal Park - County Park on North Canal Road at Townline Road; multiple hard-surface ramps, parking - no charge.
4. Widewaters Marina - Lockport City Park on Market Street near Cold Spring Road; multiple hard-surface ramps, parking - no charge.
5. Commercial ramp on Telegraph Road, west of the Bolton Road bridge; single ramp, limited parking - fee.

Orleans County

6. Launch ramp on Dublin Road between Medina and Middleport.
7. Launch ramp on Bates Road one mile east of Medina.

The New York State Barge Canal is one of the best kept fishing secrets around. Few fishermen realize that the canal offers good fishing for northern pike, bass, and walleye. Especially productive are the widewater turning basins that are located intermittently along the canal.

Monroe County

8. Town of Ogden Park - on Canal Road, west of Trimmer Road, in Spencerport; single unimproved ramp - no charge.
9. Genesee Valley Park East - on east side of the Genesee River in the township of Brighton; launch site for cartop boats and canoes at the mouth of Red Creek - no charge.
10. Lock 32 Canal Park - on south side of canal, just east of Clover Street (Route 65). Single hard-surface ramp - no charge.

Additional marine facilities, consisting primarily of canal wall tie-ups and electricity, can be found in the towns of Medina, Brockport, Spencerport, Pittsford, and Fairport.

The following article by Medina resident George Skinner provides first-hand impressions of this multifaceted waterway.

FISHING THE BARGE CANAL

By George Skinner

Ask anglers today what their major obstacle is when pursuing the sport of fishing and I'll guarantee you the majority response will be access. Too few launches, not enough parking, and crowds. There is one body of water, however, where you won't experience any of those problems and it's within easy reach of all of us: The New York State Barge Canal.

Take your choice. You can fish it on foot, by boat, by canoe, or by bicycle. The beauty of it is that access to the canal is available throughout the system. Many bridges span the canal and there is usually space for parking at least several cars at each bridge. From there you can venture in either direction on foot, by canoe, or by bike while exploring for local hotspots. Boat launches are few, but more are in the works and those that are now available are barely utilized. You'll find that launching your trailer drawn boat or car topper is no problem at all.

Water clarity in the canal has improved dramatically over the past several years and so has the fishing. This is one good side effect that can probably be attributed to the zebra mussel.

The western New York section of the canal is almost entirely man-made and only fishable from "fill up" in the spring to "let down" in the fall, which is about a seven-month season. Water for the canal is drawn from both the Niagara and Genesee Rivers, allowing an influx of a wide variety of fish species with additional fish entering the system throughout the season. Largemouth bass, smallmouth bass, bullhead, catfish, crappie, walleye, yellow perch, and various other panfish will be present in good numbers during the entire period.

As soon as the water level is up in the spring, the crappie fishing swings into high gear. Also known locally as calicos, crappie will be found in the shallows early in the season. The "widewaters" sections of the canal are choice areas at this time of year. These shallower waters will warm faster than other areas, and some form of structure, such as docks, pilings, or submerged brush can usually be found. These are favorite hangouts for spring crappie. If no such structure is available, work the shoreline until contact with a school of crappie is made. Then concentrate your efforts in that area until the school moves on or you tire of catching them. If you lose the school, drift or fancast until you locate it again or run into another batch of crappie.

It pays to check the canal for structure before the spring fill up. If you can locate a brushpile or sizeable tree branch that will stay anchored and submerged when the water is up, you have found a real future hotspot. Mentally take note, or better yet, mark its location so you can return to it after the canal has been filled.

Large crappies in the 10- to 12-inch class are not uncommon; however, expect most fish to be in the 6- to 8-inch range. Live minnows are the number one bait, especially when fished on small jigs suspended beneath a pencil bobber. Use brightly colored jigs in the 1/32- to 1/16-ounce sizes. Pink or white soft-bodied jigs tipped with small minnows are excellent baits. Adjust your bobber so the bait is suspended over the structure being fished. When fishing walls or shorelines, adjust the bobber so your bait will drift at mid-depths. Crappie are not bottom feeders, so keep your baits high.

Perch will also be encountered in the canal, but in lesser numbers than the crappie. Concentrate your fishing efforts in the bottom half of the water for perch and other panfish, such as bluegills, rock bass, and pumpkinseeds. Panfish are abundant throughout the system. Worms are your best bait, and stick close to shore with your presentations.

Bullheads and catfish are also abundant here and provide the angler with plenty of action, especially in the spring and early summer. Both species feed mainly at night and are bottom feeders. Fish on the bottom with slip sinkers along the weedy sections of the widewaters or in the main channel of canal. If you're fishing out of a boat, try the area where the main channel and widewater meets. Dew worms, gobs of cider worms, crayfish, and dead minnows are all excellent baits for these fish.

Walleyes are being caught in greater numbers every year and some real lunkers are occasionally taken. The walleyes have always been there. Fishermen have now come to realize that fact and have learned how to take them with some degree of regularity. Evening to after dark hours and overcast days are best. Most walleyes are taken by casting or trolling parallel to the rocky shorelines, which can be found throughout the western canal system. The rock-lined banks provide shelter for crayfish, small panfish, and minnows giving the walleye endless feeding areas. Cast or troll minnow-imitating stickbaits such as Rapalas and Rebels in the smaller 4- to 6-inch sizes. Color doesn't seem to be a factor as long as you're casting or trolling a properly tuned stickbait. Weighted stickbaits or diving baits can be used to explore the deeper edge of the rocks if you're not having luck shallower up. White Mister Twister jigs in the 1/8- to 1/4-ounce sizes have accounted for a lot of canal walleyes. In the spring, tip your jig with a small minnow and use a slow presentation. During the morning and mid-day hours, fish along the concrete walls on the shady side. Stillfish worms or jig up close to the walls.

Smallmouth bass seem to be the most sought after species in the canal. That's probably because they exist there in large numbers and are willing takers. Expect to encounter plenty of smallmouth in the 10- to 12-inch class. In the fall, an occasional 2 1/2- to 3-pound bass will show up in your catches.

Here again, the rocky shorelines are your best bet and both trolling or casting are effective methods. Walking the shoreline and casting small Mister Twister jigs in the evening is my favorite method for taking smallmouth. Small crankbaits and weighted spinners are also popular baits. Weekends are especially good times to cast for smallmouth. There's usually a great deal of boat traffic and you can use that to your advantage. Boat wakes along the rocky shoreline will stir up the natural bait from its hiding places. As a result, the bass will go on short feeding sprees. Let the boat go by and cast parallel to the shoreline as the wake is settling down. Fishermen usually detest heavy boat traffic, but I'm sure you'll love it in this case. Smallmouth also frequent the concrete walls and bridge piers. Live bait such as crayfish, leeches, and worms work best in these areas. Fish them suspended just off the bottom with a small bobber.

Another species inhabiting the canal system in good numbers is the popular largemouth bass. The widewater areas are excellent early in the season, but the best largemouth fishing will be along the canal banks that are tree-lined with plenty of overhang. A canoe is a great way to fish these shorelines. Cast parallel to and up under the overhangs with shallow-running stickbaits and noisy surface lures. Yellow or white spinnerbaits are good choices later in the season. Fly rod poppers in the smaller sizes will produce, especially in the evening. Large bluegills will also take small poppers and are an added bonus to an evening bass outing.

Expect the Barge Canal to offer up a few added surprises in your catch, as several other species such as sheepshead, carp, and even smelt enter the system. Who knows? Maybe there's even a trout or muskie lurking close by. With the Barge, anything's possible.

It takes approximately two hours for the eyes of a fish to adjust from daylight vision to night vision and vice versa. Consequently, the best night fishing usually occurs from two hours after sunset to two hours before sunup.

For additional information contact:

Niagara County Section

Niagara County Economic Development
and Planning Department
Niagara County Office Building
Lockport, New York 14094
(716) 439-6033
Request: I Love New York Niagara County Fishing Map

Orleans and Monroe County Sections

and New York State Department of Transportation
1530 Jefferson Road
Rochester, New York 14623-3161
(716) 272-3490
Request: New York State Erie Canal Heritage Trail for

Orleans and Monroe Counties

Rochester/Monroe County Convention
and Visitors Bureau
126 Andrews Street
Rochester, New York 14604
(716) 546-3070
Request: Fishing in Rochester brochure

New York State Department of Transportation
Waterways Maintenance Division 1220 Washington Avenue
Albany, New York 12232

OAK ORCHARD CREEK (Glenwood Lake to Lake Ontario)

Map Coordinates	43° 22′ 18″ 78° 11′ 33″
USGS Map(s)	Kent, Ashwood, Lyndonville, Medina, Akron, Oakfield
Township(s)	Carlton, Gaines, Ridgeway, Shelby
Access	Bridge crossing at Route 18 (lower section); Route 63 (upper section)
Principal Species	Chinook Salmon, Coho Salmon, Brown Trout, Rainbow Trout, Large-mouth Bass, Smallmouth Bass, Northern Pike, Bullhead, Panfish

Whether your talking about cold-water or warm-water fishing, Oak Orchard Creek rates as one of the top-producing streams in western New York. Rising out of the swamps of north-central Genesee County, it flows for approximately 20 miles through swamps, farmland, and three major impoundments before it enters Lake Ontario at Point Breeze. What follows is a consideration of this important system below Glenwood Lake. For information on the section of Oak Orchard Creek above Glenwood lake see: Genesee County - Iroquois National Wildlife Preserve.

Trout and Salmon .... Abundant; growth rate excellent

Beginning around the end of March or early April, the lower section of Oak Orchard Creek hosts an excellent run of steelhead. An early thaw and a good amount of rain, however, could bring them into the creek at any time during the late fall, winter, and spring. Steelhead can be found as far upstream as the Waterport Dam. Brown trout are also found throughout the lower creek in the spring, but not in heavy concentrations, except near the mouth. Most of them are taken from the piers at Point Breeze. The spring trout and salmon fishing usually ends by early June, although a few trout may linger in the stream for a bit longer.

Beginning in early September, chinook and coho salmon will start to school near the mouth of the creek. By mid-September, one of the best salmon runs in the entire state will be underway. Oak Orchard Creek has been very heavily stocked with salmon in recent years, as can be seen from the vast numbers of returning fish. Their spawning run will last until mid-November, with an occasional fish caught in late November and early December.

Brown trout and steelhead, which will have been staging just off shore since early fall, will begin to run up the creek by mid-November. They have not been stocked here as heavily as the chinook and coho, but the fall runs are quite good.

All the salmonids can be found throughout the lower creek in the fall. Most of the action takes place between the piers, in the bridges area, and in the area immediately below Waterport Dam. Snagging is allowed on Oak Orchard Creek from August 15 to November 15, between the bridge crossing at Route 18 and the Waterport Dam. Be sure to check for current regulations.

For stocking information on Oak Orchard Creek see section on Lake Ontario.

The following article was written by veteran Oak Orchard Creek trout and salmon fisherman Rick Kustich.

TROUT AND SALMON FISHING IN OAK ORCHARD CREEK

By Rick Kustich

The section of Oak Orchard Creek below the Waterport Dam offers excellent fishing for trout and salmon, which run up from Lake Ontario. Approximately the first mile below the dam consists of a moderate to swift current flow. The first portion of this stretch is divided into two branches. Both branches empty out of Waterport Pond. The east branch runs through an electric generation dam; the west branch begins as a waterfall at the bank of the pond. The two branches run parallel for a distance of about a quarter to a half mile before they meet.

The east branch maintains a more consistent water flow than the west branch. The west branch actually dries up or freezes during periods of low water levels in the pond. Hence, the east branch usually provides the main flow for this lower stretch. For this reason, water levels of the lower section are subject to fluctuations caused by the hydroelectric generating activity at the dam. It is this first mile stretch that offers the best opportunity for lake run trout and salmon. The main reason for this is that this stretch is comprised of a mostly gravel bottom ideal for the spawning ritual of lake-run trout and salmon. Below this first mile stretch the current slows considerably as it heads to the lake, and as a result the conditions are not as good.

The action begins in September. This is when chinook salmon begin to congregate off the mouth of the creek and make their first tentative runs. The runs intensify in late September and peak in early to mid-October. The runs can be heavy. Coho salmon will also make up a portion of the run. The numbers of coho, however, will not be nearly as great as those of the chinook.

GOLD-RIBBER HARE'S EAR (wet)

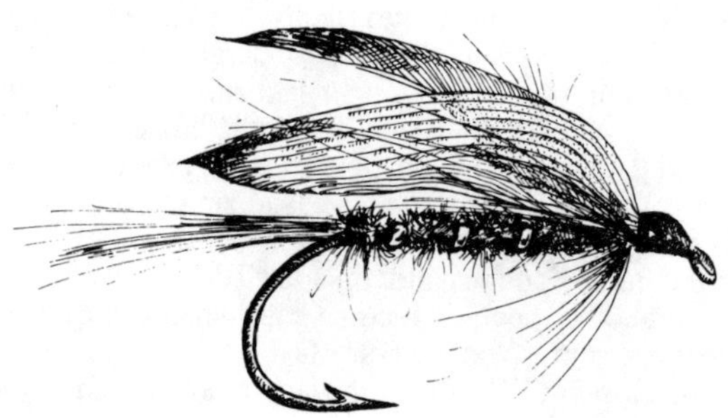

This is the emergent form of the famous Hare's Ear nymph. By varying the size of the fly it can be used all trout season. It is often productive when no hatches are occurring and fish are not feeding on the surface.

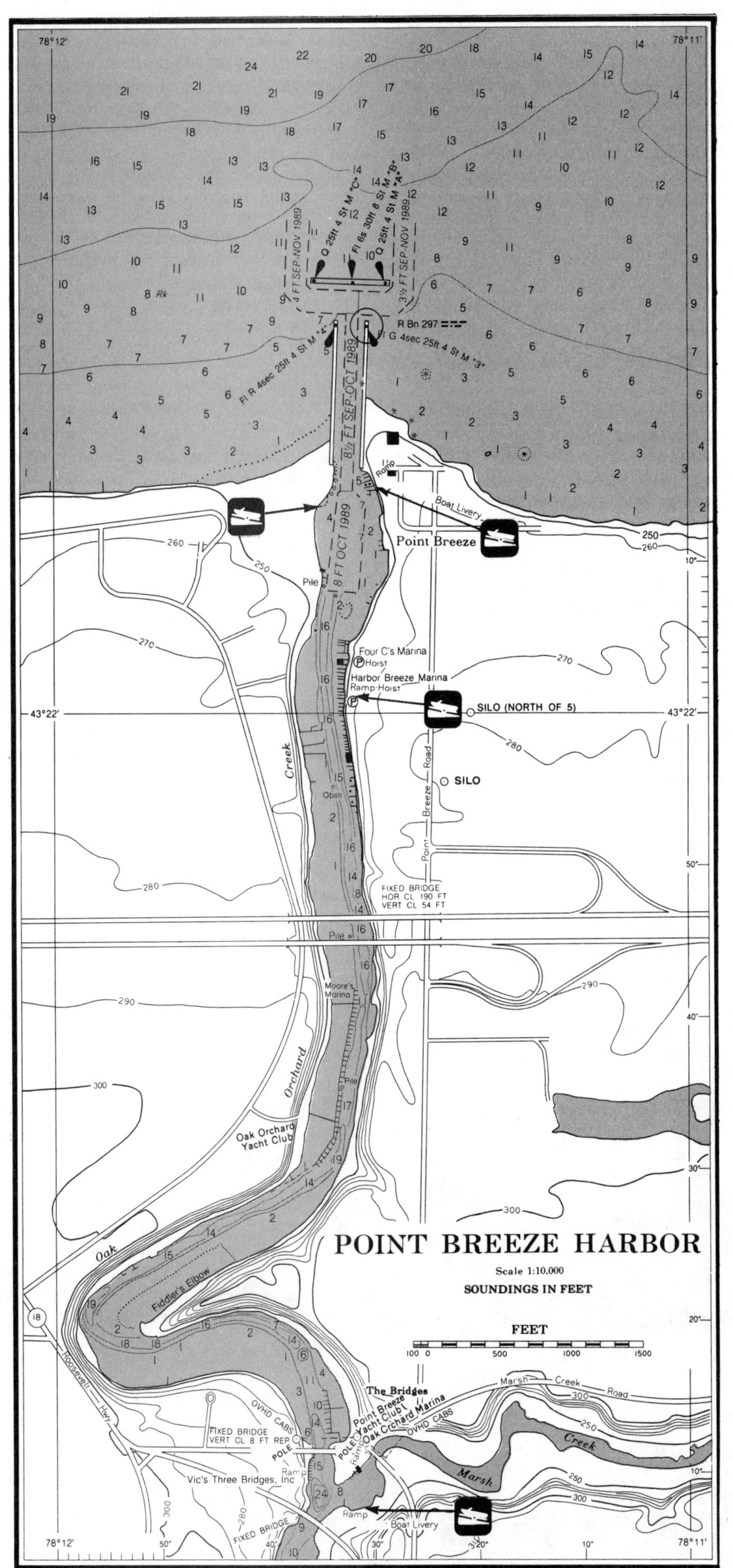
POINT BREEZE HARBOR
Scale 1:10,000
SOUNDINGS IN FEET
FEET
Point Breeze
Four C's Marina
Harbor Breeze Marina
SILO (NORTH OF 5)
SILO
FIXED BRIDGE
HOR CL 190 FT
VERT CL 54 FT
Moore's Marina
Oak Orchard Yacht Club
Fiddler's Elbow
The Bridges
Point Breeze Yacht Club
Oak Orchard Marina
Vic's Three Bridges, Inc
Boat Livery
Marsh Creek Road

Unfortunately, New York State has allowed for the snagging of chinook and coho salmon on Oak Orchard Creek for a number of years. This practice has created a following that has turned the annual salmon run into an atmosphere of mass slaughter and meat hunting as opposed to an opportunity to legitimately fish for trophies. The barbaric scene that it creates leaves little opportunity for the sportsman-like angler. Proponents of snagging justify their unethical approach based on the misconception that Pacific salmon do not hit while on a spawning run in a tributary. Although Pacific salmon do not actively feed while in the tributary, they will readily strike out of aggression caused by their spawning urge. The good news is that a plan to phase out snagging by 1994 has been introduced by New York State. Such a phase-out will most likely produce world-class Pacific salmon fishing.

As the salmon run begins to fade in late October and early November, brown trout and steelhead move into the creek. The brown trout run is the highlight of November's fishing opportunities on the lower Oak Orchard. Heavy runs of big browns can produce fast and exciting action. The browns average 4 to 6 pounds, and fish in the 10 to 15 pound category are not uncommon.

A number of brown trout remain in the creek throughout December. However, this is the month when the number of steelhead in the creek increases. The steelhead run continues to intensify throughout January and February.

Although the weather can be cold at this time of year, the fishing can be hot and heavy. The key is to select a day when the wind chill is tolerable and to properly dress for the elements. With the cold-weather gear available to anglers today there is seldom an excuse for being cold.

The steelhead run peaks in late March and early April. This time period presents an excellent opportunity to tie into trophy-size steelhead. Although the steelhead average 6 to 10 pounds, fish in the 12 to 18 pound range are not uncommon.

While the best action is found in the first mile below the dam, good action for trout and salmon can be found all the way to the lake. Access to the stretch below the dam is better than down in the slower current area. The best access to the stretch below the dam can be gained at the Niagara Mohawk access road to the dam. Anglers can park in the lot on the main road and walk down the access road to the creek. The slow-water stretch below this area, which leads all the way to the lake, is best fished from a small boat or canoe. This is due to the fact that access can only be gained through private land, and because steep gorge walls limit the angler's ability to reach the water in most of this section.

The techniques used to fish the creek for trout and salmon vary widely. In the first mile below the dam, traditional stream fishing methods work best because of the current flow. For the spin fisherman, the most popular approach is drift fishing an egg sac or skein. Bouncing the eggs along the bottom or utilizing a float are both productive. Spinners and jigs worked slowly near the bottom can also produce action. Although spin fishing is effective, this first mile of the lower Oak Orchard is also ideal for fly fishing. This stretch is not particularly deep, so the fly fisherman can get a fly down to the bottom where trout and salmon will be holding. This stretch offers an excellent opportunity for the fly fisherman to tangle with trophy-size trout and salmon. In fact, when fishing to spawning trout and salmon in the creek, it seems to be the most effective approach. Egg patterns, nymphs, and wooly buggers all work well. Dead drifting the fly or letting it swing slowly are the most effective methods.

In the slow-water stretch, the techniques used are considerably different. Utilizing a boat or canoe seems to be the best approach. Casting spinners or spoons as the boat is anchored, allowed to drift with the wind, or controlled by an electric motor are the most effective. Flies can also be cast and retrieved with results. Some anglers choose to troll this lower end; however, due to the small size of the creek, trolling may spook a significant number of fish. Actually, the quiet approach of a canoe or small boat is probably the best way to go.

Northern Pike .... Common; growth rate good

Northern pike can be caught all year long in Oak Orchard Creek, and they are well distributed throughout the middle and lower sections. Spring is a productive season for these toothsome fish, but the greatest numbers of pike are taken from Oak Orchard Creek in the late summer and early fall. Trolling in front of the mouth of Marsh Creek or along the many shallow weed beds in the lower creek are your best bet. Above Waterport Pond northerns are a bit less numerous and tend to be smaller than those below Waterport, but this stretch of the creek certainly should not be overlooked, especially if you like to fish away from the crowds. Although pike fishing begins to taper off in October, hardy anglers will continue to take them fairly consistently through the late fall and winter. Ice fishing for them is very productive on the lower section of the creek.

Smallmouth Bass .... Common; growth rate good

Good right from the opening day of bass season and peaking in late summer or early fall, exceptional fishing for these tenacious

Though trout and salmon get most of the attention, Oak Orchard Creek also offers good to excellent fishing for a number of other species, including northern pike and bass. This 6-pound largemouth was caught in the creek by Bill Fox. Photo courtesy Don Cook.

Oak Orchard Creek is renowned for the quality of its rainbow trout/steelhead fishing. The state record rainbow, shown here, was caught by Gerald Szmania just off the mouth of the creek in 1985. This fish weighed in at 26 pounds, 15 ounces. Photo courtesy Don Cook.

fighters can be found throughout the creek. Continuously replenished by large Lake Ontario smallmouth, any fast, deep water in the lower Oak Orchard should produce well. Try the channel off the mouth of Marsh Creek, Fiddler's Elbow, or Tom's Landing, as well as the fast water between Waterport Dam and the two islands for the best results.

Above Waterport Pond, smallmouth bass are well distributed and abundant, but are generally smaller than those found in the lower creek. Drift fishing is a popular and effective method for bass fishing in the middle section of Oak Orchard. Because the middle section is usually very wide, this should also be a good stretch to practice your fly-fishing techniques for bass.

Largemouth bass .... Common; growth rate good

There are largemouth bass in the middle and lower sections of Oak Orchard Creek. They are less numerous than smallmouth bass, but are usually larger. The fishing is good right from opening day and reaches its peak in late summer. It continues to be very good until cold weather turns the bass off to feeding. The sluggish, weedy areas of the middle creek seem to produce the most fish, but largemouth can be found in the lower section at the confluence with Marsh Creek, or in any of the shallow, weedy areas associated with most major creek bends. A particularly productive area is the large expanse of lily pads found about one-quarter mile downstream of the bridge crossing at Route 18. I have found plastic frogs to be especially effective in triggering a strike from the bass in this patch of lilies. Be sure to use heavy line here; you are almost certain to have to horse the fish through some thick salad.

Bullhead .... Common; growth rate good

Even before the ice is completely out of Oak Orchard Creek, tremendous numbers of large, lake-run bullhead come into the lower creek to spawn. They can be taken just about anywhere until late spring, but the piers and the pool just above the piers are best for catching full stringers of these tasty fish. Bullhead also run into the middle section of the creek from Waterport Pond. They concentrate in the area known locally as Wheelman's Rest, which is a shallow stump-filled flat just upstream of Waterport Pond. This area produces well in the spring and fall. A few bullhead are taken in the summer, primarily in the lower section. In the fall a second run of bullhead takes place in both the upper and lower creeks, and the same areas that are recommended in the spring are also productive in the fall.

Additional Species

The most important panfish in Oak Orchard Creek is the rock bass. As soon as the water begins to warm up in the spring, phenomenal numbers of these fish come into the lower section of the creek to spawn. Up until "apple blossom time", usually around mid-June, rock bass can be taken literally by the hundreds. Also plentiful are black crappies. Many locals recommend using tube jigs for both species, although worms and minnows also work well. The area between Waterport Dam and the railroad trestle, the piers, and the fast, rocky channel that runs along the creekside opposite most weed beds are the areas to concentrate on. The middle section of the creek also gets a very good run of rock bass, but they tend to be a bit on the small side.

Other fish that can be found in Oak Orchard Creek include walleyes, white perch, channel catfish, and yellow perch. None of these species are overly abundant, especially in the upper creek. However, in the lower creek you might be able to take a stringer full of them home if you fish the area between the dam and the railroad trestle, or near the mouth of Marsh Creek. The piers also provide some good perch fishing in the spring and fall. In the winter all of these fish can be taken through the ice.

For information on launch sites on Oak Orchard Creek see launch site listings for Lake Ontario.

NOTES: ______________________________

____

____

ORLEANS COUNTY LAKES AND PONDS

GLENWOOD LAKE

Location

Map Coordinates	43° 14′ 16″ 78° 23′ 37″
USGS Map(s)	Medina
Township(s)	Ridgeway
Access	Southern entrance of Boxwood Cemetery, off Route 63

Physical Characteristics

Area	93 acres
Shoreline	3.50 miles
Elevation	454 feet
Maximum Depth	Not available
Mean Depth	Not available
Bottom Type	Gravel, muck

Chemical Characteristics

Water	Clear
pH	Alkaline
Oxygen	Good throughout the lake

Plant Life

Weed beds exist along most of the shore line and in several small bays. Algal blooms do not appear to be a serious problem.

Species Information

Northern Pike	Common; growth rate good
Yellow Perch	Common; growth rate fair to good
Largemouth Bass	Common; growth rate good
Smallmouth Bass	Common; growth rate good
Black Crappies	Common; growth rate fair to good
Walleye	Uncommon; growth rate fair
Bullhead	Abundant; growth rate good

Also present are suckers, rock bass, and pumpkinseeds.

Boat Launch Sites

A small, gravel launch site and parking area is located at the end of the southern entrance road to Boxwood Cemetery. It is steep and suitable only for launching small boats.

General Information

There are no depth charts available for this 93-acre impoundment of Oak Orchard Creek, but I have fished it often enough to know that rumors that it was up to 90 feet deep are untrue. This is a fairly shallow lake, probably averaging no more than 15 to 20 feet deep.

There is good to excellent fishing here for yellow perch, crappies, bullheads, suckers, and northern pike in the spring. This is followed by bass fishing (largemouth and smallmouth), which is very good all season long. Although not overly abundant, walleyes can also be taken here in the summer months. Most walleye are taken below the Paddy Hill Dam at the southern end of the lake and along the steep drop offs along the channels that are found just to the north of the dam. Most of walleye caught here are just legal in size. In the fall, bass can still be taken in large numbers until cold weather sets in. Crappies and northern pike are caught in increasing numbers at this time and 15-pound pike are occasionally reported. Ice fishing is becoming increasingly popular on Glenwood Lake, and winter catches of northern pike, walleye, and perch are reported to be good.

NOTES: ______________________________

____

____

If you can not find a good chart of your favorite reservoir, an alternative is to check out an old topographical map of the area before it was flooded. They can often provide you with the general contour of the reservoir's bottom.

WATERPORT POND

Location

Map Coordinates	43° 19′ 35″ 78° 14′ 23″
USGS Map(s)	Ashwood, Kent
Township(s)	Carlton, Gaines, Ridgeway
Access	Kenyonville Bridge, Waterport Bridge

Physical Characteristics

Area	339 acres
Shoreline	11.93 miles
Elevation	331 feet
Maximum Depth	Approximately 85 feet
Mean Depth	Not available, but a substantial part of the lake is over 40 feet deep.
Bottom type	Gravel, muck

Chemical Characteristics

Water	Slightly turbid
pH	Alkaline
Oxygen	Good throughout the lake

Plant Life

Extensive weed beds exist along both sides of lake. Algal blooms are not usually a problem here.

Species Information

Northern Pike	Common; growth rate good
Black Crappie	Abundant; growth rate fair
Largemouth Bass	Common; growth rate fair to good
Smallmouth Bass	Common; growth rate fair to good
Bullhead	Abundant; growth rate good
Yellow Perch	Uncommon; growth rate fair
Walleye	Uncommon; growth rate fair

Boat Launch Sites

1. There is an informal launch site adjacent to the northern end of the Waterport bridge – no charge.
2. A private launch ramp is located adjacent to the southern end of the bridge in Waterport. Permission must be obtained to use this ramp.

General Information

Known also as Lake Alice, Waterport Pond is an artificial 339-acre impoundment of Oak Orchard Creek. Like Glenwood Lake, there are no depth charts for this pond. It is a long, narrow body of water, approximately 85 feet deep at its deepest point, and a substantial portion is over 40 feet deep.

With the exception of stocked trout and salmon, every species that can be caught in the lower section of Oak Orchard Creek can be taken here. In the spring, tremendous numbers of bullhead are caught in the area known as Wheelman's Rest, where the middle section of Oak Orchard Creek empties into Waterport Pond. Accessible from the Yates-Carlton Towline Road, this is a wide shallow area full of debris and stumps. A lot of big northern pike are also taken in this spawning area. Other northern pike hotspots include the mouths of most tributaries, especially Otter Creek, just west of the Waterport bridge. Crappies are another springtime favorite here, and angling for these culinary treats ranges from good to excellent. The most popular and productive areas for crappies are the bridges in Kenyonville and Waterport. They tend to run a little on the small side, but its not too difficult to fill a five-gallon pail with these scrappy fish. With a little luck, that pail might also have a few yellow perch. Perch are only caught in this pond incidentally now, but until recently, a small island a short distance downstream from the Waterport bridge was considered to be a prime perch area. This species could be heading into one of its periodic population declines, though it was never particularly abundant here to begin with.

With the coming of summer, Waterport Pond turns into a prime bass lake. For the past few years the bass fishing, especially for largemouth bass, has turned on a few weeks earlier here than in the lower Oak Orchard. From opening day until the end of the season largemouth and smallmouth bass can be taken almost anywhere in the pond. The most productive areas seem to be in the shallow western end and along the rocky slopes of the northern end. While bass fishing in the northern end, don't be surprised if you take a walleye or two. They're not very common here, but they are occasionally taken off the same rocky slopes as the bass.

As summer fades into fall, Waterport Pond comes into its most productive period. Bass fishing really picks up in the latter part of summer, and largemouth bass can be caught until the cold weather turns them off to feeding. Smallmouth can also be taken right up until the last day of the season. By mid-October crappies will again be found in large numbers near the bridges, and bullhead will be into their fall run up by Wheelman's Rest. This would also be a good time to stalk the voracious northern pike that will be cruising the flats of Wheelman's Rest or just off the mouth of Otter Creek. Winter ushers in the popular sport of ice fishing, and increasing numbers of fishermen are coming to Waterport Pond during the cold months. Northern pike, crappies, yellow perch, and an occasional walleye are all available to the hearty angler and can provide some fine winter eating. To locate the hot spots under the ice, just look for the crowds on the ice.

NOTES: ______________________________

____

____

Glenwood Lake offers fair to good fishing for many warm-water species, including largemouth bass, northern pike, catfish, walleye, and crappies.

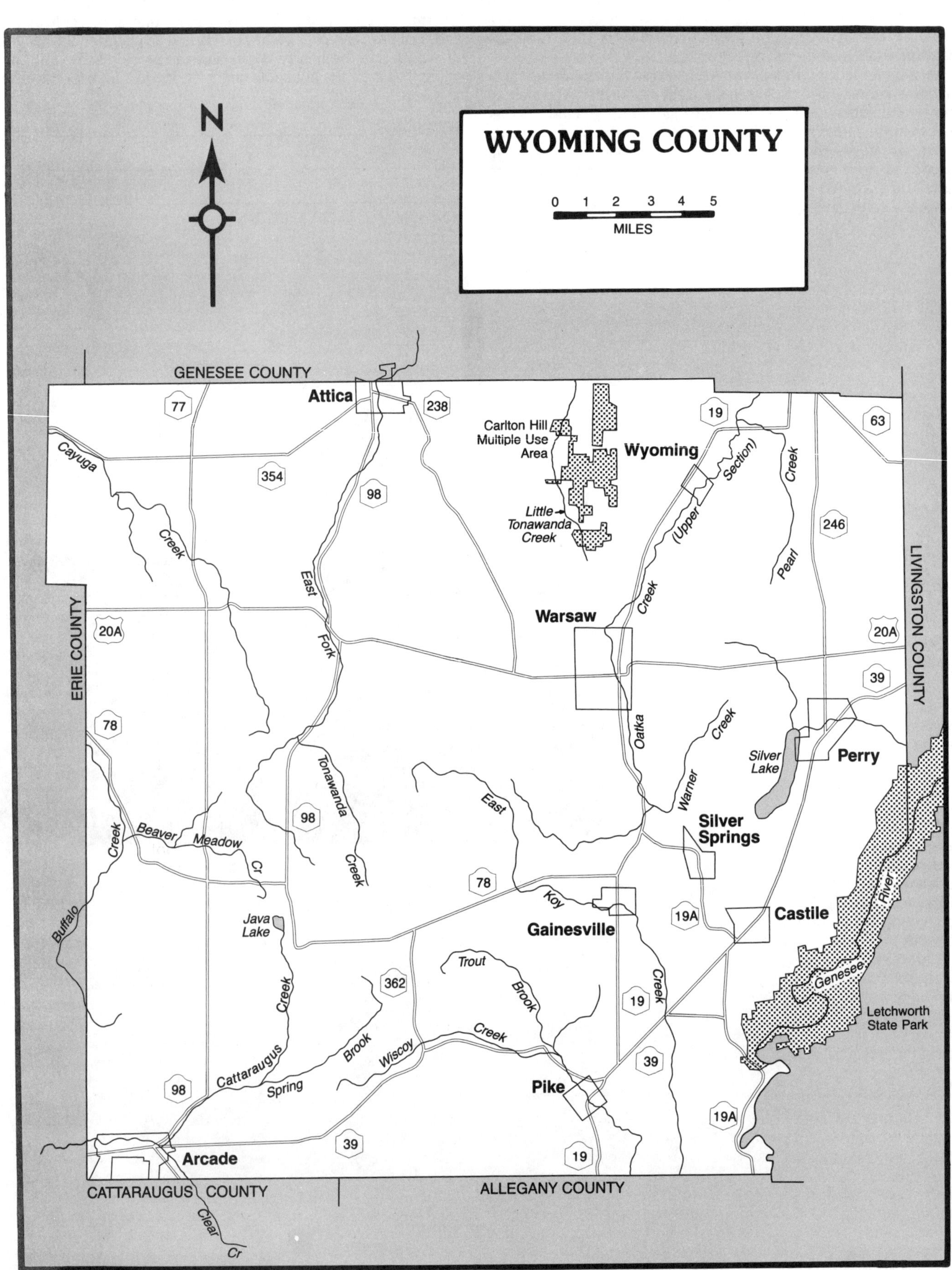
WYOMING COUNTY
0 1 2 3 4 5
MILES
N
GENESEE COUNTY
ERIE COUNTY
LIVINGSTON COUNTY
CATTARAUGUS COUNTY
ALLEGANY COUNTY
Attica
Carlton Hill
Multiple Use
Area
Wyoming
Little
Tonawanda
Creek
Warsaw
Perry
Silver
Lake
Silver
Springs
Castile
Gainesville
Java
Lake
Pike
Arcade
Letchworth
State Park
Cayuga
Creek
East
Fork
Tonawanda
Creek
Oatka
Creek
(Upper
Section)
Pearl
Creek
Warner
Creek
East
Koy
Creek
Beaver
Meadow
Cr
Creek
Buffalo
Cattaraugus
Creek
Spring
Brook
Wiscoy
Creek
Trout
Brook
Genesee
River
Clear
Cr
77
238
19
63
354
98
246
20A
20A
39
78
98
78
19A
362
19
39
98
39
19
19A

WYOMING COUNTY STREAMS AND RIVERS

BEAVER MEADOW CREEK

Map Coordinates .... 42° 40′ 19″ 78° 26′ 20″
USGS Map(s) .... Strykersville, Johnsonburg
Township(s) .... Java
Access .... Crossing at Route 78
Principal Species .... Brown Trout (stocked)

Beaver Meadow Creek is a sluggish tributary of Buffalo Creek, which it joins in the village of Java. It averages 15 feet in width and has a gravel and silt bottom. It is surrounded primarily by farmland and recreational camps. Consequently, there is limited bank cover along this stream.

Beaver Meadow Creek is heavily infested with beavers, and their numerous ponds on the stream and its tributaries tend to warm the water in the summer. Because of this, the fishing is only of marginal quality in the summer. The beaver ponds also provide breeding grounds for tremendous numbers of chubs, making bait fishing very difficult on this stream. One of the most productive spots on the stream is the pool below the waterfalls at Route 78.

In the spring, a 4.5-mile section of Beaver Meadow Creek is stocked with 800 brown trout yearlings from the stream mouth to one-half mile below the bridge at Route 78. There are a number of posted areas along this section of the stream.

NOTES: ______________________________

____

____

BUFFALO CREEK - See Erie County Streams and Rivers.

CLEAR CREEK - See Cattaraugus County Streams and Rivers.

CARLTON HILL MULTIPLE USE AREA

Map Coordinates .... 42° 49′ 35″ 78° 09′ 49″
USGS Map(s) .... Dale
Township(s) .... Middlebury
Access .... Bank Road
Principal Species .... Brown Trout (stocked and wild)

The Carlton Hill Multiple Use Area is located three miles north of the village of Warsaw. This 2,700-acre tract was purchased by New York State under the Park and Recreation Bond Act of 1962.

The area is comprised primarily of abandoned farmland interspersed with scattered small woodlots. The diversity of habitat types provides good food and cover for a wide variety of wildlife species. The area is managed jointly by the Divisions of Fish and Wildlife and Lands and Forests. Habitat management practices are being conducted to provide improvements in the quality of wildlife habitat as well as the forest resource.

Carlton Hill is managed under the multiple use concept and is available for a variety of recreational activities. Outdoor activities enjoyed on the area include hunting, trapping, cross-country skiing, bird-watching, and nature study. Of interest to fishermen is Little Tonawanda Creek, which flows through part of the area and provides angling for brown trout.

The DEC has set aside numerous tracts of land for use as wildlife management and multiple-use areas or as state forests. Many of these tracts are located in western New York. They offer a wide range of natural settings, and provide the outdoor enthusiast with many opportunities, including hiking, fishing, hunting, bird watching, camping, outdoor photography, and cross-country skiing. Information and maps for all of the state wildlife management and multiple-use areas located in western New York are found in this book.

Special regulations that apply to the use of the area include:

1. Off-road use of motorized vehicles, except snowmobiles, is prohibited except by written permission of DEC.
2. No person shall operate a snowmobile where prohibited by posting.
3. No person shall use a mechanically propelled boat or canoe in the area.
4. No person shall deposit garbage, refuse, waste, paper, or other litter in the area.

NOTES: ______________________________

____

____

EAST KOY CREEK

Map Coordinates .... 42° 30′ 44″ 78° 05′ 41″
USGS Map(s) .... Portageville, Castile, Warsaw, Johnsonburg
Township(s) .... Gainesville, Pike, Hume
Access .... Paralleled by Shearing Road (upper section), Paralleled by Lamont Road (lower section)
Principal Species .... Brown Trout (stocked and wild), Brook Trout (wild), Smallmouth Bass, Largemouth Bass

East Koy Creek is one of the finest trout streams in western New York. A heavily fished stream, East Koy Creek is also heavily stocked, with about 11,000 brown trout yearlings being released between Hermitage and the county line each spring.

In addition to the excellent trout fishing, East Koy Creek also offers unrestricted fishing for largemouth and smallmouth bass. They can be taken here any size, any number, all year.

Access to this stream is facilitated by 11 miles of public fishing access between the village of Hermitage and the county line.

The following article deals in depth with the various aspects of fishing this stream. It was prepared by Jim Keech and Al Himmel of Trout Unlimited.

EAST KOY CREEK

By Jim Keech and Al Himmel

The Headwaters

The East Koy is probably one of the most diverse of all of western New York's potential hot spots. The headwaters in Wethersfield Springs are characterized by dense overgrowth, which makes it almost impossible to fish by any means other than ultra-light spinning with small spinners or worms. The extent of the resident trout population cannot be accurately determined, since on occasion there seems to be an overabundance of trout in this section, and then when the water gets low in the summer, it appears that there are no trout at all. Fishing this section is chancy, but might prove very rewarding on the right occasion.

Hermitage to Gainesville

At Hermitage the character of the stream undergoes a drastic change, and the stream channel has a tendency to meander through pastureland. There are some good open stretches where fly fishing is possible, but the fact that in-stream cover is almost nonexistent makes it difficult to approach the open pools without spooking the trout. There are native brook and brown trout, and the annually stocked brown trout in this section. The East Koy is stocked annually on or about March 30th and May 1st with about 5,000 trout from Hermitage to Wiscoy. Several deep pools at the Hermitage bridge offer the potential for large carry-over trout, and the fireside worm fisherman should have good results. Upstream from the bridge the trout population is so great that it is almost impossible to take a step without chasing a trout. Getting the fly to them is the challenge, again thanks to the heavy overgrowth.

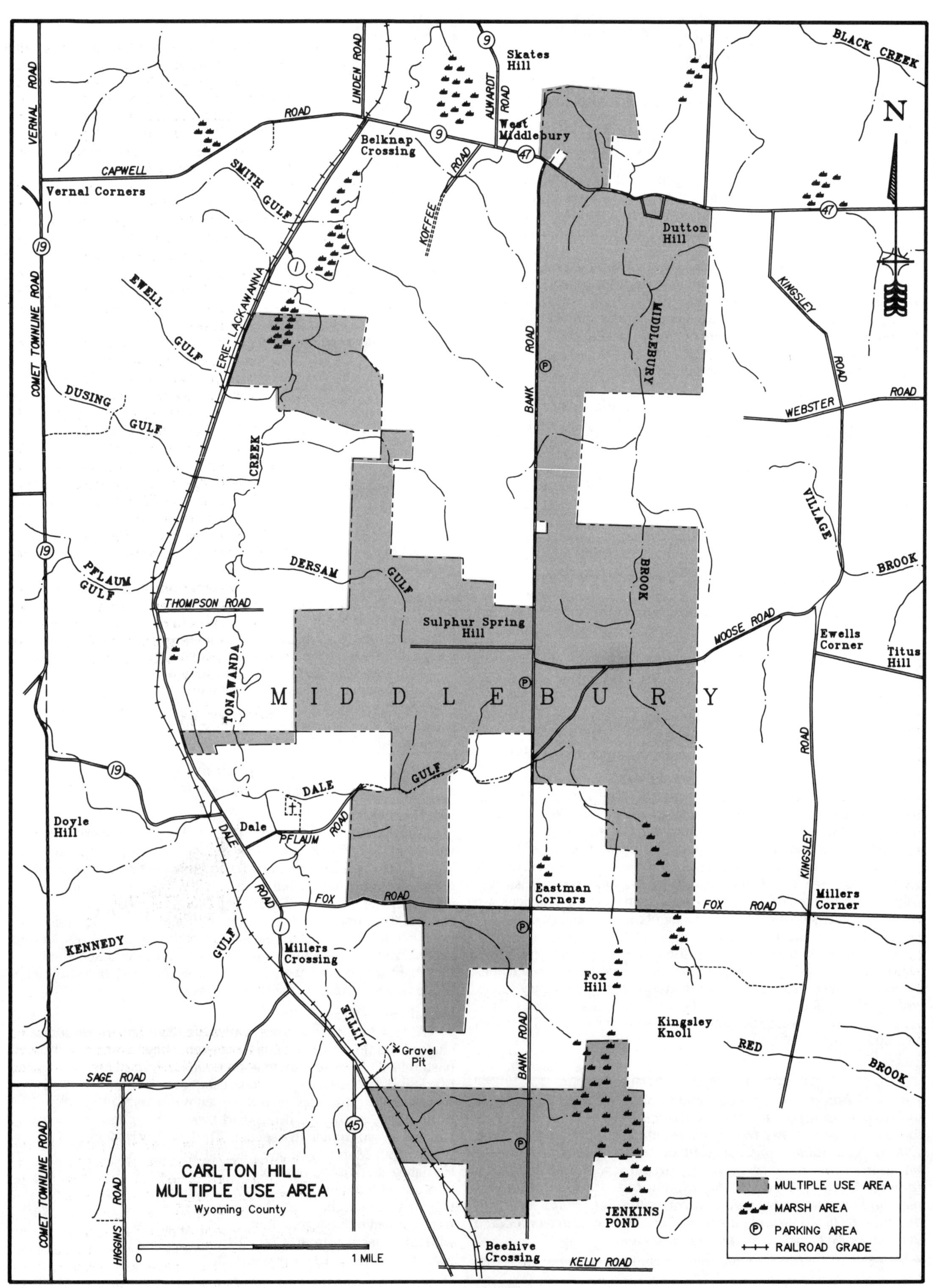
CARLTON HILL
MULTIPLE USE AREA
Wyoming County
MULTIPLE USE AREA
MARSH AREA
PARKING AREA
RAILROAD GRADE
0
1 MILE
N
MIDDLEBURY
Skates Hill
West Middlebury
Belknap Crossing
Vernal Corners
Dutton Hill
Sulphur Spring Hill
Ewells Corner
Titus Hill
Doyle Hill
Dale
Eastman Corners
Millers Corner
Millers Crossing
Fox Hill
Kingsley Knoll
Gravel Pit
JENKINS POND
Beehive Crossing
VERNAL ROAD
CAPWELL ROAD
LINDEN ROAD
AUWARDT ROAD
KOFFEE ROAD
SMITH GULF
EWELL GULF
DUSING GULF
ERIE-LACKAWANNA
COMET TOWNLINE ROAD
BANK ROAD
MIDDLEBURY BROOK
BLACK CREEK
KINGSLEY ROAD
WEBSTER ROAD
VILLAGE BROOK
TONAWANDA CREEK
PFLAUM GULF
DERSAM GULF
THOMPSON ROAD
MOOSE ROAD
DALE GULF
PFLAUM ROAD
DALE ROAD
FOX ROAD
KENNEDY GULF
LITTLE
RED BROOK
SAGE ROAD
HIGGINS ROAD
KELLY ROAD

From Hermitage to Gainesville, the creek passes through a dense swamp and through woodland, almost impossible to reach except by following the railroad for about one mile from Shearing Road. There are definitely large carry-over trout here, and some natives in the stretch from the railroad bridge to Shearing Road. Deep pools and heavy overgrowth are the rule, although the growth will not limit the spin fisherman, only the fly fisherman.

From the Shearing Road footpath the creek meanders downstream through farm and pastureland along the side of the road. Easy access and heavy stocking offers good fishing for father and son adventures. The campground waters are open to the public, and there are some deep pools containing equal numbers of chubs and trout. It is the most relaxing part of the creek to fish. This stretch continues into Gainesville. At Gainesville, the water volume and velocity seem to increase. Trout from recent stockings are usually available, although late in the summer there seems to be nothing left of these trout. As a rule, fishing in the public eye is avoided by the trouters, so perhaps this area is not fished extensively for reasons other than the limitations of fish.

Gainesville to School House Road

The best access to this one-mile section of the stream is at School House Road since there is ample parking at the bridge, and a big deep pool under the bridge is an ideal place to take the kids for some leisurely worm fishing. The pool is full of stocked trout that take worms all season long. Upstream from the bridge, there is an old crib along the left bank that holds trout that will feed in the open water and then seek cover under the crib. Fish the crib carefully and as close to the wire as possible without too much wading, and then use long casts to fish the riffles upstream for the next 50 yards. The further you can cast upstream, the more likely you will be fishing to unexcited trout. Unfortunately, once a trout is spooked and makes a mad dash for cover, all the others seem to do likewise, and what was once rise-covered water becomes like the Gobi Desert - barren. Beyond this low water riffle, the willows close in and it takes some skill to cast the fly between the willows on either side. Again, the trout are there but they hide under the willows, and it is the rule that flies and lures will be subject to numerous hang ups and break-offs. Beyond the willows the stream widens, and there is a 100-yard stretch that is exceptionally good during evening hatches. The fly fisherman must use all his skills to place the fly along the willows without hang ups or line shadows. Again, long casts usually produce the best results.

The stream follows a winding series of bends, each of which produces a pool and riffle. These hold an occasional trout, but the best spot is at the junction of the two branches that flow around a small island. Fish the junction pool, and then follow the left branch, where knee-deep water provides good fishing for a considerable distance. Once the bottom becomes sandy at the next bend, the water becomes slow and very deep so that larger trout, especially a big brown that holds under the weeping willow tree, are common. As the willows close in again, the upstream fishing becomes difficult and generally discourages the fly fisherman. However, the bait fisherman may locate more of those large trout under the bushes. Access to the stretch above this can be had by parking on the side road just outside Gainesville. Beware the dog - he barks a lot, but his bite is unconfirmed.

School Road to Metcalf Road

At the Metcalf Road bridge, there is parking for one or two cars at most, and access to the creek is made easy by either upstream or downstream entry. The bridge pool provides good fishing; however, fishing from the bridge is difficult as indicated by the number of lures and flies hanging from the overhead wires. Upstream along the rock cribbing, a few trout may be located before the willows close in and make it impossible for the fly and, at best, difficult for the spinner. The willow section lasts for about a quarter-mile, then the stream broadens again and fly fishing is possible. It is possible to avoid this closed in section by parking on Lamont Road about opposite the farm house, and walking in to the creek. Here you will find a long shallow pool that holds many trout near the willows on the opposite bank. Since the water is shallow and gin clear, it will mean long casts are necessary to prevent spooking the fish.

Further upstream there is a 100-yard stretch of willows that harbor many trout, but, as usual, casting to them is most difficult. At the end of this willow run, a large dead tree on the right bank provides cover and holding water for many large trout. Make sure you fish this undercut bank thoroughly so that the trout have time to pick up your lure from their hidden lair. The next good spot is about 100 yards further upstream, where the bend produces a knee-deep pool and a riffle, both of which always hold trout.

The upstream section for the next one-half mile is a combination of good pockets and shallow water, where the quality of fishing will depend upon the water level and the time of year. If you hook up several times, fish the entire stretch carefully; if not, proceed upstream to the Big Ben pool. This pool is frequented by the bait fisherman since it is one of the largest pools on the entire creek. Sometimes spin fishermen use small plugs on this pool, and they gain easy access by parking on Lamont Road near the farm house and walking across the corn field and down to the creek.

Proceeding upstream by climbing over the tree fall, there is a succession of small pools with usually unproductive stretches in between. Here the trout are where you find them, and it just may be that they migrate up and down this section from pool to pool as the conditions warrant. On occasion in the late season, the bottom of a pool will be black with schooled-up fish. Fallen timber, barbed wire, and meandering turns characterize the rest of the stretch to Jordan Road. This is a good section for Green Drake hatches, and the March Brown is prolific. A wooden walk bridge across the creek covers a pool that seems to hold trout all year long. Thereafter, the bushes take over, with only an occasional pool or pocket worth fishing. This section is heavily stocked at the Jordan Road bridge pool, so it is another good place to take the kids fishing, with good access and parking at the bridge.

The Woodstream Camp on the other side of the road creates a problem: Although it is stocked by DEC, there is great competition for the trout from the youthful campers in residence. The kids also enjoy rock skipping, wading, and swimming, so that fishing may be all but impossible; however, most are friendly and will tell you all about the 18-incher that was caught last week.

PICKETT PIN

The Pickett Pin is a very versatile fly. Resembling many different insects as well as sculpins, this pattern produces well under a wide range of conditions, making it a good searching pattern.

Metcalf Road to Murphy Road

Three miles south of Gainesville on Lamont Road is Murphy Road, where an old bridge provides access and parking to some of the most diverse water conditions found on East Koy Creek. Upstream from the bridge, classic rocky-bottom riffle fishing is provided for about one-quarter mile, where a rock dam produces a deep pool and small fall-off plunge pool. At times fish seem to appear from out of nowhere to take the dry fly drifted over and around the rocks. At other times, a nymph or wet fly fished deep along the bank of the pool will produce hard strikes without warning. The spin

Western New York is blessed with numerous trout streams suitable for fly fishing, and East Koy Creek ranks among the best of them. Rick Kustich, an avid fly fisherman, is shown here preparing to fish a typical stretch of the East Koy.

fisherman does not fare well due to the rocks and numerous hang-up objects in the water. Early in the season the pool above the dam is stocked with trout carried by hand from the hatchery truck in large buckets, so many anglers concentrate on this part of the stream. On occasion the DEC program calls for stocking large breeder trout in this area, and one of the prime sites is the old bridge abutment about 100 yards upstream from the dam pool. The water rushes swiftly along the left bank, which is all rocks and crevices, where hiding trout await the opportune moment to dart out and grab a salted minnow or a floated fly. Carry-over trout are also present in more than usual numbers, so that good fishing is almost guaranteed when the water conditions are right.

Further upstream, flat rock conditions prevail, and fishing over the flat shallows is spotty until a large pool located below the DEC parking area on the back road is encountered. This pool is deeper than one might think, and there is some siltation on the right-hand side. Since there is little cover provided, the fish may or may not be in the pool feeding. Most often the trout can be observed nymphing in the deep part of the pool. On other occasions there may not be a fish in the pool, but just upstream a fast riffle under the willows on the right will provide the protection and cover they seek. Fished from afar with a large Wulff fly, it is possible to take trout along here successively as though they were lined up for chow. As previously mentioned, stocking here by the bucketful can provide early season fun. Of course, some early season stocking is done in weather so cold that the only stocking done is at the bridge sites, so don't plan on this type of success; just enjoy it if you find it.

Another access to this section of the East Koy is found at a farm road, bulldozed to the stream from the back road, where the farmer lays his water pump and pipe. The two access points provide a comfortable two-hour trip during which time it is possible to determine the prevailing conditions. If success is the order of the day, by all means continue fishing all the way to Metcalf Road; however, if there is little activity going on, it is no great effort to walk back down the dirt road to the first entry point. At one point above the second entry is an old cattle watering hole, which is both deep and covered by willows. This can be most productive during late evening hatches and spinner falls. Often the hatch is so prolific that the upstream visibility seems to have a curtain being lowered. Unfortunately the number of rising fish, though impressive, does not match the hatch.

At Metcalf Road the bridge pool is so deep that generally wading is curtailed, and casting to the fish that lie under the bridge is difficult. The spin fisherman will enjoy drifting his worm or spinner along the bridge abutment, whereas the fly fisherman must rely on rising trout to reveal the feeding lanes. The entire section from Murphy Road to Metcalf can be fished in about four hours, which in late summer is just ideal for an evening's fishing.

Murphy Road to Lamont

No section of the East Koy is as generous as this lovely, short, one-mile stretch. There is access at both the bridges at Murphy Road and Lamont Road, but the Lamont access is better via a dirt road about 100 yards north of the Route 39 junction with Lamont Road. A spring enters the creek from an iron pipe just below the junction of two branches, which flow around an island. The shallow pocket created by this junction always contains a trout or two. Upstream from this pocket, fish the left side of the island and the left bank of the stream until you get to the pool in the back yard of the white house on the right. The head of this pool is best, as is the fast water created by the long stone deflector wall erected by the owner of the property. Small trout hold in the fast water behind the larger rocks.

One of the best and deepest pools is under a huge willow tree, the local swimming hole, with a rope hanging from a limb, - an excellent fly catcher. Hendrickson hatches are prolific here during May, and, almost always, trico hatches occur in July and August, which continue even into late September. This is a deep pool with excellent cover, and when fished from below the first fallen tree it is possible to take several trout without spooking or wading the pool. Reproduction here is abundant, so there are many small trout at the upstream riffle.

Other good pools, as one progresses upstream, are at the old dam site and at the bend in the creek. Fish these with attractor flies,

LEAD WING COACHMAN

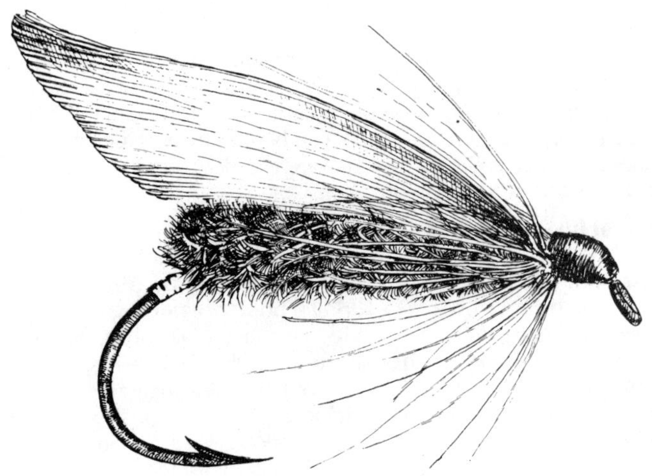

The Lead Wing Coachman is a wet fly used to imitate emerging insects. By varying the size of the fly, it can be used effectively all season.

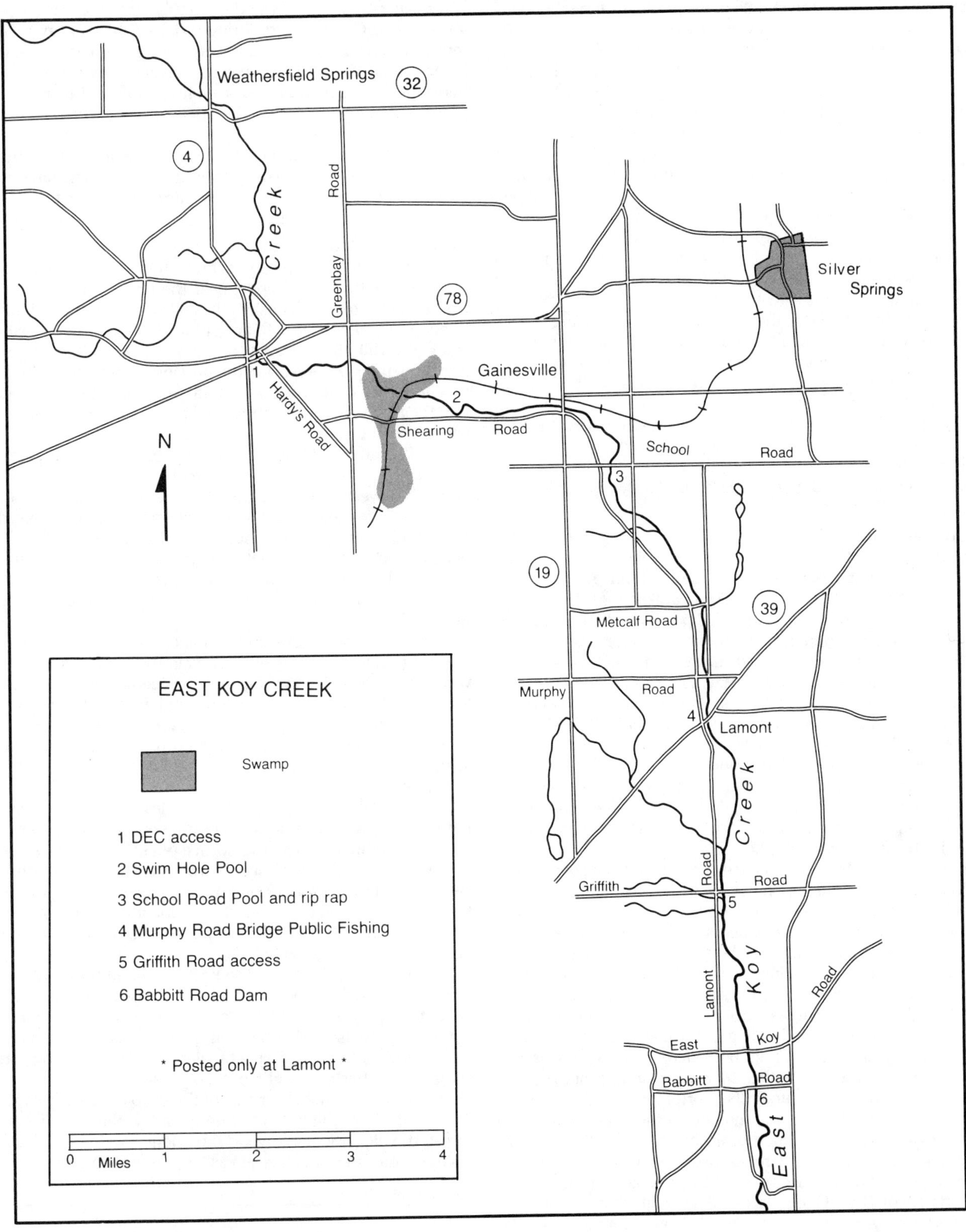
Weathersfield Springs
32
4
Creek
Greenbay Road
78
Silver Springs
Gainesville
1
2
Hardy's Road
Shearing Road
School Road
3
N
19
39
Metcalf Road
Murphy Road
4
Lamont
Creek
Griffith Road
Lamont Road
5
Koy
Road
East Koy Road
Babbitt Road
6
East
EAST KOY CREEK
Swamp
1 DEC access
2 Swim Hole Pool
3 School Road Pool and rip rap
4 Murphy Road Bridge Public Fishing
5 Griffith Road access
6 Babbitt Road Dam
* Posted only at Lamont *
0 Miles 1 2 3 4

salted minnows, or worms and spinners. The hairwing coachman, sizes 14 and 16, is particularly effective even when rising trout are not visible.

The next big event is just above the big rock in the middle of the creek. The stream divides at the rock as it leaves a small pool with a deadfall tree across the middle of the pool. The branches snag flies avidly, but the trout are always there and usually can be observed rising. One in particular is a 16-incher with a clipped adipose fin. Having been caught by at least two catch-and-release persons, he is old and wise, but catchable during the heavy hatches.

The final section of this stretch consists of a high bank on the left, which creates a holding area for the trout along this bank. They rise readily to the naturals, but are very gun shy to the artificials and poorly cast fly lines. Most of them have been caught several times by Keech and Himmel, Inc. Should you catch one with a clipped adipose fin, you might wish to remove the fin entirely, just to let the world know these fish are not exclusive. The fast water under the big tree and on upstream can be fished effectively with a small tan caddis, size 18 or smaller, and the action in this shaded portion of the creek continues well into late August.

Upstream to Murphy Road the water is shallow, with large rocks and fast runs. Wading is difficult when the water is high due to the slippery rocks, and few trout are encountered. If there is no action, it is best to go up to the bridge pool, which is heavily stocked so that trout are always present. Blue Quills, size 18, hatch in late April, Hendricksons in May, and light Cahills in June. Fish the feeding lanes on the left, as you wade upstream. Under the bridge, fish the right-side wall, and then fish the riffles above the bridge. Be careful as you wade since there is spiked half-log deflector on the left which has claimed its share of waders.

Lamont to East Koy Road

From the Lamont Road bridge downstream about one-half mile, posted signs interrupt what has otherwise been all public fishing waters. The first point of access is at a DEC walk-in sign. The stream is about one-half mile from the road at this point, and there are some marshy fields and wooded lots to traverse before reaching the stream. The solitude is worth the hike; however, the fishing is limited to a few pools that depend almost exclusively on wild trout and migrating carry-overs for occupants. The remaining five miles downstream to East Koy Road has access points at Griffith Road, an old migrant worker house, and at the East Koy Road bridge. Since stocking is usually assured at the bridge access points, one can decide beforehand what kind of fishing he seeks. At the bridge sites action will be faster, but limited mostly to fish stocked during the season, whereas at the more remote stretches, carry-over and native trout coexist, but in far fewer numbers.

Bait fishing in the boondocks areas may range from spectacular to absolute zero, depending upon how well the prospecting is done, and how lucky you are in locating a holding site. It is certain that at the end of summer, when the water is low, these fish congregate in deep holes prior to spawning, and then, as the spring thaw occurs, they move out into nearby feeding zones. As Bachman has observed, these carry-over trout will occupy the same zones from year to year; indeed, clipped-fin trout have been caught in the same pool as in the previous year. Locating these holding areas may take several days of fruitless fishing and exploration, but once onto a spot it is like paradise regained. Worms, Panther Martins, salted minnows, and grasshoppers can be drifted along the bottom in search of action. Snags and hang ups will cost you money, so the dry-fly fisherman will wait for the hatches and then begin his quest for the right fly. Riprap, bridge abutments, and rocks provide the trout cover, so concentrate your efforts there. At the Griffith Road pool there is a fantastic hatch of Blue Quills, sizes 18 and 20, during the early season. Certainly you should be prepared with imitations of the Hendrickson, March Brown, Green Drake (perhaps a Brown Drake), and light Cahill sequence of hatches. This sequence will carry you well into July, at which time the caddis and tricos, sizes 18, 20, 22, and 24, will last thru September. These hatches occur from 1 p.m. through 9 p.m., with the late evening hatches occurring later each evening as the season progresses. Only the bushes and overgrowth prevent the fly fisherman from enjoying classic dry fly conditions in this section of the East Koy, so one must seek and search, alone, methodically, and patiently until success rewards his efforts. If there is a car parked at your favorite access point, find another spot, since two in the same pot will spoil the brew.

Downstream at the corn field, a dirt road into the creek is used by the locals to fish with live bait, bass plugs, and nightcrawlers. They fish rather fast in the deep pools and progress as far as two miles above Griffith Road during a day's fishing. They report some remarkably large fish being taken during the early spring season. Later on, as the fishing pressure decreases, one can find solitary hours of fishing pleasure on seemingly unfished beaver pools and pasture streams. Again the Hendrickson-March Brown sequence of hatches is most impressive.

Your success on the East Koy will depend upon a multitude of conditions. Fish alone, fish quietly, wade sparingly, take your time, change flies or bait often, and by all means never think that there are not trout in the stream.

East Koy Road to Babbitt Road

Contrary to normal expectations, this short section of stream is more productive at the ends, near the bridges, than in the middle, where the bottom is occasionally shale and the water shallow. Each bridge area, at East Koy Road and at Babbitt Road, is usually well-stocked with hatchery trout that find little need to migrate in either direction, thereby increasing the holding trout population disproportionately. Parking and access at both bridges is easy; however, at East Koy Road, the summer cottage people would prefer that you enter where the DEC sign is.

At Babbitt Road there is a good pool under the bridge, which is knee deep, easily waded, and an excellent current carries the dry fly along the west bridge abutment, where several good trout find shelter. Above the bridge, the opposite-side abutment provides good cover under several large boulders, but a drag-free drift of the fly is difficult. More often than not, the largest of the trout in this hole will merely roll at the fly and return to his hidden lair. Bait fishermen often sit on the slope of the abutment and await their turn at "Old Reliable."

At the old dam there are trout in the fast water below, and there are trout under the wooden section in the turbulence, but finding a way to take these fellows requires considerable ingenuity. Just above the dam the pool is rather long and flat, with the larger trout concentrated in the upper two-thirds where fast water enters and provides feeding lanes. This is a good place to try a tan caddis late in the season, and this entire area is ideal to bring the kids to learn to fly fish.

Beyond the 50 or so yards of riffles, (the knee-deep water in between looks fishy, but is generally unproductive) there are two large midstream boulders that form a pocket that trout seem to love. Be sure to drop the fly above the rocks and allow it to drift into the swirl around the rocks. Beyond this spot fishing is generally poor due to low water conditions, which do not attract the stocked trout. Apparently, the shale bottom is neither conducive to reproductions nor does it provide good habitat,

About 100 yards below the East Koy Road bridge, good holding water with pockets begins again. The water is fast and a good attractor fly, like the bivisibles and hair wings, are good bets. Sometimes the Isonychia hatch is good in this section, and a size 10 Grey Wulff will produce spectacular results. Under the bridge the shale ledges harbor good trout, so be sure to fish the west bridge abutment within an inch or two of the drop-off. Finally, give the east abutment where the fast water enters a try, and then use long casts to fish the big rock just beyond the bridge carefully. A sizable brown always seems to select this site as his summer home.

NOTES: ______________________________

____

____

GENESEE RIVER - **See Allegany County Streams and Rivers (upper section) and Monroe County Streams and Rivers (lower section).**

OATKA CREEK (Upper Section)

Map Coordinates .... 42° 51′ 53″ 78° 02′ 50″
USGS Map(s) .... Wyoming, Dale, Warsaw, Castile
Township(s) .... Covington, Middlebury, Warsaw
Access .... Roughly paralleled by Route 19 above Warsaw
Principal Species .... Brown Trout (stocked and wild), Northern Pike, Largemouth Bass, Smallmouth Bass

The upper Oatka averages 15 to 20 feet in width, and has a gravel and rubble bottom. It is surrounded primarily by farmlands and some woodlands.

The village of Warsaw divides the stream into cold-water and warm-water sections. The warm-water portion, which extends from Warsaw to just above the Monroe County line, is a mediocre fishery that yields some smallmouth bass, largemouth bass, northern pike, and rough fish.

Above Warsaw, the Oatka is a lightly fished trout stream of considerable potential. Between Warsaw and Rock Glen there is little or no natural reproduction, but 1,700 brown trout yearlings are stocked here in the spring. Above Rock Glen, the stream becomes somewhat small and brushy, but is loaded with wild brown trout.

The following article will provide you with all you need to know to fish the upper Oatka.

UPPER OATKA CREEK

By Gordon Deitrick

Many western New York fishermen are familiar with the limestone waters of the Oatka Creek near Mumford, but few fishermen know about the good fishing to be found in the upper Oatka, upstream of the town of Warsaw in Wyoming County. There are abundant brown trout to be found in the approximately 6 to 7 miles of the seldom-fished upper Oatka.

To get there, you go south out of Warsaw on Route 19, which parallels the creek until Rock Glen. The first mile above Warsaw is poor fishing, so you should start at South Warsaw, at Mungers Mill Road or vicinity. There are large trout in this section of the stream, though they are less abundant than the more-numerous smaller trout to be found further upstream above Rock Glen. The water is suitable for fly fishing up to Rock Glen, though one can better use spinners. Nymphs, wet flies, and streamers all work well, and there are good fly hatches; a dry fly should work, as well. The pools in the South Warsaw area tend to be large, readily accessible from the road, and hold some large fish. The stream is usually low in the early season, and better yet, maintains an adequate flow throughout the season.

Two miles further down on Route 19 at Rock Glen, the upper Oatka becomes spinning water. You can park along Evans Road and follow the railroad tracks to the creek. It's too bushy in this section for fly fishing, so I recommend a short ultra-light spinning rod, 2- to 4-pound-test line, and 1/16- to 1/8-ounce spinners. Both gold and silver Panther Martins are deadly. Hip boots will suffice for the wading, but some prefer chest waders, for the stream is narrow, full of snags (especially since the great ice storm of 1976), and you usually hang up a spinner in water over hip boots. It's a bit mucky and marshy also, and not the easiest wading, but the 12- to 15-inch browns that you can pick up certainly make the effort rewarding.

About one-half mile upstream from Rock Glen the stream divides. The Oatka goes to the right and crosses Route 19 in about one mile. It is certainly worth fishing, but the right branch is less productive than the left. The left branch, called Warner Creek on my map, is narrow, very mucky, but with good water flow and more productive results. There are several big pools, including a very large one about 2 miles upstream where the creek goes under the railroad (you can walk back to Rock Glen along the tracks).

Trout are stocked annually in the upper Oatka, but there is certainly natural spawning in the headwaters, for you can catch trout from 4 inches to 14 inches (and if you're like me, lose even bigger ones). Perhaps the nicest feature of this stream is its solitude. On the Wiscoy there's a fellow angler met at every bend; but on this section of the Oatka you see absolutely nobody. It's seldom fished. For those of you willing to fight brush and muck, it can become a special stream.

NOTES: ______________________________

____

____

PEARL CREEK

Map Coordinates .... 42° 51′ 10″ 78° 03′ 40″
USGS Map(s) .... Wyoming
Township(s) .... Covington
Access .... Route 19
Principal Species .... Brown Trout (stocked)

A small tributary of Oatka Creek, Pearl Creek averages about 10 feet in width, and has a gravel bottom. Surrounded by farmland and fields, there is intermittent bank cover along this stream. It is fishable primarily during the early months of trout season, although there are some sections with pools that could hold a few fish all year.

In the spring, a 1.8-mile section of Pearl Creek is stocked with 400 brown trout yearlings, from the mouth of the stream to .2 mile below Lake Road.

NOTES: ______________________________

____

____

SPRING BROOK

Map Coordinates .... 42° 33′ 40″ 78° 21′ 22″
USGS Map(s) .... Bliss
Township(s) .... Arcade, Eagle
Access .... Sullivan Road
Principal Species .... Brown Trout (wild), Rainbow Trout (wild), Brook Trout (wild)

Spring Brook, also known as Flynn Brook, is a small, high-quality trout stream. It averages 10 feet in width, has a gravel bottom, and very good water quality. Surrounded by farmlands and woodlands, there is intermittent bank cover along this stream. It is fishable all trout season.

QUILL GORDEN

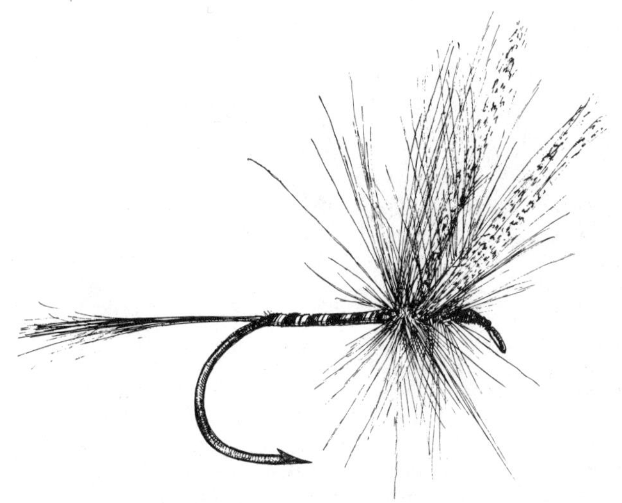

The sparse, slate-gray Quill Gordan is traditionally one of the first flies used during trout season.

Spring brook is not stocked, but does have substantial populations of brown trout, rainbow trout, and brook trout. The state has obtained public fishing rights along the quarter-mile section above the stream's confluence with Cattaraugus Creek, and along Sullivan Road, east of Allen Road.

NOTES: ____________________

TONAWANDA CREEK - See Niagara County Streams and Rivers.

TROUT BROOK

Map Coordinates .... 42° 34′ 16″ 78° 10′ 19″
USGS Map(s) .... Pike
Township(s) .... Pike, Eagle
Access .... Route 39
Principal Species .... Brown Trout (wild), Brook Trout (wild)

Trout Brook is a major tributary of Wiscoy Creek. Like the Wiscoy, Trout Brook is not stocked. Large numbers of wild brook and brown trout, however, make this a very rewarding stream to fish.

The following article on Trout Brook was originally prepared by M. T. Creel of Trout Unlimited.

TROUT BROOK

By M. T. Creel

Where does one fish when the streams are swollen with rains, running over banks and wader tops with the muddy excess of nature's bounty? The answer is Trout Brook, in Wyoming County, a small tributary that joins the Wiscoy about a mile and a half west of the town of Pike on Route 39, just east of Wing's farm and the Beardsley roadside park. When the Wiscoy runs high and muddy, Trout Brook is usually clear and just high enough for the fish to feel comfortable and safe. There's about a mile of stream that is unposted; after Hardy's Road (County Road 10) upstream it's poachers only, but that one-mile section is loaded with fish, (Mike Muldoon claims to have released a 6-pound brown from one of its small deep pools.)

Trout Brook is a small, forest stream overhung with trees, willows, and just about anything else that grows, but if you're looking for solitude and a sense of being alone in the wilderness, you can find it on Trout Brook.

You can fish the stream with ultra-light spinners (1/16- and 1/8-ounce Panther Martins or sizes 0 and 1 Mepps) upstream, running the spinner close to the willows or the numerous downed trees. Fish all the waters, even the shallow runs, for many will have a deep pocket or two that will harbor a trout. You should pick up a brookie every now and then. Try to work the spinner as slowly as possible, letting it settle a bit in the deeper pockets before retrieving; and give each small pool or run several casts before going on to the next.

If you own a short fly rod, 4 to 6 feet long, the stream frequently provides some good fly fishing for small trout. The hatches are generous, but the flies are usually smaller than those found on the Wiscoy. Seldom will anything larger than a size 16 be effective, and a size 18 is better still. There isn't much casting room, and the pools are small. Be prepared to roll cast frequently, lose a lot of flies, and curse a lot . . . but there are days on Trout Brook that make it all worthwhile. A size 16 Blue Dun in mid-May, for instance, can prove irresistible to the brilliantly colored brookies. A size 18 tan Deer Hair Caddis on a long, light leader is great in July, but it's fine and far-off fishing on low water over wild and very spooky fish.

Trout Brook can be a generous but challenging stream. It's a natural fish hatchery for the Wiscoy, and thus is an ideal stream for releasing one's catch. The trout are wild, beautiful, and far too valuable to be caught only once.

NOTES: ____________________

WISCOY CREEK

Map Coordinates .... 42° 29′ 55″ 78° 03′ 26″
USGS Map(s) .... Fillmore, Portageville, Houghton, Pike, Bliss
Township(s) .... Hume, Pike, Eagle
Access .... Paralleled by Route 39 above the village of Pike - see below
Principal Species .... Brown Trout (stocked and wild)

Wiscoy Creek is considered to be one of the top trout streams in New York State. Since it is managed as a wild trout fishery, most of the Wiscoy is not stocked. The only section that is stocked is a small 1.2-mile section just above Mill's Mills. However, incredible

Wiscoy Creek is one of the top trout steams in western New York. Much of the stream is wide and has an open canopy, making it ideally suited to fly fishing. Photo courtesy Rick Kustich.

numbers of wild brown trout make this one of the most rewarding streams you're ever likely to encounter.

Access is facilitated by extensive public fishing rights that extend from one mile above Albro Road down to one mile below the Allegany County line. From the Allegany County line upstream to one mile above Albro Road, trout can be taken from April 1 to September 30, 3 per day, minimum size 10 inches. The 1-mile section above Albro Road has the further restriction of allowing only the use of artificial lures.

The following description of Wiscoy Creek was prepared by members of Trout Unlimited.

WISCOY CREEK

By Jim Keech, Al Himmel, and Bob Janiga

Wiscoy Creek ranks as one of the finest trout streams in New York State. It is located in the heart of Wyoming County, and winds in and out of the township of Eagle. The stream has a gravel bottom nursed by cold springs. As a result, the temperature very rarely exceeds 70 degrees. This unique feature enables this stream to provide good trout fishing all season long.

The easiest way to reach the Wiscoy from the Buffalo area is to travel Route 16 south to Yorkshire, turn left (east) on Route 39 through the town of Arcade, and follow Route 39 to Bliss. At this point you will find Perry's Wiscoy Haven, a campground that offers stream as well as pond fishing. Of course there is a fee for fishing or camping, but the returns in the form of relaxation are well worth the price. Traveling along Route 39 you will find a picnic and parking area. This is the "artificials only" section, no live bait permitted. Nearby signs indicate the boundaries of this 1-mile long section.

Continuing down Route 39 to the town of Pike you will find a dam in the heart of town. From this area downstream it is all fishable water extending 10 miles or more to Allegany County.

In past years good-size trout have been caught here, ranging from 14 to 20 inches in all areas. Smaller fish are plentiful and easier to land . . . but the larger trout take all your angling skill to fool.

Special Regulations Section

The lures-only section, the 1-mile stretch from the Albro Road bridge upstream to the wooden sign on Route 39, is about 2 miles upstream from Pike. This section of once rather barren meadow stream has been vastly improved by some vegetation, fencing, willow planting, and extensive cribbing over the last few years until it is the most fished stretch in the whole Wiscoy system. Certainly a testament to the potential of stream improvement to create good wild trout fishing from mediocre waters. It's not an easy section, however, and is often infuriating evidence of the trout's selective feeding. The pool at Trout Brook in particular seems to be filled with willing, rising browns who blithely ignore anything under a fly speck in size. On those days when no flies seem to be hatching, float an attractor fly like a size 14 or 16 Hair Wing Royal Coachman or Goofus Bug alongside the cribbing. There are some good-size fish - up to 18 inches - who live underneath these cribs and can create an awesome and unexpected explosion as they dart out to take a dry fly. You usually don't see many rises and the hits are usually unexpected. But the fish are there. (Try spinners just after a thundershower has clouded the water slightly; the results can be spectacular evidence of the Wiscoy's wild trout population.)

In fishing the dry fly, float the fly as close as possible - no more than 6 inches - to the cribbing. And fish all the cribs, even those with only inches of water over them. My best fish last year (14 3/4 inches on a Hair Wing Coachman) was taken at the head of the cribbing downstream from the run of willows below Wing's Bridge in just 6 inches of water. A lot of these cribs shelter fish. Start at the tail of the cribbing above Trout Brook (a good 12-incher always seems to be there) and fish upstream past the picnic area. All of the bends seem to be especially productive, particularly the third S bend above the picnic area, the high bank bend below the cattle ford, and the bend opposite the little red summer house. You can usually count on one fish suddenly rising to the fly per bend, but if you miss him, he seldom can be persuaded to rise again. Mark the spot for later in the day, and go on to the next cribbing.

The open pools on this section of the Wiscoy are also productive, but more unpredictable. You see the rises, and the fish see you and vanish quickly. Long leaders and long casts, careful wading, and casting from your knees are usually advisable after the careless feeding of April is past. An attractor fly will also often work in the pools, but matching the hatch is much more productive. In late April try a size 20 dark Blue Dun to match the Paraleptophlebia hatch. In mid-May try a size 14 Hendrickson, and a size 16 Grey Fox at the end of the month. From mid-June on, try size 14 Light Cahills to match the usually good evening hatches. As the summer advances, your flies should get much smaller, from size 16 down to 24: size 18 Thorax Duns, size 18 to 22 Cream Variants, and sizes 18 and 20 Fluttering Grey and Brown Caddis. Size 22 Black Ants fished up against the willows are good for August, and there is usually a good early morning (7:00 a.m. to 9:00 a.m.) hatch of Tricorythodes on the upper portions of this section, matched with a black midge, size 22 to 24. In September, go back to flies you can see - size 14 in Caddis, Light Cahill, or Cream Variants, and especially the Royal Coachman. I like a parachute version for late September. All in all, this is a very generous section of a beautiful little meadow stream.

ROYAL WULFF

The Royal Wulff is considered by many fly fishermen to be the most effective attractor pattern. Brightly colored, it is an ideal choice for enticing finicky fish.

Pike to the Special Regulations Section

Above the dam at Pike there is good fishing under the willows along the right side of the creek until you reach the old riprap. Careful wading is an absolute necessity along the riprap, since the water becomes deep and slow moving, and the trout are very spooky. This section is particularly good in the late summer, from the time of the light cahill hatches until the tricos of August and September take over. It is a very demanding type of "fine and far-off" fishing.

At the fair grounds bridge, fish the cribbing on the left side going upstream, again being very careful to wade and fish slowly. Rises may also occur under the willows on the right, so it is best to wade directly up the middle, which will require chest waders. Further upstream there is a superb swimming hole pool, which harbors many young of the year that feed in the riffles above and below the pool. Continuing on upstream, one finds a variety of fishing conditions, from long, slow flats, to fast-rushing, rocky currents, all of which, or none of which, may hold trout, depending upon the conditions. Late in the season, the trout tend to congregate in the deep holes, leaving

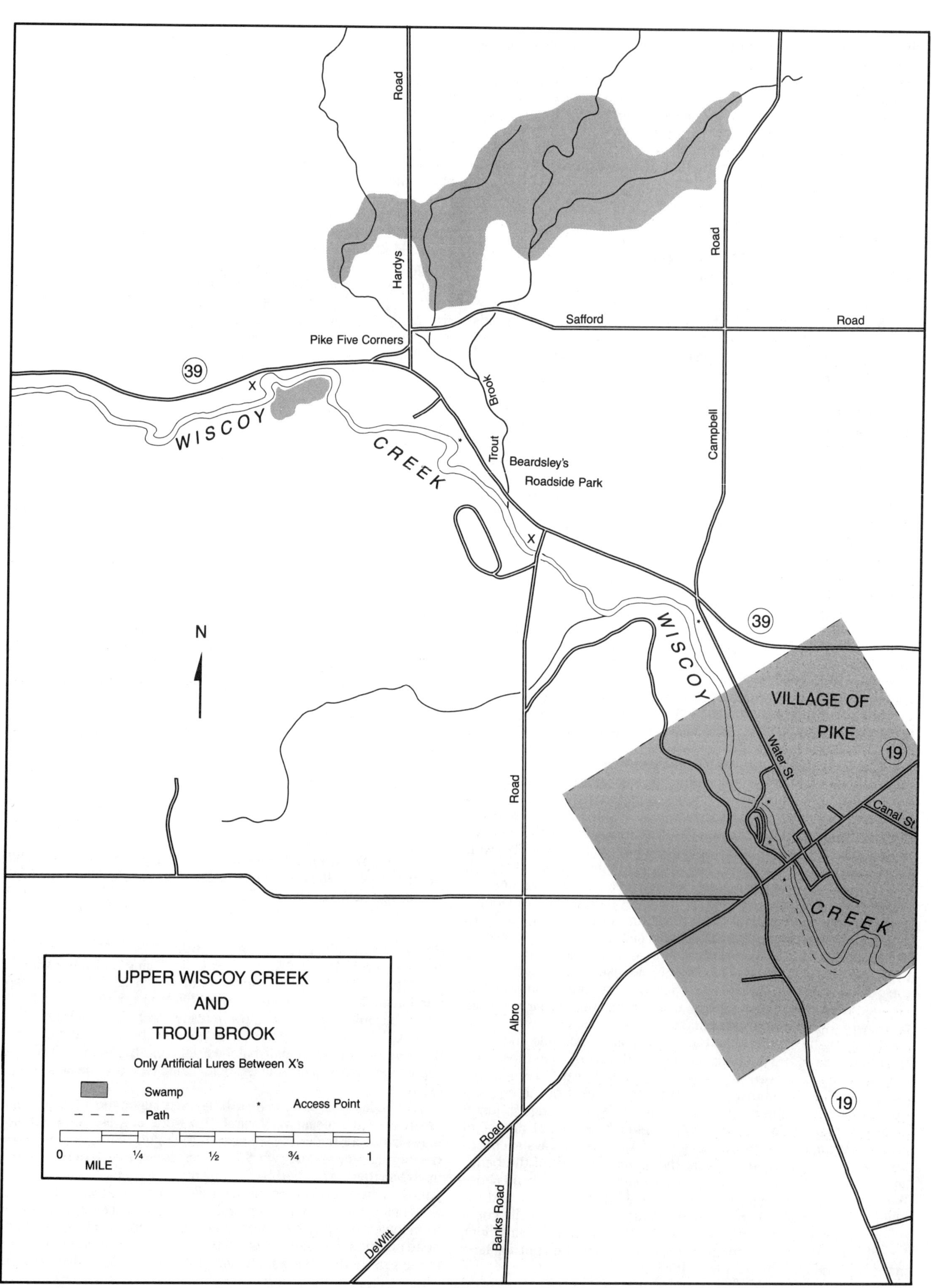
UPPER WISCOY CREEK
AND
TROUT BROOK
Only Artificial Lures Between X's
Swamp
Path
Access Point
0
¼
½
¾
1
MILE
Hardys Road
Safford Road
Pike Five Corners
39
WISCOY CREEK
Trout Brook
Beardsley's
Roadside Park
Campbell Road
X
N
VILLAGE OF
PIKE
Water St
Canal St
19
Albro Road
DeWitt Road
Banks Road

the riffles to the small baitfish, although late evenings often find fish feeding in the riffles at any time of the year. Continuing upstream there is an old crib on the left side of the stream that is a good late evening fly-fishing hole, and an all-the-time anytime spinning hole. Access to this section can also be had by parking on Water Street just off Route 39, and walking a few hundred yards through the bush.

Just beyond the crib pool there is a high bank on the right side as the stream becomes shallow and flows over table rock. This is usually unproductive for any kind of fishing; however, the pool at the head of this table rock is loaded with trout, which can be put down with a single cast of the line. These fish migrate into the riffles above the pool to feed so that it is often necessary to wade into the deeply silted pool to fish the rising trout. Needless to say, one's wading technique again becomes critical.

The next quarter mile or so is pocket-type water with some productive spots using either worms or spinners. At the end of the pocket water there is an inlet to a private pond with a deflector on the right side. The pool and the riffle hold trout that seem to take refuge in the inlet part, which is posted, but with luck it is usually possible to locate the trout without ever entering the water, and then casting to the holding fish. As one fishes upstream to Albro Road, the creek meanders through eroded pastureland, where fishing is erratic, sometimes very poor, and at other times, when mobile fish have dropped down from the Albro Bridge pool because of high water or for feeding purposes, very good to excellent. Bushes, pasture fences, cows, and siltation all act as deterrents to easy fishing. Parking and access are both available at the Albro Road Bridge.

Grey Cabin to Pike

Access to this section is obtained via a walk-in farm road by parking along East Koy Road, and walking about one-quarter mile downhill to the stream. It's the return trip that hurts. The small grey cabin at the end of the road marks the beginning of one of the best sections of the Wiscoy. Upstream, fishing is good to excellent for about one-quarter mile, where half-log shelters installed by Trout Unlimited provide habitat for native, wild trout. Fish these structures carefully, since each will harbor one or more trout. Proceeding upstream, there are three good, deep pools at bends in the creek, which invariably have large trees across the stream. The dry-fly fisherman can fish this successfully, but the spin fisherman will have problems. Either fishing technique requires that one be willing to lose a lure or two, and that casting skills be maximized. Upstream there are some good pockets and riffles, but the best by far is at an old crib on the right. The crib pool is loaded with trout, which are as fickle as any woman. Immediately after fishing the crib pool, for better or for worse, an even more impressive pool at the next bend, is encountered. Here the deep siltation on the left makes wading chancy, so that it may be necessary to stay in the middle to avoid that sinking feeling and to reach the trout, which feed in the fast water on the far side. Here is a chance for the classic dry-fly casting techniques to be utilized. The spin fisherman will also enjoy fishing the riffle with a Panther Martin or a small worm.

The last half mile into Pike has mostly slower, knee-deep water with an occasional deep pool. Several half-log deflectors have been installed by Trout Unlimited, and those that have not become silted over or destroyed by high water provide good fishing opportunities. Be careful when wading near these structures as some of the spikes could ruin the water-restraining characteristic of those new waders. From the bridge at Pike to the dam in the park, the shallow water is loaded with wary trout, and the dam pool is probably the most popular fishing spot on the entire creek. Fishermen gather here for the midnight opener on April 1, and there is always someone fishing here daily, except when school is out and the local kids swim and dive in the huge pool. Parking is ample and picnic tables make this a great place for a leisurely family fishing picnic with something for all.

Susan's Acre to Grey Cabin

The DEC access and parking area on Camp Road, about 2 miles south of Pike, is located high above the stream. Descent down the steep bank is either by a sharp rock-slide path, or by a long, sloping trail upstream. The former is a hazard to one's longevity, and the latter is terminated well beyond some of the prime trout-holding spots in the area. The pool digger dam, where the upstream trail ends, creates one of the most superb looking pools on the creek. Certainly trout must abound in this pool; however, the fact that catching those trout presents a super challenge, can be attributed to the fact that the trout hold in the turbulence under the wooden structure, thereby reducing fly fishing to mere chance. Perhaps a weighted worm at the foot of the dam is the answer.

LATEX STONEFLY CREEPER

Stoneflies are commonly found in many western New York streams and ponds that have a rock and cobble bottom. The Stonefly Creeper imitates the stonefly nymph.

Proceeding upstream there are a few good holding spots, but the long walk between spots makes it a day's outing to cover the mile or so to the grey cabin. One way to avoid the long walk is to access this stretch by parking on East Koy Road, at the edge of the woods, and walking downhill through the corn field. The pool at this access is also an excellent worm and spin fishing spot, while the riprap upstream can harbor many fine hold-over browns in the 12 inch category. Small young-of-the-year 3-inchers will rise in the riffles. Of course, these are all native trout, so handle with extreme care when releasing the little buggers.

About a half mile before the grey cabin, a high bank and several downed trees create a deep right angle pool followed by a series of riffles that hold trout during midseason. This stretch can be fished either by the "once over lightly" method, or the "slow and deliberate" approach. The flies used can be as varied as the Muddler Minnow, Hairwing Coachman, Green Drake, or the tiny tricos, ants, and beetles. For the spin fisherman, the should-be-outlawed, 1/8-ounce Panther Martin is usual.

During 1983 Trout Unlimited completed nine log deflectors in this part of the Wiscoy. Unfortunately several of these were washed out by high water in the spring of 1984. You win some, you lose some. That's what T. U. and fishing is all about. The fishing here is still good, and the log jams, although an accident, have created several deep pools that carry many large trout.

Boy Scout Camp to Susan's Acre

Access to this part of the Wiscoy is provided at the Boy Scout camp and at the Susan's Acre DEC parking area. There is no parking area at the Boy Scout camp, so you must park along Camp Road, being careful not to block the chained camp access road. Be prepared for a one-third mile hike down to the creek. Hopefully, there will be no campers present when you are fishing; however, if the scouts are there, avoid the archery range at all costs.

This is a beautiful section of the Wiscoy and probably the most secluded, thanks to the long hike back up the hill. At the scout camp the bridge pool is fascinating, since one can sit on the bridge and watch as the trout go through their daily routine. Above the bridge the riprap shelters many trout up to 16 inches. The fishing is best with dry flies drifted as close to the riprap as possible. Hang ups are

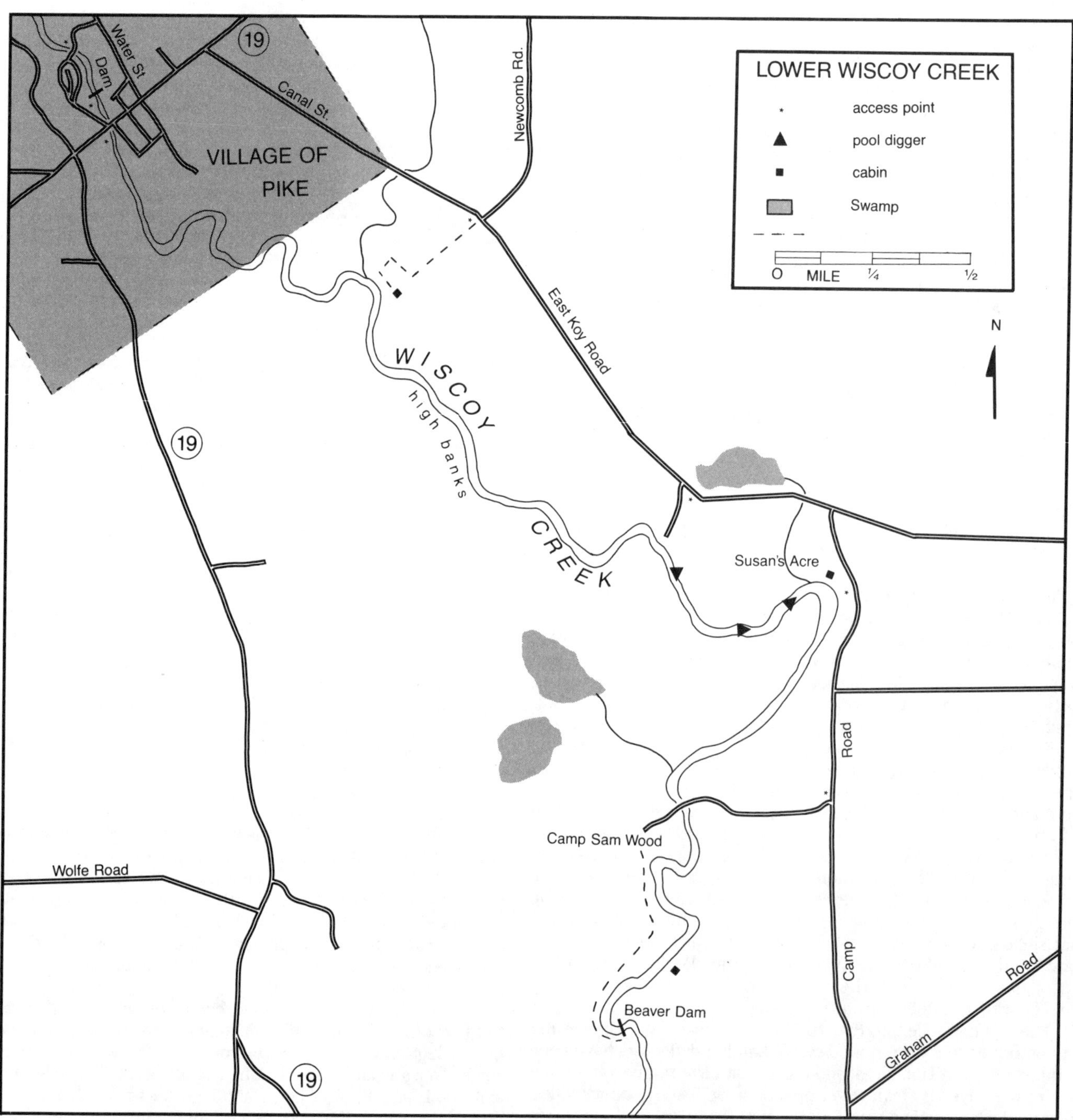
LOWER WISCOY CREEK
access point
pool digger
cabin
Swamp
O MILE ¼ ½
N
VILLAGE OF PIKE
Water St
Dam
Canal St.
19
Newcomb Rd.
East Koy Road
WISCOY CREEK
high banks
Susan's Acre
Road
Camp
Camp Sam Wood
Wolfe Road
Beaver Dam
Graham Road

best broken off so that the section can be fished carefully, since it often takes 20 or more passes to induce a rise. Beyond the scout camp area, one can find perfect solitude and long stretches of pocket water, although some slate-bottomed, shallow stretches are not very productive.

As you approach the Susan's Acre access, the stream cuts its banks along a high ridge on one side and heavy brush on the other. The water runs crystal clear over small rocks and gravel. Light lines and leaders are required to fish this gin-clear water along the high bank. Fish are spooky and so beautifully colored that one might think he has found paradise. Make sure your approach is out of the water, quiet, and perhaps on bent knees. Fly fishermen can count on good hatches of Green Drakes and March Browns in late May and early June, and excellent Isonychia hatches from mid-June through July.

Genesee River to Boy Scout Camp

This is the most lightly fished section of the Wiscoy due to limited access and posting. Access at the Boy Scout Ranger station is by permission, but the walk-in is about three-quarters of a mile. Downstream along Camp Road there is a walk-in through a farmer's pasture, but this is a 1-mile walk over two ridges. Access at the bridge below the Ukrainian camp and at the dam at Mill's Mills can be used to fish upstream; however, the campgrounds are posted. One-quarter mile below the dam, at Mill's Mills, the posting is resumed. Parking at the Rochester Power Road and walking downstream to reach the dam pool and falls may just be what the doctor ordered to locate a really large trout. Above the dam, fishing is marginal until you reach the Ukrainian camp. The swim pool and the upstream run along the bank is just loaded with trout. They are gun shy and not afraid of people. You can stand in the stream and observe them sunning close to the bank and their hideout. Step too close and, zoom, they are gone. When the campers are present it is best to avoid the camp area. (Someone is sure to let you know that you are on private land, although courteously). Once beyond the camp, public fishing begins, and fishing becomes a hunting process. The first one-quarter mile is mostly slate-bottomed shallows with crevices and drop offs serving as holding sites for the fish. Which of them has a trout is left to the wiles of the fisherman. At the end of the slate-bottomed stretch, the stream meanders and divides several times, so that pools and riffles alternate at relatively short distances. Generally, the good mayfly activity during the evenings make this section worthy of the long walk required to fish it. March Brown and Green Drake hatches are particularly impressive; however, few fishermen are willing to hike in on the chance encounter with a daytime hatch, and to remain in this section into the late evening requires a certain knowledge of the pathway out. Due to the many changes in direction one cannot rely on simply following the stream without careful planning or the use of a compass.

NOTES: ______________________________

____

____

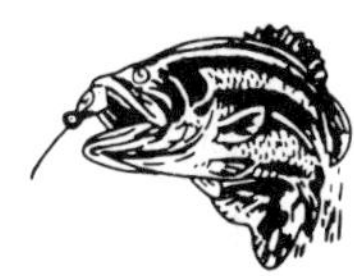

Another view of the Wiscoy. Photo courtesy Rich Kustich.

WYOMING COUNTY LAKES AND PONDS

SILVER LAKE

Location

Map Coordinates .... 42° 42′ 00″ 78° 01′ 45″
USGS Map(s) .... Castile
Township(s) .... Castile
Access .... East Lake Road, West Lake Road

Physical Characteristics

Area .... 761 acres
Shoreline .... 7.4 miles
Elevation .... 1,356 feet
Maximum Depth .... 37 feet
Mean Depth .... 25 feet
Bottom Type .... Sand, gravel, muck

Chemical Characteristics

Water .... Clear to slightly turbid
pH .... Alkaline
Oxygen .... Studies by the DEC indicate that dissolved oxygen concentrations are dangerously low in substantial portions of this lake, particularly during the summer at depths greater than 25 feet. However, this situation should be improving due to the recent construction of a perimeter sewer system around the lake.

Plant Life

There is a thin, intermittent weedline that runs almost all the way around the lake. Large solid weedbeds are found at the north and south ends of the lake.

Boat Launch Sites

1. Koziel's Inlet Boat Livery - 6882 Oatka Road, Perry - fee.
2. Silver Lake Marine - 4213 West Lake Road, Silver Lake - fee.
3. Mack's Boat Livery - off East Lake Road, Castile - fee.
4. There is a state-operated launch site (hand launch only) for small boats and canoes on West Lake Road, just south of Silver Lake Marine - no charge.

Species Information

Walleye .... Common; growth rate good

Silver Lake is at the top of the list of walleye stocking sites in the state. The ranking on this list is determined by various parameters, including the previous presence of a viable population of walleye and the survival rate of the walleye being stocked. The Wyoming County Sportsmen's Federation stocked walleye here in the 1980s, and electroshockings by the DEC indicated that a sizeable portion of the fish survived. However, Silver Lake is not going to be stocked with walleye on a permanent basis. The state is attempting to re-establish a self-sustaining population of walleye in this lake. If this can not be done after a reasonable amount of time and effort, the program will be dropped. Because of the silting over of many of their former spawning areas, it is not known if walleye will be able to successfully reproduce here. However, even if the policy of stocking fingerlings is terminated, the state will probably continue to stock the lake with walleye fry. It is believed that such a policy would now be successful in the lake given the fact that the yellow perch population is now under control.

In October 1989, the legal size of walleye in Silver Lake was dropped from 22 inches to 18 inches, and the limit set at three fish per day. The size limit had been raised to 22 inches in an effort to help control the yellow perch population in the lake, which had become overly abundant and stunted. This measure, however, did not work, and it had the side effect of adversely affecting the weight/length and length/age ratios of the lake's northern pike.

At present, the walleye are exhibiting a good rate of growth. A 5-year-old fish will typically weigh in at 4 pounds and have a length of 18 to 22 inches.

You can catch walleye here all summer by trolling deep-diving lures in 10 to 20 feet of water or using jigs in the middle of the day. The source for much of my information on Silver Lake was George Dovolos, a local angler who fishes this lake often. He recommends fishing the outside of the weedlines using perch-colored crankbaits such as Wiggle Warts and Rapalas. This method will work anywhere along weedlines. Though walleye can be taken almost anywhere on the lake, George feels that the best walleye fishing will be found

The revival of the walleye fishery is only one of several positive changes that have taken place on Silver Lake in recent years. Fish like the one held by George Dovolos are now caught on a regular basis. Photo courtesy George Dovolos.

along the windward side of the lake where the water is being churned up. A number of factors could be at work here, including increased oxygen levels in the roiled water and increased feeding activity on the part of baitfish. Also, there are a number of springs that feed the lake, and the walleye are known to congregate around these. Several are found off Buffalo Point and Country Club Point.

A lot of walleye are now being taken by anglers through the ice. Unfortunately, many undersize walleye that are caught are being kept, a situation that could hamper the development of what could eventually be a truly fine walleye fishery in Silver Lake.

Smallmouth Bass .... Common; growth rate good

Although not known for its smallmouth fishing, Silver Lake has a healthy population of smallmouth bass, some of which reach a weight of 6 pounds.

If worked properly, the outside edges of most weedlines will give up a few bass. But the best daytime fishing for smallmouth bass is found around the central portion of the east side of the lake where they are commonly taken off points, and at the north and south ends of the lake.

An important point to keep in mind when stalking smallmouth on this lake is the fact that in the summer many of the bass, especially the larger ones, will hold in relatively deep water during the day, waiting for nighttime to move onto the shallow flats to feed on crayfish and baitfish. This is fairly common on many lakes, but may be more pronounced here. The fact that many of the bass here feed at night and are unavailable to anglers during the day could account for the lack of awareness anglers have regarding the quality of the lake's bass fishery.

Many of the same methods used to take smallmouth during the day can be used to take them at night as well. Crankbaits worked along the edge of a drop off or large jigs slowly worked across the flats will take fish. But possibly the most productive method uses a top water lure. A classic piece of hardware for this type of fishing is Heddon's Zara Spook. This stickbait is made to be "dog walked" on the surface of the water. It is designed in such a way that, when you lift your rod tip, it darts first to the left and then to the right. When slowly retrieved over the flats in this manner, it is very effective for taking the big smallmouth that inhabit this lake. Jitterbugs are also very effective at night. These are cast tight up against the bank and retrieved perpendicular to the shoreline. Small plastic worms are a good choice when fishing at night for bass, especially the so-called "Do Nothing Worm" a pre-rigged 4-inch worm with a weight attached about 3 feet ahead of it. Cast up against the bank and very slowly retrieved with short sudden jerks, this worm rig can be highly productive. Another proven bass catcher is a small black flatfish trolled very close to shore. And if all else fails, don't forget what is drawing the bass to the shallows in the first place. Live crayfish, or suitable imitations, should take limits of smallmouth bass. This nighttime bass fishing is usually productive until early September.

Yellow Perch .... Common; growth rate very good

For many years Silver Lake had a well-deserved reputation for having one of the largest populations of stunted perch in the state. But changes in the management of the lake have turned this situation around. The yellow perch in Silver Lake have increased in size significantly over past years. Where a 5-year-old perch in 1986 was about 5 1/2 inches in length, the average length for a 5-year-old perch is now 8 to 10 inches. And the average size of the fish is still increasing. But as their size goes up, their numbers are going down.

In the spring, the yellow perch are going to be schooled up and moving around the lake looking for suitable spawning areas. Flats adjacent to deep water are the most productive springtime locations. Often, you can see perch churning the surface as they are chased by northern pike that cruise these flats.

Once the fish are located, there are a number of ways to fish for them. A popular and productive method for taking springtime perch is to anchor along the edges of dormant weed beds and still fish with worms, grubs, or minnows. The use of perch rigs (spreaders) will increase your catch considerably. Small deer hair jigs and small jigs dressed with Mr. Twister tails are also effective.

Silver Lake has long been known as a producer of big northern pike. There is some indication that their average size is declining, but the lake still harbors some mighty big pike. Photo courtesy George Dovolos.

Later in the year, as the summer sun warms the lake's waters, the perch school-up less and move into deeper water, making them decidedly harder to find. They will most often be found over hard, rocky bottoms and near structure associated with deep water. For the most part, yellow perch are taken incidentally in the summer, usually by anglers fishing for smallmouth bass with small spinners or jigs.

Due to the fact that, until recently, Silver Lake's yellow perch were not targeted by many anglers in the fall, I don't have much information the state of this season of the fishery. However, based on information from other lakes with similar characteristics, certain assumptions can be made.

In the fall, the perch fishing should pick up considerably. Yellow perch begin to move into very deep water by mid-October, and there is relatively little deep water in this lake. Fishing with minnows close to the bottom will probably be the most productive method. Again, use spreaders to take full advantage of the multitudinous perch just waiting for something to hit on.

Ice fishing is very popular on this lake. On any given day, as many as 100 to 200 anglers will be on the ice, each with two or three tip-ups. And the number of ice fishermen on Silver Lake could go up as a result of the decline of the yellow perch fishing on Conesus Lake.

A popular way to fish for yellow perch here is with pin head minnows on a tip-up. Small jigs or ice flies tipped with mousey grubs or perch eyes are also very effective. Productive areas for perch in the winter include the north and south ends of the lake and, later in the winter, dormant weedlines in 15 to 20 feet of water. Actually, due to the abundance of the perch and the lake's small size, they can be taken almost anywhere through the ice.

Northern Pike .... **Common; growth rate good**

The population of northern pike here is very large, possibly too large. Some of the locals feel that the pike are getting stunted as a result. The DEC, however, feels that the decrease in the weight/length ratio of this species is more likely a side effect of the walleye management policies that were in effect until recently.

Shortly after spawning, most northern pike will seek out adjacent flats in 10 to 20 feet of water, relating to rock piles, small patches of weeds, or small drop-offs. For the best early season pike action, try still fishing with live bait, preferably large shiners (8 to 12 inches). Large chubs and suckers will also work well. These baits can also be used while still fishing, backtrolling, or drifting very slowly over the flats.

In the spring, northern pike up to 15 pounds can be caught in the shallows at the south end of the lake, and, to a lesser extent, at the north end. During the first few weeks of the season, northerns will tend to be close to the bottom. To keep your bait near the bottom, be sure to use a sinker. However, by the end of May the northerns will have sufficiently recuperated from their spawning rituals to become more active and aggressive. Then you'll want to fish without a sinker, using a bobber to keep your bait off the bottom and out from the cover of emerging weeds. The late spring is also a good time to begin using spinners, such as the Mepps Aglia, Panther Martin, or Vibrax. Spinnerbaits tipped with a minnow will also produce fish.

In the summer, northern pike are usually only taken here during the first few hour of sunlight. As is the case with many lakes, the shallower you fish, the smaller the pike you catch are going to be. The smaller northerns will be found in the shallows at the north and south ends of the lake in the summer, both of which have excellent populations of small pike. The larger fish will be found off Buffalo Point, Country Club Point, or off the area known as "The Pines," which is located directly across from Buffalo Point and Country Club Point. Being a cool-water fish, the pike will also tend to congregate around the springs that feed Silver Lake.

In the fall, northern pike again begin to feed aggressively, and the daytime fishing at the north and south ends of the lake improves considerably. A very effective method for taking pike in the fall is jigging. The variety of jigs that will work in the fall is very wide, but they all have something in common - they are big. Half-ounce and 1-ounce jigs dressed with a bucktail, a 5- to 7-inch plastic waterdog, or a 4- to 6-inch Mr. Twister tail will all take pike from this lake. The fall is also a good time to use large (5- to 15-inch) minnow imitations like the jointed Rapala.

Silver Lake has always been known as a great lake for taking northerns through the ice. Fish in the 15-pound category are reportedly taken every winter. One of the most productive pike harvesting times on Silver Lake is the period immediately after the lake freezes. A majority of the northern pike will then be found in water 5 to 15 feet deep, primarily in the weedy bays or at the north and south ends of the lake. As the season progresses, however, the pike will follow the baitfish, such as the yellow perch, into increasingly deeper water. Later still, their spawning urge awakens and a majority of the pike will head for their spawning grounds.

Standard ice-fishing techniques are used on this lake. A tip-up baited with a large sucker or shiner hooked through the back is about a fancy as you have to get. Size 2 or 4 hooks are the most commonly used, and most veteran pike fishermen prefer braided nylon line terminating in either a short wire leader or a heavy-duty (40- to 60-pound-test) monofilament shock tippet. A short-handed gaff is good to have around too. A lot of pike, especially the big ones, are lost at the hole while they're being landed. A gaff will eliminate this problem.

Largemouth Bass .... **Common; growth rate good**

Silver Lake has a good population of largemouth bass, and 5- to 6-pound fish are not uncommon. Reportedly, largemouth over 7 pounds have been taken here.

There is a lot of suitable habitat for these fish, meaning that there are many sites to check out. Two of the hottest areas, of course, are the thick weedbeds at the north and south ends of the lake. But good catches of bass also come from the weedline that runs around the perimeter of the lake. In addition, there are numerous docks on Silver Lake that can provide some fast bass action.

In the late spring and early summer, largemouth bass are going to be found in shallow water along developing weed lines or adjacent to a structure, such as a boulder or piling. The latter is particularly true on sunny days. The sun warms objects that are exposed, and they in turn warm the water around them, which serves as a strong attractant to the bass. Extremely good fishing for largemouth can be had in the shallower portions of the of the lake at this time. They can be taken small (1/8- to 1/2-ounce) spinners, spinnerbaits, plastic worms, or shallow-running crankbaits.

In the summer, bass fishing typically centers around working weedlines and, where available, docks. Weedlines can be worked using jigs, spinnerbaits, and deep-diving crankbaits, while top-water spoons, weedless worms, and buzzbaits can be worked over the top of weedlines. In the summer, George Dovolos recommends throwing chartreuse spinnerbaits with white double Mister Twister tails if its bright out, and black-skirted spinnerbaits if its overcast or dark. Some of the pros that work this lake use a silver No. 6 hammered willow leaf blade in the front. If they use a tandem spinner, they go to a silver No. 6 hammered willow leaf blade in back with a No. 3 brass Colorado blade in the front.

If fished properly, docks can be amazingly productive. Accuracy is the key here. You must be able to put your lure well under the dock, not just next to it. Often it's the smaller, more aggressive fish that you pick up first. Be persistent. When the fishing is hot, it is possible to limit out on 4-pound bass in less than an hour when you're fishing under and around the docks. I know anglers who have picked up as many as 10 to 15 good-size bass from under a single dock! Jigs dressed with Mister Twister tails, plastic worms, or crankbaits are highly effective around docks, particularly at dusk and dawn.

There isn't much location change with largemouth bass in the fall. They simply move out into slightly deeper water, orienting off the deepest weedlines available. If you get an extended cold spell and then sunny weather, they often will be found relating to adjacent rocky points. If warm weather persists, the fish will usually return to their summer haunts.

When the largemouth go deep, you should consider going to smaller lures and slightly slower retrieves. Spinnerbaits are highly effective in the fall, as are deep-diving crankbaits. The fish are usually very aggressive in the fall, at least until the water temperatures drop into the mid-50s. This is due to their going on a feeding binge in late September and October. When the water temperature approaches 55 degrees F, the bass become lethargic but can still be taken on small jigs dressed with minnows or pork rind. Work these jigs slowly along deep weedlines.

Additional Species

Silver lake has an excellent population of panfish, including rock bass, bullhead, bluegills, pumpkinseeds, and crappies, which are known locally as calicos.

In the spring, there is especially good fishing for calicos in and between the inlet and outlet at the north end of the lake, in the canals at the south end, and in the cove near Silver Lake Marina. Work the brushpiles and overhanging trees using ultra-light rods rigged with light line and very small jigs tipped with a minnow. Minnows fished on a small hook also work well. The jig or minnow should be fished 3 to 6 feet below a small bobber. When fishing with just a minnow, use a small split-shot to keep the bait down. Be sure not to set the hook too hard when crappie fishing. They have soft mouths, and you can easily tear the hook right out if you're not careful.

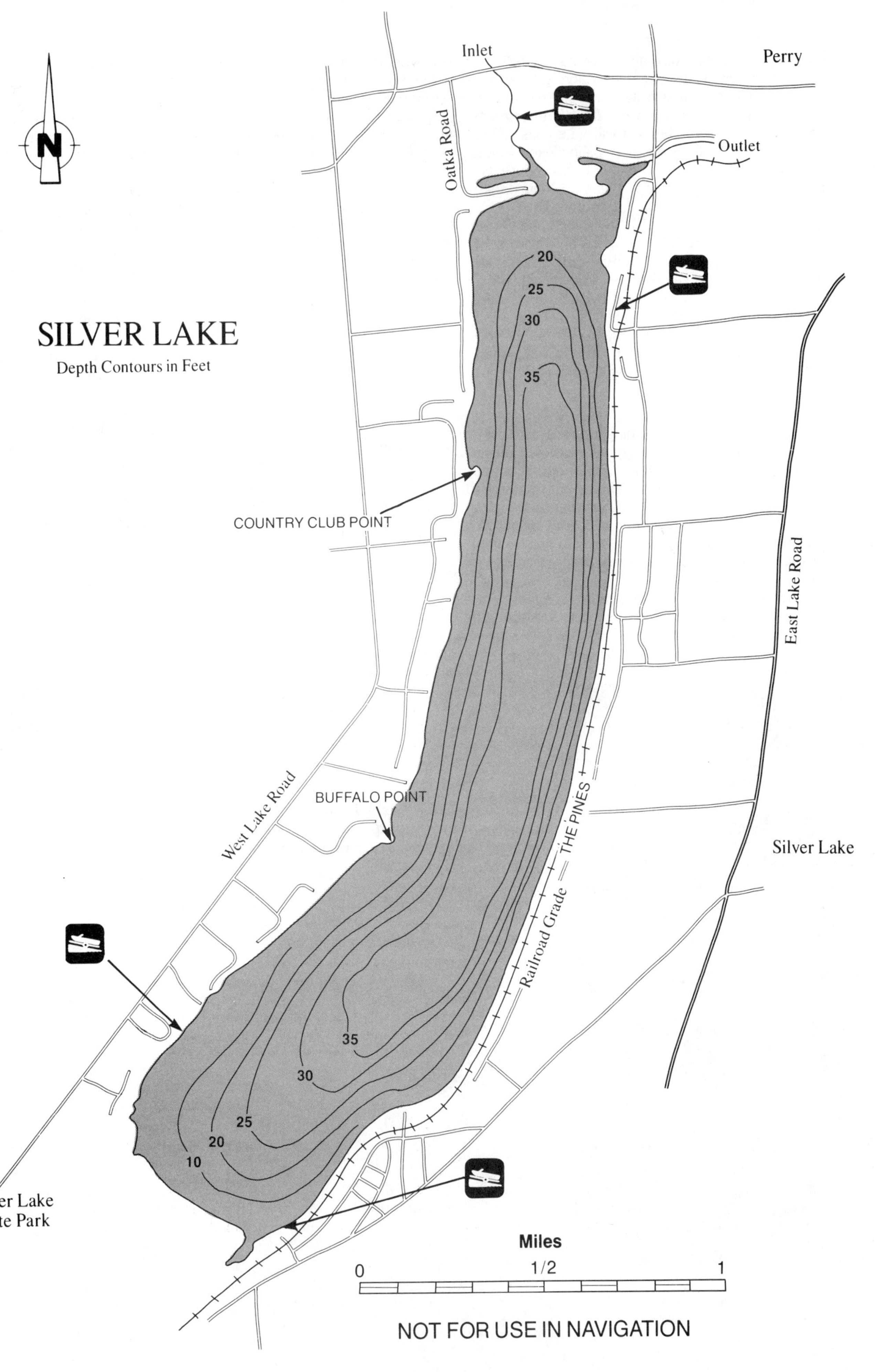
SILVER LAKE
Depth Contours in Feet
N
Inlet
Perry
Outlet
Oatka Road
20
25
30
35
COUNTRY CLUB POINT
East Lake Road
West Lake Road
BUFFALO POINT
THE PINES
Railroad Grade
Silver Lake
35
30
25
20
10
Silver Lake
State Park
Miles
0
1/2
1
NOT FOR USE IN NAVIGATION

There is also a large population of bullhead in this lake. They can be caught in large numbers in the late winter and early spring when they are concentrated in the shallows near the inlet and outlet, and to a lesser extent at the south end of the lake. Worms, dough balls, or small minnows fished on the bottom will take pails full of these fine-tasting fish. For the best results, use a slip-sinker, which allows the fish to run with the bait while it is still in his mouth. Be careful when handling bullheads; the sharp spines on their dorsal and pectoral fins can inflict a surprisingly painful wound.

Rock bass are another plentiful panfish in Silver Lake. They prefer rocky areas, but rock bass can also be taken on the edge of brushpiles and around dock pilings. Although they are small compared to their cousins, the largemouth and smallmouth bass, rock bass are tenacious for their size, and can provide a lot of sport on a fly rod or ultra-light spinning outfit. Small spinnerbaits or small jigs tipped with 2-inch Mister Twister tails cast toward shore will catch large numbers of these tasty fish. Or try fishing with small worms, using as little split-shot as possible to get the bait down to the fish.

General Information

The improvement in the quality of the fishing in Silver Lake over the past few years is incredible. A seemingly successful walleye fishery has been re-established, an overabundant population of stunted yellow perch has been replaced by a smaller (but still large) population of big jack perch, the stunting of the northern pike may have been reversed, and water clarity has improved dramatically. A number of factors have combined to make all this possible, including construction of a perimeter sewer system and new fish management and stocking policies.

This is not to say that Silver Lake has no problems. One major problem still plaguing this lake is public shore access. Although Silver Lake State Park is at the south end of the lake, it is undeveloped and swampy, and does not provide much real access to the lake. There is some shore access at the old public swimming beach near Tucker's on Walker Road.

Silver Lake is unique in that its inlet and outlet are both on the north end of the lake, and very close to each other. Normally, this would mean that the lake's waters would get very little mixing. But most of the water that feeds this lake doesn't come from the inlet. It comes from several springs that constantly feed the lake.

These springs are important to the fishery because they provide a source of clean, cool water. They are also important to the fisherman. Fish such as northern pike and walleye are attracted to areas around the springs, making them good sites to fish. To find the springs, reconnoiter the lake early in the winter just as a skin of ice is forming on it. The water from the springs will be slightly warmer than the surrounding waters, which will keep the area in the immediate vicinity ice-free longer than other parts of the lake. Several springs are known to exist near Buffalo Point and Country Club Point. Mark these locations down on a map for future reference.

Much of the information in this article was provided by George Dovolos, who owns and operates the Hole In The Wall Restaurant in Perry. Unless you are already very familiar with this lake, it would be well worth your while to stop in to the Hole and talk to George about where the current action is and what to use. He is one of the most informed fishermen I have ever had the pleasure to interview, and he is always willing to share what he knows with other anglers. You probably won't be the only person asking questions; the Hole is very popular with many Silver Lake anglers.

NOTES: ______________________________

____

____

The author's sister, Susan Prefontaine, displays a nice catch of largemouth bass from Silver Lake. Limit catches of bass are common on this lake.

PART II
MAJOR WATERS

LAKE ERIE (New York Section)

NOAA Charts 14820, 14822, 14823
Location .... Counties of Chautauqua and Erie
Access .... Paralleled by US 90 and Route 5. See launch sites listed below.

Physical Characteristics (Eastern Basin)
Area .... 3,873 square miles (584 square miles in New York)
Shoreline .... 263 miles (83 miles in New York)
Elevation .... 575 feet
Maximum depth .... 210 feet
Mean depth .... 80 feet
Bottom type .... Slate, sand, and muck interspersed with pockets of rubble

Chemical Characteristics
Water .... Generally clear; tends to be turbid after storms or periods of high wind.
pH .... Alkaline
Oxygen .... Good throughout the eastern basin all year. There is some oxygen depletion in the deepest water in the summer due to stratification, but this doesn't appear to adversely affect the fishing.

Plant Life

Most of the eastern basin, especially the New York portion, has limited rooted aquatic vegetation. This is due to the generally hard, flat lake bottom and the effects of the weather on the lake's unprotected shoreline. The few weed beds that do exist are found primarily along the Canadian shoreline, near the head of the Niagara River, and in protected harbors. Algae blooms, once the scourge of the lake, are now greatly reduced as a result of polluton control measures.

Boat Launch Sites

Erie County Section

1. Lasalle Park, foot of Porter Avenue. Multiple hard-surface ramps, parking, restrooms – no charge.
2. Erie Basin Marina, foot of Erie Avenue. Double hard-surface ramps, parking – fee.
3. Port of Buffalo Small Boat Harbor, 1053 Fuhrmann Boulevard. Multiple hard-surface ramps, parking, restrooms – fee.
4. South End Marina, 1515 Fuhrmann Boulevard. Single hard-surface ramp, repairs, parking – fee.
5. Bouquard's Boat Livery, 1581 Fuhrmann Boulevard. Single hard-surface ramp, parking – fee.
6. Sturgeon Point Boat Livery, foot of Sturgeon Point Road, off Route 5 in the town of Evans. Multiple hard-surface ramps, gas, rentals, parking – fee.
7. Point Breeze Camp, off Old Lake Shore Road, at Point Breeze. Single hard-surface ramp (small boats only), gas – fee.

Chautauqua County Section

8. Pinzel's Island Marine, foot of Exchange Street, off Route 5 in Sunset Bay. Full-service marina, single hard-surface ramp – fee.
9. Keene Marine, Allegany Road, Sunset Bay. Full-service marina, single hard-surface ramp – fee.
10. Silver Creek Town Ramp, off Route 5 on the west side of Silver Creek. Single concrete ramp (small boats only), parking – no charge.
11. Kacor's Ramp, Center Road and Route 5 in the town of Sheridan. Single hard-surface ramp, limited parking – fee.
12. City of Dunkirk Municipal Ramp, off Route 5 in Dunkirk. Double hard-surface ramps, parking – no charge.
13. M. & L. Marine (Bart's Cove), 1/2 Woodrow Avenue, Dunkirk. Single hard-surface ramp, gas, limited parking – fee.
14. D.J.'s Campground, on West Lake Road in Portland. Single ramp, gas – fee.
15. Westfield Municipal Ramp, off Route 5 at Barcelona Harbor. Double hard-surface ramps, transient dockage – no charge.

Species Information

Walleye .... **Abundant; growth excellent**

Walleye are unquestionably the most sought after species of fish in Lake Erie. The western basin is thought to hold in excess of 30,000,000 walleye. Some say that this is an underestimate. The eastern basin of the lake, though not as productive as the western basin, nevertheless has a very good population of walleye, with the New York waters estimated to harbor between 100,000 and 300,000 fish. The population of eastern basin stocks fluctuates with the number of good to excellent year-classes in the population. In 1984 the walleye spawning was extremely successful, making it the best year-class since 1971. This was one of the factors contributing to the great walleye fishing of recent years. Unfortunately, since 1984 the fish in the eastern basin have experienced only average to less than average spawning success.

Walleye growth rates generally improve as you move from west to east on Lake Erie. Thus, what the eastern basin lacks in total numbers of fish, it makes up for in their size. This is probably due to the better forage situation that exists in our end of the lake.

The most important development on the lake in recent years has been the growth of a strong summer fishery for walleye. What seems to be happening is that the western basin walleye population is expanding, spilling over into waters of the central basin and even into the eastern basin, supplementing the indigenous populations of fish in these areas during the summer months. This could account, in part, for the spectacular fishing that has been found in our end of the lake since the mid to late 1980s. This eastward migration of fish from the western basin has also been indicated by creel census figures obtained by the Lake Erie Fishery Station at Dunkirk.

In the western basin of Lake Erie, the best year-class in many years occurred in 1982. Large numbers of these fish were eventually caught in deep water off Chautauqua County. The majority of these walleye have been removed from the fishery, but other year-classes are coming up to take their place, so the great fishing of recent years should continue. There is some evidence that the 1986 year-class in the western basin is very large. These fish will become fully vulnerable to fishing in the early 1990s.

Population pressure may not be the only factor causing fish to move out of the western basin. The great walleye fishing over the past few years could also have been partly due to the excessively warm summers that we have experienced in recent years. Some fish from the western basin may have moved out of their normal haunts in search of more amenable temperatures. They would find these temperatures in the deeper, cooler waters of the eastern and central basins. Needless to say, the quality of the walleye fishing in the eastern end of the lake can fluctuate significantly from year to year as these different factors come into play.

Note that the fish from the western basin are being caught in the deep waters off Chautauqua County. The Lake Erie Fishery Station does not believe that there is much of a migration of western basin fish into the waters off Erie County. These fish have moved into the eastern and central basins in search of better forage and temperatures. In the summertime, the quality of these factors deteriorate as you move downlake of Cattaraugus Creek. This is corroborated by the fact that, compared to the great walleye fishing found off Chautauqua County in recent years, the walleye fishing in the Buffalo area has been relatively slow in terms of the numbers of fish caught and their average size.

It is unknown whether or not the walleye that migrate out of the western basin return to that area or remain in the eastern and central basins. It is known that walleye exhibit a strong homing instinct for their natal waters during spawning season. However, if these fish do return to the western basin, it is not unreasonable to assume that many of them will return to our waters later in the year given favorable conditions of temperature and forage.

When the walleye season opens on Lake Erie (the first Saturday in May) the fish are not fully spawned out, so the most productive areas initially are going to be found near spawning sites. There are only two major spawning shoals that the Lake Erie Fishery Station knows of for certain. One is located in the Hamburg area just off the mouth of Smokes Creek, and the other is found in Van Buren Bay. These areas provide much, if not most, of the walleye that inhabit the eastern basin. The fish that spawn in these areas have been shown through tagging studies to remain in the eastern end of the lake all year. However, there could be other spawning areas in the eastern part of the lake. Tradition plays a big part in the popularity of the above-mentioned areas, especially with regard to Hamburg. People tend to go with proven areas rather than try to seek out new springtime concentrations of fish. Underfished areas where walleye probably concentrate in the spring include the waters off Evangola State Park, the mouth of Silver Creek, Saint Columbans, the mouth of First Gulf, the mouth of Second Gulf, Wright Park in Dunkirk, and Battery Point. The lower reach of Cattaraugus Creek also harbors some walleye in the spring, but the fish that spawn in the eastern end of Lake Erie seem to favor spawning on lake shoals rather than in streams, as is the case in many lakes (Oneida Lake is a good example of this). To find other potential spawning areas:

1. Get out a good map of the lake and look for sites that possibly contain large amounts of rock and rubble in 4 to 6 feet of water.
2. Look at a map of the lake and identify the points. Usually these points continue on some distance underwater.
3. On a very windy day get on high ground overlooking the lake. You will be able to see waves breaking over shallow shoal areas, while the surrounding waters will look less choppy.

All of the points and shoals that you identify should be checked out as possible walleye spawning grounds. If you do find a new spawning ground, it may not be as big or productive as the two documented areas, but you won't have the crowds to contend with, either.

Temperature is another factor that plays a part in early season walleye fishing. As you might expect, the earliest consistent walleye fishing is found in those areas of the lake that warm up first. These areas include Dunkirk Harbor, both in the vicinity of the Niagara Mohawk Power Project's warm-water discharge and the area off Wrights Park known locally as "The Flats"; the shallow bay off Woodlawn; and the area around the southern half of the South Wall and the South Gap of Buffalo's Outer Harbor. These areas are often 5 to 10 degrees warmer than other near-shore waters and usually begin to produce consistent catches of walleye by mid to late May. Many people don't put their boat in the water until late May or early June, thereby missing several weeks of good spring walleye fishing in these areas.

1990 Lake Erie International Grand Prize winner Mark Damon proudly displays his winning entry, an 11-pound walleye. Photo courtesy ESLO/LEI.

Early in the season, trolling stickbaits such as Rapalas or weight forward spinner/worm harness combinations in shallow water (3 to 5 feet deep) close to shore is a very productive method for taking walleye at night. Experienced anglers often use trolling motors when fishing in these shallow waters. Trolling motors allow you to come up on the fish without disturbing them, and it avoids damage to your prop.

Initially, the fish are going to be tightly schooled up and strongly oriented to hard structures such as rocks, points, and shallow shoals. Once you get a strike, work the whole area carefully. Present the bait or lure slowly; in the first few weeks of the season, the cold water will keep the fish relatively lethargic.

Dunkirk Harbor offers some good spring walleye fishing. Its well-protected harbor can be fished on nights when the lake proper is too rough. Nearby, the flats off Wrights Park offer some fine springtime walleye fishing. Some people do go out in chest waders to fish off Wright Park, but not many.

Van Buren Bay also has very good spring walleye fishing at night. The commercial fishermen knew for years about the large concentrations of fish here in the spring, but most recreational anglers did not pick up on this fact until recently. It is possible to limit out in 1 to 2 hours in this bay.

According to Floyd Cornelius of the Lake Erie Fishery Station, a conservation officer in the Buffalo area found walleye carpeting the shallows off Smokes Creek at 2 a.m. one spring. Floyd believes that this probably happens in many shallow areas of the lake in the spring. He feels that the near-shore night fishing in the spring is very underutilized, except for the waters off Hamburg, in Van Buren Bay, and in Dunkirk Harbor.

Something to keep in mind when you're fishing in congested areas in the spring is that when large numbers of boats are concentrated in one area, the boating activity can adversely affect the fishing. This is especially true in shallow water. It causes the fish to move out of the disturbed area. Thus, fishing the outside edges of a large pack of boats can significantly increase your chances of success.

The near-shore walleye fishing usually lasts until mid to late May. After that, and depending on conditions, the fish will begin to move out in to deeper water. This outward movement starts when the water temperatures begin to exceed 45 degrees. However, it is unclear whether or not the resident walleye of the eastern basin move out into really deep water. It is possible that most of the fish found in very deep water after mid-May are actually migrating western basin fish. There is some evidence that the resident walleye do not move very far off shore. The DEC has taken good numbers of walleye in the summer in water as shallow as 18 to 36 feet.

There is a short period between the early season near-shore fishing and the setting up of the lake's thermocline during which there is a bit of a lull in the walleye fishing. The fishing becomes more random, and not directed to specific areas. The fishing pattern then becomes more consistent toward the end of June.

Lake Erie's thermocline usually sets up in early July, sometimes a bit earlier. Once this occurs, most of the walleye will not be found in any specific area. Becoming pelagic, they wander the deeper regions of the lake in search of forage and favorable temperatures. The off-shore fishing is usually good from late June to late fall, but angler effort tapers off in the fall due to weather conditions.

Usually, the best walleye fishing on Lake Erie takes place between the middle of June and the end of July. This coincides with the time when the greatest concentrations of walleye are going to be found out in deep water, but fairly high up in the water column. Look for walleye in the top 15 to 40 feet of water over depths of 70 to 150 feet. The temperatures in this depth range roughly coincide with the preferred temperature range of the walleye — 50 to 76 degrees. During this period, deep-diving plugs, crankbaits, and stickbaits in blue and silver, green, and chartreuse run behind planer boards work best. Run lures with and without weights to cover several different depths, and vary the distance between the planer board and lures until you find a combination that works. When you find a combination of depth, location, and tackle that produces strikes, work the area thoroughly.

A popular area to fish in the summer is known as "The Breaks." This is a series of drop-offs just north of Brocton Shoal, and it does produce its share of fish. Actually, any deep water area can have good fishing at this time of year. It simply depends on the location of the bait fish. Remember, though, that not all of the walleye are going to be found out in deep water. At least a portion of the resident population of fish appears to stay in closer to shore all summer.

There seems to be little or no shallow-water night fishing here in the summer such as you find on Oneida Lake. This could be due to several factors. It could be too far for the fish to travel from their deep-water daytime haunts to near-shore areas on a daily basis. It might not make sense in terms of energy spent (the effort of the trip in to the shallows) versus the energy gained (the meal eaten that night). It could also be due to a lack of angler awareness. If the resident population of walleye really do remain close to shore all summer, these fish would very likely find it energy efficient to move in to the shallows at night to feed, unbeknownst to sport fishermen. It could be well worth your while to check out some of the near-shore shoals at night for signs of fish activity.

Above I stated that the walleye are going to be stationed fairly high up in the water column at this time of year. While this is usually the case, there is one important exception to it. After the thermocline has firmly set up, most of the walleye won't venture out of the upper levels of the lake, known as the epilimnion, until the lake turns over. However, older, and consequently larger, walleye will venture into the thermocline or even below it. These fish occassionally drop down as deep as 80 to 100 feet in the water column. This is why anglers who concentrate their efforts on these depths catch fewer fish, but many of the fish caught are trophy-sized.

Beginning in early August, there is a major change in the way walleye are taken on Lake Erie. The fish can be caught in the same waters as earlier in the summer, but now most of the catches will be coming from lower in the water column, due at least in part to excessively warm temperatures higher up in the column. This means that anglers must now switch from using planer boards to downriggers.

Though the fish will be dropping down in the water column at this time, they generally will not go below the thermocline. Prior to the break up of the thermocline, the walleye and the baitfish would probably find the hypolimnion to be too cold and short of oxygen. The walleye would also be improperly positioned to feed on the baitfish, most of which ascend higher up in the water column at night to feed. However, toward the end of summer, when the thermocline breaks up creating a more homogeneous distribution of heat and oxygen in the lake, the walleye will go deeper, often close to the bottom, to feed.

By the late summer or early fall, most walleye are going to be found in deep-water habitat, usually in water over 70 feet deep. This means that most of the fish are going to be found in the waters off Chautauqua County. Flutterspoons in silver, blue, and green patterns are effective lures at this time.

Three things that can increase your chances of locating deep-water walleye in the fall are a chart-type depth finder, a Loran, and a marine radio. It is difficult to pinpoint any particular area as being consistently good during this period. In recent years the numbers of walleye have been such that they could be found even without all the hi-tech equipment, but these years have been the exception rather than the rule.

The shallow areas of the lake do offer some good near-shore walleye fishing in the fall. Walleye will be found in good numbers along the Canadian shore during this period, from Windmill Point to Erie Beach (be sure to have a Canadian license). At the head of the river, the drifts between the Middle Reefs and Limekiln Reef, and Donnelley's Wall also provide some good fall fishing. Van Buren Bay is a good location for near-shore fishing in the fall (18 to 36 feet). The walleye caught here are possibly local stocks of fish, as opposed to the fish found out in deeper water, which are believed to be excess stocks of fish from the western basin. Shorehaven, which is located just west of Barcelona Harbor, is also very productive in the fall. Both of the above areas have a good amount of structure. Battery Point is another fall hotspot. Actually, there's a good chance that any area that holds fish in the spring will also have some fish in the fall. This fall fishing can be good into November, though few anglers pursue it.

Unlike many lakes, Erie has little to offer the walleye fisherman in terms of ice fishing, although they are occassionally taken as a bonus by perch fisherman.

The following articles cover much of what you will need to know to fish for walleye successfully on this lake. They were written by veteran fishing guide Paul Cybart of Dunkirk, New York.

LAKE ERIE WALLEYE FISHING

By Paul R. Cybart

If you're a walleye fishing fanatic, you're probably aware of the claim of Lake Erie's western basin to be the "Walleye Capitol of the World." Then there's Oneida Lake's reputation for having some of the finest walleye fishing not only in New York, but in the entire United States. However, one of the best overall walleye fisheries, especially for trophy-size and fast-growing fish, is located in the waters of Lake Erie's eastern basin in western New York.

The best thing about this fishery is that we can only look forward to it improving as knowledge about walleyes and the techniques used to catch them increases. Another factor that should greatly enhance this fishery in the future is the fact that commercial fishing for walleye was all but halted by legislation in 1986 with the gill net ban in the New York waters of Lake Erie. Additional legislation was enacted in 1988 that now prohibits the sale of walleye from New York waters.

Walleye (more commonly called yellow pike by older anglers) are fast growing in Lake Erie's New York waters. They grow to the legal 15-inch size in about two years. That's quick when you consider that it takes an Oneida Lake walleye 5 years to grow to that size. A 5-year-old Lake Erie fish could weigh in at the 6 pound mark in that amount of time. Taking this into consideration, plus the fact that there are somewhere around 14 year-classes represented in the New York portion of the lake, you can see why plenty of 10-pound-plus lunkers are caught in the lake each year.

Due to their excellent growth rate, the number of year-classes present in the lake, and the legislation prohibiting the gill-netting and sale of walleye, it is my belief that you will soon see the nearly four-decade-old state record walleye fall to a fish coming out of Lake Erie.

Traditionally, most of the fishing for walleye was done along the bottom near structure. When stories of the suspending walleye of Lake Erie's western basin began reaching eastern basin fishermen, we all thought that suspending was a pattern unique to western basin fish, possibly due to the average 22-foot depth of that basin. This contrasts sharply with Lake Erie's eastern basin, which has a maximum depth of 212 feet and an average depth of 81 feet.

Discovery of the eastern basin suspending walleye fishery goes to those fishermen who first employed the use of downriggers to catch salmon and trout in New York's portion of the lake. In those early days of downrigging, it was not unusual to boat one or more walleye while fishing the thermocline for salmon and trout. At first these deep-suspending walleyes were though to be an oddball, but a very desirable, bonus catch.

Another piece of the puzzle was the fact that commercial fishermen would take a good percentage of their early walleye catch by "canning" their gill nets. With this method, the commercial fishermen would suspend the gill nets anywhere from 1 to 3 fathoms under the surface of the water. While the commercial fishermen were catching suspended walleye in their canned gill nets, it was thought that these fish were being caught at night, a period when walleye do ascend at night to feed on insects and bait fish.

The person I give credit to for putting most of the pieces of the walleye fishing puzzle in Lake Erie's eastern basin together is Dan Dietzen of Fredonia, New York. Dan ran one of the first charter boats operating on the New York waters of Lake Erie.

While Dan originally employed downriggers to target and catch suspended walleyes, it was not too long afterward that he began using deep-diving plugs run off of planner boards.

Today, besides the downriggers and planner boards, traditional bottom-bouncing techniques are still very productive for walleyes, as are other trolling equipment such as Dipsey Divers, wire lines, and sinker releases with drop weights. The one point I would like to emphasize is that, since we are still in the relative infancy of this fishery, we are still discovering new and refining old techniques and methods for catching walleyes with each passing year.

In recent years the walleye fishing in Lake Erie has been excellent. Catches such as this, boated early in the season by Scott Cybart and Captain Steve Mead, have been the norm rather than the exception. Photo courtesy Paul Cybart.

Lake Erie's walleye season opener follows the general state guidelines and opens on the first Saturday in May, and continues through March 15. The size limit is 15 inches, and the limit is 5 per day.

The New York portion of Lake Erie stays chilled longer than normal due to the giant ice cube held back in the lake by the controversial ice retention boom that is stretched across the head of the Niagara River. This delays the warming of the lake and the walleye spawning period, which usually peaks sometime after the season opener. While that can make for some difficult daytime fishing during the time of the season opener, trolling along the shoreline with shallow-diving minnow plugs is very productive at night during this period. This is also the best time of the year for the boatless angler; a set of waders will put him in reach of some of the makings for a tasty fish fry.

Access to the New York shoreline of Lake Erie is best described as limited. This is due to the fact that the great majority of the 84-mile-long New York shoreline is prominently bluffs. Along the Chautauqua County shoreline, you'll find the major access points for boat launching out of Barcelona, Dunkirk, and the mouth of Cattaraugus Creek. Smaller launches, which are ideally suited for 14-foot aluminum boats, are found at DJ's Campground in Portland, Kacor's west of Center Road in Sheridan, and at Silver Creek. Over in Erie County, your major boat access areas are Point Breeze, Sturgeon Point, and ramps in the Buffalo area.

Due to the bluffs, access for the boatless angler to the fishing is just as limited. Some of the best spots to try are off of the mouths of Lake Erie tributaries, and off some of the accessible beaches. In Erie County, the mouth of Eighteen Mile Creek may be your best choice, but parking in that area is a problem. Along the Chautauqua County shoreline, access is found along the mouths of Chautauqua Creek and Canadaway Creek, and the breakwalls and piers at Barcelona, Dunkirk, and Cattaraugus Creek. These are all good choices for nighttime spots during the first month of the season.

Whether you're fishing for nighttime walleyes from shore or from a boat, your choice of lure is basically a floating minnow plug in the straight or jointed versions. However, shoreline anglers have also done well with wide and thin bladed casting spoons such as the

Johnson Sprite and Red Eye's Evil Eye casting spoon. With regard to minnow-type baits, Rapalas, Rebel's Fastrac, and Bomber lures are popular. As to the choice of color, it seems that whatever you have confidence in will work; however, patterns that imitate the coloration of yellow perch have been a longtime favorite of mine.

At the time of the season opener, your best nighttime spots are near spawning reefs and off creek mouths where warmer water from the creeks are entering the colder lake waters. In Erie County, the area between Hamburg Town Park and Smokes Creek attracts most of the anglers. In Chautauqua County, it's the area between Lake Erie State Park and Canadaway Creek, and from Barcelona westward to Shorehaven that get the most attention. Alternative areas that are productive would include Dunkirk Harbor, Eagle Bay, and the stretch from Cattaraugus Creek eastward to Sturgeon Point.

The same areas that were productive at night are also your choice daytime spots. However, the techniques and methods to catch walleye during the day are quite different from those employed at night. While trolling was productive at night, during the daytime it would be a waste of time at the beginning of the season.

At the time of the season opener, we have to remember that the walleye spawning activity is usually beginning to peak. That peak activity is regulated by several factors, of which water temperature is the most important. Walleye begin to spawn shortly after ice-out, but spawning activity begins in earnest when water temperatures reach 42 degrees and peaks at about 48 degrees. Those temperatures are too cold to produce any algae growth. Without any algae in the water to diffuse light penetration, and knowing the walleyes aversion to bright light, you can begin to see why daytime fishing will be a bit more difficult. Algae growth will begin when the water temps reach the 60 degree mark.

So how do you catch them during the daytime? The easiest way is to fish just after sunrise and just before sunset, when the sun is still low on the horizon, especially on flat, calm days. A bit of wave action or an overcast day will help to reduce light penetration, making daytime hours even more productive.

As to the technique, slow drifting of the boat while jigging has proven to be the most effective. The weight of the jig head you will use depends on the depth of water you are in and the speed of your drift. Though there are many different types of jig bodies available, the most widely used on Lake Erie, at least in this area, is the Lindy Little Joe Fuzz-E-Grub. Of course, a small piece of worm or minnow is also added to the hook to make it more productive.

Good consistent daytime action will get underway when water temperatures reach the 60 degree mark, which usually occurs by mid-June if normal weather patterns are occurring. While most fishermen are now employing downriggers and planner boards to target walleye, those fishermen who continue to fish using traditional techniques do well at this time of the year.

By traditional, I'm referring to the bottom-bouncing method, which employs a weight dragged along the bottom with a 3- to 4-foot leader trailed behind it to which a lure is attached. Chugging irons have been the longtime favorite weight used in this method, but the bait-walker types are growing in popularity. Then there are those who still prefer a 3-way swivel arrangements where a bell-type sinker is attached to one swivel.

In the old days, the most widely used lure attached to that 3- to 4-foot leader was a June Bug Spinner and worm combination. Banana baits such as the Flatfish were also as popular back then as they are today. However, the worm harness/spinner combination is the first choice of fishermen who still fish with traditional methods for walleye. The smaller Indiana-style blade seems to work best in water up to 15 feet deep. The larger Colorado and popular Willowleaf blades work best in deeper waters. There are many color choices available in spinner blades that are productive at one time or another, but I limit myself to hammered nickel and copper, chartreuse, and green. If you like making your own worm harnesses, I recommend using pearl-colored beads.

As the water temperatures begin to increase, the walleye begin to move offshore. This is due to the fact that the main forage for eastern basin walleye is smelt. Smelt prefer colder temperatures found in the deeper offshore waters. During the daytime, smelt prefer a water temperature of 48 degrees, which is usually found in deep water. But they ascend at night to feed on surface aquatic life.

It is in this offshore fishery where the use of downriggers and planer boards become most effective. During the initial part of this fishery, when the walleye are suspending nearer to the surface, planer boards are highly productive, accounting for an average of 90 percent of the fish caught. As the lake warms and the walleye begin to hold deeper in the water column, downriggers become more effective.

Deep-diving crankbaits are the standard choice of lures to run off planer boards. Initially, fat-bodied plugs such as the Bill Norman Deep Little N are the most effective. Other proven choices include the Bagley Killer B series, Storm's Hot 'N Tot and Wiggle Wart, and Rebel's lineup of crankbaits. Shortly after this fishery gets underway, minnow-shaped deep-diving plugs such as the Bagley Bang-O-Lure DD4 and DD5, and the Bomber 25A and 26A are more widely used. Bomber has also added a smaller 24A to their lineup that should also prove to be effective. Another new introduction that has proved to be good is Storm's Deep-Diving Thunderstick.

Also effective are what I call the offspring of the marriage of the fat- and minnow-bodied plugs. These include Cotton Cordell's Wally Diver and Walleye Specialty's Wally Troll and Dive. Some anglers even claim that the Lindy Little Joe Shadlings work for them at this time of year.

You can also run your shallow-diving plugs and worn harnesses off of planer boards by adding some weight about 5 feet in front of the lure. Though more commonly used on the deep-diving lures later in the summer, added weight lets you use your shallow-diving equipment more effectively early in the season. The weight you use will vary from a large split-shot to 4 ounces or more of lead. There are those who don't like to use more than 2 ounces of weight; combining more weight than that with the action of the plug seems to take some of the fight out of the fish. If these fishermen need to run more than 2 ounces of weight, they will employ a sinker release.

When fishing with planer boards, it is very important to duplicate your set-up if you are catching fish. The length of line between the boat and lure and the trolling speed are both very important. With trolling reels it's easy to duplicate distance between the boat and the lure; just count the number of times the line guide goes back and forth. Let out too little or too much line, and chances are that your lure won't dive to the same depth as before and will be out of the fish-catching zone. If you are not catching any fish over a period of time, try shortening the leads on one side of the boat while lengthening those on the other side. Experiment with this procedure until you start catching fish.

Trolling speed is another critical aspect of planer board fishing, and it's duplication is just as important as using lures and plugs that are compatible in terms of effective trolling speeds. The Bagley Bang-O-Lure and Storm's Hot 'N Tot run best at slower speeds, while Bill Norman's Deep Little N and the deep-diving Bombers seem to catch fish best when trolled faster.

While the boards do produce a majority of the fish caught, chances are that the lunker walleye you want to hang on your wall will come off the downrigger. A general rule of thumb is to run longer leads when fishing for shallow suspending fish, and shorter leads when fishing for deep suspending fish.

Your choice of lures to run off the downriggers is limited by your imagination. My longtime favorite spoons are Red Eye's Evil Eye and Luhr Jensen's Alpena Diamond. In recent years, the Pirate has been one of the more productive lures, and newcomers like the Silver Streak and Northern King are making their presence known. Though spoons are used most often, shallow-diving minnow plugs can also be used. Some anglers even run their deep divers off the 'riggers. And if the fishing action is slow, a worm harness fished off a downrigger has been known to work when nothing else is producing.

From August through the fall turnover period (late September to early October), the walleye can be found suspending in the thermocline, which is usually located from 80 to 100 feet or more below the surface. At these depths silver-plated spoons and glow spoons are a bit more effective color choices. If the fish are found suspending this deep, a dodger-lure combination can also be very productive when run off the downrigger.

Much of Lake Erie's shoreline consists of stark bluffs such as the one seen above. Though picturesque, they are one reason that public access to the lake is so limited. Photo courtesy Mike Bleech.

I believe that there are three distinct levels of suspending walleye at this time of the year. The deepest fish are those in the colder thermocline waters that are actively feeding on smelt. A second, or middle, level of fish will suspend 10 to 20 feet above the deep fish. I also believe that these mid-level walleye had been feeding in the thermocline, have satisfied their feeding needs, and are now in temperatures of water that they prefer. While these mid-level fish are basically inactive, they are still very catchable. The last level are the shallowest fish, suspending some 15 to 40 feet below the surface. These fish are mostly active in their feeding activities, but a fair portion of their feeding is done at night when the smelt and other baitfish ascend towards the surface to feed on insects and other aquatic life.

You can see that the deep suspending walleye are easily targeted with downriggers. The mid-level fish can be caught with stacked lines or cheaters run above the deep set lines. Another way to catch mid-level fish, as well as the shallower walleyes, is to release one of your deep-set lines off the cannonball and let it flutter up. Most of the time these walleye just can't let an easy meal flutter away, so they will grab it as it passes by them. The shallowest level of walleye will generally be on the smaller side and are easily targeted off the planer boards.

While downriggers and planer boards are the main producers of suspending walleye in Lake Erie's eastern basin, there are several productive tools that will help you catch fish on slow days. One of these is a diving planer device. Although there are a few different types available, the one most widely used for this fishery is Luhr Jensen's Dipsey Diver. Because of its ability to dive and plane-off to either side, the Dipsey Diver can he fished at the same time you are using your downriggers and planer boards. Some anglers will even run the Dipsey's off their planer boards with great success. I've been a fan of Dipsey Divers since the first time I used one. It seems that they will produce numbers of fish when the downriggers and planer boards are not effective. In addition, the largest fish of the day always seem to be taken off a Dipsey.

Also proving to be effective is the use of wire line. Because of the weight of the wire line and the fact that it does not stretch, deep-diving lures run off wire will run much deeper than when run off a similar length of monofilament line. Because of this, it is possible to effectively fish those middle-level walleyes in the late summer months without the use of downriggers.

During the 1988 fishing season, my fishing partner, Captain Steve Mead, introduced me to using wire line aboard his boat, the Outlander. From the time we began using the wire line in mid-July, we caught by my estimate an average of 50 percent of our planer board walleyes on the wire. While that 50 percent figure does not seem like a lot, it is when you consider the fact that out of the six rods run off the planer boards, only two were equipped with wire line.

And where is this deep water offshore fishery located in Lake Erie's eastern basin? Essentially, it is the portion of the lake off Chautauqua County. Based on the results of fishing contests over the last few years, I have proclaimed this area to be "Lake Erie's Trophy Waters." Though those boaters who launch out of Cattaraugus Creek have accounted for a good number of winners in those contest, they have about a 12-mile westerly run before they get in 100 feet of water. Launching out of Dunkirk gives you a 4 1/2-mile ride to the 100 foot mark, while out of Barcelona the distance is even shorter.

The first anglers to fish these deep waters were seeking salmon and trout, and considered the walleye to be a bonus catch. Less than a decade later, it is the walleye that is specifically sought and salmon and trout that are considered the bonus. Lake Erie is stocked with roughly 2.5 million salmonids annually. New York's contribution is approximately 1 million fish, including chinook salmon, coho salmon, brown trout, rainbow trout, and steelhead. Since 1986 New York has even been experimentally stocking the much-desired Skamania strain of steelhead in Chautauqua Creek. In addition, nearly 200,000 lake trout from the federal hatcheries are released in the lake every year to reintroduce what was originally a native species that was wiped out by commercial over-fishing and environmental changes in the lake.

Those deep offshore waters also offer species other than walleye, salmon, and trout. Though they are considered trash fish, the freshwater drum (commonly known as sheepshead) usually provide enough action to keep things interesting. Then there are the silver bass that will tempt your patience if you inadvertently get into them, even though they make for some excellent tablefare. Then there's a good chance of catching a trophy-size bass during the mid- to late-summer months.

As the summer months slide by and Labor Day passes, increasingly stiff westerly winds make it difficult, if not impossible, to get on Lake Erie. But if you can, there's still some good walleye fishing to be had, even for the shorebound angler. A trip to the mouths of Lake Erie's tributaries after Labor Day will often yield salmon and trout. But if you want some walleye, arrive well before dawn or stay after sunset, casting the same lures you would when the season began. As for boat fishing, the majority of anglers have given up by the first week of October, not due to the lack of fish, but more to the uncertainty of getting out on the lake, the fair tributary action for salmon and trout, and in preparation for the upcoming hunting season.

However, there are some dedicated walleye anglers who continue to do well night fishing in and around the head of the Niagara River and places off the Buffalo waterfront, such as Donnelly's Wall, and the North and Middle Gaps. As with the initial night fishery, shallow-diving, minnow-type plugs trolled off flatlines yield the best results.

While this is a general guideline to the eastern Lake Erie walleye fishery, your best source of up-to-date information on what's happening will be local tackle shops. For information on the Barcelona area, try Pagano's at 716-326-3621, or Monroe Marina at 716-326-4608. For the Dunkirk area, contact Pro Angler at 716-366-FISH (3474) and Stefan's Recreation at 716-366-3386. Information on the fishing activity in the Cattaraugus-Irving area can be obtained by calling the Sunset Sport Shop at 716-934-4444 or Pinzel's Island Marina at 716-934-4861. For the Sturgeon Point area, call Herb's Tackle Shack at 716-627-7007. And for the Buffalo area, including the upper Niagara River, call Fish Tale Bait at 716-873-9457.

Another good source is the Department of Environmental Conservation's Lake Erie Hotline, which updates its information every Friday. Numbers for the hotline are 716-679-ERIE for the Dunkirk calling area, and 716-885-FISH for the Buffalo area.

As this article comes to a close, some of you may have noticed that the subject of nighttime fishing in the deep offshore waters during the summer was not mentioned, nor was ice fishing. As far as summer nighttime fishing goes, very few anglers are attempting it now, but we can expect that this type of fishing will be pursued more so in the future. Those that have fished at night have done well with shallow-diving, minnow-type lures and smaller crankbaits such as Bill Norman's Baby N series. The experience of the few fishermen fishing at night in the deep offshore waters has shown that the sunset to 11 p.m. time slot is not very productive during the summer months. After 11 p.m. the action begins to pick up and lasts till the first signs of dawn.

When it comes to ice fishing on Lake Erie, due to the inconsistent manner in which this lake freezes, I cannot in good conscience recommend ice fishing, although it is pursued by some anglers.

Whether you're a regular Lake Erie angler or a newcomer, this lake, which is indeed "Great," has to be respected. Its reputation for kicking up is well deserved and caution should be exercised when venturing out on it.

If you like participating in fishing tournaments, there are four of them worth noting. The first is America Outdoors Walleyethon, a 60-day-long, tagged-fish tournament beginning the first Saturday in June. The Southtowns Walleye Club holds their annual open tournament the third week in June. The New York Walleye Association runs their annual open tournament the second weekend of July. Finally, ESLO's Lake Erie International is held the first four-day weekend in August.

Many first-time Lake Erie anglers will hire the services of a fishing guide to help them learn about the fish and the techniques used to catch them. There are a growing number of charter services from which to choose operating out of Dunkirk and Barcelona, and a few other access areas.

TRY CHUGGING IRONS FOR LAKE ERIE WALLEYE

By Paul Cybart

The great majority of us grew up using chugging irons in order to catch walleye along the bottom. Today we target this fish with downriggers and planing boards, in addition to an assortment of tricks and gadgets I would like to share with you.

One of the tricks I like to use and promote is referred to as a three-way swivel cheater rig to run two lures off of one line. This technique has been written about before, with the writer telling you to run a deep-diving crankbait off of a short 2-foot leader attached to a three-way swivel, then a longer 3-foot leader is attached to a small flutter spoon and run off one of the other swivels on the three-way. The remaining swivel on the three-way is then attached to your reel line. This works, and believe me, you won't get as many tangles as you think.

However, I like to run my three-way cheater rig with the longer leader to the deep-diving crankbait and the shorter one to the flutter spoon. I feel you get a more natural presentation of the predator-prey relationship. With the longer leader to the deep-diving plug, it appears that the usually larger plug is chasing the smaller flutter spoon on the short lead. If you have never tried the three-way swivel cheater rig, you're only cheating yourself.

Another cheater comes into play when some of the walleye start suspending 50 feet or more below the surface. Referred to as a free-floating cheater by some, on days when the catching is slow, it could produce enough fish off your downriggers to make your fishing and catching a bit more enjoyable. To make one of these cheaters, tie a small snap swivel to a 5- to 8-foot length of leader material, but never longer then the length of the rods you're using. To the other end tie another but larger snap swivel. On the smaller swivel attach a flutter spoon, then open the larger snap swivel and pass the line off of one of your fishing, reels set to a release on the downrigger that is set at a minimum of 50 feet. Close the snap and carefully throw the rig over. This cheater will fish about half-way between the surface and where you have your downrigger set, and stays there because of a belly in the line. While this may sound a bit like asking for problems and tangled lines, it really works well, and if carefully done, a minimum of tangles will occur. The only annoying thing about using this cheater is that it also increases your catch of sheepshead.

At times you have to use weight in order to get your planer board crankbaits a bit deeper. While adding an ounce or two does not cause too many problems, when you start adding three or more ounces of weight it seems to take the fight out of the fish. So, what is the answer? Sinker releases.

A sinker release is a device that drops the weight after the fish strikes. This could be expensive if you buy your sinkers. But if you can make your own, the expense becomes bearable and the fight you get from a weight-free fish is much more enjoyable. I have tried different sinker releases, and have found the Les Davis sinker release and the Big Jon Tripper work well for me.

How many times have you set your 'riggers down deep and then mark a cluster of fish between the cannonball and surface. Chances are that these fish you're marking are walleyes, and if you react, it is possible to put one of those fish in the box. Simply release one of your lures off the 'rigger and let it float up to the surface. Don't look for a strike, but rather the added weight of a fish holding on, and then set the hook. Even when you don't mark fish, if things are slow, try popping a few lines and float them up. You'll be surprised at the number of fish you will catch even on slow days.

While the following idea won't help you catch fish, in my opinion it will make for a better tasting fish, eliminate some cleanup time, and reduce the odds that a thrashing fish will get hooks into you. When a fish is boated aboard my boat, while the fish is still in the net, and before it is even touched, a miniature baseball bat is used to strike the fish over the head, which stuns or kills them. By doing this it makes the job of getting the fish out of the net easier. If you did not kill the fish, chances are that it would jump and flop in the cooler until it died. Every time that fish flops and strikes something it is bruising its flesh, and bruised flesh does not taste as good as meat that is not.

Another advantage of killing a fish immediately is that the fillets seem to clean up a lot easier, in that the blood washes off very easily.

TEN HOT TIPS FOR LAKE ERIE WALLEYE

By Mike Bleech

In the game of competitive fishing, the angler with the biggest bag of tricks will come out on top in the long run. Of course, and thank heavens, luck also plays an important part in the game, but the odds of getting lucky are best when you can stack the deck in your favor. Following are a few additions to your bag of tricks to help you do just that.

1. **Fish Deep.** The biggest walleye are often in relatively deep water during mid- to late summer. For example, in the area between Dunkirk, New York and North East, Pennsylvania, where a large share of the biggest walleyes were caught during previous Lake Erie International Derbies, the bottom slopes rather gently out to depths of 60 to 70 feet. From there it drops more steeply into depths of 120 to 130 feet, creating a giant breakline. The most likely place to find big walleyes from mid-July through early September has been at or beyond that breakline.

Further west in the shallower Central Basin, it is common for the larger boats to run 15 to 18 miles in order to reach the larger walleyes. There, however, the productive depths are more likely to be in the vicinity of 60 to 80 feet.

Perhaps the main reason that so many big walleyes are caught by boats fishing out of Dunkirk or Barcelona, New York, is that these are the boat access areas that are closest to deep water. This allows smaller boats to reach the schools of big walleyes.

2. **Trolling Direction.** Pay attention to the direction you are trolling when you get your hits. If all, or nearly all, of the hits occur while you are moving one particular direction, then you might want to pull your lines when you finish trolling in the productive direction. Then you can make a fast run back to the other end of your trolling pattern and begin trolling in the productive direction again.

One possible explanation for getting the most hits while traveling in one particular direction is speed. Unless you are equipped with a speedometer at the depth your lures are running, you will almost certainly travel at different speeds while trolling upwind or downwind.

Another possible explanation is that the wind causes currents and the walleyes orient themselves according to the current.

3. **The Shape of Bait.** Walleyes are not notoriously selective feeders. Nonetheless, matching the shape of the predominant food of the walleyes seems to be important sometimes. According to a study done by the New York Department of Environmental Conservation (DEC) at the Dunkirk Fisheries Station, the primary foods of Lake Erie walleyes are rainbow smelt, gizzard shad, alewives, shiners, white bass, and white perch. These fishes have distinctly different shapes. Shiners, mainly emerald and spottail, and rainbow smelt are cigar shaped. White perch and white bass are relatively thicker from back to belly, similar to crappies. Gizzard shad and alewives are midway between the cigar and crappie shapes.

The relative importance of these walleye food fishes changes from year to year. Rainbow smelt were most important in 1985. The following year, they still were a major part of the walleye diet, but only about half as important as gizzard shad. In 1987, shiners, alewives, and rainbow smelt were about equally important. And last year, gizzard shad formed the largest part of the walleye diet, though shiners were still significant.

4. **Flash or Bright Colors?** Have you noticed that the most popular lures among Great Lakes anglers are bright or loud colors? The reason behind this is that visibility plays such an important part in game fish feeding in these vast waters. This applies whether you are fishing for walleyes, salmon, trout, or bass.

The highly visible lure colors can be divided into two groups: flashy and bright. Flashy includes the highly reflective lure finishes, such as the metallic colors. Bright colors include fluorescents and other loud colors.

Flashy lures are not flashy unless there is light to be reflected. There is always some light underwater and walleyes can see in lower light levels that we can, yet the flashy lures are most productive when there is a lot of light penetrating the water. As a general rule, use flashy lures when there is bright sun.

Fluorescent colors are highly visible even under low light conditions. As a general rule, use them during early morning and late evening, on cloudy days and in fog.

A choppy surface reduces the penetration of light into the water. When the sun is bright but the surface is choppy, flashy colors and bright colors are often equally effective.

5. **Structure.** As any inland walleye angler knows, walleyes are structure oriented. This is not always the case in the open water of Lake Erie, yet when the fishing is tough you can generally catch some walleyes near good structure.

Structure is the shape of the bottom. Irregular structure of various types attracts walleyes. Look for humps, drop-offs, and other rapid depth changes. Walleyes often hold right over the irregular structure or suspend adjacent to depth changes.

The main problem with fishing structure in Lake Erie is that it is very difficult to accurately present lures to structure that might be anywhere from 50 to 150 feet beneath the surface!

Snagging the downrigger weight on bottom is a major headache. To avoid this, I run my weights about 10 feet above bottom and use deep-diving lures that run several feet below the weights. I lose a few lures this way, but that is much better than snagging the downrigger weights!

6. **Use a Marker Buoy.** It is no problem staying on a school of fish if your boat is equipped with LORAN C. If it is not, then it is close to impossible to stay over a school of fish when you are more than a couple of miles from shore, unless you have a way to mark the location of the school. A floating marker buoy has some short comings, but it sure helps!

It is not practical to anchor a marker buoy to bottom in deep water, and a marker buoy that is not anchored will drift with the current and with the wind. Still, though, the floating marker will give you some visible sighting to go by.

A marker buoy for use on Lake Erie must be much larger than one used in smaller waters. It should be visible for at least a mile. I made mine with a flag on a fiberglass rod, which was intended to be used on a bicycle or a boat bumper. The rod is impaled through the bumper and lead weight is attached to the end of the rod opposite the flag to keep the flag upright. A small sea anchor is suspended 20 feet below the buoy on a light line to slow the drift of the buoy.

7. **Drift with Downriggers.** Sometimes the walleyes will not attack lures that are moving at normal trolling speeds. This is a common situation to walleye anglers, but on the central and eastern basins of Lake Erie where trolling is the predominant method of walleye fishing, it is a problem that is seldom solved.

One way to deal with this situation is to drift with downriggers if the wind is conductive to drifting.

Some lures are designed specifically for slow presentations. My most productive lure for downrigger drifting has been the night-crawler harness. Banana baits are good, too.

8. **Scents.** We have done extensive testing with scents while fishing for Lake Erie walleyes. I would not suggest that scents will make a poor angler into a great angler, nor that scents will make slow days into fast days. I am convinced, though, that scents have significantly contributed to our catches.

Our tests showed that fewer hits are missed with scented lures; we catch about 50 percent more walleyes with scented lures and the walleyes we catch are, on the average, noticeably larger than the walleyes we catch on unscented lures. There is room for error in our tests, but it seems clear that scents help.

Several interviews with charter captains revealed that most use scents devotedly.

9. **Long Lines in Calm Water.** Lake Erie walleyes are shy of boats! This is most likely related to the visibility factor. Walleyes can see farther here than in most smaller waters.

Lake Erie has always been known as a top producer of yellow perch. Jeff Rasmus caught this big perch while fishing off the city pier in Kunkirk. Photo curetey Paul Cybart.

As a general rule, the calmer the water, the further the lures should be from the boat. On overcast days when the water is choppy, it is usually not necessary to run the lures more than 50 feet behind the planer board tow lines, no flat lines more than 100 feet behind the boat. But on calm days you might have to run lures 150 feet behind the boards and 200 feet behind the boat on flat lines.

10. **Attitude.** The main idea of sport fishing is to have a good time - we all want to be winners. And we can all be winners if we behave like sportsmen. Help your fellow anglers who might have trouble catching fish. If you share your fishing knowledge, you will also share in the successes of those you help!

Yellow Perch .... **Abundant; growth rate excellent**

Several years ago, the DEC thought that the yellow perch population in Lake Erie was in decline. Now the DEC is receiving reports of anglers doing exceptionally well with yellow perch in this lake. In addition, recent deep-water trawling by the DEC has shown that large numbers of perch of many different year-classes are available.

Most of the really good perch fishing that place on this lake occurs in the spring and fall. The spring yellow perch fishing is generally good from early April to mid-May. It begins when near-shore water temperatures reach 40 to 42 degrees, and is over when these waters have reached 50 degrees. As the lake warms, the fish will move almost daily into increasingly deeper water to find these temperatures. Initially, the perch are going to be found fairly close to shore, usually at depths of 25 to 35 feet. Later in the spring, the fish will be found in water up to 50 feet deep. Check out areas that have a rock and rubble bottom. The fish use these areas to spawn.

A good way to get information on water temperatures is to call the water departments of the towns along the shore of the area you plan to fish. They draw their water from the lake and usually take a temperature reading as they do so. At Dunkirk they draw the water from a depth of 26 feet. This would give you a good indication of the near-shore water temperatures in that area. If you call other water departments, be sure to ask at what depth they are drawing their water.

Possibly the best areas overall are the spring spawning grounds along the Canadian shore, from Point Abino to the head of the Niagara River. Point Abino is several miles west of the area covered on our maps. Other good spring perch locations include the rocky shallows near the mouth of Smokes Creek, off Kellogg's Wall (about 1/2 mile east of Sturgeon Point), at Sturgeon Point in water up to 50 feet deep, from Point Breeze to Evangola State Park, off the mouth of Cattaraugus Creek, around the channel buoy (also known as the "perch buoy") out of Dunkirk Harbor (this area is good from May to December), the shoal north of Van Buren Point, and the rocky shallows due east of Barcelona Harbor.

After spawning, perch will move into increasingly deeper water, making your search area much larger. Often they will be found in large numbers on the bottom where the bottom and the thermocline meet. Under normal conditions, this corresponds to a bottom temperature of about 55 to 70 degrees, and a depth of 50 to 75 feet. What makes finding these perch difficult is the fact that this intersection is constantly moving, often on a daily basis. Because of the difficulty in finding these fish in the summer, there is little active perch fishing on this part of the lake in the summer.

All of the indicated sites on the maps will hold perch at one time or another during the summer. The most consistent summer locations include the shoals off Van Buren Point, the "perch buoy", the shoal off Fletcher Point, Seneca Shoal, and Waverly Shoal.

One way to take a few perch in mid-summer is to locate a large weed bed, such as those found along the Canadian shore, and clear out a patch with a rake. Still fishing in these clearings will usually produce a fair number of fish, but these are solitary, not schooled fish, so don't count on taking great quantities with this method.

In the fall, starting in September and peaking in October and November, the perch fishing really picks up. The reasons for this aren't clear. It could be triggered by cooling water temperatures and shortening days, the cropping down of the bait-fish population, or a combination of factors. The good perch fishing continues until weather conditions force everyone off the lake.

Start looking for yellow perch in water at least 50 feet deep at this time. They will often be found as deep as 80 feet. The areas where anglers find the most consistent fishing are those that have rather featureless bottoms — flat areas of clay, sand, mud, and shale. Good fall areas include the waters off the mouth of Cattaraugus Creek, Sturgeon Point, and Evangola State Park. Fish all of these areas in 50 feet or more of water. Closer to the head of the river, some shallower areas seem to pick up in the fall, including the North, Middle, and South Gaps of Buffalo Harbor's outer wall.

In the fall, the yellow perch are going to be found very close to the bottom. The standard way to take perch on lake Erie is to fish with a spreader baited with minnows. Slowly jig the minnows close to the bottom.

Yellow Perch are an important hardwater fishery on Lake Erie. Seemingly, the two most productive ice fishing locations are the Port of Buffalo Small Boat Harbor and the areas off Sturgeon Point. But this could be a case of accessibility determining the site of success. There is certainly some fine ice fishing available to those intrepid enough to investigate the waters between the point and the harbor.

DUNKIRK HARBOR

By Paul R. Cybart

The most productive year-round open water Lake Erie fishing is found in the waters of Dunkirk Harbor. The reason that the harbor waters stay relatively ice-free, even during the coldest weather, is due to a thermal, river-like discharge originating at the Niagara Mohawk Power Corporation's power-generating plant located at the northwestern end of the harbor.

Though you can usually target what you're fishing for rather easily, fishing in Dunkirk Harbor can yield a smorgasbord of different fish. At one time or another, it is possible to catch coho salmon, chinook salmon, brown trout, rainbow trout, lake trout, steelhead, bullhead, catfish, walleye, yellow perch, crappie, silver bass, white perch, northern pike, smelt, suckers, sheepshead, carp, and who knows what else.

Although some of the best overall fishing in Dunkirk Harbor is experienced from a boat, the shorebound angler has plenty of access and will catch his fair share of fish.

Beginning in late fall and lasting through May, the harbor waters yield good catches of many salmonid species. In October and November, mature coho and chinook salmon and brown trout spawn in the harbor, with much of this activity located in the thermal discharge area. Rainbow trout and steelhead will also be caught in the harbor at this time; they are there to gorge themselves on the eggs of the spawning fish. The rainbows, steelhead and browns, as well as an occasional lake trout, will be caught all winter long in the harbor. In March and April, coho salmon in the 2 1/2- to 4-pound range invade the harbor to feed heavily on the large amounts of baitfish that are attracted to the harbor's warm waters.

Boaters do well trolling for these fish with small floating minnow-type plugs and spoons. Fishing in the discharge area is best done with baits like egg sacs, chunk spawn, minnows, and, if available, nightcrawlers. Present the bait as you would if you were fishing a stream. Remember the discharge water is moving and is best described as a small river.

Shorebound fishermen do best at this time by casting spoons. While not very popular, bait fished under a slip bobber or even off the bottom from shore can yield good results for trout and maybe a bonus perch or bullhead.

Warming temperatures in April yield some good catches of bullhead from all of the shoreline access areas along the harbor. While nightcrawlers and minnows produce good results, the best bait in recent years has been pieces of cut shad.

In April, species such as walleye, silver bass, white perch, and smallmouth bass enter the harbor. The black bass season does not get underway until June, but it is in late April and May that a large number of these fish are caught by anglers fishing for other species. The silver bass and white perch are often caught together on both bait and hardware. The city dock yields the best catches for the shorebound angler; the boat fishermen will do best in the discharge area.

The harbor area also produces good catches of walleye. When the season opener arrives, trolling shallow-running, minnow-type plugs at night will be the best method of catching them. But if you don't like fishing in a crowd or in a confined space, you may want to try elsewhere.

During the first part of the walleye season, daytime fishing is not very productive. However, it does turn on by the end of May. The discharge area yields the better catches to those using small F4 Flatfish or a size 3 Indiana-bladed worm harness fished along the bottom.

The month of May will also yield some fair perch catches to those willing to put the time in. The action won't be fast and furious, but minnows fished off the bottom from the city dock or off Lake Front Boulevard will yield the makings of what made a Lake Erie fish fry famous.

When the bass season opener finally arrives, there's still some good fishing for smallmouth in the harbor, but the best fishing will be found in the lake. While the discharge area attracts many of the

This is a typical early morning scene in Dunkirk. A major reason Dunkirk Harbor is such a productive fishing area is the Niagara Mohawk power plant, seen in the left of this picture. The warm-water discharge from the plant warms the harbor, which serves as an attractant to every species of fish found in Lake Erie. Photo courtesy Paul Cybart.

boats, the whole harbor area is productive, especially around and along the piers and breakwaters found in the harbor. At this time of the year, the fish don't seen to be too picky about what they like to eat, as evidenced by the fact that you can catch then on a wide variety of live baits and lures. However, anglers who target smallmouth bass and fish with crabs will often catch more and larger fish than anglers using other methods.

July and August find the waters of the harbor warming into the mid-80s, especially near shore. Action for the shorebound fisherman slows down quite a bit during these months. Because the water is so warm, most fish vacate the harbor and the fish that remain usually run on the small side. The best time of day to fish would be early in the morning. Fishing from a boat in cooler offshore waters is more productive than fishing from shore at this time.

The harbor waters begin to cool in September, and that translates into some good smallmouth bass and walleye action in the discharge area. Fishing for these species will be productive until the spawning salmon arrive.

Smallmouth Bass .... Abundant; growth rate excellent

Studies by the DEC have revealed the existence of an abundant, underutilized bass fishery all along the New York shore of Lake Erie. Data from assessment surveys and creel census studies show good reproduction, excellent growth rates, and a stable age structure, suggesting a low rate of exploitation of this species by anglers.

As with many other fish species, smallmouth bass movements are mainly determined by water temperature. In the late spring, as lake temperatures begin to rise to around 50 degrees, large numbers of smallmouth will begin to move into the shallows along the shore and into connecting tributaries. They stay in these areas through the spawning season. As lake temperatures close to shore increase with the onset of summer, the smallmouth, seeking cooler water, move to the deeper shoals and reefs. These shoals range in depth from approximately 10 to 45 feet. The migration from the shallows to the shoals begins in early summer, with the heaviest concentration of fish occurring on the shoals from late July through September.

In the fall, as lake temperatures begin to cool, the groups of smallmouth will begin to break up, probably because of the fish's reduced urge to feed. Although some fish will remain near their summer shoal habitat through October, most migrate to deeper bottom areas where they remain in a semidormant state until the following spring.

Lake Erie smallmouth generally prefer cooler, clear water with gravel or rock bottoms. Areas such as gravel and bedrock shoals are especially attractive to smallmouth. Open-lake smallmouth can be found in water ranging from 60 degrees in the early spring to 75 degrees in midsummer. Yet, when possible, smallmouth tend to seek out their preferred water temperatures of 68 to 70 degrees.

Of course, the smallmouth's habitat preference is strongly influenced by its diet. Around rock strewn bottoms and shoals, schools of small minnows and crayfish are found in abundance. These two food sources make up the major portion of the smallmouth's diet.

Because the smallmouth bass is so abundant in eastern Lake Erie, the limiting factor for anglers often is access. Fortunately, proven stocks of smallmouth bass occur near all the major boat launch sites on eastern Lake Erie. The following list includes the major bass haunts located near public launch facilities.

Site 1: Seneca Shoal

Near Buffalo, a good place to start is Seneca Shoal, located about 4 miles southwest of Buffalo Harbor. Access is readily available from the Niagara Frontier Transportation Authority ramps at the inner harbor. The shoal, which is only 12 feet deep, is surrounded by waters up to 30 feet in depth. Sampling at this site by the DEC has produced abundant 1- to 4-pound smallmouth bass, especially in the deeper waters (30 feet) between Athol Springs and Seneca Shoal. Bedrock bottom seems to be the rule rather than the exception for much of this extreme eastern Lake Erie area.

Site 2: Sturgeon Point (East)

Walleye anglers using access facilities at Sturgeon Point often catch large numbers of smallmouth bass by accident. Again, bedrock substratum is the norm.

Site 3: Sturgeon Point (West)

Reef areas can be found 1.5 and 3 miles southwest of the breakwall. Depths range quickly from 12 to 30 feet here.

Site 4: Cattaraugus Creek

Little obvious structure occurs near the mouth of this major Lake Erie tributary, but smallmouth bass are nevertheless numerous. The armor stone breakwalls designed by the Army Corps of Engineers provide some structure that available even to land-based anglers, and bedrock bottom off nearby Silver Creek has proved productive.

The sandy bottom areas immediately adjacent to the harbor should be avoided. This material is prized by beach users, but provides little habitat for most fish, including smallmouth bass.

Site 5: Dunkirk Harbor

A thermal discharge from the Niagara Mohawk Power Station serves to attract forage species, predator species, and sport anglers to the harbor confines. Included in those predator fish are smallmouth bass, which on at least one occasion were caught at a rate of 1.08 fish per angler hour. Although literally thousands of bass can be caught in Dunkirk Harbor, anglers should not overlook the open-lake smallmouth bass fishery nearby. Bedrock areas occur at nearby Battery Point to the northeast of Dunkirk Harbor.

Site 6: Van Buren Bay

Patient anglers (or those with depth finders) will notice reef-type structures about 1 mile northeast of Van Buren Point on a line between Van Buren Point and the Niagara Mohawk Power Station stacks.

West of Van Buren, peaks and valleys can be found in 20 to 45 feet of water.

Site 7: Barcelona (East)

Little obvious structure occurs here, but smallmouth bass can readily be found on rock bottom areas at the preferred depths.

Site 8: Barcelona (West)

Again, little obvious structure, but ample rocky areas that provide suitable habitat for numerous smallmouth bass.

Other areas of the lake that provide good fishing for smallmouth bass include much of the Canadian side from Point Abino to Fort Erie, Waverly Shoal, Woodlawn Bar, the slag pile behind the steel plant, Eagle Bay, and the table rocks between Point Gratiot and Van Buren Point.

During the spring, many anglers catch smallmouth in shallow water casting from shore. However, once the fish migrate to deeper shoals, they become accessible only by the use of a boat.

Whether fishing for smallmouth from shore or from a boat, five basic rules should be kept in mind:

1. Fish on the bottom. Smallmouth bass rarely feed on the surface. Natural and artificial bait should be fished as close to the bottom as possible for effective results.
2. Find preferred habitat. Smallmouth prefer cool, clear water and rocky or gravel bottoms. Rock walls, submerged boulder fields, off-shore shoals and reefs are all typical smallmouth habitat.
3. Fish no deeper than 45 feet. Smallmouth are a relatively shallow water fish. In the spring, fish can be caught in less than 3 feet of water. During late summer and fall, smallmouth will range between approximately 10 to 45 feet of water. Only occasionally will these fish be found at depths over 45 feet.
4. Use light or ultralight tackle. To catch smallmouth consistently, light tackle should be used. Smallmouth are very wary; anything unnatural will scare them away. A 5- to 6-foot light or ultralight rod with an open-faced spinning reel filled with 4- or 6-pound-test line makes an ideal open-lake smallmouth outfit. When weighting the line, use only as much weight as is necessary to get bait to the bottom.

5. Use natural or natural-like bait. The smallmouth's diet is almost exclusively made up of minnows and crayfish. Consequently, these, along with the nightcrawler, are good choices for natural baits. If artificial baits are used, close imitations of minnows, crayfish, or nightcrawlers are the most productive.

There are no guarantees that any one fishing technique will produce fish consistently. Like most fish, smallmouth bass have feeding patterns closely related to their environment. Water temperature, abundance and type of food, sunlight, and weather all play a role in how actively smallmouth will be feeding on any given day. However, experienced Lake Erie smallmouth bass anglers have noted that certain techniques seem to improve chances for catching fish. Three techniques that have proved successful are described. All three are based on the five basic rules discussed above, and each technique has been developed to catch smallmouth in different circumstances.

Trolling

Trolling is a successful technique for catching smallmouth in open water, for the trolling angler is able to fish a large area. This is extremely important on two occasions. The first occasion is in early summer when smallmouth begin to move from the shallows to the shoals. Then the fish are scattered over a wide area on the shoals, and trolling increases the angler's chance of finding and catching the dispersed fish. The second occasion is for anglers fishing unfamiliar waters. They do not know the best spots where fish tend to congregate. Trolling allows them to quickly locate productive fishing spots. Some anglers find trolling to be the most successful fishing method and troll throughout the season.

When trolling, you can locate where fish may be concentrated by marking the spot where a fish hits the lure. A simple marking device can be made by tying a 45-foot, weighted string to the handle of an empty plastic bleach or milk container. Coil the string around the container. When a fish hits, toss the container off the boat toward the spot where the fish struck. The weight will automatically uncoil the string and sink to the bottom, leaving the empty container floating and anchored to the bottom. A spot under which several fish may be located is then marked.

Because of the pressure that trolling puts on equipment, tackle slightly heavier than normal is suggested. Light- to medium-weight rods and reels with 6- to 8-pound-test line make a good combination. For trolling, artificial baits that imitate small perch, minnows, or crayfish work best. Full-bodied sinking or deep-diving crankbait-type lures and large spinners all work well. Success hinges on getting the lure as close to the bottom as possible without the lure becoming hung up on weeds or the bottom. One way to ensure that the lure is deep enough is to start trolling, slowly letting line out. When the lure hits bottom, the tip of the pole will start bouncing. Crank the reel a few times until the jerking action of the tip stops. The lure should then be riding right above bottom obstructions.

Starting in June, many bottom areas of Lake Erie are covered with a green aquatic algae known as Cladophora. At that time of year, anglers should try to keep lures riding just above the algae growth and should check their lures frequently for snagged plant debris. Cladophora usually dies off by mid-August.

Drift Fishing

Drift fishing has proved to be an exceptionally successful technique for catching smallmouth. This method is most productive from late July through September when smallmouth are heavily concentrated on shoals.

Drift fishing depends upon the wind or lake waves to push the boat along slowly. Once the boat is adrift, light to ultralight tackle with 4- to 6-pound test line is used. Natural foods, including crayfish (preferably soft-shelled), nightcrawlers, and minnows, are rigged on a small (No. 4 or No. 6) single hook with just enough weight attached for the bait to reach bottom. Artificial jigs (brown, black, or chartreuse) can also be used. As the bait or jig is dragged along bottom, bass are attracted to it.

One very successful drift technique is the anchor-drag method, also known as the centerline drift method. From late July through September, the smallmouth's major food source are crayfish (crabs), which are often present in large numbers on rocky lake bottoms. A drift or drag anchor is lowered to the bottom, not for stopping the boat's drift, but rather for turning over stones on the bottom to expose the crayfish hidden beneath. This stirring up of the bottom by the anchor apparently attracts large numbers of smallmouth into the area to feed. Anglers fishing with live soft-shell crayfish or artificial jigs in the roiled waters behind the drag anchor usually experience faster action. Simple drag anchors can be made out of a cinder block, stones tied in nylon mesh bags, or a cement-filled plastic milk or bleach bottle.

Drag anchors are also useful for helping to determine the type of bottom one is drifting over. Drag anchor contact with rocky or gravel substratum areas will produce a discernable vibration in the rope that can be felt by hand. If the drag anchor is passing over mud or silt bottoms, little or no such vibration will be felt.

The angler should also be alert to catches of sheepshead (freshwater drum). If these fish are being caught in numbers, it is likely that the angler is either fishing over silt or mud bottom areas or fishing too shallow. Often moving the boat a short distance will solve the problem.

For more information on drift fishing techniques used on the Great Lakes read the section on bass fishing on Lake Ontario.

Still Fishing

Still fishing is generally used when a concentration of fish has been located or when fishing over specific bottom structures (rocks, boulders, holes, downed trees, etc.). Basic tackle used for still fishing is the same as that used for drift fishing. The boat is anchored so that it will remain stationary. Either live bait or artificial lures can prove successful. Still fishing is most effective when used in conjunction with the other two techniques. When a concentration of fish is located through trolling or drifting, the boat can be anchored in that area and the area fished. Anglers can continue still fishing until the fish leave the area and then revert to trolling or drifting until the next heavy concentration of fish is located.

The Canadian shoreline of Lake Erie offers some truly outstanding fishing for smallmouth bass. A particularly productive area are the waters around Windmill Point. Don Lindke and Jim Bergquist boated these fish in mid-October by drift fishing off the point in 12 to 30 feet of water. Photo courtesy Jim Bergquist.

Much of the preceding article was adapted from the booklet "Angling for Smallmouth Bass in Lake Erie," which is published by the New York Sea Grant Extension. Copies of this and other publications can be obtained by contacting Sea Grant at:

New York Sea Grant Extension Program
Fernow Hall, Cornell University
Ithaca, New York 14853
(607) 255-2811

The following article was written by one of western New York's top bass experts, Jim Hanley.

FISHING FOR SMALLMOUTH BASS ON LAKE ERIE

By Jim Hanley

If you want to get some strange looks from people, tell them you're a bass guide on Lake Erie. If you want to start an argument, tell them you do your guiding out of a Ranger. Most people will tell you bass boats can't run in the Great Lakes. You see, up here in the walleye capitol of the world, the smallmouth bass is considered by most fisherman to be a trash fish, but as someone once said "One person's trash is another person's treasure."

Around these parts the walleye, or yellow pike as the locals call them, are taken by trolling, trolling, and more trolling, using a spinner and worm or a worm and spinner. This leaves the smallmouth virtually unmolested, and there's not many places left in this land where that statement can be made.

Once known as a dead lake, Erie is now very much alive and well. It is the shallowest and second smallest of the Great Lakes, yet boasts a surface area of 10,000 square miles. Its average depth is approximately 40 feet, yet has areas over 200 feet deep.

Erie can almost be classified as two lakes. The eastern basin, in which I do my guiding, has a bowl-shaped configuration with long points, reefs, and shoals scattered over its otherwise featureless contour. The western half (Pennsylvania to Ohio) is hard pressed to find water over 35 feet, and islands and shoals are constant features. There's plenty of opportunity to fish whatever type structure your heart desires. The thing to remember for you fishermen that are used to impoundments is that this is a glacier-formed body of water, so obvious elements such as creek channels and road beds are not present. Instead, as mentioned before, we fish main lake humps, points, and extensive reefs that may extend for a mile or more.

The season here is short, due not only to the shorter growing season than that experienced in the South, but also due to New York's closed season on most game fish. Bass season runs from the third Saturday in June to the end of November. Further west, in Pennsylvania and Ohio, there is no closed season. Even though the shorter season is often considered a pain, the number of smallmouth we catch more than makes up for it. The two weeks following opening day often produces 25 to 50 fish for a three-man charter. New York's limit is five fish 12 inches long, so we do lots of culling. Sizes range anywhere from keepers to 5-pounders, and an opening day trip will usually produce a couple of those big lunkers. The closed season is frowned upon by many, yet the protected bass are given plenty of time to spawn and recoup before being subjected to the anglers' onslaught. These restrictions have allowed the bass to multiply into huge numbers where schools are the rule rather than the exception. It's not unusual when pulling in 2- or 3-pound fish that several (I've counted as many as 10) "cousins" will follow the hooked smallmouth to the boat. I have to say with all honesty, and I've fished all over this country, that Erie is probably the number one lake for smallmouths in the nation.

Having caught my first bronzeback at age 6, I'm the one who's been hooked ever since. I'd like to now share with you some of the techniques and patterns that have helped me locate and catch more and bigger smallmouths on my home lake.

Skill at reading a flasher or graph is very helpful, if not mandatory, because you're often fishing a mile or more from shore, and the aid of the shoreline markings is virtually eliminated. Many fishermen are now using Loran to get them back to known honeyholes. The use of floating markers is also necessary as exact positioning is critical for good catches. You have a vast amount of area to contend with and a slight breeze will blow you off your spot quickly. I don't believe you can carry too many floating markers in your boat, especially when checking out a new area. I've seen locals get lucky with a good fish now and then, and it's only luck because of haphazard trolling techniques. There have been times when we've been surrounded by trollers like a wagon train surrounded by Indians, yet they still catch nothing. Exact positioning is critical.

Once we get into the smallmouth on one of these deep-water areas, the action is usually fast and furious. Customers get so excited by the action that they fail to detect a strike while watching someone else boat a fish.

The technique I most often employ with customers is vertical jigging. It's a technique that anyone can learn in a relatively short time. I can't understand why so many fishermen are hesitant to try it. My customers are amazed when they catch their first deep-water smallmouth by vertical jigging. Generally, they never knew they got a strike and on the upswing they've accidently set the hook. I'm not ashamed to say I've caught a large number of bass this way; I'll take them any way they come.

I'll employ any number of jigging baits, including Mann-O-Lures, Strata Spoons, Silver Buddies, and my favorite, a jig 'n grub. I also use a jig 'n pig when I'm after big fish only; Uncle Josh always rides in my boat. It should go without saying, but sharp hooks are a must, and I usually change trebles on most baits to the next largest size for better hookups in deep water.

Line weights of 4-, 6-, and 8-pound test in clear Stren are employed due to Lake Erie's clear water. I favor 6-pound, going to 4-pound at tough times, and usually 8-pound for my customers for that added margin of error. I've seen more big fish break off due to excitement than I care to remember.

One of my favorite rods for deep jigging is Billy Westmoreland's Touring Special from Bass Pro Shops. I believe they've quit making that model, but a good graphite spinning rod with at least a medium action is necessary to get hooks set at the depth we fish. A quality spinning reel helps take the worry out of breakdowns. I personally back reel my fish instead of using the drag. But for my customers, I make sure the drag is set properly for the anticipated runs from the bass. I've been using the now extinct Abu Zebco Cardinal 3s.

As I mentioned before, I use a Ranger. But I did not mention that it is the 390 model. I use it because it's over 19 feet long and 7 1/2 feet wide. This big boat lists very little, even when everyone gets on one side to look into the water, and there's plenty of room for three passengers and gear. It also takes the worry out of not making it back in case of bad weather. (Always check the NOAA Weather Radio Station before going out; the weather can change quickly in this region, and Lake Erie is especially nasty when the wind is blowing hard). A 150 GT Johnson gives me plenty of power to get in, just in case we need to hurry. Last, but not least, my secret weapon is a four-blade prop. This new design wheel allows me better hole shots when carrying customers, but when it does get nasty, all I do is trim the motor up about one-third of the way, and run about 2,500 rpms and my ranger becomes an ocean liner. This keeps the front end up, actually wheel standing, allowing us to ride through the biggest swells without the worry of taking a big wave over the front end.

What we're looking for in this case are large off-shore structures. (As I'm an old Buck Perry fan, I use the term in its purest form, meaning an entire element such as a bar, hump, etc.) Structures such as humps, shoals, and extensive points having gentle slopes on at least one-third to three-quarters of the sides, with the remainder having broken or stair-step-type sides are generally the ones holding the quality fish. Broken fist- to basketball-size rocks seem to produce the best fishing. This is due to the fact that rubble of this size will usually have a large population of crawfish, who seek shelter in between the crevices. Boulders will also hold fish, but usually in the spring and fall, and since we're talking about a summer, or warm-water pattern, we'll stick to what works best during that period. I believe the crawfish population is what makes the jig 'n grub combination so productive — it imitates the crawdad so well. I'll explain more about it in a moment.

Mike Bleech boats a hefty Lake Erie smallmouth bass. Lake Erie is one of the premier smallmouth bass lakes in the country. Photo courtesy Mike Bleech

The fish will use the breaks as we use stairs. They will ascend and descend as the sun rises or sets. You'll find them on top at dusk and dawn, and generally deeper when the sun is at its apex. Of course, there will be exceptions, but this is a good rule to follow when fishing anywhere.

The effects of the sun will not only position the fish either high or low on a break; along with the wind it will also determine which way they will be facing. Imagine a bunch of birds sitting on an electric wire; they'll be facing into the wind, all in the same direction.

Sometimes, usually because of the position of the baitfish, the smallmouth will position themselves as far as 25 feet off their normal holding breaks. This is when I will utilize my spoon throwing trick. I will describe this technique shortly.

When we think the fish are shallow and on top of structure, we'll generally throw crankbaits or a jig 'n grub just to check for their presence. The tops of the humps and points are usually anywhere from 3 to 15 feet deep, so we can check them rather quickly. If we don't get any action, then we'll systematically eliminate the depth ranges or stair steps until we locate our quarry. When checking depths of 15 to 25 feet, I still stay with the jig 'n grub, but also begin to utilize the Spoon, Spinrite, and Silver Buddy. If we have to fish 25 feet and deeper, the standard lift and drop vertical jigging technique will be the best approach. Once we've located fish, the floating markers go out. Remember to place the markers at least 25 feet from your spot and then keep a mental note where to drop your bait. This is so not to scare the fish when the marker weight comes down.

Now I'm finally going to tell you the key to catching these deep-water smallmouth. I'm sure the following two tips will help you catch fish on your favorite deep-water spot, too. First lets cover the jig 'n grub.

The design of the jig head and the way the grub is rigged are the secrets to my overall success. Starting with the jig head, I generally fish a 1/4-ounce head with a Mann's 3-inch grub body. Occasionally, I also use 1/8-ounce and 3/8-ounce heads, but I have my best success with the 1/4-ounce jig head. The shape of the head is the key. Its action is what leads to the great amount of strikes. The head is a stand-up or wedge style, originally designed and manufactured by Mr. Twister several years ago. I haven't seen it marketed lately, although Rich's Right Lures of Buffalo now makes them, and they work equally well for me. Rich makes mine with a

3/0 light wire hook for better penetration. The shape of the head, with the line tie at the very tip of the jig, along with the grub body put on the hook perpendicular to the hook causes the bait to do cartwheels when the rod tip is twitched. We've tank tested it in Larry Ritcher's Hawg Trough and watched the smallmouth go crazy over it on the first cast. Strikes generally occur when the jig has gone through about three-quarters of the loop.

Keeping the bait a foot or so above the bottom as I work it up the stair steps produces great action. A rhythm of twitch, twitch, pause then twitch again (as if sending Morse code) while slowly reeling works best. When working for fish on the top of structure or for fish suspended off structure, a swimming retrieve with the same cadence also works well. Always count the bait down with a one/ one thousand count to the desired depth before beginning your retrieve for best results.

The above technique works wonders on the fish but also works a number on your line. During the course of a hard day's fishing, I might change spools as many as three times. It may seem like a nuisance, but I feel its worth the trouble.

I have no preference with regard to painted or unpainted jig heads, but I know fishermen who won't use a jig unless the eyes are painted perfectly. As to the color of the grub body, I favor smoke most of the time. If I'm not getting hits, I'll go to avocado. I also use avocado in extremely clear water. I'm not opposed to black, and have occasionally used white and yellow. Lake Erie's water color in the last five years has gotten so clear that you can see rocks 15 feet deep. This has allowed me to stick with my favorite colors.

The other tactic I use for catching fish on stair steps or that are suspended off structure is what I call ripping the spoon. With my boat positioned over the shallowest part of the structure I'm fishing over, I'll throw the spoon out a long way and engage the reel just as the spoon hits the water. This causes the spoon to swing in an arc as it falls toward bottom. As it sinks I'll be counting it down, having already predetermined the water's depth. Just before the spoon hits bottom, I'll give the rod a big sweep upward, making the spoon rip toward the surface about 10 feet or so. I'll quickly retrieve line and hang on. No self-respecting smallmouth can resist the bait getting away like that and will generally grab the spoon as it falls back down. What's really fun is when you've located a school and the pecking order takes place. The fish will try to grab the spoon out of each other's mouth, resulting in two or three strikes before a fish is finally hooked up. I've even had the bass jump and throw the spoon only to have another one grab it before the bait sinks a foot or so. Continuing to rip and retrieve all the way up the stairs allows you to cover all the depth ranges. I usually use a 1/2-ounce spoon for this technique. If the wind starts blowing and I lose my feel for what's happening at the end of the line, the 3/4-ounce spoons come out to maintain better feel; however, I've noticed my catch ratio goes down with the heavier spoons.

By carefully checking out each area in the ways described, it usually doesn't take long before you make contact with the fish. Then you can take your time and enjoy catching the best fresh-water fighter there is. Erie's fish might not reach the size of those from Dale Hollow or Pick Wick, but the sheer numbers and lack of competition seems to outweigh all other factors. The techniques I employ are a far cry from the chunkin' and windin' tactics that our buddies use to catch largemouths, but as anyone reading this knows, the reward of catching smallmouth over a largemouth is truly gratifying.

Trout and Salmon .... Common; growth rate good to excellent

Beginning with small numbers of salmon in the late 1960s, the Lake Erie stocking program has grown to include impressive numbers of coho salmon, chinook salmon, lake trout, brown trout, rainbow trout (steelhead), and palomino trout. In addition to the fish stocked by the State of New York, the Province of Ontario and the State of Pennsylvania stock a lot of rainbows in Lake Erie, and many of these fish find their way into the New York portion of the lake and run in New York tributaries. Also, pink or "humpback" salmon, which were originally introduced into Lake Superior in the late 1950s, have recently been turning up in modest numbers in Lake Erie.

Although a great many fish are being stocked in Lake Erie, the resulting fishery for trout and salmon has not developed to the degree initially expected. Since 1984 the trout and salmon fishing in the New York portion of lake Erie has not been very good. Relatively few trout and salmon are showing up in creel censuses. A thorough study to determine the cause of this has not been undertaken, but biologists at the Lake Erie Fishery Station in Dunkirk think that the problem could be that the fish are being stocked into the lake at a

Paul Cybart, a well-known charter boat captain and outdoor writer from Dunkirk, shows off a nice chinook salmon. Though the trout and salmon fishing in Lake Erie will probably never rival that of Lake Ontario, catches like this are not uncommon, especially in the spring and fall. Photo courtesy Paul Cybart.

time and place when they are very susceptible to predation by smallmouth bass and walleye. Thus, the fishery suffers a high mortality as soon as the fish are stocked. This problem does not exist in Lake Ontario.

The above problem notwithstanding, Lake Erie and its tributaries do offer some fine fishing for trout and salmon in the spring and fall when the fish are concentrated close to shore or are in the tributaries. All of the major and many of the minor tributaries of Lake Erie get substantial runs of trout and salmon. Steelhead are the bread and butter of these runs. They don't seem to be as vulnerable to predation as the other salmonids.

With the exception of the chinook, all stocked salmonids can be found in great quantity along the lake shore in spring. There is a noticeable tendency for the fish to follow the ice out of the lake in early spring, with the result that the more western shoreline turns on to fishing first. But certain areas tend to warm sooner than would be expected. The most notable early hot spot is Dunkirk Harbor. The harbor, which never freezes due to the thermal discharge from the power plant, is a strong attractant to brown trout, rainbow trout, and coho salmon. Fish can be caught here all winter long, but it really picks up in early March and lasts well into April. Other early season producers include the South Wall and South Gap of Buffalo's Outer Harbor, the bay off Woodlawn, and the mouths of most major streams. The most productive stream mouths in the spring and fall are naturally those that are stocked. These include Eighteen Mile Creek, Cattaraugus Creek, Canadaway Creek, and Chautauqua Creek. But don't neglect the areas off any other stream that has even a moderate flow of water, such as Silver Creek, Scott Creek, and Beaver Creek (the last two are known locally as First Gulf Brook and Second Gulf Brook, respectively). Barcelona Harbor, though in a heavily stocked area, is only moderately productive in the spring.

As the lake warms, the trout and salmon move into deeper water. At this time the best fishing is apparently concentrated in what is locally known as "The Breaks." This consists of a series of fairly rapid drop-offs between Dunkirk and Barcelona. A rule of thumb in finding the Breaks is to locate 100 feet of water directly out from the stacks of the Niagara Mohawk power plant in Dunkirk or the Portland water tower, just west of Van Buren Point. A similar area, known as "The East Mountains" is located just across the state line in Pennsylvania. You'll know that you are approaching Pennsylvania waters when you pass the huge Boron sign in the town of Ripley.

Following their normal pattern, the salmon will move back into near-shore waters beginning in August, just before they begin their spawning runs in the tributaries of the lake. These spawning runs will last through November. The streams where the salmon are stocked are the top producers, but many fish will stray into unstocked streams. Just as the salmon runs are dying off, the trout will move into the streams. Brown trout can be caught in most of the larger streams until late December, and rainbows can be taken through the winter and most of the spring.

The following article was written by Warren Hammond, a veteran trout and salmon fisherman and an active member of trout Unlimited.

LAKE RUN TROUT AND SALMON

By Warren Hammond

This article covers the equipment, baits, and techniques used to catch the trout (steelhead, rainbows, and browns) and salmon (chinook and coho) that make a fall and/or spring spawning run up the creeks, streams, and rivers flowing into Lakes Erie and Ontario. Not covered are the summer run of skamania steelhead. These fish are just being introduced into a few of the Great Lakes tributaries.

Most trout will make many runs up the creeks and streams to spawn before they die. The coho, or silver, salmon spawn only once, at 3 to 5 years of age, and then die. The chinook, or king, salmon only spawn once, at 5 to 7 years of age, and then die.

The spawning runs of the fish are generally as follows:

- Chinook and coho Salmon - mid-August to early November;
- Brown trout - September to November;
- Rainbow trout - October thru April; and
- Steelhead - mid-August thru April.

See the guide to the fish of western New York in the back for identification of the various trout and salmon.

Equipment

Shore and dock fishing for the salmon and trout usually requires an 8- or 8 1/2-foot fiberglass or graphite spinning rod. A medium heavy-duty or heavy-duty, open-face spinning reel is usually used. Manufacturers such as Penn, Shimano, Quick, or Daiwa make reels suitable for this type of fishing. The line used on the reels is usually 8- to 12-pound-test monofilament.

For fly fishing, an 8- to 9-foot fly rod is used. The reel should be a multiplier fly reel. The line is generally a weight-forward 7- to 9-weight sinking-tip line and a 7 1/2- to 9-foot tapered leader, ending in a 6-pound tip; 150 to 200 yards of 18- or 20-pound braided dacron line is used as backing behind the fly line.

In streams and rivers, a 6 1/2- to 7-foot spinning rod and a medium-duty spinning reel are usually used. The line is generally 8- to 10-pound-test monofilament. In streams and rivers where the water is running very clear you may want to try a 10- to 12-foot noodle rod equipped with a spinning reel and 4-pound-test line. Often the delicate presentation possible with a noodle rod, along with their sensitivity, will result in more strikes and hooks being set.

Lures

Spoons are generally used for shore and dock fishing and are at least 3/4 ounces in weight so that they can be cast a long distance. Some of the more popular spoons are the Little Cleos and the K-0 Wobblers. Popular colors for the spoons are blue and silver, chartreuse and silver, green and silver, orange and silver, and the new glo-in-the-dark colors.

When fishing in rivers and streams, stickbaits such as the Rapalas, Rebels, and Flatfish can be very effective. These lures represent baitfish that trout and salmon feed on. Spinners also work well in these waters. Popular spinners include the Mepps, Panther Martins, and Rooster Tails. Streamer flies that work well in rivers are those with blue, green, or chartreuse on the top and white or silver on the bottom. A good example of such a fly is Hawell's Coho Fly. A few steelhead flies that are popular are the yarn flies or glo bugs (in orange, red-orange, and white), Skykomish Sunrise, Green Butted Skunk, Spring Wigglers (with brown, black, or chartreuse bodies), and single- and double-egg flies tied with fluorescent chenille. Good hook sizes for these flies are sizes 2 to 8.

Baits

Bait such as fresh skein cut into small pieces, egg sacs with 4 to 5 salmon or trout eggs per snack, nightcrawlers, or a 3- to 4-inch minnow all work well.

Techniques

When fishing from a dock or shore it is advisable to make a cast and use a countdown method to locate the depth at which the fish are feeding before starting a retrieve. I generally count to myself by the thousands until the proper depth for the retrieve - usually just off the bottom - is determined. There are exceptions to this rule. When fish are actively feeding on a school of baitfish near the shore, cast to the edge of where the fish are or near the boils that indicate surface feeding fish.

When fishing rivers and creeks the fish will usually be near an obstruction such as a log jam, large boulder, or a drop-off shelf. So don't pass up these fishy spots. Usually the larger salmon will favor a deep, slow-moving pool. The largest fish will be found in the middle of the pool, medium-sized fish favor the head of the pool, and smaller fish will be found at the tail of the pool.

In the spring and fall the shoreline of Lake Erie offers good fishing for trout and salmon. The fish are often so shallow that a boat is unnecessary. Photo courtesy Mike Bleech.

Rainbow trout and brown trout will usually be found at breaks where the slow water and fast water come together. There the food is easily found and the fish do not have to work hard against the current to maintain their position in the feeding lane. Steelhead on the other hand prefer a good current in water 3 to 4 feet deep and where there is a lot of oxygen present in the water.

Studies through glass enclosures on the West Coast show that sea-run trout and salmon, coming up to spawn, stay from 8 to 24 inches off the bottom. Therefore, this is the area you want to present your lure, fly, or bait for the best results.

When fishing a pool with bait, cast close to you at first, across and slightly upstream. Fish the cast out till it is downstream of you. Use enough split-shot to keep the bait just bumping along the bottom. Then make another cast 3 or 4 feet farther out in the stream till all of the pool is covered at that spot. Then move up or downstream until the whole pool is covered in this manner. Keep out of the water as much as possible to avoid spooking the fish. Set the hook when you think you have a snag or have a bite. When a large fish takes the bait it will often feel like a snag; it is better to lose a few sinkers than a nice fish.

The same procedure for fishing bait can be used when fishing flies and lures except that the fly or lure is kept just off the bottom rather than bouncing along it.

When a big fish is hooked it will either go upstream or downstream. Apply moderate pressure after you set the hook, and just hang on. Try to get below the fish if it heads downstream. When you get below the fish you will tire it out quicker since the fish will be fighting the current as well as the rod pressure. If you keep the pressure on him, in a short time, say 15 to 20 minutes, he will tire out and can be netted or beached.

It is a good idea to preset the drag on your reel so it is about one-third the breaking strength of the line and leave it there. Tightening the drag on a big fish can result in a broken line when the fish makes a sudden lunge.

A good item to have on hand when fishing for big trout and salmon is a small sharpening stone. Check your hook points often and keep them needle point sharp. A bump on a rock can easily bend a hook point and result in a lost fish.

Additional Species

In addition to those mentioned above, there are a number of species present in Lake Erie who, by sheer weight of numbers, constitute an important, though underutilized fishery. Silver bass, a cousin of the Atlantic striped bass, are abundant in Lake Erie. They can be taken is phenomenal numbers in the spring when they come into shallows to spawn. Dunkirk Harbor is about the best silver bass area around. Freshwater drum, known also as sheepshead, are also extremely common. Although usually spurned by fishermen as a junk fish, the sheepshead is a strong fighter and quite palatable when cooked properly. They can often be found on shoals and rocky bottoms after a storm has churned up the water. Recently, large otoliths (stone-like structures found in the fish's head) have been found indicating that this species in the not too distant past reached a size of about 200 pounds. One- to three-pound sheepshead are more the norm today, though 10-pound specimens are not uncommon. Rock bass, a truly ubiquitous species, are found in the spring, summer, and fall, from shallow reefs to depths over 50 feet. The piers at the mouth of Cattaraugus Creek, Seneca Shoal, Waverly Shoal, and the walls of the Outer Harbor all produce good numbers of these fine-tasting fish. Muskellunge, although native to Lake Erie, are only rarely taken. A few are caught off Seneca and Waverly Shoals, but the only consistent muskie hole in this end of the lake is the area between Donnelly's Wall and the entrance to the Black Rock Canal. Channel catfish, though much more common than muskie, are also rarely encountered. Most catfish are taken in the waters near the mouths of major inlets, such as Cattaraugus Creek, Silver Creek, and Chautauqua Creek. Last, but not least, are the ever present carp, suckers, and bullhead.

General Information

Lake Erie is truly one of the great lakes of the world. Although only the second smallest of five Great Lakes, its relatively shallow waters have provided, over the past 150 years, more of the commercial fish harvest than the other four Great Lakes combined. The New York portion of the lake lies entirely within the deep eastern basin (mean depth 80 feet, maximum depth 210 feet). Generally less productive than the shallower central and western basins, the eastern basin has been less affected by the environmental degradation that has taken its toll on the rest of Lake Erie. Its waters are home to almost 40 species of fish. Of importance to the sport fisherman are smallmouth bass, walleye, yellow perch, silver (or white) bass, sheepshead, rock bass, trout (browns, rainbows, lakers, and palominos) and salmon (coho and chinook).

It wasn't too long ago that some people were lamenting the death of Lake Erie. Piles of rotting fish and the stench of algae blooms lent credence to their claims and clearly indicated that something was wrong. But beginning in the mid 1960s, the first hesistant steps were taken to reverse the decline of this lake and to restore it to some degree of health. By the early 1980s, Lake Erie was the cleanest of the Great Lakes, many of its species were rebounding to former levels and algae blooms were greatly abated.

The greatest success stories are return of the walleye, trout, and salmon. In recent years, the walleye fishing has been nothing short of phenomenal. The trout and salmon stocking program, which began in the late 1960s, has grown to impressive dimensions, although it has not achieved the degree of success that many had expected. All in all, Lake Erie is again one of the finest fisheries in the country.

One problem that still plagues this lake is access. Although numerous boat launch sites are listed, many are small, can handle little traffic in good weather, and are downright dangerous or impossible to use in bad weather. And bad weather is something Lake Erie sees a lot of. There is also a dearth of good bank access. Although there are several state parks (Evangola and Lake Erie State Parks) and piers (at Cattaraugus Creek, Dunkirk Harbor, and Barcelona Harbor) along the shoreline, they are wholly inadequate in terms of space and facilities. Fortunately, plans are being developed to increase both bank and boat access.

Additional information on fishing in eastern Lake Erie can be obtained by contacting:

N.Y.S. Department of Environmental Conservation
128 South Street
Olean, N.Y. 14760
(716)372-8676

Dunkirk Fisheries Station
178 Point Drive North
(716)366-0228

It should be remembered that Lake Erie is an international water and that a Canadian license is required in some of the areas covered in this guide. For information concerning Ontario fishing regulations, the locations of special sanctuaries, and where you can obtain a Canadian license contact:

The Ontario Ministry of Natural Resources
Niagara District Office
P.O. Box 1070
Fonthill, Ontario
Phone: 416-892-2656

LAKE ERIE

(New York Section)
(Contours in Feet)

NOTE A

The lines that cover the maps of Lake Erie are photographic artifacts of the Loran-C lines of position that are overprinted on all current nautical charts of this lake distributed by the National Oceanic and Atmospheric Administration.

NOTE B

The maps above listed are not to be used for navigational purposes. The navigational charts that served as the basis for these maps can be obtained by contacting:

National Ocean Service
Distribution Branch (N/CG33)
Riverdale, Maryland 20737
(301) 436-6990

For current navigation regulations on Lake Erie consult the U.S. Coast Guard Pilot 6 or the Weekly Notice to Mariners.

NOTE C

Canadian nautical charts and information pertaining to Canadian waters covered by the above maps can be obtained by contacting the following office:

Hydrographic Chart Distribution Office
Department of Fisheries and the Environment
1675 Russell Road
P.O. Box 8080
Ottawa, Ontario KIG3H6
(613) 998-4931

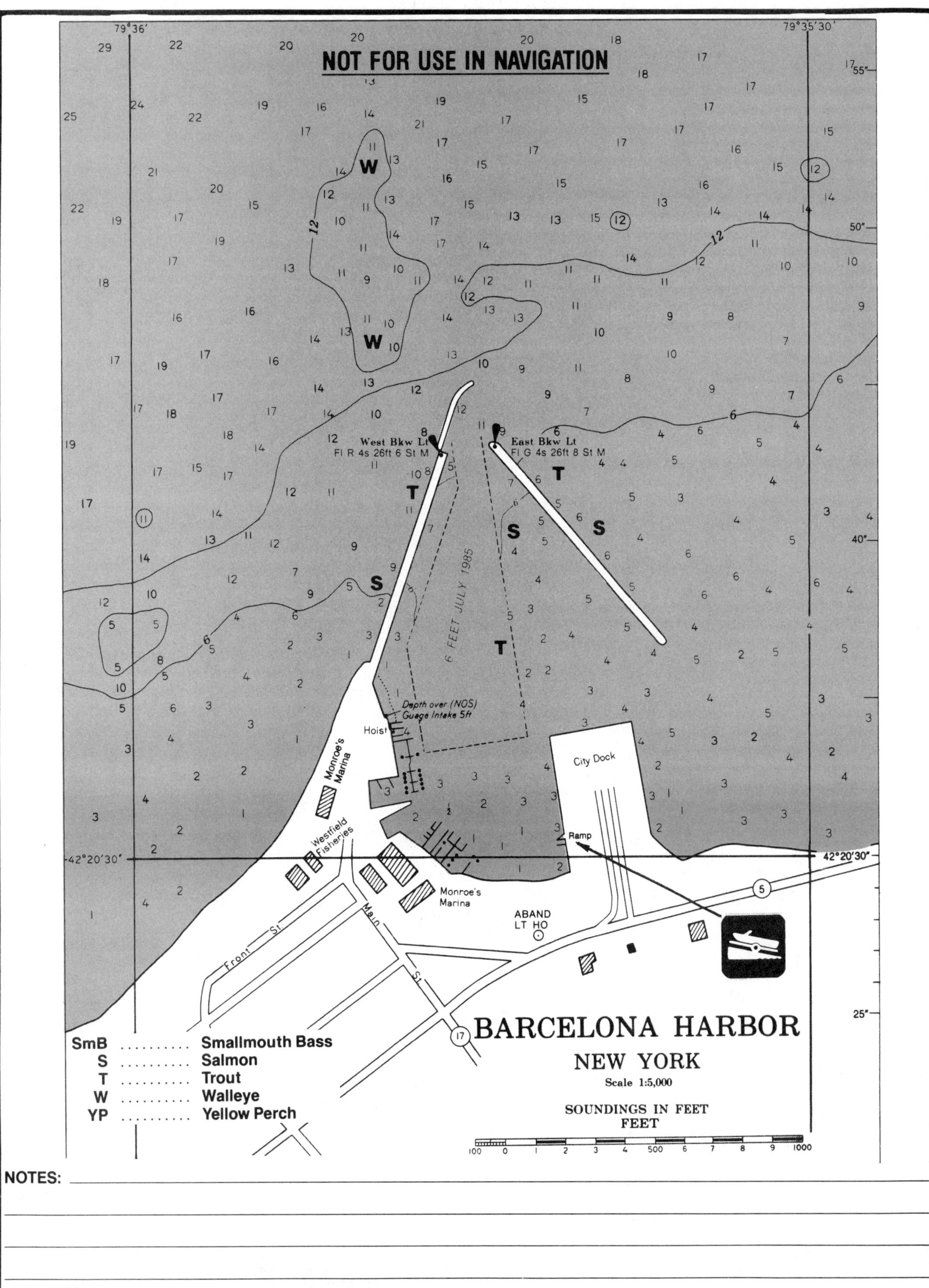

NOT FOR USE IN NAVIGATION
79°36'
79°35'30"
West Bkw Lt
Fl R 4s 26ft 6 St M
East Bkw Lt
Fl G 4s 26ft 8 St M
6 FEET JULY 1985
Depth over (NOS) Guage Intake 5ft
Hoist
Monroe's Marina
Westfield Fisheries
City Dock
Ramp
Monroe's Marina
ABAND LT HO
Front St
Main St
42°20'30"
BARCELONA HARBOR
NEW YORK
Scale 1:5,000
SOUNDINGS IN FEET
FEET
SmB .... Smallmouth Bass
S .... Salmon
T .... Trout
W .... Walleye
YP .... Yellow Perch

NOTES:

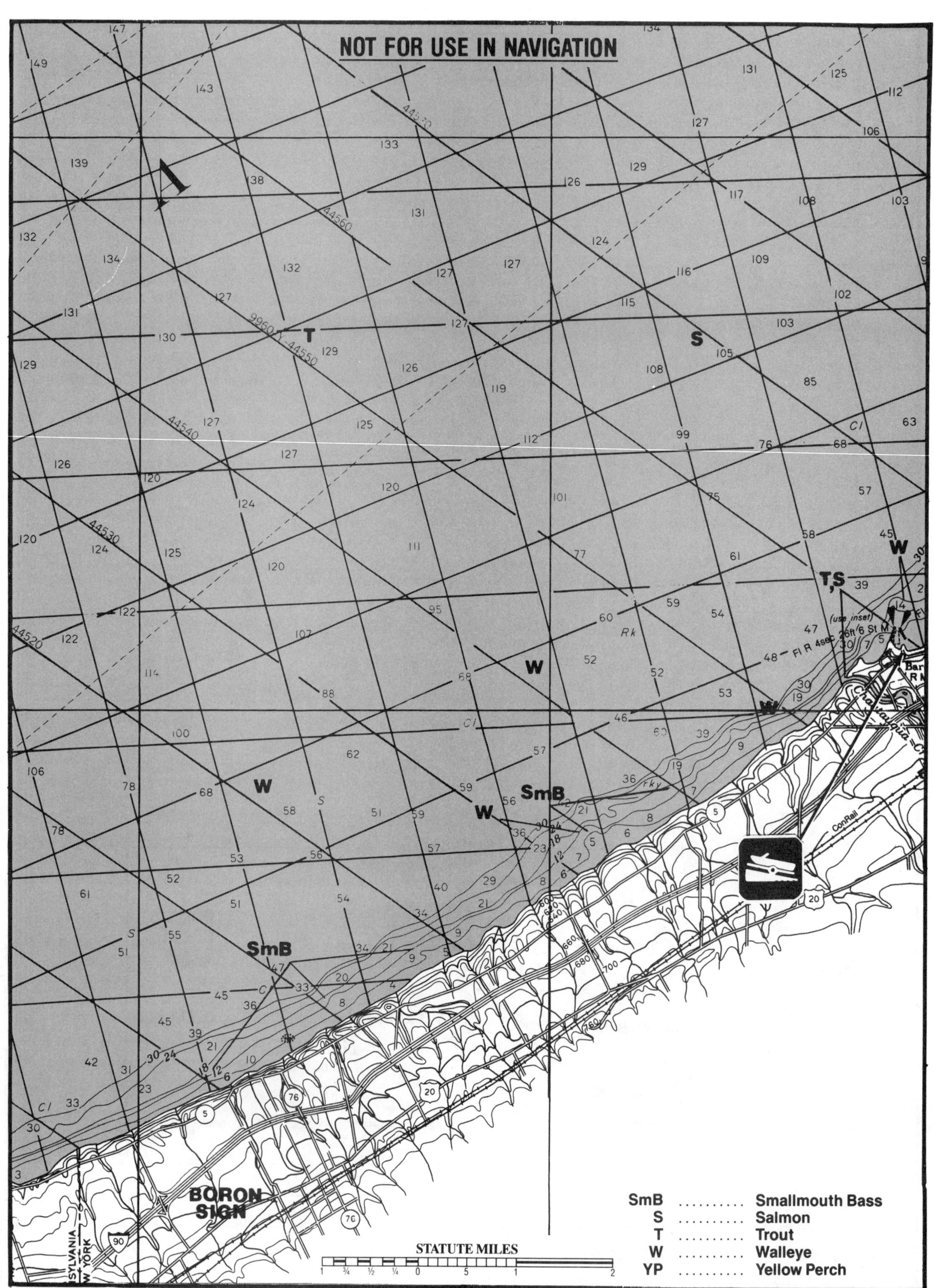
NOT FOR USE IN NAVIGATION
BORON SIGN
STATUTE MILES
SmB .... Smallmouth Bass
S .... Salmon
T .... Trout
W .... Walleye
YP .... Yellow Perch

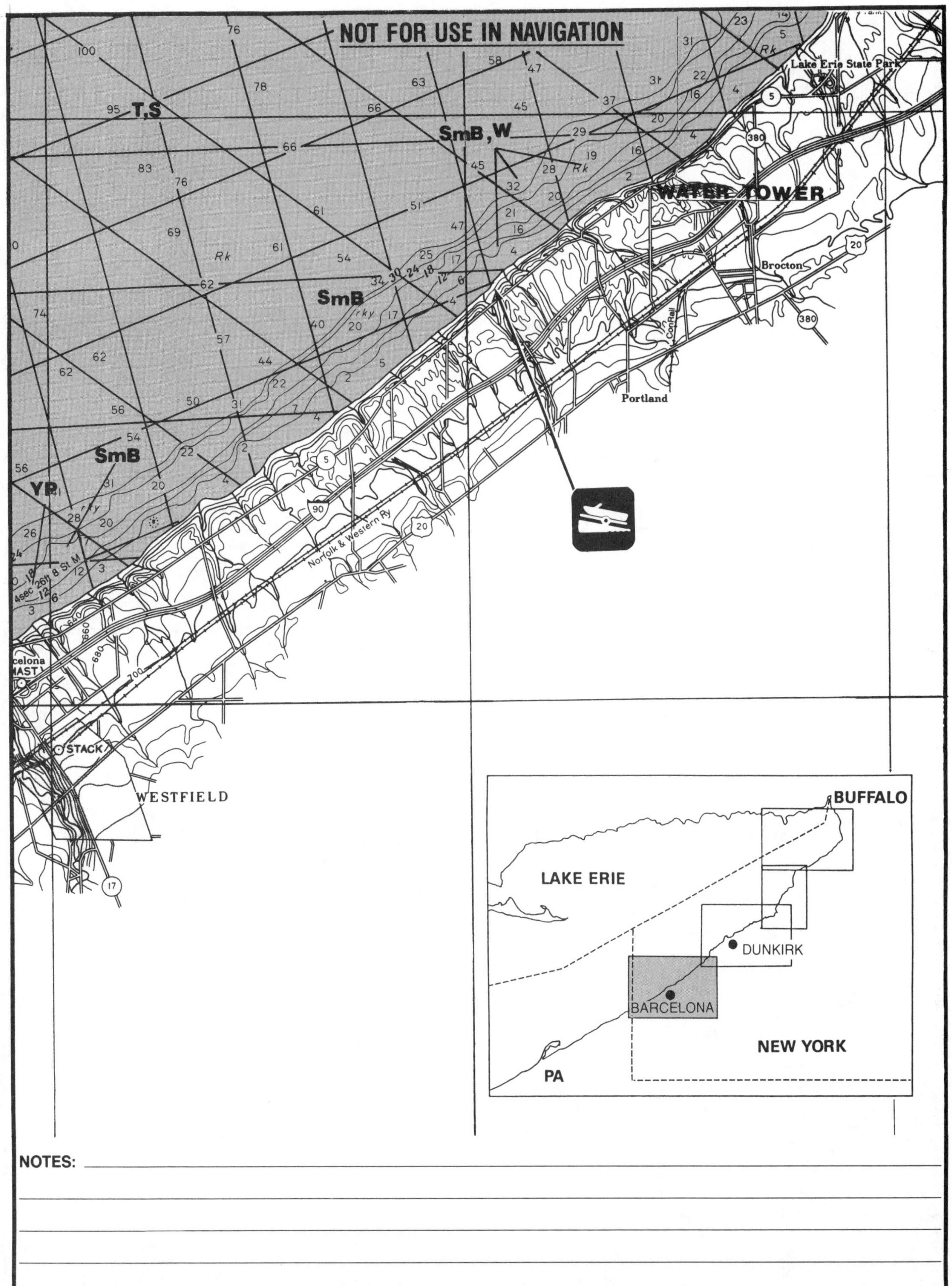
NOT FOR USE IN NAVIGATION
T,S
SmB, W
SmB
SmB
YP
Rk
rky
Lake Erie State Park
WATER TOWER
Brocton
Portland
ConRail
Norfolk & Western Ry
MAST
STACK
WESTFIELD
BUFFALO
LAKE ERIE
DUNKIRK
BARCELONA
NEW YORK
PA
NOTES:

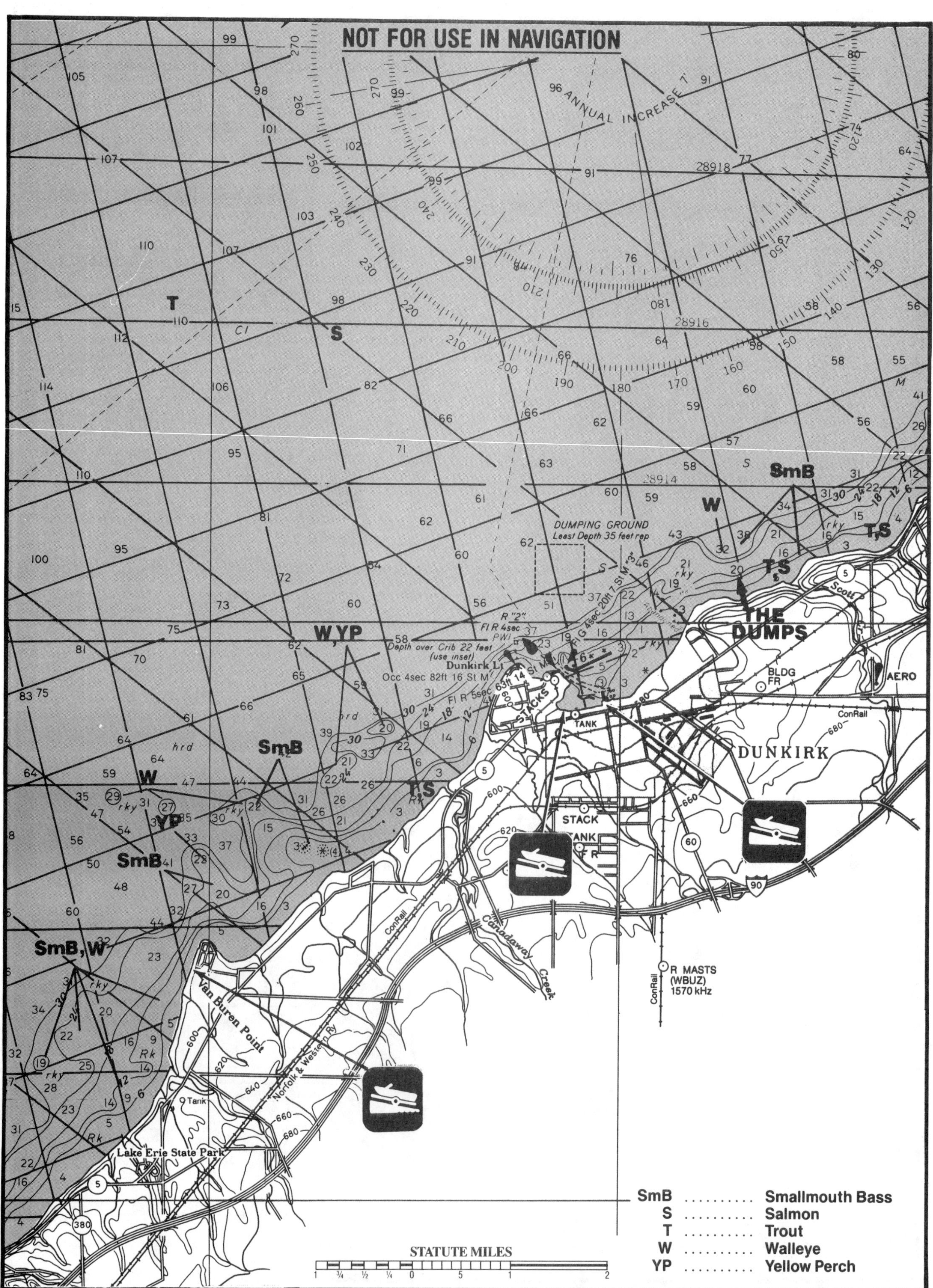

NOT FOR USE IN NAVIGATION
ANNUAL INCREASE 7'
DUMPING GROUND
Least Depth 35 feet rep
Depth over Crib 22 feet
(use inset)
Dunkirk Lt
Occ 4sec 82ft 16 St M
THE DUMPS
DUNKIRK
STACKS
STACK
TANK
BLDG FR
AERO
ConRail
Canadaway Creek
R MASTS
(WBUZ)
1570 kHz
Van Buren Point
Norfolk & Western Ry
Lake Erie State Park
STATUTE MILES
SmB .... Smallmouth Bass
S .... Salmon
T .... Trout
W .... Walleye
YP .... Yellow Perch

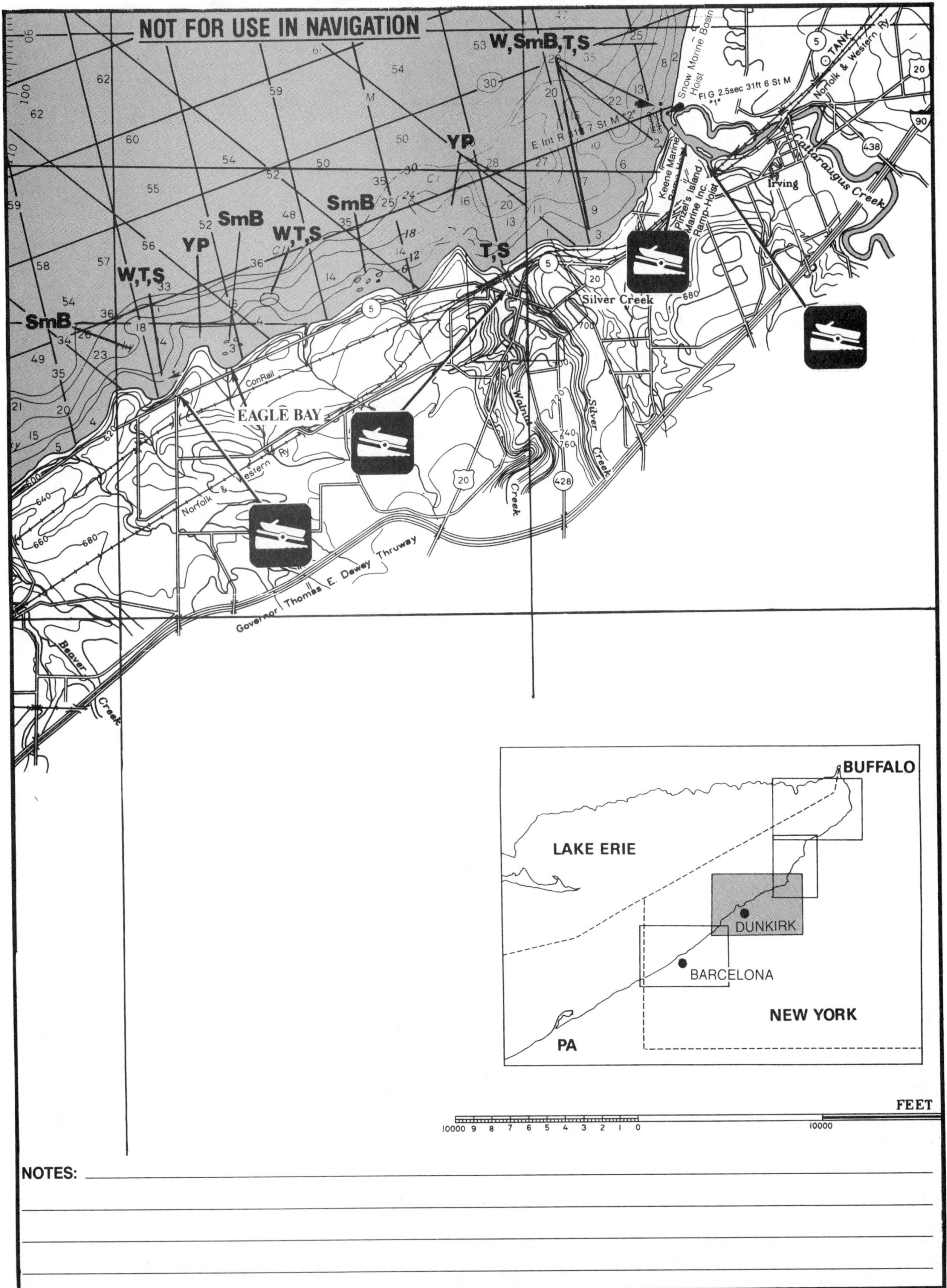
NOT FOR USE IN NAVIGATION
W,SmB,T,S
YP
SmB
W,T,S
YP
SmB
W,T,S
T,S
SmB
EAGLE BAY
Silver Creek
Irving
Cattaraugus Creek
Walnut Creek
Silver Creek
Beaver Creek
Snow Marine Basin Hoist
Keene Marine
Pinzel's Island Marine Inc. Ramp-Hoist
ConRail
Norfolk & Western Ry
Governor Thomas E. Dewey Thruway
TANK
LAKE ERIE
BUFFALO
DUNKIRK
BARCELONA
NEW YORK
PA
FEET

NOTES: ______________________________

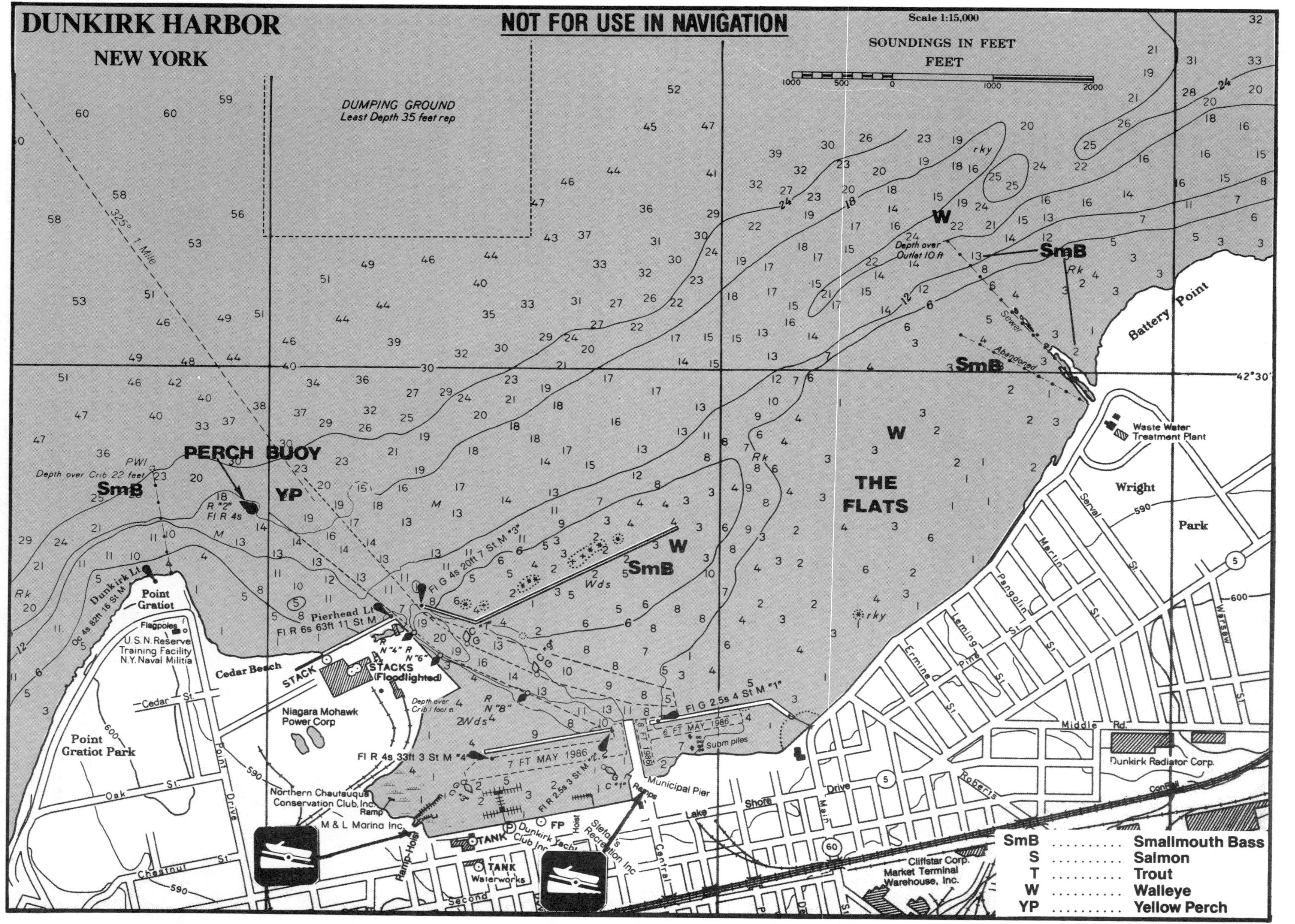

DUNKIRK HARBOR
NEW YORK
NOT FOR USE IN NAVIGATION
Scale 1:15,000
SOUNDINGS IN FEET
FEET
DUMPING GROUND
Least Depth 35 feet rep
325° 1 Mile
PERCH BUOY
YP
SmB
W
THE FLATS
Depth over Crib 22 feet
Depth over Outlet 10 ft
Sewer
Abandoned
Battery Point
42°30'
Waste Water Treatment Plant
Wright Park
Point Gratiot
Dunkirk Lt
Flagpoles
U.S.N. Reserve Training Facility N.Y. Naval Militia
Cedar Beach
Pierhead Lt
STACK
STACKS (Floodlighted)
Niagara Mohawk Power Corp
Point Gratiot Park
Northern Chautauqua Conservation Club, Inc
Ramp
M & L Marina Inc.
Ramp-Hoist
TANK
Waterworks
Dunkirk Yacht Club Inc
FP
Hoist
Stefan's Recreation Inc
Ramps
Municipal Pier
7 FT MAY 1986
6 FT MAY 1986
Subm piles
Dunkirk Radiator Corp.
Cliffstar Corp.
Market Terminal Warehouse, Inc.
SmB .... Smallmouth Bass
S .... Salmon
T .... Trout
W .... Walleye
YP .... Yellow Perch

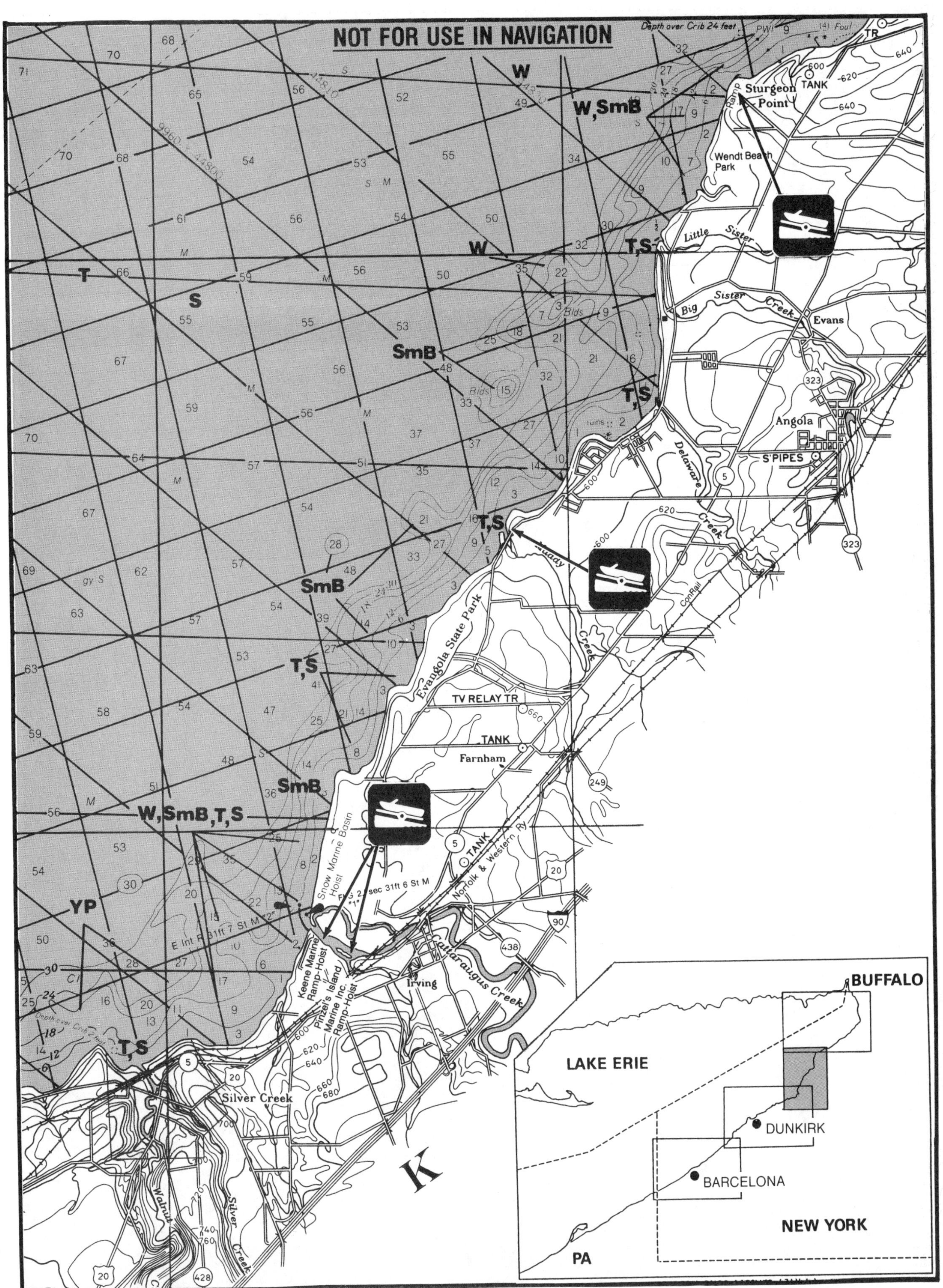

NOT FOR USE IN NAVIGATION
Sturgeon Point
Wendt Beach Park
Little Sister Creek
Big Sister Creek
Evans
Angola
Delaware Creek
Evangola State Park
TV RELAY TR
TANK
Farnham
Snow Marine Basin Hoist
Keene Marine Ramp-Hoist
Pinzel's Island Marine Inc. Ramp-Hoist
Irving
Cattaraugus Creek
Norfolk & Western Ry
Silver Creek
LAKE ERIE
BUFFALO
DUNKIRK
BARCELONA
NEW YORK
PA

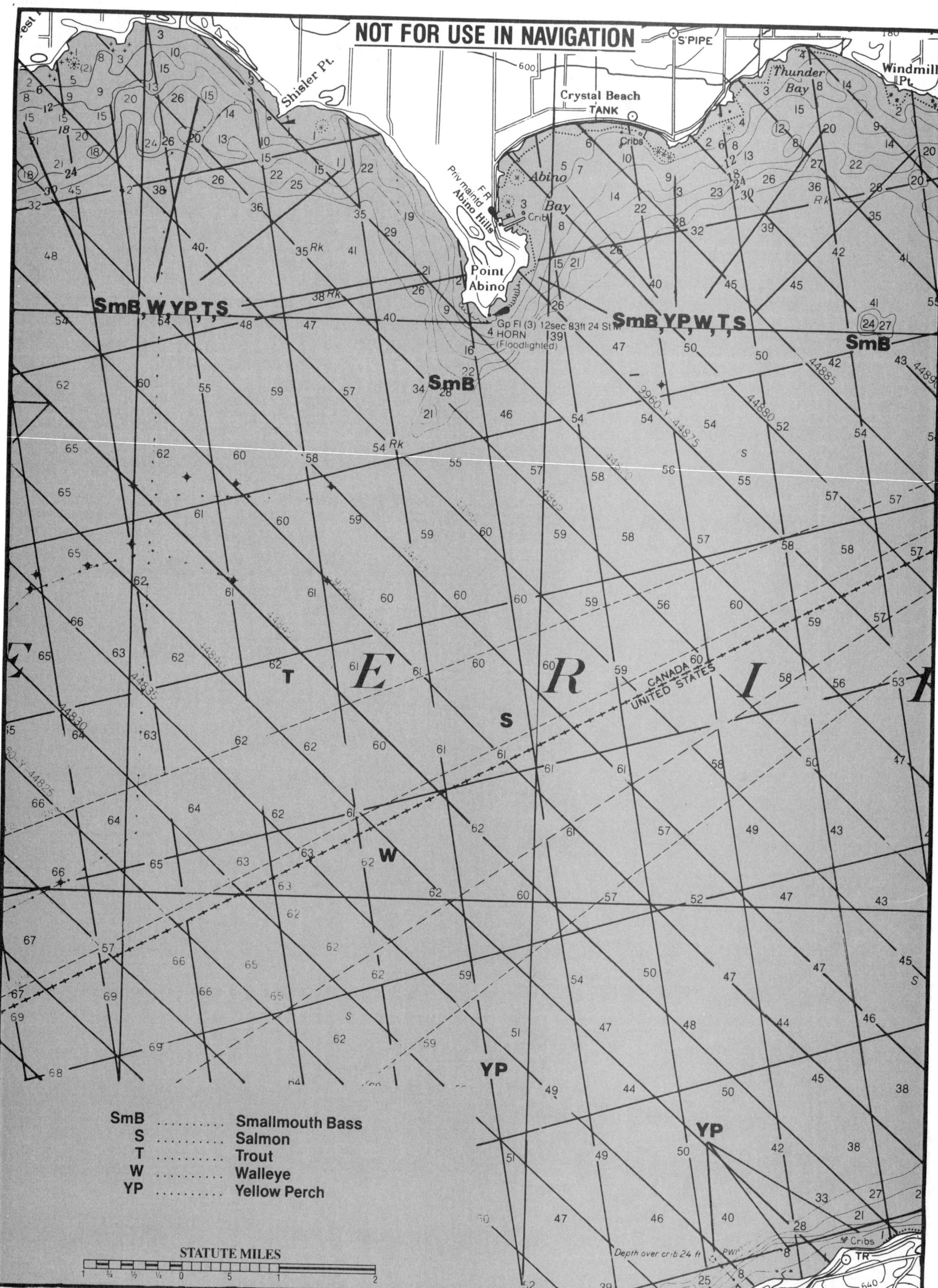
NOT FOR USE IN NAVIGATION
S'PIPE
Shisler Pt.
Crystal Beach
TANK
Thunder Bay
Windmill Pt.
Abino Bay
Abino Hills
F R Priv maintd
Point Abino
Crib
Cribs
Gp Fl (3) 12sec 83ft 24 St M
HORN
(Floodlighted)
SmB, W, YP, T, S
SmB, YP, W, T, S
SmB
T
S
W
YP
E R I
CANADA
UNITED STATES
Depth over crib 24 ft
SmB .... Smallmouth Bass
S .... Salmon
T .... Trout
W .... Walleye
YP .... Yellow Perch
STATUTE MILES

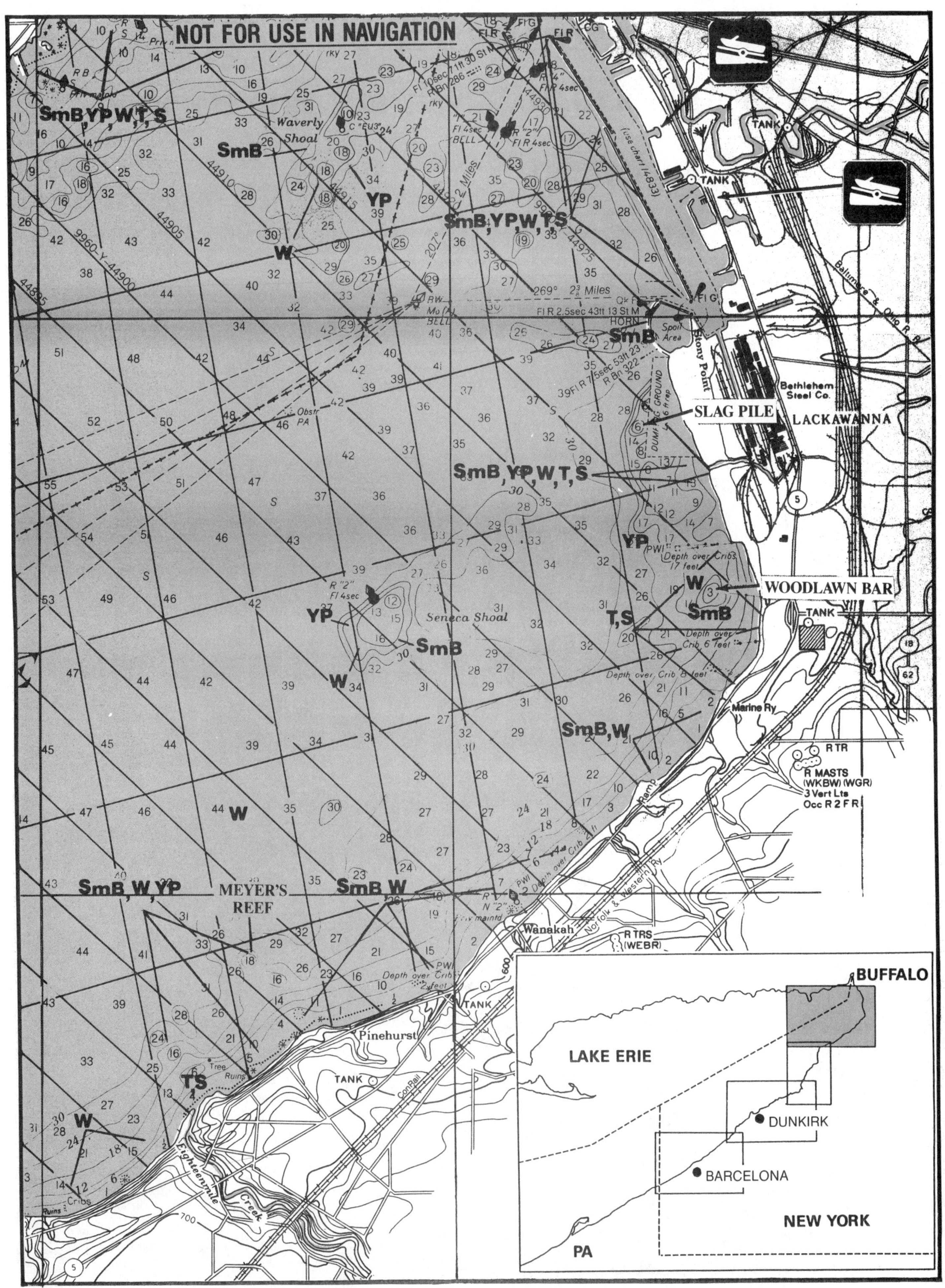

NOT FOR USE IN NAVIGATION
SmB,YP,W,T,S
Waverly Shoal
SmB
YP
SmB,YP,W,T,S
W
Stony Point
Spoil Area
Bethlehem Steel Co.
SLAG PILE
LACKAWANNA
DUMPING GROUND
SmB,YP,W,T,S
YP
Depth over Cribs 17 feet
W
WOODLAWN BAR
SmB
T,S
Depth over Crib 6 feet
YP
Seneca Shoal
SmB
W
Depth over Crib 8 feet
SmB,W
Marine Ry
R MASTS (WKBW) (WGR) 3 Vert Lts Occ R 2 F R
W
SmB,W,YP
MEYER'S REEF
SmB,W
Wanakah
Norfolk & Western Ry
Depth over Crib 2 feet
Pinehurst
TANK
ConRail
T,S
W
Eighteenmile Creek
Cribs
Ruins
Baltimore & Ohio R.R.
BUFFALO
LAKE ERIE
DUNKIRK
BARCELONA
NEW YORK
PA

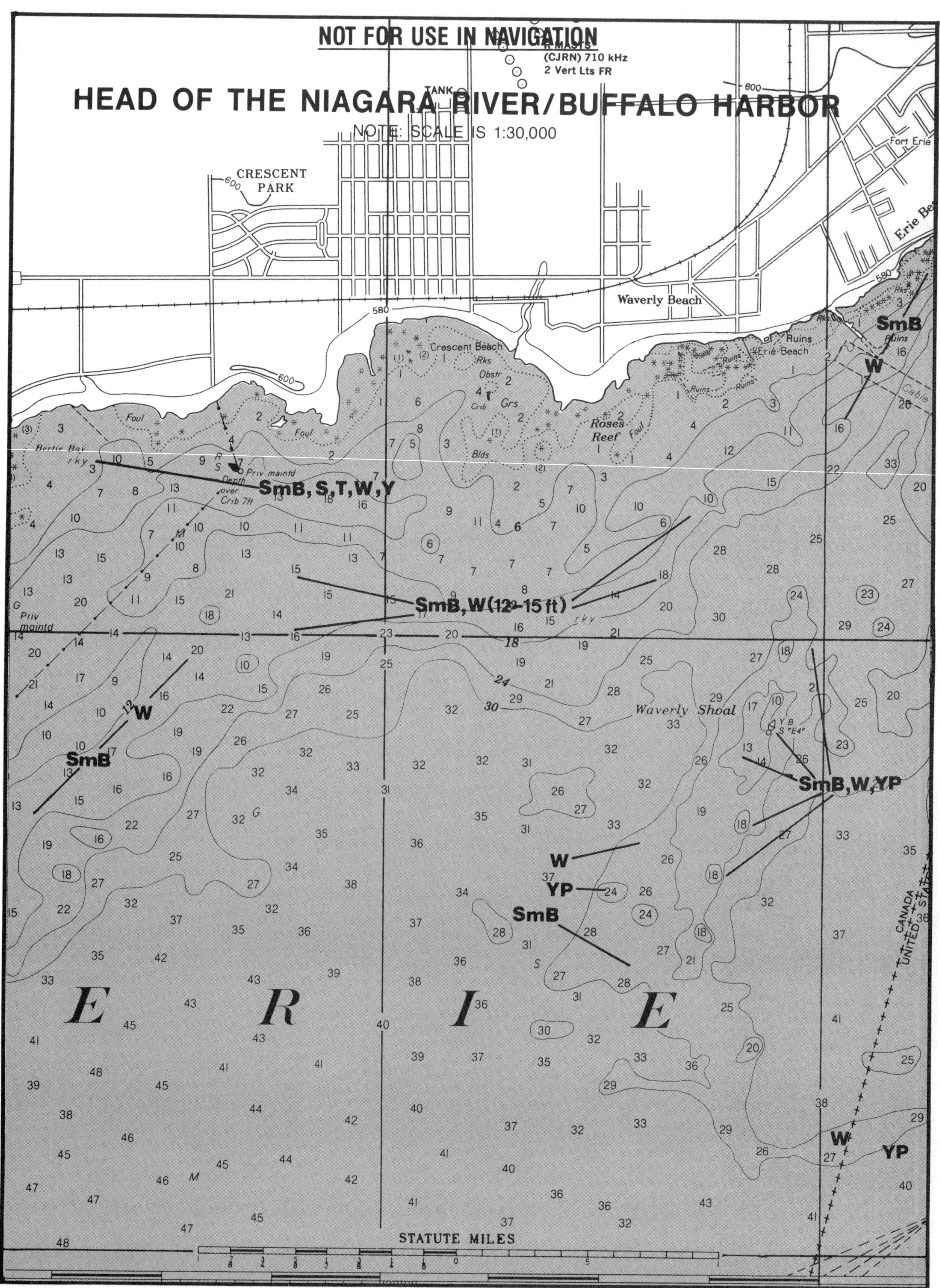
NOT FOR USE IN NAVIGATION
HEAD OF THE NIAGARA RIVER/BUFFALO HARBOR
NOTE: SCALE IS 1:30,000
(CJRN) 710 kHz
2 Vert Lts FR
TANK
CRESCENT PARK
Fort Erie
Erie Beach
Waverly Beach
Crescent Beach
Ruins
Roses Reef
Bertie Bay
SmB, S, T, W, Y
SmB, W (12-15 ft)
Priv maintd
Depth over Crib 7ft
Waverly Shoal
SmB, W, YP
SmB
W
YP
E R I E
CANADA
UNITED STATES
STATUTE MILES

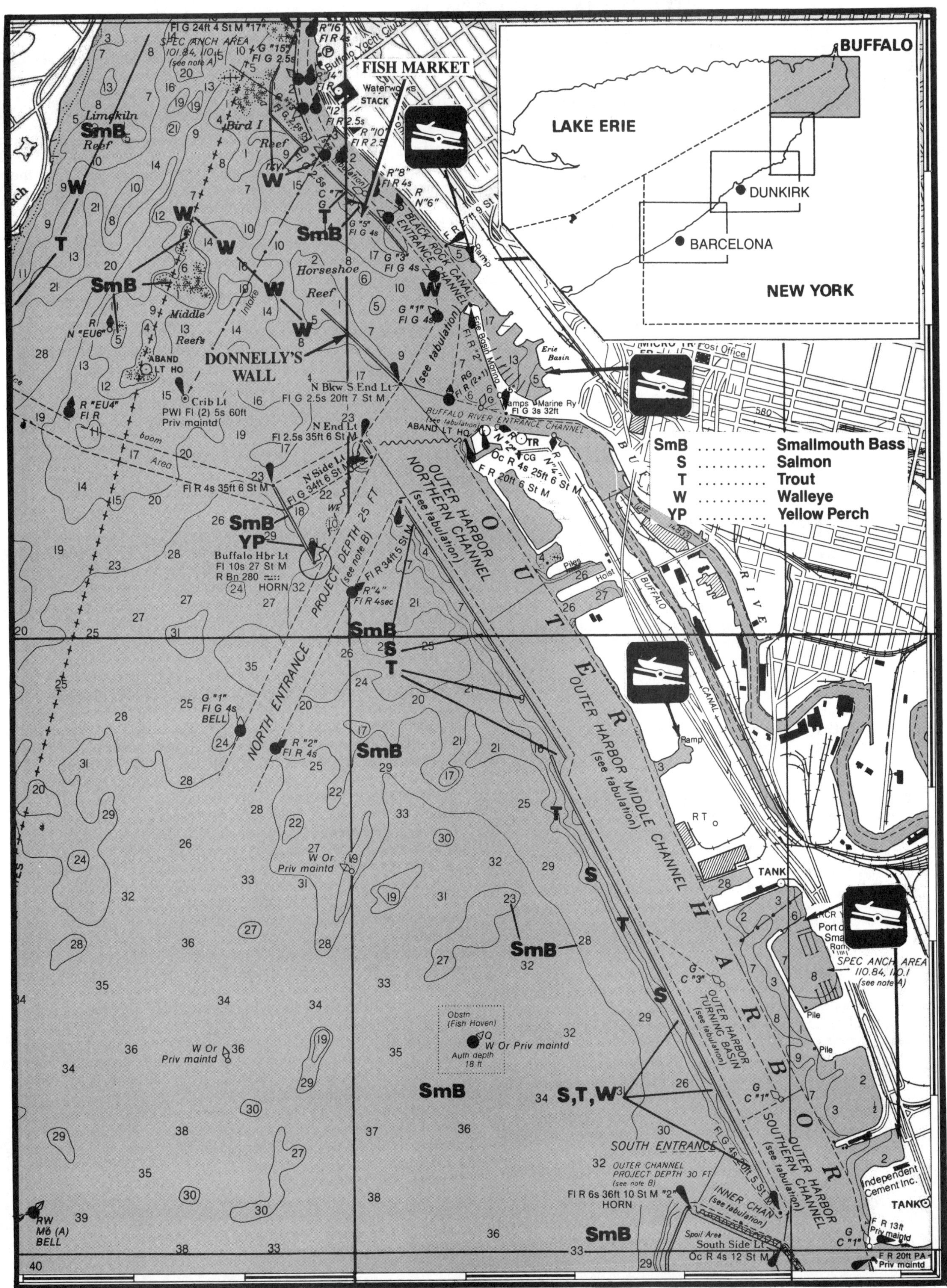
FISH MARKET
BUFFALO
LAKE ERIE
DUNKIRK
BARCELONA
NEW YORK
DONNELLY'S WALL
SmB .... Smallmouth Bass
S .... Salmon
T .... Trout
W .... Walleye
YP .... Yellow Perch
OUTER HARBOR
NORTH ENTRANCE
SOUTH ENTRANCE
OUTER HARBOR NORTHERN CHANNEL
OUTER HARBOR MIDDLE CHANNEL
OUTER HARBOR SOUTHERN CHANNEL
BUFFALO RIVER ENTRANCE CHANNEL
BLACK ROCK CANAL ENTRANCE CHANNEL
Horseshoe Reef
Limekiln Reef
Bird I
Middle Reefs
Erie Basin
Buffalo Hbr Lt
Independent Cement Inc.

NIAGARA RIVER (Upper Section)

Map Coordinates	43° 04′ 25″ 79° 04′ 15″
N.O.A.A Charts	14822 (1:80,000); 14832 (1:30,000)
Location	Erie County, Niagara County
Access	Paralleled by Route 266 and Route 384 (U.S. side); Paralleled by Niagara River Parkway (Canadian side)
Principal Species	Chinook Salmon, Coho Salmon, Brown Trout, Rainbow Trout, Largemouth Bass, Smallmouth Bass, Muskellunge, Walleye, Northern Pike, Yellow Perch, Bullhead, Smelt, Panfish

Access Sites (U.S. side going north to south)

1. Goat Island, off Buffalo Avenue right above Niagara Falls. Shore access only. Caution is advised when fishing this area.
2. Power Vista Turnoff, off Robert Moses Parkway at power plant intakes. Shore access only.
3. Cayuga Park Launch Ramps, on Buffalo Avenue at Cayuga Island. Multiple hard-surface ramps, parking for 50 cars and trailers - no charge.
4. Gratwick Riverside Park, on River Road in North Tonawanda. Multiple hard-surface ramps, parking for 50 cars and trailers, extensive shore access - no charge.
5. Fishermen's Park, on River Road, 1/2 mile south of Gratwick Park. Shore access only.
6. Niawanda Park, on Niagara Street in the City of Tonawanda. Multiple hard-surface ramps, parking for 50 cars and trailers, extensive shore access. Launching by permit only.
7. Isle View Park, on Niagara Street in the City of Tonawanda. Multiple hard-surface ramps, parking for 100 cars and trailers, extensive shore access - no charge.
8. Town of Tonawanda Ramp, at the foot of Sheridan Drive. Double hard-surface ramps, parking for 25 cars and trailers, shore access - fee.
9. Vulcan Street Foot Bridge, Vulcan Street and Niagara Street in Buffalo. Shore access only.
10. Ontario Street Ramp, foot of Ontario Street in Buffalo. Double hard-surface ramps, parking for 75 cars and trailers, extensive shore access - no charge.
11. Broderick Park, foot of West Ferry Street on Squaw Island. Shore access only.
12. Bird Island Pier (aka the breakwall), adjacent to Broderick Park (see above). Newly rebuilt. Caution is advised when fishing from this pier. Shore access only.
13. Lasalle Park, foot of Porter Avenue in Buffalo. Multiple hard-surface ramps, parking for 75 cars and trailers - no charge.
14. Erie Basin Marina, foot of Erie Avenue in Buffalo. Full-service marina, single hard-surface launch ramp, single hard-surface recovery ramp, extensive parking for cars and trailers - fee.

Grand Island Access Sites

Most of the western shore of Grand Island is public property and thus affords anglers extensive shore access. Parking is provided by several public parking areas located on West River Parkway. Additional access is found at:

15. Buckhorn Island State Park, at the northern tip of Grand Island, via West River Parkway or East River Road. Shore access only.
16. Blue Water Marine, on East River Road just north of Beaver Island State Park. Full-service marina, hard-surface ramp - fee.
17. East River Marina, on East River Road in Beaver Island State Park. Limited-service marina, seasonal use only.
18. Beaver Island State Park, at West River Parkway and South Parkway. Limited-service marina, two piers, extensive shore access, seasonal and transient dockage, no launching.
19. Big Six Mile Creek Marina, foot of White Haven Road near West River Parkway. State-operated, limited-service marina, double hard-surface ramps, parking - fee.
20. Big Six Mile Creek, off West River Parkway. At the mouth of the creek there is a small concrete pier providing limited access to the creek and the river.

Access Sites (Canadian side going south to north)

Nearly the entire Canadian shore of the Niagara River is public park land. The only notable exception is right in the town of Fort Erie, and much of this section of the shore line is also accessible to the public. Bank access is, therefore, extensive. To accommodate boaters, a number of small launch ramps are located periodically along Niagara River Parkway. They can be found at:

20. Directly across from Old Fort Erie. Single unimproved, gravel ramp, limited parking - no charge.
21. Adjacent to Nichol's Marina at the foot of Bertie Street. Single hard-surface ramp, limited parking - no charge.
22. Just above Frenchman's Creek. Single hard-surface ramp, limited parking - no charge.
23. Just above Frenchman's Creek. Single unimproved ramp, limited parking - no charge.
24. Niagara Parks Commission Marina. Limited-service marina, single hard-surface ramp, limited parking - fee.
25. One mile below Miller Creek. Single hard-surface ramp, limited parking - no charge.
26. One-eighth mile below Black Creek. Single hard-surface ramp, limited parking - no charge.
27. One-eighth mile below Usher Creek. Single gravel ramp, limited parking - no charge.

The upper Niagara River has long been recognized as one of the most diverse and productive fisheries in the northeast. The upper portion of this waterway (technically, the Niagara is not a river but a strait connecting Lake Erie and Lake Ontario) is generally trough-like, with steep banks, clear water and a rock and gravel bottom. Its depth is seldom over 20 feet, but a portion of the river off Squaw Island (i.e., Thompson's Hole) is reportedly close to 60 feet deep.

The most distinguishing characteristic of the upper Niagara is its current, which in several areas exceeds 10 knots (about 12 miles per hour). This presents something of a problem to boat fishermen who want to concentrate on a particular spot. In order to do so, many successful Niagara River anglers have had to learn a system of drift fishing that utilizes the concepts of range and cross-range. Simply put, a range (the line or position of your drift) is defined by two large objects on land and the position of your boat arranged in such a way that, as you move along your drift, the two objects and your boat remain in a straight line. It is easier to maintain your line of drift if you pick your reference objects either both fore or both aft, not one fore and one aft, of your boat. A cross-range is a hypothetical line that intersects your drift. To get a cross-range, simply select two points on shore that line up momentarily as you proceed down your drift. Thus, when you're drift fishing for bass or muskellunge, the first thing you want to do is determine your range and maintain it. Next, as soon as you hook (not land) a fish, quickly look up and get a cross-range. By doing this you can later determine accurately where you were in the river when you first hooked the fish. This is extremely important to successful fishing in this river. The areas indicated on the Niagara River fishing maps are only meant to be general guides. The actual locations where most fish will be concentrated in the indicated areas are usually very small and easy to miss if you don't have an accurate range and cross-range. After you land your fish, go back and drift over that spot again. Very possibly it holds as number of fish.

In addition to some very stiff currents, there are a number of other problems that anglers have to contend with on this river. They include: very heavy boat traffic, especially on the east branch of the river; an extremely heavy growth of moss, often lasting from the middle of May to the end of July, that can really hamper much of the fishing activity on the river; licensing and regulation differences between the American and Canadian portions of the river; pollution, which is becoming less of a problem here; and several very serious navigational hazards. This last item consists primarily of reefs that are found in the head of the river (the Middle Reefs, Horseshoe Reef, Bird Island Reef, and Limekiln Reef) and just above Niagara Falls (the Carborundum Reef). The waters between the Carborundum Reef and the falls are extremely dangerous and boat access is strictly forbidden on both sides of the river. This restricted zone is indicated by large signs on both shores.

There are a number of areas in the river that deserve special mention. Beginning at the head of the river and moving downstream we have:

Donnelly's Wall

Actually located just outside the river in Lake Erie, this wall dates back to the early days of the Erie Barge Canal. There is an excellent walleye drift running from the west side of this wall to the downstream edge of the Middle Reefs. Just inside the wall is a large weed bed that provides good fishing for walleye, smallmouth bass, and an occasional muskellunge. Boaters should note that the northern end of the wall is anchored on the Horseshoe Reef and caution is advised when approaching this end of the wall.

The Fish Market

Located just out from the southernmost leg of the Bird Island Pier, this is a very popular spot, claimed by many to be the single most productive area of the river. Nearly every species of fish found in the river can be taken here. The northern end of the Fish Market, at the Bird Island Reef, is very shallow and can be especially dangerous during periods of high wind.

The Emerald Channel

Located close to the Canadian shore between Erie Beach and the Peace Bridge, the Emerald Channel is so named because of the clarity and purity of the water. This is an excellent drift for walleye, trout, salmon, and smallmouth bass. Be sure to stay in the deeper portions of the channel, as the edges are very shallow, especially around Limekiln Reef.

Bird Island Pier

This pier forms the boundary between the river and the Black Rock Canal, and was originally constructed as a part of the western terminus of the Erie Barge Canal. The pier, which is known locally as the "Breakwall," is anchored at its northern end on Squaw Island and is accessible via Broderick Park. Several miles in length, it runs as far south as Lasalle Park. During periods of storms or high winds, water levels can rise and wash over the pier, so caution is advised. A popular area for shore-bound anglers, the river side of the breakwall provides good fishing for silver bass, yellow perch, rock bass, rainbow trout, walleye, and sheepshead. In the Black Rock Canal smallmouth bass, yellow perch, sheepshead, and rock bass are common.

Thompson's Hole

Located on the Canadian side of the river midway between the Peace Bridge and the International Bridge, this is the deepest spot in the upper Niagara river, reported to be almost 60 feet deep. The current is very fast here, but by utilizing the proper eddies it is possible to maintain a position over this large depression. Thompson's Hole is more productive on its western side. Nearly every species of fish in the river can be found here.

Strawberry Island

Situated off the southern tip of Grand Island, the shallow waters surrounding this small (and getting smaller) island are highly productive for muskellunge, yellow perch, and smallmouth bass. This is a very popular site for boaters, fishermen, and picnickers in the summer. In the winter, the backbay of Strawberry Island, which is essentially a small pond in the middle of the river, provides good ice fishing for yellow perch, smelt, and northern pike.

Huntley Station

In the spring, numerous fishing boats can be seen tied up to the wall adjacent to the warm-water discharge of this power plant, located just downstream from the launch ramps at the foot of Sheridan Drive. This is often a very productive site for rainbow trout in the spring and fall.

Beaver Island

There are some good bass and muskie drifts just off this tiny island. In the nearby harbor, two small jetties are productive for yellow perch, rock bass, and smallmouth bass in the summer, and fishermen can take yellow perch and smelt through the ice in winter.

Staley's Reef

Situated between Fix Road and Love Road on the west side of Grand Island, this reef offers excellent fishing for smallmouth bass and muskellunge.

Sunken Island

Located directly off the northern end of Baseline Road on Grand Island, this shallow reef is excellent for early season bass. Similar in nature to Staley's Reef, it could also hold a good number of muskellunge.

Navy Island

Lying off the northern end of Grand island, the waters around Navy Island are noted for their excellent bass and muskie drifts. Northern pike can also be taken in this area. Just off the northern tip of this island is a field of large boulders that should be very productive for muskie and smallmouth bass.

The waters around Navy Island are dangerous. The current is swift, especially downstream of the island, and much of the river bed downstream of the island has been scoured to table-flat rock, which won't give an anchor anything to grab on to. You should always have a backup motor on board the boat when fishing in the river, especially in the area between the north end of Grand Island and the Carborundum Reef.

The Carborundum Reef

Located just downstream of Navy Island, this is an excellent location for smallmouth bass. Shallow and very dangerous, you can only fish the upstream half of this reef. The lower half lies within the restricted zone and is off limits to all boaters.

The American Rapids

Because the waters below the Carborundum Reef are both extremely dangerous and off limits, fishing is limited to the areas where fishermen have access to the shore. Two of the best sites are found at the head of Goat Island and behind the Ramada Inn, on Buffalo Avenue in Niagara Falls. Both are excellent for rainbow trout, smallmouth bass, and an occasional palomino trout. In the summer and fall, smallmouth bass can be taken anywhere from shore between the water intakes of the Robert Moses power plant and the Ramada Inn.

What follows are individual treatments of each of the major species found in the Niagara River. This information is meant to be used in conjunction with the Niagara River fishing maps. Because of size limitations, we were forced to use N.O.A.A. Chart 14822 as the base map for the upper river. To get the full use out of the written and map information provided for the river, we strongly suggest that you obtain a current copy of N.O.A.A. Chart 14832. All N.O.A.A. charts can be obtained from the Army Corps of Engineers.

Smallmouth Bass .... Abundant; growth rate good

Smallmouth bass are by far the most important game species in the upper Niagara River. Creel census figures indicate that smallmouth account for approximately 43 percent of the catch in Canadian portions of the river and 12 percent of the catch in U.S. waters. These figures also indicate the relative productivity of the west river versus the east river in terms of this species.

Because they are so abundant in the river, smallmouth bass are usually easy to locate. In the early part of the season, most bass will be found in shallow water, on or near spawning beds. Traditional opening day hotspots include: the waters around Sunken Island and Navy Island; the Carborundum Reef; the shallow portions of Staley's Reef; the shallows off the southern tip of Grand Island; nearly the entire west shore of Grand Island, especially from Cook Point to Diamond Rock and the bay just south of Burnt Ship Creek; the east shore of Grand Island from Buckhorn Island to Spicer Creek; and the Canadian shoreline roughly from Miller Creek to the Peace Bridge.

Recently, the breakwall separating the Niagara River and the Black Rock Canal was rebuilt resulting in a much safer place to fish. Known locally as the Bird Island Pier, the breakwall is one of the most popular and productive fishing areas on the river.

How productive these areas will be is determined in part by weather conditions. If there has been a warm spring, the fish will have begun to move off the spawning grounds and into deeper water by opening day.

By the end of June, most smallmouth bass will have moved out of the shallows into deep holes, and the deeper portions of reefs and breaks. This accounts, at least in part, for the greater productivity of the west river over the east river in the summer. The west river is much deeper and has a more irregular bottom than the east river. To be productive, drift fishing is a must here in the summer. Proven bass drifts are located in the following areas: along both sides of Navy Island; the mid-channel from Diamond Rock to the head of Navy island; Hocter's Hole off Cook Point; close to the Canadian shore, from Black Creek to Bayer's Creek; the deep water off Staley's Reef; the deep water off the Clay Banks; close to the American shore, from Beaver Island to the foot of Oakfield Road; the mid-channel from Rich Marine to Strawberry Island; off the old shipyard at Miller Creek; and from the Peace Bridge to the International Bridge. The exact position of the drifts can only be learned from experience, but if you concentrate on waters 10 to 20 feet deep they should be fairly easy to find. Keep in mind that, although these drifts are often long and cover a lot of water, the actual areas where the bass will be found are usually quite small, often no larger than the average living room. When you first hook a fish be sure to get a quick bearing on your position. Once you've landed the fish, go back to a point on the drift just upstream of where the fish was hooked and try that spot again. Usually the bass will be grouped together, and where you find one fish you should find a few more. Far from being totally inclusive, the drifts listed above are simply those recognized as being consistently productive. All of the sites indicated on the Niagara River bass maps will hold smallmouth some time during the summer. Even the shallow areas traditionally considered to be early season haunts can be productive in the summer if conditions are right. At dusk and dawn bass move into these areas to feed. By drifting close to shore during these feeding periods, some anglers have had spectacular results, especially in the late summer.

Around the beginning of September, bass fishing in the east river really comes into its own. The drifts in the west river will continue to hold fish, but they will be eclipsed by the areas indicated between Sunken Island and Spicer Creek. Anglers should be able to find some truly superb bass fishing in the east river as late as October and even into November, if the weather cooperates. Smallmouth will continue to feed actively until the water temperatures fall into the low 50s.

The following article by Rick Kustich details many of the techniques used to take smallmouth from the upper Niagara River. Rick is a long-time resident of Grand Island and a veteran bass fisherman.

UPPER NIAGARA RIVER BASS FISHING

By Rick Kustich

The Upper Niagara is host to some very good smallmouth fishing. Although the average size of an upper river smallmouth is somewhat smaller than that of those living in Lake Erie, the action often times is hot and heavy, and fish in the 3 to 4 pound range are not uncommon. Typical of smallmouths is their hard-fighting and often acrobatic style, and upper river fish are no exception. They are a lot of fun to catch. Largemouth bass also inhabit the upper Niagara, but not nearly in the numbers that smallmouth bass do.

As the season opens on the third Saturday of June, the smallmouth are just leaving their spawning nests and can be found in relatively shallow water close to shore. This is a good time to take smallmouth without the aid of fishing from a boat. Wading in the water is usually required so that the angler's cast can reach the fish's holding water. The upper river can be easily waded in most areas.

Bass can be caught at this time of year by both spin casting and fly fishing. For spin fishing, a light- to medium-action 6 1/2-foot graphite rod built for 1/8- to 1/2-ounce lures is a good choice. A quality spinning rod with a smooth drag that can be adjusted easily and quickly is a must for landing big bass in the current of the river. I fill my reel with either 6- or 8-pound-test line. Although I like to use 6- or even 4-pound-test line because of its lower visibility, I generally use 8-pound-test line for its strength. This comes in handy for getting lures out of the ever present snags caused by the river's bottom structure, and its good to be prepared for the off-chance of hooking into a Niagara River muskie.

When spin fishing near the shore, a variety of lures catch bass. Various Mepps spinners in gold or pearl finish, usually in sizes 2 or 3, work well. Other lures such as CP Swings, Rooster Tails, Phoebe Fish, and Little Cleos in gold or silver finish also take fish. Cast these lures slightly upstream and work them slowly near the bottom. Jigs bounced along the bottom can be deadly at times. Again, cast slightly upstream and retrieve with a jigging action. Twister tail jigs in chartreuse, black, and purple are a good bet, while bucktail or synthetic hair jigs in purple, black, or natural deer hair to imitate a crayfish also produce well. Jig heads of 5/16 or 3/8 ounce work best.

Additional spinner baits and other conventional largemouth bass lures catch fish at this time of year and throughout the season. Drifting a worm or nightcrawler also accounts for some smallmouth. Fly fishing for upper river bass is a productive and enjoyable method for taking early season fish. I use a 9 1/2-foot graphite rod built for an 8-weight fly line, with a single action fly reel having a smooth drag system. I use a sink tip line to get near where the bass are holding. A full sinking line would also work, but the sink tip provides for better line control. I use a 5- to 6-foot leader tapered to 8-pound-test line, and I sometimes add one split-shot about 2 feet above the fly. My choice of flies includes Clouser's Deep Minnows, wooly buggers in black or brown, muddler minnows, and crayfish patterns. The flies are tied on size 4 to 1/0 hooks. The method used to fish these flies is simple. Just cast slightly upstream and allow the fly to sink. Distance is important here and that is one reason I prefer a long rod. I normally wade in the water up to my waist. Practice on getting the fly out as far as possible. As the fly sinks, retrieve it slowly as it swings in the current. Point the rod tip toward the point where the line meets the water and keep the tip low, allowing very little slack in the line. The fly should be near the bottom at all times. Hits can come as hard strikes or subtle takes, so it is important to concentrate on the point where the fly line enters the water, looking for any hesitation in movement that could signify a take. The hook should be set by striking with the line hand and raising the rod simultaneously any time the line makes an unnatural movement. If the fly hangs up on the bottom too often, then the split-slot or fly is too heavy or the sink rate of the line is too fast.

Access to the river for early season smallmouth fishing is good. Nearly the entire west branch of the river is bordered by state land. The angler can gain access from Buckhorn State Park to Alt Boulevard by parking along West River Parkway and wading the river. There is also access in Beaver Island State Park. Access to the east river of the river is much more restricted, since most of the land adjacent to the river is privately owned. However, this poses no real problem, since the west branch has better fishing and scenery. Popular spots for early season fishing include the waters off Little Beaver Island in Beaver Island State Park, the overlook parking areas at Fix and Whitehaven roads, and Buckhorn State Park, where access can be gained to the lower portion of the east river and where the fishing can be very good at times. The entire west branch of the river seems to be good, so experiment on your own to find the best locations.

Largemouth bass can also be taken at this time of year using spinnerbaits, crankbaits, and spinners. The largemouth action is found mainly along the weeds beds around Strawberry Island, the point of Beaver Island State Park, the upper part of the east river, and in any bay or creek mouth where water that has little or no current can be found. For the most part, this fishing has to be done from a boat.

Beginning around the middle of July, the fishing close to shore slows down. Although evenings can still be good as the bass move back to shallow water to feed on chubs and crayfish, activity isn't nearly as consistent as earlier in the season, since the fish are now moving into deeper, cooler water. It is during this period, about the third or fourth week of July, that the bass fishing really heats up. It is also during this time that fishing from a boat becomes almost a necessity. Although fishing close to shore from a boat can be good early in the season using the spin- and fly-fishing techniques described above, I prefer wade fishing early on. Not only does the fishing get hot at this time, but most of the bottom moss will have left the river, making fishing from a boat much easier.

When fishing from the boat, I use the same rod and reel that I use wade fishing. I spool it with 8-pound-test line for the same reasons stated above. A level wind reel would also work well.

Drift fishing is probably the most effective method of bass fishing from a boat on this river. When used in drift fishing, jigs are even more deadly than they are wade fishing. Use the same jigs when fishing from a boat as you would for early season wade fishing. I have had particularly good success with the chartreuse twister tail and the crayfish patterns. I normally tip the hook of the jig with a piece of nightcrawler or pork rind for added texture and scent. The jig should be bounced along the bottom in a slow jigging manner. Again, hits can come in the form of hard strikes or soft takes, so that concentration on your line is important. Drifted Flatfish and Quickfish are also consistent bass producers. They can be fished using a three-way swivel and dropper rig or off a straight line weighted with a split-shot. These lures should also be fished on or near the bottom. I use lures in silver, gold, and some natural colors like crayfish. I also tip these with a worm. Additionally, I replace the treble hook on these lures with a single hook. I actually land more fish on a single hook, and it does less damage to fish that I wish to release.

If the three-way swivel rig is used for fishing on this river, tie a dropper consisting of a lighter line off the swivel for the sinker. Then if the sinker hangs up on the bottom, the lighter line will break and you won't lose the lure. The leader from the swivel to the lure should be of the same Pound-test as the line on the spool and should be 2 1/2 to 4 feet long. Pencil sinkers used with this rig seem to avoid more snags than other types of sinkers. If the lead is simply added to the line it should be 2 to 3 feet above the lure and a snap swivel should be used to reduce line twist.

Drifting with bait is another effective method of taking smallmouth bass, and it often accounts for big fish. Crayfish, especially softshells, hooked though the tail using a size 4 or 2 baitholder hook and fished on the three-way swivel rig described above can be deadly all season long. Live chubs and modocks hooked through the lips and rigged in the same manner as crayfish is an exciting way to fish and is a method that consistently catches big smallmouth. This is especially true in the late summer and fall when the fish tend to move a little closer to shore to feed and to fatten up for the winter.

The upper Niagara River is a bass fisherman's dream come true. Big smallmouth like the one held by Rick Kustich are common in the upper river. Photo courtesy Rick Kustich.

While drift fishing the upper Niagara River from a boat, winds can be an important part of a day's success. Strong or gusty breezes can knock the boat off its natural drift and negatively affect the presentation of the bait or lure. A wind that pushes the boat up against the current is the worst case, since it makes it difficult to maintain contact with your lure. Other winds require adding more weight to get to the bottom. Such winds provide a good opportunity to effectively use a Flatfish or Quickfish, since the boat is moving a little faster than the current, and this gives the lure added action. Because of the winds, a well-equipped upper river boat has either an electric motor or a set of oars to try to offset the wind. A good electric motor will allow the angler to get a good drift even on windy days.

Another option for windy days while fishing from a boat is trolling. The angler can expect aggressive strikes from smallmouth bass when the lure is properly presented. Either trolling against the current at a creeping speed or across current at a slow to moderate speed can be productive. Since smallmouth will be found on or near the bottom most of the time, it is important that the lure be trolled in this area. This may require that weight be added to the line using split-shot or a three-way swivel rig. As for lures, a wide variety will take fish, from Mepps spinners to Rapalas, Rattle Traps, and Bombers.

My favorite way of fishing for bass from the boat is fly fishing while drifting. For this approach I like to locate bass in 10 to 20 feet of water. I use a very fast-sinking sink-tip line with a 6-foot leader, a little longer in very clear water conditions. I use weighted flies to assure myself that I am getting to the strike zone. As for patterns, I prefer wooly buggers in purple, chartreuse, and black, along with crayfish patterns, and my favorite, the Clouser's Deep Minnow. The technique is relatively simple. Cast enough line so that the fly can reach the bottom. Once on the bottom, I add some action. For wooly buggers and crayfish patterns, I work the fly along the bottom in a jigging fashion as the boat drifts along. When using a Clouser's Deep Minnow and other streamer patterns, I twitch the fly along the bottom for a few minutes and then begin a slow retrieve back to the boat. Sometimes the strike is subtle and other times outright vicious. A 7- or 8-weight rod is good for this type of fishing. Needless to say, bass are a lot of fun to catch on a fly rod.

As far as where to fish when fishing from a boat, this is the easy part. Over the years I have become convinced that there are bass to be found almost everywhere throughout the entire upper river. There are certainly spots that are more productive than others. This is almost always the result of favorable structure. Through experience and the use of a depth or fish finder, such structure can be readily found. Favorable structure is usually in the form of a change in bottom contour such as a reef. The change does not necessarily have to be dramatic. Even a change of one or two feet can create a good holding area. A depth finder helps determine structure, and fishing experience will tell the angler if it is good holding water or not. Once found, good structure will hold fish year after year.

I have found the west river to provide a little better bass fishing than the east river. This probably has to do with better bottom structure in the west river. As far as specific areas go while fishing from a boat, the water off Beaver Island State Park and around Staley's Reef are always good producers. One word of warning: While fishing the west river, the boundary line between New York State and Ontario runs very close to the New York side of the river. To be able to fish some of the best bass water in the river, it is advisable to obtain an Ontario license.

Muskellunge .... Common; growth rate good

Muskie fishing is fairly unique among the angling arts. Because it is common to go for several trips and not catch anything, and then have a very successful day, success has to be measured over the course of the season, not by the individual fishing trip.

A volatile mixture of speed, strength, and unpredictability wrapped in a mystique that few anglers ever even attempt to penetrate, muskellunge, or muskies as they are commonly called, are the largest game fish found in the Niagara River. Studies indicate that the potential exists here for a truly first-class muskie fishery. In terms of the quantity of fish available, this already exists. While an estimated 100 hours are spent for each muskellunge caught in North American waters, the Niagara River boasts an incredible 9 hours spent per muskie boated. But that still means the single most important factor in successful muskie fishing is putting in your time.

Unfortunately, most of the muskies caught here are relatively small. In most muskie lakes and rivers, a trophy-size muskie is at least 50 inches. A typical 50-inch fish will weigh about 30 pounds in the fall, a little less in the spring. Very few of the muskies in this river will ever attain a length of 50 inches. A 40-inch fish is considered a trophy here. The average Niagara River muskie measures about 28 to 32 inches and weighs just under 10 pounds. Specimens over 20 pounds are rare. A muskie of 36 inches is a good size fish in this river.

The principal reason for this lack of large, trophy-size muskellunge is believed to be overharvesting of the larger fish. There is a large number of local anglers who are very good muskie fishermen. Some fishermen on the Niagara River catch 100 or more muskies in a year, and they harvest a good percentage of the larger muskies in the river. However, this situation could be changing for the better due to increased angler awareness of the problem and a growing tendency for fishermen to return muskies to the river.

Another way that the average angler can help improve the muskie fishing in the river is to check each fish caught for tags, regardless of whether you intend to keep the fish or release it. A tagging study was initiated in 1977. About 400 fish were tagged near the base of the dorsal fin by Muskie Inc., in cooperation with the D.E.C. The study is still going on, though few anglers are still participating. Often the tag will be obscured by a small sore or mucus, but cleaning this off will reveal the tag's identification number. Record the number and send it to:

New York State Department of Environmental Conservation
600 Delaware Avenue
Buffalo, New York 14202

Be sure to include the length of the fish and approximately where it was caught, as well as your name and address in case the D.E.C. requires further information on the fish.

At the opening of the season on the third Saturday in June, the muskies are usually still spawning or have just finished spawning, and will be found in shallow or slack water near patches of early weed growth. The fish will often be a bit less than their normal voracious selves at this time, a result of their somewhat violent spawning habits. It takes the fish a week or two to recover from this.

The most productive waters for the first few weeks are naturally going to be the areas where spawning takes place. These include: the shallows around Navy Island, especially on the downstream side and the west side; the shallow portions of the Triangle area; the waters around Sunken Island; and the shallower portions of Staley's Reef. It is possible that many other areas of the river that have shallow, slack water will also hold at least some muskies early in the season. It is very common for people that live on the west river to see muskies resting under their docks early in the season.

The temperature of the water is usually still fairly cold when the season opens, and there are three important rules to remember when fishing for muskies in cold water: Fish slow, fish shallow, and fish with small lures.

Spinners are the most commonly used lures in the early part of the season, and the temperature of the water will determine the size of the spinner: the colder the water the smaller the spinner. Size 4 or 5 Mepps-type spinners are often used at this time of year. Some of the people at Muskie, Inc. don't feel that color is a critical factor in muskie fishing. They believe that presentation is much more important, and that people often become attached to a particular color mainly out of habit. While this may be true, there are some color patterns that are more popular than others. Spinners with silver, black, gold, and chartreuse spinner blades with or without red dots, and bucktails in brown, red, or black, or undressed hooks are all very popular with muskie fishermen.

Some anglers start the season casting in 8 to 10 feet of water, but in some areas fish can be taken in as little as 3 feet of water. Because an important ingredient in successful muskie fishing is

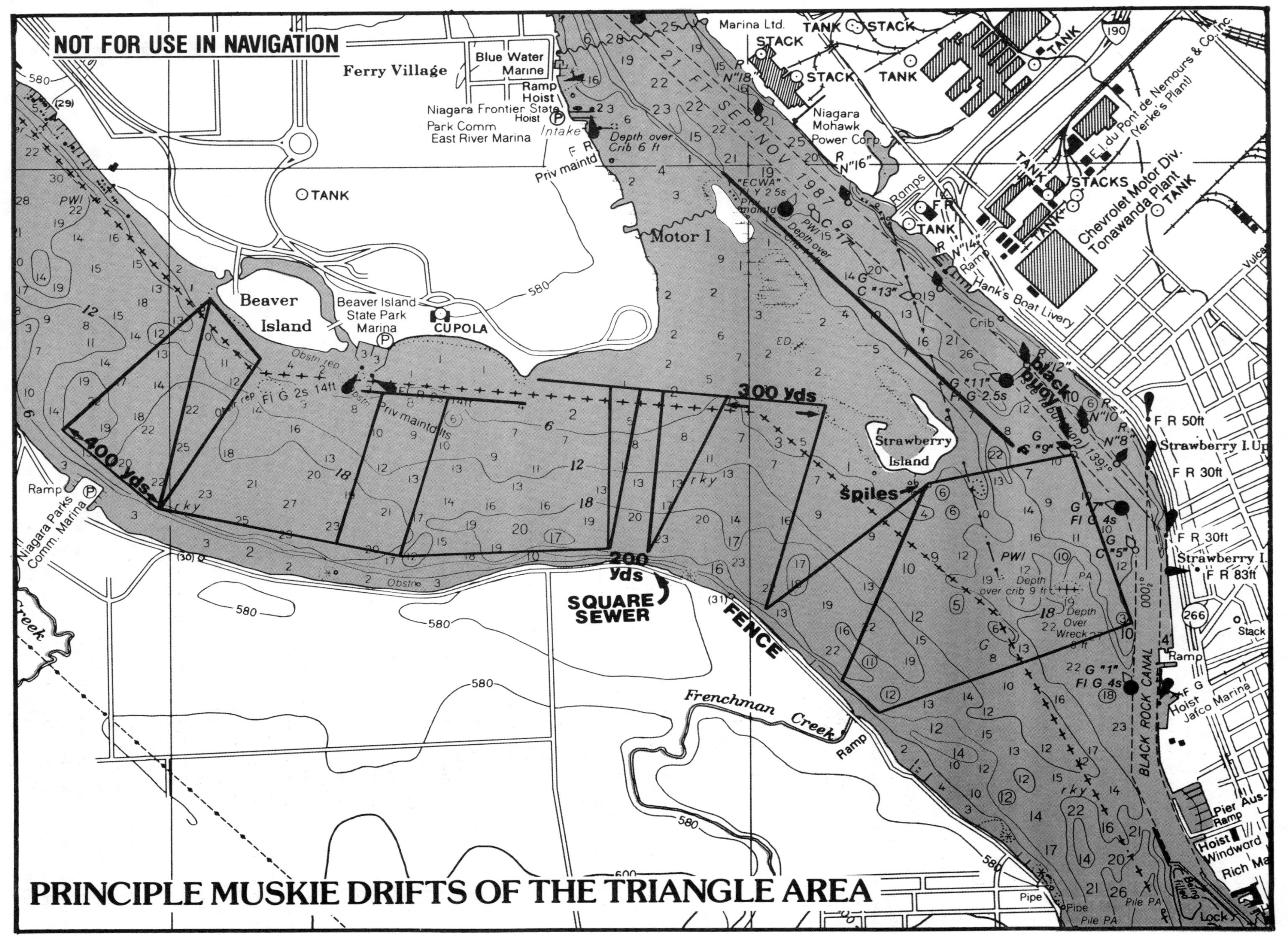

PRINCIPLE MUSKIE DRIFTS OF THE TRIANGLE AREA

The muskies found in the upper Niagara River are a different strain than those found in Lake Chautauqua. The markings on a Niagara River muskie, like the fish displayed here by Ed Bennett, tend to be broken up, giving the fish a spotted appearance. Muskies from Chautauqua Lake have a more stripped appearance. Photo courtesy Tim Herrmann.

covering as much water as possible, random casting over an area rather than concentrating on a specific spot is usually the best approach all through the season.

Many muskie fishermen on the upper Niagara River don't use leaders, or if they do they use small ones. However, leaders probably don't bother muskies very much. If they want to strike a lure, they will do so, regardless of the leader. These fish usually don't have a lot of time to scrutinize their prey or your lure.

If you don't use a leader, it is extremely important to keep your line taut when the fish hits the spinner. If you don't use a leader and the fish inhales the spinner, you stand a good chance of being cut off, regardless whether or not your line is taut. But if the fish has the spinner in the corner of its mouth, you must keep the line taut to prevent the fish from cutting you off by rolling on the line.

Another popular method for taking early season muskies is trolling. Troll in the same areas discussed above in 5 to 15 feet of water, but initially limit your fishing to areas between the first weedline and the shore. Troll in such a way that the lure stays above the emerging weeds. Navy Island, Strawberry Island, Staley's Reef, and the waters off the Holiday Inn are all good trolling areas early in the season. Spinners, small plugs such as Pikie Minnows, and Flatfish are good trolling lures. Run the lures a bit slower than you normally would in the early part of the season. The fish are usually sluggish at this time of year and have not fully recuperated from the rigors of spawning.

The rod and reel used for this kind of fishing should be capable of bringing the fish to the boat rather quickly. Use medium-size open face spinning reels, 6- to 7 1/2-foot medium-action spinning rods, and 10- to 14-pound-test line. If you attempt to bring a muskie in on light spinning gear, you are taking a big chance on killing the fish, especially the larger fish, by having to fight it for an extended period of time. The anglers I spoke with recommend using a stiff rod and heavy line to get the fish to the boat before it is entirely fought out. Muskies are known to fight so hard and long that it kills them.

Live-bait fishing is a third method of muskie fishing that can be employed here, but fortunately it is seldom done on this river. There are two reasons it is not often used. To be done properly, live bait can only be fished in slack water areas such as those mentioned above. More importantly, there is a high mortality rate associated with it. Very often the muskie will ingest the bait and be hooked far deeper than if it were taken with a spinner or plug. The ensuing fight then does considerable damage to the fish, often killing it.

By the end of June or early July, the muskies will have moved off the spawning grounds. Most knowledgeable anglers feel that muskie are well distributed in the river during the summer and early fall. They can migrate all over the river, though favoring certain areas, and will even move out into the lake. Smaller muskies tend to frequent the outside edge of shallow (8 to 10 feet) weedlines and are found in tighter groups than the larger, more solitary muskies. Larger muskies tend to be found in deeper water, up to 25 feet, and close to the bottom.

The most consistent areas in the summer include the Triangle, Staley's Reef, and the waters around Navy Island. The drifts and trolls indicated on the map of the Triangle area are all productive during the summer. Concentrate on water 10 to 20 feet deep that has some type of structure such as deep weedlines, drop-offs, points, or boulders. These will often be indicated either by current breaks or isolated patches of riffles on the surface of the water, but a good depth sounder is invaluable in locating such areas. The fish will use boulders and trenches to their advantage to keep themselves in or near feeding lanes but out of the current.

Though the best structure is found in the west river, there are some sections of the west river that muskie fishermen usually avoid. They don't usually fish the deep channel that runs between the northern end of Beaver Island State Park and Staley's Reef. It's too deep, narrow, and fast for easy trolling, and these same characteristics make it difficult for the muskies to hold in this water. It is easier for the muskies and the bait fish to hold in the wider, slower parts of the river. Also, few people fish for muskies on the west river between Big Six Mile Creek Marina and the southern tip of Navy Island. There are some muskies in that area, and some anglers do occasionally give it a pass, but it is not one of the prime muskie haunts.

For those willing to do a little investigating, the east river is a relatively unknown area in terms of muskies, and it does have some potential. Large portions of the east channel of the river are fast, narrow chutes that are too fast for the fish to hold in; thus, the east river has far fewer muskies in it than does the west river. But some areas are worth checking out. Try the break off Sunken Island, which is very similar in structure to Staley's Reef, a top muskie haunt in the west river. And near the Grand Island Holiday Inn the water widens out and slows down, making it possible for muskies to hold in this area as well.

The usual method for taking muskies in the summer is trolling, using either the traditional cross-current troll (covers a lot of area) or the upstream troll (covers less area but gives greater hooking power). Trolling downstream is not recommended. Because of the speed of the current in the river, if you try to troll downstream the lure runs too fast, too deep, and gets hung up too often. Trolling cross-current and letting the natural drift of the current work you downriver is probably the most common trolling technique. Start trolling in 16 to 18 feet of water and troll to the other side. You may drop into 20 to 30 feet of water. At the end of the drift, go directly back to the start of the drift and do it again. It is too slow to attempt to troll both cross-current and upstream at the same time.

The muskies in the river don't seem to suspend very often. They tend to be found within 2 feet of the bottom. This could be due to the fact that the current is not as strong near the bottom as it is higher up in the water column. To get the lure down to the fish many of the serious muskie fishermen on the river use color-coded 30- to 40-pound lead-core line when trolling. You must constantly change the amount of line you have out as the depth of the water changes, but trolling with lead-core line allows you to partially compensate for factors such as depth, current, and wind.

Anyone trolling on the river in the early summer is going to have to put up with a serious problem in the form of moss. The moss starts to become a factor in trolling in late June and continues to be a problem until late July. It fouls up the lure a lot; on some days, it can foul your lure in 30 seconds. You can tell if your lure is covered with moss by its lack of action. The severity of the moss in a particular area is largely dependant on the direction and speed of the wind, so what was free of moss one day might be choked with moss the next. In an attempt to keep the moss off the lure, some anglers put a treble hook on the line about 3 feet up from the lure. The hook snares some of the moss before it can get to the lure, but quite often these moss catchers don't work very well. At times there is just too much moss for trolling to be effective.

A key factor to keep in mind when muskie fishing is light intensity. In the summer and fall many of the fish will tend to be found along weedlines during periods of low light. But when it is sunny, the fish will often seek shade right in the weeds. Then trolling over the tops of submerged weed beds can be very productive.

Toward the end of summer, Niagara River muskie fishing shifts into high year. Diary studies by Muskie, Inc. show that late September and October are by far the best times for taking this toothsome predator. As the river begins to cool off, most muskies will start to move back into shallower waters, primarily those frequented in the spring (i.e., the Triangle and Navy Island). Concentrate on what shallow weed beds remain or shallow rock piles for the best results. The fishing will be good through the month of October, and if the weather cooperates, muskies can even be taken well into November.

Trout and Salmon .... Common; growth rate very good

Though the upper Niagara River is not itself stocked with trout or salmon, it has benefited greatly from the trout and salmon being stocked in Lake Erie by the states of New York and Pennsylvania, and the Province of Ontario. Rainbow trout and brown trout can be taken with a fair amount of regularity in the river, primarily along the Canadian shore above Strawberry Island. In addition, a golden-hued palomino trout, stocked in Lake Erie by Pennsylvania, is always a possibility. For those restricted to American waters, the most productive trout fishing areas include: the breakwall; the warm-water discharge of Niagara Mohawk's Huntley Station, 1/2 mile below the foot of Sheridan Drive; the waters off the Glass boat house, located one mile below the mouth of Gun Creek; and the rapids at the head of Goat Island (shore fishing only!).

Rainbow trout, and to a lesser extent brown trout, can be taken in the Niagara River all year long, with spring and late fall usually being the most productive seasons. In fact, according to recent creel census figures, rainbow trout are the fourth most commonly harvested species in the river during the summer, at least in Canadian waters.

Coho and chinook also constitute a significant fishery here, but it seems that the productive salmon areas are rather restricted, with most fish being taken between the head of the river and the International Bridge. Coho, by far the more abundant of the two species, can be found in the river from late August through early May, while Chinook are available in late summer and fall.

The following articles, originally prepared by M. T. Creel of Trout Unlimited, tells you practically everything you need to know to successfully fish for trout and salmon in the upper Niagara River.

American Side

According to Len Deletti of Trout Unlimited, browns, rainbows, cohos, and chinooks can be legally caught in the city of Buffalo itself from the breakwall along the Niagara River. You can even get there by Metro Bus! Len claims a 5 1/2-pound rainbow and says he has seen even larger fish taken. You get there via Ferry Street, where there's parking available, and you can fish from the foot of Ferry Street upstream on the breakwall to the Peace Bridge.

Though trout are not stocked in the Niagara River, brown trout pictured at left, and rainbow trout are caught regularly. Photo courtesy Rick Kustick.

The map at left, taken from a 1923 nautical chart, shows the configuration of Strawberry Island as it was before gravel mining was started. The map at right, taken from a current nautical chart, shows how the island has deteriorated as a result of such operations. The ensuing erosion is continuing apace at present and threatens the very existance of the island. Of concern to fishermen are the fertile spawning grounds for game fish (muskellunge and smallmouth bass) and panfish that lie adjacent to Strawberry Island and along the northern tip of Grand Island. These could be severely damaged or entirely destroyed if Strawberry Island was to be washed away.

Len advises that the bait fisherman using worms, minnows, or egg sacks try the wall at the foot of Ferry Street (along Broderick Park) if the kids are along because there's a very strong and swift current along the breakwall itself. Using sinkers weighing 3/4 to 2 ounces (Len uses a long lead wire, tied on with thread so that it will break free when snagged), cast out into the river and let the eddy swirl your line back to the wall, bumping along the bottom. Then lift your line and let it eddy out again. You'll hang up on the bottom frequently and loose a few hooks, but hooks are cheap and the fish are big and worth it.

For the spinning and fly fishermen, there's better fishing upstream near the Peace Bridge. It's a long and sometimes wet and slippery walk, so Len advises a hiking staff and boots. If you own a boat and want to avoid the walk, there is an alternative way. You can launch your boat at the foot of Porter Avenue and go directly to the wall, mooring your boat on the rings set into the wall, or pulling the boat up on the wall itself.

The dirtier the weather, says Len, the better the fishing. A north wind, which pushes the water back into the lake, is best for the angler. The best times to fish here are the two hours after sunrise and the last two hours of the day. For lures, he recommends a Rooster Tail spinner in fluorescent pink. Cast it upstream and work it back along the bottom. You can also use worms. A long rod helps keep the lure away from the wall.

In this area both wet and dry flies are effective, especially a large (1/2- to 3/4-inch) caddis fly, called a sand fly locally. A tan or fawn colored caddis with a yellow body is a good bet, but caddis of several colors hatch in the area and the big browns feed heavily on them. Len also advises trying large green nymphs. You might also wish to try his secret method - a walking troll. Cast your fly or spinner out and walk upstream, slowly trolling the lure through the pockets and crevices in the wall. You might just entice a lunker from his hole.

On late spring and summer evenings rainbows - some in the 4 and 5 pound category - rise to dry flies, and big brown trout are taken as well. A small size 16 or 18 brown caddis has been a very effective fish getter.

The walleye fishing in the upper Niagara River is a far cry from its former glory days, but there are times when it isn't bad. In the spring and early summer, fishing at night along the breakwall or the wall at Fort Erie can be productive, as this angler shows.

Canadian Side

To fish the Canadian side of the Niagara River, you'll need a Canadian license, but for the price you'll get the chance to catch rainbows up to 14 pounds and brown trout up to 6 pounds.

For the shore-bound angler, there's parking and good fishing available just across the Peace Bridge. The best lures, according to Wayne Hadley, (Niagara River angling expert and biologist, formerly at SUNY Buffalo) are 3/4-ounce Johnson Sprite spoons in silver and blue or plain silver, and No. 3 Mepps spinners with or without a chunk of nightcrawler on the hook. The best spots include: the wall upstream from the Peace Bridge going toward the lake and downstream from the bridge at the point where the power line crosses (good worm fishing); behind Happy Jack's, where you can wade out in chest waders and cast your spoon and spinner (and where Wayne claims a 4 1/2-pound brown); at the vacant lot and cribbing about 100 yards downstream from Happy Jack's (the back eddy at the cribbing is very productive with worms); across from Thompson's Hole and just downstream; and further downstream all the way to Frenchman's Creek. For the fly fisherman, try casting a dry caddis fly behind Happy Jack's . . . the results may be shocking!

For the man with the boat, the fishing is even better, Wayne says, with rainbows up to 11 pounds coming to the net. He recommends a 14-foot or larger boat and at least a 15-horse-power motor for fighting the strong current. Launching ramps are available at the foot of Ontario Street and at the town of Tonawanda ramp at the foot of Sheridan Drive. The best lures are Johnson Sprites and K-0 Wobblers (blue and silver). Fish upstream from the Peace Bridge (for shallow-draft boats only), about 50 to 75 yards offshore, casting both towards the wall and the river. Then try drifting downstream along the wall, keeping your lures close to the bottom.

Drift fishing for coho on the river requires a special rig utilizing a three-way swivel. Tie your line (15-pound-test mono) to one eye, and tie 14 to 16 inches of 15-pound-test mono to another eye and attach that line to your sinker with an overhand knot that will break free when hung up. To the third eye, tie 30 inches of 15-pound-test mono and attach an X-4 silver Flatfish. The secret is to fish the lure close to the bottom, as far from the boat as possible without hanging up, by bumping your weight along the bottom every couple of seconds. The amount of lead to use (from 1/2 ounce to 3 ounces) will vary according to wind speed and direction, current speed, and the drift characteristics of your boat, so you'll need to experiment to find the right weight formula. Wayne says the best drifts are: from the power lines downstream to Thompson's Hole; about 20 to 75 yards offshore; from Thompson's Hole downstream to the International Bridge, in mid-river; from the International Bridge downstream to Canadian Customs, right up against the concrete wall; and from Customs downstream 1/2 mile, from 15 feet to 50 yards offshore. The current is slower here, so Wayne recommends crawlers instead of Flatfish ... He says it's more productive, but the fish will be smaller (1 1/2 to 2 pounders).

Yellow Perch . . . . Common; growth rate fair

In the opinion of many of the older anglers we spoke with, the current population of yellow perch in the Niagara River is greatly reduced from previous levels, but these fine-tasting fish are still one of the most abundant species found in the upper river. More common in Canadian waters than American, the only really consistent perch grounds are now located along the Canadian shore, between the Peace Bridge and the International Bridge. On the American side, the waters off Squaw Island and Riverside Park are seemingly the top producers of perch. The other areas indicated on the Niagara River perch maps will all hold fish, but the action will often be spotty.

Yellow perch can be taken from the river all year, but according to Canadian creel census figures there is a marked increase in the number of perch caught beginning in the month of August. This is probably due to a concentration of the fish into the limited deep water areas of the river. Another fairly productive period is during the winter, when protected portions of the river freeze over, giving ice fishermen a chance to ply their sport. Fishing with small jigs tipped with perch eyes, mousie grubs, or small pieces of a worm can be very effective in the winter. Small minnows fished on tip-ups also work very well. Productive ice fishing areas include the backbay of Strawberry Island, the marinas at Beaver Island and Big Six Mile Creek, or any other protected harbor where anglers have access.

Northern Pike .... **Uncommon; growth rate fair**

At one time, northern pike were an important species in the Niagara River, but a number of factors have combined to reduce the quality of this fishery to the point where today it is marginal. The major culprits are probably range reduction, parasites, and the need of northerns to utilize ever-diminishing creek habitats for spawning. The few northerns that are now taken are usually found in or very near stream mouths, marinas, or bays. They are also found in most of the streams that feed into the Niagara River.

Early summer and fall are the most productive seasons for northern pike, and the bay in Strawberry Island still offers anglers the opportunity to take these voracious fighters through the ice. Overall, the best bet for northerns in this river are the areas associated with Burnt Ship Creek and Woods Creek at the northern tip of Grand Island.

Most Niagara River northerns are small (4 to 5 pounds), but occasionally a bragging-size fish of 10 to 12 pounds is taken.

Walleye .... **Uncommon; growth rate good**

Once quite common in the upper Niagara, walleye are now a marginal fishery in most of the river. The areas indicated on the Niagara River walleye map actually correspond to what were once traditionally good walleye drifts, but most of these are no longer very productive. They have been included in this guide in the hope, fed by the resurgence of walleye in the eastern end of Lake Erie, that these great-tasting members of the perch family will again be a common catch in the upper Niagara River. Of the areas that remain productive, all are located south of the International Bridge.

In the spring and early summer, shore fishermen often do especially well fishing at night from the wall on the Canadian side above the Peace Bridge. Boaters can usually take a few walleye by trolling the Fish Market or the drifts that run roughly from Erie Beach (Canadian side) to the Peace Bridge, and from the west side of Donnelly's Wall to the northern side of the middle reefs. Thompson's Hole, located directly out from Broderick Park (on Squaw Island) is also a good bet for walleye, especially from the Canadian side of this deep hole.

Additional Species

In addition to those mentioned above, a number of other species can be found in the Niagara River. Most prominent among these are rock bass. Possibly the most abundant species in the river, these tasty panfish can be found almost anywhere, from shallow, rocky shorelines to deep, cold holes. A mainstay of shore-bound anglers, rock bass are taken in abundance off the Bird Island Pier, the wall at Broderick Park, the breakwall at Beaver Island Marina, and the wall at the foot of Ontario Street. Another popular quarry of shore fishermen are white, or silver, bass. Travelling in large, closely packed schools, white bass often engage in feeding frenzies. Try the wall at Broderick Park or the Bird Island Pier for what is often some very fast action. Bullhead, one of the first fish caught in the spring, are common in stillwater sections of the river. The backbay of Strawberry Island and the wall at the western end of Buckhorn Island are both good producers of these fine tasting fish, as are most creek mouths. Later in the year, as the water warms, black crappie, pumpkinseed, and blue gill will be found in these slack waters. In the winter, many of these still-water areas freeze over, providing anglers a chance to take smelt and other panfish through the ice. The marina at Beaver Island and the backbay of Strawberry Island are the most popular locations, but almost any frozen bay or harbor should produce well. In the early spring, smelt can be dipped in the river. Good areas include around boat docks, recessed sections of the shoreline, and most stream mouths. Just off the water treatment plant on Squaw Island is often an especially good location for smelt. Rounding out the species found in the river are the very numerous carp, eels, suckers, and sheepshead.

NOTES: ______________________________

____

____

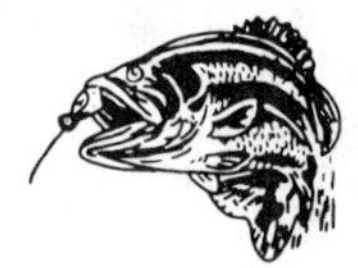

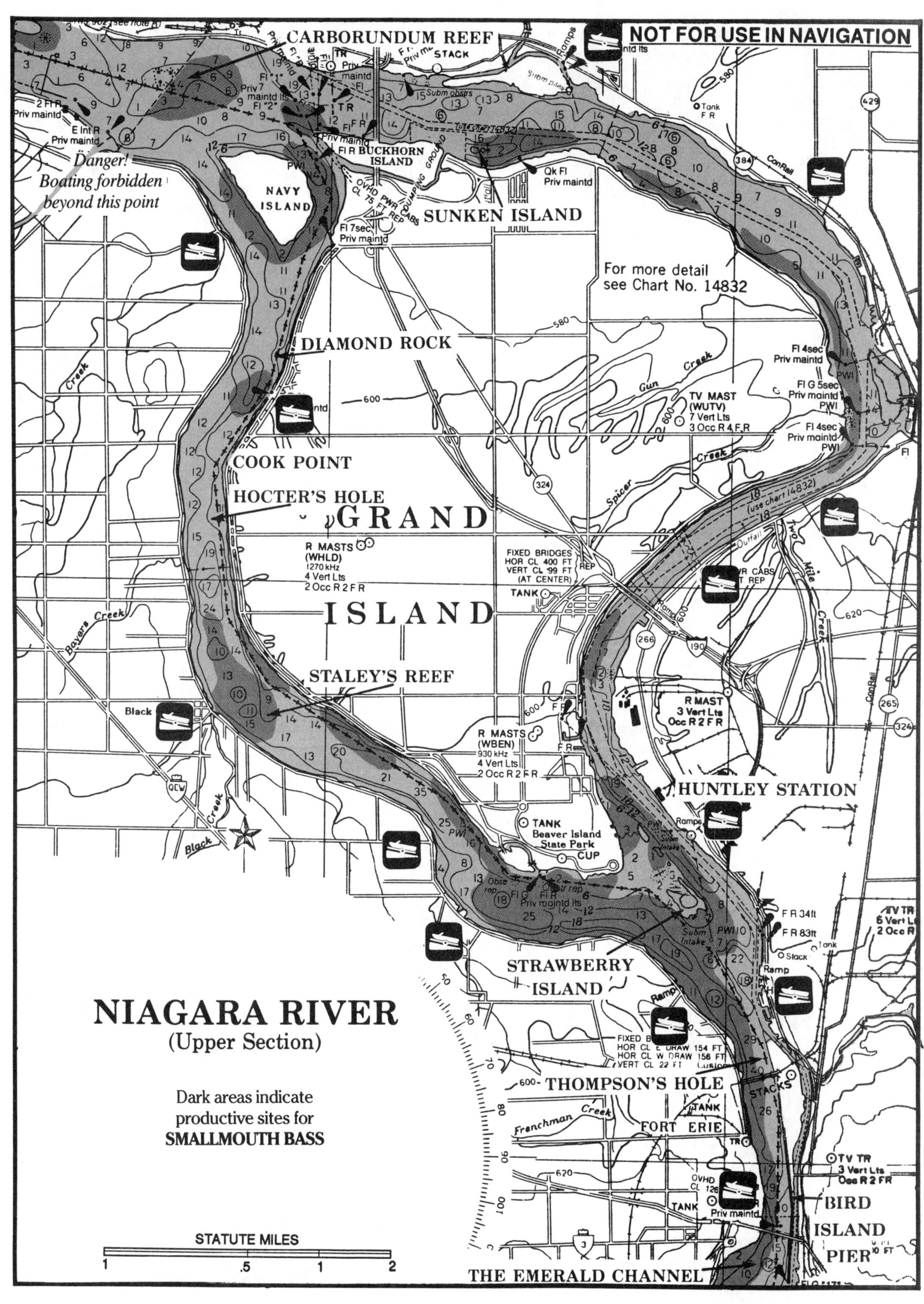
NOT FOR USE IN NAVIGATION
CARBORUNDUM REEF
BUCKHORN ISLAND
NAVY ISLAND
SUNKEN ISLAND
Danger! Boating forbidden beyond this point
For more detail see Chart No. 14832
DIAMOND ROCK
COOK POINT
HOCTER'S HOLE
GRAND ISLAND
STALEY'S REEF
HUNTLEY STATION
Beaver Island State Park
STRAWBERRY ISLAND
THOMPSON'S HOLE
FORT ERIE
BIRD ISLAND PIER
THE EMERALD CHANNEL
NIAGARA RIVER
(Upper Section)
Dark areas indicate productive sites for SMALLMOUTH BASS
STATUTE MILES
1 .5 1 2

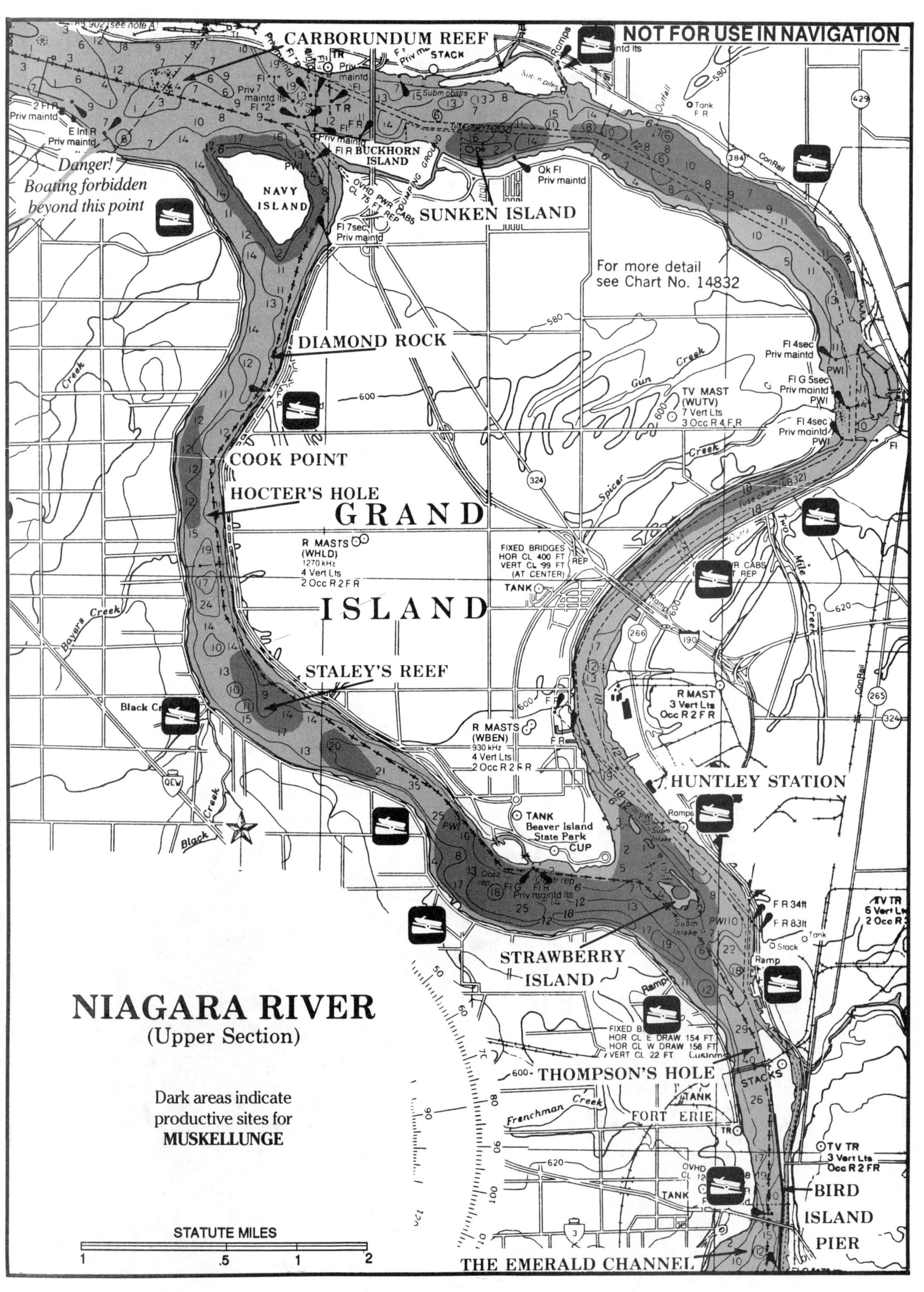
NOT FOR USE IN NAVIGATION
CARBORUNDUM REEF
BUCKHORN ISLAND
NAVY ISLAND
Danger! Boating forbidden beyond this point
SUNKEN ISLAND
For more detail see Chart No. 14832
DIAMOND ROCK
COOK POINT
HOCTER'S HOLE
GRAND ISLAND
STALEY'S REEF
HUNTLEY STATION
Beaver Island State Park
STRAWBERRY ISLAND
THOMPSON'S HOLE
FORT ERIE
BIRD ISLAND PIER
THE EMERALD CHANNEL
NIAGARA RIVER
(Upper Section)
Dark areas indicate productive sites for MUSKELLUNGE
STATUTE MILES

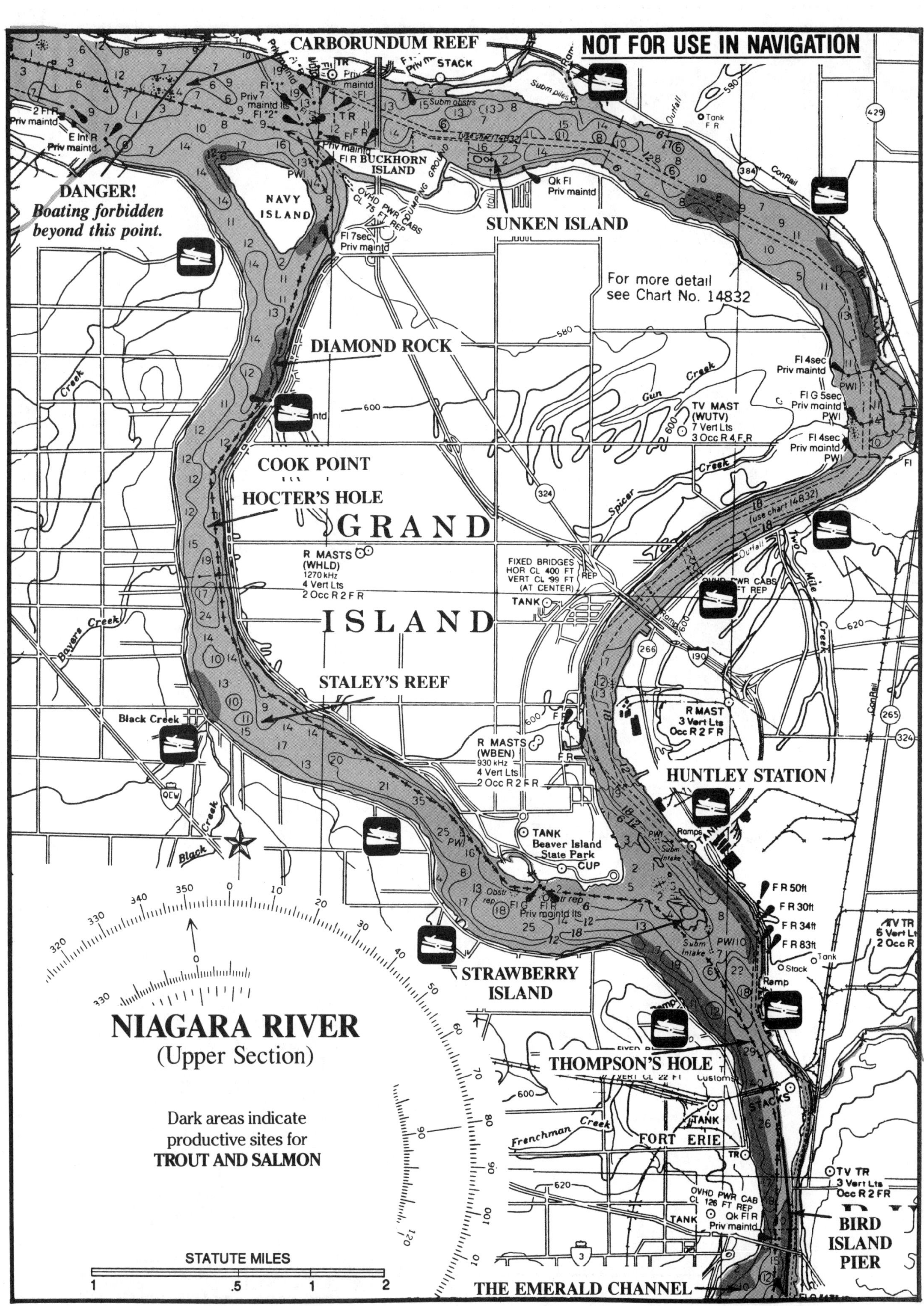

NOT FOR USE IN NAVIGATION
CARBORUNDUM REEF
DANGER!
Boating forbidden beyond this point.
NAVY ISLAND
BUCKHORN ISLAND
SUNKEN ISLAND
For more detail see Chart No. 14832
DIAMOND ROCK
COOK POINT
HOCTER'S HOLE
GRAND ISLAND
STALEY'S REEF
Black Creek
HUNTLEY STATION
Beaver Island State Park
STRAWBERRY ISLAND
THOMPSON'S HOLE
FORT ERIE
BIRD ISLAND PIER
THE EMERALD CHANNEL
NIAGARA RIVER
(Upper Section)
Dark areas indicate productive sites for TROUT AND SALMON
STATUTE MILES

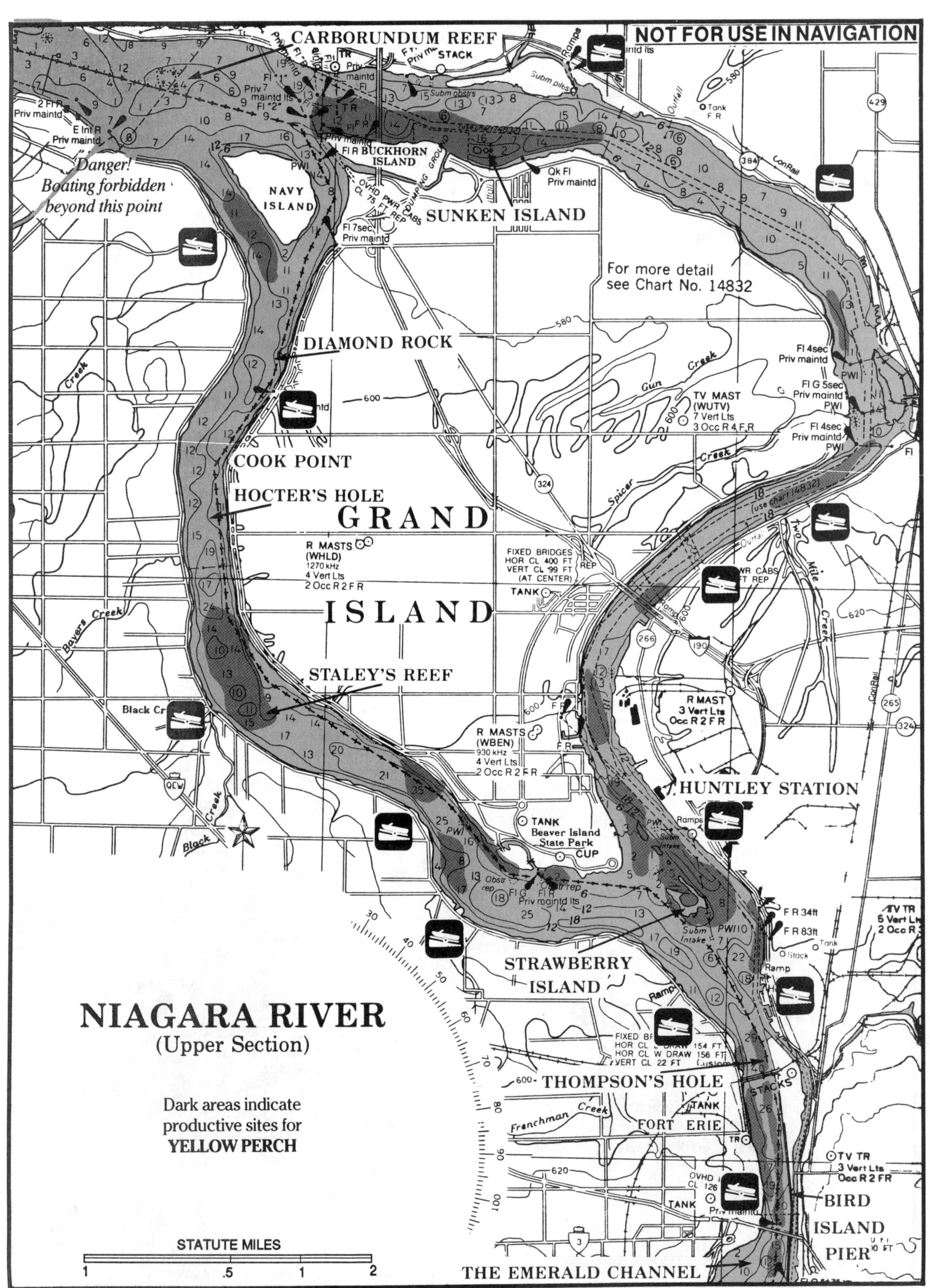
NOT FOR USE IN NAVIGATION
CARBORUNDUM REEF
BUCKHORN ISLAND
NAVY ISLAND
Danger!
Boating forbidden
beyond this point
SUNKEN ISLAND
For more detail
see Chart No. 14832
DIAMOND ROCK
COOK POINT
HOCTER'S HOLE
GRAND
ISLAND
STALEY'S REEF
HUNTLEY STATION
Beaver Island
State Park
STRAWBERRY
ISLAND
THOMPSON'S HOLE
FORT ERIE
BIRD
ISLAND
PIER
THE EMERALD CHANNEL
NIAGARA RIVER
(Upper Section)
Dark areas indicate
productive sites for
YELLOW PERCH
STATUTE MILES
1 .5 1 2

NOT FOR USE IN NAVIGATION
CARBORUNDUM REEF
BUCKHORN ISLAND
NAVY ISLAND
Danger! Boating forbidden beyond this point
SUNKEN ISLAND
For more detail see Chart No. 14832
DIAMOND ROCK
COOK POINT
HOCTER'S HOLE
GRAND ISLAND
STALEY'S REEF
HUNTLEY STATION
Beaver Island State Park
STRAWBERRY ISLAND
THOMPSON'S HOLE
FORT ERIE
BIRD ISLAND PIER
THE EMERALD CHANNEL
NIAGARA RIVER
(Upper Section)
Dark areas indicate productive sites for NORTHERN PIKE
STATUTE MILES

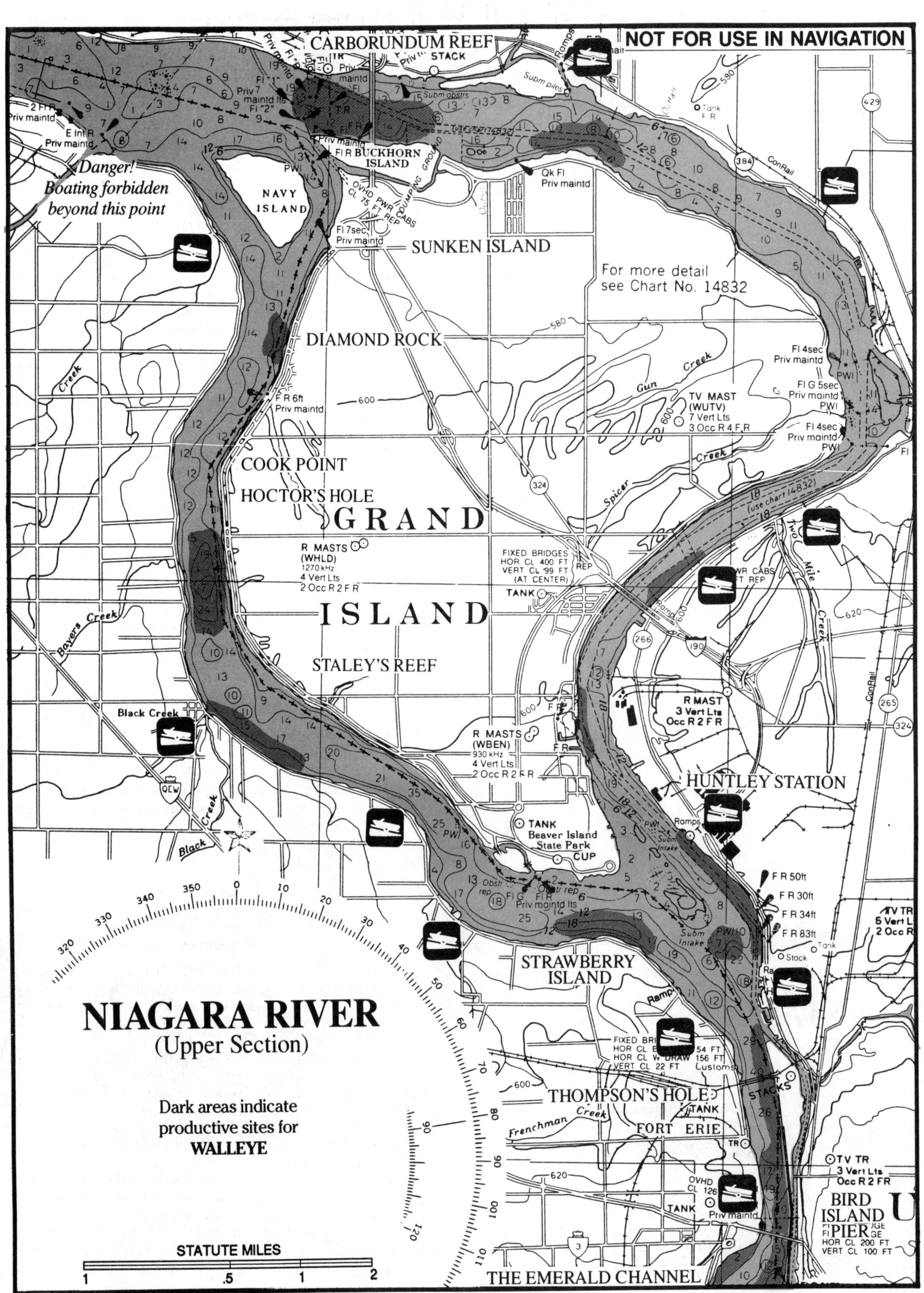

NOT FOR USE IN NAVIGATION
CARBORUNDUM REEF
BUCKHORN ISLAND
NAVY ISLAND
Danger! Boating forbidden beyond this point
SUNKEN ISLAND
For more detail see Chart No. 14832
DIAMOND ROCK
COOK POINT
HOCTOR'S HOLE
GRAND ISLAND
STALEY'S REEF
Black Creek
HUNTLEY STATION
Beaver Island State Park
STRAWBERRY ISLAND
THOMPSON'S HOLE
FORT ERIE
BIRD ISLAND PIER
THE EMERALD CHANNEL
NIAGARA RIVER
(Upper Section)
Dark areas indicate productive sites for WALLEYE
STATUTE MILES

THE NIAGARA RIVER (Lower Section)

Map Coordinates	43° 16′ 00″ 79° 04′ 10″
NOAA Chart	14816 (1:30,000 scale)
Location	Lake Ontario upstream to Niagara Falls
Access	Paralleled by the Robert Moses Parkway and Route 18F. See below.
Principal species	Brown Trout, Lake Trout, Rainbow Trout, Chinook Salmon, Coho Salmon, Northern Pike, Smallmouth Bass, Smelt, Walleye, Yellow Perch, Panfish

Access Sites (U.S. side)

1. Fort Niagara State Park, Route 18F, north of Youngstown. Double hard-surface ramps, parking, limited shore access. Park user fee mid-May to mid-September.
2. Village of Youngstown Ramp, off Water Street in Youngstown. Single ramp open to village residents only.
3. Joseph Davis State Park, Route 18F, between Youngstown and Lewiston. Convenient, but limited, access to the river via a fishing/observation pier.
4. Lewiston Guard Park, foot of Water Street in Lewiston. Double hard-surface ramp, parking, limited shore access - no charge.
5. Artpark State Park, foot of South Fourth Street in Lewiston. Extensive sections of the river are accessible from several paths that start in the park and run north and south along the river. The southern path runs almost to the Robert Moses Power Project. Stair access to the lower river is available in the park at the base of the observation tower.
6. State Power Authority Pier, located off Hyde Park Boulevard. This new fishing pier provides excellent access to the river. The road is open to foot traffic only.
7. Devil's Hole State Park, off the Robert Moses Parkway, between Niagara Falls and Lewiston. Long, steep stairways leads to a path that runs north and south, providing access to the river between the power project and Whirlpool State Park.
8. Whirpool State Park, off the Robert Moses Parkway, north of Niagara Falls. A long steep stairways leads to path that provides access to the river as far upstream as the Whirpool Rapids Bridge.

Access Sites (Canadian side)

Nearly the entire Canadian side of the lower Niagara River is public property, but access is rather limited due to terrain. The major access points include:

9. Niagara Glen, off River Road, Niagara Falls, Ontario, directly across from Devil's Hole State Park. A steep path leads to the bottom of the gorge, connecting with trails that provide shore access between the Whirlpool and the Sir Adam Beck Power Project.
10. The Queenston Sand Docks, off Niagara Parks Commission Boulevard. There is a small public launch ramp located near the sand dock. Due to the steep access road, only small boats should be launched here. There is also limited shore access - no charge.

The lower Niagara River was created on one of Mother Nature's most mischievous days. Racing through a wooded 300-foot deep gorge like a covey of runaway trains, the waters of the lower river approach 180 feet in depth, speeds in excess of 20 knots, and go every which way but straight. It begins to settle down a bit below Lewiston, but even in its lower reaches the Niagara is a river that deserves a special amount of respect from bank fishermen and boaters alike. The obvious dangers of this turbulent river are further compounded by fluctuating water levels caused by the operations of the power plants located on its banks. Water levels are lowest in the early morning and begin to rise by 8:00 a.m. The water comes up fast and it's easy to get stranded if you're not paying attention. These and other dangers (such as the stairs at Whirlpool and Devil's Hole State Parks) notwithstanding, the lower Niagara River ranks as one of the top fisheries in western New York. With respect to trout and salmon, the Niagara is, in fact, a world-class fishery with few rivals. What follows is a consideration of the major species found in this remarkable river.

Trout and Salmon .... Abundant; growth rates very good

If any single species could be said to embody the wild, robust character of the lower Niagara, the steelhead would certainly have to be the one. These sleek, silvery fighting machines are found throughout the lower river, often in fantastic numbers. They can be taken here all year long, but the peak time runs from late fall to late spring. All of the traditional drifts are productive for steelhead, especially during the winter. On the American side of the river, bank fishermen will do well if they concentrate on the shoreline anywhere between Art Park and the Whirlpool Rapids Bridge, the Lewiston sand docks and the Youngstown docks. On the Canadian side, the shore of the Whirlpool, Pebley Eddy and the Queenston sand docks all produce good numbers of steelhead.

It may seem a bit odd to talk about the good lake trout fishing that can be found in a river, but it's a fact that the lower Niagara offers anglers a chance to take these deep diving salmonids in surprisingly good numbers. Most lakers are caught in the spring (May), but only slightly diminished prospects are available in the late fall and winter. They are found throughout the river between Queenston and the Whirlpool Rapids Bridge, and Peggy's Eddy is also known to harbor lake trout.

Brown trout and palimino trout (a beautiful golden trout hybrid stocked by Pennsylvania in Lake Erie) can be found in the lower Niagara, but their numbers are relatively few in comparison to other salmonids. Browns are taken in the fall from the same locations as lake trout. Palominos are found intermittently at best, and they are taken almost exclusively in the area between Whirlpool Park and the Whirlpool Rapids Bridge.

As with most other tributaries of Lake Ontario, the river gets a fall run of chinook and coho salmon. Boat fishermen can find salmon in all of the drifts between Peggy's Eddy and Devil's Hole, while the entire shore line (both sides) above Art Park is productive for bank fishermen.

The following article was written by Rick Kustich, whose years of experience fishing the lower Niagara has made him one of the most knowledgeable anglers on the river.

LOWER NIAGARA RIVER TROUT AND SALMON FISHING

By Rick Kustich

Upon seeing the powerful flow of the Niagara River, one must agree that the term "The Mighty Niagara" is a very fitting description of this body of water. But from the perspective of the lower river angler this term can also be associated with its outstanding lake-run trout and salmon fishing.

This is a big body of water, as evidenced by its flow of 1.5 million gallons per second, making it clearly the largest of all Great Lakes tributaries. It is this size that seems to intimidate many anglers. However, it shouldn't since fish can usually be found in the traditional drifts by boat anglers and within easy casting range by the bank fisherman. In fact, trout and salmon sometimes hold in water only a few feet from shore.

Because of its relatively constant flow of water and consistent runs of trout and salmon that occur here, the lower Niagara is the premier Great Lakes tributary in the western New York area. In addition, access to the river is good. On the American side, boat launches are located in Lewiston and at Fort Niagara. Shore access can be gained at Whirlpool State Park, Devil's Hole State Park, the new pier adjacent to the power plant, Joseph Davis Park, and Artpark. Yet many times, especially in the late fall and early winter, an angler can find solitude on this productive river.

Another attribute of the lower Niagara is its breathtaking beauty. A good portion of the river runs through a deep, steep-sided gorge. When autumn turns the tree-lined gorge walls into a combination of brilliant orange, red, and yellow, it is a scene that must be experienced to be appreciated.

The steep gorge walls do restrict shore access to some degree, but by using the access points noted above, it is not a problem. Stairs exist at both Whirlpool State Park and Devil's Hole State Park. The power plant road is paved, and while no parking is allowed at the bottom, vehicles are allowed to be on the road and can drop anglers off near the river. The access at Artpark is in the form of a gradually descending fisherman's path and a set of stairs. Aside from getting a ride down the power plant road, all the shore access points require a little hike, but the rewards in terms of fishing success and spectacular scenery are well worth it.

As with all Great Lakes tributaries, fishing opportunities in the lower Niagara follow a cyclical progression, with different species occupying the river's hotspots throughout the year. A special feature of the lower Niagara, though, is that there are lake-run trout and salmon in the river almost year-round.

Many consider the chinook salmon (or king as they are also called) run as the highlight of the lower river fishing year. Hookup with one of these powerful fish in the open water of the lower Niagara and you'll see why. The salmon run starts as early as mid-August, with most the fish arriving in September and October. The peak of the run occurs between the middle of September and the middle of October. Because they're fresh from the lake, the early-run fish can put up incredible fights. This is not to take anything away from fish caught later in the run, however, for they will still give you all you can handle.

Ann Kustich proves that salmon fishing is not just for men. Ann boated this 32-pound chinnok in Devil's Hole, considered by many to be the best area of the lower river for salmon fishing. Photo courtesy Rick Kustich.

Many fisherman have been programed to think that once chinooks have entered a tributary they will not hit. That is simply not true. Limit catches of mouth-hooked salmon are not out of the ordinary at this time of year. And remember, snagging is not allowed on any part of the Niagara River.

Salmon up to 35 pounds (and occasionally larger) and averaging 22 to 25 pounds can be taken by both boat and shore anglers. While some salmon are caught in the Artpark Drift, the undisputed hotspot for fishing from the boat is the Devil's Hole area. However, one must be careful getting into the "Hole" by boat because some rough, powerful water lies between the Lewiston boat launch and the salmon. I suggest anyone going into the "Hole" for the first time do it with a professional lower river guide or with someone who has made the trip before. I also suggest a deep V boat of at least 16 feet and a 20-horsepower motor. Of course, life jackets should be worn at all times.

Once in the "Hole" the angler can concentrate on battling the salmon. The equipment must be matched properly to the quarry. Rods should have a strong lower section to muscle a fish when necessary and a long butt section to make the fight easier on the arms. The rod should also be 7 feet to 8 feet long and preferably graphite to get the feel of the bottom. Spinning and level wind reels work well. Most lower river guides prefer the level wind reels because they allow the angler to let out line easily as needed while drifting or trolling. A good drag system is a must and the reel should be capable of holding 250 yards of 15-pound-test line. Although many fisherman use 20- to 30-pound-test line, it is my feeling that 14- to 15-pound-test of quality line is sufficient.

Drifting with the river's current is the preferred boat fishing method. The drift-fishing rig is fairly simple. A three-way swivel is tied to the end of the line. A leader of 4 to 6 feet of the same test line or lower than on the reel is tied to the swivel. At times when the water is very clear or when the fish are spooky from angling pressure, even longer leaders and as light as 8-pound-test line becomes necessary. A 6-inch dropper is added to the swivel with a pencil weight heavy enough to get on the bottom. It is important to note that at this time of year the water levels will rise about 5 to 8 feet during the course of the day. Because of this, weight usually will need to be added during the day to get the rig down. Another factor affecting the required weight and the anglers presentation is the wind velocity. Any significant winds impair the boat fisherman's ability to drift naturally with the current. South winds, which push the boat downstream faster than the current, and east/west winds, which push it across the current, can be offset somewhat by adding more weight to maintain contact with the bottom. Strong north winds, however, represent a more difficult fishing condition, since the boat drifts slower than the natural drift of the current. This makes contact with the bottom almost impossible at times. Conversely, a light north wind sometimes improves presentation as it allows the egg sac or egg imitation to be presented to the fish before it is spooked by the lead. All the above problems with the wind can be eliminated, except for the gustiest days, by an electric trolling motor. This enables the boat fisherman to maintain a true drift at all times. It can also be used to get the same affect of a light north wind described above.

Large globs of both fresh and cured salmon skein account for most the chinooks taken by boat. This past year skein cured with Hot Red Procure were a hot ticket for the salmon. K9 to K11 Kwikfish in silver and a variety of other combinations including blue, chartreuse, and pink will also take fish, especially early in the run.

Trolling against the current can also be productive. It seems as though this method is best used late in the run when the salmon are bedding up on the gravel close to shore. Bombers in chartreuse and chartreuse combinations are the choice trolling lures.

A note for the boat fisherman. The lower Niagara is an international boundary water between New York State and the Province of Ontario. An Ontario license is required when fishing much of the lower river. Although the best salmon fishing lies within New York's waters, it's advisable to be familiar with the boundary line and obtain an Ontario license if you plan to fish in Ontario waters.

Plenty of opportunity exists for the shore angler to tangle with the mighty king. Through the first half of the run, the best location is the Devil's Hole and power plant area, which can be accessed by way of the stairs at Devil's Hole State Park or the power plant road. The equipment is similar to that used in fishing from a boat, except that the spinning reel is preferred by shore fisherman. Although drifted eggs do pick up some chinooks, 3/4-ounce KO Wobblers, Little Cleos, No. 5 Super Vibrex, and various size Rattle Traps worked slowly on or near the bottom produce the best results. There are big boulders along this area, and they cause many snags, so a good feel for the bottom is important to keep from losing lures.

Early mornings and evenings are good times for fishing the Devil's Hole and power plant area from shore, but by far the most productive time is at night from about 10 p.m. to 4 a.m. Night fishing is legal on the lower Niagara. The water begins to recede in the evening because of increased water usage for the generation of electricity and it continues to drop through the night. Because of this, the current slows to a point where the angler can keep his lure right on the bottom and can expect jolting hits from the salmon. Glow-in-the-dark Little Cleos and KO Wobblers, and Rattle Traps doctored up with glow-in-the-dark tape or paint work best. A bright flashlight or a camera flash should be used to charge up the lure. The brighter the light the brighter the glow. Fishing at night isn't as bad as it might seem; lights from the top of the gorge cast a dim light on the entire area allowing for some visibility; however, a good flashlight is a must when fishing here at night.

Toward the end of the run, from mid-October to the first part of November, the salmon begin to bed up near the shore from the Whirlpool area all the way down to Artpark. This is a good time for the shore angler to consistently hook chinook. Even though some have been in the river for a while and are getting pretty dark, some good fighters can still be found. Here the idea is to fish to salmon that can be seen. By getting upstream of the fish and repeatedly presenting the egg sac or lure in front of it, the salmon can often be coaxed into striking.

An important point to keep in mind about fighting a lower river chinook is that they normally do not tire themselves out. Constant pressure is required, almost to the point of horsing the fish. Without this pressure the big fish will conserve its energy and be almost impossible to land. Also, a large landing net comes in handy at the end of the fight.

Although boat fishing seems to account for more salmon, shore anglers can fare well also, and can get nearly as many hookups by fishing at night. Anglers will also hook into the occasional coho salmon at this time of year.

Fly fishing is also an effective way to take salmon. Even though I get some curious looks from other anglers while I'm fly fishing on the big open waters of the lower Niagara, with properly matched equipment it is a productive method and can add a lot of challenge and excitement to the sport.

Many fishermen who use conventional tackle seem to think that all fly rods are limber and light, but a quality rod such as a Winston or an Orvis built for a 10- or 11-weight line is powerful enough to handle a big salmon just fine. Other lower priced rods designed for 10- or 11-weight lines with strong butt sections will also get the job done. Graphite and fiberglass rods both work well. Graphite allows for a better feel for the bottom and fish, while fiberglass is usually a little stronger in the butt section, allowing the angler to muscle the fish when needed. An extended fighting butt also comes in handy by taking some of the pressure off the fly fisherman's wrist during the fight.

The reel of the fly fishing outfit is also important. It should be able to hold 200 yards of backing or running line and the fly line. A good drag system is a must. I recommend a Valentine or a Scientific Anglers System II as a quality mid-priced reel.

The fly fisherman has opportunities to take chinooks from both boat and shore. While fishing from the boat I have found a sinking shooting head line to work best. A shooting head is a short piece of flyline with sufficient weight to load up the fly rod for casting. I generally make my own sinking shooting heads using a plastic coated lead-core line. This shooting head is then attached to a flat monofilament shooting line using a nail knot and surgeon's loop knot. The shooting line is attached to the backing, which then goes to the reel spool. The leader should be about 8 feet long and have a tippet of 8- to 14-pound-test line. A splitshot or two are usually added to make sure that contact is being made with the bottom. The split-shot can be added directly to the leader about 3 feet up from the fly or a dropper can be used as discussed earlier. For flies, glo bugs or double glo bug combinations with maribou tails and wings tied on size 2 hooks work well. Flame and cheese glo bug colors seem to work best. Also, crystal bullets, which are a combination of crystal hair and chenille, also take fish. Orange seems to be the best color for this pattern. Try scenting the flies with an egg scent, especially when the water is off color.

Chinooks can also be taken by fly fishermen from the bank, especially late in the run when the fish begin to bed up close to shore. Again, fishing to chinooks that you can see is best. I try to position myself upstream from the fish and cast across and downstream, using a sink tip line. A couple of split-shots should be added to the 4- to 6-foot leader to get the fly down fast. Normally, the casts are very short and the technique is to allow the fly to drift and swing in front of the spawning salmon while maintaining a fairly tight line. Effective flies are those mentioned above in addition to small streamers such as a green over white bucktail tied on size 2 hooks. Sometimes repeated casts are required until the salmon becomes enraged enough to strike. The takes are usually rather light; normally the fly and line just stop, then the battle is on!

Rick Kustich displays a 32-pound chinook salmon caught at night. Many anglers have found the nighttime to be the most productive period to fish the salmon runs in the lower Niagara River. Photo courtesy Rick Kustich.

Before the salmon fishing has died out, steelhead, lake trout, and an occasional brown trout begin to move into the river. Actually, any of these species can be caught in September, but good numbers of steelhead and lake trout do not begin to show up until about mid- to late October. From mid-October through December is my personal favorite time to fish the river. This is a time when there is a lot of fish and a lot of action. Tying into an acrobatic, fresh-run Niagara River steelhead is an experience that is tough to beat. Steelhead average 6 to 8 pounds and 10- to 16-pound fish are not uncommon. And lake trout hooked on light tackle seem like a much different fish in the river's heavy currents. Many times the angler tires before the laker. Lake trout average about 8 to 10 pounds here. Be sure to check current regulations with respect to keeping lake trout in the lower river.

For the boat angler fish can be found in many of the traditional drifts at this time of year. The Artpark Drift is especially productive. Other good drifts include Devil's Hole, Stella, and Johnson on the New York side of the river, and Queenston, Pine, and Jackson on the Ontario side.

There are few places in the world where salmon this size can be caught, and the lower Niagara River is one of them. This fish was landed by Perry Smith, an avid lower Niagara trout and salmon fisherman. Photo courtesy Perry Smith.

Equipment for fishing from the boat at this time of year is generally lighter than that used for salmon. Graphite rods are preferred because of the feel transmitted to the angler. Both level wind and spinning reels are used, again bait casting being preferred for boat fishing. Six- to 8-pound-test line is normally used, with the water clarity determining line size.

The three-way swivel rig is used, identical to that used for salmon fishing. Normally, leaders should be 4 to 6 feet long; however, as with salmon fishing, clear water and spooky fish dictate longer leaders, from 8 to 10 feet, and sometimes even lighter than 6-pound-test lines. Fresh egg sacs, skein and K8 to K9 Kwikfish account for most of the fish caught. Mister Twister tails, bucktail jigs, and plastic eggs or egg clusters also take steelhead. Something to try when using fresh eggs or plastic eggs is to tie fluorescent yarn above the hook. Try pink, orange, or chartreuse. This works well when the water is a little off color. Also try adding the small florescent egg-sized floaters to the egg sac for visibility and improved presentation. Again, the electric trolling motor or a set of oars will improve the anglers presentation on windy days, and can prove to be the difference between a good day and a no-fish outing.

The period from mid-October through December presents some of the best opportunities for the shore angler, since many of the trout are close to shore. Fish can be found all up and down the river, but the best action seems to be concentrated in the Artpark area. This whole area has good fishable water. Here again, spinning reels and a light- to medium-action graphite rod work best. Eight-pound-test seems to be the right line for shore fishing at this time. Although 6-pound-test line can be used, due to the current and abrasive rocks near shore a little heavier line is recommended. However, water clarity may dictate lighter line here also.

Fish can be caught by drifting egg sacs on a three-way swivel rig, by casting spinners, and by working jigs along the bottom. With regard to spinners, orange and chartreuse-bodied No. 3 Super Vibrex with silver blades and similar sized Killer Spins with a pearl finish are very productive. White bucktail jigs worked slowly along the bottom also work well.

This is also a good time of year for the fly fisherman to cash in on some excellent action. A 7- to 9-weight rod is required for this type of fishing. The reel is the same as that used for salmon fishing, but loaded with a line matched to the rod. Basically, three methods are used by the fly fisherman to take steelhead and lakers during this period. The first is dead drifting egg patterns using a floating line and a long leader of about 10 to 12 feet. A split-shot or two is attached to the line for extra weight. The idea is to cast up and across the current and to allow the fly to drift naturally. Hits are detected by watching the end of the fly line, much like fishing a nymph. The second method entails using a sink tip line, and short leader of 4 to 5 feet, with a split-shot added near the fly. After an upstream cast is made, the fly is worked along the bottom in a fashion similar to that used in jig fishing. Wooly worms and woolly buggers in white and chartreuse work well with this method. The third method also utilizes the same rig as the second. After making an across-the-current cast, allow the fly to sink and swing with the current. Most of the hits come toward the end of the swing. Streamer patterns such bucktails, matukas, and zonkers work well with this method. In some parts of the Artpark area wading a couple feet from shore is possible, but extreme care needs to be taken since the river bottom drops off quickly. While wading out allows for a better presentation in the swing methods, it is not advisable when fishing this river.

For all of these methods only short casts are required, since the fish are close to the bank. Be prepared to roll cast. There isn't much room for backcasts due to the steep gorge walls. With the weight on the leader, the casting stroke should be a slow constant movement resulting in an open loop in the cast.

As the season rolls into January, the lakers will move out, but there is no reason to put away the rod, since good steelhead fishing

In April and May the lower Niagara River offers excellent fishing for lake trout. The author caught this fish on a white rabbit fur streamer, which lakers find irresistible in the spring. Photo courtesy Rick Kustich.

away from the shore. Consequently, fishing at this time is best from a boat. It can be cold fishing, but if a day is chosen that isn't too windy and the fisherman is properly dressed, it can be a very pleasurable way to spend a winters day. I recommend a one-piece suit and plenty of warm underlayers.

The traditional drifts named earlier are good all winter. The Fort Niagara (or Coast Guard) Drift near the mouth of the river begins to produce fish in February and March. Essentially the same techniques are used at this time as discussed above for steelhead fishing from the boat. The fly fisherman also has opportunities during these months. The method used is the same as discussed for fishing for salmon from the boat. A lighter rod, normally an 8 or 9 weight, is preferred and lighter leaders of 6-pound-test are required. As for flies, flame-colored glo bugs work well. Steelhead can also be taken on streamers with a little action imparted to them.

At various times during the winter, ice flows will be present in the lower river, and though the river remains fishable one must exercise care while going up river to the next drift. However, there is a period at the end of March or in early April when Lake Erie's ice is released into the Niagara River by the removal of the ice boom. This puts so much ice into the lower river that fishing is usually impossible for about a two-week period.

Most of the steelhead will have left the river by mid- to late April, but the lake trout return for an encore performance. Some hot action can be experienced in the Stella and Artpark drifts. Drifting Canadian wigglers rigged on a three-way swivel works well. Lake trout can also be found close to shore throughout the entire Artpark area until about mid-June. The water is normally clearer at this time than in the fall and winter, so the fish spook a little easier when fished from the bank. For this reason, early mornings and evenings are the best periods to fish. For the spin fisherman jigs and Super Vibrex work well. The fly fisherman should try more natural imitations such as stonefly nymphs and crayfish patterns.

After the lakers have retreated there is limited trout action during the remainder of June and July. An occasional lingering steelhead is caught and sometimes good numbers of small 2- to 4-pound rainbows can be found in the Devil's Hole and Artpark drifts. A summer-running steelhead, the Skamania strain, has been introduced to the lower river, but they have yet to make an impact on the fishery. However, there is plenty of good fishing for warm-water species through the summer until it starts all over again with those silver salmon of August.

Walleye .... Common; growth rate good

There was a time, not so long ago, when the most important species found in this section of the Niagara River was the walleye, which along with its cousin, the blue pike, constituted a fishery of spectacular proportions. Those days are probably gone for good; the blue pike is probably extinct and conditions in the lower river and Lake Ontario have changed so much over the last 40 years that walleye will never again be the dominant predator. But walleye can still be taken here, often in surprisingly good numbers. Many of the traditional walleye haunts are moderately productive when fished in the summer and fall, including the Coast Guard, Jackson, Pine, Stella, and Queenston drifts. To these can be added the Art Park/Lewiston Bridge area and Devil's Hole.

The fact that there is a viable walleye fishery in the lower river today is due in large part to the efforts of the Niagara River Anglers Association, the group that spearheaded the construction of new walleye rearing ponds devoted to raising walleye to be stocked in the river. The following article was written by one of the members of the NRAA most instrumental in bringing that project to fruition.

ON THE BRINK OF SOMETHING WONDERFUL

By John Long

One of the most often repeated arguments that my father made as he waged his relentless battle to keep me in high school and college was that an education was "something no one can ever take away from you." I was all for quitting school and living a life hunting and fishing on or near the lower Niagara River. Dad won and I earned my degree at Niagara University.

Like most college kids in those days I had to work to pay for my tuition. There were no educational loans. They, like the ball point pen, fiberglass and aluminum boats, and television had not been invented yet. So, we worked all summer to be able to pay our tuition in the fall.

My spring, summer, and fall job was fishing the lower Niagara River. My pay was the sale of the fish, blue and yellow pike. This was a thriving business on the river in those days. Commercial netting enterprises lined the riverbank at Youngstown and commercial fish traps dotted both sides of the river at the point where the gorge ends and the more navigable section of the river begins just above what is now Artpark.

The vast majority of the fish taken commercially were taken by the nets and the traps. The next substantial source of commercial fish were those taken by spearfishermen in the gorge. This activity was legal above the old Lewiston suspension bridge and catches were astronomical. Stone piers called docks extending several feet out from shore were constructed in places where the current ran close to shore and the water was 2 or 3 feet deep. A stone wall a foot or so high was placed on the bottom of the river about 4 feet out from the dock and was flared away from shore to guide fish toward the waiting fishermen. A kerosene or gasoline lantern was placed at the front of the dock and dimmed so as to cast just enough light to see the fish and not frighten them.

Although fish could be taken during daylight hours, night fishing was most productive. The view from the old bridge during the hours of darkness revealed the glow of dozens of lanterns reflecting off the swift waters. Other lights and fires further up the bank marked the location of fishermen awaiting their turn at a dock. There were far more fishermen than places to fish. Some camped in the gorge, using the same dock all summer, taking turns carrying the catches out for sale to hotels as far away as Buffalo. They brought back their supplies on the return trip.

In terms of numbers of fish harvested commercially, the boat fishermen were the least important. Since the rod and reel was the tool of the trade and outboard motors of more than 10 horsepower were almost nonexistent, these fishermen could cover only a fraction of the water that we can today. Rods were steel, level-wind casting reels were the only ones available, and braided line was the order of the day. It was well into the 1950s before the 25-horsepower motor, the fiberglass rod, the spinning reel, and the monofilament line were generally available. Equipment and tackle were primitive by today's standards.

In spite of all this, catches could be awesome. Blue pike thrived in those days and, although common in the river, concentrated in huge numbers on what we still call "The Bar". This area is simply a large sandbar created from the sediment deposited by the river's current a short distance off its mouth in Lake Ontario. Depths over the bar range from 12 to 18 feet. Catches of a hundred blues a day were not uncommon.

Yellow pike, (called pike-perch in those days and walleyes today) were most common in the river. The same drifts that produced well in those days produce other species, especially trout, today. Catches of thirty to forty walleyes were a regular event and, in fact, a fisherman needed to do nearly that well to avoid the necessity of getting a job on shore. The going price wholesale was twenty-five cents a pound live weight and the average size yellow was about 3 pounds. Allowing for rain, unfavorable winds, muddy water, and the unreliable nature of those primitive motors, it was important to get a good catch when conditions were right. At best, it was a marginal business and the hours were long when fishing was at its best.

Shortly after World War II the traps disappeared from the gorge. A few remained on the Canadian side into the very early 1950s. The commercial netters were next and, as we all know, the fish were all but gone by the end of the decade, along with the spear fishermen and the commercial boat fishermen. I caught my last blue, a monster of some eight pounds, during the summer of 1961.

Speculation regarding the disappearance of the blue and yellow pike runs rampant. At that time Lake Erie was reported to be near death and the fish disappeared from those waters at nearly the same time. After all, the theory went, Lake Erie is the source of the Niagara River. The same disease that killed the lake killed the river.

Some felt that the pike never did spawn in the lower river, but that the species received its stock from Lake Erie fish coming over Niagara Falls or through the Welland Canal.

Others figured that the appearance of two new predator species after World War II fed on the young pike. After all, smelt began their run up the river at the same time walleye were hatching, and silver bass choked the river at the time the walleye fry were growing to minnow size. Both appeared shortly after the war.

Many fishermen blamed the commercial fishing interests. In any event, the fish were gone!

Since the early 1980s, the walleye has begun to reappear in small numbers in the river. No one seems to know where they reappeared from, and speculation again runs rampant. Some feel that they are again the product of the Lake Erie fishery, which has rebounded dramatically. One or two fish have carried tags from the Ontario Ministry of Natural Resources. These fish were marked on the north side of Lake Ontario at the Bay of Quinte.

As those few walleyes began to appear, the Niagara River Anglers Association took interest. Believing that there could once again be an exciting walleye fishery in those waters, they formed a committee to explore the possibility of restocking the river with large numbers of walleye fingerlings.

A walleye rearing facility was constructed on the property of one of the members in 1985, and the first stocking of the river was done in late June of 1986. Since then ever increasing numbers of small walleyes have been caught by anglers and one lucky sportsman caught and released over twenty undersized fish on a Saturday morning in 1988.

Many knowledgeable people are predicting a blossoming walleye fishery in the river beginning in the early 1990s.

Methods of catching these fish will be nearly identical to those of the good old days. Modern Equipment should make fishing much easier. Faster and safer boats will allow the sportsman to cover much more water and change drifts in a matter of a few minutes. Modern rods and spinning reels eliminate backlashes and allow the use of a wider variety of lures, although our guess is that the old stuff will still work well. Monofilament has less water resistance than braided line and allows the use of much lighter sinkers. Fish-finders and other modern gadgetry will also give an edge to today's fisherman.

From the fish's standpoint, today's size and creel limits will help to preserve the resource, and we still have to contend with unfavorable winds and muddy water. The end of commercial fishing and the continuation of the stocking program should all help to give the fish an edge.

The most productive fishing areas will vary little from those of the old days. The major drifts going downstream on the American side and back upstream in Canadian waters begin above Lewiston at the Artpark Drift. This is marked by the high red shale cliffs above the Artpark dock and the drift runs past the "Wagon Wheels". I like to fish it fairly close to shore. It never was my favorite walleye drift, but some nice fish are caught there. It is a superb rainbow drift.

The next drift is several miles down the river at off Stella Niagara School. Again, I like to fish fairly close to shore, just far enough out to be sure the current takes you on a good drift. On days of heavy boat traffic you will have to fish in deeper water.

This drift begins where the high banks end and the Stella "Flats" begin. The Little Chapel is a good landmark. It is a long drift ending around the next major downstream point at the Joseph Davis Park fishing dock. Just below that is the Johnson Drift. It can be productive if the wind is right, but is far down on my priority list.

The Coast Guard Drift begins in front of the Fort Niagara State Park boat launch and continues past the Coast Guard Station out into the lake. It is not a long drift for walleyes, but it is a tremendous spot for smallmouth bass if you start further upstream and drift out into the lake. For walleye I like to drift it very close to the dock. It is very snaggy and must be fished with great care.

Returning up the Canadian side of the river your voyage will take you past the historic Old Fort George. Even before there was a smallmouth fishery in the lower Niagara a good fisherman could pick up the occasional bass in these waters. Now it is excellent for bass but not a good walleye drift.

The next drift upstream is above the marina. It is called the Jackson Drift and begins at the ruins of an old concrete dock extending downstream to the point above the marina. It is an excellent walleye drift and like Stella always produces big fish. Vary your distance from shore until you hit fish.

When John Long caught this 7½-pound walleye in 1958, the lower Niagara River had tremendous fishing for walleye (then commonly referred to as yellow pike) and the closely related blue pike. A number of factors, including pollution and the introduction of exotic species into Lake Ontario, combined to almost totally wipe out these fisheries by the early 1960s. Today the blue pike is considered extinct, but thanks to the efforts of sportsmen like John Long and the members of the Niagara River Anglers Association the walleye fishing in the lower Niagara River is greatly improving. Photo courtesy John Long.

The Pine Drift, sometimes called the Lone Pine Drift today, is another favorite of mine. It ends at the next major point above the Jackson Drift and begins somewhat upstream from the beginning of the Stella Drift. Fish it moderately close to shore. It holds some nice fish. I like to trade back and forth between the Pine, Stella, and the Jackson until I find the fish.

Following the river further upstream to the next big point you come to the Queenston Long Drift. It ends at that point. This is an excellent place for smallmouth when you fish the eddies near the weedlines. The drift begins several hundred feet below the Queenston Docks, just above the small boat launch. This is a very productive drift. It can be fished close to shore or some distance out. I always experiment on this drift.

The Queenston Back Drift is unique in that your drift will take you upstream towards the gorge. It is a very fast drift, fishable in nearly every wind direction. It begins some distance out from the south end of the Queenston Dock, sweeps you in toward shore off the sand piles and continues very close to shore until it swings you right out into the middle of the river. As you start out toward the center, reel in and go back to the beginning. This is an excellent backup drift if the winds are bad on the others.

Wind is a serious problem for drift fishermen on the river. A strong north wind makes things miserable, since all but the Back Drift are northbound and the wind stops your boat dead in the water. Gentle south winds are the best, but the high banks let you fish on the leeward drifts if the wind is out of the east or west.

Heavy boat traffic, especially that of the high speed variety, will drive the fish to deeper water. Start close to shore early in the morning. As you start to see more boat activity, particularly on weekends, and fishing seems to slack off, try moving out to deeper water.

The old timers never varied their terminal tackle with the exception of the color of the spinner or the fly. The time-honored rig consisted of a three-way swivel attached to the end of the line. To one eye attach an 8-pound leader with a spinner the size of your thumbnail attached to it. The spinner can vary from copper to silver to brass, and some days a hammered finish seems to work better. Flies vary from the time-honored "Yellow Sally" to White Millers, Eries, and various fluorescent shades. Don't be afraid to try a variety of them. For some reason, this can make a difference. Finally, attach an 8-inch length of 6-pound-test leader to the last eye of the swivel. Depending on the wind, add a sinker of somewhere near an ounce. Add a half of a night crawler to the hook and you are in business. Fish right on the bottom bouncing or carefully dragging with just enough line out to touch. When a fish hits I always allow it to tug at the bait for a second or two before I strike. Other fishermen disagree. You'll have to develop your own technique. Some anglers, especially on quiet days, cast and let the rig settle to the bottom then slowly reel in as they drift. This works well where there are few snags.

Some drifts have more snags than others, but all have areas where you can comfortably drag bottom. I always have the most problems at the Artpark Drift and the Coast Guard Drift, although the Stella Drift and the Back Drift also have bad spots. You'll soon learn the areas that require special care. The light leader on your sinker will allow you to break off a lot of snags without losing all of your rig. Don't let the snags keep you from fishing right on the bottom. That is where the walleyes seem to stay.

One advantage that the old timer's boats had over most of today's were oarlocks and the ability to keep the boat drifting straight by keeping one oar active in the water. An electric trolling motor can be used for the same purpose today. Modern boats have more freeboard and are higher in the water. Wind has much more effect on them. They will drift better in light winds, but much faster in stronger winds. A heavier sinker may solve the problem in these cases and some fishermen resort to backtrolling.

Walleyes are sometimes caught from shore in the lower river. Casting in the gorge results in some nice fish, but is impossible to target one species in those waters. It is not uncommon to catch walleye, lake trout, rainbows, and bass from the same place using the same lure. For those who wish to target walleyes and fish from shore, the best place is from the Artpark dock downstream past the storm water outlet. White jigs work well and some good fish are caught there.

Night fishing for walleyes was quite common forty years ago. It was accomplished by anchoring with a lantern hanging over the side of the boat. Minnows were used as bait because the light drew in schools of minnows. Most action was at the very beginning of the Back Drift and below the Lewiston sand dock. It might be interesting to try it again.

The lower Niagara River enjoys a tremendous smallmouth population. The gorge is, of course, excellent for any species, but bass cooperate all summer. It is truly a shore fisherman's bonanza, and casting lures and spinnerbaits of all kinds work well. Bait fishermen use soft-shelled crabs, leeches, and minnows with much success, although less desirable fish play havoc with live bait.

All of the walleye drifts produce smallmouth bass, but usually near eddies and close to shore. Sheepshead usually make short work of live bait, but rattling lures and other popular bass baits work well along the weedlines. Jigs and weighted Twisters are probably to most effective lures.

The best place for bass is the Coast Guard area and out into the lake on "The Bar". Fish the bar in about 18 feet of water, generally by trolling. The area around the first green buoy is excellent. Drifting the area a mile past the one-mile buoy is very productive, as is trolling about a quarter mile offshore both east and west of the river. The water is about 12 to 18 feet deep on the Canadian side. The drift along the clay banks just below the sand docks produces well if you fish just off the drop off.

Panfish are available in large numbers in the lower Niagara. Yellow Perch are available to shore fishermen off the Lewiston sand docks, Artpark, the Queenston dock, Joseph Davis Park dock, and the Youngstown dock. For boaters the "Wagon Wheels" below the foot of Tuscarora Street off Lewiston is a great producer, and lake trout and silver bass are abundant there in June. Anchor about 50 feet from shore and use worms or minnows. The same is true just below the Lewiston and the Queenston sand docks and at Peggy's Eddy near Joseph Davis Park.

Silver bass fishing is good throughout the river, but nothing short of spectacular at the Power Authority plant in the gorge in late June and early July. These fish can be a real pest to perch fishermen.

The Power Authority has constructed a new fishing pier. It offers truly superb fishing in the spectacular setting of the Niagara Gorge. This facility is truly the "icing on the cake" for the already tremendous lower Niagara River fishery. It provides excellent bass and walleye fishing in addition to the superb salmonid fishing already enjoyed there.

My father was right when he told me that no one could ever take my education away. But he missed another treasure that will never leave me either. That is my memories of the old days on the river. They remain vivid and I can only speculate on the memories the young people of today will have of the rebirth of the lower Niagara River. We are on the brink of something wonderful.

Smallmouth Bass .... **Common; growth rate good**

Smallmouth are an important species in the lower river, though their numbers are certainly limited when compared to the bass population of the upper river. There is a limited migration of bass into the river from Lake Ontario in May, but this doesn't seem to enhance the fishery. The greatest concentrations of smallmouth are found in the Whirlpool State Park area, especially on either side of the point, in the upstream half of Bullhead Bay, along the quarter-mile stretch of shore immediately upstream of Fort George and in the Coast Guard area. With a little persistence, though, they can be taken sporadically almost anywhere along the rocky shore lines above Lewiston and Queenston.

Silver Bass .... **Abundant; growth rate good**

These scrappy fish are in the river year 'round, but they're taken in the greatest numbers in the late spring and early summer. Indeed, its not uncommon to catch these fine-tasting fish by the hundreds at this time. The number one spot for silver bass is the shoreline on either side of the Robert Moses Power Project. Other productive areas include the Youngstown docks, the sand docks at Lewiston and Queenston, Peggy's Eddy, and the shore along Whirlpool State Park and Devil's Hole State Park. They readily take small silver-colored spoons worked near the surface or small minnows fished 1 to 3 feet under a bobber.

Smelt .... **Abundant; seasonal**

Every spring, the lower Niagara is host to a tremendous run of smelt. Moving off the bottom at night, they head upstream along the shore and fall prey to fishermen with nets, often in amounts that are staggering. During the peak of their run it would be no problem for one man with a net to take a ton or more of these tasty fish each day. Such availability often leads to gluttony, so keep in mind that you should only take what you can reasonable expect to clean and eat. The most popular areas to dip for smelt are the Lewiston and Queenston Sand Docks, and at Artpark near the base of the stairway adjacent to the observation tower.

Yellow Perch .... **Common; growth rate good**

The perch population in the lower river is still in good shape. Perch are probably distributed all through the river below Whirlpool State Park, but they tend to be concentrated in specific areas. The most popular locations for taking these fine-tasting fish include the Youngstown Docks, Joseph Davis Park, Peggy's Eddy, and the sand docks at Lewiston and Queenston. The perch run in the spring is quite good and any of the above mentioned site are sure to be productive. There is also some very good perch fishing here in the fall. Fish with small minnows or worms along the edges of dying weedbeds in 15 to 25 feet of water.

Northern Pike .... **Uncommon; growth rate good**

The section of the river between Fort Niagara and Youngstown is a major spawning ground for northern pike from Lake Ontario. These fish move into the area in the early spring in great numbers, but are usually gone by the time their season opens. A few pike may linger in this area, but more productive are the Queenston long drift and the Pine drift, both of which are best in the spring.

Additional Species

Other species that you might encounter in relative abundance in the lower Niagara River include rock bass, sheepshead, suckers, and, in the early spring, American eels. Sturgeon and muskellunge are also present here, but the sturgeon are illegal to possess and the muskies are taken only rarely.

NOTES: ______________________________

____

____

Recently, the New York Power Authority constructed a fishing pier next to the Robert Moses Power Project. This new pier provides excellent access to the river. Photo courtesy New York Power Authority.

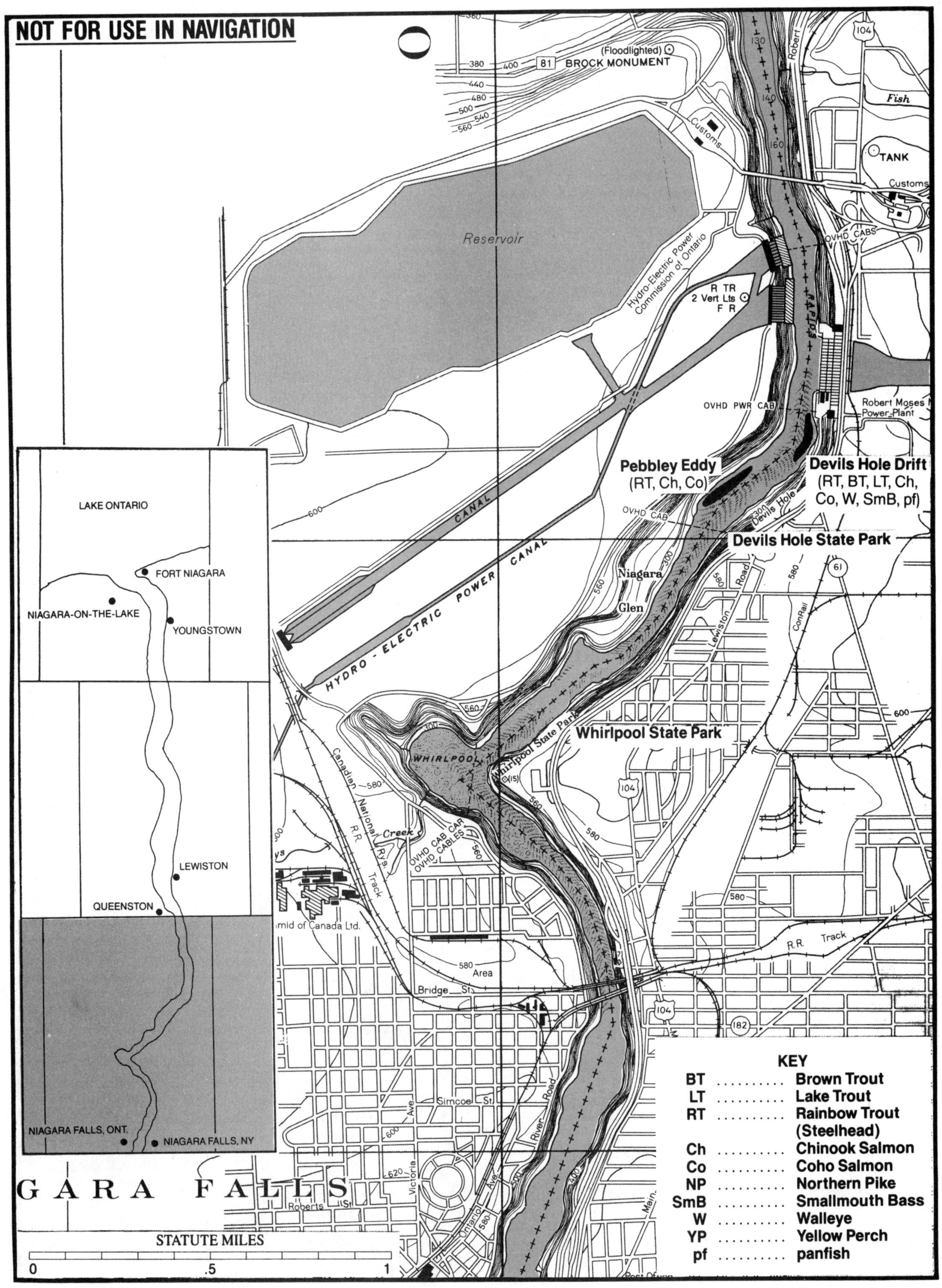
NOT FOR USE IN NAVIGATION
Pebbley Eddy
(RT, Ch, Co)
Devils Hole Drift
(RT, BT, LT, Ch, Co, W, SmB, pf)
Devils Hole State Park
Whirlpool State Park
Reservoir
HYDRO-ELECTRIC POWER CANAL
Robert Moses Power Plant
BROCK MONUMENT
Niagara Glen
WHIRLPOOL
LAKE ONTARIO
FORT NIAGARA
NIAGARA-ON-THE-LAKE
YOUNGSTOWN
LEWISTON
QUEENSTON
NIAGARA FALLS, ONT.
NIAGARA FALLS, NY
GARA FALLS
STATUTE MILES
0
.5
1
KEY
BT .... Brown Trout
LT .... Lake Trout
RT .... Rainbow Trout (Steelhead)
Ch .... Chinook Salmon
Co .... Coho Salmon
NP .... Northern Pike
SmB .... Smallmouth Bass
W .... Walleye
YP .... Yellow Perch
pf .... panfish

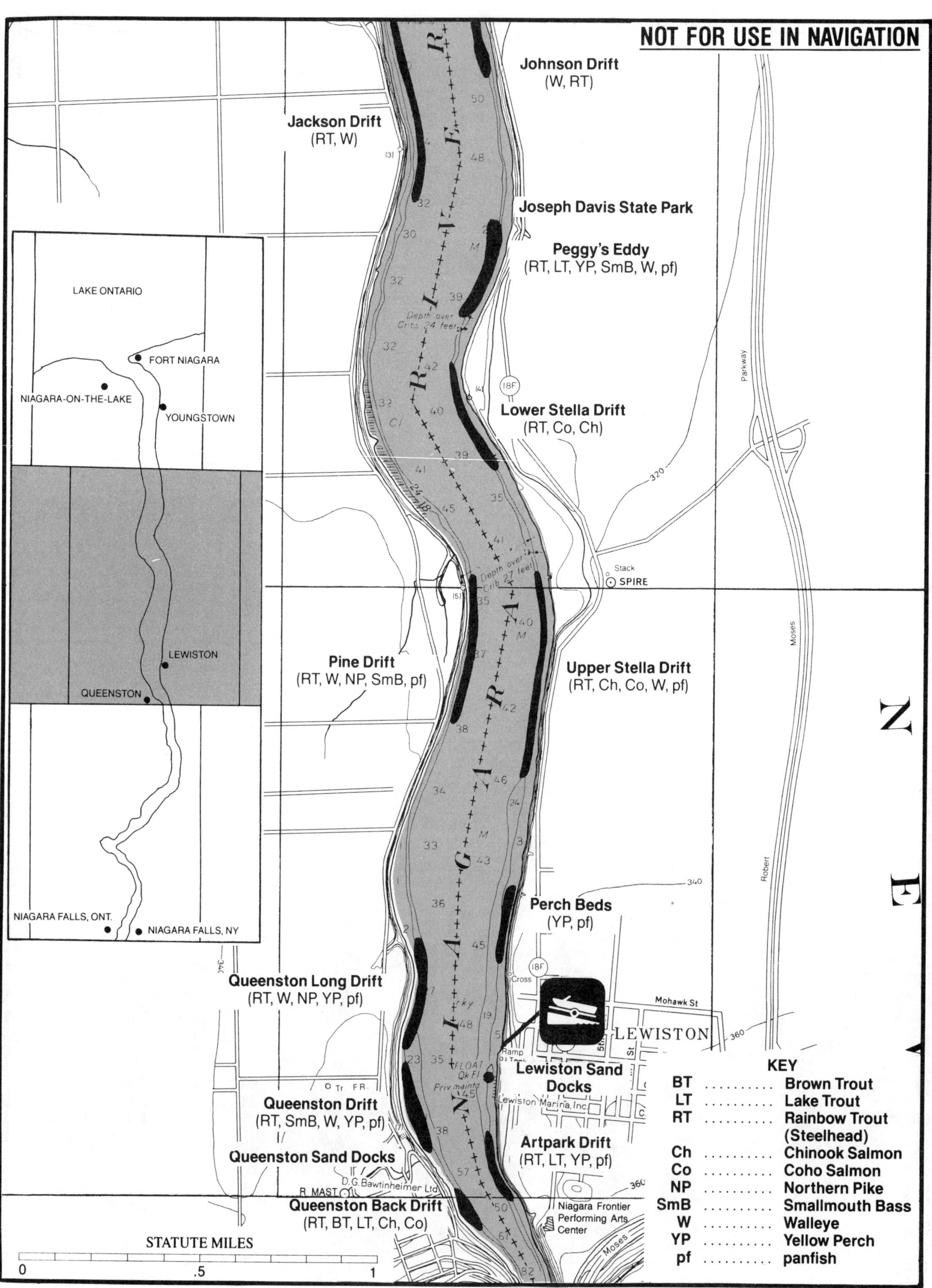

NOT FOR USE IN NAVIGATION
Johnson Drift
(W, RT)
Jackson Drift
(RT, W)
Joseph Davis State Park
Peggy's Eddy
(RT, LT, YP, SmB, W, pf)
Lower Stella Drift
(RT, Co, Ch)
Pine Drift
(RT, W, NP, SmB, pf)
Upper Stella Drift
(RT, Ch, Co, W, pf)
Perch Beds
(YP, pf)
Queenston Long Drift
(RT, W, NP, YP, pf)
Lewiston Sand Docks
Queenston Drift
(RT, SmB, W, YP, pf)
Queenston Sand Docks
Artpark Drift
(RT, LT, YP, pf)
Queenston Back Drift
(RT, BT, LT, Ch, Co)
LAKE ONTARIO
FORT NIAGARA
NIAGARA-ON-THE-LAKE
YOUNGSTOWN
LEWISTON
QUEENSTON
NIAGARA FALLS, ONT.
NIAGARA FALLS, NY
NIAGARA RIVER
Depth over Cribs 24 feet
Depth over Crib 27 feet
Stack
SPIRE
Robert Moses Parkway
Mohawk St
LEWISTON
Lewiston Marina, Inc.
D.G. Bawtinheimer Ltd
Niagara Frontier Performing Arts Center
STATUTE MILES
0
.5
1
KEY
BT .... Brown Trout
LT .... Lake Trout
RT .... Rainbow Trout (Steelhead)
Ch .... Chinook Salmon
Co .... Coho Salmon
NP .... Northern Pike
SmB .... Smallmouth Bass
W .... Walleye
YP .... Yellow Perch
pf .... panfish

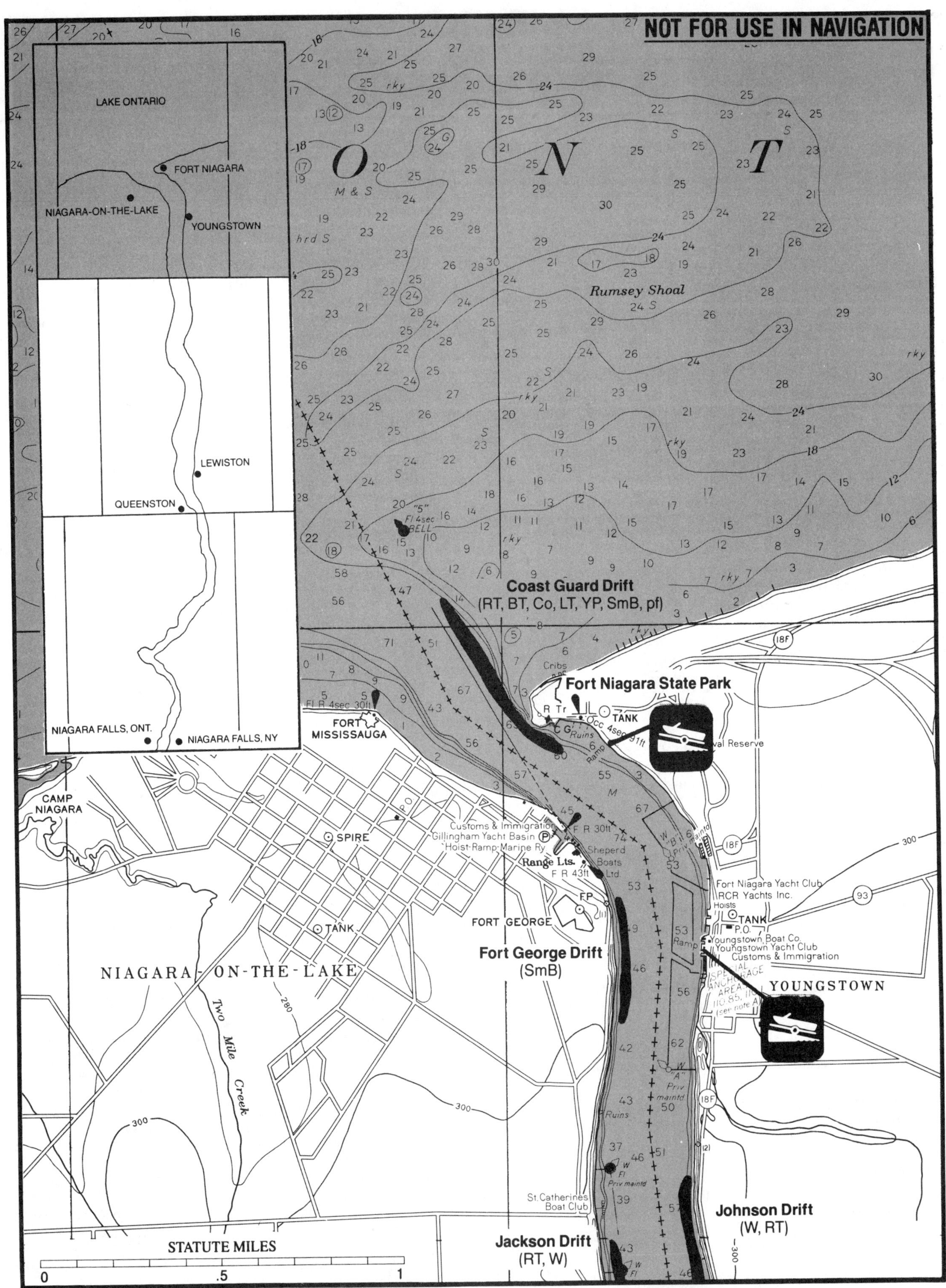
NOT FOR USE IN NAVIGATION
LAKE ONTARIO
FORT NIAGARA
NIAGARA-ON-THE-LAKE
YOUNGSTOWN
LEWISTON
QUEENSTON
NIAGARA FALLS, ONT.
NIAGARA FALLS, NY
Rumsey Shoal
Coast Guard Drift
(RT, BT, Co, LT, YP, SmB, pf)
Fort Niagara State Park
FORT MISSISSAUGA
CAMP NIAGARA
SPIRE
TANK
Customs & Immigration
Gillingham Yacht Basin
Hoist-Ramp-Marine Ry.
Range Lts.
Sheperd Boats Ltd.
FORT GEORGE
Fort George Drift
(SmB)
Fort Niagara Yacht Club
RCR Yachts Inc.
Youngstown Boat Co.
Youngstown Yacht Club
Customs & Immigration
YOUNGSTOWN
NIAGARA-ON-THE-LAKE
Two Mile Creek
St. Catherines Boat Club
Jackson Drift
(RT, W)
Johnson Drift
(W, RT)
STATUTE MILES
0
.5
1

LAKE ONTARIO

N.O.A.A. Charts 14806, 14805, 14804
Location .... Counties of Niagara, Orleans, and Monroe
Access .... Paralleled by Route 18 between Youngstown and Point Breeze; paralleled by the Lake Ontario State Parkway between Point Breeze and Rochester. See boat launch sites listed below.

Physical Characteristics

Area .... 3,560 square miles (U.S. waters)
Shoreline .... 356 miles (New York section)
Elevation .... 245 feet
Maximum Depth .... Approximately 780 feet
Mean Depth .... Unknown; approximately by 80% of the New York portion of the lake is over 100 feet deep.
Bottom Type .... Slate, gravel, and sand interspersed with pockets of rocks and boulders.

Chemical Characteristics

Water .... Generally clear; near-shore areas are often muddy after storms.
pH .... Varies with location
Oxygen .... Good throughout the lake all year due to the seasonal turnover of top and bottom waters. Some bays and harbors might experience some oxygen depletion, but this is not generally a problem.

Plant Life

Due to its relatively hard, featureless bottom, unprotected shoreline, and great depth, Lake Ontario has little rooted aquatic vegetation. Weed beds that do occur are usually found in harbors, bays, or off the mouths of streams. Algae, in the form of Cladophora, a hairlike seaweed, is often a problem in the shallow (5 to 25 feet) portions of the lake in May, June, and July.

Boat Launch Sites

Niagara County Section

1. Fort Niagara State Park, off Route 18, at the mouth of the Niagara River. Multiple hard-surface ramps, parking - no charge (a park user fee is required from mid-May to mid-September).
2. Six Mile Creek, off Route 18 at Willow Beach Campground. Single ramp - fee.
3. Town of Wilson Ramp, on Twelve Mile Creek (west branch), on Riverview Drive off Route 18, Wilson. Single ramp - no charge.
4. Wilson-Tuscarora State Park, on Twelve Mile Creek (east branch), off Route 18. Multiple hard-surface ramps, transient tie-ups, parking - no charge.
5. Beccue Boat Basin, on Beccue Island in Twelve Mile Creek (east branch). Full service marina, single hard-surface ramp - fee.
6. Wilson Boat House, on Twelve Mile Creek (east branch), Harbor Street, Wilson. Full service marina, double hard-surface ramps - fee.
7. Newfane Town Marina, on Eighteen Mile Creek at the foot of West Main Street, Olcott. Multiple hard-surface ramps, parking - fee.
8. Golden Hill State Park, off Route 18, on Lower Lake Road. Single hard-surface ramp - no charge.

See also launch sites on the lower Niagara River.

Orleans County Section

9. Green Harbor Campsites, 12813 Lakeshore Road, Town of Yates, 6 miles west of Oak Orchard Harbor. Single ramp - fee.
10. Oak Orchard State Marine Park West, at Point Breeze on west side of Oak Orchard Creek. Multiple hard-surface ramps, parking - no charge.
11. Oak Orchard State Marine Park East, at Point Breeze on the east side of Oak Orchard Creek at the north end of Route 98. Multiple hard-surface ramps, parking - no charge.
12. Bald Eagle Marina, at mouth of Bald Eagle Creek, off Lake Ontario Parkway (exit for Route 237), in Kendall. Full-service marina, multiple ramps - fee.

See also launch sites on Oak Orchard Creek.

Monroe County Section

13. Hamlin Beach State Park, on Route 19, off the Ontario State Parkway. Launching of cartop boats is permitted in designated areas of the park at no charge, but there is a park user fee after mid-May.
14. New York State launch site on Sandy Creek, off the Ontario State Parkway on the east side of Sandy Creek. Multiple hard-surface ramps, parking for 60 cars and trailers - no charge.
15. Braddock Bait and Tackle, 372 Manitou Beach Road, Hilton. Tackle, hard-surface ramp - fee.
16. Parkway Marina, 320 Manitou Road, Hilton. Full service marina, single hard-surface ramp - fee.
17. Braddock Bay State Park, 194 Braddocks Road, off East Manitou Road, Greece. City-owned, full-service marina, double hard surface ramps - fee.
18. Monroe County launch site, on the west side of the Genesee River, at the north end of Lake Avenue. Multiple hard-surface ramps and parking facilities. There is a modest fee during the height of the fishing season. When the launch closes "officially" you can launch without charge.

See also listings for the Genesee River and Irondequoit Bay.

* Navigation through some of these channels may be impaired by shifting gravel bars, especially at times of low water. Channel conditions may vary daily. Check with facility owner/operator before attempting to use these facilities.

Species Information

Rainbow Trout/Steelhead Common; growth rate excellent

NOTE: Lake Ontario and its tributary systems contain several strains of rainbow trout, including domestics, Skamania, Canadian strain, Washington strain, Lake Ontario strain, and an increasingly significant number of wild fish. They are often referred to as steelhead, the name commonly given to lake-run rainbows. However, the true steelhead is a specific strain of rainbow trout, and it too is stocked in several Lake Ontario tributaries. Because most rainbows found in the lake are almost indistinguishable from true steelhead in terms of anatomy and habits, I have used the terms steelhead and rainbow trout interchangeably when discussing lakes Erie and Ontario, as well as those tributaries recognized as "steelhead" streams.

The major change in the Lake Ontario rainbow trout fishery since 1985 is the dramatic increase in the number of fish being caught. Rainbows now rank second in the yearly creel census; only chinook salmon are caught more often. There are several reasons for this, including increased angler knowledge about where and how to catch rainbows, a decrease in the popularity of brown trout, and the slot limit now imposed on lake trout, which formerly held the number two spot.

Another change to the fishery was the introduction of Skamania steelhead to the lake. This highly prized strain was developed through the efforts of fishery scientists at the Skamania Hatchery, which is located on the west branch of the Washougal River in the

State of Washington. There are two distinct types of steelhead in the State of Washington: Winter steelhead, which re-enter freshwater from November through the following June, and summer steelhead, which re-enter freshwater from May through September. Skamania are a genetically selected strain of the summer steelhead. Selective breeding resulted in a strain that matures at an older age and spawns two months earlier than wild fish, enabling hatcheries to produce one-year-old smolts. Thus, returning Skamania steelhead are larger than wild rainbows because they are older. Tolerant of warm water, they begin to show up off the mouths of their natal streams by June or early July. Except for when they move inshore, they will be found with other strains of rainbows near thermal structure (breaks, thermal bar, etc.)

Studies over the past several years have indicated some interesting differences between the Chambers Creek strain of steelhead (also known as the Washington strain and the Skamania steelhead. In 1989, 24.7 percent of the Skamania steelhead caught were 30 inches or larger, while only 8.5 percent of the Chambers Creek strain of fish were that large. Also, Skamania steelhead are being harvested at a slightly higher rate than they were stocked compared to the Chambers Creek steelhead, which may be due to either a higher surviaval rate of the Skamania fish or to differences in distribution. In 1989 Skamania steelhead comprised 7.9 percent of the rainbow/steelhead catch in Lake Ontario.

In the early spring (March to early April), great numbers of rainbow trout will be found spawning in all of the major tributaries of Lake Ontario, as well as in a surprising number of smaller streams that all but disappear in the summer. Streams with good to excellent spring runs of rainbows include: the lower Niagara River, Four Mile Creek (Niagara County), Twelve Mile Creek (east branch), Eighteen Mile Creek, Keg Creek, Johnson Creek, Bald Eagle Creek, Oak Orchard Creek, Sandy Creek, the lower Genesee River, Irondequoit Creek, Mill Creek, Four Mile Creek (Monroe County), and most of the streams that feed Braddock Bay and the Greece Ponds. While these streams get a majority of the fish, they also get a majority of the fishermen; so don't neglect some of the smaller tributaries if solitude is something you desire. After a good spring rain even the most unlikely looking streams will hold enough rainbows to make your trip worthwhile.

Because of selective breeding in the hatcheries, not all rainbow trout spawn in the spring. Many of those that don't will be found close to shore in search of forge fish and warm temperatures. The preferred temperature range for rainbows is 50 to 65 degrees. These fish tend to orient off rocky points, piers, sudden drop-offs, along the edges of shoals, and near areas of thermal mixing such as the mouths of streams, power plant discharges, and sewage outfalls. Watoma Shoal, the drop-offs at Oklahoma Point (east of Irondequoit Bay), The Flats, which are located 2 1/2 miles east of Point Breeze, and the thermal discharges at Russell Station (Slater Creek) and Somerset are all examples of productive near-shore areas, both in the spring and in the fall.

By the end of April, rainbow trout will begin to move off shore. Before they can break out into deep, open water, they become corralled behind what is referred to as a thermal bar. The thermal bar is a temporary interface between waters of different temperatures. It is characterized by a rapid change in surface temperature over a very short distance, with warm near-shore waters quickly giving way to a steep "wall" of cold (approximately 39 degrees), dense water. Rainbows are strongly attracted to this thermal structure and stack up along the shoreward edge of the bar as it moves toward the center of the lake, finally disappearing around the middle of June. While it lasts, the trout fishing near the bar can be spectacularly productive. In fact, this is probably the premier rainbow trout fishing in the whole world!

Once the thermal bar dissipates and the thermocline sets up, rainbows break out into deep, open water, roaming the lake at least 3 to 5 miles from shore. They exhibit little apparent pattern other than the fact that they are often found anywhere from 10 to 200 feet down in waters between 200 and 500 feet deep.

In the late spring and early summer, locating thermal breaks is of paramount importance in locating and catching rainbow trout. An example of such a break are the occasional cold-water upwellings that take place in the western and central portions of Lake Ontario. As prevailing west winds push warm surface waters toward the eastern end of the lake, it is displaced by relatively cold water from the bottom. When this cold mass comes in contact with warm surface waters, marked temperature differences can be observed, often as much as 20 degrees over a distance of a few yards. Rainbow trout, as well as coho salmon, are greatly attracted to this narrow transition zone, which can last anywhere from a few hours to a few days. Recently, commercially available surface temperature maps of the lake have come on the market. Taken by satellite and updated twice-weekly, these maps can be valuable aids in locating rainbows.

Rainbow trout and steelhead rank second only to chinook salmon in importance on Lake Ontario. These silvery battlers are well-known for their magnificent leaps and strong runs when hooked. Photo courtesy John Kowalczyk.

Regardless of their origin, most rainbows exhibit similar behavior in the summer and can be caught with similar methods. The key elements are locating the thermal breaks, brightly colored lures, and fast trolling speeds.

In the early fall, rainbow trout begin to move closer to shore, searching for more favorable water temperatures. They can be found within a quarter mile of shore from late September to early November, and are readily taken by conventional trolling methods. By the middle of November, these fish will begin moving into streams, some to spawn, most simply to spend the winter. All of the streams that have good spring runs of rainbows will get some influx of fish in the fall. An impression formed by conversations with a number of experienced anglers is that in the fall many of the unstocked streams don't get quite the number of rainbows trout that they do in the spring. Why this would be so, if it is true, is unknown. Whatever the case may be, after a good fall rain, most, if not all, of the tributaries of Lake Ontario will harbor rainbows. In the stocked streams especially, the angling can be good to excellent from the middle of November right through to the middle of April, if the weather cooperates.

Streams and rivers that usually have open water all winter include: the lower Niagara River, the Burt dam area of Eighteen Mile Creek, below the Waterport dam on Oak Orchard Creek, the lower Genesee River, and the lower portions of Irondequoit Creek. All of these waters are heavily stocked and produce good numbers of rainbows through the winter. For the ice fisherman, your best bets would be Braddock Bay, Long Pond, and Irondequoit Bay, all in Monroe County. Wilson Harbor and Olcott Harbor will also give up an occasional rainbow trout through the ice.

The following article is a guide to cashing in on Lake Ontario's summer rainbow trout/steelhead fishing bonanza. It originally appeared in the July 1989 issue of Great Lakes Fisherman magazine.

OFFSHORE STEELHEAD

By Bill Hilts, Jr.

"Steelhead!" It's a cry becoming more frequently heard on the seemingly magical waters of Lake Ontario, the current Great Lakes hotspot when it comes to salmonids. It wasn't until the last couple of years that the testy steelhead became a popular quarry for anglers willing to tackle the deeper waters off the shores of New York during the hot summer months. And July is the absolute best time frame for wrestling these silver bullets of the deep.

The steelhead population in Lake Ontario consists of Washington strain steelhead, domestic rainbow trout, some naturally produced wild rainbows, and since 1986, Skamania steelhead. For 1988 alone, New York assisted the lake's natural production with the stocking of 943,400 steelhead/rainbows - fish that are paying back anglers now in big dividends.

With anglers making longer trips in search of the popular king salmon during the summer months, the super July steelhead fishery became an added bonus, especially in Lake Ontario's western basin - often regarded as any areas west of Rochester. The three most popular ports: Wilson, Olcott Beach, and Point Breeze. It's these three ports that may be most-often influenced by the powerful Niagara River current, one of the primary reasons why spring and summer salmon fishing is so productive in this part of the lake. For those of you who don't believe in the magic ... it's worth the trip - no matter where you are. But back to the steelies.

Tips from the Pros

Fishing for steelhead - specifically targeting those fish - is not always an easy proposition, especially if you're a novice at Great Lakes angling adventures. Once you get the knack, though, and you know what to look for on the water, using the right equipment and perfecting your presentation are the keys to successful fishing. No one knows the tricks of the trade better than the professional fishermen that troll the big water as their livelihood. Day in and day out, the full-time charter fisherman has usually done it all in the way of trial and error. He knows what works and what doesn't under certain weather conditions. He'll be able to take short cuts in finding out what will work best for him on any particular day. And most importantly, he's always learning, willing to adapt and change with the fishery. Here's a few tips from three well-respected charter fishing operators in the western basin of Lake Ontario. Take note that this is what works for them, and by applying similar methods and patterns, these same techniques can work for you, too.

Wilson's Heffernan

Situated in the confines of the small community of Wilson, Captain Jeremiah Heffernan of North Tonawanda unties his 34-foot Silverton from Wilson Boat Yard and heads north from the harbor. Heff, on his boat Bull Frog, has been an institution here, fishing for hire for more than a decade. His list of accomplishments is a long one, sounding out his fishing competence.

"Personally, I never target for steelhead," notes Heffernan. "When I go out fishing ... I target for fish! During the July time frame, I'll head north or what ever direction I came from the day before until I find a pocket of bait fish. For me, bait fish are the key during the summer months, especially when I've found bait to be absent from my Lowrance electronics screens for long distances.

He may put down sooner if he finds a pronounced temperature break, scum line, or feeding sea gulls. His forte on the water is the ability to put down loads of junk — plenty of hardware for fish to make that decision of what they want to hit on that particular day. Predominant colors may include hot pink, red, kelly green, green/red combinations, and/or silver combinations.

During the summer, Captain Jeremiah will gear most of his lures and sets toward king salmon, but he'll often find kings and steel head stacked together, with the latter on top. This is why he starts off with a godawful conglomeration of spoons, with his downriggers set up in a V pattern — salmon lures down deep, steelhead hardware closer to the surface. The preferred temperature zone for Heff and the fish is 56 to 62 degrees.

Lure selection is critical. "Steelhead are usually attracted to smaller spoons," emphasizes Heffernan. "Lure size should correspond with the size of the bait in the area you're fishing." He prefers (as do the fish) smaller Flutterchucks, Northern King, and Pirate spoons. "You want a lure with forgiving speeds, something that can handle a faster troll - especially if you're using planer boards."

Heff likes using planer boards for summer fishing, and July is a month when the water is most-often flat. Any set of good double boards will do the trick. "Cannon collapsible weighted boards work well, but so do Wille and Super Ski products."

Using side surface planers accomplishes much for the wily veteran. He's able to diversify with Deep Six divers or drop weights, using the latter primarily for kings, incorporating dodger techniques. Experimenting with different lead lengths off the boards will also help him dictate what leads to run off the downriggers.

Heffernan developed the Deep Six pattern off his planer boards a couple years ago, and since then, more times than not, Deep Sixers will out-produce his downriggers during the hot summer months.

Jeremiah uses three sizes of Deep Sixes. Early summer, he'll go with the smaller size. With up to 100 feet of line (maximum), Heff will attain depths of up to 26 feet, with a flutterspoon and 20-pound-test line. If he uses the medium-size diving plane, he'll get nearly 50-foot depths.

One of the biggest reasons for his Deep Six success is that Heff uses a release that allows him to extend his lead longer than the length of his rod. He also incorporates the use of rubber bands. Primary colors of the Deep Six will be chrome/silver, but red and chartreuse have worked well, too.

"I refer to steelhead as pack fish. Once you find them, you've got to stay on them and hit them with everything you've got. Once locating steelhead, I'll run a W pattern off my downriggers. Once I determine what the fish want to eat, I'll double and triple up my sets with that type of lure. I'll also experiment with 6- or 8-inch dodgers on effectiveness."

Olcott's Cinelli

Captain Bob Cinelli of Lockport has been working these productive waters off Olcott Beach for the better part of a decade. Currently, he's running a 28-foot Chris Craft, Trout Hunter II, under the name of Lake Ontario Charter Service out of Hedley Marina.

"My most productive method for July steelhead is use of Dipsy Divers, followed by free-floating sliders," notes Cinelli as we head out to deep water. "What I look for are current rips or thermal structure with bait on it."

Since Olcott is only six miles from Wilson, he'll often see Captain Jeremiah out trolling in deep water. They communicate with one another and compare notes often, especially during this July time frame.

During this time of year, wind direction (if any) dictates where the Niagara River current will travel. "You're looking to fish the back side of the current," points out Cinelli. "It might be 3 or 15 miles (out) ... working cold-water upwellings for steelies up high. These steelhead will be on the edge of a current rip or thermal plumb where baitfish are present. Once you locate those ingredients, you're cooking."

No sooner had those words emitted from Captain Bob's mouth when there was an explosion in the water off the back of the boat - a big steelhead. The fight lasted 10 seconds before the battling silver streak was off.

"There's a big difference between hooking them and catching them," laughed Cinelli, "Especially the trophy fish over 15 pounds. Some days, you lose half the steelhead you hook up with because of their explosive power and acrobatic abilities. And when these Skamania get bigger who knows what will happen."

Skamania steelhead were first stocked in 1986, with the intent of creating a close-in shoreline fishery for the small boater during the early summer months. But Cinelli and other captains have frequented these spectacular fish during the summer while hitting other steelies. Skamania are identified by an adipose and left pectoral fin clip. Last year, some fish topped 11 pounds. This year, they should be over 15 pounds for the four-year-old fish.

Cinelli is very specific about his equipment. Not because he's a Daiwa/Luhr Jensen pro-staffer, but because it's what really works for him. For Dipsy fishing, he stresses a Daiwa Diver Rod, a rod designed specifically for diver fishing stresses. The reel is none other than the Daiwa 47 LC, sporting a line counter to give you exact distances. The line he uses for Dipsy fishing is 20-pound Prime Plus, and his reason is a simple one. "Most monofilament will have a tendency to stretch. The further out your dipsy is, the harder it is to release the clip. With cofilament line, I've got less stretch, less problems with releases, and more hook-setting power."

During July, Cinelli will run four Dipsy Divers - two off the outriggers and two off the sides. He'll dial in 2-1/2 on the outside divers, and 2 for the inside, choosing colors based on water clarity, sunlight, and how deep the fish are. Gold, silver, green, chartreuse, and white will all produce their share of fish.

Cinelli will be consistent with his baits, running the same spoons on the Dipsy Divers that he runs off his downriggers and sliders. For example, if he runs black with green off his downriggers, he'll have the same color combination off the sliders and the divers.

"Generally, I'll run silver-plated spoons, such as the Diamond King, Pirate, Northern King, or Fin Weaver, or colored baits, like the Yeck or Southport Slammer - all in the small to medium-size ranges for steelies."

Cinelli varies his course when pulling divers, allowing them to rise and fall with an S troll. He'll start with 50 and 70 feet off the reel counter on each side, with lead lengths from Dipsy to lure never more than 10 feet.

"Steelhead will come up for baits, and it's been my experience that this is what they prefer. I fish above the targeted temperature zone for steelies." Like Heffernan, he'll run a deep set for kings, and a shallow set for steelhead off the 'riggers.

"The key to running divers successfully is to stick with them," echoes Cinelli. "They can't work for you if they're in your tackle box." It's a lesson he learned from captain number three.

Oak Orchard's Pierleoni

Near the mouth of Oak Orchard River, where it empties into Lake Ontario at Point Breeze, docks Captain Vince Pierleoni, of Kent, another popular fishing fanatic that's made his mark on the lake-wide fishing scene. We had just come in off the lake after a productive morning of fishing — 17 steelhead, 7 kings, and a sunburn — not unlike the days we had with Heffernan and Cinelli. In fact, Cinelli tag-teamed on this particular outing.

To describe Pierleoni's fishing attitude in a word: intense. Even when he's just out fun-fishing. He pays extreme attention to detail, and he's very meticulous about even the smallest thing, such as sharpness of his hooks. For steelhead in July, Pierleoni covers as much water as possible to locate the fish. When he does pinpoint a location that harbors fish, he likes to stay on them. He swears by his Loran C to not only stay on his fish, but to also use it as a navigational tool when poor visibility might crop up as a result of unexpected fog or storm conditions.

As far as keeping on the fish, a hand-made marker buoy can be every bit as effective. All three captains agree on the versatility of the new Lowrance LMS 300, which combines Loran, plotter, and graph with temperature and speed - all rolled up into one.

Because of the high ratio of dead to fertile water in the summer, he trolls at a faster pace mimicking a school of baitfish off his downriggers with a set of spoons that can, once again, tolerate faster trolling speeds. "Many times," reflects Captain Vince, "the faster troll will actually help the steelhead into triggering them to hit." The spoon names of Yeck, Northern King, and Pirate are all reiterated, with color depending on the day and depth, as well as water clarity.

"We've seen the past few years that the hottest tape one year will produce little or nothing the following year. You need to experiment and learn to adapt to the changing conditions of the lake."

His trolling speed, which will vary from two to four knots, will be a zigzag-type pattern over a current edge, once he establishes one. Most of his spoon set will be the same color, with an odd one or two thrown in for good measure when fish decide to change their feeding preferences.

Pierleoni, too, runs Dipsy Divers, but he differs from Cinelli in that he likes to run a different pattern or different-size lures off the diver than he runs in his V set. That V set will be set up in such a way so that the middle of it will focus in on his targeted zone.

"Colors that will work for me for steelhead will often not catch kings."

Unlike Heffernan, Pierleoni specifically targets steelhead and develops patterns directed at these leapin' lunkers. He agrees that spoon size is critical, matching size to the available bait. He also believes in heavier line. It offers anglers every bit as much of a sporting challenge, and smaller fish can be brought in much more easily - and released to fish another day. It also gives you more of a chance at catching the trophy steelhead. He prefers Trilene Big Game in 20-pound test.

For steelhead fishing, Pierleoni stresses quality hardware - from hooks to split rings. "Sharp hooks are essential. Steelhead are quick to find fault with inferior hooks. For my boat, more steelhead are lost than any other species of fish. I prefer treble hooks."

That latter lesson was a pay-back by Cinelli. Pierleoni's favorite hooks are VMC and Eagle Claw.

"Keep an eye on those split rings. Don't let them bend. Replace them at the first sign of fatigue. And if you really want to improve your trophy steelhead chances, pay attention to your reel drag. If your drags are too tight, even a hair, the initial jolt may be too much. The greatest challenge steelhead fishing provides is that even if you're doing everything right, it still won't ensure you'll catch that fish."

"As far as reading the lake's current and thermal structure, the only accurate way to learn is with time on the water," notes Pierleoni.

Now that you've heard it from the professionals, you should be able to go out and tackle these underwater magicians. Right? These tricks should help catch steelhead that will average in size from 5 to 10 pounds. But the only condition that these three captains give for lending you a helping hand is that you practice catch-and-release, especially on the smaller fish. This is a finite resource, and they've seen the average size of the fish decline a bit from fishing pressure. They're not seeing the seven- and eight-year-old fish any more. They seem to be four to six years old. It's no crime to take some for table fare, but never take more than what you can use - and please, put the small ones back!

All three captains can be very accommodating when it comes to on-water educational lessons in the way of a charter. Just let them know beforehand, and they'll take you step-by-step along the way. Here's how you can contact them:

Captain Jeremiah Heffernan
Heff's Charter Service, 133-12th Avenue
North Tonawanda, NY 14120
(716) 694-6315;

Captain Bob Cinelli
Lake Ontario Charter Service
The Harbor, Olcott, NY 14126
(716) 434-2189

Captain Vince Pierleoni
Thrillseeker Charter Service
1197 Transit Road North
Kent, NY 14477
(716) 682-1287

Chinook Salmon .... Abundant; growth rate excellent

One of the biggest changes on Lake Ontario in the past few years has been the development of a great spring and summer fishery for chinook salmon. Previously, the spring was a period when relatively few chinook were caught, and the summer offered only spotty action for these sleek, powerful denizens of the lake. Fishing for chinooks is now excellent from April through September.

There are several reasons for the growth of the spring chinook fishery. First and foremost is the tremendous number of chinook stocked in the lake by the state of New York. Since 1983 the state's stocking recommendation for Lake Ontario has remained at 2.7 million chinooks per year. Because these fish do not return to their natal streams to spawn for 2 to 3 years, the full impact of this stocking program was not felt until the mid-1980s. The situation has continued to improve as anglers' experience develops and techniques are refined.

The spring salmon fishing is especially good in the near-shore waters between Braddock Bay and the mouth of the Niagara River. The reason or reasons why this particular area is so good in the spring is unknown, but it probably involves a fortuitous combination of temperatures, structure, and forage. Within this area local hot spots occur. These include the waters off Sandy Creek, Golden Hill Creek, Eighteen Mile Creek, and Twelve Mile Creek. But the best salmon fishing by far is found on the Niagara Bar at the mouth of the Niagara River. The waters off the mouth of the Genesee River also provide some good spring salmon fishing, but it is not nearly as good as areas to the west.

In the spring, the chinook fishing takes place close to shore early in the day. As the day progresses, though, the fish usually move into increasingly deeper water. Depending on conditions (light, wind, available forage, etc.), midday will find the salmon in water as shallow as 15 feet or as deep as 60 feet.

In the late spring, the salmon will begin a migration out into the deeper regions of Lake Ontario. This signals the start of the great summer salmon fishing.

Until the mid-1980s, relatively few chinooks were caught in the open lake. Since that time, increasing numbers of available chinook salmon, the development of more effective techniques for finding and taking salmon, and a greater willingness on the part of anglers to fish far from shore has made the summer a great time to experience Lake Ontario's trophy salmon fishing.

By the middle of July, the fish will be found off the bottom and at least 3 to 5 miles off shore. Often they are found out as far as the shipping lanes in water over 500 feet deep and suspended anywhere from 20 to 200 feet down. Their temperature range is 50 to 58 degrees, with a very strong preference for 55 degrees. They will wander far and wide over the lake in search of this temperature or something very close to it. Unlike coho salmon, chinook are not strongly attracted to thermal structures such as the transition zone around upwellings.

Chinook fishing in western Lake Ontario really comes into its own in mid to early August. For most of this month, sexually mature salmon are engaged in a shoreward migration, seeking out their natal streams. They become much more temperature tolerant at this time and can be found in water as cold as 40 degrees or as warm as 60 degrees. Initially they are prey only to boat fisherman, but by the end of August, as phenomenal numbers of fish stage just off the mouths of streams or cruise very shallow near-shore waters, shore-bound anglers can also engage in this fishing bonanza. These fish will normally be found in deeper water during periods of high sun, moving closer to shore during the early morning and evening, and on overcast days. By early September, the greatest concentration of salmon will be found in or just off the mouth of stocked streams (the lower Niagara River, Eighteen Mile Creek, Oak Orchard Creek, and the Genesee River). But a sizable portion of these fish will stray into many unstocked streams that have good water flow. Twelve Mile Creek, Johnson Creek, Bald Eagle Creek, Salmon Creek/Braddock Bay, the Greece Ponds, Slater Creek, and Mill Creek are all known to have good fishing for chinooks in the fall. Spawning runs usually continue until the end of November, but the peak runs will be over by early November. There is no winter fishery for chinook salmon.

Brown Trout .... Abundant; growth rate excellent

The only significant change in the Lake Ontario brown trout fishery since 1985 is the fact that far fewer anglers are pursuing this species. This is due to the dramatic increase in the popularity of chinook salmon and steelhead fishing during the months when, prior to 1985, browns were the primary quarry.

In 1985 and 1988 the fishing for brown trout in Lake Ontario was poor. This had nothing to do with the number of browns in the lake. The number of fish has remained fairly constant over the years and will probably remain so for the foreseeable future. The problem had to do with the number of yearling alewives in the lake. Because of a very successful spawning the previous year, tremendous numbers of these baitfish were available as food for species such as trout, and they provided such an abundance of forage that the trout were always well fed. Any offering from an angler had to compete with thousands or millions of free-swimming baitfish for the trout's attention. It is impossible to predict when such an explosion in the baitfish population will occur.

Soon after ice-out, brown trout will be found very close to shore as they seek forage fish and favorable water temperatures (50 to 65 degrees). Compared to other salmonids, browns are rather sedentary and tend to remain in the general area in which they were stocked. This is particularly true if that area has significant shoals, boulders, or other underwater structure. For this reason, the shallow water off stocked creeks and shore lines will be the hottest areas for browns in the spring. In western Lake Ontario these include: Twelve Mile Creek (east branch), Eighteen Mile Creek, Point Breeze, the jetties at Hamlin Beach State Park, Braddock Bay, the Genesee River, the shallows off Irondequoit Bay, and the waters off Webster Park (Mill Creek). Structure areas that are especially productive in the spring are limited to "The Flats", which are located 2 1/2 miles east of Point Breeze, Watoma Shoal, and the drop-offs east of Irondequoit Bay.

Brown trout are much more tolerant of high water temperatures than other salmonids. Consequently, good numbers of browns will be found fairly close to shore after the rainbows, lakers, and salmon have headed for deeper water. Its not until the end of June, when the thermocline has set up, that most brown trout will have moved out into deeper, cooler water, preferring summer temperatures of 56 to 62 degrees. They tend to remain fairly close to the area in which they were stocked. However, their preference for the upper levels of the thermocline, coupled with the tendency to remain in relatively near-shore waters, will at times force brown trout to move parallel to shore, often great distances, to meet these requirements.

Because they do exhibit a strong preference for specific conditions, and because they are so abundant in Lake Ontario, browns are very susceptible to downrigging techniques. Although they can be taken through June, July, and mid-August, the most productive period is from early July to early August. Usually by the first week of August, brown trout begin to enter their spawning phase

Once rarely caught in the spring, chinook salmon began turning up in significant numbers along the western shore of Lake Ontario in the mid-1980s. Twenty-pound chinooks like the one displayed by Mike Bleech are now commonly caught in the spring, especially near the mouth of the Niagara River. Photo courtesy Mike Bleech.

and for a while turn off to feeding. They begin to move closer to shore as water temperatures drop, and by the end of September or early October will be abundant in most near-shore waters. Shortly thereafter they begin their spawning runs up streams and rivers. They will be concentrated in the streams that are stocked; however, unlike the spring fishery, almost any tributary that has a good flow of water will get at least a fair run of browns. Approximately 80 percent of these fish will die after spawning. Those that survive will return the following year as a significantly larger fish. Brown trout in the 10- to 20-pound category will have survived several spawnings. Browns that do survive spawning can be taken through the late fall and winter. Burt Dam (Eighteen Mile Creek), Oak Orchard Creek, and the Genesee River all have significant numbers of carry-over trout. For those who enjoy ice fishing, Wilson Harbor, Olcott Harbor, Braddock Bay, Long Pond, and Irondequoit Bay all provide fair to good fishing for brown trout in the winter.

The popularity of brown trout fishing has decreased significantly in recent years; anglers are now seeking out larger, more aggressive species such as steelhead and chinook salmon. But the quality of the brown trout fishery is still very good. Feeding voraciously, Lake Ontario browns grow rapidly and are relatively easy to catch. Photo courtesy Tim Herrmann.

The following article by veteran Lake Ontario charter boat captain Roger Lowden will give you a handle on catching these hard-fighting trout in the summertime.

FINDING AND CATCHING SUMMERTIME BROWN TROUT

By Roger Lowden

Where do you find brown trout in Lake Ontario in the summer and how do you catch them? ... Anglers who were unable to answer that question gave up on browns during this warm-weather season. Now, however, due to the efforts of researchers and the success of an increasing number of fishermen who have applied advanced deep-trolling techniques, we know where and how to fish for summertime browns.

Summertime, as defined for brown trout fishing purposes, is the period when the lake has warmed to the point where stratification (the formation of the thermocline) occurs. It lasts until brown trout "turn off," as they near their spawning phase, usually beginning in early August.

Researchers, led by Dr. James Haynes at SUNY College at Brockport, have shown that browns in Lake Ontario have a strong association with the thermocline when that magic band of cooler water is located within 3 miles of shore. If the thermocline is located 40 feet down, for example, brown trout will be there, especially where the thermocline intersects bottom. But the thermocline moves due to wind and weather and a few days later it may be 90 feet down. The browns will still be there if the bottom intersection is within about 3 miles of shore. If the bottom intersection is farther offshore, evidence indicates that brown trout will move laterally, paralleling the shoreline until they find the thermocline closer to shore. Haynes has documented lateral movement of individual brown trout up to 70 miles.

Using vertical gill netting techniques coupled with temperature profiles, Haynes found that 75 percent of brown trout were netted in or within 10 feet of the thermocline. Thirty percent were netted within 10 feet of the lake bottom, but 80 percent of those were caught there when the thermocline intersected bottom. These nettings showed that browns are distributed in fairly equal numbers from about 48 degrees to about 68 degrees, that is, throughout the thermocline. Angling success, however, indicates that the most catchable fish — those that are feeding-active — are most often located in the warmer end of the zone. Experienced brown trout trollers concentrate their efforts in water from 56 to 62 degrees, although some fish are caught in water as warm as 70 degrees.

Based on this information, here is a game plan that will put you on summer browns. First, you'll need a boat equipped with tackle that will take your lines deep. Downriggers have the edge over other deep-trolling devices because they offer the most precise depth control. With the downriggers, you'll need line release devices to connect your line to the trolling weight or downrigger cable. Stacking releases (Roemer, Clipper, Walker, Offshore) are an advantage because they allow lines at various depths to cover the entire preferred temperature zone.

Next in importance is your choice of temperature sensing devices. Constant read-out units, such as the Temp-Trol, Fish Hawk, Fishmate, or Combinator (which measure the temperature at the trolling weight) are a definite advantage over hand-held units because the thermocline is constantly moving and changing.

A good depth finder is another important aid to summer brown trout fishing. In addition to showing fish and bait, the depth finder will help you locate bottom structure and will enable you to fish close to bottom without hanging up tackle if the occasion calls for tight-to-bottom fishing.

Your boat should also be equipped with a VHF or CB radio for safety's sake, as well as to share information. Many lake trollers are friendly fishermen who will help others find the daily pattern of depth, lure selection, and color necessary for success.

Begin your brown trout trolling day by heading offshore until you are over a depth where you can find the thermocline. If there is any extensive bottom structure in the area, fish offshore from it as a starting point. Lower your temperature sensor (at trolling speed if it's a constant read-out type) until you find 56 degree water. For brown trout that should be your deepest lure. Now raise the sensor slowly until it just reads 70 degrees and you've got the depth for your shallowest lure. In most cases, this range will be found in a relatively narrow band seldom exceeding 20 feet in width and often much narrower. Troll this temperature zone from the point where it intersects bottom to deeper water until you locate fish. Trolling speed should be moderate and, of course, turns and speed changes will often trigger strikes. Most of the time, browns prefer smaller lures, such as No. 2 and No. 3 Andy Reekers, the Sutton West River, No. 1 Mepps spoons, No. 44 Flutterspoons, and small Alpena Diamonds and Evil Eyes. Brown trout seem to have a marked preference for green or chartreuse color combinations with white or silver, but like all fish, on certain days they can be very selective. So, it's wise to experiment with color combinations until you find the best one for that day. Combinations of yellow and red are good, and sometimes black variations can be deadly. While spoons are currently the most popular brown trout offering, don't rule out small plugs. Some days they make the difference necessary to catch fish. Line test for brown trout should be fairly light, usually no more than

- SPECIAL INSERT -

EMPIRE STATE/LAKE ONTARIO DERBY

Nothing demonstrates the success of the state's rejuvenation program for Lake Ontario any more than the phenomenal growth of the Empire State/Lake Ontario Trout and Salmon Derby, Inc. Known simply as ESLO, this tournament was founded in 1976 by Dick Schleyer, a former Rochester area biology teacher and fishing enthusiast.

ESLO's beginnings were modest. Competing for a grand prize worth $2,500, a total of 2,884 entrants participated in the first derby. In 1977 disaster struck when the contest had to be cancelled due to the DEC's ban on fishing on Lake Ontario that year. But Schleyer was not to be denied his dream. Convinced that the lake could once again support a viable sport fishery, he and other businessmen and sportsmen pushed to have the fishing ban lifted. It was, and as they say, the rest is history.

As the quality of Lake Ontario's trout and salmon fishing grew, so did ESLO. Today, Schleyer and his son Rick manage what is recognized as the world's largest fishing derby operation. ESLO now runs four derbies: The Spring ESLO Derby held in late April; the Busch Summer Derby, which runs from early May to mid-April; the Fall King Salmon Derby, which runs from mid-August to early September; and the Lake Erie International Derby, which runs from the end of July to early August. More than 36,000 anglers from all over North America compete annually for over $400,000 in guaranteed prizes, as well as for thousands of dollars worth of manufacturer's incentive prizes.

One of the many reasons that ESLO has been so successful is the fact that everyone who enters the contest has a very good chance of winning something, whether you're fishing from a pier, a dinghy, or a fully outfitted charter boat. And you don't have to be an expert angler to win either. The rank and file fisherman often walks away with the top prize, which can be worth more than $50,000.

There are an incredible number of ways to win in these derbies. Aside from the grand prizes, there are scores of awards for the largest fish in the major divisions: salmon, brown trout, lake trout, and rainbow trout/steelhead. Then there are prizes handed out by the Kidney and Easter Seals Foundations, numerous manufacturer and dealer prizes, and special awards. All totalled, there are over 8,000 chances to be a winner in the ESLO derbies!

It doesn't cost a fortune to take part in this exciting tournament. In 1991 the entry fee for an individual derby was only $14. The entry fee also entitles you to receive the ESLO Newsletter, an information-packed brief that reviews past derby events and discusses important happenings on the lake.

Then there is The Derby Gazette, which is put out twice a year and available free at many tackle shops and marinas ($3.25 by subscription). This newspaper is so filled with information on various aspects of Lake Ontario that it would take days to read it all. Many of the articles are written by some of the best anglers on the lake. In fact, many of the guest articles that appear in this book are reprints of articles that have appeared over the years in the Gazette. They are valuable sources of information on how to fish Lake Ontario successfully.

The positive impact that Lake Ontario's rebirth has had on the state's economy is tremendous. A significant part of this is due directly to ESLO. In a report prepared by the Wayne County Public Information Office and Sea Grant, it was shown that in 1986 the spring ESLO Derby generated over $4,800,000 in revenue for the lakeshore region of the state. Significantly, over half of this money was spent by anglers not residing in the lakeshore region (16.5 percent were from out-of-state). A total of 12,845 fishermen participated in the 1986 spring derby. When you consider the fact that over 36,000 anglers participate in the derbies now held annually, the economic impact of ESLO assumes truly amazing proportions.

Although ESLO is a fishing-for-profit business, money is not the only concern of the people who run the operation. As early as 1970 Dick Schleyer was lobbying state agencies to recognize the economic and recreational value of Lake Ontario. This sense of commitment to upgrading one of the state's greatest natural resources has remained a part of ESLO throughout its existence. In 1985 it resulted in the formation of the ESLO Fishing Advisory Council (FAC). The FAC is funded entirely from derby entry fees and membership is free to all entrants. Designed to represent the broad-based interests of its members, which number well over 30,000, its board of directors is manned by charter boat associations officers, county representatives, commercial interests and fishing organizations. The lobbying of the FAC has been instrumental in getting federal, state, and county aid for various waterfront projects, for the banning of gill nets on Lake Ontario, and in getting the state to introduce Skamania steelhead into the lake.

To participate in one of the ESLO Derbies all you need to do is register. Walk-in registrations can be obtained at many tackle shops along the lake and in major cities of the state. Mail in registrations and other information about ESLO can be obtained by contacting:

ESLO
P.O. Box 23746
Rochester, New York 14692
(716) 272-0130

The ESLO Derbies are the largest fishing contests in the world. The popularity of the derbies is due to their total prize package worth about $500,000! John Allen, grand prize winner of the 1990 Spring ESLO Derby, collected cash and merchandise worth $53,500 for his entry, a 30.5-pound chinook salmon. Photo courtesy ESLO.

10 pounds — lighter if you can handle it. The distance from the lure to the downrigger weight is a matter of personal choice. Browns will hit lures fairly close to the weight in deep water. If you prefer to run long lines, remember that some lures will run deeper as line is let out so it will be necessary to raise the downrigger weight to keep the lure in the strike zone and off the bottom.

Lake Trout .... **Abundant; growth rate excellent**

Lake Ontario originally had an excellent population of native lake trout. Their eventual demise began in the 19th century with the settlement of large numbers of people on the southern shore of the lake. By the early 20th century, a combination of commercial overharvesting and predation by lampreys had all but wiped out this once thriving population. The last recorded sport catch of native lake trout occurred in the 1930s.

In the 1960s advances in artificial rearing techniques and a commitment on the part of the state and federal governments to reestablish sport fishing in Lake Ontario resulted in a program for stocking lake trout here. Coupled with an ongoing lamprey control effort, the long-term purpose of this stocking program is to reestablish a self-sustaining lake trout population. Naturally produced lakers have, in fact, been reported in recent years. If the program is successful, it will be a major step toward the rehabilitation of Lake Ontario.

The preferred temperature range of lake trout is 45 to 55 degrees. In the spring they move into shallow near-shore waters, drawn in by amenable temperatures and abundant forage fish. This takes place just after ice-out, which is important to remember, because ice-out does not occur on all areas of the lake at the same time. In a typical year the shoreline of the lake will be ice-free by late March in areas west of the Salmon River.

Lake trout are a mainstay of Lake Ontario's summer fishery. This fish weighed in at just over 14 pounds. Photo courtesy Tony Arlauckas.

For information on fishing in central New York, obtain a copy of Sander's Fishing Guide No. 2 - The Finger Lakes Region. This comprehensive guide to over 250 lakes and streams is available in most tackle shops and book stores or can be obtained by using the order form in the back of this book.

Nettings by the DEC have shown that lake trout can be found almost anywhere along the shore in the spring and can be taken by shore fishermen and boat fishermen alike. West of the Salmon River, lakers are not harvested in numbers that are indicative of their abundance. This could be due to a number of factors. The fish could be moving a little further off shore during the daylight hours due to their sensitivity to light. Or possibly the fishermen are concentrating their efforts on the more popular brown trout, rainbow trout, and chinook salmon.

Lakers are very active feeders when found at their preferred temperatures, and can be taken by shore fishermen and boat fishermen alike. Although they can be found almost anywhere along the shore in the spring, especially productive areas include: the stretch of shoreline between the mouth of the Niagara River and Four Mile Creek (Niagara County); off the mouths of all major tributaries (Twelve Mile Creek, Eighteen Mile Creek, Oak Orchard Creek, and the Genesee River); any warm-water discharges (Somerset Station and Russell Station); the jetties at Hamlin Beach State Park; the piers at Sandy Creek; the pier at Webster Park, east of Rochester; and on major sand bars and rocky points.

This spring fishery lasts roughly until the middle of May, when near-shore temperatures become too warm and the fish are forced to move into deeper, cooler waters.

During the summer, lake trout are relatively easy to catch using modern downrigger techniques. They tend to school at known water temperatures (45 to 55 degrees) at or very near the bottom, in water up to 300 feet deep. Because of the tremendous number of lake trout now being stocked in the lake in recent years, any location that meets these requirements is almost certain to be productive. Lake trout return to near-shore waters in the late fall to spawn over gravel or rocky bottoms. Unlike other salmonids, they spawn in the lake and only rarely venture up past the mouth of a stream (the lower Niagara River is an exception). Most of their spring haunts will again be productive at this time. Lake trout survive spawning and will remain in the shallows until they are forced to move into deeper water in favor of more favorable temperatures.

Beginning on October 1, 1987, new regulations went into effect for lake trout in Lake Ontario. The season now runs from January 1 to September 30. Possession is limited to fish less than 27 inches in length and greater than 30 inches. All other lake trout must be released. The daily limit is 3 lake trout per day. Be sure to check current regulations.

Coho Salmon .... **Abundant; growth rate excellent**

Coho salmon, also known as silver salmon, are not nearly as abundant in western Lake Ontario as chinook salmon. In some years they comprise as much as 50 percent of the spring catch, but in most years they are a relatively minor fishery. The main problem is the fact that the fishery consists essentially of a single year-class. These salmon are stocked in the lake at an age of 18 months, and 18 months later they spawn and die. Unlike chinook salmon, there is almost no overlap of year-classes with cohos.

In the spring, soon after ice-out, coho will be found close to shore in search of baitfish and water temperatures that most closely approximate their preferred range of 50 to 58 degrees. Areas that warm up first, such as the mouths of major streams, warm-water discharges from power plants, and large piers near harbors, serve as attractants and are very productive early on. Unlike their cousin the chinook, coho are a schooling fish, tending to concentrate in the spring along particular sections of the lake shore. The following areas should be the most productive locations for spring coho: Eighteen Mile Creek/Olcott Harbor, Oak Orchard Creek/Point Breeze, and Sandy Creek/Hamlin Beach. In fact, the stretch of shore from Point Breeze to the Genesee River provides the bulk of the spring coho catch for the entire lake. Trolling close to shore or fishing from piers in these areas will be very productive. Also, don't overlook the shoreline from the Genesee River to Oklahoma Point or the jetty at Webster Park, both of which are known to attract spring salmon.

As near-shore waters begin to warm into the mid-50s, coho begin to migrate toward deeper water. This takes place in late May and June. By July, the fish will be far off shore, at least 3 to 5 miles out. During the months of July and August, coho roam the open lake at random, showing little pattern other than preferring, when temperatures permit, the top 10 to 30 feet of water. They are also strongly attracted to the same cold-water upwellings described in the section on rainbow trout. Generally speaking though, summer coho are elusive and require a good deal of luck and persistence to locate.

Around the middle of August, coho begin to migrate back toward shore in anticipation of their spawning runs. At this time they again congregate in massive schools. Initially, these schools will be found anywhere from near-shore waters to several miles off shore, depending on weather conditions. But by the first week of September, they will be located very close to the spawning streams. They will remain stacked up off the mouth of these streams for several weeks, waiting for the right conditions to trigger their spawning run. It is during this period that boat anglers experience the tremendous salmon fishing for which Lake Ontario has become renowned. The same general areas that are productive in the spring will also be good in the fall, with the difference that by the end of September coho will be found not only near shore, but also in the streams. Naturally, the greatest number of fish will be found in stocked streams (Eighteen Mile Creek, Oak Orchard Creek, and Sandy Creek). But good numbers of coho will also stray into many nonstocked streams that have a good flow of water. Streams such as the lower Niagara River, Twelve Mile Creek (east branch), Johnson Creek, Salmon Creek (Braddock Bay), Slater Creek, the Genesee River and Mill Creek all get fair to good runs of coho each fall. The spawning runs last until the end of November, with a few fish being taken into December. There is no winter fishery for coho salmon.

NOTE: In September 1989, a new world record coho salmon was caught in Lake Ontario. The fish, caught by New Jersey angler Jerry Lifton, weighed in at 33 pounds 4 ounces. This broke a record set 40 years ago in British Columbia

Atlantic Salmon .... Uncommon; growth rate good

At one time, Lake Ontario had a bountiful population of landlocked Atlantic salmon. Unfortunately, during the late 1800s an abundance of mill dams on spawning streams, parasitic sea lamprey, and industrial pollution dealt a swift and fatal blow to these magnificent gamefish.

In an attempt to reestablish a viable Atlantic salmon fishery, the DEC developed an experimental stocking program. The goal of the program was to determine the feasibility of reestablishing the fishery through natural reproduction. Beginning in 1983, three potential nursery streams – Irondequoit Creek in Monroe County, Little Sandy Creek in Oswego County, and Lindsey Creek in Jefferson County – were identified and stocked annually with a total of 49,000 yearlings. During the spawning season, these streams were closed to fishing to protect the returning salmon. These streams were periodically monitored in the fall for returning adults and during the summer to determine if any natural reproduction occurred. A few adult salmon survived to return to Irondequoit and Lindsey Creeks and fewer yet returned to Little Sandy Creek. A handful of wild juveniles were produced in Little Sandy Creek, but no successful reproduction could be documented in the other two potential nursery streams.

It was determined that the overriding limiting factor in establishing wild populations in these high-quality Lake Ontario tributaries was not stream habitat quality but extreme competition from other salmonids, most notably rainbow trout, for spawning and nursery areas. DEC biologists also found chinook and coho salmon successfully reproducing in the study streams. Stream-resident wild brown trout were also a serious competitor in Irondequoit Creek.

Another factor limiting the success of this stocking program was the relatively low number of Atlantics that survived to maturity to spawn. This fact was borne out by DEC creek census figures, which showed that the number of Atlantics harvested by anglers each year was low compared to the numbers being stocked. This low survival rate may have been due to predation, especially in regard to the fish stocked in Irondequoit Creek and Little Sandy Creek. Before dropping down into Lake Ontario, the smolting Atlantics had to pass through Irondequoit Bay and Sandy Creek, both of which are full of warm-water predators.

The experimental stocking of the streams provided conclusive data that some Lake Ontario tributaries contain sufficient quality habitat to produce significant numbers of wild salmonids. It suggests that New York cannot rehabilitate the once native Atlantic salmon by stocking the modest numbers utilized in this study. Also, because other trout and salmon are firmly established in many streams, it would be necessary to limit their access to spawning areas by

Once native to Lake Ontario, Atlantic salmon were wiped out by numerous environmental changes wrought on the lake by man. Since 1983, Atlantic salmon have been stocked in the lake in an effort to re-establish their population, but the program has had limited success. Fish like 12-pound salmon shown here are a real bonus. Photo courtesy John Kowalczyk.

selective fish passageways. The Ontario Ministry of Natural Resources is managing the middle Credit River for Atlantic salmon in this manner since they have barrier dams with fish traps that allow the flexibility of passing only desired species.

Given this set of circumstances, the DEC has set as its goal the establishment of a trophy Atlantic salmon sport-fishery based on a put/grow/limited-take management policy, while at the same time maximizing any potential for rehabilitating the fishery via natural reproduction. To reflect this change in policy, the stocking program was also modified. The state terminated the stocking of Atlantics in Irondequoit Creek, Little Sandy Creek, and Lindsey Creek in 1990 (recently, the summer-to-fall fishing restrictions on Irondequoit and Lindsey Creeks were removed because natural reproduction of Atlantics was not occurring. Only Little Sandy remains closed to all fishing from June through November to protect spawning Atlantics). In 1991, the DEC began stocking 200,000 Atlantic at various points in Lake Ontario. The DEC believes that survival will be improved because lake life tends to be less rigorous than stream residency, where competition for food and space is markedly higher, and because the salmon will be spared the hazardous out-migration through embayments populated with a host of warm-water predators. This stocking program will be supplemented by fish from the U.S. Fish and Wildlife Service and by the 350,000 salmon stocked by the Province of Ontario.

DEC's Fishing Boat Census indicated that New York lake anglers caught about 1,000 Atlantics during a typical April through September fishing season. Of note were the two state record Atlantics that were caught during the experimental years. The standing record is an Atlantic caught by a Pennsylvania angler off Braddock Bay on May 17, 1987. This 24-pound 9-ounce specimen eclipsed the old record by about 5 pounds. When New York and the Province of Ontario get their Atlantic programs in full swing, anglers should find 20 pounders with regularity!

Smallmouth Bass .... Abundant; growth rate good to excellent

Lake Ontario has long been known as a superb smallmouth bass fishery. But most, if not all, of the attention directed toward this species has been in the far eastern portion of the lake, in places such as Chaumont Bay and Henderson Harbor.

Recently, however, studies by the DEC and the Sea Grant Extension have shown that smallmouth bass can be found along much of Lake Ontario's shoreline. The really productive areas are rather localized, especially west of Rochester, but they are quite good and very underutilized.

Beginning in late spring, when water temperatures are nearing 50 degrees, smallmouth bass begin to school up in shallow water along the lake shore and in the lower reaches of many tributaries. They remain in these areas through the spawning season. Later, around the middle of June, rising temperatures force the bass to seek out cool, deeper waters. Their preferred water temperature range is from 68 to 70 degrees, though they will at times be found in water as warm as 75 degrees. Actively feeding fish will usually be found in water less than 50 feet deep. They favor areas with a cobble or rocky bottom and are especially attracted to structures such as boulder-strewn shoals and submerged ledges. The greatest concentrations of smallmouth occur in these areas during the months of July, August, September, and October. By the end of October most bass will have migrated into deeper waters and will not feed very aggressively. Unlike some of the Finger Lakes, Lake Ontario has never developed a winter fishery for bass.

There are three basic methods used to take smallmouth bass from Lake Ontario: trolling, drift fishing, and still fishing. Some anglers consider trolling to be the most productive of these techniques and troll throughout the season. But there are two occasions when trolling is especially successful. The first is in the early summer when the bass are moving out of the shallows and on to the shoals. For a period of a few weeks they are well dispersed on and between the two areas, and locating their precise location is difficult. Trolling allows the angler to cover a great deal of ground, improving the chances of finding fish.

The second occasion when trolling is particularly called for is when an angler is fishing in waters he is unfamiliar with. Even though it has been possible to identify individual areas as "hot spots," some of these areas are themselves the size of small lakes. Usually an angler working over a new location is not going to know exactly where the fish tend to congregate. Trolling is a good way to locate these spots.

Once you've located a productive area by trolling, don't just try to commit it to memory. On a lake the size of Ontario this usually isn't feasible. Instead, mark the spot with a buoy (a plastic bleach bottle will serve the purpose) attached to 45 feet of heavy line and a weight. When a fish hits while trolling, toss the marker buoy overboard immediately, in the direction of where the fish hit. This will give you a pretty good idea of where a school of feeding smallmouth are located.

Because trolling, even at very slow speeds, puts extra stress on equipment, use slightly heavier equipment than you normally would. Light- to medium-weight rods and reels should be used with 6- to 8-pound-test line.

The major portion of the smallmouth's diet in Lake Ontario consists of crayfish and small minnows. Thus, you want to troll with artificial baits that imitate these foods. Full-bodied sinking or deep-diving lures will produce the most fish if worked properly, but jigs and spinners will also take smallmouth. They can be trolled using flat lines or on short lines behind a downrigger weight.

A critical element in successful trolling is getting and keeping the lure as close to the bottom as possible without getting hung up on rocks or weeds. The smallmouth in this lake are seldom far from the bottom. One way to ensure that the lure is at the proper depth is to start trolling, slowly letting out line. When enough line has been played out to get the lure to the bottom, the rod tip will start dipping repeatedly as the lure bounces along the bottom. Don't let it do this too long or you could lose it. Reel in just enough line to make the rod tip stop jerking. The lure should then be just above the bottom.

In some portions of the lake a green algae known as cladophora carpets the bottom from mid-June through mid-August. If you're fishing in such an area, be sure to keep your lures riding above the algae and check them often for snagged plant debris.

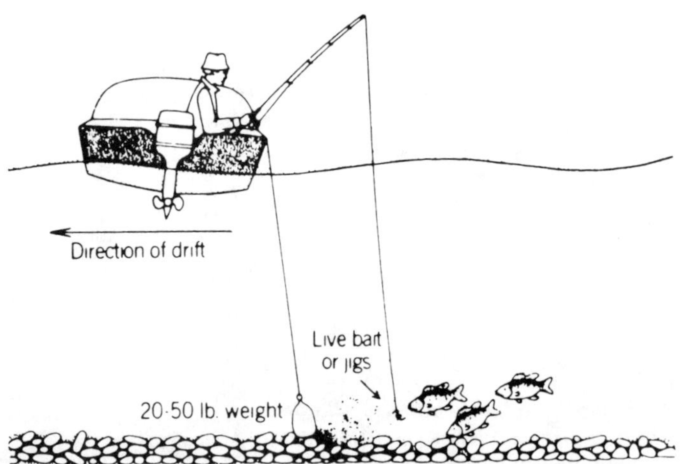

One very successful drift technique is the anchor-drag method. From late July through September, the smallmouth's major food is crayfish (crabs), which are often present in large numbers on rocky lake bottoms. A drift or drag anchor is lowered to the bottom, not with the intention of stopping the boat's drift, but rather for the purpose of turning over stones on the bottom which expose the crayfish hidden beneath. This stirring up of the bottom by the anchor apparently attracts large numbers of smallmouth into the area to feed. Anglers fishing with live soft-shell crayfish or artificial jigs in the roiled waters behind the drag anchor usually experience faster action. Simple drag anchors can be made out of a cinder block, stones tied in nylon mesh bags, or a cement-filled plastic milk or bleach bottle.

The second technique used to take smallmouth on this lake is drift fishing. There are several variations to this method, all of which can be fantastically productive. This is especially true from late July through September when smallmouth are heavily concentrated on the shoals. Because drift fishing depends on the wind and the waves for speed and direction, you are somewhat hostage to the whims of the weather. If the lake is too calm, obviously you're not going to have a drift. If it's too windy and choppy you're going to be blown off the lake. Anglers I spoke to who specialize in drift fishing recommend a south, southwest, west, or west-northwest wind just strong enough to kick up a 1 1/2- to 2-foot chop. Typically, ultra-light tackle and 4- to 6-pound-test line is used. Artificial baits, primarily jigs in black, brown, or chartreuse, can be used, but live baits get more action. Crayfish (soft-shelled if at all possible), nightcrawlers, and minnows, in descending order of preference, are the natural baits to use. Rigged on a size 4 hook with just enough weight to reach the bottom, the bait is dragged along the rocks and cobbles attracting the bass.

Charter boat captain Charlie DeNoto, who operates out of Port Bay (40 miles east of Rochester), has developed a technique of drift fishing that he calls "center-line drifting." At times this method can be almost sinfully productive. More than once I've heard of parties coming back from a charter with Charlie having boated in excess of 50 smallmouth!

DeNoto's method takes advantage of the fact that from late July through September the smallmouth rely primarily on crayfish for food. These small crustaceans are often found in great numbers on bottoms that consist of rock and cobble. The key to center-line drifting is a 20- to 50-pound weight, which is attached to the gunwales amidships and allowed to drag along the bottom. This churns the bottom up, exposing crayfish and creating what amounts to a chum line. The best smallmouth action occurs when you fish in the freshly roiled waters right behind the weight. Soft-shelled crabs are by far the best bait to use with this method, followed by worms, jigs, and minnows.

A secondary function of the weight is to serve as a drag anchor, helping to control the speed of the drift. With a 1 1/2-foot chop you can drift with the weight almost straight down. But if the wind picks up, causing you to drift too fast, feed rope out, letting the weight drag further and further behind the boat until your drift has been sufficiently reduced. Remember, though, that you want to be fishing on the far side of the weight, regardless of where it's positioned.

Center-line drifting is most productive in the waters just off the mouth of Port Bay, where the conditions are ideally suited to this technique. It can, however, be used on other parts of Lake Ontario that have a gravel or cobble bottom. It probably wouldn't be very productive in areas with a silt or sandy bottom, and it can't be done in areas covered with large rocks or boulders because the weight would hang up.

The third method used to take smallmouth from Lake Ontario is still fishing. This is used when a concentration of fish has been located, or when fishing over specific structures, such as boulders, ledges, etc. Ultra-light rods and reels with 4- to 6-pound-test line should be adequate. Live bait or artificials can be used, depending on how and where you are fishing. Still fishing is most effective when used in conjunction with trolling. Once a concentration of fish has been located through trolling, the boat can be anchored and the area fished until the bass leave the area or stop feeding. Then resume trolling.

Much of the information used in this article was taken from the pamphlet Angling for Smallmouth Bass in Lake Ontario, which was put together by Robert Buerger and Michael Voiland of the New York Sea Grant Extension Program. For information on how to obtain this and other Sea Grant publications see General Information.

Yellow Perch .... Common; growth rate good to excellent

Western Lake Ontario has long enjoyed a substantial fishery for yellow perch. Although this species regularly undergoes large swings in its population, there is always some good perch fishing to be found in the western portion of the lake.

In the spring and early summer, these great tasting fish will be found in or near every major harbor or stream mouth. Especially productive areas include: the mouth of the Niagara River, the piers at Wilson Harbor, the pier at the end of Route 425 (you'll have to get there early for a spot on this pier), the shoal off the mouth of Hopkins Creek, the Olcott Piers, the piers at the mouth of the Genesee River, and the mouth of Mill Creek, east of Rochester.

Captain Charlie DeNoto with a fine stringer of Lake Ontario smallmouth bass. DeNoto developed a technique he calls "Centerline Drifting." His technique has proven to be one of the most effective methods for catching smallmouuth bass in Lake Ontario. Photo courtesy Charlie DeNoto.

In the summer, schools of perch are often found on the Niagara Bar, at the mouth of the Niagara River. They can be encountered almost anywhere on this undulating alluvial plain, but most perch seem to be taken in 20 to 30 feet of water, just out from Rumsey Shoal. Good numbers of perch can also be found between the mouth of the Niagara and Four Mile Creek. This particular stretch is often very productive in the late summer and early fall. Another summer hotspot is located east of the Genesee River, in the waters between Mill Creek and Nine Mile Point. The perch fishing here can be quite good in the early summer and, again, you'll be looking for fish in 20 to 30 feet of water. Between the Niagara River and the Genesee River, there are some very localized areas that offer excellent perch fishing. If you look carefully at the maps of Lake Ontario, you'll notice that most of these areas are located at or near potable water intakes, which are marked as PWI on nautical charts. The reason for this may be the fact that Lake Ontario has so little natural bottom structure in its warm-water zone that the perch are attracted to the cribbing at the end of each intake. Whatever the reason, these intakes can be very productive in the summer, especially when located in 20 to 30 feet of water. Those located just off Round Pond and Little Round Pond (Slater Creek) near Rochester, and just off the Albion Water treatment plant, one mile west of Point Breeze, are often spectacularly productive. Perch should be found in these areas until they begin to move into really deep water in the fall.

In the winter, fishing opportunities on Lake Ontario are minimal due to the rough weather and lack of safe ice (very little of Lake Ontario ever freezes). But many of the small harbors along the shore offer some excellent ice fishing opportunities for perch. Wilson Harbor, Olcott Harbor, Bald Eagle Harbor, Braddock Bay and Irondequoit Bay all offer some fine hard-water angling for perch and other panfish.

Walleye .... Uncommon; growth rate good

Traditionally, walleye were an important fishery in western Lake Ontario, but changes in the ecology of the lake have resulted in a drastic reduction in their numbers. There was a fairly successful spawning of walleye in 1978, and this year-class has provided the bulk of the walleye caught in recent years. But their numbers are now greatly diminished. At present, there is very little open-water walleye fishing in western Lake Ontario. Most of the walleye are now taken in or near the mouths of major streams, primarily those that have a healthy indigenous populations of walleye. These include the lower Niagara River, Oak Orchard Creek, and the Genesee River. Less productive sites include Olcott Harbor, the lowermost reaches of Golden Hill Creek, Bald Eagle Harbor, and Braddock Bay, all of which will give up an occasional walleye.

Northern Pike .... Common; growth rate good

Northern Pike are quite common in the western portion of Lake Ontario, as evidenced by the tremendous spawning run of pike in the lower Niagara River in the spring, almost all of which are gone by the time pike season opens. Very few pike, though, are encountered in the open lake. Instead, they are most often taken in the mouths of streams or in marshy estuaries along the lake shore. The most consistently productive areas include Wilson Harbor, Olcott Harbor, the lower reaches of Johnson Creek, lower Oak Orchard Creek, Braddock Bay, the Greece Ponds, and Irondequoit Bay. Waters that are somewhat less productive, but certainly worth investigating, include Four Mile Creek (Niagara County), Sandy Creek, and the lower Genesee River. All of these areas provide exciting pike fishing in the spring and fall. Northerns can also be taken through the ice in Wilson Harbor, Olcott Harbor, Braddock Bay, and the Greece Ponds (with the exception of Round Pond).

Smelt .... Abundant; growth rate good

Much of the success of Lake Ontario's rejuvenated salmonid fishery can be attributed to the huge forage base that exists in the lake. A large portion of this forage base, the smelt, are themselves an important sport fishery. Every spring, usually several weeks after ice-out, unbelievable numbers of these small, very tasty fish move in close to shore. They hug the bottom during the day, but at might move into very shallow water (1 to 3 feet) and swim parallel to shore in schools that number in the millions, seeking out streams in which to spawn. Anglers armed with dip nets and fishing at night can harvest almost unlimited quantities of smelt at the height of the runs. Almost any stream mouth, pier, or stretch of shoreline will be productive, with angling opportunities limited more by accessibility than by the availability of fish.

Additional Species

Aside from the major species found in Lake Ontario, a number of lesser fisheries exist whose combined importance can not be overestimated. Prominent among these secondary fisheries are the white perch, crappies, bullhead, and rock bass. These fish all spawn in the spring and can be found in most harbors, bays and major streams.

Excellent spring fishing for white perch can be found in the Greece Ponds and Braddock Bay west of Rochester, and to a lesser extent in and near Wilson Harbor. In the summer, good catches of white perch are often taken from shoal areas at dusk and dawn, and from deep-water areas in the daytime. They are a schooling fish, and when one is caught it is almost certain that great numbers of others are nearby.

Bullhead, which can be taken immediately after ice-out in most streams, are especially abundant in Four Mile Creek (Niagara County), Twelve Mile Creek (east and west branches), Eighteen Mile Creek, Johnson Creek, Oak Orchard Creek, Braddock Bay, the Greece Ponds, and the Genesee River. Later in the summer, they can be found over shallow sandy-bottomed areas of the lake. A unique fall run of these fine tasting members of the catfish family occurs in Eighteen Mile Creek, Johnson Creek, and Oak Orchard Creek.

Crappies, like bullhead, are found in almost all bays and harbors in the spring. In early May, large schools of these excellent tasting fish can be found in the back bay of Wilson Harbor, in the pool below Burt Dam, throughout Oak Orchard Creek, Braddock Bay, the Greece Ponds, and the lower Genesee River.

In late May, around "apple blossom" time, rock bass will move into most bays and larger streams to spawn. Spectacular angling for these scrappy fighters is found in the lower Oak Orchard Creek. Later in the summer, rock bass can be found in the lake over the same rocky bottoms frequented by smallmouth bass.

Other species of lesser importance include largemouth bass, which are found in limited numbers in the lower Niagara River, Wilson Harbor, the mouth of Johnson Creek, Oak Orchard Creek, Braddock Bay, the Greece Pond, the Genesee River, and Irondequoit Bay. Channel catfish, though probably fairly common, are not often sought by Lake Ontario Anglers. They can be found off the mouth of major streams as well as in Braddock Bay, the Greece Ponds, and Irondequoit Bay. Last, but certainly not least, are the ubiquitous carp, suckers, and sheepshead, all of which are quite common throughout the shallow portions of the lake.

General Information

Lake Ontario is truly a little giant. Though the smallest of the Great Lakes, it has nevertheless developed a well-deserved reputation as one of the finest sport fishing waters in all of North America. It's deep, well-oxygenated waters, productive littoral zone, and numerous tributaries offer anglers outstanding fishing opportunities for a wide range of cold- and warm-water species.

Historically, Lake Ontario was a fishery of monumental proportions. Indians and early white settlers harvested vast quantities of the lake's native species, including Atlantic salmon, walleye, blue pike, and lake trout.

Unfortunately, this bounty was doomed by a long series ecological disasters, all of which were man-made. The destruction of spawning areas, overharvesting, and the introduction of exotic species combined to wipe out nearly all of the lake's game species. Those that remained were assaulted by toxins from industrial and municipal sources. By the late 1960s, all that was left of this once great fishery was a bittersweet memory. In the words of Bill Abraham, a senior aquatic biologist for the DEC Region 8 office, "Before 1973, Lake Ontario was a good place get your drinking water and dump your garbage."

In the late 1960s, the first tentative steps were taken to turn this situation around. Programs were initiated to bring the problem of the sea lamprey under control, which was critical to the success of any stocking program. Then, taking their cue from the successful pioneering efforts of Michigan's early salmon program, the State of New York and the Province of Ontario began stocking the lake with trout and salmon in 1968. Encouraged by the success of these early plantings, the scale of the program has increased steadily ever since. By 1986, over 8,000,000 trout and salmon were being stocked in the lake by New York and Ontario each year, and the dream of re-establishing a world-class fishery had been achieved. Lake Ontario is now arguably the best lake for brown trout and rainbow trout fishing in the world, and the quality of the chinook and steelhead fishing draws anglers from all over North America. And the miracle isn't over yet. In the near future, biologists hope to establish a significant fishery for Atlantic salmon and the Skamania strain of steelhead.

Overshadowed by the spectacular trout and salmon fishing is Lake Ontario's warm-water fishing. The narrow littoral zone of the

Sea Lampreys are still a problem in Lake Ontario. Using their sucker-like mouth to attch to a large fish, such as the lake trout shown here, the rasp a wound in the side of the fish and suck fluids out of it, retarding the growth of the fish and often killing it. Photo courtesy DEC.

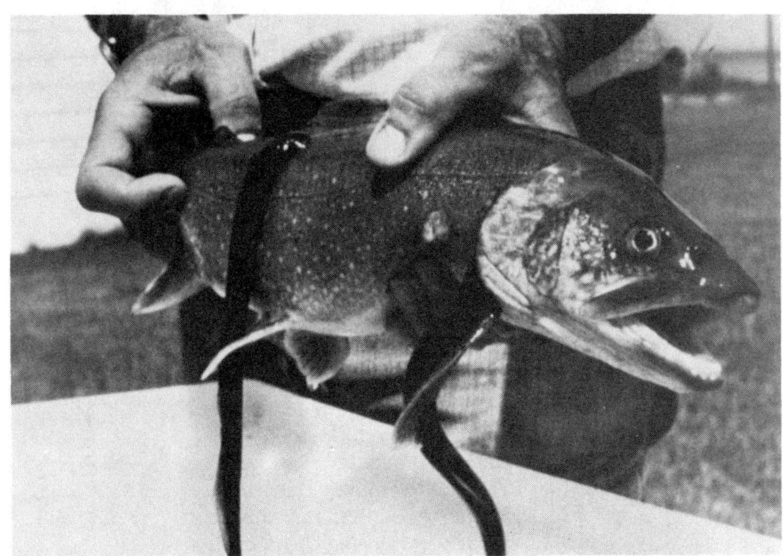

lake has very good fishing for smallmouth bass, rock bass, bullhead, black crappies, and white perch. If conditions are right, the lake can also have some pretty respectable fishing for yellow perch. The many bays and creek mouths along the lake also provide good fishing for these and other species, and in the winter provide the bulk of the ice fishing on the lake.

Although the situation in Lake Ontario has vastly improved over the past two decades, it would be wrong to presume that all of the problems have been eliminated. Pollution is still a major problem here. The levels of pollutants in the lake have been declining for a number of years, but the levels of toxins found in many of the fish are still a concern to health officials. The state strongly recommends limiting your intake of most of the species caught in Lake Ontario. For a current summary of the state health advisory regarding this lake consult your fishing regulations guide. For information on how to reduce the amount contaminants found in the fish contact your regional office of the DEC or county cooperative extension.

Another problem that besets Lake Ontario is the lack of adequate public access, especially boat access. With the phenomenal growth of boating and fishing on the lake, the state has for a number of reasons been unable to keep up with demand for additional facilities. And some areas of the lake will never have adequate launching capabilities due to the topography of the shoreline. County, state, and federal agencies are looking into the problem, and new access sites are constantly being considered. But for the moment, access to some portions of lake are not adequate.

To accommodate those not familiar with the techniques of trout and salmon fishing on Lake Ontario, or who don't have the necessary equipment, a booming charter boat industry has developed. Operating out of every port on the lake, there several hundred charter boat captains licensed by the Coast Guard to take you out in search of some of the finest fishing in the world. Many of these captains are bonafide fishing pros who will not only help you catch fish, but will also teach you a great deal about how it's done. They can provide you with an experience you're not likely to forget.

There are far too many licensed charters to list here, but many of them are affiliated with regional organizations. For information on what charters are available try contacting local marinas, area chambers of commerce, or regional tourism boards.

Additional information on fishing in central and western Lake Ontario can be obtained by contacting:

NYS Department of Environmental
Conservation Region 8
6274 East Avon-Lima Road
Avon, New York 14414
(716) 226-2466

NYS Department of Environmental
Conservation Region 9
600 Delaware Avenue
Buffalo, New York 14202
(716) 847-4565

NYS Department of Environmental Conservation
Olean Sub-office (Region 9)
128 South Street
Olean, New York 14760
(716) 372-8676

Sea Grant Extension Program
SUNY/Brockport
Brockport, New York 14420
(716) 395-2638

Cooperative Extension of Niagara County
4487 Lake Avenue
Lockport, New York 14094
(716) 433-8839

Lake Ontario Fishing Hot Lines

1. Jefferson County .... (315) 782-2663
2. Oswego County .... (315) 342-5873
3. Wayne County .... (315) 483-4454
4. Monroe County .... (716) 987-8800
5. Orleans County .... (716) 682-4223
6. Niagara County .... (716) 433-5606

The equipment and techniques used to locate and catch trout and salmon on Lake Ontario are subjects worthy of a separate book. Rather than taking on such a task, I have chosen instead to reproduce a number of previously written articles, which can be found in the appendices of this book. Written by some of the best anglers on the lake and by biologists studying the dynamics of this fishery, these are reliable sources of information on various aspects of fishing for Great Lakes trout and salmon. These articles originally appeared in various magazines or as separate publications issued by Sea Grant.

LAKE ONTARIO

(Niagara River to Smokey Point)
(Contours in Feet)

NOTE A

The lines that cover the maps for Lake Ontario are photographic artifacts of the Loran-C lines of position that are overprinted on all current nautical charts of this lake distributed by the National Oceanic and Atmospheric Administration.

NOTE B

The maps above listed are not to be used for navigational purposes. The navigational charts that served as the basis for these maps can be obtained by contacting:

National Ocean Service
Distribution Branch (N/CG33)
Riverdale, Maryland 20737
(301) 436-6990

For current navigation regulations on Lake Erie consult the U.S. Coast Guard Pilot 6 or the Weekly Notice to Mariners.

NOTE C

Canadian nautical charts and information pertaining to Canadian waters covered by the above maps can be obtained by contacting the following office:

Hydrographic Chart Distribution Office
Department of Fisheries and the Environment
1675 Russell Road
P.O. Box 8080
Ottawa, Ontario KIG3H6
(613) 998-4931

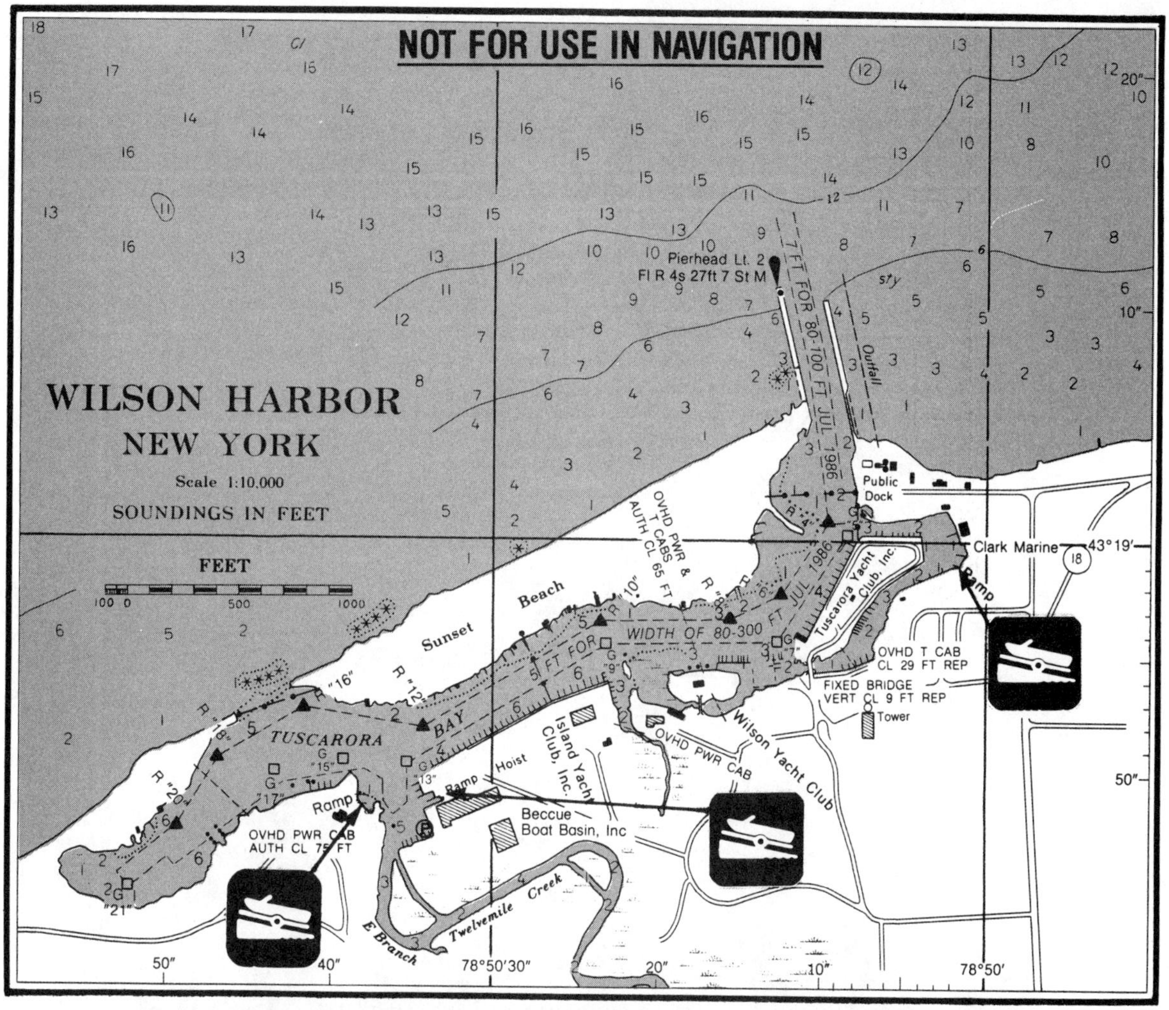

NOT FOR USE IN NAVIGATION

WILSON HARBOR
NEW YORK

Scale 1:10,000

SOUNDINGS IN FEET

FEET

100 0 500 1000

Pierhead Lt. 2
Fl R 4s 27ft 7 St M

7 FT FOR 80-100 FT JUL 1986

Outfall

Public Dock

Clark Marine

43°19′

Ramp

Tuscarora Yacht Club, Inc.

OVHD T CAB
CL 29 FT REP

FIXED BRIDGE
VERT CL 9 FT REP

Tower

OVHD PWR & T CABS
AUTH CL 65 FT

WIDTH OF 80-300 FT JUL 1986

5 FT FOR

Sunset Beach

TUSCARORA BAY

Island Yacht Club, Inc.

OVHD PWR CAB

Wilson Yacht Club

Hoist

Ramp

Beccue Boat Basin, Inc

OVHD PWR CAB
AUTH CL 75 FT

Twelvemile Creek

E Branch

50″ 40″ 78°50′30″ 20″ 10″ 78°50′

50″

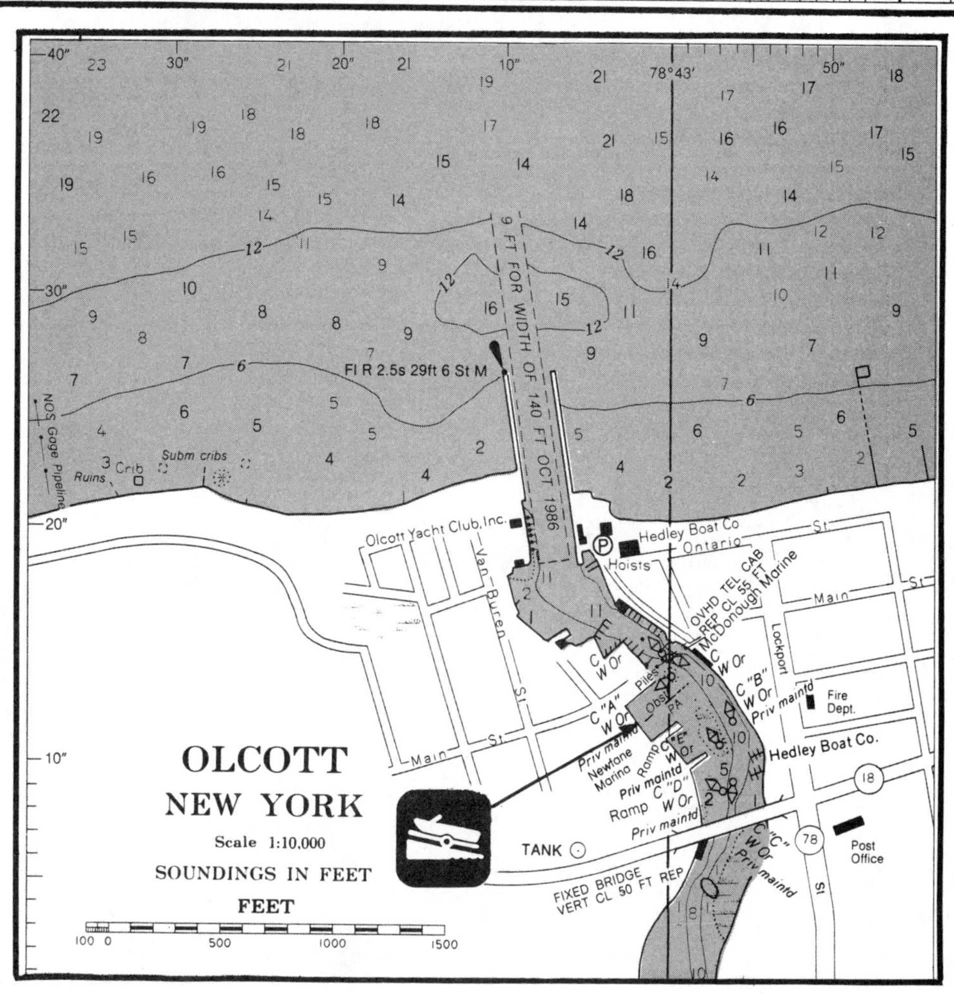

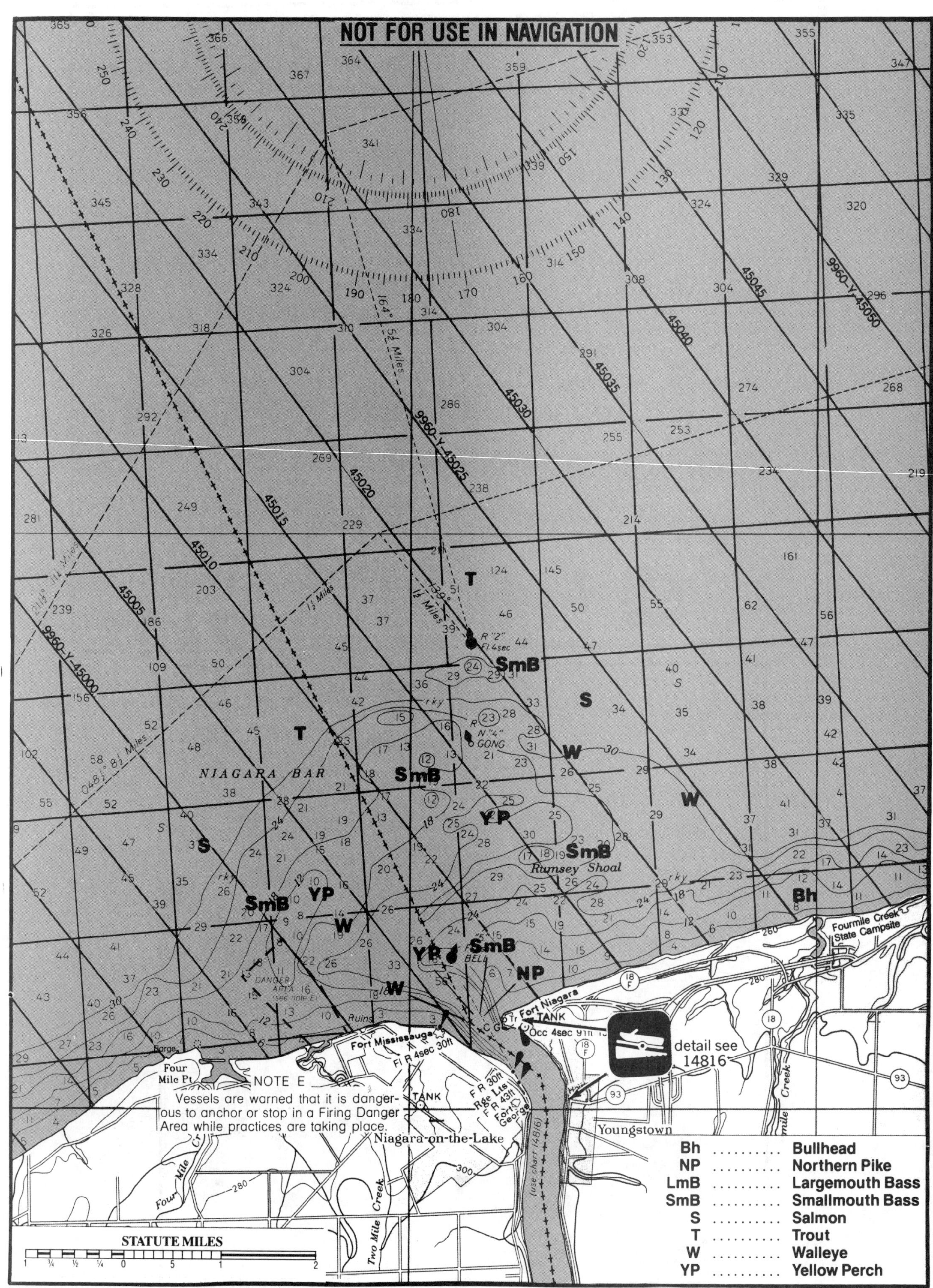
NOT FOR USE IN NAVIGATION
NIAGARA BAR
Rumsey Shoal
Four Mile Pt
Fort Mississauga
Fort Niagara
Niagara-on-the-Lake
Youngstown
Fourmile Creek State Campsite
Two Mile Creek
Four Mile Cr
Fort George
detail see 14816
NOTE E
Vessels are warned that it is dangerous to anchor or stop in a Firing Danger Area while practices are taking place.
STATUTE MILES
Bh .... Bullhead
NP .... Northern Pike
LmB .... Largemouth Bass
SmB .... Smallmouth Bass
S .... Salmon
T .... Trout
W .... Walleye
YP .... Yellow Perch

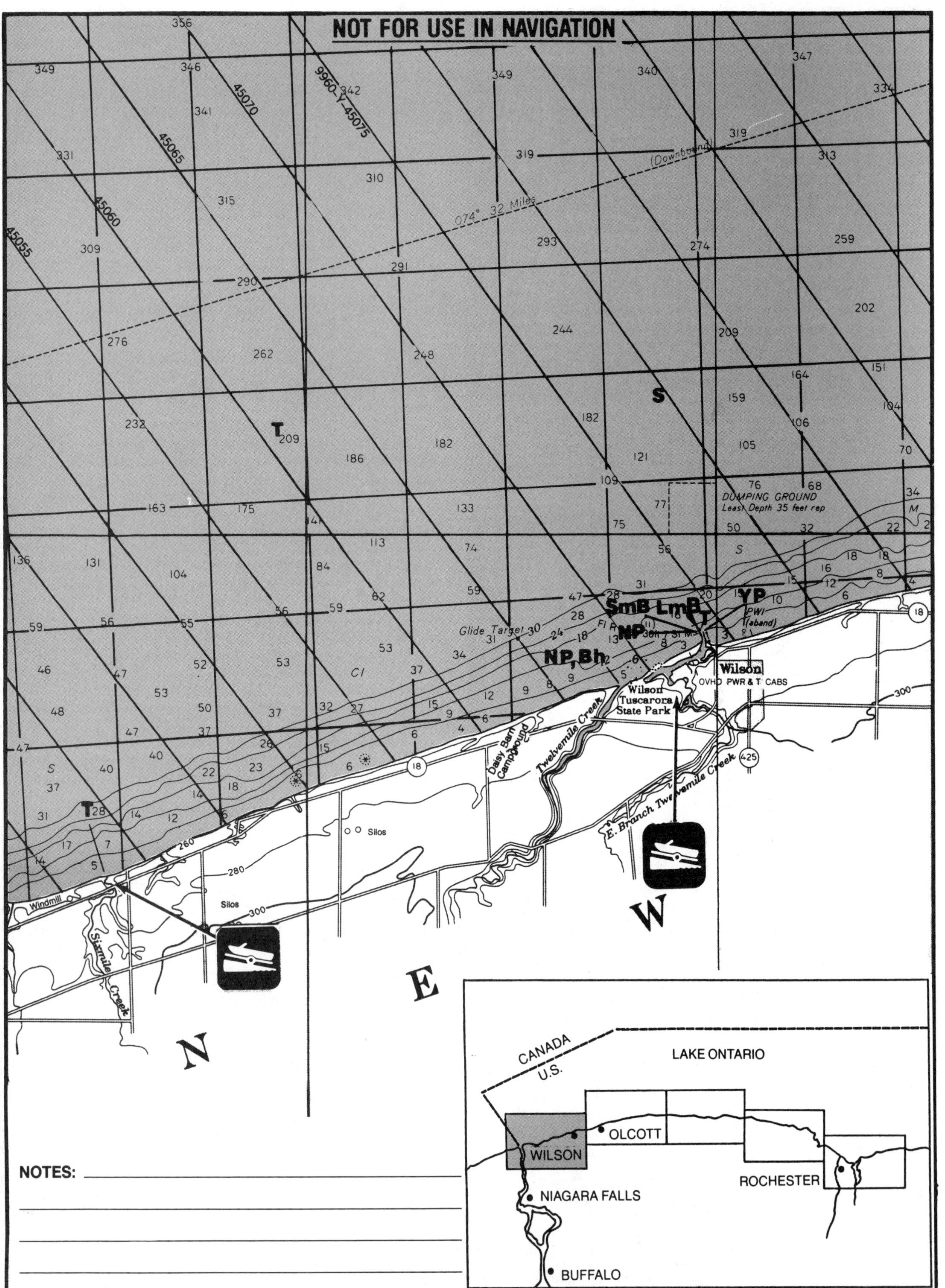

NOT FOR USE IN NAVIGATION
074° 32 Miles
(Downbound)
DUMPING GROUND
Least Depth 35 feet rep
Glide Target
Wilson
OVHD PWR & T CABS
Wilson Tuscarora State Park
Twelvemile Creek
E. Branch Twelvemile Creek
Daisy Barn Campground
Silos
Windmill
Sixmile Creek
N
E
W
CANADA
U.S.
LAKE ONTARIO
OLCOTT
WILSON
NIAGARA FALLS
ROCHESTER
BUFFALO

NOTES:

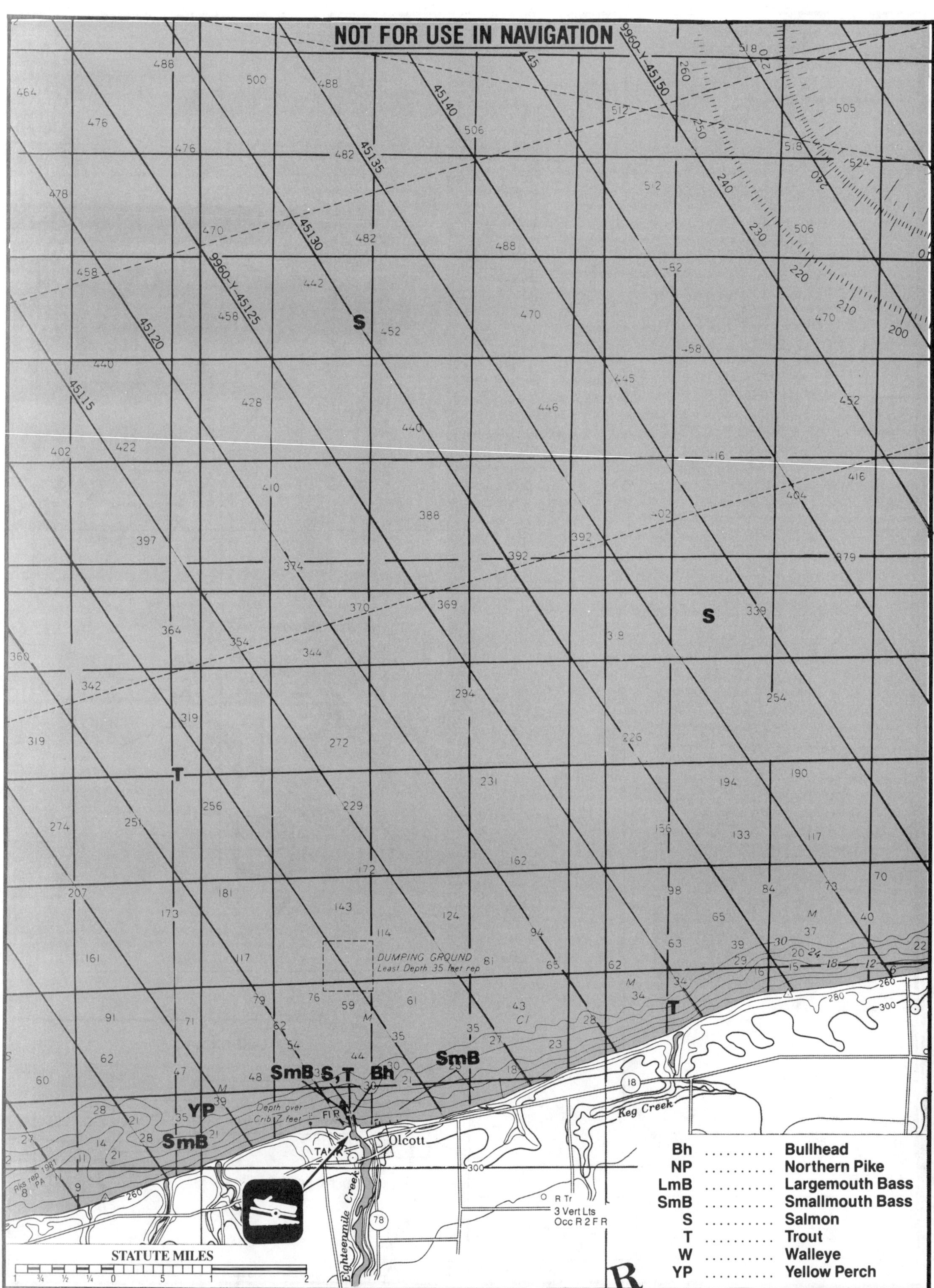
NOT FOR USE IN NAVIGATION
9960-Y-45150
45140
45135
45130
9960-Y-45125
45120
45115
DUMPING GROUND
Least Depth 35 feet rep
Depth over
Crib 2 feet
Olcott
Keg Creek
Eighteenmile Creek
R Tr
3 Vert Lts
Occ R 2 F R
Rks rep 1981
STATUTE MILES
SmB
S, T
Bh
YP
Bh .... Bullhead
NP .... Northern Pike
LmB .... Largemouth Bass
SmB .... Smallmouth Bass
S .... Salmon
T .... Trout
W .... Walleye
YP .... Yellow Perch

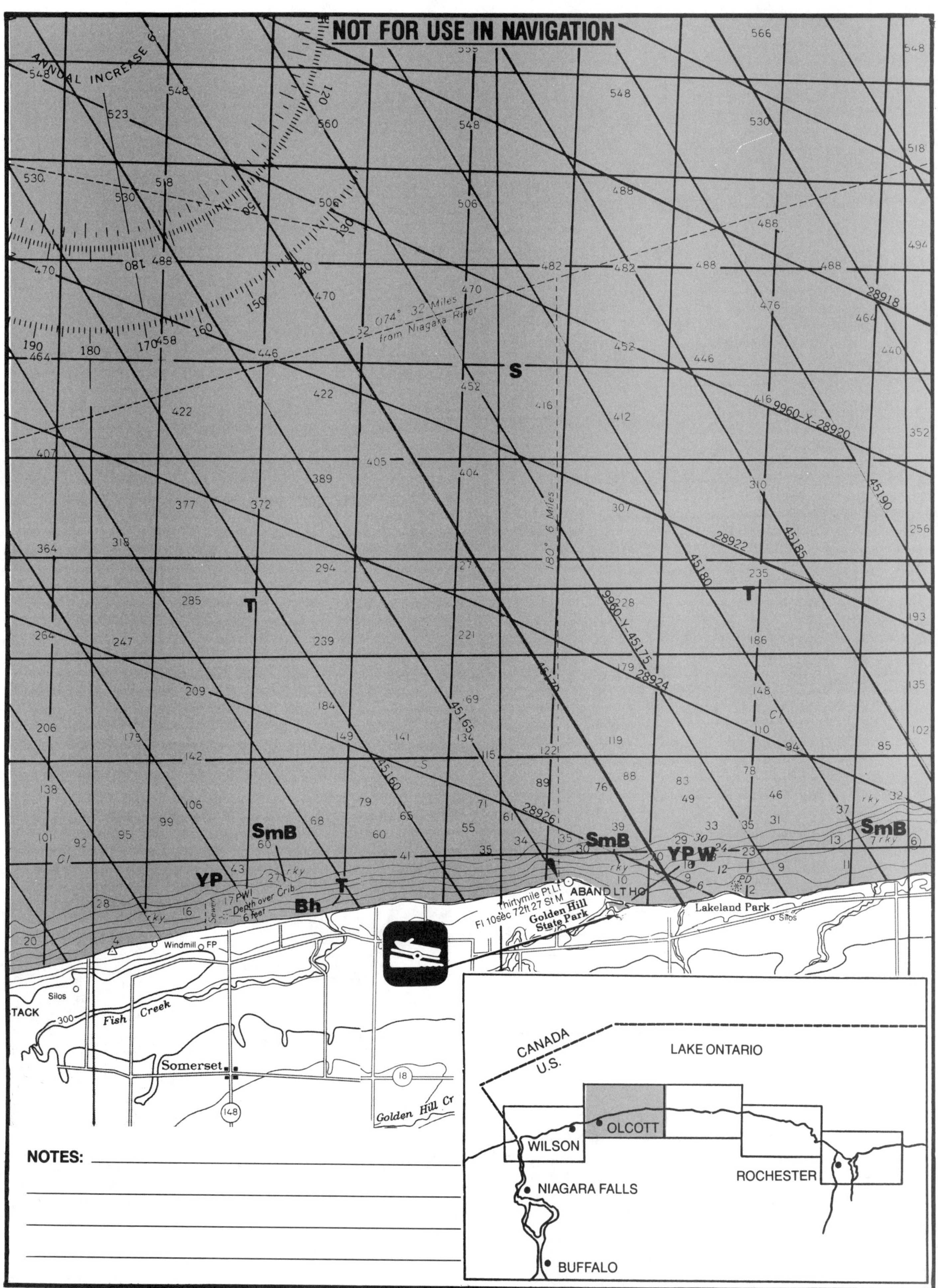

NOT FOR USE IN NAVIGATION
ANNUAL INCREASE 6'
074° 32 Miles from Niagara River
180° 6 Miles
9960-X-28920
9960-Y-45175
Thirtymile Pt Lt Fl 10sec 72ft 27 St M
ABAND LT HO
Golden Hill State Park
Lakeland Park
Silos
Windmill
FP
Depth over Crib 6 feet
Fish Creek
Somerset
Golden Hill Cr
STACK
CANADA
U.S.
LAKE ONTARIO
WILSON
OLCOTT
ROCHESTER
NIAGARA FALLS
BUFFALO
NOTES:

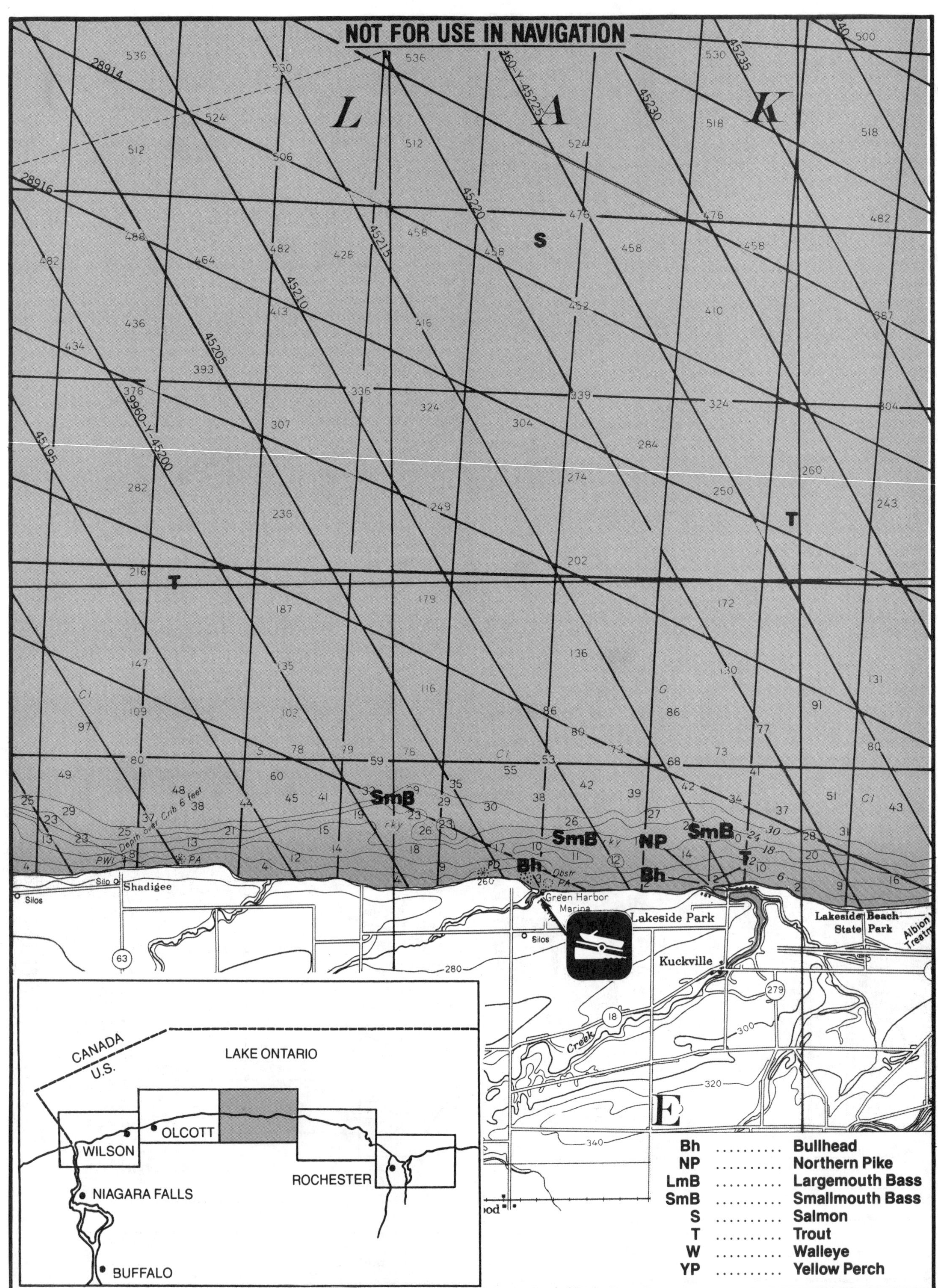
NOT FOR USE IN NAVIGATION
L A K E
Shadigee
Silos
Green Harbor Marina
Lakeside Park
Kuckville
Lakeside Beach State Park
Creek
Depth over Crib 6 feet
LAKE ONTARIO
CANADA
U.S.
WILSON
OLCOTT
ROCHESTER
NIAGARA FALLS
BUFFALO
Bh .... Bullhead
NP .... Northern Pike
LmB .... Largemouth Bass
SmB .... Smallmouth Bass
S .... Salmon
T .... Trout
W .... Walleye
YP .... Yellow Perch

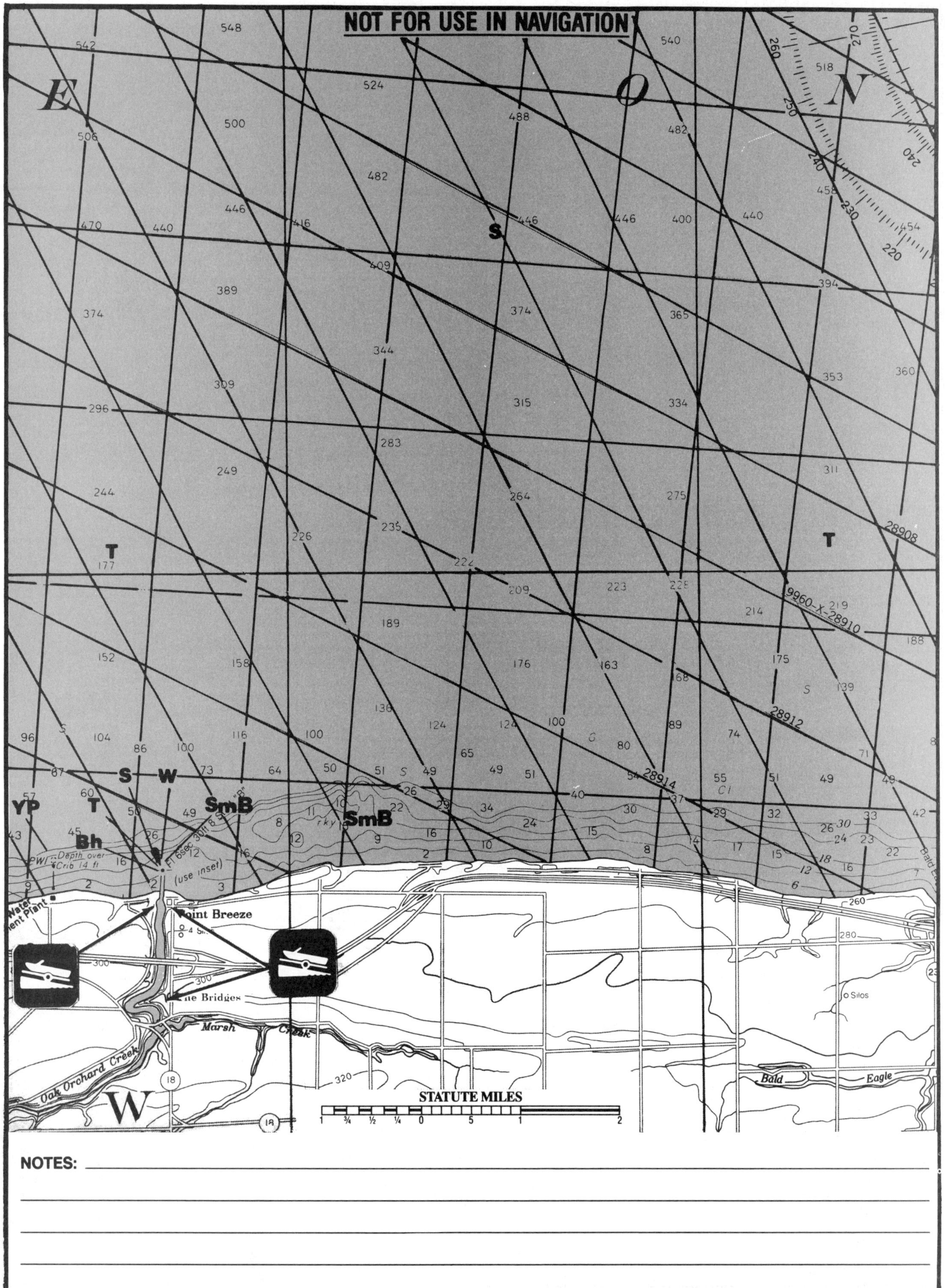
NOT FOR USE IN NAVIGATION
Point Breeze
The Bridges
Marsh
Creek
Oak Orchard Creek
Bald
Eagle
Silos
STATUTE MILES

NOTES:

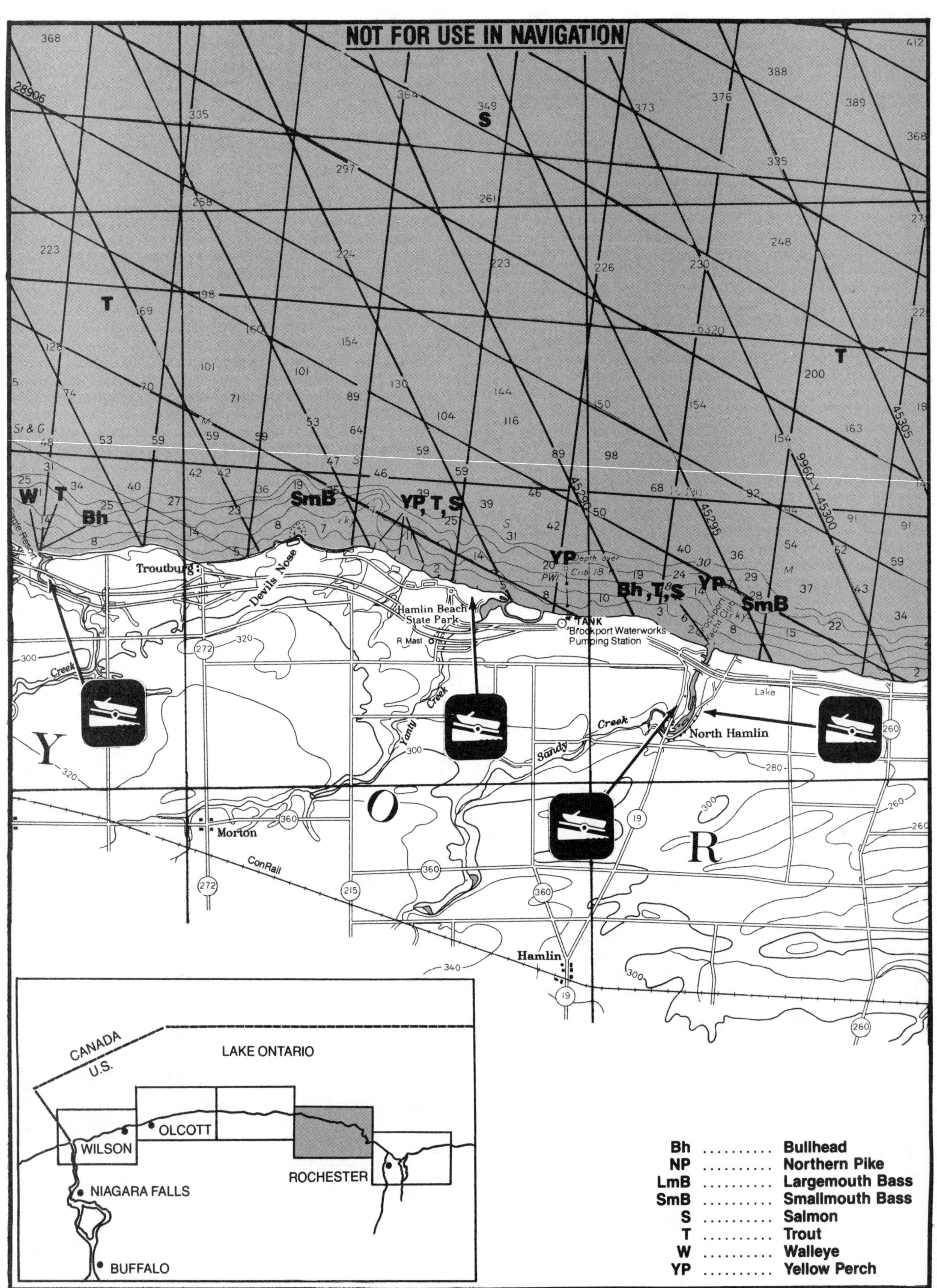

NOT FOR USE IN NAVIGATION
Troutburg
Devils Nose
Hamlin Beach State Park
R Mast
TANK
Brockport Waterworks Pumping Station
Lake
North Hamlin
Morton
ConRail
Hamlin
Creek
Sandy Creek
Yanty Creek
CANADA
U.S.
LAKE ONTARIO
WILSON
OLCOTT
ROCHESTER
NIAGARA FALLS
BUFFALO
Bh .... Bullhead
NP .... Northern Pike
LmB .... Largemouth Bass
SmB .... Smallmouth Bass
S .... Salmon
T .... Trout
W .... Walleye
YP .... Yellow Perch

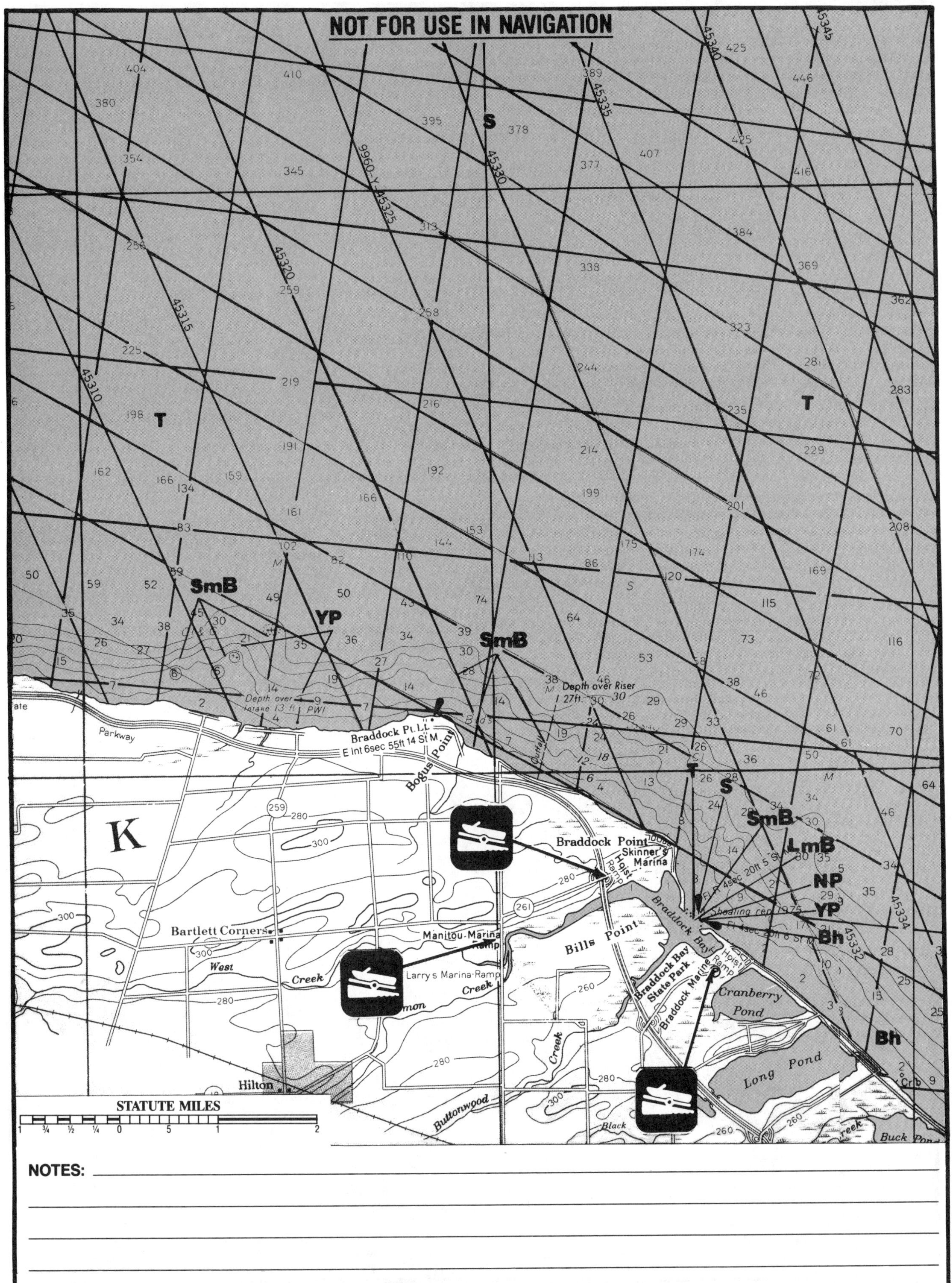
NOT FOR USE IN NAVIGATION
9960-Y-45325
45310
45315
45320
45330
45335
45340
45345
45334
45332
SmB
YP
LmB
NP
Bh
Depth over Intake 13 ft PWI
Depth over Riser 27ft.
Braddock Pt.LL
E Int 6sec 55ft 14 St M.
Bogus Point
Parkway
K
Braddock Point
Skinner's Marina
Hoist Ramp
Bartlett Corners
Manitou-Marina Ramp
Larry's Marina-Ramp
West Creek
Bills Point
Braddock Bay
Shoaling rep 1975
Fl R 4sec 20ft 5 St M
Braddock Bay State Park
Braddock Marine Hoist Ramp
Cranberry Pond
Long Pond
Hilton
Buttonwood
Black
Buck Pond
Crib
STATUTE MILES
1 ¾ ½ ¼ 0 .5 1 2

NOTES:

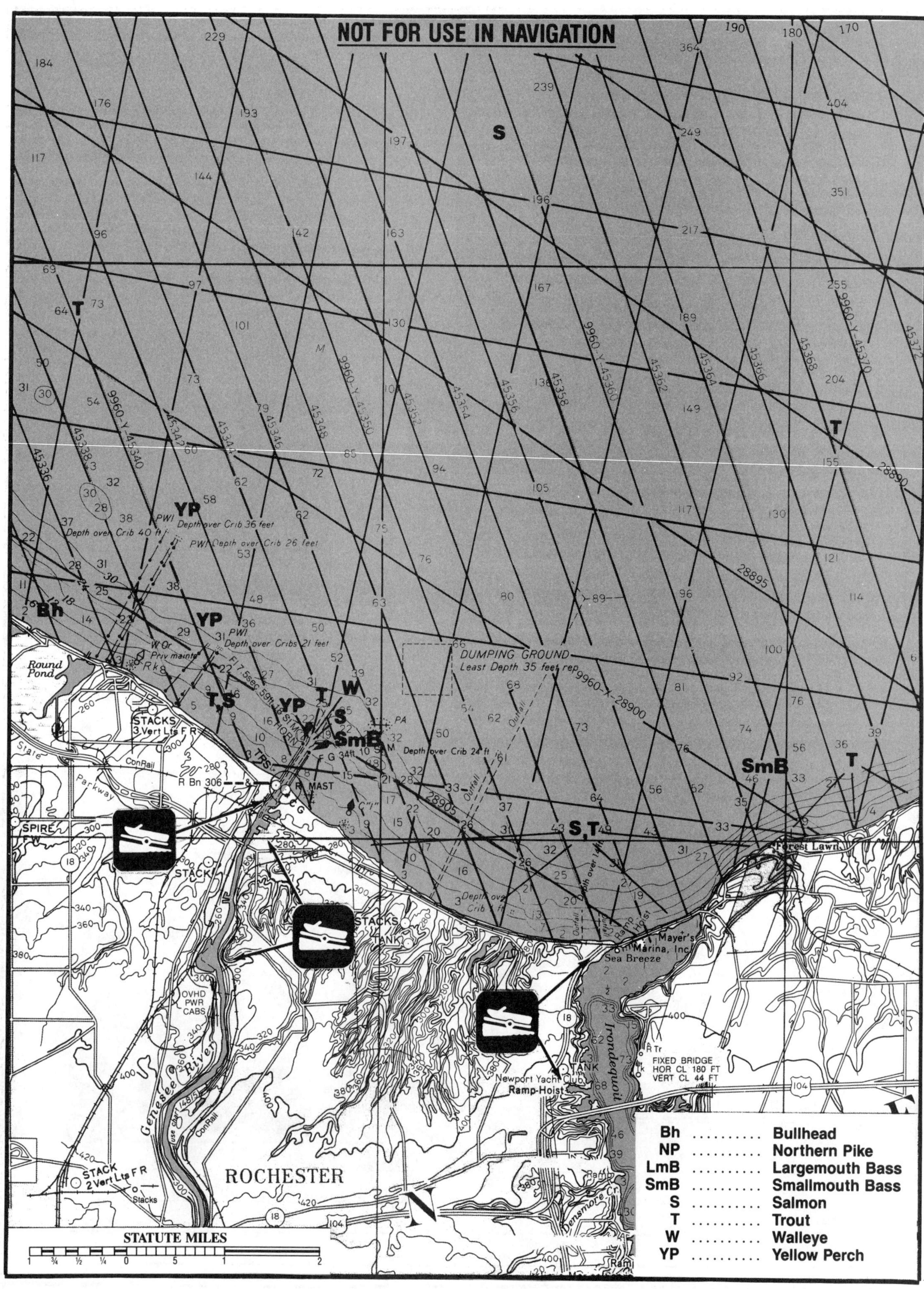
NOT FOR USE IN NAVIGATION
DUMPING GROUND
Least Depth 35 feet rep
Depth over Crib 40 ft
Depth over Crib 36 feet
PWI Depth over Crib 26 feet
PWI Depth over Cribs 21 feet
Depth over Crib 24 ft
Round Pond
STACKS 3 Vert Lts F R
ConRail
Parkway
R Bn 306
R MAST
SPIRE
STACK
STACKS
TANK
OVHD PWR CABS
Genesee River
ROCHESTER
STACK 2 Vert Lts F R
Stacks
Mayer's Marina, Inc.
Sea Breeze
Newport Yacht Club
Ramp-Hoist
FIXED BRIDGE HOR CL 180 FT VERT CL 44 FT
Irondequoit
Densmore Cr.
Forest Lawn
STATUTE MILES
Bh .... Bullhead
NP .... Northern Pike
LmB .... Largemouth Bass
SmB .... Smallmouth Bass
S .... Salmon
T .... Trout
W .... Walleye
YP .... Yellow Perch

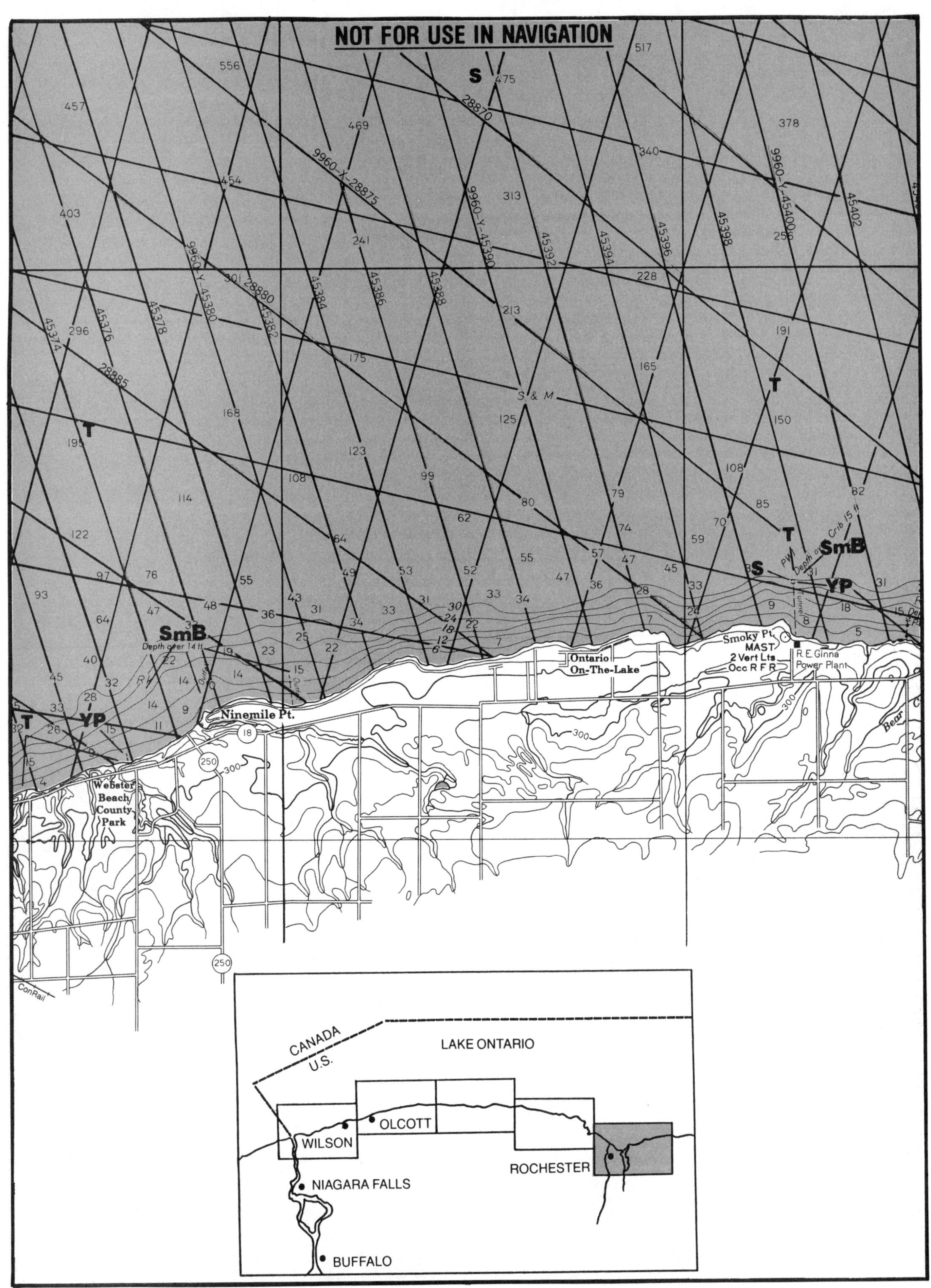
NOT FOR USE IN NAVIGATION
Ninemile Pt.
Ontario On-The-Lake
Smoky Pt.
MAST
2 Vert Lts
Occ R F R
R.E. Ginna Power Plant
Webster Beach County Park
Depth over 14 ft
Depth over Crib 15 ft
ConRail
CANADA
U.S.
LAKE ONTARIO
WILSON
OLCOTT
ROCHESTER
NIAGARA FALLS
BUFFALO

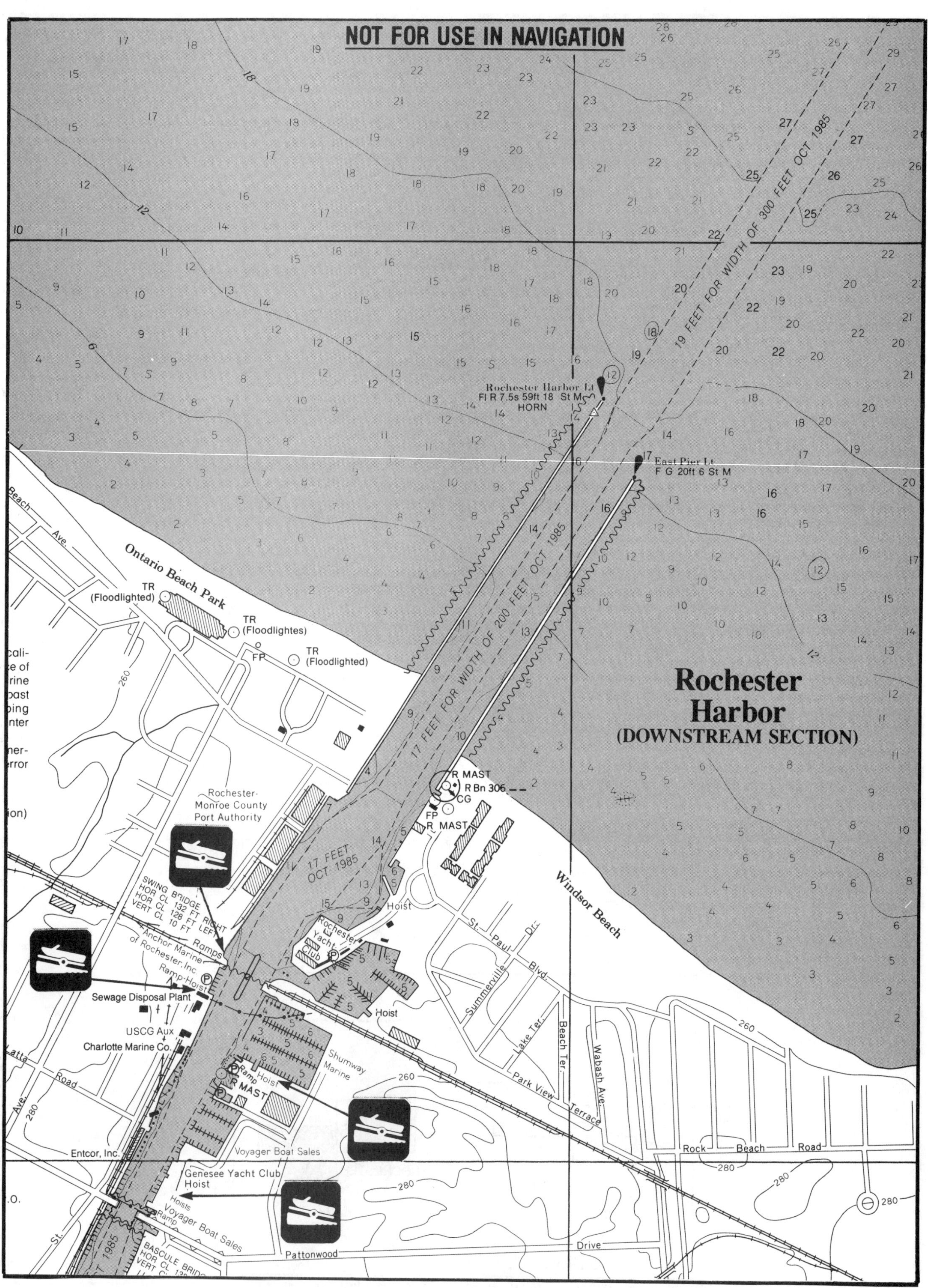

NOT FOR USE IN NAVIGATION
Rochester Harbor
(DOWNSTREAM SECTION)
19 FEET FOR WIDTH OF 300 FEET OCT 1985
17 FEET FOR WIDTH OF 200 FEET OCT 1985
17 FEET OCT 1985
Rochester Harbor Lt
Fl R 7.5s 59ft 18 St M
HORN
East Pier Lt
F G 20ft 6 St M
R MAST
R Bn 306
CG
FP
Ontario Beach Park
TR (Floodlighted)
TR (Floodlightes)
Rochester-Monroe County Port Authority
SWING BRIDGE RIGHT HOR CL 132 FT LEFT HOR CL 128 FT VERT CL 10 FT
Ramps
Anchor Marine of Rochester, Inc
Ramp-Hoist
Sewage Disposal Plant
USCG Aux
Charlotte Marine Co.
Rochester Yacht Club
Hoist
Shumway Marine
Ramp Hoist
Voyager Boat Sales
Entcor, Inc.
Genesee Yacht Club Hoist
Hoists
Ramp
BASCULE BRIDGE
Windsor Beach
St. Paul Blvd.
Summerville Dr.
Lake Ter.
Beach Ter.
Wabash Ave.
Park View Terrace
Rock Beach Road
Pattonwood Drive
Beach Ave.
Latta Road

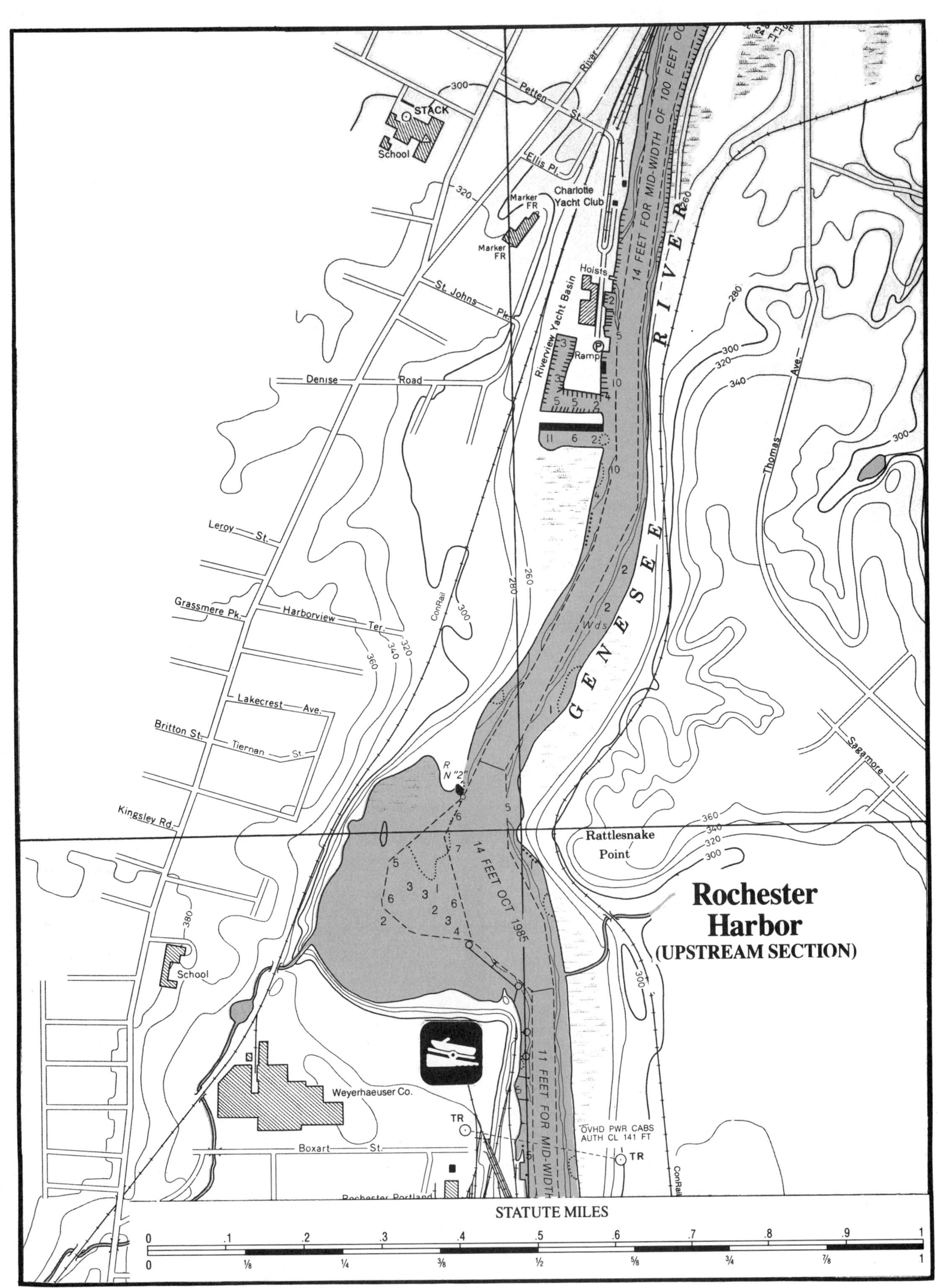
Rochester Harbor
(UPSTREAM SECTION)
STATUTE MILES
GENESEE RIVER
14 FEET FOR MID-WIDTH OF 100 FEET
14 FEET OCT 1985
11 FEET FOR MID-WIDTH
Charlotte Yacht Club
Riverview Yacht Basin
Hoists
Ramp
Marker FR
STACK
School
Petten St.
Ellis Pl.
St. Johns Pk.
Denise Road
Leroy St.
Grassmere Pk.
Harborview Ter.
Lakecrest Ave.
Britton St.
Tiernan St.
Kingsley Rd.
Boxart St.
Weyerhaeuser Co.
Rochester Portland
ConRail
Thomas Ave.
Sagamore
Rattlesnake Point
OVHD PWR CABS AUTH CL 141 FT
TR
R N "2"

APPENDICES

PROP WASH: SALMON MAGNET

By Mike Bleech

With the emphasis on long lines, planer boards, and other means of getting the lines as far from the boat as possible, many salmon anglers are overlooking an important attractor - the prop wash. Something about the swirling water behind a trolling boat brings in salmon like a magnet! During my first few years of Great Lakes salmon fishing I moved my lures further and further back from the boat, trying to trick the "spooky" salmon. Fortunately, a twist of fate set me straight.

Everyone who fishes for trout and salmon out of my boat knows about "Whitey and the Plug." Whitey is the white Fenwick "Flippin' Stik" that I customized into a trolling rod. When the plug is run off this rod, 30 feet or so behind the boat in the prop wash, fish get turned on!

"The Plug" is a size 3, fluorescent yellow Bomber Model A. I found my first one floating off the mouth of Trout Run (PA) in Lake Erie. The first time I tied it on, two years later at almost the same exact spot, we clobbered the salmon with it! Furthermore, we were the only boat in a group of about 30 to catch any salmon at all. One other boat employing the same tactic with another lure did catch a nice batch of rainbows. As far as we could see, every other boat drew a blank.

The Plug was our top producer until it was stolen by a monster chinook off Cattaraugus Creek in Lake Erie!

Whitey and the Plug (I now carry plenty of spares!) are standard gear in my boat whenever we head for the Great Lakes, but other rods and lures are now part of our prop wash trolling system, too. The heart of the system is not the gear, but rather the prop wash.

Why are salmon and trout, or any other fish for that matter, attracted to the prop wash. I have a few theories that satisfy my mind, but it is hard to think like a fish. Whether it's the sound of the propeller or the churned up water, it really doesn't matter anyway. The important point is, some fish are attracted to the prop wash! It is tempting to say that the prop wash turns fish on, because the action in the wash frequently gets hectic, but who knows how many nonstriking fish come into the prop wash?

My observations indicate that the propeller may play a large part in attracting fish to the prop wash. I base this on my experience that fish come in behind some props, but not others. The main powerplant on my boat is a 70 hp Evinrude outboard and it attracts fish like a magnet! In some of my earlier attempts to slow my trolling speed I tried a 4-hp, a 9.9-hp, and an 18-hp motor. But I noticed that the action in the wash stopped when these smaller motors were used, and started again when I switched back to the 70-hp motor.

Was it the small motors that scared the fish off? To some extent, maybe yes, but I think the key is the speed of the prop. When the smaller motors are used with smaller boats they do not have to work as hard to push the boat, so the propeller slows down and fish come into the prop wash. The lesson appears to be, don't use a smaller motor to troll with a large boat if you want to catch salmon in the prop wash!

To keep the proper perspective for anglers who must use small motors, it does appear that the small motors, even on small boats, do not bring in the fish as good as larger motors. There is no dividing line between big and small motors, but success increases as engine rpms drop. There may also be some connection to the size of the prop wash, with bigger being better. The prop wash, to make things perfectly clear, is the swirling water extending back from the transom of a boat, caused by the thrust of the turning propeller. Lures run in this turbulent water will dance and dart from side to side. When you get fish in the prop wash you'll know it - they can't resist those dancing lures!

Most fast prop wash action comes from cohos. They seem fascinated by the swirling water. Browns, rainbows, and chinooks are also attracted. And while it is not a consistent lake trout tactic, they are also occasionally caught in the prop wash.

There are two basic methods of trolling in the prop wash: with flat lines and with downriggers. Both catch fish but different lures are used, although the principle is the same.

Flat line rigs like Whitey and the Plug utilize a crankbait. Besides the plug (a Bomber or Rebel), other proven lures for flat lines in the prop wash are the Tadpolly and Hot'N Tot. Fluorescent yellow and chartreuse have been our most consistent colors, followed by fluorescent orange and fluorescent red. The latter two colors are tops when the water temperature is below the mid-40s. Chartreuse is outstanding in dark water.

The crankbaits are run 10 to 35 feet behind the boat. Since the lures should be right in the wash, there is room for only one or two flat lines. But when you get a school of cohos in the prop wash that will be plenty of lines!

Be sure to keep the rod in the rod holder at a right angle to the line, to cushion the shock of the strike. Since there is very little stretch in the short length of line, the strikes will test the strength of the line. Without taking full advantage of the rod as a shock absorber, you'll break off a lot of fish, or at least tear the hooks out of their mouths.

Again because of the short line shock, it pays to keep the reel drags lighter than usual, and pay special care to tie good knots. (This does not imply that less care should be taken at other times!) The short-line shock also applies to prop wash lines run off downriggers.

Many salmon anglers do not see the logic in using downriggers in the prop wash since the lures are down less than 12 feet. Probably the best argument for it is the measure of control that the downriggers give. While two is the maximum number of flat lines that can be run in the prop wash, it is no problem running four lines off the downriggers. By staggering the lines both in depth and length, they will not tangle even in tight turns!

A typical spread of downrigger lines in the prop wash would be: a line down 4 feet and back 35 feet; one down 6 feet and back 15 feet; a line down 9 feet and back 25 feet; and another down 11 feet and back 10 feet.

It may be necessary and it is certainly easier to maintain that control by using the traditional downrigging lures. Ace and 7-11 flutters, colored chartreuse with red dots and Rebels are consistent producers. In the spring of 1983, we tried some soft vinyl lures, called Clouts. The cohos went crazy over the pearl yellow and fluorescent orange, 3 1/2-inch-long models! J-Plugs also do the trick, especially when there are chinooks in the area. The J-Plugs and Rebels should be run only on the deepest lines when more than two lines are used, since these lures may dive well below the depth of the downrigger weight.

In actual practice I rarely fill up the prop wash with four lines. Two downrigger lines and one flat line is a compatible spread with my 16-foot boat. Not every fish in the area will be attracted to the prop wash, so I run additional long lines or planer boards.

Trolling in the prop wash is effective whenever the salmon are near the surface, say less than 15 feet deep, which makes it primarily a spring and fall tactic.

While lures run beneath the prop wash will not have the dancing action of lures in the wash, they will still be productive on fish attracted to the turbulence. We have had little success trolling to the sides or behind the prop wash (and we haven't tried above it), but lures run just below the prop wash are in danger of being hit by salmon!

Try this tactic the next time you find salmon in the near-surface waters. It does not replace the long lines or planer boards, but it will be a valuable addition to your bag of tricks. The prop wash can indeed be a salmon magnet!

DODGERS AND FLIES/SQUID PROVIDE GOOD CATCHES

By George Richey

Most people now recognize the fact that using dodgers and flies or squid will often double your catch of salmon and trout. The problem is, however, that doesn't mean everyone will use them. Many folks assume there is some sort of dark magic involved when it comes to running dodgers and flies. Oftentimes, all that's involved is some common sense, and trying them.

I've heard, "There is too much drag, the fish doesn't fight well with a dodger hanging off its nose." To a degree, I'll agree. But the use of an attractor (dodger) will usually generate more strikes, and that's a dandy reason to use them.

Question - Why do you see charter boats in July, August, and September with dodgers and flies or squid hanging off the rods on their boats? Answer - Because they produce fish for the skippers. In two words, THEY WORK!!

During the last three months of the salmon fishery, the dodgers and flies or squid will probably put more fish in the coolers than any other methods of salmon fishing. Oh sure, some days the J-Plugs, NKs, or Yeck spoons may do the job. But day in and day out, the attractors with a fly/squid behind will put most of the fish in the box.

There are lots of theories on why the dodgers work. You have to realize that the dodgers provide the action for the fly or Michigan Squid. The attractors also provide lots of flash and sonic noise at the salmon's level. A combination of flash, noise, and action will help draw the fish into your spread.

It seems that when running attractors such as dodgers, the rules aren't written in stone. There are general rules of thumb, but as in most facets of fishing, if it works - run it! I'll list a few general rules of dodger/fly fishing, and why we do it this way.

First of all, when using a dodger, the boat speed must be slower than when you run a J-Plug, for example. The proper boat speed differs from side to side, with an occasional turn-over. If the dodger is constantly turning over, or spinning, then your boat speed is too fast. While spinning the dodger does occasionally work, most of the time the rig will spook the fish when spinning out.

A nice, snappy rocking back and forth action of the attractor is what your looking for, especially when trolling for coho salmon. Most of the time, we will run the dodger from 4 to 12 feet behind the cannonball. For kings, we generally drop back further behind the ball. The kings seem to prefer a bit "lazier" action, so we'll run the dodger from 10 to 30 feet behind the ball. This slows the action of the dodger down. This works well when the water is super cold, as well.

For the most part, we run dodgers and flies/squid anytime the salmon or trout are deeper than 35 feet down. However, we have taken fish just below the surface by increasing our boat speed to maximum dodger speed, running the attractor back 25 to 40 feet and then lowering the cannonball down until the dodger just goes under the surface.

The general "rule of thumb" on leader length is a length and a half of the dodger length for the leader. We primarily use the "O" size dodger, which is 8 inches long. That means using a leader of some 12 inches. This might be a tad short for most fishing applications. We have taken fish on leaders of 6 inches, but that's too short most of the time.

For coho, the snappier action of the dodger can best be transferred to the Michigan Squid or Dazzler trolling fly with a leader from 14 to 1 8 inches long. For the slower action required by kings and lake trout, try lengthening the leader to its fullest. Often, we run a leader of 20 to 24 inches long behind the dodger. Several years ago, I fished with Captain Mark Price aboard his boat "Obsessed", during the Lowrance Derby. Mark is from Ludington, Michigan, and we finished in third place. During our stay fishing out of Olcott, we really hammered the lake trout and kings. Most of the lakers were right on bottom, and the kings were just about 15 feet above the lakers. Our program was using either white, chrome fluted, or yellow/white dodgers. Combined with those colors in attractors, we used laser, black laser, glow green, and yellow/white Michigan Squid. It was almost sinful what we did to the fish with those squid and attractors. Mark was moving right along with the Obsessed, so we dropped the dodgers back about 30 feet, and with a leader of some 20 inches the action wasn't a bit too fast.

As an attractor, the dodger will definitely "draw" fish into your spread, often taking the bulk of the strikes. Sometimes, all or most of the strikes will come on the other lures or spoons that you also have down. Don't make the common mistake of taking the dodgers off, and replacing them with more spoons or plugs. The reason the fish are hitting the plugs and/or spoons is that the dodgers drew them in, and then they hit the other baits. Take the attractors off, and the strikes also fall off. If your boat has at least four downriggers, leave a minimum of two dodgers down to attract the fish. You'll take the fish on them as well. Other times, the dodgers and flies or squid will take almost all the fish. When they are really on the "bite", the smart skippers will have dodgers all across the back of the boat. Why? They have to produce fish for their clients, and attractors are the best way to accomplish that.

Remember when I said there wasn't really any rules to using attractors? We have taken lake trout in 12 feet of water on dodgers and Sparkle flies. The dodger was only 6 feet behind the cannonball. We have also taken some great catches of brown trout using a chrome fluted dodger and laser Michigan Squid. I've had other folks tell me, "There are too many different color combinations, and I don't know what to use, or when." One day, due to light penetration or fickleness, the fish will want a black fly or squid. The next day, the color may be blue or a glow.

In recent years, the use of the flies or squid that glow has been well documented. I pioneered the use of glow-in-the-dark pigments in my Michigan Squids. Since then, we have also had fantastic success using the Glo-Fly and a glow Sparkle fly.

The glow colors in the Michigan Squid seem to work anytime the fish are deeper than 40 feet down, in low-light conditions, or after dark. We have had good luck using fluted or hammered chrome and the glow squids, and a chartreuse dodger coupled with the glows also has proven itself to be effective.

Myself, I really like the white dodger with the laser tape insert and either the laser glow or the green frog glow (Kermit) Michigan Squid. Some fishermen have told me the yellow/white dodger works the best for them with the glows.

Black is another good low-light color, such as first thing in the morning or during a foggy day. Gradually, as the sun starts getting a little higher up in the sky, we may switch to a kelley green. We may take a couple fish on kelley, and as the sun continues to climb that color slows down, and we switch to lighter and brighter colored dodgers and squid.

During the bright part of the day, we will use the chrome or chrome fluted dodger, and chartreuse, laser, or silvery colored flies or squid. The Dazzler trolling fly has lots of followers, and for a simple reason. The Dazzler has five colors in its skirt, and works under almost any conditions, from light to dark. Try a chrome fluted or yellow/white dodger with the dazzler. We have taken tons of coho, kings, and lakers and some fishermen I've talked with say its deadly on steelhead on Lake Ontario.

Gradually, as you work from the bright part of the day back toward dark, gradually reverse the color schemes and end up with the blacks or the glow in the darks.

Some of the very best charter skippers on Lake Ontario pull the dodgers and flies or squid faithfully. I know that I don't know all the good ones, and for that I'm sorry, but folks like Captains Ron Penna, Dan Dietzen, John Oravec, Butch Tiberio, Howard Zeitlin, Dave Siegfried, and Vince Pierleonie all use dodgers and flies or squids with great results.

It pays from time to time to experiment. Sometimes, a color combination will work for days or weeks - and then die. Now what? The good fishermen I know will get busy and work at lots of different colors in dodgers and flies until they find a pattern that works.

Once you find something that works, get more of the same down. Mark Price is a top charter skipper, and he seldom has less than 12 of each color dodger and squid that has produced for him. "If something gets hot, I can't afford to only have just one hot bait down there. I've got six downriggers and I want the hot bait on each downrigger," says Mark.
salmon and trout? Obviously, colors may change from locale to locale. These have worked for me on Lakes Huron, Michigan, and Ontario: chrome fluted or hammered chrome and laser Michigan Squid or blue green Sparkle fly, and a white dodger coupled with a black or black laser Michigan Squid. Other combinations include: green/yellow dodger and green Metallic fly, or a green/white dodger and green/white Michigan Squid or green Sparkle fly. Try a yellow/white dodger and a Dazzler trolling fly when the fish are up high. The same dodger and a yellow/white Michigan Squid produced well for us in the Lowrance Derby.

The glow Michigan Squids include: glow green, glow blue, green or blue frog glow, laser glow, and laser glow 2. Most of these have been teamed up with the following dodgers: chrome, fluted chrome, white, white/laser tape inserts, chartreuse, and yellow/white. The new glow dodgers have produced fish as well. When all else fails, "Go with the Glow."

What dodgers work best? We have had good success using Luhr Jensen, Side Kicks, and Yeck. I understand that Red Eye makes one that is quite tolerant as to speed. If you can find any of the old Grizzly dodgers, buy a bunch of them. We call them "stubbles" because they are shorter and fatter than most. You can run them quite a bit faster than others.

We often stack other lures above the dodgers. Running at slow speed, the small, thin flutter-type spoons stack well above the dodger/squids. If you're moving along at a faster speed, we have had good luck stacking Grizzly plugs, Silver Streaks, NKs, and other spoons and plugs. Put a spoon or plug down and make sure it is compatible with the attractors. Make sure that all the dodgers and other baits are working properly. Get a bait that isn't tracking straight, and you can have a horrible tangle in a hurry. Tangles cost you fish, and time. The bait needs to be in the water to take salmon.

I've only dented the surface of running dodgers and flies or squid. The use of the attractors will put additional fish in your boat. You just have to have faith in them, and keep them down in the water. Give the dodgers and squid a chance, and they may just make a convert out of you.

POWER PLANTS: YEAR-ROUND "HOT SPOTS"

By Dick Schleyer

If you're brave at heart and can't wait for mid-April when the lakes actively begin to come to life, you might consider the power plant "hot spots" as a major source of winter fishing activity.

Many serious, and indeed hearty, fishermen will have taken large numbers of trout and salmon throughout the winter months from the heated discharges of power plants on all the Great Lakes. These hot spots hold large concentrations of salmonids, bait fish and other forms of aquatic life.

Warm power plant outflows create a winter environment that sets the stage for an artificial ecosystem that is alive and active during the winter months. The normally cold inshore water has dispersed the salmonids and slowed their metabolism to the point where they feed infrequently, making fishing poor at best. The exception to this occurs during winter thaws when runoff attracts steelhead, domestic rainbows, browns, and immature salmon to the mouths of rivers and streams.

Increased water volume and temperature following thaws brings a run of steelhead into the rivers and streams providing exciting inshore winter fishing. Power plants that discharge directly into the lake from the shoreline create a high volume stream within the lake itself. The strong currents maintain a steady, regular flow into the lake. There is a minimal amount of dispersion from the area where it leaves the shoreline until it reaches 80 to 100 yards into the lake. That is where you want to fish. Anchor your boat at the edge of the stream current in the lake and fish much the same as you would fish a big stream. Cast your small- to medium-size spoons, plugs, egg sacs, or bait (try jigging) and retrieve them to the boat through the current.

Spawning rainbows and browns are fooled into reacting to these currents as they do when seeking streams in which to spawn. They will also respond to the current even when the plant is shut down and the water being pumped into the lake is nearly the same temperature as the lake water. Some inshore warm water releases are located so that wading and pier fishing are possible as well.

Feeding salmonids, primarily brown trout, generally use the flow only when power is being generated and the water is warm. It is important that you fish for this species at plants (preferably nuclear) that are on-line and discharging a large volume of warm water. These outflows periodically produce excellent fishing for smallmouth bass, lake catfish, and silver bass after the lake warms in the spring.

The offshore discharging plants release their heated water from huge pipes well offshore and below the surface. This water is also released under great pressure and "boils" to the surface and disperses there. "Boils" or "bubbles," as they are sometimes referred to, are terrific fish attractors. You can fish this type of flow from anchored boats, casting, jigging, or trolling though the bubbles. As with the shoreline discharge plants, the trout and salmon for the most part leave for more bountiful waters as soon as the lake temperature warms in April.

The good or bad of nuclear and fossil fuel power plants on the Great Lakes has been argued for years. Fishermen have come to accept this major intervention by man as an attractor and concentrator of various species of fish and have learned to capitalize on them to augment and extend their fishing seasons.

Fortunately, the game fish seem to move in and out of the temperature changes at will with less traumatization than was predicted by some biologist early on. The damage, which has been minimal, seems to occur when there are sudden shut downs at power plants during inshore cold water periods. The detrimental impact of power plants, especially nuclear, that discharge into river systems are another story and should not be confused with the results to date in the Great Lakes.

While launching can be a problem because of ice on ramps, some areas are sanding their ramps for better winter lake access. If the idea of dragging a small aluminum boat across the ice, when necessary, to gain access to the lake appeals to you, don't forget that small boats afford little protection from the elements. The outdoor experts recommend a number of layers of clothing over heavier single layers to provide insulation and insurance against hypothermia. Use good judgement and caution.

There are a few charter guides available for this kind of fishing. Telephone calls to the ESLO/LEI weigh-in stations along Lake Ontario's and Lake Erie's shorelines, or tackle stores on the other big lakes, can alert you to the times when fish concentrations are at their peek and whom you might contact to arrange a winter charter.

FINDING A GREAT (LAKES) GUIDE

Reprinted by Permission of Sea Grant

The number of fishing guides offering services on Lake Ontario (and Lake Erie) has mushroomed over the last few years. This presents a problem to many potential charter customers: How do you evaluate and select a charter service?

The key to making the wisest choice in the selection of a charter captain is simple: ASK QUESTIONS! Most good captains are open and willing to answer any questions and concerns you might have about a fishing trip. Don't hesitate to "talk turkey" (or chinook or brown trout) with a charter operator - it's the only way both you and the operator can hash out each other's expectations and responsibilities of the fishing trip.

Some basic questions should be answered before you decide on retaining a captain's services. These include:

Is the captain validly licensed by the U.S. Coast Guard to carry passengers for hire? Operators are required to possess and carry a Coast Guard license to carry six or less passengers for hire. Since there is no state licensing system, a federal license is the only way (and an easy way!) to determine if your captain is working legally and has passed the Coast Guard captain's exam. If there are any concerns, ask to see the license.

Is the charter boat properly outfitted with the required safety equipment? There is no required annual inspections that a charter boat must pass. As such, it is important to ascertain that the boat has the required flotation devices and emergency equipment. Look to see if the boat has a U.S. Coast Guard Auxiliary Courtesy exam sticker. It's not legally required, but does indicate that the captain has taken the time to have this voluntary inspection carried out.

Is the boat adequately insured? Again, there is no requirement here, but it may make you feel better to know that the boat and its operation is insured against passenger accidents. It also indicates that an insurer has screened the captain and the vessel to some degree and considers the charter business worthy of coverage.

Does the boat carry a radio telephone? It is not required, but a VHF-FM marine radio telephone is perhaps the safest and most reliable common communication device on the water. Radio channels are continuously monitored by the Coast Guard and most radios have a weather-band channel that constantly receives U.S. Weather Service broadcasts. CB radios do not offer these advantages and are limited in their broadcast range.

Is the captain a member of any fishing, community or professional trade organization? A captain who gives up time to be a member of a fishing group, a community board or professional charter boat association suggests by his involvement that he is responsible. For example, one charter boat group, the Lake Ontario Charter Boat Association has requirements of its members regarding licensing, insurance, vessel safety, and radio equipment.

Is the captain a skilled fisherman? Obviously, not a question a customer would want only to ask of the captain. Ask around at tackle stores, talk to other fishermen, and maybe some previous customers.

There are numerous other questions that might be asked, including those related to price, payment and deposit, departure time, bad weather contingencies, refreshments, and other boat rules. It's your money, so don't hesitate to ask. The good captain will want to answer these questions and have his potential clients understand all arrangements fully.

LOCATING MID-SUMMER BROWNS

By Ernie Lantiegne

The nearest boat was two miles away and we were just five minutes out of port as the Fish Doctor settled into the water from an easy plane. It was July 19, 1988, and at 2:00 o'clock on a hot midsummer afternoon, Dave Nettles was all smiles. No one could have been more confident. We were looking for brown trout and were sure we would find them because we had an ace up our sleeve.

We had teamed up to take on midsummer browns in Lake Ontario, Dave as a fishery researcher with an interest in practical information for anglers, and I as a full-time charter captain who had specialized in summer brown trout fishing since 1977. Dave is an avid angler himself and had done his master's thesis, "Ecology of Lake Ontario Brown Trout" for the primary purpose of helping Ontario anglers find browns after they move offshore in late spring.

The proof is in the pudding, as they say, and as Dave explained brown trout temperature preferences, one of his study's most important findings, my first mate and youngest son, Jeff, was already lowering the temperature probe. Seventy-three degrees all the way down to 40 feet. Sixty-five degrees at 60 feet, 55 degrees at 80 feet, and 50 degrees at 100 feet. We had half the information we needed.

The other half, according to Dave's findings, was the location where the broad, 30-foot-wide thermocline we had just found intersected the lake bottom. As Jeff nosed our 26-foot sport fisherman toward shallower water, Dave and I set four downriggers at depths of 60 to 80 feet to cover the 55 to 65 degree temperature range. We also Set two diving planers to run at about 55 feet. We were fishing the same gear I had been using successfully for brown trout in recent weeks, but per Dave's instructions we would be fishing warmer temperatures than I was confident with. Curiosity was killing me.

As we headed for one of our Loran C waypoints marking some nice structure in 65 to 75 feet of water, Dave explained more about his brown trout research, and why it was so important to fishermen.

The brown trout fishery in Lake Ontario originated following the first successful stocking of yearling browns in 1973. Fishermen found the fast-growing, heavy-bodied browns easy to catch in early spring when they were inshore. Later, as spring temperatures warmed the brown trout seemed to disappear. Biologists were concerned that harvest was not reaching expectations, and anglers wanted to extend their brown trout fishing season. With that in mind, Dave Nettles and several fellow researchers went to work to unlock the secret of locating midsummer brown trout.

Using radio telemetry gear and 25-foot-wide vertical gill nets suspended at various depths from-near shore to 14 miles out, Dave and his crew conducted the study from 1980 to 1982. The study area stretched from Point Breeze to Port Bay along Ontario's New York shore. Telemetry findings pinpointed the location of 36 radio-tagged browns in spring and fall when the fish were in shallow. The tags also relayed back the temperature at which the browns were located. When the water temperature warmed above 65 degrees, however, browns moved to water deeper than 36 feet and Dave lost contact with the tagged fish. Gill nets along with carefully recorded water temperatures and depths at which browns were netted were then relied on to precisely locate fish. Along with the browns, data was collected on forage fish such as alewives and smelt. As Dave and I talked Jeff rudely awakened us as he barked "Small fish on the number three rigger!" The 12-inch brown had taken a chartreuse and red Dynamite fished close to the weight 60 feet down in 65 degree water. Stocked two months earlier at about 8 inches, it was growing fast and weighed close to a pound. As we released the fish carefully the starboard diving planer rod doubled over and the screaming drag of the level-wind reel gave rude notice that something was trying to tear the gears out of it. With a pencil in one hand and note pad in the other I got there too late and the fish was gone. Dave chuckled, but the look from my first mate yelled, "Come on. Pay attention!" As Dave reeled in the diver to reset it he told me more about the results of his study.

The gill netting results had shown conclusively that brown trout are commonly found in and just above the thermocline, often at temperatures much warmer than most anglers fish. Eighty-eight percent of the browns Dave netted during his study were taken within 15 feet of the thermocline, and more than a third were taken at the point where the thermocline intercepted the bottom. Seventy-five percent of the browns netted were inside the 100 feet contour. Almost none were netted outside the 150 feet contour even though some nets were suspended in the thermocline over depths up to 420 feet. No brown trout were netted more than 2.0 miles from shore. Unlike other pelagic species such as steelhead, cohos, and to a lesser extent, chinooks, the study showed conclusively that brown trout tend to be homebodies, strongly associated near-shore with the thermocline.

A slight breeze was blowing from the west under an overcast, hazy sky - good conditions for midsummer browns. I noticed the boats on the horizon three miles away, outside good brown trout water. This time we were ready. I heard the stern downrigger rod snap free as Jeff yelled, "Fish on!" It was Dave's fish and he snatched the rod from the holder setting the hook. The brown fought hard even after reaching the surface and the chrome flasher and brilliant spectra fly made a great picture as Dave held the football-shaped 6-pounder. The brown had hit the rigger at 80 feet in 55 degree water as the downrigger weight barely skimmed the bottom. "We're only two-tenths of a mile from the waypoint", Jeff announced, again his tone saying, "Come on you guys, that's enough of that biologist talk. Let's hammer some fish." Dave and I agreed.

As we slid the brown into the fish box we noticed the tail of a freshly eaten alewife between its jaws. Dave had found that baitfish make up the bulk of the diet of Ontario browns in summer. Most of the alewives netted during his study were in and above the thermocline with a preferred temperature of 65 degrees. Interestingly, in both the summer of 1981 and 1982, smelt were found in brown trout stomachs only during the second and third weeks of July. The smelt were found to occupy the depth zone in and below the thermocline and preferred a water temperature of 47 degrees. Alewives, because of their temperature preference, are the most available forage for summer browns.

" Hey you guys, take a look at this graph," our on-his-toes mate beckoned excitedly. We could see why. The structure beneath us, dropping sharply from 65 to 75 feet, was lined with small, dense schools of alewives. Larger marks on the graph paper betrayed the brown trout and occasional chinooks there. We knew we were in the brown trout zone.

The next two hours were wild, with fish on most of the time. The light tackle gave the browns a sporting chance, and provided more than one groan as some good fish parted company with us. At the end of the flurry we had boated a total of 15 browns up to 6 pounds and lost a beautiful, deep-bodied male at the net. His light amber sides and slightly hooked jaw were a clear sign spawning season was not far away. A bonus chinook added some weight to the fish box. An 8-pound lake trout and all but three of the browns were released.

All information had been duly recorded in the Fish Doctor diary, including depths at which the fish were taken. Four of the browns were caught in 65 to 70 degree water, and all but two browns were taken at temperatures above 55 degrees. Dave had proven his point. Even though Jeff and I had been consistently taking good catches of browns in early July in 50 to 60 degree temperatures, there wasn't any question that many browns were much closer inshore, well inside most of the boats.

Once midsummer brown trout are located, they aren't hard to catch, except on occasion in very bright, sunny, midday conditions. However, some of our best catches in 1988 came in just such situations. Contrary to what some of the books say, browns are not spooky or leader shy at normal midsummer depths. As a matter of fact, spoons like Locos, glow chartreuse Flutter Chucks, Evil Eyes, Northern Kings, and others are extremely effective in low light conditions fished 4 to 6 feet behind large, chartreuse-painted, fish-shaped weights.

Although rotating flashers like those used on the West Coast by commercial salmon trollers are not a traditional Lake Ontario rig, they are extremely effective not only for chinooks, but also for midsummer browns. One of my hottest brown trout takers in 1988 was the large F-4 chrome flasher with spectra prism trailed by a green-glow silver streak squid. Some of the browns weren't much bigger than the flasher, but they weren't a bit shy. Another hot item was a chrome Martin flasher trailed by a purple, green, and silver Spectra fly.

A variety of spoons fished above the flashers on cheaters were also effective. When browns don't take a liking to your flash and dash offerings or spoons trailed close behind a weight, try running spoons further back, say about 25 feet. Diving planers fished with a variety of flutter spoons are also deadly for summer browns when the thermocline is shallow enough to reach. My favorite diving planer spoons are Flutter Devles, especially in lemon-lime, and Suttons in sizes 38, 71, and 44.

As we docked the boat, Dave Nettles commented that the biggest problem he had with his brown trout study was getting the word out to Lake Ontario anglers. With his help, locating midsummer browns isn't difficult at all.

MAGNUM SPOONS FOR BIG KINGS

By Ernie Lantiegne

My wife Carol and I sat silently in the big wooden skiff, alone in the remoteness of the 80-mile-long Canadian lake. In our minds, we were surrounded by giant lake trout. Four days of fishing had fulfilled our every hope for trophy brook trout and northern pike. The small lakers we had taken so far had been fun on light tackle, but monsters like the 35-pounder we had seen an old-timer with back at the dock had eluded us.

It was time for a strategy session. As we pondered our pleasant dilemma, the old adage, "Big fish, big bait" broke the stillness. That was it! As we dug through the tackle box a No. 09 Elmer Hickley caught my eye. This silver-plated flutter spoon measures 9¾ inches long, not counting the hook! As it disappeared into the depths dressed with a white bucktail and single hook, we saluted it with an optimistic premonition: If a laker hits that, it will have to be a monster!

Unbelievably, the first laker we caught on it was only 21 inches long - hardly twice the size of the lure itself. By the end of the day the largest laker the big spoon had enticed was only 10 pounds. Another adage coined: "Hungry fish, big bait."

A thousand miles away and 10 years later I watched an excited angler from Pennsylvania on his first charter fishing trip for big chinook miss his second fish. We were fishing the big kings in the murky depths of a recent storm. The same downrigger at 135 feet had produced two hits, but we didn't connect. The Pennsylvania angler was apologetic. As I looked him in the eye, I responded, "You didn't do a thing wrong, but I may have."

He and his friends were a jumble of questions as we inspected the rig responsible for the action. One of my Great Lakes favorites for deep-water lakers and kings, the silver-plated No. 09 Elmer Hinkley - used as a flasher - was followed by a smaller Flutterdevle on an 18-inch leader. After a quick strategy session the same rig went back in the water with one addition: a 4/0 hook on the 09 Hinkley. To make a long story short, by the end of the day, three big kings in the fish box stood out from the rest. Each had fallen prey to the 9-inch flutter spoon.

Big spoons, generally referred to as "Magnums," are nothing new to Great Lakes anglers today. In the last two years these big baits have really come into their own for chinook salmon, especially from midsummer to early autumn. Magnum spoons also take big browns, lakers, cohos, and even steelhead. Most spoons that lure manufacturers label "Magnums" or "Super Magnums" are actually about 4½ inches in length, not counting the hook. A few manufacturers produce spoons 5 inches or more in length. Then you have what I call the "Monster Mags" of 6 inches and larger.

Many anglers think standard 4½-inch magnum spoons are big lures, bordering on oversized. Putting things in perspective, however, many of the alewives eaten by trout and salmon in the Great Lakes are 4 inches to 6 inches long, and I've seen alewives as large as 9 inches in some fish. Where big kings are chowing down on smelt, ciscoes, or other forage fish, bait as small as 6 inches in length is often uncommon. Anglers may have just started to explore the frontier of big baits for big chinook.

A number of lure manufacturers market magnum spoons 4½ inches long or larger. This includes spoons like the Northern King, the Diamond King made by Luhr Jensen, the Avery Assassin, Yeck Zipper, Dynamite, Pirate, Producer, Southport Slammer, Steffey Spoon and others. Other manufacturers produce spoons from 5 inches long and up. These include Red Eye's 5-inch No. 7F Evil Eye, Eppinger's 6-inch Big Ed, Mooselook Wobbler's Jag spoon, Sutton's No. 38 flutter spoon, and Nos. 06, 07, and 09 Elmer Hinkley flutter spoons. Generations of West Coast commercial chinook salmon trollers have used large spoons like the Kach-Moi and Superior to take Pacific kings that commonly feed on big herring.

In the Great Lakes, magnum spoons are a proven producer now, especially when mature chinook salmon are staging before September and October spawning runs. Big baits take prespawning kings more as the result of an aggressive reaction to the lure than an urge to feed. This is common knowledge, but are anglers using large enough spoons? The trend has been to bigger lures rather than smaller ones for late season kings. "Monster mags" may be on their way.

What about the rest of the year for Great Lakes trout and salmon? Well, one of my favorite spoons for the past 13 years has been the No. 38 Sutton in hammered finishes. Some the largest early spring brown trout taken aboard my boat, the Fish Doctor, have been seduced by this old spoon made in the Finger Lakes region of New York State for many years. It works great through the entire lake fishing season when fished from downriggers, wire line, drop sinker rigs, and diving planers. One of my favorite Monster Mag downrigger techniques for midsummer kings is an Eppinger "Big Ed," a 7F Evil Eye, or the big No. 09 Hinkley about 4 feet behind the downrigger weight with a standard size Flutter Chuck or Evil Eve stacked 4 to 6 feet above it on a 5-foot-long leader. Summer kings seem to say "Wow, there's a meal and a half! Sure looks good, but can I handle something that big? Aha, there's a smaller one. Wham!" Apparently, the big spoon excites or aggravates fish into striking the smaller one.

There is no question about it. Magnum spoons have made their mark on the Great Lakes' chinook salmon fishing. Magnums, Super Magnums, and maybe even the Monster Mags will probably find their place in more and more big-water tackle boxes - and rightfully so!

FAVORITE BAITS

By C. Scott Sampson

Ask my wife, Sonni, what her favorite bait is and there is no hesitation - "worm." If you qualify that and say, artificial lure, her response is just as fast - red and white Dardevle.

There is little reason behind her answers, except that she has caught fish on both and has total confidence in them.

We all react this way. As we gain more experience we may widen our choices, but often they are still made because we previously caught fish on that particular lure.

Catching fish is the name of the game, but the selection of lures is something that should be accomplished with more thought than a popularity contest.

The difference between a successful bait and an also-ran is action. The action is imparted by the speed of the troll or retrieve, but it may also be modified by the style and quality of the rigging. Each bait has an optimum speed and most baits were designed to work within specific speed ranges. For example, light, thin flutter spoons are designed to provide action at slow speed.

The action of any light flutter spoon, which is good for shallow-water trolling in the spring of the year, can be killed with the wrong rigging. Use a heavy snap swivel and you dampen the movement or the effective action of the spoon. If you are using the small size spoons to match the small natural baits of spring, you may need to tie the spoon directly to the line or use only a snap. If you are concerned about line twist you can put in a swivel 5 or 6 feet above the lure. The swivel might be an advantage, especially after a storm, in that it will stop algae from collecting on the bait. If a swivel is necessary to prevent line twist, perhaps you are trolling too fast. Few spoons are designed to twist and roll; they are normally meant just to rock back and forth.

Less hardware allows me to fish water as shallow as 3 and 4 feet without hanging the bottom, a distinct advantage in searching for a potential winning brown trout in the early morning hours.

Even large baits such as the Rebel should not be attached with the same heavy duty snap-swivels that you use on fall terminal tackle. If You carefully read the directions for any of these stickbaits, you are advised to attach the lure with a loop knot that allows the lure its full range of dodging back and forth. Many anglers, myself included, will opt for a high-quality but small round snap. Notice, I did say round. Snaps that have a sharp fold on the bend tend to inhibit lure action as much as a tight knot.

Excessive line weight can also dampen the action of light trolling baits. Too heavy a line will tend to hold a bait and not allow it to work as it was designed. In the spring of the year, I generally go no more than 10-pound-test even when I am looking for a 30 pound derby winner. This may sound reckless, but the light line significantly increases the number of fish that take my baits.

As the season progresses and you expect to catch salmon or steelhead, you may need to entice them with a faster trolling speed. The faster speed will also let you cover more water, but you must select the heavier baits that can withstand the speed without spinning. The Northern King spoon is a good example. In plugs, the Rebel Fastrac is a good choice for fast trolling.

With every lure, you need to test the bait and perhaps tune it, following the manufacturers' instructions. These tests take place at the side of the boat and should be a continuous activity throughout your fishing day, generally each time you change lures or start a new trolling direction. Let out just enough line so that the bait is capable of full movement. You can easily see the effects of the speed. Too slow and the bait seems to just drag through the water. Too fast and the bait is rolling or walking off to one side and perhaps breaking the surface.

Some baits are very speed sensitive. Others have a wider tolerance. I would suggest to you that the more popular a bait is on Lake Ontario, the more tolerant it is to changes in speed.

Speed instruments or even a tachometer can be used to judge your engine settings for a particular bait or lure. However, if you are using a tachometer, be sure to check the lure action for each direction of trolling because the engine rpm rate does not consider the effects of wind and currents. Actually the only really accurate speed measurement is one that is taken at the level of the lure that can show the effects of deep currents that are found in Lake Ontario.

Most successful anglers set baits that have the same speed tolerance in order to maintain the optimum lure action. Using the same baits or lures has an added advantage of imitating a school of bait, generally considered to be a more effective means of attracting fish.

If you are catching fish that is fine, but if the trout and salmon are selectively feeding it may take you a significant period of time to solve the puzzle. Working with other anglers in a cooperative effort can help to minimize this drawback.

Adding an attractor such as a dodger or Dipsy Diver can affect the fish-catching action of your favorite baits. These devices by themselves are designed to provide action and they must complement the action of the terminal bait. Again, testing is the answer.

Changing the length of the leader between the attractor device and the bait may also affect the combination's performance. As little as an inch can make a difference, especially with dodgers where the baits may be less than 15 inches from the attractor.

It's no mystery that we each have our favorite baits; the mystery is how they got to be the favored lure. The challenge is to expand your lure friendships. Watch the action and you may develop a whole tackle box of choice baits, a distinct advantage on any fishing trip, including the Spring ESLO Derby.

DOWNRIGGER FISHING: MORE FISH FOR YOUR FUEL

By Robert B. Buerger and Christopher F. Smith

Fishing is more exciting than ever with the variety of modern equipment available for today's sport angler. From video screen depth finders to computer-assisted navigation aids, the sportfishing industry has kept up-to-date on the latest technological advancements. The age-old quandary still faces the modern angler, however: How to get the fish to bite. For the boat sportfisherman, the problem can be more than just coming home empty-handed. Fuel and maintenance costs of operating a boat have risen drastically. The more time spent trying to locate and catch fish, the higher the cost of a day's sportfishing outing in energy and dollars. The successful angler today is the one who returns to port, not only with a well full of fish, but also with fuel remaining in the tank.

Innovations in sportfishing technology now enable you to increase your chances of finding and baiting certain fish. One technique that has proven successful for fish species sensitive to specific water temperatures is downrigging.

Most fish actively feed at or near a precise temperature range. The angler who knows and can gear his bait to the optimum range for his intended catch stands the greatest chance of success. When fish are in deep water, however, traditional flat lining will not hold the bait to the depth at which the fish are feeding. For years, some anglers have solved this problem by attaching heavy weights to their lines or using lead core line. Although this technique has proven effective, the excessive weight needed to lower the line to the appropriate depth minimizes much of the sporting "fight" of catching a fish; and even when the line is weighted, it becomes difficult to determine how deep it is running. Downrigging allows you to fish at specific depths without sacrificing the excitement of catching fish on light or medium tackle.

Downrigging: How it Works

The downrigger is a winch-type mechanism that feeds cable off a rotating reel through a guide system along an extension arm. A weight attached to the end of the cable draws it to the appropriate depth. Located near the bottom of the cable is the line release. The fishing line from an independent rod is attached to the release mechanisms on the downrigger cable.

By lowering the weight you can drop the line down to the desired depth. A meter is usually connected to the reel unit to provide a specific count of the amount of cable that has been released. At the desired depth the reel is locked into place.

The independent fishing rod is set in a holder either attached to the downrigger or placed directly behind it on the gunwale. A bow is placed in the rod by tightening the line between it and the release on the downrigger cable. When a fish strikes, it pulls the line from the release on the cable and thereby sets the hook. As tension on the line is released, the rod appears to snap straight up and allows the angler to play the fish without excess line weight.

The downrigging unit is typically mounted on the stern or along the rear side of the boat. Figure 1 depicts a fully-rigged system.

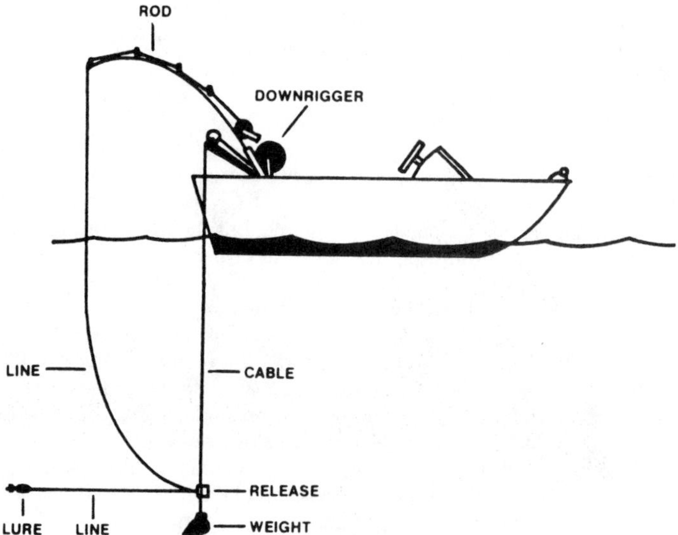

Figure 1 - Downrigger System

Basic Equipment

Downrigger designs and construction vary with the manufacturer; however, all downriggers have some similar components (see Figure 2).

A. **REEL** - The wheel device on which the cable is coiled. Cable length capacity is usually up to 600 feet.

B. **CRANK HANDLE** - Device used to rotate the wheel to shorten or extend cable length. Manual cranks are standard, but more sophisticated units use electrically-powered cranks. Electric units raise and lower weight via a 12-volt motor. Power required to operate electric downriggers is minimal, usually about 6 amps for a 12-pound weight. Some electric units shut off automatically when the weight reaches the arm on retrieval.

C. **CLUTCH** - Drag system that adjusts tension on the wheel. This allows cable to unravel when weight becomes entangled or caught on an obstruction. On some manual units it allows the weight to be lowered quickly without the use of a crank handle.

D. **CABLE** - Stranded stainless-steel wire (approximately 150-pound-test) is used to connect weight and reel. Line releases are placed on this cable. Special coaxial cable can be used that provides water temperature sensing (see temperature sensing section).

E. **ARM** - Extension tube or rod, usually between 1 to 6 feet in length, along which the cable runs and is supported. Some units have arms that are adjustable to various lengths. Arms that can be tilted up to the vertical position are available on some models.

F. **GUIDE HEAD AND PULLEY** - Located at the end of the arm, the guide head and pulley ensures smooth lowering and retrieval of the weight.

G. **MOUNTING** - The mounting provides for quick securing or release of the downrigger unit. Many mounts have a swivel base that slides in or bolts down to a mounting plate to allow for different positioning and ease in connecting lines to release. Lock-in security mounts are an option available on some units.

H. **WEIGHTS** - Used to submerge line to desired depth. Weights are usually 6 to 12 pounds and come in numerous shapes and colors.

I. **RELEASE** - Mechanisms used to attach line from fishing rod to downrigger cable.

J. **COUNTER** - Usually attached to the reel, this provides accurate measure of the amount of cable that has been let out.

K. **ROD HOLDER** - The fishing rod attached to the downrigger is placed in this unit, which may be single or double rigged.

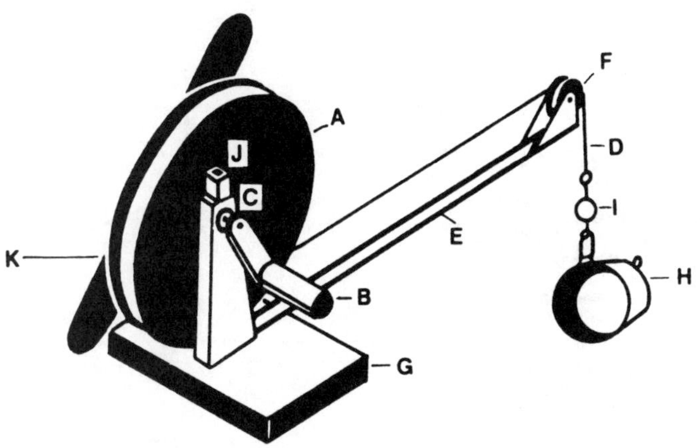

Figure 2 - Downrigger Components

Using the Downrigger System

Releases

Correct application of line release systems is essential for successful downrigging. Releases can be mounted (1) between a cable and a downrigger weight, (2) directly to a weight, or (3) at any location along the wire. The ability to attach the release at any point affords placement of more than one line on a single downrigger cable. "Stacking," illustrated in Figure 3, must be attempted with caution, as multiple hookups may cause line crossing.

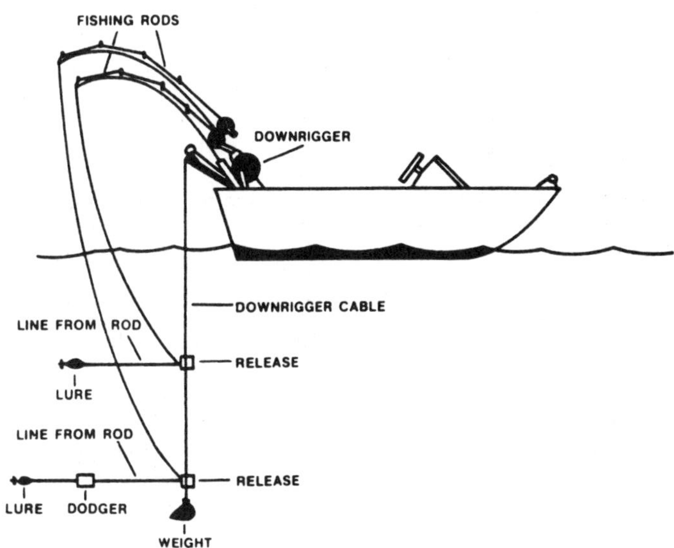

Figure 3 - Stacking Technique

Release designs vary in complexity, from a simple rubber band to plastic-molded, spring-set, adjustable tension mechanisms. Choice of type and design are dependent upon application. Adjustable tension releases are appropriate when high and slow speed trolling of lines having varying weights is expected over the course of a season, whereas less sophisticated releases are suitable for slow speed, light lure trolling. Correct release tension, best learned through experience, allows for release only when a fish bites the bait, and not when normal lure resistance occurs while trolling.

Releases should also be evaluated in terms of potential line wear. Some designs with flat, nonpointed surfaces, tend to distribute the "pinching effect", a feature that minimizes line wear over greater lengths of line.

With the variety of downrigger releases on the market today and the continual influx of new designs, you should consult an expert before choosing a release for your fishing needs.

When manufactured releases are not available, a rubber band may be substituted in the following way:

— Pull one end of a No. 12 rubber band through the other until it clinches down on your fishing line.

— Attach the rubber band loop to a snap-swivel located above the downrigger weight.

— If stacking lines, then repeat above and attach the other end of the swivel to the downrigging cable, using a second rubber band and snap.

Line from Release to Lure

The amount of line from the release mechanism to the lure is an important consideration when downrigger fishing. When you are fishing in shallow water, the boat may spook the fish; therefore, it may be necessary to locate the lure a greater distance behind the weight to enable fish to reenter the troll alley following passage of the boat. Generally, if you think fish are disturbed by boat movement, move the lure further from the release.

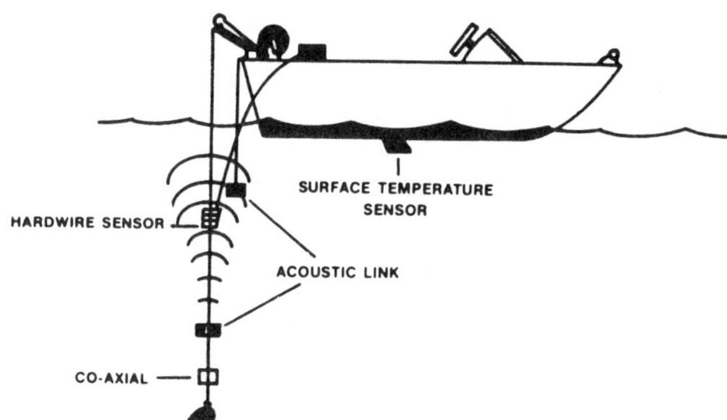

Figure 4 - Water Temperature Sensing Equipment

The greater the distance between lure and release, the greater the line drop after a fish strikes. Line drop describes the slack period from the time the line is pulled free of the release to the time it comes taut to the tip of the fishing rod. At this time the lure is free-falling, possibly simulating prey that has been stunned as the result of an attack. If you are fishing for game fish that stun their prey and return to consume crippled bait, this could be to your advantage. If bait does not stall in the water after line drop, the game fish may think its prey has not been injured and is not catchable.

You may wish to use a dodger (see Figure 3) between the lure and release to attract attention and impart movement to the lure or bait.

Lure Action

Another important consideration in downrigger fishing is the action of the lure. If your lure is of the diving type, the distance it will dive must be considered if stacking it next to nondiving lures or if fishing close to the bottom. A diving lure that would normally dive 10 to 15 feet if free trolled, will also dive 10 to 15 feet from the release point, with a downrigger. This should be taken into account when setting release position and weight depth.

Trolling Speed and Cable Angle

Trolling speed should vary according to type of lure, depth fished, and species sought. When trolling live or rigged baits, you should allow them to move as naturally as possible; therefore, a slower trolling speed is usually preferred. A faster speed can tear the hook, if not adequately secured, from the bait.

Artificial lures are normally trolled faster than live bait. As trolling speed increases, the angle of the downrigger cable off the stern also increases. As the boat moves through the water, the cable and weight tend to trail behind, which produces cable deflection.

To make accurate depth determinations for weights and lines, you might wish to use a paper-recording, fish-finding fathometer when downrigger fishing. Metal weights often appear as a solid black line on the paper. Consult a marine electronics dealer for details.

Temperature Sensing Equipment and Use

Water temperature is a primary determinant of fish distribution. Temperature may act to concentrate food organisms that attract fish, or may be a physiological barrier through which fish will not move. Generally, water temperatures decrease with increasing depth. As wind keeps the surface water layer well mixed and uniform in temperature, the temperature decreases rapidly within a subsurface layer of water called the thermocline. During midsummer months, the thermocline contains favorable dissolved oxygen and nutrient levels for fish and prey.

Knowledge of fish temperature preferences, coupled with the ability to measure temperature at various depths, can contribute to angling success.

Many types of water temperature sensing equipment are available. The simplest is a thermometer, used only to measure surface temperature, that can be hand-held over the side of a boat. A variation of the thermometer is a temperature sensor permanently mounted to the hull.

To measure temperatures at various depths, other instruments must be used. The coaxial temperature sensor system utilizes a special kind of downrigger cable that conducts an electrical signal from a sensor placed near the downrigger weight. As the weight is lowered, temperatures are read off a display unit on the boat. The hard wire sensor is similar to the coaxial sensor, but in this case the unit can be mounted at any point along the downrigger cable, and the signal is conducted along a separate wire. Several of these can be mounted on a cable to provide continuous temperature measurements at various depths. A third unit, the acoustic link, telemeters the temperature signal through the water from a dry cell-powered sensor on the downrigger cable to the display unit on board. No wire joins the sensor and display unit in this system. Yet another system uses insulated, coated, downrigger cable to transmit temperature information from a dry cell-equipped sensor attached to the cable, with water itself acting as the circuit ground. All of this equipment is flexible enough for practically any application, whether you are taking an isolated survey of the water column or a continuous reading at various depths while trolling.

Figure 4 illustrates types and uses of temperature sensing equipment. Consult marine and boating buyers guides to find equipment manufacturers.

Mounting Boards

Downrigger bases are sometimes attached to mounting boards, usually placed atop the transom of a boat and containing four downrigger units and associated fish-finding electronics and equipment. Because each downrigger is equipped with its own mountable base located at any point on the gunwale or transom of the vessel, mounting boards are not essential for downrigging.

Figure 5 illustrates two popular patterns for mounting four downriggers on a moderate-size fishing boat. In general, downriggers

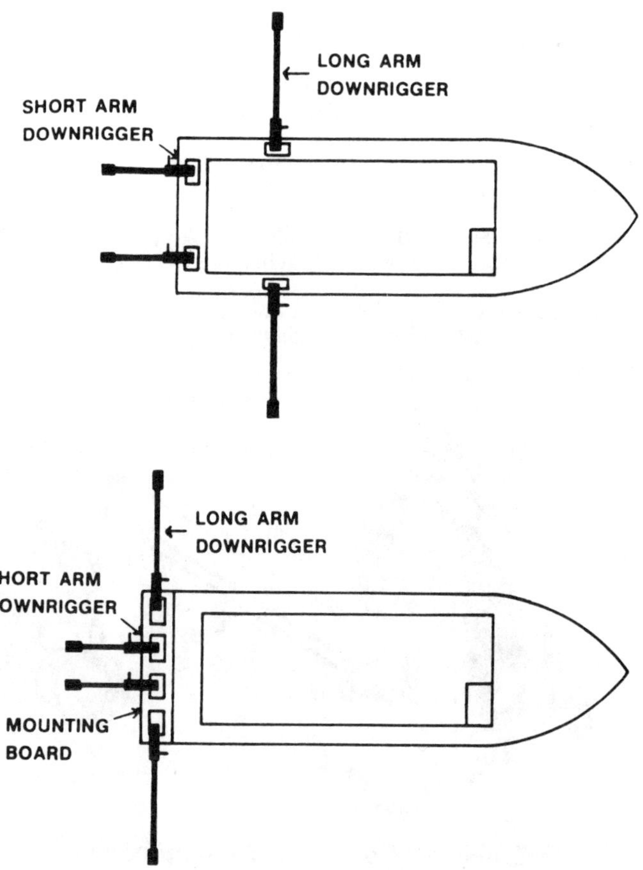

Figure 5 - Downrigger Layout Options

with long arm extensions are used for side downrigger positions, and short arms are used for stern mounting. Common sense should be exercised when locating downriggers, so as to minimize potential interference with adjacent lines. When mounting electric downrigging units, you might wish to consult a qualified boat electrician.

Maintenance

Manufacturers generally outline any necessary maintenance required for various downrigger models. Because downriggers have moving and often electrical components, visual maintenance and upkeep should be part of the cleanup routine following a fishing trip. Cables should be inspected for frays and kinks and replaced as necessary. Electrical cables should have no cracks and remain waterproof. Lubrication of pulleys, swivels, and snaps should be done often to prohibit corrosion and ensure smooth working characteristics.

Conclusion

Today's boat angler is faced with increasing operating costs due to rising fuel and maintenance expenses. The longer the time spent angling for fish the higher the costs. Downrigger fishing provides a way of locating and catching fish faster and thus saving fuel and money.

BROWN TROUT TACTICS MADE SIMPLE

By Capt. Chris Michaels

Lake Ontario offers some of the finest brown trout action in the country. With a little practice and patience consistent catches of sizable browns can be taken from ice-out through mid-July. Here are two techniques commonly used for catching spring browns.

When browns are located in areas of less than 15 feet of water, surface lines rigged with body-baits or stickbaits, can be deadly. I prefer to run similar plugs throughout my set, creating a schooling effect. The most productive models of stickbaits are the shallow-running minnow imitations 4 to 5 inches in length.

If lake conditions and boat traffic allow, a rule-of-thumb is three rods per planer board. Don't be afraid to run long leads behind side-planers, 100 to 150 feet back. Since body-baits float, they can be quickly free-spooled to the desired distance behind the boat without the worry of snagging bottom. Floating plugs also allow a boat operator to slip the vessel in and out of neutral to help an angler battle a stubborn brown without the problem of hang-ups.

With all the work involved in running six lines properly, I seldom use downriggers when fishing shallow for spring browns. Working a planer board set is much easier without rigger lines to get in the way, and with the back of the boat open netting is a breeze.

In most situations, plugs in black-on-silver and blue-on-silver work best. If forced to fish off-color or dirty water, try red-on-chartreuse or combinations of white. If the trolling area is heavy with floating debris, try placing a small split-shot or knotting a piece of rubberband a few feet ahead of the bait; this will help keep lure action intact.

Trolling speeds should remain on the slow side - 1.6 to 2.2 mph seems to work best. Before dropping a plug back to the set, observe its action along the side of the boat. Many plugs, even those fresh out of the package, require tuning to insure a proper swimming action. To adjust the lures action, simply bend the nose of the plug in the direction you wish it to favor until the bait swims true. Make adjustments slight at first until you become familiar with the process.

As inshore water temperatures warm to the high 50s, brown trout head for structure in lake depths of 20 to 50 feet. During low light conditions, browns may come into shallow areas to feed, but as a rule they spend most of their time in deeper water.

To cash in on subsurface brown trout action, a spoon pattern run behind downriggers and diving planers works best. Using a graph recorder or fish-finder can save time when locating structure oriented browns. Look for schools of bait fish near shoals or drop-offs.

The ideal temperature range for deep-water browns is 56 to 58 degrees. Combine a comfortable temperature zone with bottom depths of 20 to 50 feet, schools of forage fish, and an irregular bottom contour and brown trout action shouldn't be far behind.

Once an area is found, select single-hook flutter spoons in the 2½ to 3 inch range. The best color patterns are black-on-white with green trim for deeper sets and hammered brass and black-on-silver for lines run closer to the surface. As with the stickbait pattern, spoon speeds vary from 1.6 to 2.2 mph.

When setting-up for structure-oriented browns, I run my downriggers in a V pattern. Dropping the deepest lines with the center rigger and setting each outward rigger nearer to the surface. An example of this would be: setting the center rigger at 35 feet, corner riggers at 32 and 29 feet, side riggers at 27 and 25 feet and diving planes behind outriggers at 15 and 18 feet. I prefer to run one rod per rigger until I begin fishing depths greater than 50 feet, at which time I stack one additional rod per rigger. My usual distance between the bottom rod and stacker is 8 feet.

Running figure-eight patterns over drop-offs and shoals seems to trigger more strikes than simply trolling in a straight course over a structure-filled area. If the graph recorder is showing activity and temperatures are favorable, work the area several times before moving to new water. Many times a change in trolling speed, a different lure color, or new leader length is all it takes to start rods popping.

I have to credit Captain Roger Lowden, of Hilton, New York, for putting me on to deep-water browns. One June afternoon seven years ago, Roger and I headed out of Braddock Bay to work Braddock point shoal. I had never been able to catch browns consistently after they left the 10- to 15-foot shallows, but that was all to change that spring day. The spoon pattern Roger recommended produced several big browns in a short four hour trip and convinced me of the fact that good brown trout fishing can continue long after the planer boards are stowed away.

Both the surface stickbait pattern and the deep-water spoon set are proven producers. If presented properly, the two techniques can provide reliable brown trout catches from April through July.

DEADLY FLIES FOR CHINOOKS

By Ernie Lantiegne

The town hall was jam-packed with angry fishermen locked in controversy over the recent announcement by New York State's Bureau of Fisheries that all snagging for Pacific salmon in Lake Ontario tributaries would be banned by 1991.

On one side were the proponents of snagging, convinced after years of indoctrination that Pacific salmon could not be taken using traditional hook and line techniques. On the other side were anglers convinced from their own experience in rivers and streams of the Great Lakes and West Coast that cohos and chinooks could be taken with rod and reel without resorting to snag hooks.

As the controversy raged and tempers flared, my mind wandered back to a more tranquil setting in early November on a gravel bar in the Big Salmon River above Pulaski. Overcast skies made early morning even darker as I sensed a perfect bottom-scratching drift toward the barely perceptible silhouette of what I thought was a monster steelhead. As the fish inhaled the Oregon Cheese Glow Bug, I felt the tell-tale pause in the drift and drove the needle-sharp No. 6 hook home hard with the 10½-foot noodle fly rod. The graphite fibers held together under the pressure, but the aerial acrobatics I expected never happened. Instead, after a freight train run and a 15-minute toe to toe battle, I beached a surprisingly silver, late-run female chinook. It took longnosed pliers to unhook the firmly imbedded barb from the big chinook's tongue. The female righted herself and continued her upstream journey, hardly the worse for wear.

A movement to my right brought me back to the reality of the noisy meeting. Fran Verdoliva sat next to me shaking his head as anglers argued. Fran, at the age of 36 years, is a master Lake Ontario fly fisherman, fly tyer, rod builder, and renowned river guide. He may know more about fly fishing for Pacific salmon in Lake Ontario tributaries than any man alive. As he listened to some of the comments from the crowd that salmon would not take an artificial lure, he knew well that much of the controversy was fueled by years of indoctrination by New York's Department of Environmental Conservation and their misleading policy that the only way Pacific salmon could be harvested was by snagging.

Verdoliva knew better. He caught his first Pacific salmon on a Mepps spinner in the Oswego River when he was only a teenager. He took his first chinook salmon on a fly two years later in 1973, well before most fishermen were even aware of spawning salmon in Lake Ontario streams. Since then, Verdoliva and the fly fishermen he guides have taken many hundreds of fair-caught chinooks and cohos on flies. His original technique, fine-tuned over the years, is still deadly in the right conditions.

The first step in gearing up to fly fish for Pacific salmon is selecting the proper equipment. Polaroid glasses for spotting fish, good waders with cleats, a vest to carry accessory paraphenalia, and warm, lightweight clothing are a must. A 9- to 10-foot, 9- to 10-weight graphite fly rod, and single action reel with a smooth disc drag and capacity to hold 200 yards of dacron backing is the proper combination.

Fly lines may be the most critical ingredient in the Verdoliva fly fishing formula. Three basic lines are required: A floating line with a 5-foot sink tip is perfect for fishing pocket water and shallow riffles where salmon spawn; a floater with a 24-foot sink tip works well in deeper pools and runs where water averages 3 to 5 feet deep; and level floater for use in short, fast runs when split shot must be attached to the leader to get the fly down to bottom-hugging fish. A 10-foot leader tapering to a 15-pound-test tippet completes the system.

Surprisingly, the assortment of flies deadly for salmon is not extensive. Three basic patterns - Comets, Teeny nymphs, and stone fly nymphs - will take fish in most situations.

Comets are a gaudy fly especially effective later in the spawning season. They have chain eyes, a chenille body wrapped with tinsel, a long tail, and a light wrap of hackle. Chartreuse and hot pink are good colors for this fly. Heavy size No. 2 and No. 4 hooks plus metal bead eyes provide weight to get the fly down to the fish. The eyes provide built-in flash and a very slight jigging action. Fran Verdoliva's personal version, the King Comet, incorporates a copper tinsel body, orange tail, white wing mixed with silver flashabou (a marabou-like tinsel), and an orange chenille head with bead chain eyes.

Stone fly nymphs and Teeny nymphs in black or hot pink on size No. 8 to No. 2 hooks are also favorites. Interestingly, salmon actively engaged in digging gravel to build a spawning redd will often take one of these black nymphs, perhaps mistaken as the real thing flushed from the gravel.

In September, 1976, on the Big Salmon River in a shallow riffle spawning area, Verdoliva was casting a flashy streamer to actively spawning chinooks. As he cast the fly, it would swing downstream and across the current in front of the fish. As the fly came into view, aggressive males chased it as far as 15 feet before hitting it savagely. At the end of the swing, if the fly had been ignored, it was retrieved with a 6-inch stripping motion, often aggravating fish into striking. This is still the basic Verdoliva technique.

When chinook and coho salmon are actively spawning, the males especially are aggressively territorial. Anything in the vicinity of their spawning redds, including other salmon, small minnows, and artificial lures, are intruders to be attacked and driven away. Salmon will commonly seize small minnows in their mouths and carry them away from redds before dropping them. Small jack salmon with chunks bitten from their backs by larger males bear witness to this protective nature. This is surmised to be the primary reason why nonfeeding salmon strike artificial lures in a spawning stream. Spawning chinook and coho salmon returning to a natal stream are in a strange environment compared to the cold depths of the lake or ocean where they grew to adulthood. The typically clear water and shallow depths of a river expose them to a variety of new dangers and make them extremely spooky. Even false casts by a fly fisherman will often scare them to the nearest holding water. Even a small fly presented in the path of an upstream moving fish can stop them dead in the water and turn them back downstream.

Needless to say, crowds of fishermen lined up along a stream spook fish. Under these conditions Pacific salmon can be almost impossible to take on a fly or any other type of artificial or bait. When this happens, look for quiet water, away from the crowds, especially pocket water where fish may be holding unseen by most fishermen. On busy streams like the Big Salmon River, which flows through Pulaski, try fishing on Tuesdays, Wednesdays, or Thursdays when pressure is lightest and the fish have returned to normal behavior.

Because of this spookiness, Pacific salmon should be approached carefully from above so that a quartering downstream cast will swing the fly at the level of their eye or lateral line. Flies presented well above fish pose no territorial threat and are generally ignored. If repeated casts to fish produce no hits, move on and locate fresh fish. When a chinook or coho strikes, the fish will commonly turn its body or move upstream slightly. Unless the angler strikes instantly, the fish will spit the fly.

The ideal stream to fly fish for Pacific salmon has a good run of fish and reasonable access, either public or by permission. Such a stream will have areas of pools and riffs where a fly can be easily presented to spawning fish with little or no weight.

If, as the New York State Department of Environmental Conservation has announced, snagging of Pacific salmon is discontinued by 1991 in Lake Ontario tributaries, the number of streams ideally suited for fly fishing will increase. As this happens, anglers will quickly learn how deadly and enjoyable fly fishing technique for Pacific salmon can really be.

DIPSY DIVER TECHNIQUES

By Capt. Monte Chilson

If you have ever been involved in some form of a love/hate relationship with a lover or spouse, then you know how I relate to Dipsy Divers. They can be the most frustrating piece of equipment on your boat and can also be the most productive fish-catching equipment you have. I often hear fishermen say "I don't use Dipsy Divers, they're too hard to control and always giving me tangles or breaking off." Welcome to the club!

There are times when the Dipsy Divers will provide the majority of fish for the day. There are also times when I've pulled them over the length of Lake Ontario (or so it seems) without a single strike. They are a prime example of one of Murphy's laws, which states "If anything can go wrong, it will." I have hooked them on bottom, around other lines and downriggers, and even on a 35-foot sailboat, which gave me quite a battle for a while, but got away. If you aren't currently using Dipsy Divers, you need to begin immediately. You can't consider yourself an 'all-around' fisherman if you aren't willing to do battle with them.

If you are currently dragging Dipsies around and are beginning to be comfortable with how they work and feel, let me give you a couple of more options that will probably drive you crazy. Remember, no pain, no gain!

First, I've heard several fishermen on the radio comment on how frequently the Dipsies break off. They also said they were using heavy line, 15- to 20-pound-test! Well, Dipsy Diver draggers, 15- to 20-pound-test line on Dipsies isn't heavy. You should never use less than 25-pound-test line and most successful Dipsy fishermen use 30-pound-test or more. During the 1990 fishing season, I used 30-pound-test braided dacron line. Give it a try. There is no stretch and you can release the Dipsy with 150 to 200 feet of line out with no problem. Even though it doesn't stretch when a fish strikes, it hooks up solid and doesn't break. I also recommend using dacron between the Dipsy and lure during salmon season. This keeps the salmon from breaking the line off the Dipsy and the salmon don't seem to be line-shy when they're feeding.

For the last two years, I've been using a Dipsy with a long line between the Dipsy and the lure. By long line, I mean whatever length of line you want. You can run 20, 50, or 100 feet behind the Dipsy. This practice is sometimes very productive when fish aren't hitting the normal Dipsy setup. They seem to be less spooked by this and it can also be used in a manner similar to the "drop sinkers" without the need of dropping of additional lead sinkers into the lake. It also might soon be illegal to use drop sinkers, so here is an alternative. When fishermen ask how this is done, I say "You just need a real long pole." Not really. I will describe how it's done.

Just like almost everything we buy lately, some assembly is required. Make sure you try the setup and practice with it before you try it on the lake or it will drive you crazy. You will need the following items:

— Two snap swivels capable of handling 15 to 20 pounds of stress. Make sure they are good quality.
— One Big Jon sinker release.
— One barrel swivel, large size. Also make sure it's of good quality.

1. Cut off a length of line from your Dipsy Diver set up that is a little shorter than your rod. I use 9-foot Dipsy rods, so I use approximately 7 feet of "heavy" line.
2. Attach one of the snap swivels to one end of this cut line (this will be where the lure will be attached) and the barrel swivel to the other end of this cut line.
3. On the line coming from the rod (not the piece you cut off), slide the sinker release and remaining snap swivel over the line and tie the line to the barrel swivel (see Diagram A).
4. Add a number 7 split ring to the Dipsy Diver (see Diagram B). Use the large size Dipsy. I also leave the ring on the Dipsy, but that's a personal choice. If you do leave the rings on, I recommend that you "super glue" them on so you won't have any more problems with the rings coming off.
5. Now comes the fun. Remember to practice this before you try it in front of others to avoid being laughed at or maybe even be accused of being a little crazy. It takes a little getting used to. With the Dipsy rod in a holder, the reel in free spool and the clicker on, let out line while hanging onto the snap swivel and sinker release. I hold the snap swivel and sinker release in one hand and pull line out with the other. If you are using a reel with a counter, you can let out the line to any exact length. (I've assumed you've already attached your favorite lure before letting the line out.)
6. When enough line has been let out, hook the snap swivel to the back ring of the Dipsy Diver (see Diagram C).
7. Latch the Dipsy Diver and hook the sinker release through the number 7 split ring that you installed earlier on the Dipsy. Make sure the line is wrapped a couple of times around the sinker release to avoid having the Dipsy trip from the drag. This also allows you to trip the Dipsy from the boat for retrieval (see Diagram C).
8. Let the Dipsy out to the desired depth. If using a counter reel, it can reset to zero and then let out to the desired depth. I usually set the Dipsy on a setting of two or three to get it out far out to either side. That's all there is to it!

When the fish strikes, the Dipsy will release and slide down the line to the barrel swivel. This keeps the Dipsy away from the fish. Salmon especially don't like getting banged on the nose by a Dipsy!

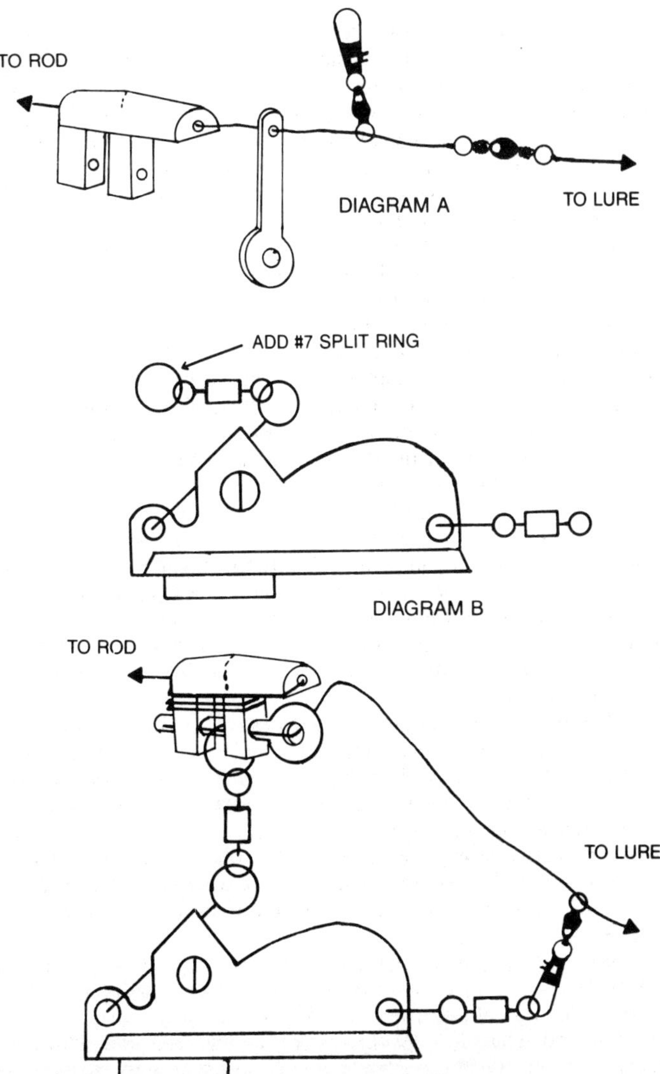

If you want to release the Dipsy, jerk the rod sharply and the Dipsy will release. Reel in the Dipsy until it can be reached, pull the sinker pin and unhook the snap swivel from the Dipsy. The lure can now be reeled in. Remember to hang on to the Dipsy so it doesn't drop into the lake (I'll bet you'll lose at least one).

If you haven't had enough of Dipsy Diver problems, let me give you a couple of more ways to drive yourself crazy. Dipsies off of downriggers! Well, I thought those fishermen who told me about them were on something stronger than smoked salmon. But, I am also one to try almost anything. The first technique is one I learned about from Roger Looker, a friend and charter boat captain from Fair Haven, New York. He explained that he was using the small Dipsy with the normal length of line between the Dipsy and the lure but was letting out 20 to 30 feet and hooking the line to a downrigger. The Dipsy was set between the one and two setting to spread out and away from its respective side of the boat. The smaller Dipsy doesn't create too much drag and most downrigger releases can be adjusted to hold them. This technique seems to work well during the transition from shallow water spring fishing to the formation of the thermocline. My theory is that the fish are a little cannonball shy at this time and the spread of the Dipsy moves the lures further away. But then, many of my theories have been proven wrong, so you can make up your own theory. Give it a try. It does work.

Now! You thought I was crazy before! Read on! These techniques have been explained to me by several excellent fishermen and I must confess, I'm still learning how to fish them. I do know, however, that they can be deadly on fish, especially salmon. The technique is one of running the large Dipsies off downriggers. This requires the Dipsy to be set so that it tracks "down and out" from the downrigger. A setting of one to two works well, although you might want to try other settings. The first problem is one of keeping the releases from letting go as soon as the Dipsy hits the water. Many releases can be set to hold the Dipsy, like the Black release. But an easier technique is to hook the line to a release that has been really tightened, using two rubber bands. The rubber bands will hold the Dipsy and also break when a salmon hits the lure. The Dipsy also releases, usually prior to the rubber bands breaking. Remember, the tension release on the Dipsy can be set a little lighter as the downrigger cable is taking up much of the drag.

In addition to running the Dipsy off the downrigger, try putting a dodger and lure on the Dipsy. There are times that this combination is so productive that you will need very few lines in the water when the salmon are hitting. The line is usually run short off the downrigger, but experiment with different lengths and colors of Dipsies, dodgers, and lures. Remember, when fishing there are no "hard and fast rules."

Well, I hope I've given you a couple of more things to think about for the new fishing year. If you try these techniques, I'm sure you will add to your catch. Good fishing!

FISHING FOR SPRING BROWNS ON LAKE ONTARIO

By Capt. Victor A. Malambri

Spring fishing for brown trout on Lake Ontario can be fun; it can also be a trying experience. I know that these statements are contradictory, but bear with me. Spring browns feed on crustaceans and whatever the waves turn up on the shoreline. This means fishing close to shore in 10 feet of water or less, and the invention of side planer boards has greatly simplified this type of fishing.

Another factor that tends to draw brown trout in close to the shoreline in the spring is water temperature since the lake warms from the shoreline out. This warmer water attracts the bait that browns feed on, and let me tell you, browns will have the feed bag on in April and May.

The source of warmer near-shore water in the spring is the many small creeks, rivers, and swamps that flow or leech water into Lake Ontario. These are the areas you want to fish if you're after browns. Watch the water; you'll see pockets of brownish coloration (stained water) around these areas.

Lure selection in the spring will vary, but generally your best choice of lures will be the smaller sizes. Last spring there were a lot of complaints about the brown trout fishing in the eastern basin of Lake Ontario. Up until the beginning of the ESLO Derby in late April, browns were being taken with consistent regularity, but due to a hatch of emerald shiners, the catches ceased. The fishermen who caught onto this and switched to smaller-size spoons and plugs off planer boards experienced limit catches.

In nature, predator fish prey or feed on the most prolific bait available. They will not look for a specific species of bait fish; it takes too much energy to hunt for a favorite type. This is also nature's way of keeping a species from being hunted to extinction.

As far as lure colors go, I've had browns take a multitude of different colors. I have found that a Color C-Lector helps in making your choice of colors, too. Some important points for successful planer board fishing include the type of line you use. Side-planer line or surveyor cord will give your lure a jigging action. By running the planer boards off a downrigger cable, you lose most of this action. When fishing in windy conditions, you will find that the side-planer on the windward side will run almost 90 degrees off the side of the boat. The planer board that's on the opposite side will trail and/or even fall down if it's a single board. If I run side planers in windy conditions, I only run one board on the windward side of the boat.

If you happen to hang up a lure while using side planers, don't stop. If you do, you'll hang your other lures. Break the lure off instead. If you stop your boat in an area where you're surrounded by other boats using planer boards, you will cause them problems as well. Many seasoned fishermen will run over your lines and even cut off your planer line if need be. Use some common sense. While side planers can be run out to 100 feet on each side, when fishing in congested areas, you'd better suck them in. That's another good way to lose your planer boards.

When fishing for browns in the spring, lure speed will have a lot to do with your catch. They prefer slow speeds; the slower the troll, the bigger the browns is one school of thought. How slow? I can't say. Speed is relative to your boat and the weather conditions on any given day. But I can give you a good example of how not to fish for browns.

When I first placed a surface speed indicator on my boat, I tried to go by the speed the manufacturer suggested. I suffered through two months of the worst fishing I have ever had. And I'm here to tell you, it was caused by my following these recommendations. I found that out by chance, and since that time, I have done quite well.

Shallow-water fish have a tendency to be boat shy. That's why small boats tend to do better when fishing the shoreline, and side planers were designed for this reason. As you troll across the water, the fish will move out to the sides as you pass over them. This puts the fish under your lures off the side planers.

Lure drop-back should be relatively short when using side planers, 50 feet or less in shallow water. When fishing temperature breaks in deeper water, you can let out considerably more line. The further back the line, the deeper the lure. In 4 to 5 feet of water 20 to 30 feet of drop-back will generally be far enough. Any deeper than this and your lures will snag bottom. of course, this will depend on lure weight.

When using stickbaits or plugs, you must pay close attention to the depth. Snagging bottom can be an expensive proposition, and when it comes to speed, you will have to experiment on your own boat. Checking your lure action occasionally will prove productive.

There are many types of side planer releases on the market. You can also use rubber bands and shower curtain hangers, but the major problem with this setup is that rubber bands can cut the line. Your local tackle shop should have a supply of planer board releases.

If you're fishing close to shore and the fish have quit hitting, move out a little further into the lake. Heavy boat traffic can drive the fish out and down deep. Pounding the same area will cause this, too. It's better to fish a longer troll than to circle right back to the same spot. Once you've located the fish, why scatter them? And here's a tip that might save your fishing trip. When you buy snap swivels, spend the extra money on the ball bearing ones with rounded ends. They allow the lure to work better. Ball bearing swivels also help to keep your line from tangling.

Now let's get to the serious side of spring fishing. Keeping an eye on the weather is paramount. Fishing for brown trout in the spring puts you close to the shoreline. If you have engine trouble, you will be on the rocks fast. The water is cold at this time of year and it doesn't take long for hypothermia to set in.

Warm winter clothing is a normal requirement, too. Wind, however slight, can blow right through you. You have to remember that the lake's water temperature in the spring can be in the high 30s to low 40s. I have seen times when we went out with our warmest clothes on and froze. But by one o'clock, we were changing into shorts. Then by nightfall, we were back into winter clothes again and wishing for 10 gallons of hot coffee. A quart to drink, and the rest to stick our cold feet into.

TROLLING SPEED CAN BE THE DIFFERENCE

By Mike Bleech

Trolling speed is but one of many variables that the salmonid troller must deal with. Any seasoned angler knows that a change in speed of less than one-half-mph can spell the difference between a number of hookups and just a few. Yet trolling speed is taken casually by some anglers and is misunderstood by even more.

To deal with trolling speed in an efficient manner, the angler must: 1) understand what trolling speed is; 2) understand how to match terminal tackle to trolling speed; and 3) know how to control trolling speed.

Trolling speed is the speed that the lures are moving through the water, but not necessarily the same speed the boat is moving. Currents, either on the surface or below, can cause the relative speeds of boat and lures to be different. For that matter, the lures in the spread may be traveling at different speeds, relative to the water. The wind, for example, can cause a surface current that would mean that lures run in that current, say from planer boards, would be traveling at a different relative speed than lures run below that current from downriggers.

Trolling speed for Great Lakes salmonids varies from the slowest possible speed to over 4 miles per hour. Any trolling speed over 5 mph is usually too fast. The standard trolling speed, if there is such a thing, is between 1 1/2 and 3 mph. This is an oversimplification, however, since the various salmonids react differently to trolling speed.

As a general guideline, salmon (especially in the spring) and steelhead are most likely to be turned on by faster trolling speeds, while browns and lakers are more likely to be taken by a slower troll. Another general guideline is that trolling speeds for salmon and steelhead should also be slowed in water colder than 50 degrees.

It is important that you understand that speedometers and knot meters are not calibrated the same. You must understand your own instrument and not try to relate it to what you read or hear, just as you must match lures and attractors to the trolling speed. Few, if any, lures will perform acceptably throughout the salmonid trolling speed range. Most have an optimum speed range of somewhere in the neighborhood of 1 1/2 mph. The most versatile lures in this context are the action plastic lures.

Dodgers are meant to wobble, but when they spin they are being trolled to fast. Spoons generally can be evaluated in the same way, while plugs tend to have a broader operating range than lightweight spoons. The exception to this is the class of plugs commonly called the banana baits, which give great action with the slowest trolling speeds.

It is important that you remember that all plugs must be perfectly tuned to achieve desired action under maximum trolling speeds. A few plugs are factory-tuned while many others include tuning instructions in the package. Lures should be tested alongside the boat with a minimum of 6 feet of line between the lure or dodger and the rod tip to allow freedom of movement similar to what it will have during use.

It is easy to understand what trolling speed is; control of the trolling speed is more difficult. Matching tackle to trolling speed takes time, effort and a good assortment of lures and attractors, but the end result is worth the effort.

In order to control trolling speed there must first be some way to measure trolling speed! The only accurate way to measure trolling speed is to have a speedometer at the same depth as the lures in question. Such devices are on the market, but everything has a price - in addition to dollars and cents. There are speed devices that attach to downrigger balls that afford precise speed control down where the lures are, and some very good trolling speedometers that meter the speed of the boat. Granted, relative speed of lures may be different from boat speed, but these devices give the troller the ability to accurately gauge small changes in trolling speed. The ability to measure changes in trolling speed is far more important than measuring the actual relative speed of lures.

Why is it more important to measure change than the actual speed? Because the troller does not really care how fast the lures are traveling. What matters is how the fish react to the speed. If they're hitting, then it is important to measure absolutely no change in trolling speed. If the fish are not hitting, it is important to measure small increases or decreases in trolling speed until a productive speed is found.

Tachometers are commonly used to measure changes in speed and some trollers watch the angle of the downrigger cables, while others rely on some mystical ability to sense speed. These methods are of limited reliability at best. Still, just knowing that minor trolling speed adjustments can be critical to success is an important bit of knowledge!

Many anglers have sadly learned that measuring the trolling speed is not enough - large motors will often not troll slow enough for salmonids. However, the new Evinrudes with big horses troll unbelievably well, and auxiliary motor mounts are available, as is steering linkage, to allow the small motor to be steered from helm.

SUMMER DEEP-TROLLING TIPS

(Adapted from Summer Salmonids in Lake Ontario, NYSDEC)

Often the difference between an empty cooler and a satisfying catch of trophy Lake Ontario salmonids can be attributed to seemingly minor details. Not specific to Lake Ontario is the often heard statement: 10 percent of the fishermen catch 90 percent of the fish. If you would like to be part of the 10 percent that get 90 percent, study and practice these secrets of the happy minority!

Lures

Since the major forage of summer salmonids in Lake Ontario consists of smelt and alewives, spoons and full-bodied plugs imitating bait fish are the logical choice. Silver is apparently the key color. Catches have been enhanced by the addition of red or green stripes, either painted or the stitch-on variety. One expert has recently found that luminescent (glow in dark) lures may make all the difference, especially when favorite silver varieties fail to produce. After talking with several experts, no one lure can be suggested as the lure to stock in your tackle box. The key points on lure selection are: color, trolling speed, action imparted by boat maneuvering and, importantly, the confidence you place in a particular bait. In short, an angler fishing with a lure in which he has little faith tends to fish sloppily. He does not pay attention to the fine details that separate the fish catching minority from the unsuccessful majority.

Line

Because the visibility at summer preferred depths is often limited, line diameter is not as important as during the spring nearshore fishery. The experts recommend a line from 10- to 17-pound-test. The actual line test will, in the end, depend upon the quality of line, individual skill and the downrigger line release. Breakage is most likely to occur at the time of a strike, just before the release trips. The amount of line trailing between the release and lure is a subject of much discussion. Unfortunately, there is no subject of exact formula for fishing success, but there are a few general guidelines that should be heeded. First, the shallower the water, the more line that is required between the lure and boat. Most seasoned anglers feel this is simply a matter of the boat spooking fish. Secondly, the type of lure will govern the amount one can play out before he loses depth control. Flutter spoons track straight but full-bodied plugs may dive or rise far enough to send them out of the zone of preferred temperatures if line length is excessive. Frequent turns will cause a change in lure action and running depth. The more line out, the less control.

In summary, a compromise between a "long line" and control must be reached. As a starting point, try these suggestions with your particular rig:

Water Depth	**Lure Distance from Release**
Surface	150 feet
20 feet	100 feet
50 feet	75 feet
75 feet	50 feet

Temperature Preference

Species	**Range** (°F)
Brown Trout	56 - 60
Rainbow Trout	56 - 62
Lake Trout	45 - 52
Coho Salmon	55 - 62
Chinook Salmon 55 - 62	

Relation to Thermocline

The thermocline is that layer of water in which a rapid change of temperature takes place. This layer occurs in Lake Ontario beginning in late June and can be found until September or October. Typically, the thermocline is about 10 feet wide and reflects a temperature change or drop of about 5 degrees F. The salmonid species generally orient to the summer thermocline as follows:

Brown Trout .... No distinct orientation; can be found below or above the thermocline.
Rainbow Trout .... Above.
Lake Trout .... Below.
Coho Salmon .... Probably in and above.
Chinook Salmon .... In and above.

Speed

The experts interviewed could not pin down a specific trolling speed that would guarantee success. Some days the fish seem to prefer a faster or slower presentation than other days. If one speed fails, try another. Don't get stuck in a grove. It is important that the lure is traveling at the speed for which it was designed. Remember that boat speed downwind is different than that upwind. However, they all agreed on the importance of one technique - TURNS. The action imparted to many lures by turning apparently is irresistible to many lunker salmonids. Trolling in figure 8s or turning abruptly often brings strikes on slow summer days.

The Downrigger

Precise temperature/depth fishing has been stressed. The careful angler must be aware that his key piece of summer equipment, the downrigger, may inject serious bias into an otherwise carefully calculated approach. First, check your counter to insure its accuracy at all depths. Prepare a correction chart if the actual depth does not correspond to metered depth.

Secondly, the angle of the downrigger wire line while being trolled will produce another source of bias. The faster you go and/or the more cable that is fished, the greater the deflection. A deflection from the stern of 30° will impart a 13 percent error in the actual fishing depth. A trolling weight of 10 pounds (standard weight 8 pounds) will alleviate some deflection. A recognition and understanding of this variable will allow the angler to adjust accordingly.

TOP BAITS FOR STAGING KINGS

By Jo Victor

As chinook start to stage off the streams they were stocked in throughout the Great Lakes, a new season starts for trollers. Actually, fishing staging kings is much like a cumulative effort of earlier parts of the season - a combination of spring and summer tactics sometimes are required to take fish - and the truly remarkable catches during this time of year will come just as dawn is breaking or just as last light leaves the western horizon.

Remarkable from several standpoints, the first being the simplicity of the tactics utilized. As in the spring, this will be the time when shallow-set lines, utilizing baits that antagonize and trigger instinctive - rather than feeding - strikes, will be productive. This is probably the time of year when the faithful J-Plug and its many copies will shine when the sun is not.

At river mouths, pier heads, and in protected harbors, running J-Plugs on flat lines or set off downriggers just below the surface will prove very effective prior to the sun's getting up - or after it drops. Much like the spring fishery, this requires long leads behind the balls - 50 feet or more - and long flats. It can be a frustrating tactic in heavy boat traffic, but by fishing the outside edges of patterns being fished by others, it can be effectively fished.

Colors that will prove effective on staging chinook are from the warm spectrum: reds, golds, yellows, as well as black. Also quite effective are the glow models, either those that work when light is applied to them or those that contain light sticks.

Staging fish are not actively feeding; keep that in mind when trolling for them. You must trigger an instinct to attack to hook them, and I've found the best way to do that is to speed up. By running the plug by the fish fast - 3.5 to 4.0 mph - there is little time for it to do anything other than react instinctively.

Another tip involves a slight alteration to the harness on the J-Plug-type lures. I found that a lot of hits resulted in missed fish at this time of year - until I took a hint from an old friend, Dick Swan of Clare, Michigan, famous for his light-line tactics.

Because of the lack of hook-setting power when using line as light as 2-pound test, Swan modifies all his J-Plug harnesses by extending the harness to 8 to 10 inches long and replacing the rear treble with a No. 8 wire hook. For staging kings that have a tendency to slap at a bait rather than take it in their maws, this little "stinger" often delivers a hookup. Even for those fish that chomp down on the front trebles the little stinger usually ends up in the cheek as a backup. Because of its smaller size it will not pull out. All of my harnesses have been altered to this system.

I never run more than four lines when fishing close-in for staging fish. If the action is hot and heavy, I'll usually drop to only two sets. It is tough enough to fish long leads in heavy traffic with a limited number of lures out. Fishing more than four lines only makes the problem worse. Then when you get everything right and everything goes right with the fish cooperating - sometimes to the extreme with multiple hookups - trying to cope with more than two lines can be impossible. With up to four kings on, all trying to go different directions, and boats all around, the morning's or evening's fun quickly becomes frustrating work.

Another top bait for this close-in fishing are the minnow-immitating plugs like the Rebel Fastrac, especially the larger sizes in their special salmon glow finishes. Many times, when I'm running four lines, I'll run J-Plugs off two shallow-set downriggers and compliment them with flats towing Fastracs. Unlike some minnow imitators, I've found these baits run true at fast speeds. Another lure to try is Yakima's Hawgboss Super Toad deep diver, which is capable of diving down to 15-plus feet even at fast speeds. It is one of the few baits with a long bill, delivering a tight wiggle, that is capable of speed trolling. I really like their metallic finishes, and as the fish start moving offshore with increased light, I've found them ideal replacements for the J-Plugs and Fastracs. If, as the fish move out to deeper water, I choose to add a diver rod or two to the arsenal when moving out, I prefer the Super Toad to any other body bait behind the dipsy diver.

As mentioned earlier, especially this month (August), staging kings require the angler to be able to adjust tactics in a day's trolling. As the day brightens, the fish will move out of the shallows for deeper haunts. Although on overcast days toward the end of August the shallow patters will work long after daylight, there will come a time to move to deeper water and adjust the pattern being fished.

It still doesn't hurt to keep a couple of the standby plugs in the water - J-Plugs, Fastracs, Super Toads, or other body baits - but I'll usually put those behind divers. Although I don't like to slow down, even when I move to deeper water, I cannot dispute the fact that those who slow to dodger/fly or dodger/squid combinations catch a lot of fish.

Because I favor the faster troll, I opt instead for magnum-size spoons and long enough leads to permit me at least a 3-mph troll without causing the big spoons to spin. Color choices are a contradiction here because I've done equally well, even on bright sunny days, on both ends of the color spectrum. Silver plate with blue, green, or chartreuse tape and blacks with yellow, red, or orange trim have all worked well during the same trolling pattern.

Again, I believe this is because the fish are not actively feeding but merely reacting out of anger at the imitation bait- school going by their noses, which is why I prefer the magnum sizes (the bigger the spoon the more the irritation).

In contrast to the close-in pattern of predawn and postsunset, I really "load the mule" when I move off to deeper water during the middle of the day: I run the maximum number of lines permitted. I want as much irritation moving through the water as possible and find that staging kings act similar to those of late June and early July when they move out. They seem to scatter as they retreat to deeper water.

The combination of their physical state causing them to stop feeding, and the scattering effect, make midday fishing for staging chinook a challenge. Again, this is why I prefer baits that I can zip through the water as opposed to slower patterns utilizing dodger/fly combinations. I want to pull my baits by as many of these uncooperative kings as possible.

Probably the one exception to this scattering pattern is in areas where there are sharp structural changes in deep water near shore. These areas will hold tight schools of fish and can be worked quite effectively with a slow troll and the big attractor baits.

Catching staging kings can run easy to tough, all on the same trip. For the angler willing to use knowledge gained over the entire season, the fishery can be much more than one of fishing only close-in or off-shore. The day can actually reflect certain characteristics of both, and that means changing tactics to deal with both situations. Being willing to adapt is the key to tackling staging kings.

CATCHING SPRING KINGS

By Capt. Jerold R. Felluca

It's finally here, SPRING! Time to gather new lures, along with your old favorites, and invade the south shore of Lake Ontario in hopes of picking up where you left off last year. Here are a few tips on how to make this year better than any other.

There are many so-called "Hot Spots" that traditionally produce springtime fish in any normal year. Last year, however, was not normal. Large amounts of extremely cold, ice-ridden water flowed down the Niagara River into Lake Ontario, forcing the fish to move east, towards the eastern basin of Lake Ontario. In late April, when thousands of fishermen converged on the great lake in hopes of cashing in on the many fishing derbies and tournaments, they found the so-called "Hot Spots of Spring," the Niagara River, Wilson, Olcott, Point Breeze, and even Sandy Creek to be literally ice cold. By giving you this scenario, I can't emphasize enough the importance of talking to local fishermen at area tackle shops and marinas. Although many fishermen tend to stretch the truth, much useful information is exchanged. In the spring, ask what the most recent temperature is. Once you locate a warm-water port, chances are you may have also located a "hot" fishing spot.

Let's face it, it's much easier to call a few different tackle shops or marinas than it is to spend hours, days, and even weeks fishing out of ports in spring that are consistently not producing any fish. Another option you might want to try is a charter boat captain. A fishing trip with a professional will fill your mind with a whole inventory of fishing facts, tricks, and proven local hot spots. Make sure you ask a lot of questions while on board. You're not just paying him to help you catch fish on that given day, you're paying him to help you to catch fish everyday.

Now that you have found a preferred fishing port for a starting point this spring, hopefully, by word of mouth rather than by trial and error, you're ready for a couple of early season tips.

Trophy spring kings are the most sought after spring battlers but are rarely caught with any consistency. Most juvenile kings (also known as jacks and weighing 2 to 18 pounds with an occasional 20 pounder) are found close to shore in spring. Smaller kings tend to school up with smaller kings in spring. They roam the shore line hunting bait fish in packs. When these packs are located, the juvenile kings are relatively easy to catch with simple trolling tactics. These tactics include running long lines, 75 to 250 feet, with small spoons or small- to medium-size plugs. I emphasize presenting smaller size bait to these jacks because the baitfish (alewife, smelt) that these spring kings are feeding on are generally smaller in size in spring. Matching lure size with bait size this time of year presents a more natural offering to these fish. Once a jack is hooked, start turning the boat around immediately back to the area where the fish hit. By the time that fish is boated, chances are great that you will have another one or two fish on. Repeat this tactic until no more fish are caught. Remember, fish are easily spooked in spring, mainly due to boat traffic in shallow water. Sound carries 4 to 5 times faster in water than in the air. So unless another pack of kings are found, return to this spot 2 to 3 hours later.

Enough on how to catch small kings. After all jacks are jacks and kings are kings. The secret to catching trophy kings weighing 20 to 30 pounds in spring is putting in a lot of time on the water and patience. I'm sorry I can't offer a miracle lure or surefire tactic to catch these brutes. But lets look at the problems with catching the kings.

The trout and salmon in Lake Ontario are cold blooded. This means that whatever the water temperature is around these fish, that's the temperature of the fish. The bigger fish can withstand colder water longer simply because they have a larger body mass. A 30-pound spring king could suspend in 39° F water for months burning off its body fat to survive, whereas an 8-pound king with very little fat will run into shallow, warmer water to feed. This in turn makes him easier to catch. To find larger kings, you must head out into deeper, colder water. As the water temperature gets colder, so does the king's body temperature. This slows down their metabolism greatly making these normally aggressive fish very sluggish and inactive. To catch these 30-pound zombies, we put our small- and medium-size lures away. We now troll all 5 1/4-inch J-13 Rapalas. After all, we are no longer trying to imitate smaller bait fish because these kings are not feeding yet on any size bait. Large Rapalas work well because they have terrific action trolled at low speeds. You must troll slow and sometimes several times over the same fish on your graph in order to entice a hit. Another advantage of trolling slow for sluggish kings is that inactive kings like to expend the least amount of energy possible when chasing bait. A jack king will normally eat a dozen 4-inch alewives, for example, whereas a large King will prefer to swim after fewer but larger 6-inch alewives. This is due to the sluggish nature of the king this time of year and the cold water as well. Another personal theory is that small lures catch small fish and larger lures catch larger fish. In the spring of 1988, the temperatures in which we caught our kings ranged from 39° to 49° F at the surface. The 41° to 44° temperature range was the most productive.

When you leave the house to go fishing this spring, the most important weapon you can have for a successful trip is confidence. And confidence comes from having a set game plan before leaving on a fishing trip. Most of your game plan can be accomplished at home on a telephone.

A typical game plan in spring includes: What is the most active port for catching fish at this time of year? Which direction, east or west, will I troll in the morning? What set of lures, colors, and sizes will I use? Now that you have a confidence-building plan in effect, whether it's a complex or basic plan, you must give that plan time out on the water. Try spending as much time as possible on the water in order to fine tune your plan. After all, you can't catch fish unless you are out there fishing.

PLOT YOUR OWN COURSE TO TROUT AND SALMON

By Mike Bleech

Do not follow the crowd unless you are satisfied with being one of them! When most boats are catching fish, it takes a tremendous amount of luck to come out on top by doing what everyone else is doing. When the crowd is not having much success, it makes no sense to mimic their efforts.

A lure change is one of the easiest ways to break with the crowd. Most tackle shops along the salmon coast carry an impressive assortment of lures. There is good reason for this - five species of salmonids in the Great Lakes that numerous anglers pursue. All five may be most receptive to completely different lures at any given moment and the most effective lure for any of those species may change a few times each day. Moreover, even when a particular lure gets hot, there may be some other lure that would be more attractive to larger fish!

Even a small boat can easily troll at least six lures, so it is simple to be both conservative and bold with your lure choices at the same time. With six lines out, for example, you can run four of the currently "hot" lures and two oddballs.

During a spring outing in 1983, Craig Littlefield and I had been smacking the fish on floating minnow lures, but on a couple of lines we experimented with screw-tail jig bodies.

The first few cohos and most of the fish we caught that morning fell for the screw-tails! The fish were less fussy about what they hit after a couple of hours. But, if we had not experimented with lures from the beginning we would have missed the early action. No matter how effective a lure has been, don't put all of your faith in it!

Boats tend to bunch up and do the same thing when a few fish are caught after a long spell of poor fishing. Word spreads fast about the method used to take the first few fish, and soon most anglers are copying that method. It is easy to see why that method accounts for nearly all fish caught for awhile. And the situation compounds itself. The action slows, while the rare fish caught is still taken with that method. This leads many anglers to believe it is the only method that works.

It is the trap of following the crowd! It is also a situation that puts the innovative angler at the advantage!

The crowd will continue to use the most recent productive method until the next successful method becomes common knowledge. The anglers who discover what it takes to turn the fish on will ride the gravy train alone, for a while.

During the first ESLO Brown Derby I met some new friends from my home state, Pennsylvania, while fishing out of Olcott. They were new to Lake Ontario fishing, and were full of questions. I supplied all the answers I could, while my strongest advise was to keep changing until something worked.

We had fair fishing that day as did most boats in our area, but nothing spectacular. Then we ran into our new friends. They were trolling at least twice as fast as any other boat. I headed my boat in their direction to inform them they were going too fast. They hooked and lost two fish before I could get within shouting distance!

While we trolled alongside them to get the story, they had a couple of more hits. They informed me that they had done as I suggested, changing every variable until something happened. It was when they tried to fast troll that the rods started popping. Lucky for them they were too new to the game to realize they were trolling too fast!

One of the most consistently productive methods of breaking with the pack is trolling around the outside perimeter of a pack of boats. There are two lines of thought behind this. First, schools of fish move while packs of boats tend to stay in the same area. Second, fish are believed to shy away from heavy boat traffic.

A pack of boats may be so large during a derby that it takes an hour or more to troll around the pack. The fish can be concentrated in one area, making most of the loop unproductive. Once fish contact is made, concentrate on that area working away from the pack. You may have located the route that the school is taking to leave the heavy boat traffic.

You may also find a clue to the direction the fish are taking by watching the pack of trolling boats. Most often catches will come from one area of the pack. If the action is happening in the outer, west end of the pack for example, this may be a signal that the school of fish is moving west and possibly deeper. Remember, though, that the result of such logic is merely an educated guess, not something to take to the bank!

"Don't be too sure of anything," advised one of my earliest mentors in Lake Ontario fishing. "Let those fish pick out what they want."

This applies to the depth factor, also. Salmonid anglers are very aware of the importance of temperature in fish location. In fact, many fish-finding formulas have their basis in temperature. Preferred temperature charts are printed on the back of lure packages, in magazines, and in government literature. Unfortunately, fish cannot read!

The thermocline makes a good starting place in the search for trout or salmon, but that is all it is - a starting place.

In Lake Ontario, the thermocline has usually formed by early July. Before this time, the thermal bar (or thermobarriers) are the angler's primary temperature factor. Two and three years ago this factor was a hot thing. Savvy trollers were reaping big rewards by trolling along these thermal "fences," but it was a different story in the spring of 1985.

Numerous theories exist about why the thermal bar was less productive that spring; it really does not matter. Better to worry about where the fish are than to worry about why they are not somewhere else.

Still, temperature can be a big factor in locating trout and salmon, with two essential tools for taking full advantage of the temperature factor: a surface temperature gauge and a temperature probe. These tools will aid in locating fish, then help you stay with the fish as water temperature characteristics change.

Neither the thermocline nor thermal fences are constants. The exact location of a thermal fence or the depth of a thermocline can change significantly in the course of a day.

During a May 1984 outing at Olcott, we located a huge school of cohos and lakers off the power plant over 180 feet of water. After steady action all morning, we returned to port for lunch, then we headed back to the same area we had fished in the morning. A pack of boats marked the location, but it was soon apparent that the action had ceased. There was no mystery to it. The surface temperature gauge showed that there was no longer a thermobarrier in the area.

We headed out, finding a thermobarrier over 240 feet of water. Even before the gauge revealed the fence, a coho slammed a lure off the planer board. We caught and released a dozen fish before the first boat broke from the pack and headed our way. By the time a dozen boats had joined us, the school had moved or dispersed.

We did not relocate the fish again that afternoon, but by breaking from the pack, we had action the other boats missed! The boats that had waited for someone else to find the fish experienced a dull afternoon.

There is a time to join the crowd. When everyone is catching fish, the high percentage shot is to do what everyone else is doing. But if you want to go for the gold, break with the crowd and set your own course for trout and salmon action!

Trolling plates are also popular on the Great Lakes. These devices attach to the lower units of motors. A metal plate is positioned behind the propeller, effectively reducing the thrust to the propeller. For many boats, this may be the best way to achieve desired trolling speeds.

Propellers can also play a part in speed control and most boat motors can operate with a variety of propellers. Generally, propellers with a large pitch are meant for speed while those with less pitch give more power. A propeller with pitch at the lower end of the range that a motor will safely handle will produce the slowest trolling speeds. For example, if a 70-horsepower motor can be used with 15, 17, or 19 pitch props, then the 15 pitch would be best used for trolling. Be sure to carefully watch the tachometer with low pitch props, as too small a prop with too little pitch can allow an engine to develop to many rpms.

One simple way to slow a boat's trolling speed is to drag a sea anchor. An effective trolling drag can be made by cutting a 5-inch hole in the bottom of a plastic bucket. Some anglers drag a bucket from each corner of the transom, but care must be used to keep trolling drags clear of lines and propeller.

Serious Great Lakes salmonid anglers know the importance of matching trolling speed to tackle, and of making minor adjustments until a productive speed is found. But fishing remains a game of man against nature. No matter how carefully we handling the trolling speed factor, wind and waves will take much of the control away from us! No matter how scientific the angler gets, fish are still fish and nature has a way of reminding us that we are just men when we get too cocky.

THE LURE SPREAD

By Mike Bleech

One of the big keys to consistent success on Lake Ontario is a good spread of lures that gets all the lures you are allowed to run into the water without tangling. This spread covers a broad range of depths, distances from the boat, lure style, and color to help the anglers zero in on the hot patterns. It catches the fish!

There are millions of salmonids in Lake Ontario - certainly one of the finest sport fisheries in the world. But there is a lot of water out there! The angler's job is to get a lure in front of a fish. Even with all the modern tools at the anglers' disposal - sonar, temperature probes, and so on - it still boils down to covering as much water as possible.

The basic tools for attaining a maximum lure spread are: downriggers, planer boards, and diving planes. The other ingredients of a good lure spread are accessories such as releases or rigging, and a thorough knowledge of the characteristics of the various lures.

What is the purpose of the downrigger? Most anglers would probably answer, "To get the lures deep." Dick Julylia, a respected field tester and innovator, taught me a better answer a few years back - an answer that gives the downrigger more than glorified sinker status. The downrigger, Dick pointed out, is a controlled depth trolling tool that provides precise depth control. It is the nucleus we will build the lure spread around.

Most small boats are equipped with two downriggers. Start the lure spread out right by mounting these with the arms pointed outward. With swivel bases they can be swung in for high-speed running or trailering. Using this setup on my 16-foot boat and 4-foot booms on my downriggers, I get a spread of about 13 feet between the cables and I can run 1 or 2 more downriggers in between. The balls are set at different depths for two reasons. First, various depths are tried until fish contact is made. Second, even after the fish-producing depth band is found, depths of the balls are staggered by at least a couple of feet to avoid tangling. Deep-diving lures are usually run on the outside downriggers when three or four lures are used, and in any case, on the deepest.

Dropper lines can be a major improvement to the lure spread by doubling the number of lures run from the downriggers. One dropper per downrigger is the maximum that can be run without constant tangling. Droppers are attached to the main line, but are free to slide up and down. Set in position, they are attached to the downrigger cable by a special release.

Length of the droppers should be about 5 feet and they should be set at least 5 feet above the main line at the ball. The best lures for the droppers track straight, causing very little drag. Flutter spoons are a good choice. During midsummer when most of the salmonids are deep, a dropper run well above the thermocline, using a bright red lure, is a good bet for steelheads.

Planer boards are the principle tool for the horizontal lure spread. With a pair of boards and a number of lines, a boat can troll a 200-foot-wide strip of water. This distance should only be attempted when the boat traffic is at a minimum, and up to six lines can be run off each board if conditions are right. Most use three lines off each board and cover about 100 feet and all about the same distance behind the release, approximately 10 to 15 feet. Since the tow line angles back, the outside lure will be furthest behind the boat. In most cases, when a fish is hooked it will swing clear of the other lines.

Many anglers look at diving planes as a tool for anglers who cannot afford downriggers. While they can be used successfully in place of downriggers, they are much more than a substitute. Diving planes give the lure spread versatility.

Diving planes can get a lure at least as deep as 100 feet. Not with the control downriggers afford, but down there. Recent arrivals on the market are diving planes that go both down and out. When you want to get most of your lures down deep, but do not have enough downriggers to handle them all, the down-and-out divers can supplement the vertical spread, by giving the deep lures horizontal mobility.

Small diving planes can be run off the planer boards. This setup can be used to get lures down to about 35 feet, according to Capt. Jim Shouey, who introduced me to this tactic during a productive outing last August. Thus, diving planes give the planer boards vertical mobility. Bead chain weights are also very effective in accomplishing this.

Horizontal mobility for the deep lures and vertical mobility for the wide lures is certainly a lot more than a mere substitute for downriggers! A growing number of innovative deep trollers are using diving planes off their two downriggers to give a better deep troll.

So far in our treatise on the lures we have covered the tools that spread the lures. Now we will look at a sample spread. In this example the boat carries three anglers and is equipped with two downriggers and all the other tools mentioned so far. The thermocline is between 60 and 70 feet.

Since we are dealing with three anglers, we have six rods to work with, and since the thermocline is deep, we want most, but not all, of the lures to be deep. Many trollers would approach this situation by stacking two rods on each downrigger, and this is fine. However, by placing just one rod on each downrigger and adding a dropper, we have as many lures on the downriggers and two extra rods to play with.

Down-and-out diving planes will take these two lines down into position. They will be covering water that cannot be reached with the downriggers. The two remaining rods can be run as flat lines or off a planer board. Since there are only two lines, one board will be sufficient. A good setup would be to run a small diving lure on the inside line. When one of these lines pops from its release, a steelhead will likely be the culprit.

Now, let's look at another example. This time the fish are near the surface, a typical spring situation. We will use the same boat and anglers as in the previous example.

One line is run from each downrigger, but there is no room for droppers in shallow water. While looking for a pattern, one of these lines should be short, 15 feet behind the ball, and down about 8 feet. The other line will be longer, say 50 to 70 feet back and down 5 feet. All lines should be changed (distance, depth, lure color, and type) about every 15 minutes until a pattern is established. If cohos are in the area, an additional flat line can be added in between the downriggers.

The remaining lines go out on the planer boards. Keep a variety of lures out there until fish contact is made. Some should be shallow-runners, and some deep-divers. With two rods on the downriggers, two lines would be run from each board. Four lines could be run off one board, but this cuts the width of the spread, which means only half as much water would be covered.

Too many trollers hold back on the purchase of the tools used in this work and adoption of these rather involved methods, thinking it too much effort for a Great Lakes' method. The more adventurous have perfected these tactics, and found that they can be applied to almost all trolling situations in any large body of water.

Got the idea? Catching fish is like solving a puzzle, and there are many pieces to the fishing jigsaw. The good lure spread is only one piece of the puzzle, but it ties in other equally important parts. Pay careful attention to your lure spread. It will reward you with many fish!

THERMAL FRONTS: MAGNETS FOR GREAT LAKES SALMON AND TROUT

By Michael Voiland and Diane Kuehn

INTRODUCTION

Since 1982, many serious trollers have significantly improved their spring catch of steelhead, salmon, and lake trout in offshore waters of Lake Ontario. One reason behind their increased success has been research and educational efforts carried forth by the New York Sea Grant Program. Through a comprehensive program of radio- tracking fish, synthesizing past research data, and organizing offshore boat trolls among fishermen, Sea Grant researchers and educators have helped Lake Ontario anglers fit many pieces of the springtime fish location puzzle together into a new and productive body of fishing knowledge.

How productive, you might ask? Well, by 1985, over 90 percent of lake charter skippers questioned indicated that they had used the new information and improved their catch accordingly. This new information is based on scientists' improved understanding of the nature and behavior of thermal fronts in Lake Ontario and how the movements and locations of trout and salmon may correspond to these fronts. A "thermal front" is defined as any interface between water masses of significantly different temperatures where relatively rapid water temperature changes occur. "Thermal bar", "thermocline", and "thermal break" refer to different types of thermal fronts.

The following information on fishing Great Lake springtime thermal structure relates specifically to studies conducted on Lake Ontario, and experiences reported there. But as our basic understanding of Great Lake limnology (the study of lakes) suggests, this new knowledge developed on the smallest Great Lake should be easily transferable and adaptable to the bigger lakes. If use of the new information has the same impact as it has had on Ontario, then spring salmonid catches may be greatly improved on its "bigger sisters."

Before we proceed, one note of clarification. In terms of improved catches likely to be realized when applying this information, experiences on Lake Ontario indicate that the biggest payoff likely will come in catching more steelhead (rainbow) trout, followed (in descending order of catch) by chinook, lake trout, and lastly, coho. With very few exceptions, catches of brown trout have not occurred in association with the thermal phenomena described below.

THE WINTER-SUMMER TRANSITION

Everything discussed in this article pertains directly to how one can locate and fish Great Lake thermal fronts present during the period from about April 1 to about mid-June. Within this 75-day time frame, Lake Ontario undergoes a dynamic transition from winter mode to summer mode. This period sees the lake change from a very cold water body, having frozen or near freezing (32 degrees F) surface waters underlaid with warmer waters between 33 and 39 degrees, to a relatively warm water body, having surface temperatures exceeding 50 degrees and underlaid by cooler water temperatures down to near 39 degrees. Obviously, in the case of the other Great Lakes, the warming process and features may be slightly different in degree and timing, given contrasts in the lakes' water volume and regional climate. But all the lakes do undergo the winter-summer transition.

It is important for Great Lake anglers to understand that they will be fishing in waters that are highly dynamic - thermally speaking - during this transition time. The Lake Ontario experience suggests that those who apply an understanding of these dynamics are likely to make more productive fish-location decisions on a daily basis.

THE THERMAL BAR

Probably no single thermal front has captured more press in recent years than one referred to as the thermal bar. Similarly, it is likely that no thermal feature has been more often misidentified or incorrectly described. We'll try here to give the most accurate and understandable explanation we can of the bar, its action, and its function in the lake.

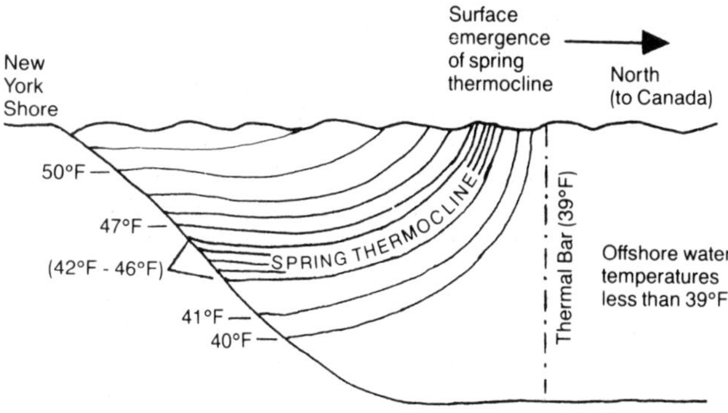

Figure 1. Idealized representation of spring water temperature profile on Lake Ontario, including the thermal bar and the spring thermocline. Note the pocket of warmer water formed inshore of the spring thermocline. Anglers on the lake have had greater success catching rainbow and other salmonids at the bar's surface and the surface emergence of the thermocline.

The spring thermal bar on any larger lake in the cooler latitudes is a relatively short-lived, migrating temperature feature within which lake turnover takes place. It is, so to speak, a surface-to-bottom vertical wall that is located where 39-degree water temperature first occurs on the surface as you move away from shore. Inside, or nearshore, of it, surface and subsurface temperatures are above 39 degrees; outside, or offshore, of it, surface and subsurface temperatures are below 39 degrees (see Figure 1).

What's so magical about 39 degrees, and where does lake turnover come into play? Well, at 39 degrees, water is at its densest or heaviest. This is the part of natural law that dictates why ice (at 32 degrees) can float (it's lighter). In fact, all water with temperatures above or below 39 degrees is lighter (less dense) than water right at 39 degrees.

This process drives springtime turnover in lakes in cooler climes. To wit, as nearshore waters first rise to 39 degrees in early spring, they get heavy and sink to the bottom. This heavier water is replaced with warmer water from inshore and cooler water from offshore which, when mixed, reaches 39 degrees and sinks. This unalterable process takes place at the bar, powering the turnover of all lake waters.

As spring progresses, more warm water collects in the adjacent nearshore zone due to stream inflows and solar heating. This zone expands and the bar moves offshore as more and more cold offshore lake core water is being warmed and turned over (see Figure 2). This offshore migration runs its course during the 75-day transition period referred to earlier, until no water having a temperature of 39 degrees or less exists on the lake surface - usually in early to mid-June (see the insert, "Predicting a Disappearing Act" at the end of this article). At that time, the lake assumes the character of its summer mode as described earlier.

The thermal bar migrates offshore at a slow rate before mid-May on Lake Ontario and at a much faster rate after that, again due mainly to the warming power of the late spring sun. On average, the Ontario bar moves about 1/3 of a mile per day during the transition period. Also, the bar migrates more quickly over areas having slight depth changes, and much more slowly over bottoms having steep offshore gradients. Lastly, the bar's general offshore progression is fairly consistent and predictable year to year, except when extreme weather conditions advance or delay migration to some extent (see Figure 3).

THE SPRING THERMOCLINE

Just a few years ago, scientists had no real inkling of the existence and importance of another spring thermal front now known as the spring thermocline. For years, the characteristics and functions of this feature were simply attributed to the thermal bar. Both the bar and the spring thermocline usually occur in close proximity to one another, possibly masking each other's distinct role and qualities from earlier scientific investigations.

In any case, the spring thermocline is, as its root word "cline" connotes, a zone of rapidly declining water temperatures. According to studies done in the early 1970s on Lake Ontario, the spring thermocline represents that strata of water temperature change between 46 and 42 degrees. Yet, unlike the generally horizontal summer thermocline, the spring version is inclined and has an emergent offshore end at the water's surface (see Figure 1). Thus, it is both a surface area and a subsurface layer. Also, it is a zone of sharp changes in many measures of water quality, including biological productivity, turbidity (muddiness) and current (see Figure 4), as well as density and temperature.

Given their nature as places of change, the spring thermocline and the thermal bar are very much what ecologists define as ecotones or, in lay terms, edges or fronts. Like a hedgerow abundant with wildlife, the thermocline and bar have demonstrated their attractiveness to trout and salmon on Lake Ontario. Like a suspended reef, these features have shown the ability to concentrate salmonids in the lake's offshore regions.

PUTTING THERMAL KNOWLEDGE TO WORK: A RECIPE FOR FISHING GREAT LAKE THERMAL STRUCTURE

Finding the Features

Of course, the definitive way to locate the thermal bar and the emergent spring thermocline is to use a water surface temperature system. Moving offshore, you have found the bar when the temperature meter first intercepts 39-degree surface water. Then, as you move inshore of the bar, your gauge should detect the relatively rapid thermal gradient between 46 and 42 degrees that constitutes the surface edge of the spring thermocline. A surface temperature meter is not always an absolute necessity, however. The downwelling created atop the bar and corresponding upwelling and current effects occurring near the upper and lower sides of the spring thermocline (see Figure 4) frequently cause the formation of surface slicks of collected debris, such as insects, bird feathers, grass, dead forage fish, and other materials. Also, the same factor often creates distinct differences in water surface tensions and ripple effects that are especially noticeable to the eye on calmer days. Another way to eyeball the bar and spring thermocline is to look for sharp water color or turbidity changes. Generally speaking, waters offshore of the dynamic duo tend to be less biologically productive and darker in color than inshore waters.

How wide is the surface zone making up the two features? Over the last few years on Lake Ontario, zone widths exhibiting the full temperature gradient of 39 to 46 degrees have been reported to range from a few hundred feet on some days to a half mile or so on others.

Planning and Predicting Daily Movements of Features (and Fish!)

As a rule, the bar and spring thermocline tend to parallel the shore as prevailing onshore winds help to maintain a temperature profile and ribbon much as seen in Figures 1 and 2. If strong offshore winds arise, however, the ribbon of warmer nearshore waters can literally be blown offshore in the form of an island or bubble. If winds of this nature occur before and during your fishing trip, you'll probably find yourself running farther offshore in pursuit of the moving bubble and fish. Remember, too, that both the bar and spring thermocline will run their migratory course and be found farther and farther offshore with each passing week, as spring progresses toward summer.

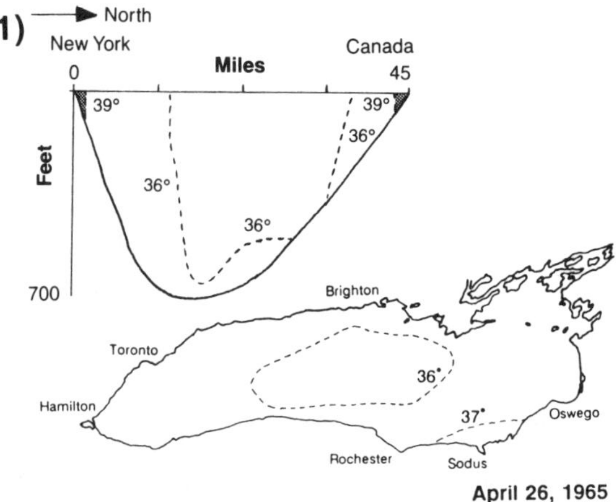

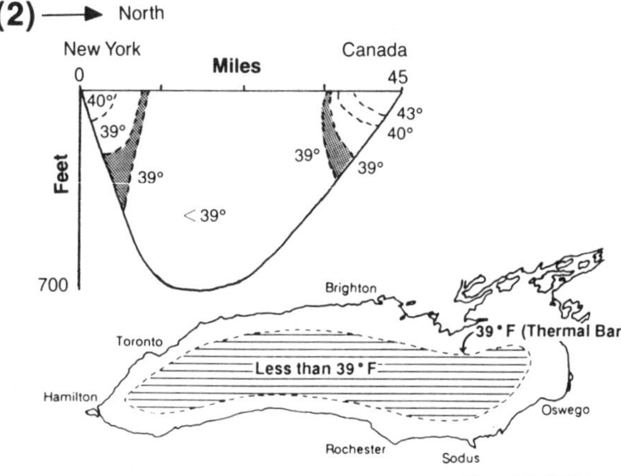

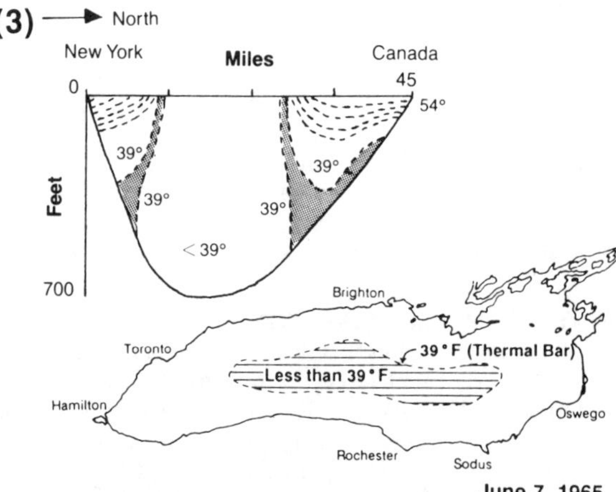

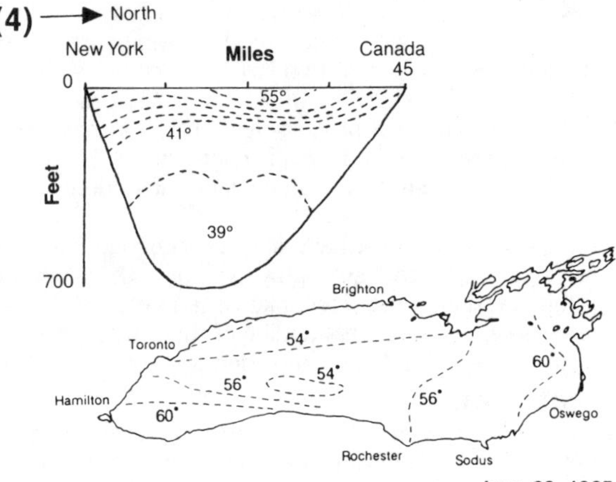

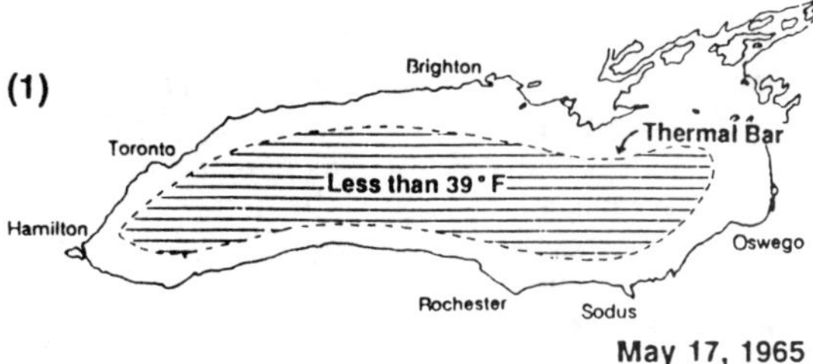

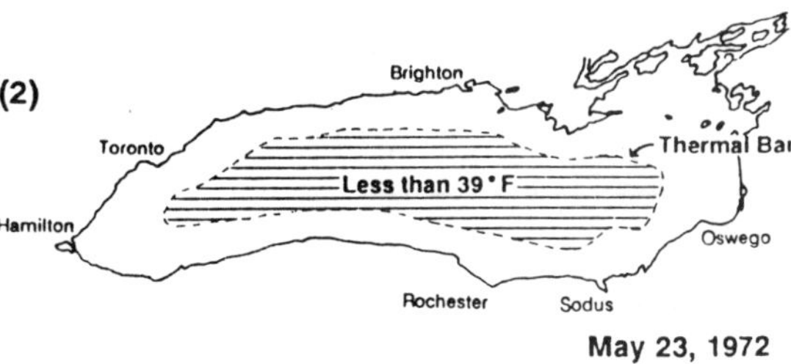

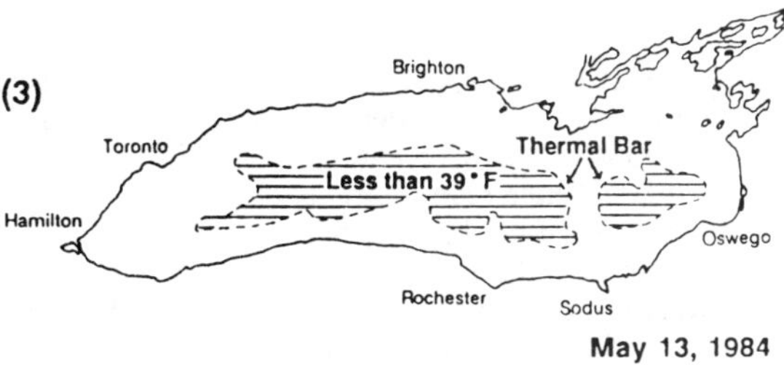

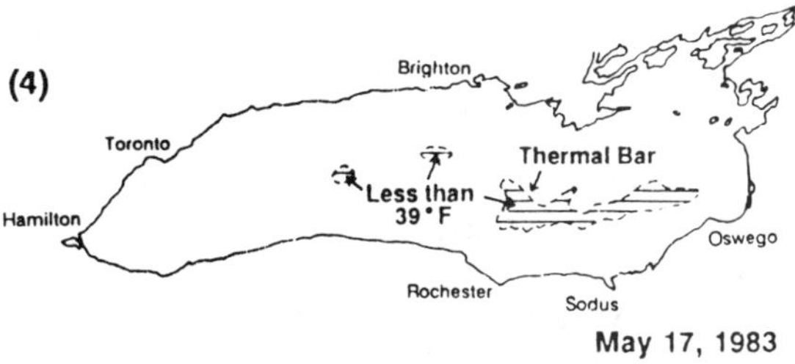

Figure 3. General consistency in the thermal bar's location (and the extent of lake warming) from year to year is evident in surface temperature maps from late May in 1965, 1972, and 1984 (Maps 1 to 3). In contrast, Map 4 shows how one of the mildest winters on record in the Northeast advanced the warming process on the lake, so that, on about the same date, much less water at 39 degrees or lower was found on the surface in spring 1983.

Finding and Hooking Fish

An approach suggested by "tried and true" application of thermal information by charter skippers and ardent anglers on Lake Ontario in recent years is as follows:

1. Head offshore, locating the bar (39 degrees) with your surface temperature gauge. Longline on the surface preferably using planer boards to spread your pattern. Keep lures well behind the boat (50 to 150 feet). The major portion of the catch at the bar on Ontario has been steelhead and lake trout.
2. Next, particularly if the bar is not producing that day, troll inshore until you locate the spring thermocline (46 to 42 degrees) manifesting on the surface. Again, longline on the surface within this temperature band for steelhead and some cohos and chinooks.
3. If your main target is chinooks, try downrigging, using your subsurface temperature system to keep lures between 46 and 42 degrees within the submerged portion of the spring thermocline. On Lake Ontario, many spring chinook are taken by anglers deep trolling near this feature. Remember the temperature band constituting the thermocline will likely incline deeper as your boat moves toward shore, as seen in Figure 1.
4. Experiment! Try fishing atop the thermal bar and spring thermocline, then just inshore and offshore of these two features. Why? Two reasons. First, the track record from Lake Ontario indicates that, each year, a slightly different fish aggregation pattern will develop in association with these thermal features. For example, in 1982, most catches were reported right atop the bar. In 1983, most catches seemed to occur smack within the 46 to 42 degree spring thermocline surface edge. In 1984, best catches were at the warm (46 to 45 degree) edge of the thermocline, and in 1989, fishing well inshore of the 46 to 42 degree thermocline was most productive for many anglers.

   The second reason to experiment is because localized winds and an irregular coastline that has spits, peninsulas, points, and shoals can produce indentations, oxbows, and bulges in the normally parallel-to-shore thermal features. Paying attention to where catches are best and adjusting your trolling pattern and location accordingly can often make for a fuller cooler.
5. Don't ignore other thermal fronts. In late spring, randomly occurring surface temperature gradients generically known as "thermal breaks" often occur. These breaks appear well inshore, usually between 50 and 60 degrees. Depending on the day, break gradients can be as slight as three degrees (say, 53 to 56 degrees) or as severe as 10 degrees, and can occur over a relatively short trolling distance. Lake Ontario experiences have suggested that these breaks hold fish and tend to be most productive when they represent the sharpest break to be found that day. They're definitely worth exploring.

Predicting a Disappearing Act

Offshore boat anglers on Lake Ontario may be able to get an early fix on how long that lake's springtime warming phase will run, and when the thermal bar might disappear. Thanks to research done at the Canada Centre for Inland Waters and an educational fact sheet produced by New York Sea Grant Extension, Lake Ontario anglers can calculate an approximate thermal bar submergence date. Armed with this information, fishermen can estimate if the surface thermal

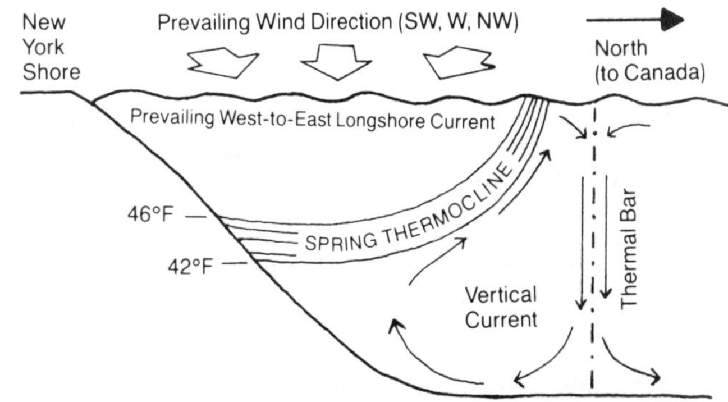

Figure 4. Idealized representation of some water movement at the thermal bar and spring thermocline. Note the sinking actions taking place at the bar. Also, note how corresponding upwelling along the bottom edge and longshore current shear along the top edge of the submerged spring thermoclime may occur, creating a variety of current effects that may be attractive to salmonids.

fishing season will run late into June (or even July), or will likely run out of gas in early or mid-May. Fishing techniques and search patterns can be adjusted accordingly.

The calculation is based on average winter (December 1 to March 31) air temperature data generally available from a local National Weather Service office, college science departments, or other sources. The bar's disappearance date, given in number of days beyond April 1, can be computed using tables in the fact sheet "Predicting When Lake Ontario's Thermal Bar Disappears?", by David MacNeill. For copies of this fact sheet contact:

Sea Grant
52 Swetman Hall, SUNY,
Oswego, NY 13126.

Private Company Markets Surface Temperature Charts

In 1989, Offshore Services, Inc. (2679 Route 70, Manasquan, NJ 08736) began offering subscription service for Lake Ontario and Lake Michigan surface temperature charts. The company's information, provided to subscribers through the mail or by fax machine, is based on heat-sensitive imagery generated from the NOAA-11 weather satellite. At the time this fact sheet was published (August 1990), no other commercial company was providing Great Lake surface temperature chart services to the public.

OSI offers its service from mid-May to about mid-September. According to president Len Belcaro, subscribers opting for OSI's facsimile service can look forward to having surface temperature data in their hands at least twice a week, and within a few early morning hours of the satellite's nighttime pass. "Outside of when cloud cover blocks our 'eye in the sky,' anglers can consistently have a real edge by using the charts to find offshore thermal breaks," claims Belcaro.

TO CATCH A STEELHEAD

Abstracted from pamphlets of:
The Oregon Wildlife Commission
By Milt Guymon and Luhr Jensen & Sons, Hood River, OR 97031

There are some slight differences in angling for winter steelhead and the summer-run fish. As an example, summer steelhead will take flies much more readily, either wet or dry, than will winter steelhead. Furthermore, summer fish prefer slightly different water flows.

Water conditions more often than not influence success or failure, so it behooves the angler to keep informed on stream levels and turbidity, then do his fishing when the rivers are "right." Generally, the best steelheading takes place following storms or freshets during the time the rivers are dropping and clearing.

The Plunker or Still Fisherman

All he has to do is cast out, anchor his bait or lure on the bottom, then sit and wait. His main objective is to place his offering smack in the middle of a steelhead travel route and wait for the fish to come along.

Generally, these plunking areas are the large, deep holes in the river. The most productive portion will be from about midpoint in the hole downstream to where the hole shallows and breaks into rapids below. Steelhead travel upstream through these rapids, and upon reaching the slick or apron above will sheer off to one side or the other into the quieter water. Usually they rest here a bit before continuing the up-stream journey. Plunkers recognize this characteristic of steelhead and attempt to anchor their bait just to one side of the heavy water.

The Drift Fisherman

He has a few more problems to consider. First, steelhead have definite travel routes that they use consistently on their journey upstream. These routes will vary depending on water stages. If the angler is to be successful he must recognize "steelhead runs" at all water levels.

Steelhead will not remain long in the deeper holes, nor will you find him often in the eddies or quiet pools. This big fish prefers a strong flow of water and will seek and follow these flows throughout the river.

Water depths are extremely important. Steelhead prefer to travel and hold in water ranging from about 4 feet to 8 or 9 feet. Deep holes and riffles are preferred only when water temperature is high or oxygen content lower than normal. Summer steelhead will consistently seek out the fast chutes and even white water simply because of the higher water temperatures during the summer months. Dissolved oxygen is also at maximum in such areas.

Steelhead will hold at certain locations along these travel lanes. These "slots" may be immediately ahead of or behind a sunken boulder, below a slight drop-off, near the tail of a pool just ahead of the apron, in a slight bend along the bank where a change in water velocity occurs, alongside an underwater ledge or channel cutbank, and other locations of a similar nature. Recognizing steelhead slots is an art in itself, but once learned the angler can return to the same spot time after time and be reasonably sure a steelhead will be there. The basic drift-fishing technique consists of casting across and slightly upstream and then allowing your drift bobber or bait and accompanying lead to naturally drift downstream in the river current, the lead gently bouncing along the bottom. When your lure has drifted back near the bank, it is reeled in and another cast and drift made.

A good rig for drift fishing is to attach your bait - egg cluster, drift bobber, or egg fly - to an 18- to 24-inch leader connected to the line by a three-way swivel. A weight, preferably pencil lead, should he attached to the third loop of the swivel by a dropper 3 to 4 inches in length. The dropper should be of lighter line strength so that it will break first in case of snags.

The Spin Fisherman

Casting with weighted spoons and spinners provides several distinct advantages over other fishing methods including: A minimal amount of terminal tackle is needed (you can tie your main line directly to the lure via a snap or other attachment device, eliminating the need for leader, weights, and extra knots); spoons and spinners are deadly in low and/or clear water; lighter rods, reels, lines, and lures can be used; both spoons and spinners represent natural fish foods (baitfish); because of the vibration patterns these lures send off underwater, strikes are often vicious.

In learning and mastering hardware casting techniques, the most important aspect is to become completely familiar with the feel and action of individual lures under a variety of water conditions. A hardware fisherman who knows a lure's vibrating or wobbling action by heart can, by watching his or her rod tip, determine the necessary speed of retrieve and whether or not a lure is working properly. A spoon should swim and wobble from side to side, a spinner should have a constantly revolving blade. If your spoon is spinning, you are reeling too fast and should slow the retrieve. If the blade on your spinner is not constantly revolving, you are reeling too slow and should speed up the retrieve. You can go as slow or as fast as you wish within these confines. Spoons should be fished near the bottom, however. When spoon fishing in a river, if you feel a tap now and then from rocks or the bottom you are fishing the correct depth and reeling at the correct speed.

Do everything you can to prevent a lure from running at a constant speed and in a straight line. Twitch the rod tip every few seconds, speed up and then slow down the retrieve, stop the lure dead in the water and then start it up again, reel extremely fast for a few seconds and so on. The more variety in speed and action you impart to the lure with your rod and reel, the better your chances of enticing a strike.

Rivers have built-in currents and it becomes more difficult to present a spinner or spoon properly than in a lake setting. In fishing spoons the most common casts will be across the stream from your position or just slightly upstream, allowing the spoon to sink a moment or two before beginning a retrieve. As the spoon works downstream and gets caught in the river current, you should slow your retrieve and as the lure works across the stream back towards your position, stop reeling altogether. Once the lure has reached quiet, soft water and has begun settling toward the bottom (vibrations at the rod tip will fade) then it's time to reel the lure slowly in and take another cast. Tailout areas are favorites for feeding, resting, and holding fish. These areas are at the tail end of a hole or drift where the water shallows and begins picking up speed. Because of their shallowness they are difficult to fish with cross-stream casts and are best worked with downstream casts. Position yourself above the tailout you wish to work and then cast across and downstream into the edge of the tailout. When the spoon or spinner hits the water take a few turns of your reel handle and then let the current do the work for the rest of the way, pushing and activating the lure as it crosses the river back to your bank.

Extremely deep holes or fast water requires still another kind of casting technique called upstreaming. The lure is cast upstream and then allowed to settle toward the bottom as you reel in line very slowly. By the time it has reached a position across from you it should be near the bottom and can then be slowly reeled in until the current catches it, and then the cross-stream technique is used.

By following all the techniques discussed ... in time you are sure to take steelhead.

A QUICK GUIDE TO THE FISH OF WESTERN NEW YORK

ATLANTIC SALMON
(Salmo salar)

Other Common Names
Landlocked, sebago salmon

Identifying Characteristics
- Back and sides are grayish brown, grading to olive on the sides.
- Large dark spots resembling x's are scattered over the body, but are rarely on the tail.
- Bears a strong resemblance to brown trout, but the upper jaw extends only to the rear edge of the pupil, and there is only a single row of bottom teeth and no teeth on the roof of the mouth.

Habits and Habitat
- Prefers cold, oxygen rich waters.
- There are populations of Atlantic salmon that have been cut off from the ocean and thus spend their entire lives in fresh water.
- Starting in September they move into their natal streams, but don't spawn until October or November.
- Atlantic salmon do not always die after spawning.

Tackle and Techniques
- Use medium to heavy tackle and 14- to 25-pound-test line.
- Spoons and spinners work very well, as do flatfish and J-Plugs. A change in color can often make a big difference.
- Caught off flatlines in the spring and fall, and off downriggers in the summer.
- If water is too cold, try the warmest water available.
- When the salmon are spawning in streams and rivers, egg sacs and yarn flies are very effective.

Local Hot Spots
Hemlock Lake (landlocked); experimental stockings are currently being made in Lake Ontario.

Current State Record
24 lbs. 9 oz.

CHINOOK SALMON
(Oncorhynchus tschawytscha)

Other Common Names
Chinook, king salmon, tyee

Identifying Characteristics
- Blue to bluish green on back, grading to silver on the sides and white on the belly; almost black during spawning season.
- Mouth is black.
- Large black spots found on back, dorsal fin, and entire tail.

Habits and Habitat
- Preferred temperature range is 50 to 58 degrees; 54 degrees is ideal.
- Less of a schooling fish than coho salmon.
- Often found where the bottom and thermocline meet.
- Fish areas and depths where preferred temperatures are found.
- Spawn in fall in area streams and rivers; this is the best time of year for catching big salmon.

Tackle and Techniques
- Use medium to heavy tackle and 14- to 25-pound-test line.
- Spoons and spinners work very well, as do flatfish and J-Plugs. A change in color can often make a big difference.
- Caught off flatlines in the spring and fall, and off downriggers in the summer.
- If water is too cold, try the warmest water available.
- When the salmon are spawning in streams and rivers, egg sacs and yarn flies are very effective.

Local Hot Spots
Lake Erie, Lake Ontario, the lower Niagara River, all streams stocked with chinooks; see Lake Erie and Lake Ontario stocking information for streams that are stocked with chinook salmon.

Current State Record
47 lbs. 0 oz.

COHO SALMON
(Oncorhynchus kisutch)

Other Common Names

Coho, silver salmon

Identifying Characteristics

- Dark blue to green back, grading to bright silver on sides; turns reddish during spawning.
- Black mouth with white gums.
- Small black spots found on back, dorsal fin, and upper half of tail (no spots on lower half of tail).
- 13 to 15 rays in anal fin.

Habits and Habitat

- Preferred temperature range is 50 to 58 degrees; 54 degrees is ideal.
- Often a schooling fish that prefers surface waters when temperatures permit.
- The first salmonid to move shoreward in fall.
- Spawns in the fall in area streams and rivers.

Tackle and Techniques

- Use medium to heavy tackle and 14- to 25-pound-test line.
- Spoons and spinners work very well, as do flatfish and J-Plugs. A change in color or speed, can often make a big difference.
- Caught off flatlines in the spring and fall, and off downriggers in the summer.
- If the water is too cold, try the warmest water available.
- When the salmon are spawning in streams and rivers, egg sacs and yarn flies are very effective.

Local Hot Spots

Lake Erie, Lake Ontario, lower Niagara River, all streams stocked with cohos; see Lake Erie and Lake Ontario stocking information for streams that are stocked with coho salmon.

Current State Record

33 lbs. 4 oz.

BROOK TROUT
(Salvelinus fontinalis)

Other Common Names

Speckled trout, native trout, speckled char, squared-tailed trout, eastern brook trout

Identifying Characteristics

- Body is dark olive to brown, with light spots scattered along its length.
- Spots are irregular and wavy along the back, becoming progressively more circular towards the belly.
- A few bright red spots surrounded by a blue ring are found on the sides.
- Bottom fins are orange to pink, with a white leading edge followed by a dark stripe.
- 9 to 10 rays in anal fin.

Habits and Habitat

- Prefers cold, clear waters; seldom found in water over 65 degrees.
- Usually found in headwaters of streams and rivers.
- Has very low tolerance for warm water or pollution.
- Feeds on insects, worms, and crayfish.
- Spawns in fall.

Tackle and Techniques

- Use ultra-light spinning or fly-fishing tackle.
- Excellent quarry for fly fishing. Can be taken on a variety of dry flies, wet flies, or nymphs.
- Small spoons and spinners, and live bait such as worms and crayfish also work well.

Local Hot Spots

Hemlock Lake, Allen Lake, upper Cohocton River, Mill Creek (Livingston County), East Koy Creek, Wiscoy Creek. Brook trout are found in the headwaters of most of the larger trout streams listed in Cattaraugus County and Chautauqua County.

Current State Record

8 lbs. 8 oz.

LAKE TROUT
(Salvelinus namaycush)

Other Common Names

Laker, togue, mackinaw

Identifying Characteristics

- A dark background of bluish gray to olive green with light spots scattered over the head and sides.
- Lower fins are faintly edged in white.
- Tail is deeply forked.
- 10 to 12 rays in the anal fin.

Habits and Habitat

- Preferred temperature range is 44 to 55 degrees; 50 degrees is ideal.
- Often found in very deep water (down to 300 feet), particularly in summer.
- When water temperatures approach freezing, they can be taken in the shallows.
- Spawn in the fall in shallow areas of lakes, and rarely venture into rivers. The exception to this is the lower Niagara River.

Tackle and Techniques

- Use medium to heavy tackle and 8- to 14-pound-test line.
- In the early spring and late fall, cast from shore or troll in shallows.
- A variety of spoons and spinners work well, as do flatfish and fireplugs. Lake trout also hit well on white streamers.
- Live bait such as a small sucker, chub, or minnow, is also productive.
- In the summer, troll deep using the above lures in combination with dodgers or cowbell attractors.

Local Hot Spots

Lake Erie, Lake Ontario, Hemlock Lake, the lower Niagara River

Current State Record

32 lbs. 0 oz.

RAINBOW TROUT/STEELHEAD
(Salmo gairdnerii)

Other Common Names

Bow, rainbow, steelhead, Kamloop trout

Identifying Characteristics

- The migratory, lake-dwelling variety (steelhead) tend to be silver and are often confused with coho salmon. The lateral color line of pink or red is often very faint in the lake-dwelling fish.
- Stream-dwelling fish have many small, dark spots on body and upper fins, especially on the tail. Body color varies from bluish silver to brown to olive green. Lateral line of pink or red can be very pronounced, especially during spawning season.
- The mouth is white. The tail is square.

Habits and Habitat

- Preferred temperature range is 50 to 65 degrees; 60 degrees is ideal.
- Prefers moving water.
- Spawns primarily in the late winter and spring. Some hatchery-raised fish will enter streams in the late fall.
- Often found near piers, rocky points, sharp drop-offs, and thermal breaks.
- Stream and small pond rainbows feed on worms, crayfish, and insects; lake-run fish feed on alewives and smelt.
- One of the hardest fighting gamefish in North America.

Tackle and Techniques

- Use light to ultra-light spinning or fly-fishing tackle for stream fish and medium to heavy tackle for lake fish.
- Natural baits work well for stream fish.
- Spoons and spinners are good in the fast water of streams and rivers.
- Egg sacs are very effective when the lake-run fish are spawning in streams.

Local Hot Spots

Lake Erie, Lake Ontario, the lower Niagara River, Cattaraugus Creek, Oak Orchard Creek, the upper Genesee River, Allen Lake, Case Lake, Harwood Lake, Quaker Lake, Redhouse Lake

Current State Record

26 lbs. 15 oz.

BROWN TROUT
(Salmo trutta)

Other Common Names
German brown trout, brown, brownie, Lochleven trout

Identifying Characteristics
- Usually tan to golden brown in color, with dark spots on the entire body, but few or none on tail. Spots are often surrounded by a light halo. A smaller number of red or orange spots are scattered along the body.
- The tail is square.

Habits and Habitat
- Found in a variety of waters, from streams and rivers to ponds, lakes, and reservoirs.
- Preferred temperature range is 50 to 65 degrees; 60 degrees is ideal.
- Normally doesn't wander far from its home waters.
- Spawns in late fall, toward the end of the salmon runs.
- Slightly less tolerant of warm water than rainbow trout.
- Large browns are often active at night, particularly in summer.

Tackle and Techniques
- Use light to ultra-light spinning or fly-fishing tackle for stream fish and medium tackle for lake fish.
- Live baits such as worms, minnows, insect larvae, and small chubs, work well.
- Flies such as wooly worms, muddler minnows, and big millers, work well, especially at night.
- Lures such as spoons and spinners, in silver and fluorescent colors, and minnow plugs also work well.
- Night fishing is often very good, especially in fall.
- Eggs, single and sacs, produce well when lake-run fish are spawning in streams.

Local Hot Spots
Lake Erie, Lake Ontario, Cattaraugus Creek, Eighteen Mile Creek (Erie County), East Koy Creek, Ischua Creek, Mill Creek (Livingston County), Oatka Creek, Wiscoy Creek

Current State Record
30 lbs. 5 oz.

BLACK CRAPPIE
(Pomoxis nigromaculatus)

Other Common Names
Crappie, calico bass, strawberry bass, Oswego bass

Identifying Characteristics
- Back is green or olive, quickly grading to cream or silver on sides and belly.
- Irregular dark blotches on sides and fins.
- Anal fin nearly as large as the dorsal fin.
- 5 to 7 rays in the anal fin.

Habits and Habitat
- Found in lakes and ponds; prefers quiet waters.
- Holds in weedy areas with generally clear water.
- A schooling fish.
- The best action occurs in the late winter and early spring, when large schools spawn in shallow water.

Tackle and Techniques
- Use light or ultra-light spinning or fly-fishing tackle and 4- to 6-pound-test line.
- Small, live minnows work best. Put a bobber a few feet up from the bait and cast out.
- Small spinners also work well, as do small jigs dressed with Mr. Twister tails.
- In the spring, when the fish are in the shallows, fan cast with small spinners or drift with minnows until a school is found; then anchor and still fish.

Local Hot Spots
Wilson Harbor, Waterport Pond, Chautauqua Lake, Oak Orchard Creek, Rushford Lake

Current State Record
3 lbs. 2 oz.

PUMPKINSEED
(Lepomis gibbosus)

Other Common Names
Common sunfish, sunny

Identifying Characteristics
- Body is olive to golden brown, grading to yellow or orange towards belly.
- Black gill flap with red tip.
- Large pectoral fins.
- Small mouth.
- Sides are mottled or lightly striped.
- Light blue-green lines radiate back from mouth and eye region.

Habits and Habitat
- Prefers warm, weedy waters, especially in lakes and ponds.
- Usually found close to shore near weeds, logs, docks, etc.

Tackle and Techniques
- Use ultra-light spinning or fly-fishing tackle.
- Small spinners and jigs work well, but natural baits such as small worms are the most productive.
- Good fishing for children in the summer.

Local Hot Spots
Bonds Lake, Wilson Harbor, Chautauqua Lake, the Greece Ponds

Current State Record
1 lb. 7 oz.

BLUEGILL
(Lepomis macrochirus)

Other Common Names
Bluegill sunfish, bream

Identifying Characteristics
- Body is dark green to brown, grading to yellow or orange on breast.
- Dark blue to almost black gill flap.
- Dark blotch on the back of the dorsal fin.
- Irregular vertical dark bars on sides.

Habits and Habitat
- Prefers quiet, weedy waters similar to pumpkinseed, but tends more towards open areas.
- Holds close to shore, hiding under docks and among vegetation.

Tackle and Techniques
- Use ultra-light spinning or fly-fishing tackle.
- Small spinners and jigs work well, but natural baits, such as small worms, are the most productive.
- Good fishing for children in the summer.

Local Hot Spots
Bonds Lake, Chautauqua Lake, Wilson Harbor, the Greece Ponds

Current State Record
2 lbs. 4 oz.

ROCK BASS
(Ambloplites rupestris)

Other Common Names
Goggle-eye bass, redeye

Identifying Characteristics
- Body is dark olive with black mottling.
- Eyes are red.
- Faint horizontal lines on sides, particularly towards belly
- Dark spot on gill flap, often edged with white.
- 5 to 7 rays in the anal fin.

Habits and Habitat
- Frequents deep, rocky streams and cool, clear lakes.
- Often found in same areas as smallmouth bass.
- Abundant in many areas; if you get one, you can get a stringer full.
- Scrappy fighters.

Tackle and Techniques
- Use ultra-light spinning tackle and 4- to 6-pound-test line.
- Will take flies, small spinners, and live bait.
- Fish around old pilings and along rocky shorelines.

Local Hot Spots
Upper and lower Niagara River, Oak Orchard Creek, Tonawanda Creek, Wilson Harbor

Current State Record
1 lb. 15 oz.

LARGEMOUTH BASS
(Micropterus salmoides)

Other Common Names
Bigmouth bass, black bass

Identifying Characteristics
- Dark olive-green sides.
- A dark band runs along both sides the length of the body.
- Deep notch between front and rear portion of dorsal fin.
- Upper jaw extends beyond the back of the eye.

Habits and Habitat
- Prefers warm, sluggish streams or shallow, weedy lakes and ponds.
- Prefers mud bottoms.
- Feeds on insects, frogs, worms, crayfish, and small fish.

Tackle and Techniques
- Use light to medium tackle and 6- to 10-pound-test line.
- Live baits such as worms, frogs, and crayfish work well.
- Try spinners or buzzbaits on the surface, plastic worms on the bottom.
- The best action is on light tackle unless pursued in heavily vegetated areas, in which case heavier tackle and line should be used.

Local Hot Spots
Oak Orchard Creek, Bear Lake, Case Lake, Chautauqua Lake, Irondequoit Bay, Conesus Lake

Current State Record
11 lbs. 4 oz.

SMALLMOUTH BASS

(Micropterus dolomieui)

Other Common Names

Black bass, bronzeback

Identifying Characteristics

- Body is pale green to golden bronze in color.
- Dark, wavy bars run vertically along the body.
- The upper jaw does not extend back beyond the back of the eye.
- Shallow notch between the front and rear portion of dorsal fin.

Habits and Habitat

- Prefers cold, clear water
- Found in rock- or gravel-bottomed lakes and streams.
- Often found in fast water or riffles.
- Usually stays near the bottom in water no deeper than 45 feet. In some large lakes such as Erie and Ontario, some smallmouth bass will become pelagic.
- Spawns in the spring.

Tackle and Techniques

- Use light to medium tackle and 6- to 10-pound-test line.
- Live baits such as crabs, minnows, and worms work well.
- Small plugs and spinners work well.
- Fish the shallows in spring; fish further out in summer and fall.
- Fish near the bottom.
- Trolling, drifting, or still fishing are all productive methods.

Local Hot Spots

Upper and lower Niagara River, Lake Erie, Lake Ontario, Oak Orchard Creek, Bear Lake, Chautauqua Lake, Cazenovia Creek

Current State Record

9 lbs. 0 oz.

WHITE BASS

(Morone chrysops)

Other Common Name

Silver bass

Identifying Characteristics

- Back is silvery green, quickly grading to silvery gray on the sides.
- Small head.
- Deeply forked tail.
- Thin, dark lines run horizontally across body.
- Protruding lower jaw and yellow eyes.
- Deeply forked dorsal fin.

Habits and Habitat

- Prefers large, deep streams, rivers, and medium to large lakes with clear, quiet waters.
- Usually found in deep waters in daytime, shallows at twilight.
- Often feeds in dense schools in shallow water right at the surface.
- Feeds on insects and small fish.
- Spawns in streams from May to August.

Tackle and Techniques

- Use light to ultra-light spinning tackle.
- Live minnows or worms are the preferred baits.
- Imitation minnow lures and Mr. Twisters produce well, as do small spinners.
- The best time to catch white bass is when they are feeding in schools, often just off shore.

Local Hot Spots

Lower Niagara River, upper Niagara River, Lake Ontario

Current State Record

3 lbs. 3 oz.

CHAIN PICKEREL
(Esox niger)

Other Common Names
Pickerel, grass pickerel, mud pickerel

Identifying Characteristics
- Body color varies from green to bronze.
- Dark, chain-like markings along the length of body.
- Long, thin snout.
- 14 to 16 branchiostegal rays (slender bones that support the soft part of the gill cover; best seen from belly side of fish).
- Cheeks and gill cover are completely scaled.
- Dark vertical bar below eye.

Habits and Habitat
- Prefers weedy, quiet waters.
- Eats insects, worms, crayfish, and small fish.
- Similar to northern pike, but not usually found where larger relatives (muskellunge and northern pike) are present.

Tackle and Techniques
- Best taken on light spinning or fly-fishing tackle.
- Use of a steel leader is recommended.
- Prefer natural baits such as minnows and crayfish.
- Spoons, spinners, and bucktail jigs work well.
- Can be taken through the ice.

Local Hot Spots
Lime Lake, Hemlock Lake, Conesus Lake

Current State Record
8 lbs. 1 oz.

MUSKELLUNGE
(Esox masquinongy)

Other Common Names
Muskie, maskinonge, lunge

Identifying Characteristics
- Body is green to light brown with grading to cream yellow on the belly.
- No scales on lower half of cheeks or gill covers.
- Sides often have dark vertical bars or spots on lighter a background.
- Head is shaped like a duck's bill.
- 6 to 9 sensory pores on each side of the lower jaw.

Habits and Habitat
- Preferred temperature range is 60 to 70 degrees; 68 degrees is ideal.
- A solitary, non-schooling fish.
- Frequents clear, quiet, shallow areas of rivers and medium to large lakes.
- Usually hangs near submerged weed beds or structure.
- Most often found in shallow water (20 feet or less).
- Tend to be territorial, though some individuals will wander.

Tackle and Techniques
- Use heavy bait-casting gear and steel leaders.
- The most productive muskie fishing is in the spring and fall.
- Suckers and frogs are good as live bait.
- Spinners and jigs work well, but think B-I-G.
- Muskies are not very numerous and are difficult to catch; it's said a veteran angler can average about 30 hours of fishing per catch. If you are serious about catching a muskie, consider hiring an experienced guide.

Local Hot Spots
Lake Chautauqua, Findley Lake, and the upper Niagara River

Current State Record
69 lbs. 15 oz.

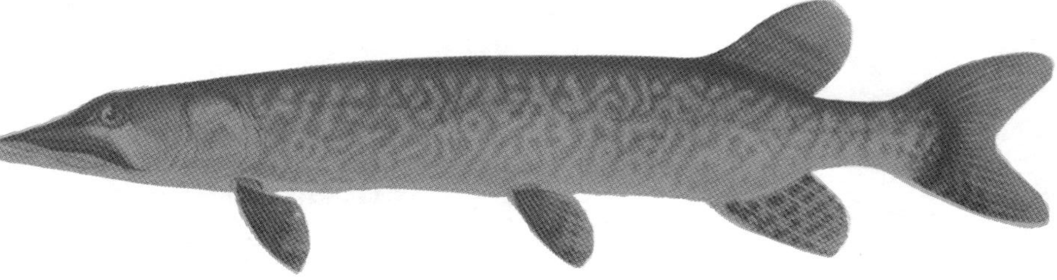

NORTHERN PIKE
(Esox lucius)

Other Common Names

Pike, great northern pike, pickerel

Identifying Characteristics

- Body color varies from green to brown.
- The sides have light spots on a dark background.
- Entire cheek has scales, but only the upper portion of gill cover does.
- Fins are heavily spotted or mottled.
- 5 sensory pores are found on each side of the lower jaw.

Habits and Habitat

- A solitary fish that frequents cool, sluggish waters of lakes and streams.
- Often found in shallow water over weed beds or structure.
- Feeds primarily on fish such as perch and suckers, but also eats insects, crayfish, frogs, and snakes.
- Spawns in spring.

Tackle and Techniques

- Cast or troll using medium to heavy bait-casting tackle.
- Steel leaders will prevent a lot of cutoffs.
- Still fish with live suckers or chubs.
- Medium-size spinners, spoons, and plugs work well.
- Often caught through the ice on live chubs or dead smelt.

Local Hot Spots

Twelve Mile Creek, Tonawanda Creek, Braddock Bay, Oak Orchard Creek, the Greece Ponds (Buck, Cranberry, Long, and Round), the New York State Barge Canal, the Allegheny Reservoir

Current State Record

46 lbs. 2 oz.

WALLEYE
(Stizostedion vitreum vitreum)

Other Common Names

Walleyed pike, yellow pike, yellow, pike perch

Identifying Characteristics

- Big, glassy eyes that reflect light at night.
- Body is brassy to olive green on sides, and white on the belly.
- Dark, narrow bands run vertically on back and sides.
- Silver or white tip on lower fork of tail.
- Sharp spines on first dorsal fin.
- Sharp canine teeth on jaws and roof of mouth.
- Considered by many to be the best tasting freshwater fish.

Habits and Habitat

- Preferred temperature range is 55 to 70 degrees.
- Can be either a pelagic fish, following schools of baitfish in the open lake, or a bottom dweller that is frequently found near drop-offs and shoals.
- Often found in large schools, which tend to be dominated by a single year-class.
- Spawn in early spring in or near the mouths of streams and in areas that have a rocky bottom.

Tackle and Techniques

- Fishing is best at night, especially during late spring and fall.
- Use live baits, or deep-diving plugs that resemble bait fish.
- Weight-forward spinners dressed with a worm, brightly colored spoons, and worm harnesses work well.
- Troll slowly or drift with the wind in shallow areas in the spring, moving to deeper waters in the summer and fall.
- Walleye will often take just the tail end of the bait at first. Wait a few seconds before setting the hook to give the fish time to take in the whole bait.
- Bottom bouncing with jigs works well through the ice.

Local Hot Spots

Chautauqua Lake, Lake Erie, Allegany Reservoir, Silver Lake

Current State Record

15 lbs. 3 oz.

YELLOW PERCH
(Perca flavescens)

Other Common Names
Perch, jackperch

Identifying Characteristics
- Body is golden yellow on sides with vertical olive green bars.
- Two separate dorsal fins.
- Slight humpbacked appearance.
- Moderately forked tail.
- Many tiny teeth.
- An excellent tasting fish, especially if caught through the ice.

Habits and Habitat
- Prefers clear, weedy lakes and the quiet parts of large streams.
- A schooling fish; the schools are usually dominated by a single year-class.
- Eats insects, crayfish, and minnows.
- Usually found in shallow water in the spring, yellow perch move to deeper water in the summer and fall.
- Do not feed at night.

Tackle and Techniques
- Use ultra-light tackle and 4- to 6-pound-test line.
- Most often taken on live bait just off the bottom. Minnows are the top bait.
- Troll or drift with small spinner and worm combinations to locate schools, then still fish with worms and small minnows.
- Fish through the ice with grubs, perch eyes, or small jigs.

Local Hot Spots
Upper and lower Niagara River, Lake Ontario, Lake Erie, Silver Lake, Chautauqua Lake

Current State Record
3 lbs. 8 oz.

WHITE PERCH
(Morone americana)

Other Common Name
Silver perch

Identifying Characteristics
- Body is olive to blackish green on back, grading to silvery green on the sides.
- Superficially resembles white bass, but usually has no stripes and is darker in color.
- Has a compressed body and small head.
- Dorsal fin is deeply notched.

Habits and Habitat
- Prefers large, deep streams, rivers, and medium to large lakes with clear, quiet waters.
- Usually found in deep waters in daytime, shallows at twilight.
- Often feeds in dense schools in shallow water right at the surface.
- Feeds on insects and small fish.
- Spawns in streams from May to August.

Tackle and Techniques
- Use light to ultra-light tackle and 4- to 6-pound-test line.
- Live minnows or worms are the preferred baits.
- Imitation minnow lures and small jigs dressed with Mr. Twister tails produce well, as do small spinners.
- The best time to catch white bass is in the spring when they are feeding in schools, often just off shore.

Local Hot Spots
Lake Ontario, the Greece Ponds (Buck, Long, Cranberry, and Round), Braddock Bay

Current State Record
lbs. 14 oz.

BROWN BULLHEAD
(Ictalurus nebulosus)

Other Common Names

Bullhead, common bullhead, speckled bullhead, horned pout, bullhead catfish

Identifying Characteristics

- The body is chocolate brown to almost black on top and sides
- Vague, dark mottling on back and sides. grading to cream yellow on the belly.
- There are strong, sharp spines on the back edge of the pectoral fins.
- Has a square to slightly rounded caudel fin.
- The head is flat and has soft barbels on the bottom and sides.
- Excellent table fare.

Habits and Habitat

- Prefers weedy areas of lakes and deep, sluggish streams.
- Found over both muddy and gravelly bottoms
- A bottom feeder with a diverse diet, including insect larvae, mollusks, algae.
- Feeds primarily at night.

Tackle and Techniques

- Use light to ultra-light tackle and 4- to 6-pound-test line.
- Can be caught in great numbers very early in the spring along the shores of lakes.
- Fish on the bottom with slip sinker using worms, crabs, minnows, or dough balls.
- Handle with care; the spines are sharp.

Local Hot Spots

East and west branches of Twelve Mile Creek, Tonawanda Creek, Johnson Creek (Orleans County), Oak Orchard Creek, the Greece Ponds (Buck, Long, Cranberry and Round), Braddock Bay, Chautauqua Lake

Current State Record

3 lbs. 6 oz.

CHANNEL CATFISH
(Ictalurus punctatus)

Common Names

Catfish, channel cat, lake catfish, silver catfish, spotted catfish

Identifying Characteristics

- Dark blue or olive on back, grading to silvery gray on the sides.
- Small, dark, irregular spots on body.
- The tail is deeply forked.
- Four barbels on the chin, two on the snout, and one on each side of the upper jaw.
- 24 to 30 rays in the anal fin.
- Excellent table fare.

Habits and Habitat

- Inhabits lakes and large rivers; often found just downstream of dams.
- Not usually found in weed beds; prefers open waters with bottoms of sand or gravel.
- Feeds primarily at night.
- A bottom feeder, channel catfish eat small fish, insects, and crustaceans.

Tackle and Techniques

- Use light to medium tackle and 6- to 14-pound-test line.
- The best fishing is at night.
- Drift bait such as a strip of fish belly or gob of worms, or fish on the bottom with slip sinker using stinkbait.

Local Hot Spots

New York State Barge Canal, Allegany Reservoir, Genesee River, Lake Erie, Dunkirk Harbor

Current State Record

28 lbs. 0 oz.

RAINBOW SMELT
(Osmerus mordax)

Other Common Name
Smelt

Identifying Characteristics
- Body is greenish gray on back, grading to silvery gray on the sides.
- Small and slender with forked tail.
- The mouth is very large.
- Adipose fin between dorsal fin and tail.

Habits and Habitat
- Inhabit cool, deep waters of large lakes.
- Spawn in the spring, at which time they run up streams and rivers in great numbers.
- Spawn primarily at night.
- A schooling fish.
- Often migrate inshore at night to feed.

Tackle and Techniques
- The best time to catch smelt is during their spring spawning runs.
- Fish at night in the lower ends of streams that feed into Lake Erie or Lake Ontario.
- Use dip nets.
- Can also be taken through the ice using a strip of perch belly or small pieces of worm.

Local Hot Spots
Most tributaries of Lake Ontario, especially the lower Niagara River and lower Genesee River, and Dunkirk Harbor

Current State Record
Not available

WHITE SUCKER
(Catostomus commersoni)

Other Common Names
Sucker, white sucker, common sucker, mullet

Identifying Characteristics
- The body is olive brown to grey.
- Long, cylindrical body.
- Blunt snout; upper lip thinner than lower lip.
- Large scales.
- Their flesh is good for patties and smoking.

Habits and Habitat
- Found in almost any water condition - clear or muddy, fast or slow, clean or polluted.
- Widely distributed.
- Seems to prefer large streams and deep water impoundments.
- A bottom feeder whose diet consists of insect larvae, crustaceans, and algae.
- Spawns in the spring, often in trout streams.

Tackle and Techniques
- Use light to medium tackle and 4- to 6-pound-test line.
- Fish on the bottom with worms, dew worms, or dough balls.
- Suckers hit very lightly.

Local Hot Spots
Upper and lower Niagara River, Genesee River, and most tributaries of Lake Erie and Lake Ontario

Current State Record
1 lb. 6 oz.

CARP
(Cyprinus carpio)

Other Common Names
Carp, German carp, European carp

Identifying Characteristics
- The body is olive green to bronze in color.
- Long dorsal fin.
- A pair of fleshy barbels on each side of upper jaw.
- Large scales, each with a dark spot at its base and dark edge.
- Has cross-hatched pattern on sides.

Habits and Habitat
- Can tolerate a variety of aquatic environments, but prefers warm streams or lakes with muddy bottoms.
- Bottom feeders, carp eat both plant and animal material.
- Tolerant of pollution.
- A hard-fighting fish that can get quite large.
- Spawns in the spring.

Tackle and Techniques
- Use light to medium tackle and 6- to 8-pound-test line.
- Fish on the bottom using a slip sinker.
- Dough balls and worms work well.

Local Hot Spots
Lake Erie, Lake Ontario, Chautauqua Lake, and the lower portions of almost any large stream.

Current State Record
41 lbs. 2 oz.

FRESHWATER DRUM
(Aplodinotus grunniens)

Other Common Names
Sheepshead, croaker, grunt, drum

Identifying Characteristics
- The body is silver gray and somewhat opalescent.
- Humped back and blunt snout.
- Rounded tail.
- Deep notch in dorsal fin, with very long rear section.

Habits and Habitat
- Found in large rivers and lakes.
- Prefers clear waters, but tolerates turbid, silty areas.
- Stays near bottom in 10 to 40 feet of water.
- Usually feeds on snails, mollusks, and crayfish.

Tackle and Techniques
- Use light to medium tackle and 6- to 14-pound-test line.
- Live baits, such as worms, minnows, and crayfish work well.
- Occasionally, drum will hit on small spinners and spoons.
- Keep bait and lures near the bottom.
- Drum are strong fighters, especially if large.

Local Hot Spots
Lower Niagara River, upper Niagara River, Lake Erie, Lake Ontario

Current State Record
18 lbs. 12 oz.

A QUICK GUIDE TO ICE FISHING

The sport of ice fishing becomes more popular each year. Participants are no longer thought of as deranged individuals looking for a quick case of frostbite. Ice fishing is now a favorite pursuit of men, women, and children, and often, whole communities. Ice fishing is not just a lot of fun, it's also very sociable, it promotes companionship, it's often competitive, and it's productive. Trout, salmon, bass, pike, pickerel, perch, walleyes, and panfish can all be pulled through the ice. Hard-water angling takes as much skill and knowledge as open-water angling. Anyone, however, can ice fish successfully if they do their homework. This would include learning about the water to be fished, the equipment and its capabilities, and all safety factors involved. Study this guide, dress warm, and head out for a day of exciting ice fishing.

ICE FISHING REGULATIONS

Ice fishing is permitted in the following waters:

1. All non-trout waters
2. Certain trout waters including Lake Ontario and Hemlock Lake.

Refer to your fishing regulations guide for laws pertaining to the water you intend to fish. Unless otherwise noted, fish may be taken where ice fishing is permitted as follows:

November 15 - April 30	Those species for which there is no closed season.
November 15 - March 15	Northern pike, pickerel, walleye
During open season	Other species

Two hand lines and five tip-ups may be used except for Lake Ontario, where 15 tip-ups may be used. All tip-ups must be marked with the name and address of the operator; the operator must be attendance when lines (either tip-ups or hand lines) are in the water.

Ice fishing is permitted on all non-trout waters and certain trout waters mentioned above. Ice fishing is prohibited in all other trout waters. If you are unsure whether a water is considered trout or non-trout, contact the local DEC office or the local Environmental Conservation Officer.

Names and telephone numbers of all ECOs are presented in the New York State Fishing, Small Game Hunting, and Trapping Regulations Guide. ECOs are also listed in local telephone directories under New York State Department of Environmental Conservation.

GEAR AND GADGETS

Tip-ups

A tip-up is a device designed to let the angler set his bait without having to constantly handle the tackle. It is constructed so that a signal alerts the angler when a fish takes the bait. There are many variations, but most have the standard red flag to signal when a fish strikes. The common tip-up consists of a pair of wooden support braces that span the hole. A vertical mast is attached to the braces with a reel on the submerged end and a flag on top. When a fish strikes, the reel turns, triggering the flag to spring up.

Jigging Rods

These are used for all types of fish. A light, flexible rod is used for panfish, while a stiffer, longer rod is better for the bigger sport fish.

Ice Auger

The two conventional designs for augers are the spoon and drill. These come in diameter sizes of 4 inches to 8 inches. The drill auger also has a gasoline powered cousin. Power driven augers are convenient and fast on thick ice.

Ice Spud

This is essentially a heavy pipe with a sharpened piece of iron welded to one end. It is recommended that you attach a heavy gauge rope or leather loop to the top of the spud. Secure this rope around your wrist while chopping so your spud doesn't end up on the lake bottom.

Ice Sled/Ice Basket

Both sled and basket serve as equipment transporters on and off the ice. The sled is constructed on a pair of runners (old skis, sled, or wooden staves) that provide for smooth ride. The box is usually big enough to hold tip-ups, a stove or heater, jigging rods, and other equipment. Also, the box serves as a seat, and, with a few poles and a tarp, can be converted into a useful windbreak. A pack basket is sufficient with less gear. Most people who jig use these baskets.

Minnow Bucket

Various types of buckets are available, including styrofoam, nonfloatable, and floatable. Floatable are the most popular. The floating section can be removed from the bucket and placed in the water you are fishing. The circulating fresh water will keep your minnows much livelier. A minnow net is essential to protect your hands from the cold when taking bait from your bucket.

Skimmer

A skimmer is used to remove chunks of ice and slush after drilling holes. A skimmer looks very similar to a soup ladle with holes in it.

Sounder

This is a weight attached to some line and lowered into the water to check depth before fishing. Any type of small sinker that is easily detached can be used.

Ruler or tape

These are used to measure your catch to see if its within legal size limits.

Jaw Spreader

Spreaders are used to help prevent injury to your hands when removing your hook from a sharp-toothed fish. A jaw spreader can be homemade from spring steel or bought commercially.

Needlenose Pliers

These can be used to extract a hook lodged deep in a fish's mouth. There are also special tools sold at fishing tackle stores that are manufactured exclusively for this purpose.

Ice Creepers

Creepers are usually strap-on steel soles with sharp metal spikes. Attached to a fisherman's boots, these give the person superior footing when running to a tip-up or just walking.

Ice Awls

These are two short pieces of dowel with a pointed spike in one end. They are generally connected by a piece of twine and worn around the person's neck. They help the person pull him/herself out should the person break through the ice.

TYPE OF BAITS AND LURES

The two most commonly used baits used for ice fishing are minnows and grubs.

Minnows

Shiners and creek chubs are the most popular minnows for ice fishing. Small minnows in the one inch to one and one-half inch length range are generally used for panfish (e.g., perch). Larger minnows, three to five inches in length, are used for predatory fish (e.g., pickerel).

Grubs

Fly larvae, often called "mousies", are the most commonly used grubs. Mayfly nymphs, often called "Michigan wigglers", are a close second. Grubs are usually attached to a small weighted lure or jig, which is then moved up and down in the water to attract fish.

Lures

Usually artificial imitations of a natural food, ice fishing lures have become increasingly popular and varied in design. The size and shape of the lure is chosen in accordance with the species of fish you want to catch. For large fish such as pike and walleye, a minnow imitation, often with up to five hook points, is used. For smaller perch and panfish, a single hook lure or jig is used. Jigs come in a variety of colors and fishermen often tip them with a live bait, such as a grub, to improve their fish attracting potential. It is not unusual to catch small fish on bigger lures and vice versa. Finding the right combination is the trick. Local tackle shops are usually happy to provide information on the most effective baits, lures, and jigs for use in nearby waters.

To make your bait or lure most effective, just add action. By jigging your offering up and down, you will attract more fish. Vary your jigging motion until you find a pattern the fish like.

METHODS OF ICE FISHING

Yellow Perch

During the winter months perch are found in water as shallow as 5 to 6 feet deep and to depths of 40 feet or more. Perch are schooling fish, so once located many are often caught. A 2- to 4- foot light rod and an ultralight reel filled with 2- to 4-pound- test line is the ideal outfit for perch. Tying a lead sinker to the end of the line gets your bait to the desired depth fast. Above the sinker, small, brightly colored jigs are tied to the line one to two feet apart. Bait, such as minnows, grubs, or perch eyes, is put on the jigs to improve their attractiveness. In some cases, the larger the bait, the bigger the perch you catch. A small bobber placed on your line at the waters surface will help you *detect the slightest nibble.

Bluegills

These fish prefer shallow water areas, seldom going deeper than 20 feet. Like the perch, the bluegill is usually found in schools. A very sensitive rod with 2- to 4-pound-test line will let you detect the delicate nibble followed by the aggressive fight of a fat bluegill. Small tear-drop jigs are used, baited with mousie grubs, spikes, or oak leaf grubs. By finding the right water depth and jigging your bait up and down, bluegills will afford you fast panfish action.

Crappie

These fish are minnow eaters. Like perch and bluegills, they travel in schools and are found suspended over submerged cover. Crappies are generally light strikers. Tiny bobbers are often useful in detecting their faint nibble. Hand lines and tip-ups are used and, as with other species, fishing should be done from the bottom of the ice to the bottom of the pond to determine the level of the fish. Do not "under fish" this species. Crappies will rise to your bait but seldom will they take an offering below them.

Walleye

Walleyes are highly prized by winter anglers. This species is generally found on or near the bottom. Bottom structures, such as spring holes, brush piles, gravel bars, or drop offs, are productive fishing areas. Medium shiners are the usual baits used on tip-ups set for walleye. Spoons, jigs, and imitation minnow lures are best when jigging.

Northern pike and pickerel

These predatory fish usually spend the winter months lurking in and above shallow water weedlines. Tip-ups or jigging poles are both satisfactory for these fish. Tip-ups should have a strong main line of 20- to 30-pound-test braided nylon. The leader attached to the main line should be of at least 15-pound test monofilament, wire, or steel leader. Some fishermen find steel leaders superior to monofilament because of the pike and pickerel's sharp teeth. Treble or English hooks, baited with a common or golden shiner or chub 3 to 6 inches long, are preferred. With the treble hooks, the bait should be attached under the dorsal fin to allow the minnow movement. When using English hooks, the bait is threaded on just behind the minnow's head using a bait needle, with the hook points facing the tail. When placing your bait, set it just above the weedbed, allowing the fish a clear view of your offering. Spoons and jigs are good lures for use with hand lines.

Bass

Jigging rods and tip-ups are used to catch both largemouth and smallmouth bass through the ice. A weighted, minnow imitation lure is used with the jigging rod. A braided nylon main line with an eight- to ten-pound test monofilament leader four to five feet long works best. Tip-ups are rigged in a similar manner, but with a baited English hook. Bass are usually light hitters under the ice and do not usually attack the bait like a pike or pickerel. By using an English hook, it ensures you a better success rate as more fish are hooked.

Trout

Again, both the jigging rod and the tip-ups are used to catch these sport fish. Brown trout and rainbow trout are usually found at various depths beneath the ice, ranging from 3 to 20 feet. Lakers spend most of their winter near the bottom so you often have to fish for them in 60 to 100 feet of water or deeper. With a jigging rod, a light leader attached to a braided nylon main line is best. Some popular jigging lures include Swedish Pimples, Rapalas, spoons, and other flashy, artificial baits. A minnow or piece of minnow attached to one of these is often deadly. When jigging deep for big lakers, look for drop-offs, gravel bottoms, and rocky shoals. When tip-up fishing, use eight- to ten-pound test with a small split shot 12 to 18 inches above the bait. A single hook with a live minnow is the number one bait. Frozen minnows will work if live bait cannot be found. To help add some "life" to your dead bait, a piece of styrofoam packing material can be sewn in the body cavity or, simpler yet, a piece of sponge can be pushed down the throat.

CLOTHING

No outdoor sport can be fully enjoyed if the participants are not comfortable. Ice fishing is no exception. Because most people are stationary while ice fishing, clothing is critical. Experienced outdoorsmen know that it is easy to take off excess clothes when they are warm, but it is difficult to get warm if additional clothing is not available. Don't be unprepared on the ice. Winter weather can change rapidly.

Keeping you hands, head, and feet warm is the key to comfort. Approximately 80 percent of your body's heat can be lost through those areas. Insulated gloves or mittens work well for hands. Insulated hoods or wool knit hats with a heavy scarf will protect the susceptible head and neck region. Because your feet are in constant contact with the ice, quality boots are a must. Thick rubber bottoms, leather uppers, and felt insoles are preferred. Waterproofing is also a good feature since there is often slush and water on top of the ice.

Your main outerwear should consist of insulated coveralls, a jacket/pants combination, or a snowmobile suit. The more waterproof and wind-proof your outfit is, the better.

SAFETY

Safe ice is the number one consideration in this sport. A minimum of three to four inches of solid ice is the general rule for safety. Ice thickness, however, is not uniform on any body of water. Be wary of areas with fluctuating water levels, such as rivers and reservoirs. Pay special attention to ice thickness near the mouths of tributaries and near warm water discharges. Also, avoid "black-ice" dark patches that indicate weak, unstable ice. Using the buddy system while ice fishing has saved many lives.

Accidents do happen and having someone near-by to pull you out or get help is a must. If you or someone else does fall through, use a sturdy rope, long pole, or even a ladder laid on the ice to aid them. Whether rescuer or victim, sprawling out on the ice to distribute your weight until you've reached safe ice is important.

If you fall through the ice while fishing alone, keeping your head can save your life. While awaiting rescue, relax and keep your movements to a minimum, thus keeping trapped air inside your clothing. When alone, carry along a pair of ice awls. These are handles with a sharp point or points. You can make them easily enough by cutting a pair of four inch lengths of one inch diameter wooden doweling and then pounding a thick nail into one end of each. Cut the nails to a length of two inches and sharpen the points. Connect the awls with a 15 inch length of rope and cover the nail points with corks. Carry them around your neck when ice fishing and, if you fall in, use them to pull yourself back on to the ice.

Once someone is pulled from the water, they must be treated for hypothermia, a condition caused by a drop in body temperature below the normal 98.6°F. Protection from further heat loss must be provided immediately. Getting the victim out of the wind, into a warm shelter, into dry clothes, and, if conscious, feeding warm fluids are all effective actions to take. If problems are severe, medical help should be sought.

Remember, falling through the ice is not the only cause of hypothermia. This condition results from exposure in any form, and can be brought about by inadequate clothing. Symptoms to watch for include severe shivering, coordination problems, slurred speech, and muscular weakness. Frostbite is another exposure condition to protect yourself against. Wind chill is a big cause of this problem. If it does occur, warm the affected area, but do not rub the frozen tissue. Again, for severe cases, medical attention should be obtained. As long as ice conditions are safe and you take proper precautions, accidents can be avoided. However, being prepared for accidents can turn tragedy into just a wet, uncomfortable experience.

LOG SHEET

Date: / /

Time: ____________

Stream/Lake Name: ____________ Species Name(s): ____________

Access Used: ____________ No. Caught: ____________

Section Fished: ____________ Size (lbs./in.) ____________

SITE CONDITIONS

Water Level/Flow: ____________

Clarity: ____________

Weed Growth: ____________

pH: ____________

Bottom Type: ____________

Insect Hatches: ____________

WEATHER CONDITIONS

Barometer: ____________

Wind Speed & Direction: ____________

Humidity: ____________

Cloud Cover: ____________

Air Temp.: ____________

Recent Rain Fall: ____________

Range (Drift): ____________ Cross Range: ____________

Tackle Used: ____________

Method Used: ____________

Rigger Settings: ____________

____

Comments: ____________

____

LOG SHEET

Date: / /

Time: ____________

Stream/Lake Name: ____________ Species Name(s): ____________

Access Used: ____________ No. Caught: ____________

Section Fished: ____________ Size (lbs./in.) ____________

SITE CONDITIONS

Water Level/Flow: ____________

Clarity: ____________

Weed Growth: ____________

pH: ____________

Bottom Type: ____________

Insect Hatches: ____________

WEATHER CONDITIONS

Barometer: ____________

Wind Speed & Direction: ____________

Humidity: ____________

Cloud Cover: ____________

Air Temp.: ____________

Recent Rain Fall: ____________

Range (Drift): ____________ Cross Range: ____________

Tackle Used: ____________

Method Used: ____________

Rigger Settings: ____________

____

Comments: ____________

____

LOG SHEET

Date: / /

Time: ______

Stream/Lake Name: ______ Species Name(s): ______

Access Used: ______ No. Caught: ______

Section Fished: ______ Size (lbs./in.) ______

SITE CONDITIONS

Water Level/Flow: ______

Clarity: ______

Weed Growth: ______

pH: ______

Bottom Type: ______

Insect Hatches: ______

WEATHER CONDITIONS

Barometer: ______

Wind Speed & Direction: ______

Humidity: ______

Cloud Cover: ______

Air Temp.: ______

Recent Rain Fall: ______

Range (Drift): ______ Cross Range: ______

Tackle Used: ______

Method Used: ______

Rigger Settings: ______

______

Comments: ______

______

LOG SHEET

Date: / /

Time: ______

Stream/Lake Name: ______ Species Name(s): ______

Access Used: ______ No. Caught: ______

Section Fished: ______ Size (lbs./in.) ______

SITE CONDITIONS

Water Level/Flow: ______

Clarity: ______

Weed Growth: ______

pH: ______

Bottom Type: ______

Insect Hatches: ______

WEATHER CONDITIONS

Barometer: ______

Wind Speed & Direction: ______

Humidity: ______

Cloud Cover: ______

Air Temp.: ______

Recent Rain Fall: ______

Range (Drift): ______ Cross Range: ______

Tackle Used: ______

Method Used: ______

Rigger Settings: ______

______

Comments: ______

______

LOG SHEET

Date: / /

Time: ____________

Stream/Lake Name: ____________ Species Name(s): ____________

Access Used: ____________ No. Caught: ____________

Section Fished: ____________ Size (lbs./in.) ____________

SITE CONDITIONS **WEATHER CONDITIONS**

Water Level/Flow: ____________ Barometer: ____________

Clarity: ____________ Wind Speed & Direction: ____________

Weed Growth: ____________ Humidity: ____________

pH: ____________ Cloud Cover: ____________

Bottom Type: ____________ Air Temp.: ____________

Insect Hatches: ____________ Recent Rain Fall: ____________

Range (Drift): ____________ Cross Range: ____________

Tackle Used: ____________

Method Used: ____________

Rigger Settings: ____________

____

Comments: ____________

____

LOG SHEET

Date: / /

Time: ____________

Stream/Lake Name: ____________ Species Name(s): ____________

Access Used: ____________ No. Caught: ____________

Section Fished: ____________ Size (lbs./in.) ____________

SITE CONDITIONS **WEATHER CONDITIONS**

Water Level/Flow: ____________ Barometer: ____________

Clarity: ____________ Wind Speed & Direction: ____________

Weed Growth: ____________ Humidity: ____________

pH: ____________ Cloud Cover: ____________

Bottom Type: ____________ Air Temp.: ____________

Insect Hatches: ____________ Recent Rain Fall: ____________

Range (Drift): ____________ Cross Range: ____________

Tackle Used: ____________

Method Used: ____________

Rigger Settings: ____________

____

Comments: ____________

____

LOG SHEET

Date: / /

Time: ____________

Stream/Lake Name: ____________ Species Name(s): ____________

Access Used: ____________ No. Caught: ____________

Section Fished: ____________ Size (lbs./in.) ____________

SITE CONDITIONS

Water Level/Flow: ____________

Clarity: ____________

Weed Growth: ____________

pH: ____________

Bottom Type: ____________

Insect Hatches: ____________

WEATHER CONDITIONS

Barometer: ____________

Wind Speed & Direction: ____________

Humidity: ____________

Cloud Cover: ____________

Air Temp.: ____________

Recent Rain Fall: ____________

Range (Drift): ____________ Cross Range: ____________

Tackle Used: ____________

Method Used: ____________

Rigger Settings: ____________

____

Comments: ____________

____

LOG SHEET

Date: / /

Time: ____________

Stream/Lake Name: ____________ Species Name(s): ____________

Access Used: ____________ No. Caught: ____________

Section Fished: ____________ Size (lbs./in.) ____________

SITE CONDITIONS

Water Level/Flow: ____________

Clarity: ____________

Weed Growth: ____________

pH: ____________

Bottom Type: ____________

Insect Hatches: ____________

WEATHER CONDITIONS

Barometer: ____________

Wind Speed & Direction: ____________

Humidity: ____________

Cloud Cover: ____________

Air Temp.: ____________

Recent Rain Fall: ____________

Range (Drift): ____________ Cross Range: ____________

Tackle Used: ____________

Method Used: ____________

Rigger Settings: ____________

____

Comments: ____________

____

LOG SHEET

Date: / /

Time: ______________

Stream/Lake Name: ______________ Species Name(s): ______________

Access Used: ______________ No. Caught: ______________

Section Fished: ______________ Size (lbs./in.) ______________

SITE CONDITIONS

Water Level/Flow: ______________

Clarity: ______________

Weed Growth: ______________

pH: ______________

Bottom Type: ______________

Insect Hatches: ______________

WEATHER CONDITIONS

Barometer: ______________

Wind Speed & Direction: ______________

Humidity: ______________

Cloud Cover: ______________

Air Temp.: ______________

Recent Rain Fall: ______________

Range (Drift): ______________ Cross Range: ______________

Tackle Used: ______________

Method Used: ______________

Rigger Settings: ______________

____

Comments: ______________

____

LOG SHEET

Date: / /

Time: ______________

Stream/Lake Name: ______________ Species Name(s): ______________

Access Used: ______________ No. Caught: ______________

Section Fished: ______________ Size (lbs./in.) ______________

SITE CONDITIONS

Water Level/Flow: ______________

Clarity: ______________

Weed Growth: ______________

pH: ______________

Bottom Type: ______________

Insect Hatches: ______________

WEATHER CONDITIONS

Barometer: ______________

Wind Speed & Direction: ______________

Humidity: ______________

Cloud Cover: ______________

Air Temp.: ______________

Recent Rain Fall: ______________

Range (Drift): ______________ Cross Range: ______________

Tackle Used: ______________

Method Used: ______________

Rigger Settings: ______________

____

Comments: ______________

____

LOG SHEET

Date: / /

Time: ____________

Stream/Lake Name: ____________
Species Name(s): ____________

Access Used: ____________
No. Caught: ____________

Section Fished: ____________
Size (lbs./in.) ____________

SITE CONDITIONS

Water Level/Flow: ____________

Clarity: ____________

Weed Growth: ____________

pH: ____________

Bottom Type: ____________

Insect Hatches: ____________

WEATHER CONDITIONS

Barometer: ____________

Wind Speed & Direction: ____________

Humidity: ____________

Cloud Cover: ____________

Air Temp.: ____________

Recent Rain Fall: ____________

Range (Drift): ____________
Cross Range: ____________

Tackle Used: ____________

Method Used: ____________

Rigger Settings: ____________

____

Comments: ____________

____

LOG SHEET

Date: / /

Time: ____________

Stream/Lake Name: ____________
Species Name(s): ____________

Access Used: ____________
No. Caught: ____________

Section Fished: ____________
Size (lbs./in.) ____________

SITE CONDITIONS

Water Level/Flow: ____________

Clarity: ____________

Weed Growth: ____________

pH: ____________

Bottom Type: ____________

Insect Hatches: ____________

WEATHER CONDITIONS

Barometer: ____________

Wind Speed & Direction: ____________

Humidity: ____________

Cloud Cover: ____________

Air Temp.: ____________

Recent Rain Fall: ____________

Range (Drift): ____________
Cross Range: ____________

Tackle Used: ____________

Method Used: ____________

Rigger Settings: ____________

____

Comments: ____________

____

SAMPLE ENTRY

RESERVOIR CREEK

Map Coordinates .... 42° 43′ 36″ 77° 24′ 44″
USGS Map(s) .... Naples
Township(s) .... Naples (Ontario County), Prattsburg (Steuben County)
Access .... Crossing at Route 21 – see below
Principal Species .... Rainbow Trout (wild), Brook Trout (wild)

Reservoir Creek is a small tributary of Naples Creek, which it joins just south of the town of Naples. The stream averages 10 feet in width, has a gravel and rubble bottom and has a good seasonal flow of water. It can get very low in the summer. Flowing through agricultural land and woodlands. Reservoir Creek is loaded with a lot of natural cover. Numerous log jams, pools, undercut banks and overhanging trees provide hiding areas for the wild rainbows that run here in the spring. This run of fish is very good and is repeated in the fall if the rains are sufficient. Reservoir Creek is such that it does not get fished out quickly in the spring. There are so many places for the fish to hold over in that, if fished properly, the stream will be productive all spring. It is a little too small for fly fishing, but this is an ideal stream for drifting worms, egg sacs or very small spinners.

The upper reaches of Reservoir Creek, while very small, do provide some fishing for wild brook trout.

To guarantee public access to this stream, the state has purchased a total of 241 miles of public fishing easements on Reservoir Creek, near Route 21.

Reservoir Creek is not stocked.

NOTES: ______________________

SANDER'S Fishing Guide No. 1

Covering Hundreds of Lakes, Streams, Rivers, and Ponds in

The Western New York Region